THE
HISTORIC
HOUSES
HANDBOOK

THE HISTORIC HOUSES HANDBOOK

Neil Burton

photographs by A.F. Kersting

Facts on File, Inc
460 Park Avenue South
New York, N.Y. 10016

The British Historic Houses Handbook

Second edition published in the USA in 1982 by
FACTS ON FILE, INC.
460 Park Avenue South
New York, N.Y. 10016

Second edition published in the United Kingdom
1982 by PAPERMAC
a division of Macmillan Publishers Limited
London and Basingstoke
Companies and representatives throughout the world

ISBN 0-87196-627-1

CONSULTING EDITOR: Klaus Boehm

RESEARCH ASSISTANTS: Stephen Bate, Chezel Bird, Caroline Dakers, Ruth Owens,
Carol Procter, Peta Ree, Fay Sharman

DRAWINGS by Charlotte Ellis

THE DESCRIPTIONS of many of the houses in the 'Houses Open by Appointment'
section are taken from the annual reports of the Historic Buildings Council for
England and the Historic Buildings Council for Wales by kind permission of Her
Majesty's Stationery Office and the Welsh Office, Crown Copyright reserved.

NOTE: All information in this work is given in good faith and every effort has been
made to ensure accuracy but entrance charges and facilities available at houses are
liable to change at short notice; no responsibility can be accepted for resulting
inaccuracies in the *Handbook*.

Typeset by Leaper & Gard Ltd., Bristol, England
Printed in Great Britain

Contents

Introduction	page	vii
How to use the *Handbook*	page	ix
Season tickets and organizations	page	xii
A guide to the leading architects, gardeners, furniture makers and painters	page	xvii
Glossary	page	xxii
List of counties, England and Wales	page	xxxvi
Houses regularly open to visitors (in alphabetical order by counties)		
England	page	1
Wales	page	475
Houses open by appointment (in alphabetical order by counties)		
England	page	501
Wales	page	559
Maps	page	569
Index of houses	page	587

Introduction

There are more houses open to the public in Britain than in any other European country. Nearly every one has some quality about it, whether of architecture, furnishing, historical association or scenery which makes it, in the strict sense of the word, incomparable and it is precisely this diversity which makes house visiting so enjoyable. The purpose of this *Handbook* is to describe every historic house and castle in England and Wales which is open to visitors for more than 20 days in the year. The descriptions are brief, but they are all based on first-hand experience of the house in question and every effort has been made to get the facts right.

Nowadays, historic houses are a major part of what has come to be called 'The Heritage' — in other words the Tourist Industry — and the actual tour of the house is only one part of a ritual which usually includes tea-eating and souvenir shopping and may include exhibitions, spectacles and sideshows additional to the house. Since these things usually have to be paid for, it seems a good idea to describe them and the main description of each house is supplemented by information about the other facilities.

At the back of the book is a section devoted to houses that are only open for a few days in the year, or by appointment with their owners. Many of them are buildings whose owners have agreed to allow some public access in return for a government grant towards repair costs. Such houses seldom have special facilities for visitors but can be very rewarding, especially for the architectural enthusiast.

It may seem artificial to confine the coverage of the book to houses when there are many gardens, museums and magnificent cathedrals open to visitors. The reason is simply that it is just possible to deal with all the houses in a single volume; to include other places would make the book too large and too long.

This year the *Handbook* has been enlarged by the addition of houses in Wales. The 1981 text has also been thoroughly revised. Historic houses are not like restaurants, where staff, decor and menu can all change in a short time. In general, the most important things about them are also the most permanent and it seems pointless to re-write descriptions merely for the sake of novelty. Some of the descriptions of English houses in this edition are brand new, some have been altered and amended, some have been left completely unchanged. The descriptions of the facilities available to visitors have been revised on the basis of further visits and in the light of comments made by the owners or managers of the houses concerned.

How to use the Handbook

The entries in the main part of the *Handbook* deal with houses open on a regular basis or on stated days. They are listed alphabetically under the appropriate county. A list of the counties in the order they appear in the book and a map showing their location can be found on pages 00 and 00. Individual houses can also be located by using the index and the regional maps at the back of the book. Each entry contains a brief description of the house with the basic facts and dates. It will usually say how much of the house can be seen and whether or not there are guided tours. Attention may be drawn to particular treasures or to other items of interest. The rest of the information is arranged under a series of standard sub-headings which are shown below.

Opening times: The basic qualification for inclusion is that a house shall be open for at least 20 days in the year. The open days may be distributed throughout the year or concentrated into a few weeks. In the case of the more popular houses it is worth remembering that there are always more visitors at weekends than during the week and more visitors on Sundays than on Saturdays. Sunday afternoon is the worst possible time to visit if you want to see a house in comfort. On a weekday you may have the place to yourself.

Entrance charges: Wherever possible these are correct for the 1982 season. If the information for 1982 was not available at the time of going to press, last year's charges are given with the date thus: (1981). The letters HHA in this section mean that the house belongs to the Historic Houses Association and Friends of the Association are given free admission.

Parking: Where car parks are provided the main considerations are the distance between car park and house and whether an additional charge is made.

Wheelchair access: 1981 was the International Year of Disabled People. Some praiseworthy improvements were made by the National Trust and other owners to provide access for wheelchair users and special facilities where necessary, but such improvements were not general and there are still many historic houses where there is no direct access to the interior. It is sometimes almost impossible to adapt an old building to allow wheelchair access, but there are many houses where a single flight of steps is the only barrier between the outside and the main interior rooms and there seems no reason why anyone in a wheelchair should not, with assistance, negotiate a moderate flight of steps. This section of each entry contains basic information about steps and ramps or the lack of them.

It must be admitted that visitors in wheelchairs can cause problems, especially where it is necessary for them to go against the direction of flow, or where circulation is along narrow, roped-off walkways. For this reason it is a sensible precaution to avoid Sundays when a house is likely to be crowded and, wherever possible, to telephone beforehand to make sure that access will be possible.

The National Trust publishes a small booklet entitled 'Facilities for the Disabled and Visually Handicapped' which covers those properties which are considered especially suitable for the disabled. It is very good as far as it goes, but there are many properties which do not appear at all. The Trust also gives free admission to anyone necessarily accompanying a disabled person.

Guidebook: Most houses in this *Handbook* have guidebooks of their own. There are two main types: the Souvenir Guide, which usually consists of colour pictures with a small amount of text, and the guidebook proper. I prefer the latter. A good guidebook should contain an outline of the history of the house and its owners and a description of the furniture and paintings inside. The description is best arranged as a room-by-room tour so that it is convenient to read whilst going round the house. Illustrations always improve a guidebook and so do plans which show how the rooms fit together. Very often the architect will have spent more time on designing the layout of the building than anything else and only a plan can reveal this design. Taken as a whole, the best guidebooks available are those produced by the National Trust which are clear, well-written and full of information.

Catering: A refreshment room serves the double purpose of providing sustenance and also a place to sit down, which is usually very welcome after an hour or more on one's feet. A substantial number of houses have a restaurant serving at least a light soup-and-salad lunch, but the meal most closely associated with house visiting is tea, with its simple elements of tea and scones, cakes or sandwiches. Even within these narrow limits there is enormous variation in quality and quantity, though the advent of the deep-freezer has made stale rock buns something of the past. A good tea should not only be composed of good ingredients, but needs to be properly presented, with china plates and cups – not those sordid plastic abominations which create an instant litter problem. Not surprisingly, the best teas can often be had at the smallest houses, where the cakes and scones have been specially prepared, but the National Trust tea rooms are usually pleasant places and their food is of a reliable standard. There seems to have

x

been a slight improvement in the standard of catering in historic houses in 1981, though this may be just an opinion based on a series of lucky visits, and, of course, there is a select group of houses like Churche's Mansion in Nantwich and Sheldon Manor in Wiltshire where the food is a major consideration.

WCs: There is no need to say much about lavatories, except to note their existence, and perhaps to warn against those which are best avoided. The phrase 'Not for Wheelchair Users' means that there is no cubicle with an outward opening door and the extra space required inside.

Shop: Historic house shops remain depressingly uniform, probably because the things which apparently sell best are small and trashy objects. The National Trust and some private owners make an honourable attempt to stock their shops with good quality things, but the Trust suffers a little from the fact that all their shops stock the same basic range. Some houses offer produce from their garden or home farm, or cider from their orchards and these are often very good value for money.

Extras: This section deals with anything for which an additional charge is made. Some extra attractions which are free have also crept in because there was no space for them in the main description.

Houses which are open only for a few days in the year or by appointment are listed in a separate section towards the back of the *Handbook*. Many of them are buildings whose owners have agreed to allow limited public access in return for a government grant towards the cost of repairs. Most of these houses have no special facilities for visitors. There is a brief description of each building and the name and address or telephone number of the person to contact.

Season tickets and organizations

One way to save money when visiting houses is to buy a season ticket. Unfortunately, there is no single season ticket which covers all houses open to the public, but three of the national organizations involved with historic buildings (The Department of the Environment, The National Trust and The Historic Houses Association) offer their own season ticket equivalents which give free access to a large number of houses and other properties. Details of these are given below. The English Tourist Board and The Wales Tourist Board are useful as sources of information about everything to do with historic houses and other places to visit. The details of the various regional offices are given here.

The Department of the Environment (DOE) is the government department which looks after most royal buildings and a large number of ancient monuments. These include the Tower of London, Hampton Court, Windsor Castle and a large number of other castles. The Department also maintains Stonehenge and many prehistoric monuments which are not covered by this *Handbook*. At many of these buildings and monuments it is possible to buy a 'Season Ticket to History', which gives free admission for a year to all properties in the Department's care, with the exception of some royal residences like Sandringham and Windsor Castle. The same ticket may also be purchased by post only from The Department of the Environment, AMHB Store, Room 32, Building 1, Victoria Road, Ruislip, Middlesex. The cost of the 1982 Season Ticket to History is £6, OAPS and children £3. It is particularly good value for visitors to London, where many of the most expensive monuments are concentrated. The ticket comes with a booklet giving a list of all monuments in Britain with their opening times and also a location map. Most of the monuments conform to standard opening times which are as follows:
Standard Hours (S)
16 Oct to 14 March, weekdays 9.30–4, Sun 2–4.
15 March to 15 Oct, weekdays 9.30–6.30, Sun 2–6.30.
(Some of the smaller or less important monuments close for lunch 1–2.)
Standard Hours (SM)
As above but also open on Sunday mornings from 9.30, April to September.

The National Trust was founded in 1894 for the preservation of places of historic interest or natural beauty in England, Wales and Northern Ireland (there is a separate National Trust for Scotland). Today the Trust is the largest private landowner and conservation society in Britain. It also has in its possession more than 200 historic buildings which are open to visitors. Anyone can become a member of the National Trust; the cost of single adult membership for a year is £10 and there are reduced membership fees for additional members of a family living at the same address or for family group membership. Members have free admission to all National Trust properties open to the public and may take part in the various social and educational activities organised by the regional centres. An annual booklet called *Properties Open*, which is sent to members, contains the necessary details of all Trust properties. It is possible to join the National Trust at many of their houses or by post through the membership department. General enquiries should be addressed to:

National Trust Headquarters,
42 Queen Anne's Gate, London SW1H 9AS
Tel: (01) 222 9251

Applications for membership and membership enquiries should be addressed to:

P.O. Box 30, Beckenham, Kent BR3 4TL.
Tel: (01) 650 7263

The Historic Houses Association (HHA) is primarily an association for the owners of historic houses. It acts partly as a pressure group to secure tax and other concessions from the government and partly as a vehicle for the exchange of information about such things as insurance or the best way to go about opening a house to the public. Those who do not own historic houses can become Friends of the HHA for the sum of £10 per year. Friends have free admission to over 200 of the houses whose owners belong to the Association, and since these include many of the larger and more expensive stately homes this is an attractive proposition. Houses whose owners belong to the Association are indicated by (HHA) in the 'Entrance Charges' section. All enquiries should be addressed to:

The Historic Houses Association,
38 Ebury Street, London SW1.
Tel: (01) 730 9410

The English Tourist Board is a body whose primary function is to provide information. Any questions which this *Handbook* does not answer can usually be solved with the help of the appropriate ETB regional office.

Cumbria Tourist Board (Cumbria)
Ellerthwaite, Windermere LA23 2AQ.
Tel: (096 62) 444/7

Northumbria Tourist Board (Northumberland, Tyne & Wear, Cleveland, Durham)
9 Osborne Terrace, Jesmond, Newcastle upon Tyne NE2 1NT.
Tel: (0632) 817744

Heart of England Tourist Board (Herefordshire, Shropshire, Staffordshire, Warwickshire, Worcestershire, West Midlands)
P.O. Box 15, Worcester, Worcestershire WR1 2JT.
Tel: (0905) 29511

North West Tourist Board (Cheshire, Greater Manchester, Lancashire, Merseyside)
Last Drop Village, Bromley Cross, Bolton BL7 9PZ.
Tel: (0204) 591511

East Midlands Tourist Board (Derbyshire, Leicestershire, Lincolnshire, Northamptonshire, Nottinghamshire)
Exchequergate, Lincoln LN2 1PZ.
Tel: (0522) 31521

Yorkshire and Humberside Tourist Board (Humberside, North, West and South Yorks.)
312 Tadcaster Road, York YO2 2HF.
Tel: (0904) 707961

Thames & Chilterns Tourist Board (Berkshire, Bedfordshire, Buckinghamshire, Hertfordshire, Oxfordshire)
8 The Market Place, Abingdon, Oxon OX14 3UD.
Tel: (0235) 22711

East Anglia Tourist Board (Cambridgeshire, Essex, Norfolk, Suffolk)
14 Museum Street, Ipswich IP1 1HU.
Tel: (0473) 214211

Southern Tourist Board (East Dorset, Hampshire, Isle of Wight)
The Old Town Hall, Leigh Road, Eastleigh SO5 4DE.
Tel: (0703) 616027

London Tourist Board (Greater London)
26 Grosvenor Gardens, London SW1.
Tel: (01) 730 0791

West Country Tourist Board (Avon, Cornwall, Devon, West Dorset, Somerset, Wiltshire)
Trinity Court, Southernhay East, Exeter EX1 1QS.
Tel: (0392) 76351

South East England Tourist Board (East & West Sussex, Kent, Surrey)
Cheviot House, 4-6 Monson Road, Tunbridge Wells, Kent TN1 1NH. *Tel:* (0892) 40766

The Wales Tourist Board fulfils similar functions for the Principality. Its address is 3 Castle Street, Cardiff (personal callers only), *Tel:* Cardiff 27281. The address for correspondence is PO Box 151, WDO, Cardiff CF5 1XS.

A guide to the leading architects, gardeners, furniture makers and painters

ADAM Robert (1728–92). A Scot who became the most fashionable architect in Britain in the 1760s and 1770s. He created a light and elegant kind of decoration which has been widely imitated. Among his best works are Syon Park in London, Newby Hall in Yorkshire and Saltram in Devon. His brothers John and James were also architects.

ARCHER Thomas (1668–1743). A gentleman-architect who was familiar with the latest developments in the Italian architecture of his day and imitated them in his buildings, which include part of Chatsworth in Derbyshire and Chettle in Dorset.

BARRY Sir Charles (1795–1860). Best known for the Houses of Parliament, which he designed in 1840, but Barry also designed a large number of houses, usually in the Gothic or Italian styles. Cliveden in Buckinghamshire and Harewood in Yorkshire were both rebuilt or re-fronted by him.

BRIDGEMAN Charles (died 1738). The leading landscape gardener in England in the 1720s and 1730s and one of the first to introduce informal garden layouts. He worked at many houses, including Stowe in Buckinghamshire and Wimpole in Cambridgeshire, but most of his work has been destroyed.

BROWN Lancelot – nicknamed 'Capability' (1716–83). The most famous landscape gardener of the 18th century; his parks, with their clumps of trees and serpentine lakes, still survive at many houses. Brown was also an architect and he designed Claremont in Surrey and altered Broadlands in Hampshire.

BURGES William (1827–81). A wealthy and eccentric architect with a love of the bold forms and bright colours of the Middle Ages. His best works are those for himself or for other rich men like the Third Earl of Bute, for whom he built Cardiff Castle and Castell Coch in South Wales.

BURLINGTON Lord – otherwise **Richard Boyle, Third Earl of Burlington** (1694–1753). A noble enthusiast for architecture and sometimes an architect as well. He was one of those who introduced the Palladian style into Britain in the early 18th century.

CAMPBELL Colen (1626–1729). A Scottish architect, one of the first to use the Palladian style. He designed Stourhead in Wiltshire and Houghton in Norfolk, but exerted a wider influence through his three-volume book on architecture *Vitruvius Britannicus*, published 1715–25.

CARR John (1723–1807). Sometimes known as 'Carr of York', the principal architect working in the north of England between 1760 and 1800. Houses by him include Harewood in West Yorkshire, Constable Burton in North Yorkshire and Cannon Hall in South Yorkshire.

CHIPPENDALE Thomas (1718–79). The best-known English furniture maker. He moved from Yorkshire to London in 1748 and built up a large firm which furnished many important houses, including Nostell Priory in Yorkshire. He also published *The Gentleman and Cabinet Maker's Director* in 1754, which spread his influence still further.

FLITCROFT Henry (1697–1769). Began his career as a carpenter, but was taken up by Lord Burlington and became a successful architect. Among his buildings are Woburn Abbey in Bedfordshire, and he also worked at Wimpole in Cambridgeshire.

GAINSBOROUGH Thomas (1727–88). A leading painter of portraits and landscapes in the later 18th century; his portraits are always softly painted and flattering.

GIBBONS Grinling (1648–1741). The leading sculptor in England in the late 17th and early 18th cen. ury. He is most famous for his exquisite carving in wood, especially the swags of fruit and flowers popular in the interior decoration of his time. Examples of this work can be seen at Hampton Court, Windsor Castle and Petworth in Sussex.

GIBBS James (1682–1754). A successful early 18th century architect whose *Book of Architecture*, published in 1728, was thought the best general work on the subject. Gibbs's buildings include St Martin's in the Fields, London, the Radcliffe Camera at Oxford and the magnificent hall at Ragley in Warwickshire.

GILLOW OF LANCASTER. The principal furniture makers of northern England in the late 18th and early 19th century. The work of the firm is spread widely throughout the north, especially in the houses of Roman Catholics since the Gillows were also Catholics.

HEPPLEWHITE George (died 1786). Famous solely because of his book *The Cabinet Maker's and Upholsterer's Guide*, published in 1788. No furniture made by him is known.

JONES Inigo (1573–1652). The father of classical architecture in Britain. He was Surveyor General to King Charles I and his Banquetting House in Whitehall and his Queen's House at Greenwich were among the very first buildings which brought the classicism of Palladio and other European architects to this country.

KENT William (?1685–1748). He began his career as a painter (and decorated the inside of Kensington Palace) but turned to architecture at the age of 30. He followed the Palladian style in his buildings, which include Holkham Hall in Norfolk and the interior of Houghton nearby. Kent was also a landscape gardener, one of the first to use informal layouts.

KNELLER Sir Godfrey (1646–1723). A German painter who settled in England. He was the leading portrait painter in the reigns of William and Mary, Anne and George I.

LELY Sir Peter (1618–80). A Dutch painter who became the leading portraitist in the reign of King Charles II.

LUTYENS Sir Edwin (1869–1944). The last great English architect working in the classical tradition. Among the many country houses he designed or altered are Castle Drogo in Devon and Lindisfarne Castle in Northumberland. His other works include the Cenotaph in London, The Viceroy's Palace at New Delhi and Queen Mary's Dolls' House at Windsor Castle.

NASH John (1752–1835). The favourite architect of the Prince Regent, later King William IV, for whom he laid out Regent's Park in London and other new streets. His best-known house is the Royal Pavilion at Brighton.

PALLADIO Andrea (1508–80). One of the greatest Italian architects. His finely-proportioned villas built for the nobility of Venice provided the patterns for the English Palladian movement of the 18th century.

PUGIN Augustus Welby Northmore (1811–52). In the early 19th century when classical architecture was failing, Pugin was an ardent worker for the establishment of the Gothic style, which he considered the only true one.

As both architect and designer his output was enormous, but his life was cut short by overwork.

REPTON Humphrey (1752–1818). Repton took Capability Brown's place as the leading English landscape gardener. Each of his clients was given a 'Red Book' containing proposals for improvements to be made. Repton favoured a more picturesque and overgrown appearance than Brown's bare lawns and lakes provided.

REYNOLDS Sir Joshua (1723–92). The most distinguished and respected portrait painter working in England in the second half of the 18th century.

ROSE Joseph (1723–80). One of the leading plasterers in England between about 1750 and 1770. He did most of the Robert Adam's interiors and those of other leading architects.

SALVIN Anthony (1799–1881). Born in County Durham, he preferred the Gothic and the Castle styles and restored many houses in these two styles.

SHAW Richard Norman (1831–1912). One of the most successful late Victorian architects. He turned from the Gothic to the Old English style and among the houses he designed in this style are Cragside, Northumberland, Adcote in Shropshire and Flete in Devon.

SHERATON Thomas (1751–1806). Sheraton gave his name to the elegant furniture style of the late 18th century. He made no furniture himself but published several influential books of designs.

SMITH Francis (1672–1738). Often known as 'Smith of Warwick', this master-builder and his brother William designed a very large number of country houses in the Midlands in the first 30 years of the 18th century.

SMYTHSON Robert (1535–1614). Perhaps the most talented Elizabethan architect whose works include Wollaton Hall, Nottingham, Hardwick and Bolsover in Derbyshire and parts of Longleat in Wiltshire. His son John continued his work.

SOANE Sir John (1753–1837). A talented neurotic, one of the most original English architects and a great collector. He became successful after his appointment as architect to the Bank of England in 1788. His house in London, which he left to the nation, contains his collections and many drawings of his buildings.

VANBRUGH Sir John (1664–1726). Gentleman playwright who turned to architecture in mid-life with no training at all. A friend and colleague of Sir Christopher Wren. His works include Blenheim, Oxfordshire and Castle Howard, Yorkshire.

VASSALLI Francesco (1724–63). An Italian plasterer who worked in northern England in the mid-18th century.

WREN Sir Christopher (1632–63). The most famous English architect, also a distinguished mathematician. He was Surveyor of the Royal Works to King Charles II, William and Mary and Queen Anne. His best known works are St Paul's Cathedral, Hampton Court and the 52 City churches rebuilt after the Great Fire of London in 1666.

WYATT James (1746–1813). The most successful of this large family of architects. With Robert Adam he was considered the most fashionable designer of the 1770s. His classical works include Heaton Hall, Manchester and Doddington, Avon, but he also had a great liking for the Gothic style and used it for many of his buildings.

Glossary

ARCADE: a series of arches.

ARTISAN MANNERIST: a term to describe the vigorous but ignorant classical style of the mid-17th century in England.

ASHLAR: squared blocks of stone.

BAILEY: a courtyard of a castle.

BALUSTRADE: a series of small vertical columns (balusters) supporting a handrail.

BARBICAN: a fortified outwork defending the entrance to a castle.

BAROQUE: a style in which massiveness is combined with vigorous ornament; the literal meaning of the word is 'irregularly shaped'.

BELVEDERE: either a turret on a building or a separate tower built to give a good view.

BUTTERY: a room used in mediaeval and Tudor houses for the storage of provisions, especially beer or wine.

BUTTRESS: a mass of stone or brickwork built against a wall to give it additional support.

CAPITAL: the head of a column or pilaster.

CASCADE: waterfall.

CHINOISERIE: a style imitating Chinese arts and buildings.

CLASSICAL: copied or adapted from ancient Greek or Roman buildings.

COLUMN: the main vertical support in classical architecture; a row of columns forms a colonnade.

COLONNADE: see column.

CORBEL: a bracket projecting from a wall, intended to support something.

CORNICE: a projecting ornamental moulding at the top of a wall, either inside or outside a building.

CROSS-WINDOW: a window whose opening is divided by one vertical and one horizontal member of stone or wood; cross-windows were usual in late 17th century buildings.

CUPOLA: usually a small domed turret built upon a roof.

CURTAIN-WALL: a wall between two towers in a castle; also used for a wall enclosing a courtyard.

DIAPER: all-over decoration, usually in a criss-cross pattern.

DORMER WINDOW: window standing up vertically from the slope of a roof.

DRESSINGS: smoothly-finished stone used to decorate and strengthen the corners, window openings or any other part of the building.

EAVES: the overhanging edge of a roof.

ELIZABETHAN: anything built or made during the reign of Queen Elizabeth I (1558–1603).

ENTABLATURE: the collective name for the three horizontal members (architrave, frieze and cornice) supported by a column in classical architecture.

FACADE: the face or main front of a building.

FINIAL: a decorative ornament at the top of a gable, spire, roof etc.

FRIEZE: a horizontal band of ornament.

GABLE: the upper part of a wall at the end of a pitched roof; usually triangular, but sometimes with curved sides (shaped gable) or with a pediment on top (Dutch gable).

GARDEROBE: latrine or privy in mediaeval buildings.

GEORGIAN: strictly-speaking, the Georgian period stretches from 1714 (the accession of King George I) to 1830 (the death of King George IV), but the word is often used loosely to mean 18th century.

GIANT COLUMN OR PILASTER: one which is two or more storeys high.

GOTHIC: the style or period of mediaeval architecture in which the pointed arch was used. The word can also be used to describe later imitations of the style, although 19th century imitations are usually called 'Gothic Revival'.

GOTHICK: this word is often used to signify the pretty fanciful version of the Gothic style found in the later 18th century; sometimes called 'Strawberry Hill Gothick'.

HALF-TIMBERED: may be either another word for 'timber-framed' or used to mean those 19th century buildings with a false timber frame applied to the outside wall.

HALL: in mediaeval houses the hall was the largest and most important living room. It has become steadily less important since the 16th century.

HIPPED ROOF: a roof where the ends are sloped inwards instead of being gabled.

HOUSEBODY: the name given in the north of England to the great hall or main room of a house.

JACOBEAN: anything built or made during the reign of King James I (1603–25); the Jacobean style often mixes the late Gothic and the classical styles.

JACOBETHAN: a mixture of Elizabethan and Jacobean, often used to describe 19th century imitations of the architecture of these two periods.

JETTY OR OVERHANG: the projection of an upper storey beyond the storey below, almost always in timber-framed buildings.

KEEP: the main tower of a castle, also called a donjon; sometimes containing the main living rooms.

MATHEMATICAL TILES: tiles made to look like brickwork.

MOULDING: a general term for thin projecting bands of continuous ornament on walls and other surfaces.

MULLION: vertical bar dividing a window.

NEO-CLASSICAL: there have been several revivals of the classical style, but this word usually refers to the mid-18th century revival, which included a Greek Revival about 1800 and continued well into the 19th century.

NORMAN: the Norman period in Britain includes most of the 11th and 12th centuries; the Norman style of architecture precedes the Gothic and uses the round arch, not the pointed arch.

ORDER: in classical architecture, a column with its base and entablature proportioned and decorated according to accepted rules. There are five orders (Tuscan, Doric, Ionic, Corinthian and Composite) all with their own proper forms.

ORIEL: a projecting window, usually on an upper floor.

PALLADIAN: a style dervied from villas built by the architect Andrea Palladio (1500–80) for Venetian noblemen producing plain but well-proportioned buildings with classical ornament. Palladian houses are usually symmetrical, and often have wings and a pedimented central block.

PANTRY: a room in a mediaeval or Tudor house for the storage of food, especially bread.

PARAPET: a wall for protecting any sudden drop, for example on the sides of a bridge, or in front of a roof.

PARTERRE: a level space in a garden occupied by ornamental flower beds or low hedges.

PEDIMENT: in classical architecture, a shallow gable like that of a Greek or Roman temple; also used over doors and windows.

PELE TOWER: a square fortified tower house, most common in the border counties of England.

PERPENDICULAR: a shorthand term for the last phase of the English Gothic style (15th and early 16th centuries) with its strong vertical emphasis. One of the best-known examples of the style is King's College Cambridge.

PIANO NOBILE: an Italian phrase to describe the main storey of a house; usually raised above a basement or ground floor and taller than the other storeys.

PIER: a square column.

PILASTER: a flat representation of a column against a wall.

PORTICO: a covered colonnade at the entrance to a building.

POSTERN: a back door in a castle.

QUOINS: dressed stones that run up the corners of a building.

RENDERING: the process of covering an outside wall with a waterproof skin of plaster or cement.

RETICULATED TRACERY: literally 'net-like' window tracery, formed by the repetition of small regular openings.

ROCOCO: a light and elegant style of decoration with much use of natural forms, plants and animals, which began in France and reached England in about 1730.

ROUGHCAST: rendering with a mixture of plaster and gravel.

ROUNDEL: a circular panel.

RUSTICATION: the deep channels on a wall meant to look like joints between large blocks of stone; most often used on the lower storeys of buildings.

SCAGLIOLA: an artificial stone, often made to resemble coloured marble.

SCREENS PASSAGE: the screened-off entrance passage of a mediaeval or Tudor house, dividing the hall on one side from the service rooms (buttery and pantry) on the other.

SEGMENTAL: in the shape of part of a circle.

SHELL KEEP: a massive wall encircling the top of a castle mound and serving instead of a keep.

SOLAR: the upper living room or withdrawing room of a mediaeval house, usually reached from the high-table end of the hall.

STRING COURSE: a projecting band running horizontally across the facade of a building.

STUCCO: very smooth plaster rendering.

SWAG OR FESTOON: an ornament in the form of a piece of cloth or a garland of flowers suspended at both ends and hanging down in the middle.

TIE-BEAM: the main beam which ties together the bottom ends of a pitched-roof.

TIMBER-FRAMED: a method of construction in which the main structure of a building is made of wood; the spaces between the timbers may be filled with bricks, wattle-and-daub or another material.

TRANSOM: horizontal bar dividing a window.

TUDOR: strictly-speaking, the Tudor period runs from 1485 (the accession of King Henry VII) to 1603 (the death of Queen Elizabeth I), but the word is often used to mean the first half of the 16th century.

TUSCAN: the simplest and most massive of the Five Orders of classical architecture.

UNDERCROFT: a vaulted room below an upper room such as a church or chapel.

VAULT: an arched roof; the arch may be either pointed or semi-circular.

VENETIAN WINDOW: a triple window whose central section is heightened and arched at the top.

WAINSCOT: wooden interior wall-covering.

WARD: a courtyard of a castle.

WATTLE AND DAUB: woven branches covered with mud or plaster; a common material for walls in mediaeval and Tudor houses.

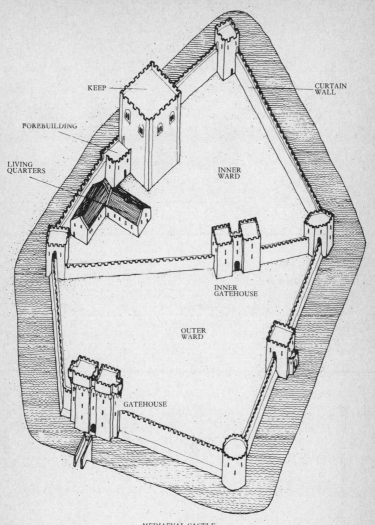

KEEP

CURTAIN WALL

FOREBUILDING

LIVING QUARTERS

INNER WARD

INNER GATEHOUSE

OUTER WARD

GATEHOUSE

MEDIAEVAL CASTLE

xxvii

A MEDIAEVAL HALL HOUSE OF ABOUT 1400

SMOKE LOUVER

HOOD MOULD

ORIEL WINDOW

MULLION

TRACERY   BUTTRESS

ENTRANCE FRONT

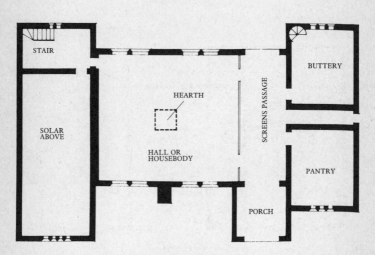

STAIR

SOLAR ABOVE

HEARTH

HALL OR HOUSEBODY

SCREENS PASSAGE

BUTTERY

PANTRY

PORCH

GROUND FLOOR PLAN

xxviii

A TIMBER-FRAMED HOUSE OF 1577

GABLE

BARGE BOARD

BRACE

JETTY

LEADED LIGHTS

ENTRANCE FRONT

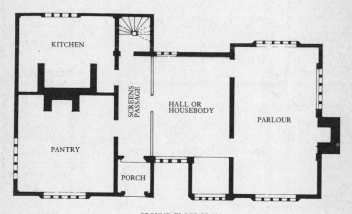

KITCHEN

SCREENS PASSAGE

HALL OR HOUSEBODY

PARLOUR

PANTRY

PORCH

GROUND FLOOR PLAN

xxix

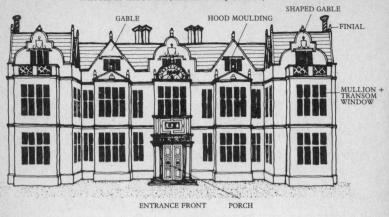

A HOUSE OF ABOUT 1600 (ELIZABETHAN/JACOBEAN)

GABLE   HOOD MOULDING   SHAPED GABLE

FINIAL

MULLION +
TRANSOM
WINDOW

ENTRANCE FRONT   PORCH

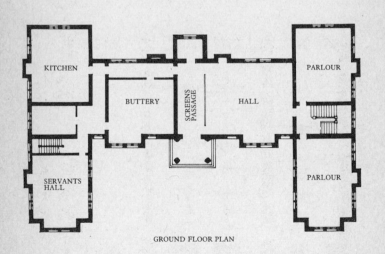

KITCHEN

BUTTERY

SCREENS PASSAGE

HALL

PARLOUR

SERVANTS
HALL

PARLOUR

GROUND FLOOR PLAN

XXX

A HOUSE OF ABOUT 1680 (LATE STUART/CAROLINE)

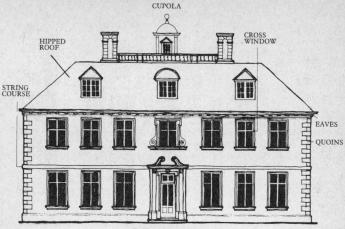

CUPOLA

CROSS
WINDOW

HIPPED
ROOF

STRING
COURSE

EAVES

QUOINS

ENTRANCE FRONT

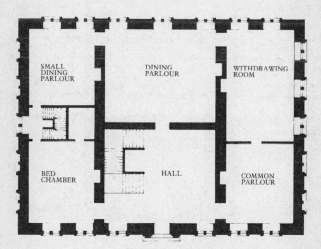

SMALL
DINING
PARLOUR

DINING
PARLOUR

WITHDRAWING
ROOM

BED
CHAMBER

HALL

COMMON
PARLOUR

GROUND FLOOR PLAN

xxxi

A HOUSE OF ABOUT 1715 (EARLY GEORGIAN/ENGLISH BAROQUE)

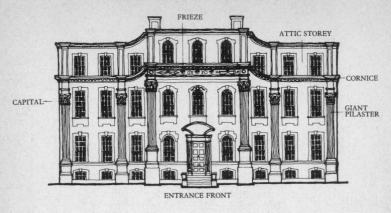

FRIEZE

ATTIC STOREY

CORNICE

CAPITAL

GIANT PILASTER

ENTRANCE FRONT

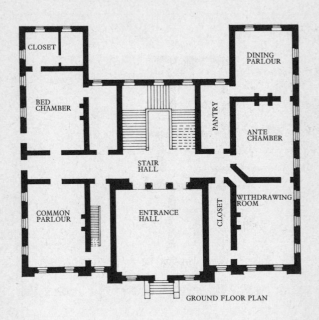

CLOSET

BED CHAMBER

DINING PARLOUR

PANTRY

ANTE CHAMBER

STAIR HALL

WITHDRAWING ROOM

COMMON PARLOUR

ENTRANCE HALL

CLOSET

GROUND FLOOR PLAN

xxxii

A HOUSE OF ABOUT 1740 (MID GEORGIAN/PALLADIAN)

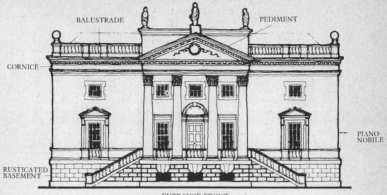

BALUSTRADE

PEDIMENT

CORNICE

PIANO NOBILE

RUSTICATED BASEMENT

ENTRANCE FRONT

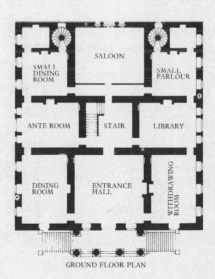

SALOON

SMALL DINING ROOM

SMALL PARLOUR

ANTE ROOM STAIR LIBRARY

DINING ROOM

ENTRANCE HALL

WITHDRAWING ROOM

GROUND FLOOR PLAN

xxxiii

A HOUSE OF ABOUT 1790 (LATE GEORGIAN)

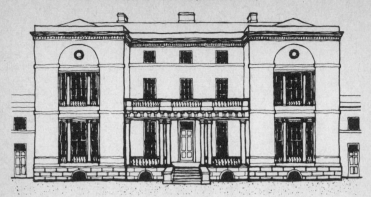

ENTRANCE FRONT

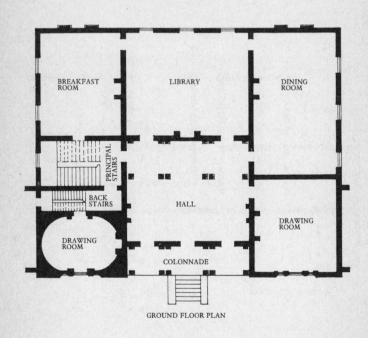

GROUND FLOOR PLAN

xxxiv

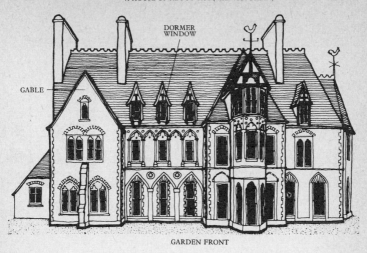

A HOUSE OF ABOUT 1850 (MID VICTORIAN)

DORMER
WINDOW

GABLE

GARDEN FRONT

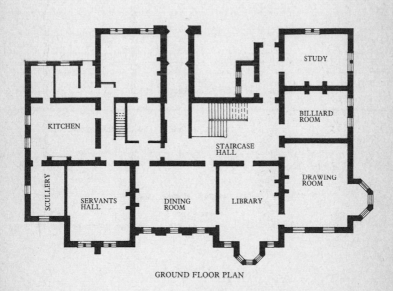

STUDY

BILLIARD
ROOM

KITCHEN

STAIRCASE
HALL

DRAWING
ROOM

SCULLERY

SERVANTS
HALL

DINING
ROOM

LIBRARY

GROUND FLOOR PLAN

XXXV

List of counties

England

Avon
Bedfordshire
Berkshire
Buckinghamshire
Cambridgeshire
Cheshire
Cleveland
Cornwall
Cumbria
Derbyshire
Devon
Dorset
Durham
Essex
Gloucestershire
Hampshire
Hereford and Worcester
Hertfordshire
Humberside
Isle of Wight
Kent
Lancashire
Leicestershire

Lincolnshire
Greater London
Greater Manchester
Merseyside
West Midlands
Norfolk
Northamptonshire
Northumberland
Nottinghamshire
Oxfordshire
Shropshire
Somerset
Staffordshire
Suffolk
Surrey
East Sussex
West Sussex
Tyne and Wear
Warwickshire
Wiltshire
North Yorkshire
South Yorkshire
West Yorkshire

Wales

Clwyd
Dyfed
Mid Glamorgan

Gwent
Gwynedd
Powys

Houses regularly open to visitors

England

Avon

BATH: 1 ROYAL CRESCENT (The Bath Preservation Trust)
Tel: Bath (0225) 28126
Directions: About ½ mile N.W. of the Abbey

The Royal Crescent is perhaps the most spectacular street in Bath and was the first crescent to be built in England. It was designed by John Wood the younger and was built between 1767 and 1774. The fronts of the houses are punctuated by massive Ionic columns (over 100 in all) between each bay of windows and the crescent overlooks what is now Victoria Park. Houses in Bath were rented for the Season, as we all know from Jane Austen, and No. 1 had a series of different occupiers. By 1967 the building was much decayed, but it was rescued and given to the Bath Preservation Trust, who have restored the interior, taking great pains to make the decoration historically accurate. The hall, for example, has been marbled and the staircase painted to simulate stonework. The drab colour of the library walls may not seem attractive but apparently it pleased 18th century residents. The rooms of the ground and first floors are suitably furnished with later 18th century items and contain portraits of well-known figures of the period. Each room is viewed from a roped enclosure at one end and the guides are eager to explain the contents and enlarge on the general history of Bath.

Opening times: March to end Oct, Tues to Sat 11–5, Sun 2–5; last admission 4.40.
Entrance charges: (1981) 50p; students and children under 18 30p; no dogs.
Parking: No car park, but there is sometimes parking space in the Crescent adjacent.
Wheelchair access: Eight steps to the front door; two rooms on ground floor accessible.
Guidebook: An excellent little illustrated guide, foreign language sheets are available and there are information boards in each room.
Catering: None.
WCs: None.
Shop: None.

BLAISE CASTLE HOUSE Henbury, Bristol (Bristol Corporation)
Tel: Bristol (0272) 506789
Directions: 5 miles N.W. of Bristol centre, on the outskirts of the city;
   signposted from the A4018

The grounds at Blaise are of great interest as an example of picturesque
garden layout. Two famous talents were involved; Humphrey Repton
suggested the landscaping and John Nash designed most of the garden
buildings. The house is a dull stone box designed by the Bristol architect
William Paty and built for a Quaker banker named John Harford in 1796. A
picture room was added to one side of the house by C.R. Cockerell in 1832
for the collection of John Harford Junior. Since 1949 the house has
contained an interesting museum of West Country life from the period
1750–1900. All the original furniture and fittings have gone and the interior
is like any municipal gallery with a colour scheme that is worse than most.
Visitors make their own way round. The park has suffered badly from
vandalism and is enclosed on all sides by 20th century housing. The estate
was deep in the country when Repton made his landscaping suggestions in
1795, and he created a dramatic approach to the house through the Combe
Dell gorge. This entrance is now disused, but it makes a good walk. The
garden buildings include the gothic Blaise Castle on top of Henbury Hill
(designed by Robert Mylne in 1766 for a previous owner of the estate)
Nash's conservatory next to the house and his thatched dairy nearby with its
charming water garden. A short walk from the house is the celebrated Blaise
Hamlet, nine outrageously picturesque cottages round a miniature village
green. The hamlet was designed by Nash in 1811 to house John Harford's
old retainers.

Opening times: All year, Sat, Sun, Mon, Tues, Wed 2–5; closed Christmas, Boxing and New
   Year's Day, Good Friday, May Day and Spring Bank Holiday Mon and Tues. Blaise
   Hamlet always open.
Entrance charges: Free.
Parking: Free municipal car park 250 years from house.
Wheelchair access: Possible to ground floor of house and part of park.
Guidebook: An excellent guide to the park and buildings, with plans and illustrations;
   separate guide to 18th century women's costume display with a free mantua pattern.
Catering: There is a café in the park.
WCs: Near the car park, and by the stables near the house; neither adapted for wheelchairs.
Shop: Museum publications only.

BRISTOL: THE GEORGIAN HOUSE 7 Great George Street (Bristol
Corporation)
Tel: Bristol (0272) 299771
Directions: From College Green in the centre of Bristol go up Park Street
   and Great George Street is a turning on the left

This 18th century town house is part of the development of the Brandon

Hill area in which a local dynasty of architects, the Patys, were deeply involved. No. 7 Great George Street was designed by William Paty in 1789 for John Pinney, who had returned to Bristol after 20 years of managing his sugar plantations in the West Indies. The house is now administered by the City Art Gallery and is arranged to recreate the atmosphere in which a wealthy Bristol merchant lived. It is a great success. The interior decoration is in the Adam style, with delicate plasterwork and carved ornament and there is some good English furniture, including a collector's cabinet attributed to the Exeter cabinet maker John Channon. The portraits include several of the Pinney family and there are a number of local views. The basement is interesting for the kitchen layout and the various pieces of obsolete domestic equipment. Here too is a cold water plunge-bath of the type recommended by Dr. Oliver of Bath as a stimulus to the nervous system; such baths were especially popular with merchants who had lived in the tropics. Visitors are free to wander round and the staff are very helpful and justly proud of the house which they maintain beautifully. The garden is not open.

Opening times: All year, Mon to Sat 10–1, 2–5; basement closes 12–2, 3–4.
Entrance charges: Free.
Parking: No car park, there is a municipal car park behind the Council House.
Wheelchair access: Three steps to front door; ground floor only accessible.
Guidebook: A cheap and well-written booklet.
Catering: None.
WCs: None.
Shop: None.

BRISTOL: RED LODGE Park Row (Bristol Corporation)
Tel: Bristol (0272) 299771
Directions: From the centre of Bristol follow Colston Street and turn left into Park Row

The Bristol merchant John Yonge built himself a great mansion in 1570 and he later built two smaller houses or lodges. The mansion was demolished in 1861 and the White Lodge was pulled down in 1868 to make room for Perry Road, but the Red Lodge survives and it contains the oldest interiors in Bristol. It has an unattractive exterior of rubble masonry and its upper parts were rebuilt in the early 18th century. Visitors enter the house by what was once the back door and, because of the steeply sloping site, descend a flight of stairs to reach the main ground floor rooms. This floor was remodelled in about 1720 and the rooms contain early Georgian furniture, including a fine English walnut bureau. On the first floor are the three original rooms of about 1590. All are handsomely panelled, one has a very fine carved and panelled internal porch, and two have contemporary plaster ceilings. The Great Oak Room has a richly carved stone overmantel with the coat of arms of Sir John Yonge and his wife, whose sister-in-law founded Wadham

College Oxford. The rooms contain good 17th century furniture. The garden of the house is not accessible and one cannot see the original main front.

Opening times: All year, Mon to Sat 10–1, 2–5; closed on public holidays.
Entrance charges: Free
Parking: There is a multi-storey car park adjacent in Park Row.
Wheelchair access: Not possible, far too many steps.
Guidebook: A good and thorough illustrated guide to the building and its contents.
Catering: None.
WCs: In the house.
Shop: None.

CLAVERTON MANOR nr Bath (The American Museum in Britain)
Tel: Bath (0225) 60503
Directions: 2½ miles E. of Bath via the A36 (Warminster Road) and Claverton Village

Claverton Manor was built in about 1820 for John Vivian. His architect was Sir Jeffry Wyattville who is best known for his Gothic work at Windsor Castle, but this house is of a completely different character. It is a fine classical villa of Bath stone with a pedimented south front and two bold bay windows on the east front. The house now contains the American Museum and the whole interior has been remodelled for this purpose. All the fixtures and fittings — even the floorboards — have been brought over from the United States and the rooms are laid out to show the history of North America up to 1860. Every aspect of life seems to be covered. There are sections on the Wild West, New Mexico, The Shakers, and a room from a Massachusetts tavern of the 1770s where a piece of fresh baked gingerbread can be had. The excellent collection of American quilts and textiles deserves a special mention. Guides in each room bubble over with enthusiasm and information about their particular subject. The only drawback is the comparatively large number of visitors. There are more exhibits outside the house, including marvellous figureheads and shop signs in the Folk Art Gallery. Elsewhere in the grounds is a milliner's shop and a model of an Indian tepee. Homesick Americans can console themselves in the Mount Vernon Garden, which is modelled on George Washington's garden in Virgina. There is also a herb garden which supplies the herb shop in the museum.

Opening times: 27 March to 31 Oct, daily except Mon 2–5; Bank Holidays and preceding Sun 11–5. Other times by arrangement. No parties of children during normal hours.
Entrance charges: (1981) House and grounds £1.30; OAPs and children under 16 £1.10. Grounds only 50p, no reduction.
Parking: Free parking 5 mins from the house.
Wheelchair access: Possible to the ground floor and part of the garden.
Guidebook: More a souvenir than a guide, with lots of colour pictures.
Catering: Self-service tea room with very good selection of American cookies and cakes; it is

possible to eat on the lawn outside.
WCs: Next to the tea room; unsuitable for wheelchairs.
Shop: Herb shop and country store, both part of the museum themselves, selling herbs, publications and Americana.

CLEVEDON COURT Clevedon (The National Trust)
Tel: Clevedon (0272) 872768
Directions: Clevedon lies on the coast, 11 miles W. of Bristol; the house is 1½ miles E. of Clevedon on the Bristol Road (B3130)

Clevedon is a delightful small manor house, built in about 1320 for Sir John de Clevedon. The tower and the Old Hall or 'Museum Room' on the east side are the remains of an earlier building of the 13th century and the windows to the right of the porch look like 16th century work. The most striking feature of the entrance front is the large window with reticulated tracery, which lights a small first floor chapel. Apart from the chapel, the house follows the usual mediaeval layout, with a central great hall flanked by a screens passage and service rooms at one end, and the parlour and solar at the other. The hall now has an 18th century ceiling and screen. An Elizabethan doorway was inserted in the 19th century. The contents of the house belong to the Elton family,. who have lived here since 1709. In the small number of rooms shown, family portraits are mixed with 17th, 18th and 19th century furniture. The stairway is hung with prints from Sir Arthur Elton's collection of the history of technology and the Justice Room to the right of the porch contains examples of the local Nailsea glass. Sir Edmund Elton was widely known in the 1890s as a potter, and examples of his distinctive 'Eltonware' pottery can be seen in the Museum Room and elsewhere in the house. Visitors make their own way round and there is a guide on each floor. A terraced garden has been formed in the hillside behind the house, giving fine views across the Clevedon Moor; the only drawback is the noise from the M5.

Opening times: April to end Sept Wed, Thurs, Sun and Bank Holiday Mon 2.30–5.30; last admission ½ hour before closing.
Entrance charges: £1.00; children under 16 50p. No unaccompanied children under 15.
Parking: In a field 200 yards from the house.
Wheelchair access: The mediaeval irregularities of the house make access for wheelchairs difficult.
Guidebook: A chronological account of the building and its owners which is a bit confusing to read; also a list of furniture in each room, some photos and a good plan. There are very useful information boards in each room.
Catering: Tea and shortbread dispensed from the kitchen door [3.30–5.30]. There is no formal tea room.
WCs: In the car park field, signposted behind a hedge; not for wheelchairs.
Shop: None.

DODINGTON HOUSE nr Chipping Sodbury (Sir Simon Codrington)
Tel: Chipping Sodbury (0454) 318899
Directions: 10 miles N. of Bath, off the A46 near its junction with the M4
  (Motorway exit 18)

'Capability' Brown provided a landscape setting for an Elizabethan house which still stood at Dodington in 1764, but there is no trace of that building now. Between 1796 and 1816 it was replaced by the present house which was designed for Christopher Codrington by James Wyatt. It is Wyatt's outstanding neo-classical house and also his last, for while he was driving from Dodington to London with Codrington in 1813 their carriage overturned and the architect was killed. The three main fronts of the house are all different; on the west is a colossal Roman Corinthian portico, on the south a centrepiece with a giant order of Corintian pilasters and a raised attic, and on the east two projecting bows. The interior is magnificently solemn, especially the entrance hall with its coffered ceiling and porphyry scagliola columns; the floor of the hall is paved in stone, marble and brass. Bethell Codrington's library is unaltered, but the four other rooms shown to the public have been redecorated recently. Although the furniture is attractive, the fittings — doors and fireplaces — are more splendid. In the centre of the house is a handsome staircase whose three great flights lead to a first floor gallery. North of the house is the church also by Wyatt, which is now an exhibition room. The charming dower house, once the dairy, is also on this side. The stable block north of the church contains a collection of carriages, many still in regular use. Adventureland offers various activities for small children, and there is a miniature railway and nature trails. Because of all these attractions the area north of the house gets crowded, but the house itself usually remains fairly quiet. Most of the large park is open for walks and a trip on foot to the lake is advised to see 'Capability' Brown's Gothic cascade and fishing house.

Opening times: 16–26 April weekends only, 25 May to 4 Sept daily 11–5.30.
Entrance charges: (1981) house, park and exhibitions £1.50; children and OAPs £1.00.
  Carriage museum 50p; children and OAPs 30p.
Parking: Free parking in a field west of the house.
Wheelchair access: Possible to the main rooms of the house and to exhibitions.
Guidebook: Lavish and full of superlatives and colour photos, but without a proper plan.
  There will be a revised edition for 1982.
Catering: Self-service restaurant and licenced bar which tend to get rather crowded.
WCs: Near the restaurant, and elsewhere; facilities for wheelchairs.
Shop: There are shops selling souvenirs, pottery and plants.
Extras: An extra charge is made for rides on the miniature railway.

Dodington House, Avon

DYRHAM PARK   nr Chippenham (The National Trust)
Tel: Abson (027 582) 2501
Directions: 8 miles N. of Bath off the A46; signposted locally

The mansion, stables and parish church form a close group in a steep-sided valley so narrow that one end of the house is jammed into the hillside. The present house was built for William Blathwayt, a civil servant of modest means who married Mary Winter, the heiress of Dyrham, in 1686. Five years later he set about altering and extending her family home and added the long two-storey west front across the old Tudor house. His architect was an obscure Frenchman called Hauduroy and this front, facing the church, has a definite French look to it. Blaythwayt prospered under King William III and between 1700 and 1704 the architect William Talman added what amounts to a second house, back to back with Hauduroy's and linked to it by the rebuilt Tudor Hall. Talman's front is Italianate with a first floor *piano nobile* and a great deal of carved ornament. The stables next to the house are a bold but crude piece of architecture and are probably by Talman's general foreman Edward Wilcox. Visitors are free to wander round the interior, where there are guides in each room and no barriers. The rooms have not greatly altered since Blaythwayt's time. Their dark panelled walls are rich but not gaudy. Most of the furniture dates from the period 1690 to 1710 and includes the Dutch paintings and the blue and white pottery which were fashionable at that time. There is also a sprinkling of furniture belonging to later Blaythwayts. The garden was once very elaborate, with parterres and a cascade and canal like those at Chatsworth, but only the bare outlines survived the landscaping carried out in the 18th century.

Opening times: Park all year 12–6 or sunset; house and garden April, May and Oct, daily except Thurs and Fri 2–6; June to Sept daily except Fri 2–6; last admission ½ hour before closing.
Entrance charges: House, garden and park £1.60; children 80p. Park only 40p.
Parking: Free parking next to the house.
Wheelchair access: Possible to the whole ground floor, about 75% of rooms shown; access to the gardens and the church is difficult.
Guidebook: A good, recently revised guide with plan, photos, history, room-by-room guide and lists of the pictures.
Catering: Teas in the greenhouse (also designed by Talman); a pleasant setting and reasonable food, accessible to wheelchairs.
WCs: Next to the stable yard; unsuitable for wheelchairs.
Shop: None.

HORTON COURT nr Chipping Sodbury (The National Trust)
Tel: Written communication only.
Directions: 3 miles N.E. of Chipping Sodbury, ¾ mile N. of Horton; not signposted; when in Horton take the road for Hawkesbury and the house is on the right before the church

The National Trust guide classifies Horton Court as 'of specialist architectural interest' and there is not very much to see. It is a pleasant mediaeval manor house of Cotswold stone, over-restored in 1937. The north wing is the hall of a house built about 1140. Only this hall and the garden are shown to visitors. 12th century houses are not common and although altered Horton is a valuable survival; the walls are largely original but the roof was replaced in the 14th century and a chimney added in Tudor times. The hall now contains a 17th century table, some pewter plates and miscellaneous objects. Conducted tours take about five minutes. The main house has an unusual carved porch of 1521, built by William Knight, later Bishop of Bath and Wells. He was involved in the discussion with the Papacy over King Henry VIII's divorce, and his visits abroad probably inspired him to build the ambulatory or covered walk in the garden, which is clearly modelled on an Italian loggia.

Opening times: April to end Oct, Wed and Sat 2–6 or sunset.
Entrance charges: 30p, no reductions.
Parking: In front of the house.
Wheelchair access: Possible to the garden and to the hall with assistance.
Guidebook: A leaflet with no plan and no illustration of the building.
Catering: None.
WCs: None.
Shop: None.

PRIOR PARK Bath, Prior Park College
Tel: Combe Down (0225) 835353
Directions: 1 mile S.W. of Bath centre; from the station cross the river, take Claverton Street, turn right up Prior Park Road to Ralph Allen's Drive and take second entrance on left

Prior Park is one of the great Palladian houses of England, splendidly sited at the top of a steep combe looking down towards the city. The house was built for Ralph Allen, who owned the quarries which supplied the stone for the 18th Century rebuilding of Bath. One of Allen's reasons for building Prior Park was to advertise the high quality of the stone from his quarries, and he took care that it should be bigger than other great houses of the day, especially the famous Wanstead House near London. The house was designed by John Wood the elder, who also designed Queen's Square and the Circus in Bath. Work began on the house in 1734. The massive central block, with its deep pedimented portico, was linked by sweeping colonnades to pavilions on the east and west. The east pavilion was altered from the original design by Richard Jones, who finished the building after Wood had been dismissed. In 1829 the house became a Roman Catholic school and the west wing was partly rebuilt to give more rooms and enormously enlarged by the addition of a new chapel, designed in 1844 by J.J. Scoles, but not finished until 1863. The house itself was gutted by fire in

Prior Park, Avon

1836; of the original rooms only Ralph Allen's chapel survives, but plasterwork and carving from another 18th century house, Hunstrete, were used in the reconstruction. Prior Park is now a school. Four rooms in the main house and Scoles' impressive chapel are shown to visitors, who should introduce themselves at the school office. After the splendid exterior, the house inside is disappointing and the contents of no interest. A famous feature of the grounds is the Palladian Bridge, magically sited on a lake half-way down the combe. It was built by Richard Jones in 1755 and is copied from a design by Andrea Palladio.

Opening times: Chapel and grounds all year daily 11–4. House open May to Sept, Tues and Wed 2–5; Aug only Mon to Thurs 2–5.
Entrance charges: Free.
Parking: Free parking behind the house.
Wheelchair access: Possible to ground floor and part of the grounds.
Guidebook: A scholarly work, giving much space to the Roman Catholic occupants; no plan, but several of Wood's original drawings are reproduced.
Catering: None.
WCs: In the house.
Shop: None.

ST CATHERINE'S COURT Bath (Mrs Katherine Christophers)
Tel: Bath (0225) 858159
Directions: 4 miles N.E. of Bath centre, off the main A4 at Batheaston; access is by a narrow lane impassable for coaches; house not signposted

This is a house of great charm in a lovely setting on the slope of the steep St Catherine's valley. It was built in 1490 by Prior Cantlow, who built the nearby church at the same time. Some of his work in the house survives, but the present north front, with its three gables and fine two-storey porch is the result of a rebuilding in about 1600 and the south and west fronts were much altered in 1919. The interior has been redecorated recently and has a slightly Mediterranean flavour. The drawing room has panelled and carved decoration of about 1690, while upstairs there is some 16th century panelling and painted wall decoration. The house contains excellent early needlework collected by the present owner. Visitors are shown round in a tour which can last over two hours. The tours are conducted by the owner, who makes the visitor feel like a guest, not an economic unit. The gardens to the north of the house are a long series of terraces formed in about 1600. On the south side is a pleasantly decayed Italianate garden.

Opening times: 17 April to 27 Sept, Mon, Sat, Sun and Public Holidays 2.30–5.00.
Entrance charges: (1981) £1.20; children under 16 60p. Coaches not accepted.
Parking: Free parking in front of the house.
Wheelchair access: Not practicable.
Guidebook: In preparation, temporary leaflet available.

Catering: Tea in the drawing room is an integral part of the tour.
WCs: In the house.
Shop: None.

Bedfordshire

HOUGHTON HOUSE Ampthill (Ancient Monument)
Directions: 6 miles S. of Bedford, 1 mile N. of Ampthill on the E. side of the A418

Houghton is the ruined and battered shell of a grand 17th century house. Despite the openness of the sloping site, which overlooks a landscape interrupted only by the distant chimneys of the largest brickworks in Europe, the house has an air of mystery. It was begun in 1615 for Mary, Dowager Countess of Pembroke, and building continued until her death in 1621. Her house was built of red brick with the standard H-shape plan, but it had some unusual features. For one thing, the main door in the south front led into the middle of one side of the great hall, not into a screens passage at one end. Even more extraordinary were the spectacular three-decker stone centrepieces on the north and west fronts with their Renaissance ornament. The Countess was the sister of Sir Philip Sidney and among her friends were some of the most cultivated members of the Court. It has been suggested that Inigo Jones, the Court architect, was responsible for the design of the centrepieces, but there is no proof. Tradition has it that John Bunyan, who lived nearby, took Houghton as the model for the House Beautiful in *Pilgrim's Progress*, but as the building was largely dismantled by the Duke of Bedford in the 1790s, it takes imagination to recreate its original glory from the remains. There are no roofs or floors, but the outside walls still stand to a good height.

Opening times: Open at all reasonable times.
Entrance charges: Free. Dogs must be on a lead.
Parking: Free parking at the end of the access road, 7 minutes walk away.
Wheelchair access: Possible to all parts of the building.
Guidebook: None.
Catering: None, but picnics allowed.
WCs: None.
Shop: None.

LUTON HOO Park Street, Luton (The Wernher family)
Tel: Luton (0582) 22955
Directions: 2 miles S. of Luton, between the A6 and A6129, M1 exit 10

The main attraction of Luton Hoo is the magnificent Wernher collection of works of art, the creation of a South African diamond magnate and his daughter-in-law, a member of the Russian royal family. The architecture takes second place. Visitors must approach the house through the bushes and enter by a door at one end of the main front. The building is a mongrel product of several builds. The Earl of Bute employed Robert Adam to rebuild an older house here in the 1760s. In about 1820 the house was altered by Sir Robert Smirke, who also added the portico on the entrance front. Fire gutted the building in 1843 and it was reconstructed by Sidney Smirke. When Sir Julius Wernher purchased Luton Hoo in 1903 he employed the firm of Mewès and Davies, architects of the Ritz Hotel, to redecorate the house again. They also gave the building a new roof. The white marble staircase is one of their best efforts, and the Dining Room, faced with marble and hung with Beauvais tapestries, is typical of their rich Beaux Arts style. After World War II half the house was converted into a private residence for the family, and this wing is now used for conferences and banquets; the rest of the house contains the art collections. There are beautiful French tapestries and furniture, and a series of small collections. Each is select enough not to tire the visitor who is unfamiliar with, for example, mediaeval ivories, Renaissance bronzes or salt-glazed pottery. There are important Old Master paintings and a large collection of English porcelain, but most stunning are the jewelled trinkets made by Fabergé. In the basement are photographs and relics of the Russian royal family. The large and noble park was landscaped by 'Capability' Brown, but the formal garden is later work by Romayne Walker. There is also a terraced rose garden on the only surviving Robert Adam front.

Opening times: 3 April to 10 Oct, Mon, Wed, Thurs and Sat 11–5.45, Sun 2–5.45 (garden 6).
Entrance charges: House and gardens £1.25; children 50p; gardens only 50p; children 25p. (HHA)
Parking: Free, near the house.
Wheelchair access: Six shallow steps to entrance, ground floor on the level, lift to the first floor and basement.
Guidebook: Good, but better on the collections than on the house itself, many colour illustrations, no plan. There is also a separate leaflet (10p) on the Russian collection.
Catering: The cafeteria in the basement is adequate; there is an unattractive picnic area behind the car park.
WCs: In the basement, near the cafeteria; unsuitable for wheelchairs.
Shop: On main floor.

WOBURN ABBEY nr Leighton Buzzard (Trustees of the Bedford Estate)
  Tel: Woburn (052 525) 666. Catering enquiries: Woburn 662
  Directions: 8 ½ miles N.W. of Dunstable, off the A528; M1 exit 12

The Duke of Bedford and his family have been in the stately homes business since 1955 and have turned Woburn into a thoroughly professional and commercial entertainment centre. The house is only one of the attractions. Before 1950 the house was in the form of a quadrangle, perhaps on the site of the cloister of the original Abbey. The north side is a 17th century building, the west side with its central pediment was added by Henry Flitcroft between 1747 and 1761, and the south side by Henry Holland in 1787. The east side was also by Holland, but it was pulled down in 1950, together with part of the north and south sides. Some of the outbuildings were destroyed at the same time. Despite these losses, Woburn is still interesting; the outside of the house is dignified and the interiors are sumptuous and contain many treasures. The house lacks an imposing main entrance or grand staircase. Visitors enter by the north wing, and follow a route through the rooms on the first floor of this wing and the state rooms on the west side. Most of the rooms have rich mid-18th century plaster ceilings, many of them picked out in gold, and some have their original wall coverings. The wallpaper in the Chinese Room of the north wing is particularly good. There is an excellent collection of paintings, including some fascinating 16th and 17th century portraits, works by Velasquez, Reynolds and the Dutch masters, and a notable collection of continental porcelain. Curiosities range from etchings by Queen Victoria to a miniature dinner service made for the Czar of Russia. There are guides in each room who will supplement the guide book if required. There is an extra charge for the private apartments (when open); they include the Canaletto Room and the Ante-Library, a fine room with good paintings. The Library is not open in the morning. Besides the house there are a number of curious outbuildings, including the lakeside Chinese Dairy, a Chinese pavilion in the centre of a maze, and the enormous park, which contains a wildlife centre.

Opening times: 1 Jan, Feb to Easter and Nov (closed Dec), Park 12–3.45, Abbey 1–4.45; Good Friday to end Oct, Park 10–4.45 (Sun 10–5.45), Abbey 11–5.45 (Sun 11–6.15). Last entry to Abbey 45 mins before closing time.

Entrance charges: Abbey and park, adults £2.00, children 5–16 and OAPs £1.00; family ticket for 2 adults and up to 4 children £5.25. Private apartments, adults and OAPs 30p; children 10p. Park only, cars and motorcycle combinations inc. passengers £1.50; motorcycles £1.00; pedestrians and cyclists 40p. (HHA)

Parking: Free parking, 200 yards from house.

Wheelchair access: No wheelchairs are allowed in the Abbey.

Guidebook: Large format with copious colour illustrations. It contains a detailed family history, a little architectural history and a room by room description of the house.

Catering: Buffet open from 10.30, Oak & Pine Restaurant open on Sun only from 12.00. There is also the Duke's Head pub. Banqueting facilities in the Sculpture Gallery. The picnic area is a delightful piece of parkland near the house.

WCs: Near the car park; suitable for wheelchairs; there are also lavatories at the entrance to the Abbey.

Shop: There are four shops, including an Olde English sweet shop, and a pottery with a sales section.

Extras: An extra charge is made for admission to the antique market, rides on the model train, and the fairground amusements (both open only in summer). The Safari Park costs

£4.60 for each car and its occupants; the price includes a guide book. Dogs must be left in the kennels at the entrance.

Berkshire

BASILDON PARK nr Pangbourne (The National Trust)
Tel: Pangbourne (073 57) 3040
Directions: 7 miles N.W. of Reading on the A329 between Pangbourne and Streatley

Sir Francis Sykes, who had made a great deal of money in India, began to build this elegant house on the slopes of the Thames Valley in 1776. Sir Francis came from Yorkshire and he employed a Yorkshire architect, John Carr, to design his new house. Basildon is one of Carr's best works and the excellent Bath stone has kept the ornament crisp. The house is nearly square with a portico in the centre of the entrance front, and a bay at the back, overlooking the garden. On either side of the main block are compact wings flanked by courtyards containing the kitchens, drying yards, and other necessary facilities.

As in most Palladian houses, the principal rooms are on the first floor. Twin staircases lead up from behind the low arches in the middle of the entrance front into the tall and airy space behind the portico, which makes an excellent introducton to the rest of the rooms. Much of the interior decoration is contemporary with the house; the hall, dining room and green drawing room have good plaster wall decoration of the 1770s. The octagon room in the centre of the garden front was not finished until 1840. Its heavy plaster ceiling and richly coloured wall (now red but originally purple) are surprisingly successful in this otherwise coolly classical house. At the centre of Basildon is the great staircase, best seen on a sunny day with the light streaming down from the roof. Basildon stood empty for 30 years before World War II and during the war it suffered the fate of many other houses in being requisitioned for military purposes. It was rescued from dereliction by Lord and Lady Iliffe, who brought in doors and fireplaces from Panton Hall in Lincolnshire (another house by Carr, now gone) and filled the rooms with 18th century pictures and furniture, much of it brought at post-war house sales. The bedrooms on the first floor are chiefly interesting for the furniture they contain, especially the Crimson Bedroom, with its magnificent bed from Ashburnham House and the Bamboo Room with its bed from Stoneleigh in Warwickshire. Visitors can wander at will around the edges of the principal rooms and into the bedrooms.

Opening times: April to end Oct, Wed to Sun, 2–6 (Oct 2–5), Bank Holiday Mon 11–6; closed Good Friday.
Entrance charges: £1.50; children 75p.

Parking: Free car park but with ¼ mile stiff uphill walk to the house.
Wheelchair access: The principal rooms are reached only by a winding staircase, the tea room and shop are on the ground floor.
Guidebook: Excellent value with a history of the house and its owners, a room-by-room guide, a plan and many black and white illustrations.
Catering: The tea room is on the ground floor, in what would have been the family entrance hall. An elegant setting for the sound National Trust teas.
WCs: Free and clean lavatories in one of the wings; also at the car park with facilities for wheelchairs.
Shop: On the ground floor, next to the tea room, sells sweets, jams, books, games and all the usual National Trust material.

DONNINGTON CASTLE nr Newbury (Ancient Monument)
Directions: 1½ miles N. of Newbury off the A34 in the village of Donnington

All that remains of Donnington Castle is a tall gatehouse with twin towers, standing on top of a grassy mound. The gatehouse was added to an existing building in 1386 as part of a programme of fortification carried out by Richard Abberbury, the owner of the house. It is possible that his architect was William de Wynford who also built New College, Oxford, and the nave of Winchester Cathedral. Donnington is one of those buildings which bridges the gap between proper castles and country houses; it was a comfortable residence inside walls of moderate thickness. The great time for the castle was during the English Civil War when Donnington was held for the King by John Boys; he and his men managed to hold out against the forces of Parliament for almost the whole of the war. The stone walls of the castle were flattened by artillery but Boys built elaborate earthworks which can still be seen on the side of the castle away from the gatehouse. By the time Boys surrendered in March 1646 there was not much left of his stronghold, and it has not been lived in since that time.

Opening times: Open at all reasonable times.
Entrance charges: Free.
Parking: Free car park about 100 yards from the castle.
Wheelchair access: This would be difficult; a rough track leads from the car park to the monument.
Guidebook: The Official Handbook to the Castle, which can be obtained from Donnington Post Office, contains a stirring account of the Civil War siege and a description of the gatehouse with a plan of the castle.
Catering: None.
WCs: None.
Shop: None.

SWALLOWFIELD PARK nr Reading (The Mutual Households Association
Tel: Reading (0734) 883815
Directions: 6 miles S. of Reading off the A33 on the edge of Swallowfield village

Swallowfield has a rather dull exterior of buff-coloured Roman cement but under this 19th century coating are the walls of a red brick house which was built for the second Earl of Clarendon in 1690. The architect was William Talman, who was then working on Chatsworth House in Derbyshire. The basic shape of Talman's house has not been altered, but the building changed hands several times in the 18th century and a number of alterations were made both inside and out. The red brick stables were probably added in 1717 and the house was given a major overhaul by the architect William Atkinson in the 1820s. He lowered the roof, changed the appearance of the east front, put in a new main staircase and covered the building with cement. He also removed Talman's elegant doorway into the house, which now stands by itself in the garden. In 1965 the house was converted into a number of flats, but the main downstairs rooms have been preserved. They function as common rooms for the occupants and contain few furnishings of special interest. The rooms have a 19th century appearance, with some plaster decoration which may date from 1690. There is also a very pretty little oval room, part of the original house, which has been restored to its original appearance. Visitors are conducted around by one of the tenants.

Opening times: May to Sept, Wed and Thurs, 2–5.
Entrance charges: 40p; children and OAPs 25p; no dogs.
Parking: Free parking in front of the house.
Wheelchair access: All rooms shown are on the ground floor and accessible to wheelchairs.
Guidebook: The free leaflet and the booklet contain exactly the same information about the architectural history.
Catering: None.
WCs: In the house; not for wheelchair users.
Shop: None.

WINDSOR CASTLE (H.M. The Queen)
Tel: The Superintendent, Windsor (075 35) 68286
Directions: In the centre of Windsor old town

The Castle at Windsor is the largest in England, covering nearly 13 acres. It is also one of the principal residences of the Queen and the 'home' of the Order of the Garter. The first castle on the site was set up by William the Conqueror in about 1070, on the edge of a steep slope down to the river Thames and with an excellent view over the surrounding countryside. His fortifications of earth and timber were replaced by stone buildings in about 1170 at the direction of King Henry II. In later years other major additions were made to the castle by Henry III, Edward III, Edward IV (who began St George's Chapel), Henry VIII and Charles II who rebuilt the State Apartments. The present appearance of the castle is mainly due to King George IV, who employed the architect Jeffry Wyatville to turn Windsor into a romantic place. The famous silhouette is the result of Wyatville's work and many of the walls and other buildings were either totally rebuilt or 'improved' by him.

The castle is divided into three sections or 'wards'. The public entrance leads into the lower ward, which contains St George's Chapel and a maze of cloisters and domestic buildings, only a few of which are open to the public. The middle ward was the defensive heart of the castle and contains the famous round tower (not open to the public). The bottom half of the tower dates from about 1170 but the top 33 feet were added by Jeffry Wyatville, to prevent the old keep being dwarfed by his other new buildings. The upper ward is a large quadragle with buildings on three sides. To the north are the state apartments, i.e. the main ceremonial rooms, which are usually open to the public. On the south and east sides are the private apartments of the Royal Family, which are never open, nor it is usually possible to see the outside of these ranges, except from a distance. The state apartments have been in their present position for 800 years and a good deal of the mediaeval and 17th century buildings still survive, but the older work is hidden underneath Wyatville's Gothic of 1830. After the entrance hall one ascends the grand staircase of 1866 to a series of large and rather dull rooms decorated in the 19th century, but re-using bits of 17th century carving. There are some excellent paintings, especially in the Waterloo Chamber, but it is often difficult to see them properly because of the crowds of visitors and the roped-off walkways. After the great rooms come the King's and Queen's private apartments, which are a little smaller and jollier, especially the King's Dining Room with its wall paintings and carved woodwork.

Opening times: Castle precincts: open daily from 10; closes 5.15 (mid-March to 30 April & 1 Sept to late Oct), 7.15 (late Oct to mid-March); closed Mon 15 June.

Hours of opening of Castle buildings (except as stated below): late Oct to mid-March, weekdays 1.30–3, closed Sun; mid-March to late Oct, weekdays 10.30–5, Sun (10 May–18 Oct) 1.30–5.

The State Apartments will be *closed* as follows: Main rooms 1 Jan, mid-March to June, Dec. Queen Mary's Dolls' House 1 Jan, 17 April, 18 June, 25–26 Dec. Exhibition of Drawings 1 Jan, 17 April, 15 June, 25–26 Dec.

The Castle is always subject to closure, sometimes at short notice.

Entrance charges: Precincts free. State Apartments £1.00; children and OAPs 50p. Queen Mary's Dolls' House 40p; children and OAPs 10p. Drawings 40p; children and OAPs 10p. St George's Chapel 80p; children and OAPs 30p.

Parking: There is no car park for visitors. Limited on-street parking is available near the castle and there are several car parks in the town.

Wheelchair access: Access to the precincts is straightforward. Access to the State Apartments can be arranged with the staff of the ticket office in the North Terrace.

Guidebook: The elderly official guidebook is good value and contains a reliable history, a room-by-room guide of the State Apartments and information on other parts of the castle which are open. The handlist of pictures is very out of date. There are sound-guides in several languages which may be hired at the entrance to the State Apartments.

Catering: None within the castle.

WCs: On the North Terrace.

Shop: In the Lower Ward sells books, slides, postcards and souvenirs.

Extras: St George's Chapel, one of the most famous examples of the late mediaeval 'Perpendicular' style. Begun in 1475 by Edward IV and not completed until 1511. The chapel has been substantially restored since the 19th century.

Queen Mary's Dolls' House, a huge elaborate minature palace, designed by Sir Edwin Lutyens and given to Queen Mary in 1923. There is also a collection of dolls and miniature pieces, and other toys.

Exhibition of Drawings, some superb drawings from the Royal Collection, especially those by Holbein.

Buckinghamshire

ASCOTT   nr Wing (The National Trust)
Tel: Wing (029 668) 242
Directions: 2 miles S.W. of Leighton Buzzard, ½ mile E. of Wing on the S. side of the A418

Ascott is one of several Buckinghamshire houses which belonged to the Rothschilds (Waddesdon and Mentmore are the others) and architecturally it is the least interesting. The original small farmhouse of 1606 has been completely swamped by the half-timbered additions made in 1874 (by George Devey) and in 1938. The interior was completely redecorated in the 1930s for Anthony de Rothschild and it is his superb art collection that makes the house worth visiting. The rooms on the ground floor which contain the collection are laid out like a elegant museum and almost everything can be examined from close range. The strength of the collection lies in Dutch 17th century paintings, richly-coloured Chinese porcelain dating from 1400 to 1700, 18th century French furniture and a small but very good collection of 18th and 19th century English paintings. All this excellence attracts many visitors and the house is usually full. Tickets have a printed entry time, so visitors may have to wait in the large garden, which is a fine example of late 19th century planting, with many specimen trees and also a superb view of the countryside of the Vale of Aylesbury.

Opening times: April to end Sept, Wed and Thurs, also Sat in Aug and Sept and Mon 30 Aug 2-6; last admission 5.30.
Entrance charges: House and grounds £1.80; children £1.30. Grounds only £1.00; children 50p.
Parking: Free car park at the entrance to the grounds, which is some distance from the house. Disabled visitors may drive to the door.
Wheelchair access: All the rooms open are on the ground floor; there are a few shallow steps; part of the garden is also accessible.
Guidebook: A detailed catalogue to the collection with a few paragraphs about the house and garden.
Catering: None.
WCs: In the garden near the house; unsuitable for wheelchairs.
Shop: None.

CHENIES MANOR HOUSE Chenies (Lt Col and Mrs Macleod Matthews)
Tel: Little Chalfont (024 04) 2888
Directions: 4 miles N.W. of Rickmansworth, off the B484 in Chenies village

The village has that trim uniform appearance which suggests a rich landlord. Until fairly recently the owners of Chenies were the Russell family, better known as the Dukes of Bedford. John Russell bought the estate in about 1530 and enlarged the house so that he could entertain Henry VIII and his court. What now remains is one long brick range and a shorter gabled range set at right angles to it which the guides call the great hall, but which looks more like a gatehouse. The original layout of the house is still a puzzle, it seems. The guided tours take in three ground floor rooms, a good 16th century staircase, and most of the first floor rooms. Some of the downstairs rooms have a Victorian appearance for not only are many of the fittings and decorations of that period, but much of the present owners' furniture is 19th century too. The upstairs rooms in the long south range were intended as a series of apartments for visitors, and each one has a dark little closet opening off it in the thickness of the chimneystack. The tours take about half an hour. There is a pleasant garden, from which one gets a good view of the back of the south range, with its six massive chimney breasts and their magnificent Tudor brick shafts.

Opening times: April to end Oct, Wed and Thurs 2–5, also Spring and Summer Bank Holidays 2–6.
Entrance charges: (1981) £1.00; children 50p.
Parking: Free parking in the approach to the house, outside the church.
Wheelchair access: Might be possible to the downstairs rooms, but the best things are inaccessible upstairs; garden accessible.
Guidebook: A brief illustrated history and description which duplicates what the guides tell visitors during the tour of the house.
Catering: Tea by the cup and home made biscuits or cake served in a ground floor room.
WCs: In the outbuildings, adequate but unsuitable for wheelchairs.
Shop: There is a small souvenir shop in the last upstairs room visited.

CHICHELEY HALL nr Newport Pagnell (Trustees of the Hon Nicholas Beatty)
Tel: North Crawley (023 065) 252 or 336
Directions: 2 miles N.E. of Newport Pagnell on the A422

Chicheley's main front is one of the best surviving examples of the English Baroque style. It is built of the red brick typical of the eary 18th century and the main cornice is swept up to make room for a richly carved frieze over the three central bays, which have round headed windows. The door has a wild-looking pediment. Chicheley was built between 1719 and 1723. The architect was Francis Smith of Warwick, but the owner, Sir John Chester, may have taken a part. Each side of the house is different and many of the windows still have their original glass and thick glazing bars. The front door leads directly to the entrance hall, designed by Henry Flitcroft in 1722 with a triple-arched screen opening onto the staircase. Visitors are guided in tours which take about an hour. The main rooms are intimate in scale and many have good original ceilings and panelling; the furniture is a mixture of comfortable modern sofas and chairs and older pieces. The present occupants are the descendants of the famous naval commander Earl Beatty, and the study contains many things connected with his career, as does the naval museum on the second floor. In the 18th century one of the second floor rooms was fitted out as an ingenious library, in which all the books were completely hidden from view behind hinged panelling. Like most houses of its date, Chicheley exudes a comfortable feeling, which is taken up in the straightforward lawns and herbaceous borders of the garden.

Opening times: Good Friday to 27 Sept, Sun and Bank Holidays, 2.30–6.
Entrance charges: £1.30; children 65p; OAPs £1.00 (HHA).
Parking: Free parking in the stable yard.
Wheelchair access: All the ground floor rooms are accessible; the garden presents no problem.
Guidebook: A brief but accurate history of the building with a room by room guide.
Catering: A small clean room in the stable block serves cups of tea and commercial cakes etc.
WCs: Ladies' in the house, basic gents' next to the stable. There is a separate W.C. in the house which is suitable for wheelchair users.
Shop: In the stable block, a sizeable stock of tea towels, jams, recipe books and souvenirs.

CLAYDON HOUSE Middle Claydon (The National Trust)
Tel: Steeple Claydon (029 673) 349
Directions: 13 miles N.W. of Aylesbury, 3½ miles of S.W. of Winslow, near Middle Claydon village, signposted locally

Claydon is the seat of the Verney family, who still live in the rear part of the house. The second Earl Verney was a colourful character (his coach was always accompanied by two negroes blowing silver trumpets) and he was fond of building. In 1754 he began a huge new house, to be built in front of the old brick manor house. The first part to be finished contained four main rooms and a grand staircase, but then, with the help of the gentleman-architect Sir Thomas Robinson, Lord Verney went on to add a huge rotunda with a ballroom beyond it. He went bankrupt in 1783, most of the contents of the house were sold, and the rotunda and ballroom were pulled down in 1792. Only the west end of the house survives. The exterior is elegant, but the interior has some of the most extravagant decoration in England. Lord Verney's carpenter, Luke Lightfoot, set out to make Claydon 'such a Work as the World never saw'. In the four main ground floor rooms Lightfoot decorated the doors, windows, chimneys, walls and even the ceilings with lavish carved rococo ornament, executed with the greatest skill. The rooms upstairs received similar treatment. In the Chinese room the decoration of the pagoda-like alcove and doors fills an entire wall. The famous parquetry staircase, beautifully constructed by Lightfoot and with a wrought iron balustrade so delicate that its gilded husks of corn rustle as one goes up or down, can be seen but is too fragile for daily use. There is a new and stronger back staircase. The ground floor rooms are large, and can seem bare despite their furnishings; the walls have new coverings in something like the original colours. The smaller rooms upstairs seem cosier. Some are used to exhibit a collection of oriental musical instruments and material about the Verneys and Florence Nightingale, who was related to the family by marriage and spent much time at Claydon. Her bedroom is one of the rooms on view. There are no guided tours, but there are guides on hand to answer questions. Outside the house the 18th century landscaped grounds are used as farmland, but they provide a peaceful setting.

Opening times: April to end Oct, daily except Thurs and Fri, 2–6 or sunset, Bank Holiday Mon 12.30–6; last entry 5.30.
Entrance charges: £1.20; children 60p.
Parking: Free parking next to the house.
Wheelchair access: Possible to the ground floor rooms and the staircase. Also to the tea room.
Guidebook: A history and room-by-room guide with illustrations and a plan.
Catering: The tea room is now under new management and greatly improved.
WCs: In the outbuildings, free; there are facilities for wheelchair users.
Shop: Only a small selection of National Trust goods.

CLIVEDEN HOUSE nr Maidenhead (The National Trust)
Tel: The Administrator, Burnham (062 86) 5069: shop and restaurant Burnham 61406
Directions: On the N. bank of the Thames, 3 miles upstream from Maidenhead, 2 miles N. of Taplow on the B476

Most of Cliveden's owners have been very rich. The first house on this magnificent site by the river was built in the 1660s for the Second Duke of Buckingham. It was burnt down in 1795, rebuilt and burnt again in 1849. The present house was built in 1850 by the architect Charles Barry for the Duke of Sutherland, one of Britain's richest men. It passed from him to the Duke of Westminster and finally, in 1893, to William Waldorf Astor, the American millionaire. Barry designed the house in the 16th century Italianate style and coated the outside with cement render to match the small wings left over from the first house. On one side is a large stable courtyard with an enormous clock tower built in 1861. The interior of the house was completely refitted for William Astor in the 1890s by J.L. Pearson. Cliveden is now used by an American college and only four rooms are open to the public. Of these, the best have fittings which were imported from France: The long dark entrance hall which serves as a sitting room has a huge French 16th century stone chimney piece and the dining room is lined with carved

Cliveden House, Buckinghamshire

rococo panelling of about 1750, which Astor bought from the Château d'Asnières near Paris. The plaster ceiling is a copy of an original which is still at Asnières and the furniture and mirrors were made to suit the room. The large and small libraries beyond the dining room are of less interest, though they have splendid views. The grounds are magnificent. There are formal gardens on both sides of the house, studded with the antique sculpture which William Astor bought in Italy. Beyond the garden stretches the park, laid out and planted in the early 18th century and now fully mature. The whole park is open to visitors, and a walk including Canning's Oak with its famous view of the Thames is recommended.

Opening times: Grounds all year, daily 11–6.30; House April to end Oct, Sat and Sun 2.30–5.30; last admission 5.00.

Entrance charges: House and grounds £1.50; children 75p. Grounds only £1.30 and 65p.

Parking: Lage free car park inside the grounds but about ½ mile from the house.

Wheelchair access: Disabled visitors may drive to the house; all rooms shown are easily accessible, as well as the shop and tea room.

Guidebook: A very full guide, mainly concerned with the grounds, but covering the history of the house; many illustrations and plan of the grounds.

Catering: Large tea room in the old conservatory, which can get extremely hot in full summer. Self-service, morning coffee, lunches and teas.

WCs: In the car park with facilities for wheelchair users; secondary facilities adjoining the tea room.

Shop: At one end of the tea room is a large shop selling the complete National Trust range.

DORNEY COURT   Dorney, nr Windsor
Tel: Burnham (062 86) 4638
Directions: 2 miles W. of Eton, off the B3026; the approach is tricky because the house lies between the river and the M4 and is difficult to locate

It is said that the first English pineapple was grown at Dorney Court and presented to King Charles II in 1661. The Palmers of Dorney also supplied Charles with his favourite mistress, who became Duchess of Cleveland. The house itself dates originally from about 1500. At first sight it looks almost too good to be true – a rambling building of mellow red brick and old beams with irregular roofs and plenty of gables, all set in an English garden with box hedges and herbaceous plants. Some of the present exterior is, in fact, Victorian; it was reconstructed when a classical front was removed in the last century, but old materials were re-used wherever possible and behind the façade the late mediaeval house survives more or less intact. The principal rooms are the dark panelled parlour on the ground floor, the great chamber on the first floor, now a bedroom, and the great hall, which is hung with an impressive collection of family portraits. The furniture in these and the lesser rooms on show is a fine and varied mixture of 17th and 18th century work; some of it is slightly battered and some of the decoration is slightly dingy but this all contributes to the 'lived-in' feeling of the house. Visitors make their own way round and there are guides on hand in most rooms. At the end of the prescribed route is the dining room, an elegant early Georgian panelled interior, nothing like the other rooms in the house and a piquant reminder of the 18th century.

Opening times: Good Friday to Easter Mon (9–12 April); 18 April – 24 Oct, Sun and Bank Holiday Mon; also Mon and Tues 31 May – 28 Sept, 2–5.30.
Entrance charges: £1.50; children 80p.
Parking: Free parking on grass near the house.
Wheelchair access: Disabled visitors may park by the house; access is possible to the ground floor rooms; gravel paths in the garden.
Guidebook: A jolly little book with much family history, not a great deal of information about the house itself, colour pictures, no plan.
Catering: A small and cheerful tea room in the house.
WCs: In the house; not suitable for wheelchair users.
Shop: A small shop selling some pretty souvenirs and local honey (Dorney means 'Island of Bees') and home-grown vegetables.

DORTON HOUSE nr Brill (Ashford School Trust Ltd)
Tel: Brill (0844) 238 237
Directions: 11 miles W. of Aylesbury, 6 miles N. of Thame on the edge of Dorton village; not signposted

Dorton is a large Jacobean house built of pleasant red brick, with long wings projecting on either side of the entrance front. Some alterations were made in the 1780s when many of the mullioned windows were replaced with wide sashes, but the interior still has many original features. The house is now used as a school. The front door leads into a screens passage and thence to the hall, which had a good early carved screen and fireplace. There are two original staircases; the larger has the date 1626 in the plaster decoration. Two of the upstairs rooms have decorated plaster ceilings of the same period and the north wing contains a long gallery, now converted into dormitories.

Opening times: May to July and Sept, Sat and Sun 2–5, but closed 30 May to 3 June.
Entrance charges: (1981) 25p; children free.
Parking: Free parking next to the house.
Wheelchair access: Flight of steps to front door, but a enthusiast could see the hall and main staircase.
Guidebook: None.
Catering: Tea is available during term time only in the house.
WCs: In the house.
Shop: None.

HUGHENDEN MANOR nr High Wycombe (The National Trust)
Tel: High Wycombe (0494) 32580
Directions: 1½ miles N. of High Wycombe on the W. side of the A4128 to Gt Missenden

The house at Hughenden is most interesting as a Tory party shrine.

Benjamin Disraeli, Earl of Beaconsfield, Prime Minister from 1874–80, lived here for the last 33 years of his life. When Disraeli bought Hughenden it was a plain late 18th century house set at the top of a beautiful sloping park. In 1862 his wife set about making improvements. With the help of the architect E.B. Lamb she gave the house a thoroughly Victorian red brick skin. Many of the rooms were redone in a Gothic style, perhaps to conjure up the Good Old Days of the Middle Ages. Some of the downstairs rooms still contain pictures and furniture which belonged to the Disraelis, arranged as though the family were still in occupation, but the house is really a museum of Lord Beaconsfield's life and career. There are pictures of all his allies and friends, including Queen Victoria, as well as trinkets, letters and locks of hair. Visitors have free run of most of the house. The rooms are rather small and it is best to avoid the weekend crowds. The park is still very attractive; the garden next to the house is planted with bedding plants in the correct Victorian way; the plants are changed thrice yearly.

Opening times: April to end Oct, house and garden Wed to Sat 2–6, Suns and Bank Holiday Mon 12.30–6 or sunset (closed Good Friday and 26 April); March and Nov, Sat and Sun 2–5 or sunset. Last admission ½ hour before closing.

Entrance charges: £1.30; children 65p.

Parking: Free car park to one side of the house, near the shop.

Wheelchair access: Possible to all ground floor rooms, which are the most rewarding; disabled visitors may be driven to the front door.

Guidebook: Contains a brief history and a description of each room, but is mainly a catalogue of the exhibits. There is also a braille information sheet.

Catering: Tea and biscuits are served upstairs in the house on Sat, Sun and Bank Holidays.

WCs: Hidden away on the upper floor of the house; totally inadequate for the usual weekend rush.

Shop: Quite a good version of the standard National Trust shop upstairs in the stables.

MENTMORE   (The World Government of the Age of Enlightenment)

Tel: Cheddington (0296) 668008

Directions: 7 miles N.E. of Aylesbury, 5 miles of Leighton Buzzard, near Mentmore village

The recent history of Mentmore has been colourful. The entire contents were sold at a famous auction in 1977 and raised several million pounds. The house is now the British Seat of World Government of the Age of Enlightenment, the organisation dedicated to creating an ideal society through the Transcendental Meditation and TM-Sidhi programme founded by His Holiness Maharishi Mahesh Yogi. Originally one of the mansions of the wealthy Rothschild family, it was built in 1852–4 for Baron Meyer de Rothschild. The architect was Joseph Paxton, who designed the Crystal Palace. Paxton used the Jacobean style and Mentmore is partly a copy of Wollaton hall in Nottinghamshire. It has the same large corner towers, the same carved decoration, and is built of the same Ancaster stone. The rooms are arranged round a huge central hall which contains the large black and white marble fireplace brought from Rubens' house in Antwerp. The decoration of all the main ground floor rooms is very rich, with plenty of gilding. The dining room has gilded carved ornament brought from the Hôtel de Villars in Paris. The rooms have recently been redecorated and renovated. One contains the mattresses on which the meditators practise the TM-Sidhi technique for levitation. The guided tours, conducted by immensely polite young men last about one hour and take in most of the main rooms, the first floor gallery round the hall, and finish with a visit to the servants' rooms where visitors are given a short lecture on current scientific research into Transcendental Meditation.

Opening times: 4 April to 17 Oct, Wed, Sun and Bank Holidays 1–5, last admission 4 30; rest of year Sun 1–4.
Entrance charges: House and grounds £1.50, children half price. (HHA)
Parking: Free parking near the house.
Wheelchair access: There is a flight of steps up to the hall, but from there the main rooms could be reached easily.
Guidebook: None at present, apart from a small free hand-out.
Catering: Teas by the cup and home-made cakes and biscuits served in a small room by the entrance. In summer home-made cream teas served in former conservatory with fine views over the Vale of Aylesbury.
WCs: Inside the house, very acceptable, but unsuitable for wheelchairs.
Shop: Sells literature about Transcendental Meditation, home-made confectionery, and giftware.

MILTON'S COTTAGE Chalfont St Giles
Tel: Chalfont St Giles (024 07) 2313
Directions: 3 miles N. of Gerrards Cross off the A413 in Chalfont St Giles village

This timber and brick cottage, of which the oldest parts date back to the late 16th century, was lent to the poet John Milton in 1665 as a refuge from the Great Plague which was then raging in London. Whilst here, Milton finished his great poem 'Paradise Lost' and on this account the cottage was purchased by subscription in 1887 and dedicated to his memory. After an introductory talk by the curator, who goes out of his way to interest children, visitors may see two small rooms on the ground floor. One contains a miscellaneous collection of old things, the other has portraits and busts of Milton, books by him (including a first edition of *Paradise Lost*) and by his Quaker friends and, inevitably, a lock of his hair. There is a small pretty garden which is densely packed with English flowers.

Opening times: Feb to Oct, Tues to Sat 10–1 and 2–6, Sun 2–6. Nov weekends only.
Entrance charges: 50p; children 15p.
Parking: No car park, there is a limited amount of space at the roadside nearby.
Wheelchair access: Two steps down into the cottage, otherwise no difficulty except lack of space.
Guidebook: A small booklet about the poet, the house and the museum.
Catering: None.

WCs: None.
Shop: Milton souvenirs, including reprints of some of the books, are sold in one of the rooms.

NETHER WINCHENDON HOUSE   (Mrs John Spencer Bernard)
Tel: Haddenham (0844) 290101
Directions: 6 miles S.W. of Aylesbury, 4 miles N.E. of Thames, 1 mile N. of the A418 in Lower Wichendon village; the house is reached by a dead end road

The house and its picturesque village lie deep in the country. The first impression is of a screen of grey arches, with a red brick courtyard and Tudor chimneys behind. The screen itself and the battlements and windows of the courtyard date from about 1796, and are part of the Gothick improvements carried out by Scrope Bernard. There are more Gothick windows and battlements on the garden front which is haphazard in appearance but extremely pretty. Beneath these ornaments is a mediaeval house with Tudor alterations, once owned by the nearby Abbey of Notley. The old house had a walled front courtyard, with square corner towers which survive, although altered and petrified. The house is still occupied by the Bernards and visitors are guided round the main ground floor rooms by a member of the family. The first room is the entrance hall, added by Scrope Bernard in about 1800, and now containing a selection of the many charters relating to the house. Next is the drawing room, an addition made to the mediaeval house in Tudor times by Sir John Daunce. Its walls are lined with linenfold panelling, painted white; Sir John's portrait and initials form part of the decoration of the frieze, carved in about 1530. The great hall of the mediaeval house is now the family dining room; it has later panelling and a Georgian Gothick ceiling. The fine 16th century fireplace was probably brought from elsewhere. All four of the rooms shown are in daily occupation. Much of the furniture dates from the 18th century or earlier and there is a good selection of family portraits from the same period. The gardens, sloping down to the river Thame, have been replanted in recent years.

Opening times: May to Aug, Thurs, also Bank Holiday weekends, Sat, Sun and Mon; second Sat and Sun in June; first Sat and Sun in July; 2.30–5.30.
Entrance charges: £1.00; children under 12 50p; OAPs 50p on Thurs. (HHA)
Parking: Limited parking next to the house, or in the road outside.
Wheelchair access: Possible to all rooms; one or two steps inside.
Guidebook: Mainly a history of the owners with some description of the main contents; little is known about the history of the building.
Catering: None.
WCs: None.
Shop: None.

Nether Winchendon House, Buckinghamshire

WADDESDON MANOR Waddesdon (The National Trust)
Tel: Waddesdon (029 665) 211 or 282
Directions: 5 miles N.W. of Aylesbury on the A41; main entrance in Waddesdon village

Waddesdon is formidable, in both the English and French senses of the word. Baron Ferdinand de Rothschild bought the hillside in 1874; he levelled the ground, planted the woods and employed Hippolyte Destailleur to design him a large château in the French 16th century style. The exterior is a powerful mixture of French elements, copied from Blois, Chambord and elsewhere, with tall roofs, towers and chimneys. the interior contains some of the best French rooms outside France. Many of the main ground floor rooms have genuine 18th century boiseries (carved wooden decoration) brought from various French houses and skilfully refitted here by Destailleur. These dark-coloured richly-decorated rooms contain collections of 18th century French furniture, carpets, porcelain, sculpture and other art objects of the very highest quality. There are also 17th century Dutch and 18th century English paintings, all by the best painters of the time. Almost the whole house is open and some of the upstairs rooms contain more specialized collections, including musical instruments and costume, all well displayed by the National Trust. Visitors are given a brief introduction to the house in the first two rooms then left to wander through the house as they like; this is an excellent arrangement which more houses should follow. The only criticism is that it is difficult to see some smaller items, like the Clodion terra-cotta busts, either because they are too far from the rope barrier or because the light is not good enough where the curtains are drawn to preserve the colour of fabrics. There is a large park with a herd of deer, some formal gardens, fine trees and continental statuary, an elaborate aviary and a play area for young children, who are barred from the house under 12 years of age.

Opening times: 24 March to 31 Oct, House Wed to Sun 2–6; grounds Wed to Sat 1–6, Sun 11.30–6, Good Friday and Bank Holiday Mon, House and gardens 11–6, but both closed Wed after Bank Holidays.
Entrance charges: House, grounds and aviary £1.50, including Good Friday and Bank Holiday Mons; children 12–17 75p; Fri (extra rooms shown) £2.00; no reductions. No children under 12 in house. Grounds and aviary only 60p; children under 12 25p.
Parking: Free parking off the approach, close to the front of the house.
Wheelchair access: Some steps to entrance (stewards will assist) then all ground floor rooms accessible; these contain the cream of the collection. The tea shop is also accessible.
Guidebook: Contains a good plan of the house and a few words of history; otherwise it is entirely concerned with the contents of the rooms. Some of the collections are fully catalogued in separate publications.
Catering: Tea room in the ground floor of the bachelor's wing; waitress service, tea by the pot.
WCs: Near the tea rooms, free; suitable for wheelchairs.
Shop: There are two counters in the house selling books, slides and souvenirs: plants and other produce from the estate on sale near the tea rom.

WEST WYCOMBE PARK (The National Trust)
Tel: High Wycombe (0494) 24411
Directions: 3 miles W. of High Wycombe, off the A40 in West Wycombe
   village

The first Sir Francis Dashwood built himself the small brick house which
forms the core of the present building soon after 1698. His son, another Sir
Francis, spent much of his youth touring the Continent. He was one of the
founders of the Society of Dilettanti, dedicated to the study of Classical
Antiquity, but he is better known as the founder of a Hell Fire Club dedicated to drinking and whoring. He was always adding to the house and
park, and employed a series of architects and artists. Each front of the house
is different; the north is Palladian, the east has a Doric portico, the south
has a long two-storey colonnade, probably inspired by Palladio's Palazzo
Chiericati at Vicenza. These fronts date from the 1750s and were designed
by an obscure architect called John Donowell. The west front has a severe
Greek portico of 1771 by Nicholas Revett, which was copied from the Temple of Bacchus at Teos. The entrance for visitors is through the colonnade
on the south front. Most of the rooms on the ground floor are included in the
guided tour and on Sundays visitors are free to wander as they please. The
styles inside are as mixed as the outside. The hall and dining room are
painted to imitate various different coloured marbles in the neo-classical
fashion and are of the same date as the west front. The Red Drawing room
has slightly less formal decoration of the 1760s and the Saloon, Blue Drawing room and music room all have overpowering painted ceilings in the
Baroque taste by Guisseppe and Giovanni Borgnis, who came over from
Italy in the 1750s. Most of the paintings collected in Italy by Sir Francis
seem to be copies by lesser artists. The furniture is almost entirely 18th century English and includes some very fine commodes by Langlois. The park
is quite small and very prettily laid out round a lake, with a scattering of
18th century garden buildings including the Temple of the Winds,
Daphne's Temple and the Temple of Venus, which is being reconstructed.

Opening times: House and grounds, June, Mon to Fri 2.15–6, July and Aug daily except Sat
   2.15–6. Grounds only open Easter and Spring Bank Holiday Sun and Mon 2.15–6.
Entrance charges: House and grounds £1.60; children 80p. Grounds only 60p, no reduc-
   tions.
Parking: Car park inside entrance gate, about ¼ mile from the house.
Wheelchair access: House considered 'unsuitable for wheelchairs'; the park is mostly grass.
Guidebook: An excellent booklet with history, room-by-room guide, many illustrations and
   plans of house and grounds.
Catering: None.
WCs: Gents' in the stable block facing the south lawn, ladies' beneath portico of east front
   neither suitable for wheelchairs.
Shop: None.
Extras: Across the valley from the house are the church with its golden ball, the mausoleum
   built by Sir Francis and also the Hell Fire Caves, now a commercial thrill with separate en-
   trance charge.

WINSLOW HALL Winslow (Sir Edward and Lady Tomkins)
Tel: The Administrator, Winslow (029 671) 2323
Directions: Winslow is 9 miles N.W. of Aylesbury on the A413; the house is on the edge of the town

Winslow is probably one of the very few houses by Sir Christopher Wren, the architect of St Paul's Cathedral. It was built in 1700 for William Lowndes, Secretary to the Treasury. Some of the best craftsmen in London were employed on the brickwork and carpentry, but Winslow is quite a modest building. It is more a town than a country house, built of brown and red brick, only seven windows wide and with a fairly small garden. The two main fronts are tall, and made to seem even taller by their steep pediments and the four enormous chimneys lined up along the roof. The plan is simple; chimneys in the middle, rooms all round and staircases at each end. Most of the rooms have their original panelling some of it painted, and original chimneypieces. The walls of the one of the first floor rooms are covered with engagingly clumsy murals. The mixture of comfortable armchairs and more distinguished furniture and paintings complements the sensible plan of the building. The tours include the ground floor and most of the first floor rooms and are conducted by the owners, who are happy to show the original building accounts, corrected by Wren himself. The garden is beautifully kept.

Opening times: July, Aug and Sept, daily except Mon, also Bank Holiday Mon except Boxing Day, 2.30–5.30.
Entrance charges: 75p; children under 12 free. (HHA).
Parking: Free parking next to the house, or in a large lay-by in the road outside.
Wheelchair access: Possible to all the ground floor rooms, about ⅔ of the tour.
Guidebook: None yet.
Catering: A cup of tea and fresh scones and cakes cost 75p in 1981.
WCs: In the house by the front door, clean and spacious; not suitable for wheelchairs.
Shop: A small selection of souvenirs; there are usually plants from the garden as well.

Cambridgeshire

ANGLESEY ABBEY Lode, nr Cambridge (The National Trust)
Tel: Cambridge (0223) 811200
Directions: 6 miles N.E. of Cambridge on the B1102 in the village of Lode

Anglesey Abbey was originally a house of Augustinian monks, which was founded in the 12th century and thrived until the mid-16th century, when most of the buildings were destroyed. In the early 17th century the remains were acquired by Thomas Hobson (who gave us the phrase 'Hobson's choice'). He adapted the old buildings into a mansion and it was probably

Hobson who added the south front with its five gables and mullioned windows (not accessible to visitors). The house was later owned by Sir George Downing, whose estate financed Downing College in Cambridge. The house was restored in 1861 but the larger part of the present house is the result of alterations carried out between 1926 and 1938 by the architect Sidney Pavin for Lord Fairhaven. He added a fourth bay to the common room, a new library and a picture gallery. The house contains a very diverse collection of *objets d'art*, a reflection of Lord Fairhaven's cosmopolitan upbringing and cultivated taste, and for most visitors the collection will be of much more interest than the house. Lord Fairhaven's greatest contribution to Anglesey was the laying out of the grounds, which are on a grand scale rare in the 20th century and have now reached a mature state. There are a number of smaller gardens linked by avenues, giving long vistas enlivened with sudden surprises.

Opening times: House and gardens, 1 April to 10 Oct, Wed, Thurs, Fri, Sat, Sun and Bank Holidays, 2–6. Gardens only 24 May to 5 Oct, daily, 2–6; closed Good Friday and Easter Mon.

Entrance charges: House and gardens £1.40; children (5–17) 70p. Gardens 80p; children 40p; no dogs.

Parking: Free and ample, 400 yards from the house.

Wheelchair access: Wheelchairs are provided at the entrance gate, but only the first three rooms of the house are easily accessible. The paths in the grounds mostly have reasonable surfaces.

Guidebook: Very little on the history and architecture, a confusing plan showing the monastery buildings but not the present house and a full description of the collections, room by room, and the gardens.

Catering: Tea room by the car park with an ample lawn outside; home-made cakes and cream teas.

WCs: Near the car park; facilities for wheelchair users.

Shop: A large modern shop with the full National Trust range.

BURGHLEY HOUSE Stamford (The Marquess of Exeter)
Tel: Stamford (0780) 52451
Directions: 1 mile E. of Stamford, off the B1443

Burghley was one of four houses built for William Cecil, who was Chief Secretary of State and Principal Adviser to Queen Elizabeth I. It was meant for show, and the enormous stone palace, with its fantastic silhouette of towers and chimneys, is an unforgettable sight. Building work began in the 1550s, broke off in the 1560s while Cecil attended to one of his other houses, and was completed by about 1587. The house is built round a courtyard with the great hall and kitchen on the east side, and the other principal living rooms on the first floors of the other three sides. Visitors can see the exterior of the south and west sides of the house from a distance. A brief glimpse of the great courtyard, which is an important example of Elizabethan architecture, may be had from the ante-chapel inside the building. The tour starts in

Burghley House, Cambridgeshire

the great kitchen, with its array of cooking pots, and continues up the Roman Staircase to the chapel, which has some pretty woodcarving, perhaps by Grinling Gibbons. From here the route takes in all the main rooms on the north, west and south fronts, before returning to the great hall on the east. The interiors were extensively redecorated in the 1680s by the 5th Earl of Exeter, probably with the help of the architect William Talman. The long gallery on the west side was converted into a series of smaller rooms with panelling and ornamental plaster ceilings. The south side contains the State Rooms, whose ceilings are covered with late 17th century paintings by Antonio Verrio. The climax is reached in the Heaven Room where the paintings completely cover the walls and ceiling. The Cecils still live at Burghley and their collection of furniture is excellent, but most astonishing is the very large number of paintings in every room. All the paintings are numbered and there is a complete picture list in the *old* guide book to the house, which is still on sale. This list is indispensable on Sundays and Bank Holidays when there are no guided tours, and these are the best days for picture-lovers. The large park was landscaped by 'Capability' Brown.

Opening times: 1 April to 3 Oct, Tues, Wed, Thurs, Sat and Bank Holidays 11–5; Good Friday and Sun 2–5.

Entrance charges: (1981) £1.35; children 60p; no dogs in house.

Parking: Free car park for visitors to the house, about 100 yards from the building. A charge is made for those not intending to visit the house.

Wheelchair access: Permitted but awkward; there are stairs to the first floor, all in straight flights. Access to the tea room presents no problems.

Guidebook: Either a glossy souvenir guide with many colour pictures and basic historical and room by room information or the cheaper, older booklet which is a little out of date with its information, but contains a full list of pictures. Translations of the souvenir guide are available in French, German and Italian.

Catering: In the Orangery which was designed by 'Capability' Brown, or on the lawn outside; waitress service or self-service, homemade cakes and tea by the cup.

WCs: In the courtyard, free but small; unsuitable for wheelchairs.

Shop: Souvenir kiosk in the outer courtyard and another in the Goody Rudkin museum close by.

Extras: The Goody Rudkin room in the outer courtyard is a museum of ancient charters and other material relating to the family (no charge).

HINCHINGBROOKE HOUSE Huntingdon (Hinchingbrooke School)
Tel: Huntingdom (0480) 51121
Directions: ½ mile W. of Huntingdon on the A604

Horace Walpole described Hinchingbrooke as 'old, spacious and irregular' which sums up very well this rambling house of brick and stone formed out of the ruins of a small Benedictine nunnery. After the nuns had left, Richard Cromwell acquired the property in 1538 and began the work of converting the buildings into a house. His son Henry added the north range which contains the main entrance and the service wing next to the dining room. He also brought the mediaeval gatehouse from Ramsey Abbey to make a suitable entrance to his new house. His son Oliver added a large bow window to the east front in 1602, to celebrate his marriage to an heiress, but spent all her money in entertaining and was forced to sell up in 1627 to Henry Montagu, Earl of Manchester. The house remained in the Montagu family until 1962. Edward Montagu, first Earl of Sandwich, made improvements in the 1660s. Samuel Pepys gives an account of the work in his diary and comments that 'the house do please me infinitely beyond Audley end'. In 1830 fire damaged a large part of the house and that boring but reliable architect Edward Blore was called in to restore it. He moved the great bow window from the east to the south front and re-fitted the rooms in a thin Gothic style. The house is now part of Hinchingbrooke Comprehensive School and contains mostly school furnishings, but it is still in use and alive. Tours of the house, in small groups, are conducted by well-informed pupils. Most of the ground and first floor rooms are open.

Opening times: March to end July, Sun 2–5.
Entrance charges: 50p; children 30p.
Parking: Free parking near main entrance.
Wheelchair access: Possible to all ground floor rooms (with a few steps).
Guidebook: Hinchingbourne is very well served, with a excellent and concise account and a
    more expensive and informative guide. Both contain plans and room-by-room descriptions.
Catering: Good, cheap home-made teas.
WCs: Free, well-maintained.
Shop: None.

PECKOVER HOUSE North Brink, Wisbech (The National Trust)
Tel: Wisbech (0945) 3463
Directions: In Wisbech, on the north bank of the river Nene (B1441)

The North Brink is a row of substantial Georgian houses with the river directly in front of them. Peckover House is the largest house in the row, but the yellow and red brick front makes no great impact. The house dates from the 1720s, and from 1777 until 1948 it was owned by the Peckover family of Quaker bankers. After the quiet exterior the elaborate mid-18th century plasterwork and carving inside come as a surprise. The carved overmantel in the drawing room especially shows the very high standard of English provincial craftsmanship in the 1750s, but even the small details like the door locks are worth looking at. Only five rooms are shown, all on the ground floor. They are filled with pleasant furniture and paintings of the later 18th century. By contrast, the large garden behind the house is thoroughly and delightfully Victorian, with many evergreens and exotic trees.

Opening times: April to end Oct, Tues, Wed, Thurs, Sat, Sun and Bank Holidays 2–6; closed
    Good Friday.
Entrance charges: 90p; chilren 45p; no dogs.
Parking: Free car park to rear and limited on-street parking nearby.

Wheelchair access: Possible to garden only; steps at front and rear of the house. The tea room is not accessible.

Guidebook: Brief coverage of architecture and history, room-by-room guide, black and white illustrations, no plan.

Catering: In the old kitchen of the house, tea and home-made cakes.

WCs: Free, adequate.

Shop: None.

WIMPOLE HALL Orwell (The National Trust)

Tel: Arrington (022 020) 257

Directions: 8 miles S.W. of Cambridge off the A6023 near the hamlet of New Wimpole

Some of the most famous architects and landscape gardeners of the 18th century were employed at Wimpole. The huge park makes an immediate impact, even though the three-mile long avenue of elms fell victim to disease. The florid Victorian stables by the car park are striking but the qualities of the house are less obvious. Although Wimpole is large, the architecture is not dramatic: a tall central block faced with red brick in a quiet mid-Georgian style is flanked on each side by wings of the same style and material.

In brief, the main block was built by 1670, and the wings were added between 1719 and 1721 by James Gibbs for Edward Harley. The main block was refronted and some of the rooms improved between 1742 and 1745 by Henry Flitcroft for Lord Hadwicke. Further improvements to the interior were made between 1791 and 1793 by Sir John Soane for the Third Earl of Hardwicke. A final enlargement was made in 1849 to 1851 by the architect Henry Kendall, but much of his work has been demolished, It is impossible to give an impression of the rich variety of the interior but some of the highlights are Jefferin Alken's carving in the south drawing room and elsewhere, Soane's dramatic yellow drawing room with its domed ceiling and the chapel filling the east wing, whose walls are covered with painted decoration by Sir James Thornhill, finished in 1724. The whole of the ground floor and a part of the first floor are open to the public and these rooms are filled with fine 18th century paintings and furniture collected by Mrs Elsie Bambridge, the last owner of Wimpole, who was also the daughter of Rudyard Kipling. The park provides almost a case-book history of English gardening from 1590 until 1830, starting with a formal layout with long avenues, which was gradually made more informal. Charles Bridgeman, 'Capability' Brown, and Humphrey Repton were all involved in the work at different times.

Opening times: April to end Oct, Tues, Wed, Sat, Sun and Bank Holidays 2–6; closed Good Friday.

Entrance charges: £1.40; accompanied child 70p.

Parking: Large car park next to Henry Kendall's stable block.

Wheelchair access: Difficult; gravel paths and steps up to and inside the house.

Guidebook: An excellent full account with room-by-room guide, illustrations and a plan of the main floor.

Catering: In the dining room of the main house with a view over the garden; very acceptable tea and cakes.
WCs: Free, excellent condition; suitable for wheelchairs.
Shop: Also inside the house, well laid out, with the usual National Trust stock and a few local products.

Cheshire

ADLINGTON HALL nr Macclesfield (Charles F. Legh Esq)
Tel: Prestbury (0625) 829206
Directions: 5 miles N. of Macclesfield off the A523

The house at Adlington is an attractive mixture of brick and timber buildings grouped round a quadrangle. They are all the work of various members of the Legh family, who have been at Adlington since 1315. The timber buildings on the north and east sides are mostly of the 16th century, the brick buildings on the south and west sides of the 18th century. Part of the west side was removed in 1928. Following the usual route, visitors see some cosy little rooms on the first floor of the north range, then two very pleasant early 18th century panelled rooms in what is left of the west range, and finally the Great Hall in the north range. The hall was completed in 1505 and improved with new and bigger windows in 1581. the first date is on the carved canopy at the high end while the second is on the porch facing the courtyard. As well as a splendid hammerbeam roof and some curious wall paintings, the hall also has one of the finest 17th century organs in England, built by 'Father' Smith and decorated with elaborate carving. On coming out of the house it is worth going round to look at the south front, with its portico looking uncomfortably large beside the rest of the buildings. This part of the house was added 1757 and the nearby stables in 1749. Across from the front of Adlington, hidden among trees, is a delightful little summerhouse whose walls are lined with sea shells, but few visitors ever seem to find this gem.

Opening times: Good Friday to 3 Oct, Sun and Bank Holidays 2.30–6; July and August as above plus Wed and Sat.
Entrance charges: (1981) 90p; children 45p. (HHA)
Parking: Free parking a short way from the house
Wheelchair access: Only to the ground floor rooms, i.e. the hall and dining room. The tea room is not accessible.
Guidebook: A brief history of the house, room-by-room guide and an account of the family; some illustrations; no plan.
Catering: The tea shop upstairs in the stable block sells tea by the pot and very good cakes.
WCs: In the stable block, free, clean and modern. Not suitable for wheelchairs.
Shop: A small souvenir shop in the stable block.

BRAMALL HALL Bramall, Stockport (Metropolitan Borough of Stockport)
Tel: (061) 485 3708
Directions: 3 miles S. of Stockport off the A5102 in Bramall Park, 1 mile N. of Bramhall village, badly signposted

An enormous timber-framed house built at various times for the Davenport family. The oldest part is the south wing which dates from the late 15th century, and most of the rest was added between 1500 and 1600. Originally there was an open courtyard in the centre, but one whole side of it was removed in the 18th century. A Victorian owner, Charles Nevill, repaired and restored the house, so there is quite a lot of 19th century work. Long (75 mins) and chatty guided tours. There are some splendid rooms, including what is called the ballroom in the south wing with its mediaeval wall-paintings and the drawing room which has a splendid Tudor plaster ceiling. The house is not lived in and the furniture is scanty, but good of its kind and in keeping with the building. Altogether one of the most solidly impressive timber houses in the country.

Opening times: Guided tours only, April to end Sept, Tues to Sun, schools and organizations only 10–12; general public tours at 12, 1, 2, 3 and 4; Oct to March, Tues to Sun, 10–12 and 12, 1, 2 and 3; closed all December.
Entrance charges: (1981) 60p; children 30p.
Parking: Free asphalted car park about 50 yards from the house.
Wheelchair access: Wheelchair users are welcomed but access to the first floor rooms would be difficult
Guidebook: Fully illustrated, room-by-room guide and brief history, but no plan, which is a pity for such a complicated house.
Catering: The café in the adjacent stable building is open every day for tea, coffee, biscuits, etc.
WCs: None in the house. There are WCs near the cafe in the park; not suitable for wheelchairs.
Shop: None.

CAPESTHORNE HALL nr Macclesfield (Lt Col Sir Walter Bromley-Davenport)
Tel: Chelford (0625) 861221
Directions: 6½ miles N. of Congleton on the A34

Capesthorne looks very striking from a distance, a long spiky silhouette by the lake, seen across the rolling park. The core of the house dates from the 18th century, but it was rebuilt by Edward Blore in 1837 and again by Anthony Salvin in 1861. Both of these architects favoured the Tudor style and turned the house into a Elizabethan palace. The ground floor rooms are tall and cold, the walls painted in strong colours which overpower the paintings and furniture and the collection of Roman sculpture. A splendid staircase leads to the upper floor where one can peer into all the bedrooms without being able to get close enough to see anything properly. One of the rooms contains what looks, from a distance, like an interesting collection of Americana. The furniture is a mixture of old and new and the old is of good average rather than outstanding quality. There is a lot to see and almost every room in the house is on show: even the cellars are open and contain documents and photographs about the estate. There is also a small late 18th century chapel next to the house with lush late Victorian fittings. The park is huge.

Opening times: 28 March to 26 Sept, Sun, Good Friday and Bank Holidays 2–5, also May to Sept, Wed and Sat 2–5, 1 July to 30 Sept, Tues and Thurs 2–5. Park and gardens noon–6.

Entrance charges: Hall, gardens and park £1.40; children 70p. Park and gardens only 70p; children 35p. (HHA)

Parking: Free parking near the house.

Wheelchair access: Wheelchairs are admitted; several steps to the main entrance, but ground floor rooms on the flat. First floor and basement not accessible. Tea room, shop and park all accessible.

Guidebook: There is a choice: the 'Guide to Capesthorne Hall' is a room-by-room guide with details of the pictures; the 'History of Capesthorne' contains a general history of the building and the family, has many illustrations and is signed by the owner.

Catering: Set lunches, teas and high teas are served in a room beside the house; solid traditional fare.

WCs: In the house near the craft shop or adjacent to the tea rooms; neither are suitable for wheelchair users.

Shop: A craft shop with aprons, and commercially produced 'home-made' jam.

CHURCHE'S MANSION Nantwich (Mr and Mrs R.V. Myott)
Tel: (0270) 625933
Directions: In Nantwich, at the bottom of Hospital Street

An inscription on the front of the house reads *Rychard Churche and Margerye Churche his wife Mai IIII Thomas Clease made this worke, anno dni MCCCCCLXXVII in the XVIII yere of the reane of our noble queene elesabeth.* Richard Churche was a wealthy local man and the house which Thomas Clease finished for him on 4 May 1577 is a very good example of a Tudor merchant's house. It is timber-framed and the timbers of the upper floor are formed into the elaborate patterns which were popular in the Midlands. The internal arrangements are the usual ones, with a hall in the middle, kitchen to the left and drawing room or great chamber to the right. These rooms now house a restaurant. The upstairs rooms are sparsely furnished with 16th and 17th century oak furniture. As so often with timber buildings, the fascination lies in the way in which the house was put together out of a set of numbered parts; at Churche's mansion the timber beams with their carpenters' marks can be closed examined. The house has been well restored over the last 30 years with old timber brought from elsewhere, and one original piece of furniture, a buffet with the initials of Richard Churche and his wife, has been brought back to its original place in the hall after a 360-year absence.

Opening times: April to 31 Oct daily 10–5.
Entrance charges: For visitors 40p; children 30p. (HHA)
Parking: Free car park next to house.
Wheelchair access: Possible to downstairs (i.e. restaurant) rooms.
Guidebook: A chatty little book which starts with a plan, narrates the history of the house and concludes with an account of the restoration work.
Catering: This is one of the few historic houses in the *Good Food Guide*. Restaurant open 10–11.30 (coffee), 12–2 (lunch), 7–8.30 (dinner – not Sun).
WCs: Downstairs, but not suitable for wheelchairs.
Shop: None.

DORFOLD HALL nr Nantwich (Mr R.C. Roundell)
Tel: Nantwich (0270) 625245
Directions: 2 miles W. of Nantwich on the A534. The house is visible from the road at the end of its drive, but is not signposted

Dorfold Hall is a Jacobean house, built for Ralph Wilbraham in 1616, of smoky red brick with diaper patterns. The little buildings at the outer corners of the forecourt are also of 1616 but the other buildings here date from 1824 and the lime avenue leading up from the main gates was not planted until 1862. The first builders of the house were determined to make the front symmetrical and concealed the off-centre front door by turning it at right angles to the front wall, but they were less concerned with the rest of the house which has a jumbled and irregular appearance. Visitors are guided round four of the main rooms. The dining room was redecorated in 1757, and the library has a ceiling with two love-birds designed by Samuel Wyatt in about 1772. The upstairs room or great chamber has a fine plaster ceiling with interlacing patterns dating from 1621. This room has also kept its original panelling. The rooms are filled with pleasant but not outstanding furniture, mostly of the 18th century and later. There is only one guide, so delays may occur.

Opening times: April to Oct, Tues and Bank Holidays Mon 2–5.
Entrance charges: £1.00; children 50p. (HHA)
Parking: Free parking on the drive immediately in front of the house.
Wheelchair access: Not really practicable as there are steps up to the front door and between each room.
Guidebook: A small leaflet with a brief history of the house and a description of the principal objects in each room; the descriptions add nothing to what is said by the guide.
Catering: None.
WCs: None.
Shop: None.

GAWSWORTH HALL   Gawsworth, nr Macclesfield (Timothy Richards Esq)
Tel: North Rode (02603) 456
Directions: 3½ miles S.W. of Macclesfield off the A536 in Gawsworth village

A picturesque rambling timber-framed house, largely built in the late 15th century but, like all such houses, with a number of later additions. There is one long show front with a splendid three-storey bay window, but otherwise the place is not much to look at from outside. Originally the house was nearly twice as big as it is now. Visitors thread their way through most of the rooms on both floors, which are low and packed with furniture, pictures and sculpture some of which is of good quality and some only average. The small size of the rooms means that one can get closer than usual, except in one or two cases where only peering from the doorway is allowed. There are several people dotted about the house who are willing to answer questions about the furnishings. Gawsworth Hall is a popular house, and its small rooms and passages can get too crowded as a result. In the outbuildings is a collection of 19th century double-decker horse-drawn buses and other vehicles. The house and its park are a part of one of the prettiest villages in the country.

Opening times: 1 March to 25 Oct, daily 2–6; Christmas week 2–4.30.
Entrance charges: £1.00; children 40p. (HHA)
Parking: Free parking in a field 135 yards from house.
Wheelchair access: Not a easy house for wheelchair users; circulation inside the house is cramped and there are many steps.
Guidebook: Packed with information, including a plan of the house, room-by-room guide, details of every picture.
Catering: One of the best features of the place is the splendid old-fashioned tea room in the pavilion at the top of the car park. Morning coffee, tea by the pot, toasted tea-cakes; high teas as well.
WCs: Rather inadequate, tucked behind the garage. Not suitable for wheelchairs.
Shop: Souvenir shop inside the house.

LITTLE MORETON HALL   nr Congleton (The National Trust)
Tel: Congleton (02602) 2018
Directions: 4 miles S.W. of Congleton on the A34. The house is clearly visible from the road

Little Moreton Hall is perhaps the best-known timber-framed building in England; the elaborate patterns of its walls appear on National Trust tea towels in thousands of homes. The countryside hereabouts is flat and the higgledy-piggledy outlines of the house can be seen from some distance away. As it stands today, Little Moreton Hall is the creation of three generations of the Moreton family, who owned the property from about 1250 until the present century. The buildings are grouped round a courtyard. Across the yard from the main entrance is the Great Hall and the

Gawsworth Hall, Cheshire

rooms on either side, completed in about 1480. The accommodation here was later improved by the addition of two bulging bay windows to light the high end of the Hall and the Withdrawing Room. A carved inscription at the top of these bays records that they were built for William Moreton by the carpenter Richard Dale in 1559. The other sides of the courtyard, including the front range with its long gallery crazily perched on top, were complete by 1580. Since that time very little has been altered. The house is now almost empty of furniture, except for a few items in the great hall which have remained in place since the 1550s, but there is rare 16th century glass in the great bay windows, painted decoration in the parlour and a quantity of fine early panelling. These things give the empty rooms a magic of their own. Around the house is a knot garden, based on a design published in 1688 and both house and garden are enclosed by a water-filled moat.

Opening times: March, Sat and Sun 2–6; April to Sept, daily except Tues, 2–6; Oct, Sat and Sun 2–6 (or sunset, if earlier). Closed Good Friday.

Entrance charges: £1.20; children 60p.

Parking: Free parking directly in front of the house.

Wheelchair access: Possible to great hall, drawing room and parlour and also to the tea room off the great hall.

Guidebook: Recently revised, with a tour of the rooms, and sections on the building and the family. There is a plan of all floors.

Catering: Small tea room in the oldest part of the house. Cream teas, log fires in the colder months.

WCs: Free, adequate; facilities for the disabled.

Shop: In the west wing of the old house, very much the standard National Trust package with sweets and souvenirs.

LYME PARK Disley (The National Trust and Stockport Borough Council)

Tel: Disley (066 32) 2023

Directions: 1 mile W. of Disley on the A6 going towards Stockport

Lyme is a very large and splendid stone house, partly of the 16th and partly of the 18th century, with some impressive rooms. It was built by various members of the Legh family. The Tudor house of Sir Piers Legh is still standing, but all one can see of it is the curious ornament over the gateway. The rest was faced with stone by the architect Giacomo Leoni in 1725, when he was called in to modernise the old building. He added the impressive west front which faces the lake, and refronted the walls of the courtyard in the middle of the house to make it look like an Italian palace. He also improved some of the rooms inside. Nearly 100 years after this, in 1816, the squat tower on top of the south front was added to house the servants. Visitors have access to about half of the house and the rooms on show include the saloon with the very lovely carved decoration, which might be by Grinling Gibbons, and the drawing room which is in the old part of the house and has some of its original decoration. Though fine, the rooms are rather bare of furniture.

The house has an enormous park which still contains deer and in the woods to the east of the house is the tower from the top of the Tudor house which was removed in 1725 and set up as a folly.

Opening times: Park and gardens, all year daily, 8–dusk. House, April to end Sept, Sun, Good Friday and Bank Holiday Mon 1–5.30, Tues to Sat 2–4.30; Oct, Sun 1–4.30, Tues to Sat 2–4.

Entrance charges: 60p; children 30p (subject to review).

Parking: An inescapable 60p. The large car park is about 5 minutes from the house.

Wheelchair access: Not absolutely forbidden, but there are stairs to *all* interior rooms.

Guidebook: Contains a plan, history of family, description of house with room-by-room guide.

Catering: None in the house, but the cafeteria in the stable block by the lake serves tea ad also meals.

WCs: In the house itself. There are also lavatories in the stable block, not so good; facilities for wheelchairs.

Shop: There is a small National Trust shop in the house.

PEOVER HALL Over Peover, nr Knutsford (Randle Brooks Esq)
Tel: Lower Peover (056 581) 2404
Directions: 4 miles S. of Knutsford, off the A50 near Over Peover village: badly signposted and difficult to find

Peover is an Elizabethan house of 1585 built for Sir Ralph Mainwaring. In the mid-1960s a large 18th and 19th century wing was taken down, leaving the older house behind. The rooms inside are mostly quite small and low; the only exception is the huge kitchen with its heavy timber-framed ornamental ceiling which is most unusual. The conducted tour takes in rooms on all floors of the house, including a long thin gallery on the second floor and the comfortably furnished drawing room on the first floor. Three of the ground floor rooms have panelled walls, but visitors should be beware! Much of the panelling which seems to fit the rooms so well was brought from elsewhere quite recently. The stables are at least as fine as the house. This long range of brick buildings near the house was built in 1654 and the original stalls fo the horses still survive inside. They have arched entrances, carved decoration and an ornamental plaster ceiling. Near the house is the church of St Laurence, a building of 1811 containing some splendid alabaster tombs of the Mainwarings.

Opening times: Hall and stables, May to Sept, Mon (except Bank Holidays) 2–5; stables only, Thurs 2–4.30.

Entrance charges: £1.00; children 50p. (HHA)

Parking: Free parking on the road near the outbuildings.

Wheelchair access: Too many steps inside the house, but possible to the stables.

Guidebook: A small pamphlet is available.

Catering: Teas in the stables.

WCs: Facilities at the house.

Shop: None.

STANLEY PALACE Watergate Street, Chester (The English Speaking Union)
Tel: Chester (0244) 25586
Directions: In Watergate Street, just beyond the inner ring road

Stanley Palace was the town house of the Stanley family of Alderley. It was built in 1591 (the date is on the front of the building) and is one of the most elaborately decorated Tudor houses in Chester. The main front is at right angles to the street and until fairly recently looked onto a narrow courtyard. Road improvements have cleared away the buildings which stood on the other side of the court. The palace was very thoroughly restored in the 1930s and both the right hand gable and the front to Watergate Street date from this time. This is one of the few houses in Chester which is open to the public and although the rooms contain little furniture of interest there are still a lot of early timbers to be seen; one ground floor room has early 18th century panelling.

Opening times: All year, Mon to Fri except Bank Holiday Mon, 10–12, 2–4.30.
Entrance charges: Free.
Parking: There is no car park for visitors, who are advised to use the official pay car parks in the city.
Wheelchair access: Difficult, even to the ground floor rooms.
Guidebook: A guidebook will be available in 1982.
Catering: Only by prior arrangement.
WCs: Upstairs and downstairs; neither for wheelchair users.
Shop: None.

TATTON PARK Knutsford (The National Trust and Cheshire County Council)
Tel: Knutsford (0565) 3155 or 52748
Directions: 3½ miles N. of Knutsford. Entrance by Rostherne lodge on Ashley Road, 1½ miles N.E. of junction of A5034 and A50: M6 junction 19, M56 junction 7

The owners of Tatton until 1958 were the Egertons, who became extremely wealthy in the middle of the 18th century and spent a great deal of money in building and furnishing the present house. Tatton has a calm and elegant stone exterior in the neo-classical style; there is no indication that the two halves of the house were built at different times, although the western half was built to the designs of Samuel Wyatt between 1780 and 1790 and the eastern half to the designs of his nephew Lewis Wyatt between 1808 and 1813. Amongst it all is the dining room which was part of a house built in 1760. The interior is richly decorated and full of fine furniture. Many of the rooms have been redecorated in colours like the original ones. There is an exhibition of the paintings from which the evidence for this decoration comes. The entrance hall and the staircase in the centre of the house, with its unusualy domed vestibule, are perhaps the best rooms, though all the rooms on the ground floor are impressive. The furniture is almost all of the late 18th and early 19th centuries and most of it was made for Tatton by Gillow of Lancaster (later part of Waring & Gillow). Visitors can take their own time to wander through. There are guides on hand to answer questions. Outside the house are pleasure gardens, including a orangery with real oranges and lemons and a thousand acres of deer park, all open to visitors.

Opening times: Every day except Mon; but open Bank Holiday Mon and Mon in Aug. Closed Christmas Day. Sun and Bank Holiday times in brackets. Easter to mid-May and Sept to early Oct, House 1–4 (1–5); Garden 12–4.30 (1–5); Park, pedestrians 9–7, others 11–6 (10–6). Mid-May to end Aug, House 1–5 (12–5); Garden 11–5.30 (11–6); Park, pedestrians 9–8, others 10.30–7 (10–7). Old Hall, Easter to mid Oct, Tues to Sat 12–4 (12–5); July and Aug 12–5; Farm, Easter to mid-Oct 11–5.

Entrance charges: (in addition to road toll) House 80p; children 40p. Garden 50p; children 25p. Old Hall 70p; children 35p. Farm 60p; children 30p. (HHA). Charges subject to revision.

Parking: Road toll at entry 80p for all cars (other vehicles accordingly). Car park adjacent to outbuildings.

Wheelchair access: There are steps up to the main entrance, but once inside, all main rooms are on the flat. The cafeteria is accessible.

Guidebook: Very good value. A room-by-room guide and sections on the architecture, family and park. Black and white and colour illustrations and a plan of the house.

Catering: Cheap and cheerful self-serve cafeteria in the stable block serves tea and cakes as well as hot meals. Unexciting food.

WCs: In the stable block, free and well-maintained. WCs for wheelchair users in the stable yard.

Shop: The shop in the stable yard sells books, sweets, souvenirs, etc.

Extras: Admission to the garden is 50p and this is the only way to see the outside of the house from close-to. A mile from the main house is the Old Hall, dating from about 1450, with a display about the history of Tatton and also a museum of farming implements. Newly opened in 1981 is Tattondale, the home farm, shown as a working 1930s farm.

Cleveland

ORMESBY HALL Ormesby (The National Trust)
Tel: Middlesborough (0642) 324188
Directions: Ormesby is 3 miles S.E. of Middlesborough on the A161 to Whitby; if you by-pass the city centre on the Middlesborough Parkway, leave at the Marton interchange

Ormesby Hall is not a spectacular house, nor one of great architectural distinction, but it offers an insight into the style of life of the ordinary country gentry in the 18th century. The house was built in the 1750s for Dorothy Pennyman and completed by her nephew Sir James Pennyman, who went bankrupt shortly afterwards. It is a plain and sensible classical block of three storeys, built of stone, with a tall hipped roof and a central pediment.

Behind and to one side is an earlier house of about 1600, which was retained as a kitchen wing. The main house is organised around the entrance hall, a large elegant space with a screen of columns at either end. The principal rooms leading off this hall are a quiet corner study and the drawing and dining room with plaster ceilings in the Adam style which are probably the work of craftsmen from York and may have been designed by the architect John Carr of York. The dining room also boasts a small portrait of Sir James Pennyman by Sir Joshua Reynolds. A few of the first floor rooms are open to visitors; they are not of particular interest but one contains a display of costume. The Hall is still occupied by a Pennyman and the public rooms are still in use. This reinforces the air of homely gentility and contributes to the charm of the house. The grounds are pleasant, at least for Middlesboro'.

Opening times: April to end Oct, Wed, Sun and Bank Holidays 2–6.
Entrance charges: 70p; children 30p.
Parking: Free parking at the house.
Wheelchair access: Possible to part of the property; a wheelchair is available.
Guidebook: A short, inexpensive account with one illustration and no plan.
Catering: None, but the National Trust ladies recommend the cafeteria in Captain Cooke's Museum nearby.
WCs: There are facilities for wheelchair users.
Shop: Guide books only.

Cornwall

ANTONY HOUSE Torpoint (The National Trust)
Tel: Plymouth (0752) 812191
Directions: 5 miles W. of Plymouth via Torpoint car ferry; 2 miles from the ferry on the N. side of the A374

Antony is a plain but distinguished classical building of cool grey stone, with a forecourt and wings of rich red brick covered with roses. The house stands near the sea in the placid countryside of Torpoint. The estate has been owned since the late 15th century by the Carew family, who still live here and the present house was built in 1718 by Sir William Carew. The mason in charge of the building was John Moyle; the architect is unknown, although James Gibbs may have provided the design for the forecourt. The front porch was added in 1838. The interior still has its original panelling of Dutch oak and is rather dark. There is a very fine collection of portraits of members of the family and also some excellent sporting paintings. Some of the rooms, especially the saloon, still have the furniture which was made for them in the 1720s. Most of the main ground floor rooms and several upstairs bedrooms are shown in the guided tour which lasts about 40 minutes. The tours can get very crowded in high summer. The garden was 'improved' in about 1800 by Humphrey Repton and many trees were planted to enhance the natural beauty of the site sloping down to the river Lynher. Some of these trees have now grown to enormous size. To the west of the house massive yew hedges line a wall that leads to a Burmese temple bell, brought back by Sir Reginald Pole-Carew after the Burma Wars. There is also a woodland garden.

Opening times: April to end Oct, Tues, Wed, Thurs and Bank Holiday Mon 2–6, last tour 5.30.
Entrance charges: £1.20; children under 16 60p; parties must book; no dogs.
Parking: At entrance, 250 yards from the house, free.
Wheelchair access: Possible to the ground floor and the gardens.
Guidebook: An adequate history and room-by-room guide; rather small pictures and no plan.
Catering: None.
WCs: In the wing to the left of the entrance; unsuitable for wheelchairs.
Shop: The usual National Trust shop with sweets, tea towels, toys, etc.; there is also a garden centre selling plants from the estate.

COTEHELE nr St Dominick (The National Trust)
Tel: St Dominick (0579) 50434
Directions: On the W. bank of the River Tamar, 8 miles S.W. of Tavistock, signposted off the A390

Cotehele is a romantic grey granite manor house. The Edgcumbe family owned the house and estate from 1354 until 1948, when it was given to the National Trust, but Cotehele has been attracting visitors ever since King George III came here in 1789. Although the Edgcumbes did not use the house much after about 1700 they did not neglect it. The house is built round a series of small courtyards. It dates mainly from the 15th and early 16th centuries, although the lower parts of many of the walls are earlier than this. The tower was built in 1627. The east side of the house was rebuilt internally in 1862 but the later work fits in well with the original. Inside, the great hall is an impressive room whose walls are decorated with armour. The other rooms on the ground and first floor are small and dark, with highly polished oak floors and walls hung with rich tapestry. The bedrooms have four-poster beds. The ground floor chapel contains a very early clock of about 1485, before the invention of the pendulum. Visitors make their own way through the house and there are guides in the rooms to answer questions. A free film about the house and estate is shown. The whole house has a marvellously romantic atmosphere but it can get very crowded in midsummer and at weekends. The slope down from the east front of the house is laid out as a series of gardens. Besides the house, the estate includes a water mill and a riverside quay on the Tamar with docks and warehouses. The quay and buildings are being restored and there is a very good little maritime museum in one of the buildings, with some excellent ship models.

Opening times: House April to end Oct, daily including Bank Holidays 11–6; last admission 5.30.

Cotehele, Cornwall

Entrance charges: House, garden and mill £2.00; children £1.00. Garden, grounds and mill only £1.00; children 50p; no dogs.
Parking: Two car parks, one nearer the house, both free.
Wheelchair access: Possible to most ground floor rooms; shop and restaurant also accessible, but garden difficult.
Guidebook: A good and thorough booklet with a plan and full page illustrations; there is an excellent free leaflet which describes the contents of the room.
Catering: Lunches and teas served in the barn restaurant, which is mentioned in the Good Food Guide.
WCs: Suitable for wheelchairs.
Shop: A large shop selling books as well as the usual National Trust range and a good selection of plants.
Extras: The Maritime Museum on the quay, open April to Oct, costs 20p.

EBBINGFORD MANOR Bude (Mr and Mrs Dudley Stamp)
Tel: Bude (0288) 2808
Directions: In Bude, south of the town centre across the river and canal, signposted

Ebbingford is a snug little stone manor house of the 15th century with some 16th century additions. From the 15th to the 18th century the house was owned by the Arundell family who were powerful Cornish landlords. In 1953 the house was acquired by Sir Dudley Stamp (who swapped it for his own nearby) and his family still live there. The furniture is not outstanding but the present owner has created an interesting exhibition about the house and the families associated with it. There are fascinating details of local history and customs, as well as an attempt to make Bude seem less dull than is often thought. There is also some information about the Bude and Holsworthy canal, which passes the house and which enthusiasts are hoping to restore. Much thought and imagination has gone into the exhibitions to find things of interest for children. A nature trail and quiz have also been organised.

Opening times: Ebbingford will be open by appointment only in 1982.
Entrance charges: (1981) 40p; accompanied children 5–14 20p.
Parking: On grass verge inside entrance gates, free.
Wheelchair access: Possible to all main rooms.
Guidebook: Mostly about the Arundell family, with a bit about the building; no illustrations and no plan.
Catering: Tea and good home made biscuits.
WCs: Next to the tea room; unsuitable for wheelchairs.
Shop: A small shop selling craftwork.

GODOLPHIN HOUSE   Breage, nr Helston (S.E. Schofield Esq)
Tel: Germoe (073 676) 2409
Directions: 5 miles N.W. of Helston, 2 miles N. of the A394, between
Townshend and Godolphin Cross

The Godolphin family made a fortune from tin mining in the 16th century
and the remains of the mines can still be seen in the woods near the house. In
the 18th and 19th centuries the buildings were badly treated and only one of
the two original courtyards has survived. On two sides are long ranges which
date from about 1475 but have been altered. They have large windows facing the courtyard and small windows in the outer walls. A third side of the
court is occupied by the ruins of the Tudor great hall, pulled down in 1805,
while the battlemented range containing the main entrace was rebuilt in
1635. This very unusual range is supported on stout granite Tuscan columns and was the first stage in a programme of rebuilding which was interrupted by the Civil War and never re-started. The rooms inside have original plaster ceilings and friezes, with carved doorways and overmantels. The
furniture includes some good oak tables and furniture and there are tapestries on the walls. The present owner, who bought the house in the 1930s,
has been largely responsible for preserving and restoring the house and he
has also managed to bring back portraits and other items belonging to the
Godolphin family.

Opening times: May and June, Thurs 2–5; or by appointment; parties may visit throughout
the year.
Entrance charges: (1981) 70p; children 30p.
Parking: Free parking next to the house.
Wheelchair access: Possible to the ground floor rooms with assistance; there are two shallow
steps.
Guidebook: A cheap information sheet about the family and the buildings; visitors are issued
with a printed guide to be returned at the end of the tour.
Catering: Teas in the courtyard, excellent value with cups of tea and home-made cakes.
WCs: In the grounds; unsuitable for wheelchairs.
Shop: Pottery, made on the premises, for sale in the tea shop and in the pottery itself.

LANHYDROCK HOUSE   nr Bodmin (The National Trust)
Tel: Bodmin (0208) 3320
Directions: 2½ miles S.E. of Bodmin, signposted from the A38 and B3268

There is a contrast between the exterior and interior of Lanhydrock which
visitors may find disconcerting. The mansion house is built of silvery-grey
granite and is set into the hillside with the church tucked behind it; there are
dark woods beyond and the parkland in front slopes down the Fowey valley. The land was bought in 1620 by Sir Richard Roberts (or Robartes as he
became), a merchant from Truro. He and his son built the house between
1630 and 1642. It was originally planned round a courtyard, with a charm-

ing small gatehouse standing by itself to the east. The east wing containing the great rooms was removed in about 1780 and the gatehouse now stands in front of an open court. In 1881 a major fire destroyed the whole house, except for the north wing, the porch and the gatehouse. It was at once rebuilt to designs by the London architect Richard Coad. Only local materials were used and the Victorian granite walls look like the Jacobean ones, but Coad's interior decoration is very obviously Victorian. Visitors follow a set route through most of the main house on both floors; much of the furniture is also 19th century, notably that in the splendid billard room in the south wing. The main rooms in the east wing were probably on the first floor in the north wing is taken up by the magnificent long gallery with its original rich plaster ceiling illustrating scenes from the Old Testament. As well as rebuilding the house, Coad added a large servants' wing which is open to visitors. All the elaborate processes of Victorian country house cookery are on show. The formal gardens around the house are part of a series of improvements carried out by Giles Gilbert Scott in 1857 and the wooded parkland, which is open for walks, was mostly planned at about the same time.

Opening times: House and gardens, April to end Oct, daily 11–6, last admission 5.30; Nov to March, garden only open during daylight.

Entrance charges: £2.00; children £1.00. Garden and grounds only £1.00 and 50p. Dogs on leads in park only.

Parking: At the edge of the park, 600 yards from the house, free.

Wheelchair access: The whole house is accessible for those who can cope with a few steps; there is a lift to the first floor. Disabled visitors may be driven to the house.

Guidebook: An excellent guide on all counts, with two good plans; there are separate leaflets describing the contents of the house and kitchen wing; some foreign language leaflets are available.

Catering: A licensed restaurant serves coffee, snacks, lunch and tea 11–5 and there is also a tea room in the stable yard. Both open April to Dec.

WCs: In the stable yard; suitable for wheelchairs.

Shop: A large National Trust shop selling the full range of standard products.

LAUNCESTON CASTLE Launceston (Ancient Monument)
Tel: Launceston (0566) 2365
Directions: In the centre of Launceston

A fort of some kind existed here before the Norman Conquest. The wooden defences of the Normans were rebuilt in stone between 1227 and 1272. All that remains of the large outer bailey of the castle are two gateways. At one end of the bailey is a very steep mound, topped by the keep. The keep is a cylinder, like that of Restormel or of Carisbrooke in the Isle of Wight, but it is unusual because another cylindrical tower was later built inside the first wall. The keep is ruined, but still spectacular, and is reached by a very steep flight of steps which was originally defended by walls and covered with a roof.

Opening times: Standard hours (S), see page xii, closed 1–2.

54   *The Historic Houses Handbook*

Entrance charges: (1981) 40p; children under 16 and OAPs 20p.
Parking: Municipal pay car park opposite.
Wheelchair access: Part of the outer bailey is accessible.
Guidebook: An Official Handbook, with a ground plan.
Catering: None.
WCs: In the Castle Street car park.
Shop: Postcards only.

LAUNCESTON: LAWRENCE HOUSE 9 Castle Street (The National
Trust and Launceston Borough Council)
Tel: Launceston (0566) 2833
Directions: In Launceston, signposted from the castle on the N. side, 5
mins walk

This modest 18th century brick house bears the name of the family who
lived here for many years. The outside is plain but some of the rooms inside
are quite elegant and the 'Mayor's Parlour' has good 18th century plasterwork, like that in the nearby Eagle Hotel. Lawrence House now contains a
fascinating museum, built up from local donations. Among the items on display are some of the feudal dues the borough must offer the Duke of
Cornwall (Prince Charles). They include a faggot, a salmon spear, and a
pound of pepper. In the same room can be seen a 17th century sporting gun,
a cake of soap with the face of George V on one side and Queen Mary on the
other, and caricatures made from animal bones by French prisoners who
were confined in the house during the Napoleonic wars. All the exhibits are
clearly labelled, and the guides are very friendly.

Opening times: April to Sept, Mon to Fri 10.30–12.30, 2.30–4.30, not Bank Holidays.
Entrance charges: Free, but donations requested towards museum funds.
Parking: Very limited on-street parking outside, pay car park opposite the castle.
Wheelchair access: Possible to ground floor rooms.
Guidebook: A very long-winded account of the history of the house, no plan.
Catering: None in the house.
WCs: Unsuitable for wheelchairs.
Shop: None.

MOUNT EDGCUMBE nr Plymouth (City of Plymouth and County of
Cornwall)
Tel: Plymouth (0752) 82311
Directions: The best approach is by the pedestrian ferry from Admiral's
Hard, Stonehouse in Plymouth to Cremyll, or by car ferry from
Plymouth to Torpoint. The park lies just across the Hamoaze from
Plymouth

Mount Edgcumbe is one of the great 18th century gardens of England, occupying a magnificent promontory overlooking Plymouth Sound. The
house at its centre, looking like a toy fort, was built between 1547 and 1553

by Sir Richad Edgcumbe of Cotehele. The round corner toweres were made octagonal in the 18th century and other alterations were made, but in 1941 the building was completely gutted by incendiary bombs. It was rebuilt for the Sixth Earl of Mount Edgcumbe by the architect Adrian Gilbert Scott, who kept to the old plan but simplified the decoration of the rooms. The family furniture, including a large collection of portraits by Sir Joshua Reynolds, was lost in the fire and the present furniture is pleasant enough but not outstanding. There are guided tours of the house every half hour. The gardens were created by the First and Second Earls between 1761 and about 1800 and a great variety of effects have been created on this beautiful site; by the Cremyll entrance there are small formal French, Italian and English gardens, and an orangery which is now the tea room. The rest of the large grounds are scattered with monuments and buildings.

Opening times: Park open all year 8 to dusk; house open May to end Sept, Mon and Tues 2–6.
Entrance charges: (1981) Park free; house 50p; children 25p.
Parking: Free car park near Cremyll entrance about ½ mile from the house; cars with disabled or young children may enter by the west entrance and park by the house.
Wheelchair access: Difficult; the steps inside leading up to the main floor are very steep.
Guidebook: A very meagre history, which does not mention the furniture but does contain a plan of the grounds with suggested walks. It is not on sale at the house, but may be bought at the Tourist Information Cenre in Plymouth.
Catering: In the Orangery café, municipal food.
WCs: Behind the cafe, also inside the house on request; neither suitable for wheelchairs.

PENCARROW Washaway, nr Bodmin (The Molesworth-St Aubyn Family)
Tel: St Mabyn (020 884) 369
Directions: 4 miles N.W. of Bodmin, signposted off the A389

In the 1760s the Molesworth family enlarged their old house with the help of Robert Allanson, a little-known architect from York. He added the south and east fronts, which are both in the Palladian style, but parts of the older building can still be seen on the north and west fronts. The guided tour of the house (which lasts about 40 minutes) begins in the Music Room which combines a pretty stucco ceiling of the 1760s with maple-grained walls done in 1844 to produce a powerful effect. The Music Room is the odd one out in a delightful series of mid-Georgian rooms, all with good chimneypieces, excellent furniture and first rate contents. Pencarrow is noted for its fine collection of 18th century paintings, including portraits by Sir Joshua Reynolds, who came from Plymouth. Upstairs the two bedrooms, a dressing room and a boudoir, and the tour ends in the ante-room with its 19th century linen wall-paper patterned with butterflies and birds. The gardens are largely the work of Sir William Molesworth who created the Italian garden and rockery in the 1830s and began the planting of specimen conifers for which the garden is famous. Past neglect of his two gardens is being amended by clearance and new planting, but the woods are still burgeoning. Walkers in the wood should buy the 'Guide to the Trees' because they will need the map it contains to find their way in the jungle, which has no signposts.

Opening times: Easter Sat to end Sept, Tues, Wed, Thurs, Fri and Sun 1.30–5.30; 1 June to 6 Sept and Bank Holiday Mon 11–5.30, last tour 5.00. Grounds open daily during season.
Entrance charges: House and garden £1.30; children 70p. Grounds only 70p; children 35p. (HHA)
Parking: Free parking in stableyard, near to house; disabled visitors can park closer; watch for signs.
Wheelchair access: Possible to the ground floor, which contains the best rooms; much of the garden is also accessible.
Guidebook: Lacks a plan of the house but is otherwise very good value. The 'Guide to the Trees' is a serious catalogue of the species in the grounds, complete with a location map.
Catering: The tea room serves simple teas and light lunches; there is also a picnic ara near the car park.
WCs: Suitable for wheelchair users.
Shop: A plant shop selling plants grown on the estate. A craft shop sells work by members of the Cornwall Craft Association. Soft fruit may be picked from the walled garden in season.
Extras: Childrens area near the car park with Wendy house, climbing frames, rabbits etc.; free.

PENDENNIS CASTLE Falmouth (Ancient Monument)
Directions: On the south edge of Falmouth, on Pendennis Head

The core of Pendennis Castle was built in about 1540 by Henry VIII to strengthen coastal defences against attack from the Continent. The King used some of the money seized from the monasteries to pay for the work at this castle, and at many others along the coasts. The castle is a squat building intended to house cannons and men to fire them. It is circular in plan and has a moat, a portcullis and ramparts from which there are fine views across the Carrick Roads. The large outer ramparts were added in the reign of Queen Elizabeth I. During the Civil War Pendennis was beseiged by the Parliamentary forces for several months; only Raglan Castle held out longer. The garrison were allowed to leave with honour and marched out 'with bullets in their mouths'. The rooms inside are empty, except for an exhibition explaining King Henry's castle-building programme. The 19th century hospital block near the entrance to the castle enclosure contains another exhibition, this time of arms and armour.

Opening times: Standard hours (SM), see page xii.
Entrance charges: 50p; children and OAPs 25p.
Parking: Free parking inside the walls.
Wheelchair access: Possible to the grounds, and the ground floor of the keep with assistance.
Guidebook: A useful combined guide to Pendennis and St Mawes Castle on the opposite side of the sound; history, description and ground plan.
Catering: None.

WCs: In the castle, but not adapted for wheelchairs.
Shop: Small selection of postcards, slides etc.

RESTORMEL CASTLE nr Lostwithiel (Ancient Monument)
Tel: Lostwithiel (0208) 872687
Directions: 1 mile N. of Lothwithiel on an unclassified road, signposted off the A390 in the centre of Lothwithiel

Restormel is the best piece of military architecture in Cornwall. What remains is the shell keep, a massive circular wall, like those at Launceston and Totnes, built on a natural hill on the west bank of the river Fowey. There was an earthwork on the site before the Norman Conquest and a timber castle with a stone gateway was built here in about 1100. The present outer wall dates from about 1200. The final additions were made by Edward, Earl of Cornwall, who built a continuous ring of living quarters inside the great wall in about 1280. His buildings are now ruinous but their original use can easily be made out with the help of the guide book. The setting of the castle is trim and the flower beds have received a lot of love and attention.

Opening times: Standard hours (SM), see page xii.
Entrance charges: 50p; children and OAPs 25p.
Parking: Free car park near the castle.
Wheelchair access: Castle and grounds both accessible.
Guidebook: An informative 20p leaflet with a ground plan.
Catering: None.
WCs: Next to the ticket office; unsuitable for wheelchairs.
Shop: Postcards and official publications only.

ST MAWES CASTLE St Mawes (Ancient Monument)
Tel: St Mawes (032 66) 526
Directions: In St Mawes, 2 miles from Falmouth via the King Harry Ferry or 19 miles S. of Truro by way of the A3078

The castles of St Mawes and Pendennis face each other across the wide inlet known as Carrick Roads, guarding the way to Falmouth and Truro. They were built by King Henry VIII as part of his coastal defence system. Amongst these many coastal castles St Mawes, built 1540-3, is held to be the finest. It has a large central tower topped by a little turret, and three bastions on the seaward side, forming in plan the shape of an ace of clubs. The curving walls were designed to deflect gunshot and also provided maximum visibility for the castle gunports. The whole building is in an excellent state of preservation. The exterior is decorated with carved coats of arms and Latin inscriptions. St Mawes was only attacked once, during the Civil War, when it promptly surrendered — in marked contrast to the spirited resistance of Pendennis. Although now empty of contents, there are various levels to explore and stairways to climb. Below the castle is a small garden planted with colourful shrubs.

Opening times: Standard hours (SM), see page xii.
Entrance charges: 40p; children and OAPs 20p.
Parking: Beside the castle; there is a charge.
Wheelchair access: Not practicable.
Guidebook: An interesting booklet, with plans, which also covers Pendennis Castle.
Catering: None, although this would be a good picnic spot.
WCs: In the gardens below the castle.
Shop: Only postcards and slides.

ST MICHAEL'S MOUNT   nr Marazion (The National Trust)
Tel: Marazion (0736) 710507
Directions: ½ mile off the coast at Marazion; which is 3 miles E. of Penzance. The causeway can be crossed on foot at low tide; at high tide in the summer months only there are ferry boats – 30p, children 15p, each way

The rocky island of St Michael's Mount is the twin of Mont St Michel in France though the buildings are less dazzling than their French counterparts. From 1135 until 1424 there was a Benedictine Priory on the Cornish island under the control of the Abbot of Mont St Michel. After the monks were expelled, the island had a succession of owners until it was bought by the St Aubyn family in 1659. Over the years the monastery buildings were adapted for use as a private house. Large additions were made between 1873 and 1878 by Piers St Aubyn, an architect member of the family with a bad reputation as a church restorer, but he took great pains not to alter the island's romantic silhouette. Visitors make their own way round the rooms at the top of the mount. The best are the mediaeval refectory, now called the Chevy Chase Room – from the plaster hunting frieze – the 14th century chapel, and the Lady Chapel which was converted in about 1750 into charming drawing rooms with rococo plaster decoration. All are furnished and the drawing rooms have a good set of Chippendale Gothic chairs. Some of the rooms are reached by crossing the terraces which form the roofs of the rest of the house from which there are excellent views.

Opening times: Nov to end March, Mon, Wed and Fri by guided tour only at 11, 12, 2, 3 and 4 weather and tide permitting; April to end May, Mon, Wed and Fri, including Good Friday 10.30–5.45, last admission 4.45 at visitors' entrance on island; June to end Oct, Mon, Tues, Wed and Fri 10.30–5.45, last admission 4.45.
Entrance charges: £1.50; children 75p.
Parking: There are pay car parks in Marazion adjacent to the ferry.
Wheelchair access: The house is not suitable for wheelchairs.
Guidebook: Written by John St Aubyn, Lord St Levan, whose family live on the Mount. It includes a plan, good photographs and lots of information. There is also an excellent free leaflet describing the contents.
Catering: In the Island Café at the foot of the Mount; open all day during summer serving hot meals as well as teas; very ordinary food.
WCs: Clean and free.
Shop: A National Trust shop selling the usual assortment and an island souvenir shop.

TINTAGEL: THE OLD POST OFFICE (The National Trust)
Directions: In the centre of Tintagel, which is on the coast 13 miles north of
 Bodmin

Beneath a crazily undulating roof of massive slates, this long low stone cottage seems to be growing out of the earth. It was built in the 14th century,
probably as a small manor house, and is a rare example of a mediaeval Cornish domestic building. The rooms inside follow the usual mediaeval layout
of hall and parlour. Between 1844 and 1892 the cottage served as the village
post office and one of the ground floor rooms has now been furnished as a
Victorian post office. The other rooms have few furnishings.

Opening times: April to end Oct, every day, including Good Friday, 11–6 or sunset.
Entrance charges: 60p; children under 16 30p.
Parking: There is a pay car park opposite the house.
Wheelchair access: Would be possible to the three ground floor rooms.
Guidebook: Included in entrance charge; a good little booklet with a plan.
Catering: None but there are many tea shops in the village.
WCs: None; there are some in the car park opposite.
Shop: Standard National Trust shop.
Extras: Further down the street, behind a very ordinary front is the curious Hall of Chivalry
 and King Arthur's Hall built in the 1930s for Fred Glasscock, a instant pudding millionaire
 who had founded a Fellowship of the Order of the Round Table. Why he chose to build his
 great hall behind this Victorian house is not clear. The ante room is hung with large paintings by William Hatherall telling the story of King Arthur. The main aisled hall, built of
 more than fifty different types of Cornish stone, has really excellent stained glass windows
 by Veronica Whall. The symbolism of the windows is explained in the guide book, which
 describes King Arthur as 'a World-Wide Asset'. Open daily 10–5.30; admission charge.

TRELOWARREN Mawgan in Meneage, nr Helston (Sir John Vyvyan
 and the Trelowarren Fellowship)
Tel: Mawgan (032 622) 366
Directions: 6 miles S.E. of Helston, signposted off the B3293

Sir Richard Vyvyan erected a pair of gate piers, like totem poles, to mark the
restoration of King Charles II. These piers, dated 1660, mark the entrance
to the drive which passes through dense woods (planted by Sir Vyell Vyvyan
in the 1820s) on its way to the house. Trelowarren is a low spreading building, now divided between the Vyvyan family (whose rooms in the north
wing are only open by appointment) and the Trelowarren Fellowship who
use the rest of the house for residential courses. The history of the building
is confusing. There was a house of some kind here in the 15th century, and
the walls of the main block may be of about 1450. The south wing contains
the chapel, which may be old in part but much was rebuilt in the mid-18th
century, while the north wing used to house the kitchens. If there was a west
range enclosing the front courtyard, it has now disappeared. Most of the exterior is covered with rendering, which hides the evidence of alterations.
The best thing in the house is the interior of the chapel which is Strawberry

Hill Gothick. Its lightness and gaiety contrast strongly with the gloomy library next door, panelled with wood from wrecked ships (the Vyvyans held the wrecking rights on the Manacles). All of the five rooms shown in the main house were redecorated in the early 19th century and have been handsomely repainted but apart from a fair selection of Vyvyan family portraits the contents are sparse. The music room upstairs is used for exibitions.

Opening times: Easter Mon, 14 April, 3 and 31 May; June and July Wed and Sun; Aug daily except Fri and Sat, 5, 6, 7, 8, 15, 22 and 29 Sept, 2.30–5.
Entrance charges: 60p; children 5–16 25p.
Parking: Free parking next to the house.
Wheelchair access: Possible to chapel and three ground floor rooms.
Guidebook: Almost totally useless as a guide to the house, concentrates on family history. There is also a free leaflet about the contents.
Catering: None in the house but coffee is served in the craft shop (see below).
WCs: On application to the housekeeper, not adapted for wheelchairs.
Shop: The Cornwall Craft Association has its exhibition centre in the stable block (built in 1698); open mid-July to mid-Sept, weekdays 11–5, Sun 2–5; admission charge.

TRERICE Newlyn East, nr Newquay (The National Trust)
Tel: Newquay (063 73) 5404
Directions: 3 miles S.E. of Newquay via A392 and A3058; signposted at Kestle Mill

Only three miles from Newquay, Trerice lies secluded in the depths of the country. It is a delightful grey stone building and doubly valuable because few substantial Elizabethan houses have survived in Cornwall. The house was built for Sir John Arundell in 1572. It has the common Elizabethan E-shaped front, with gaily curving gables and a massive window lighting the great hall which still contains some of the original 16th century glass. The gable of the north wing was taken down in the last century but was restored when the rest of the wing was rebuilt in 1954. The Arundells became great landowners in Cornwall, and at the beginning of the 18th century they ceased to live at Trerice, which was let out as a farmhouse and so escaped 'improvements' and alterations. The great hall is two storeys high and both this room and the great chamber or drawing room on the first floor have outstanding plaster ceilings; both rooms also have their original dated fireplaces. Other rooms open are the library in the south wing and a series of smaller rooms in the north wing, which are reached by a corridor which gives onto the gallery overlooking the hall. The house was purchased empty of contents by the National Trust and the present furnishings have been brought from various places. They are a very happy mixture, mostly dating from the 17th and 18th centuries, and all of good quality; the embroideries are especially interesting. The house is pleasantly compact, which means that it can get crowded in high summer. Visitors make their own way round and there are guides in each room. There is a small garden, recently formed, and a comprehensive collection of old lawn mowers on display in the barn.

Opening times: April to end Oct, daily 11–6, last admission 5.30.
Entrance charges: £1.20; children 60p; no dogs.
Parking: Free car park, 250 yards from the house.
Wheelchair access: Possible to the two ground floor rooms only; garden unsuitable.
Guidebook: Good historical account with black and white pictures but no plan; an excellent free leaflet describes the contents.
Catering: Light lunches and teas served in the converted barn, where photos of the house before restoration are displayed; restaurant open 11–6.
Wcs: Near the barn; suitable for wheelchairs.
Sho: Standard National Trust shop.

TREWINT: WESLEY'S COTTAGE (The Methodist Church – North Hill Circuit)

Tel: Pipers Pool (056 686) 561
Directions: 8 miles W. of Launceston, ½ miles S. of Altarnum, on the S. side of the A30 down a narrow signposted turning

In the 18th century the London to Penzance coach road passed this plain stone cottage, where lived Digory Isbell and his wife. In 1743 they gave hospitality to two strangers who turned out to be Methodist preachers and the Isbells soon became converts. Inspired by a passage in the Bible, Digory Isbell built a 'Prophet's Chamber' to house other travelling preaches. There were similar chambers elsewhere in Cornwall, but only this one remains intact. It was used by many preachers, including John Wesley himself, and the two rooms are simply furnished, as Wesley might have known them. The building was restored in 1950.

Opening times: All year, daily, 9 to dusk.
Entrance charges: Free.
Parking: Limited space by the house.
Wheelchair access: Not practicable.
Guidebook: Exhaustive history of the house and of local Methodism, also a brief illustrated booklet.
Catering: None.
WCs: None.
Shop: None.

TREWITHEN nr Probus (Mr and Mrs A.M.J. Galsworthy)

Tel: Grampound Road (0726) 882418: Head Gardener 882764
Directions: 6 miles E. of Truro, 1½ miles E. of Probus, signposted off the A390

Trewithen is internationally famous for its gardens, created in the 1920s by George Johnstone; the house is worth visiting too. Soon after Philip Hawkins bought the estate in 1715 he employed the architect Thomas Edwards of Greenwich to rebuild the old house. Edwards' building has a plain but stately front of brick, but now rendered. The two small stable blocks which flank this front and the stone garden front are still as Edwards designed them. In 1763 Sir Robert Taylor was brought in to make improvements, notably the redecorating of the dining room. This is certainly the best room in the house, filling five bays on the garden front. It has arcades at each and the walls have light-hearted rococo plasterwork. The rest of the house is on a more intimate scale and every room is panelled. The strange arrangement of staircases suggests that the original house still survives, buried behind the 18th century exterior. There is a very varied collection of furnishings, most of high quality and associated with the Hawkins, Mudge and Raffles families, including a number of Reynolds, Opie and Ramsay portraits and a magnificent Jacobean four-poster bed, complete with its hangings. Visitors are guided round the limited number of rooms on view. The tours take about half an hour. The gardens contain a very wide collection of flowering shrubs. Camellias, rhododendrons and magnolias were brought from the Himlayas in the 1920s and are still grown here. To the south of the house is the Long Lawn bordered with massive rhododendrons which merge into the woodland gardens behind.

Opening times: House April to end July, Mon and Tues 2–4.30, incl. Bank Holidays; Gardens March to end Sept, weekdays including Bank Holidays but not Sun 2–4.30.
Entrance charges: House £1.50, no reductions; Gardens March to June 80p; OAPs and children 70p; July to Sept 70p; OAPs and children 50p.
Parking: Free parking beside garden centre.
Wheelchair access: Possible to most of the garden.
Guidebook: Available for the garden only.
Catering: None.
WCs: Beside the plant shop. Special facilities for wheelchair users.
Shop: Plant shop open all year round.

Cumbria

ABBOT HALL Kendal (Lake District Art Gallery and Museum Trust)
Tel: Kendal (0539) 22464
Directions: In Kendal, next to the parish church and the river, signposted locally

Abbot Hall is a small 18th century house in a very pleasant setting beside the river Kent. It was designed by John Carr, one of the leading architects of northern England, and built in 1759 for Col. George Wilson. The house is built of rough local limestone and the entrance front is very plain and forbidding, but on the garden side the projecting bays and large palladian windows make a more elegant effect. Abbot Hall was purchased by Kendal Corporation in 1897 and the park has been open to the public since then. Lack of money kept the house closed until 1962, when it was turned into an art gallery. The ground floor has been restored to its 18th century appearance and furnished to look as if it were still occupied, with pictures of local interest on the walls, furniture by Gillows of Lancaster, and carpets on the floors. Many of the furnishings have local associations. The upper floor has been stripped of all its fittings and functions solely as a gallery for 20th century pictures. The stable block across the yard from the main house has been turned into a Museum of Lakeland Life on quite a large scale.

Opening times: 2 Jan to 19 Dec, House, Mon to Fri, 10.30–5.30, Sat and Sun 2–5. Lakeland Life Museum, Mon to Fri, 10.30–5, Sat and Sun, 2–5. Both closed Good Friday.
Entrance charges: House and museum 65p; children 25p. House or museum 40p; children 15p.
Parking: Free parking in front of the house, which is reached through a pay car park.
Wheelchair access: There is access by lift to the main floor of the house on Mon to Fri only.
Guidebook: A brief history of the house and the collection. There is a separate history of the Museum.
Catering: A minute but immaculate café in the outbuildings serves tea, good coffee and a limited range of snacks.
WCs: In the house, or near the café, free.
Shop: The ticket counter in the house sells postcards and publications only. A shop in the museum sells a fairly wide range of 'craftsman-made' items.

APPLEBY CASTLE Appleby (Ferguson Industrial Holdings)
Tel: Appleby (0930) 51402
Directions: In the centre of Appleby, at the top of Boroughgate

The grounds and moat of Appleby castle are stocked with exotic birds and rare breeds of domestic animals. For most visitors the wild cattle and Tamworth pigs will be the main attraction, but the castle buildings are worth at least a brief examination. At one end of the castle enclosure stands the tall square keep which was built in about 1100; the top of the keep was added at a later date and the walls inside the building are also later. There are two main rooms on each floor and some attempt has been made to furnish various rooms in the styles of the 14th, 17th and 19th centuries. Visitors can climb right on to the roof where there is a splendid view of the country around Appleby, and of the range of domestic buildings on the eastern side of the castle. A great deal of the stonework of these buildings dates from the 14th century and the postern gate on the side facing the river Eden is probably as old as the keep. The front which faces the keep was built in 1686, to the designs of the Reverend Thomas Mascell, who was the first man to bring the classical style of architecture into the north of England. The interior of this range of buildings is not open to the public.

Opening times: Good Friday to Easter Mon, then 1 May to 30 Sept daily 10.30–5.
Entrance charges: £1.00; children and OAPs 50p.
Parking: Free parking inside the castle gates, about 50 yards from the house.
Wheelchair access: Impossible to interior of the keep but otherwise fine.
Guidebook: Contains 2 pages of information about the castle and 20 pages about the animals; plenty of colour pictures.

Catering: Inside the castle a small but pleasant room serving good coffee, salads, etc.
WCs: In the stable block outside the castle proper, newly built but very cramped; not suitable for wheelchairs.
Shop: In the ground floor of the keep; not a wide range of goods, and surprisingly little material about the rare animals.

BELLE ISLE   Bowness on Winderemere (E.S.C. Curwen Esq)
Tel: Windermere (096 62) 3353
Directions: The house is on an island in Lake Windermere. Boats leave from the far end of Bowness Promenade near Cockshott Point; the landing-place is well signed

Belle Isle is an appropriate name for this highly unusual circular house. It stands on the largest island in Lake Windermere, about a mile in circumference, which is planted with mature trees that now conceal the house from the mainland. The building was designed for a Mr English by a young architect called John Plaw, and built in 1774. English was apparently the first person to visit the Lake District for its scenery. The circular plan of Belle Isle, which was Plaw's first building, was copied in a few other houses, including Ickworth in Suffolk. The architect wanted the house to look perfect from every side and he concealed the kitchen and other rooms for the servants in a sunken basement. His house is not quite so perfect now because a new kitchen has been built on to the back of the house. Belle Isle is built of a rough stone and is three storeys high, with a portico on the east side facing towads Bowness. The Curwen family have owned the house since 1776 and a portrait by Romney of Isabella Curwen shows the house in the background. Visitors to the inside of the house are guided round the ground floor only, and it is interesting to see how the architect coped with the difficulties of a house where all the outside walls are curved. An elegant staircase rises in the middle of the building and there are three principal rooms, quite small, but with Adam style plaster decoration. Some of the furniture comes from the Curwen's other house in Cumbria, at Workington, and was made in the 18th century by Gillow of Lancaster, the best furniture makers in the north west of England at that time. There is a small garden and the whole of the island is available for exploration.

Opening times: 22 May to 18 Sept, Sun, Mon, Tues and Thurs, 10.30–5. Guided tours of the house at roughly hourly intervals.
Entrance charges: Ferry to island return fare £1.00; children 60p. House 50p extra. (HHA)
Parking: There is a large pay car park near the embarkation point at Bowness.
Wheelchair access: Not possible.
Guidebook: A slim booklet giving a brief history of the house and of its owners.
Catering: In an airy room behind the house with seats and tables outside in good weather. Tea, coffee, salads, etc. of a good standard.
WCs: Next to the café, free and clean.
Shop: In the same building as the café, very much the usual run of souvenirs.

BRANTWOOD Coniston (The Ruskin Museum)
Tel: Coniston (09664) 396
Directions: 6 miles S.W. of Ambleside off the B5285, on the edge of Coniston Water

The principal attractions of Brantwood are its superb setting, backed by a wooded hillside and looking across the lake towards Coniston and the Old Man, and the associations with John Ruskin. The house itself is not very striking. At its centre is a cottage built in about 1797, which was extended at intervals during the 19th century. Ruskin himself added the turret on the front of the house and the dining room with its seven arched windows. The lumpish extension at the back of Brantwood was also built in his time. John Ruskin, who lived at Brantwood from 1872 to 1900, was one of the most famous writers on art and architecture of the 19th century and books like *The Stones of Venice* were to be found in every cultured household. He was also a great watercolour painter. The interior of Brantwood is something between a shrine and a museum. Some of the rooms have kept most of their original furniture, but they look only a little like the paintings in the house which show the rooms in Ruskin's lifetime. The paintings themselves, especially those by Ruskin, and his teacher Prout, are some compensation. Visitors can wander round as they please in the ground floor rooms and in one first floor bedroom. Ruskin's carriage, his boat and his travelling bath are preserved in the coach house by the side of the drive.

Opening times: Good Friday to end Oct, Sun to Fri, 11–5.30.
Entrance charges: House and nature trail, £1.00; children and OAPs 50p. Nature trail only 30p; children 20p. Family day-ticket £2.50.
Parking: Free car park about 100 yards from the house.
Wheelchair access: Possible to the ground floor (i.e. all but one room).
Guidebook: A short history of Brantwood and Ruskin, and a room-by-room guide which is mostly concerned with the pictures.
Catering: Coffee, tea and biscuits.
WCs: On the drive up to the house, free and well-maintained; suitable for wheelchairs.
Shop: Inside the house sells mostly books relating to Ruskin, some postcards and souvenirs, and bottles of Ruskin sherry.
Extras: Brantwood has one of the finest nature trails in the country laid out in the hills behind the house, best seen when the rhododendrons and azaleas are in flower.

BROUGH CASTLE Brough (Ancient Monument)
Directions: Brough is on the A66 about 30 miles west of Scotch Corner. The castle and the church are on the south side of the road, near the junction with the A685. The castle is signed from the village square

Brough is a ruined castle, but its walls still stand to a good height. The site is dramatic and commands excellent views across country. The Romans had a fort here and the present castle is built inside the Roman earthworks. The first keep was built by King William Rufus in about 1095, destroyed by the Scots in 1174 and rebuilt soon after. The outer walls survive almost complete but the inside is gutted. Some stretches of the wall encircling the keep survive from William Rufus' time but they have been rebuilt several times, the last time by Lady Anne Clifford in the 1660s. The great hall and the other domestic buildings inside the curtain wall are in a worse state than the keep.

Opening times: Standard hours (S) see page xii.
Entrance charges: 40p; children and OAPs 20p.
Parking: Free parking in the charming village square, about 200 yds from the castle.
Wheelchair access: Would be possible, but some energetic pushing along grass paths would be required.
Guidebook: A leaflet with a history and description the castle and a ground plan, no illustrations.
Catering: None.
WCs: None.
Shop: Postcards only.

BROUGHAM CASTLE nr Penrith (Ancient Monument)
Directions: 2 miles S.E. of Penrith just S. of the A66

The red stone ruins of Brougham Castle have been in the care of the state since 1928. They stand in a peaceful spot by the side of the River Lowther. This river crossing has always been important and long before the castle was built there was a strong Roman fort here of which some remains can still be seen. Visitors enter the castle by the outer gate, which was built in about 1300, pass through the inner gate which is ten years older, and enter the large courtyard now paved with small round stones set in cement which makes walking uncomfortable. On one side is the tall keep, the centre of the castle, built in about 1170. The two gateways and the keep are next to each other and gave Brougham a formidably strong entrance. On the south side of the courtyard are the living quarters, including the Great Hall and the kitchen. All these parts of the castle are ruinous and must be viewed from ground level but the south west tower can be climbed if the key of the door is obtained from the custodian. Although the castle was allowed to fall into decay in the late Middle Ages, it was thoroughly repaired in 1651 by Lady Anne Clifford, a lady of strong character who also restored her other castles of Appleby, Brough and Skipton and lived in them all in grand style. An inscription in the outer gatehouse records her work.

Opening times: Standard hours (S) see page xii.
Entrance charges: 50p; children and OAPs 25p.
Parking: Free parking available at castle gate.
Wheelchair access: Difficult because of the rough stone path leading from the road to the castle.
Guidebook: A small leaflet containing a full history and description of the castle and a plan.
Catering: None.

WCs: None.
Shop: None.

CARLISLE CASTLE (Ancient Monument)
Directions: In the centre of Carlisle, next to the inner ring road

The castle at Carlisle was one of the strongest in the noth of England; it was also an important royal residence. Unfortunately, many of the mediaeval buildings of the castle have been destroyed. In the last century the ground of the great outer ward was raised to make a parade ground and new barracks were built. The barracks are still used by the military and only the inner ward of the castle is open to visitors. The walls of the inner ward have been rebuilt several times in their life. This can be seen clearly on the inside of the gatehouse where an ornamental doorway has been half covered by additions made when the walls were strengthened to take artillery. The wall-walk is open to the public. In the centre of the inner ward is the Norman keep, built in about 1160. The top of the keep and the inside walls are later additions. The whole of this building is open to visitors but apart from the exhibition area on the ground floor the staircases in the thickness of the walls lead to empty rooms. On the second floor there are some small rooms which were once used as prison cells. Their walls are covered with mediaeval graffiti of animals, knights in armour, and other subjects. Close to the keep is a 19th century building which houses a museum of the history of the Border Regiment.

Opening times: Standard hours (S) see page xii.
Entrance charges: Summer 90p; children and OAPs 50p; Winter 50p; children and OAPs 25p.
Parking: Free parking inside the castle, in the outer ward.
Wheelchair access: Not possible to interior of keep or upper floor of museum.
Guidebook: An elderly (1937) work with a history of the castle, a description, and a plan of the keep; rather dry reading.
Catering: None.
WCs: Adequate; not for wheelchair users.
Shop: Postcards and souvenirs.

DALEMAIN nr Penrith (Mr and Mrs Bryce McCosh)
Tel: Pooley Bridge (085 36) 450
Directions: 3 miles S.W. of Penrith on the A592 (M6 exit 49)

Dalemain stands in rich wooded country on the northern edge of the Lake District. The oldest parts of the building are a 12th century tower and great hall, probably of the 15th century. In 1679 the old house was bought by Sir Edward Hasell. In about 1740 his son added a long new front on the east side and continued it round to enclose the hall and tower, which are now at the back of the house. The new front is long and low, built of pinkish stone, with very little decoration; the name of the architect is not known. Visitors may see the staircase, hall and three rooms on the ground floor of the 18th century house, and almost all of the older buildings. There are information boards in the rooms with text in English, French and German. The staircase is simply but elegantly carved. The Chinese drawing room is decorated with an elaborate Chinese wallpaper and a very pretty fireplace carved in the Chinese style; the drawing room has plain panelling and some good portraits. The ground floor of the tower contains the Regimental Museum of the Westmoreland and Cumberland Yeomanry but the rest of the older rooms are furnished with 17th and 18th century furniture. Two of these rooms have 16th century panelling and the Fretwork Room has a good plaster ceiling; there is also a nursery and a housekeeper's room. The garden is not large, but attractively combines formal and informal planting. Dalemain is still a working estate and to one side of the house is a large yard, enclosed on the north side by a very large 17th century barn. The first floor of the barn is open to the public and is worth a visit. It contains a display of farm machinery.

Opening times: Easter Sat to mid-Oct, daily except Fri, 2–5.15.

Entrance charges: Houses and gardens £1.40; children and registered disabled 70p, wheelchair-users free. (HHA)

Parking: Free car park about 50 yards from the house.

Wheelchair access: Possible only to ground floor rooms, and to the great hall which serves as the tea room.

Guidebook: Principally a room-by-room guide; rather thin on information about the house. Many illustrations, no plan.

Catering: Small self-service tea room in the old hall, tea by the cup and good home-made cakes.

WCs: In the yard, modern spacious; suitable for wheelchairs.

Shop: On two levels, rather cramped; sells china, craft goods and home-made jam. There are usually plants for sale in the yard.

DOVE COTTAGE Grasmere (The Dove Cottage Trust)

Tel: Grasmere (096 65) 464 or 418

Directions: ½ mile S.E. of Grasmere village centre, just off the A592

William Wordsworth lived here from 1799 until 1808 and during that time he wrote some of his best-known poetry. The building was acquired as a Wordsworth Memorial in 1890 and has been open to the public ever since. The cottage contains three small rooms on the ground floor, two of them panelled, and four on the upper floor, one of them newspapered. Most of the furniture belonged to the Wordsworth family and a successful attempt has been made to recapture the flavour of the simple domestic life which Wordsworth lived here. A doorway opens off the staircase landing to the rocky garden which the poet formed behind the house. Near to the cottage are a museum, which contains manuscripts and other material relating to

Wordsworth, and the new Heritage Centre.

Opening times: March and Oct, Mon to Sat, 10–1, 2–4.30; April to Sept, Mon to Sat, 9.30–1, 2–5.30; last admission half an hour before closing. Sunday opening 1–5 and lunchtime opening 1–2 are to be tried as an experiment in July and August.

Entrance charges: (1981) £1.00; children 50p (to cottage and museum).

Parking: Free car park of limited size next to the heritage Centre.

Wheelchair access: Possible to ground floor rooms of thecottage.

Guidebook: A brief history of the house and room-by-room guide, larded with Wordsworth quotations.

Catering: None.

WCs: In a separate building near the cottage, free but basic; not suitable for wheelchairs.

Shop: Called a bookshop; the emphasis is on the works of the poet, with other books of literary criticism.

Extras: Visitors might like to be reminded that Wordsworth is buried in the churchyard at Grasmere. A new Grasmere and Wordsworth Museum was opened in October 1981 which explains the development of and interest in the picturesque landscape.

HILL TOP Near Sawrey (The National Trust)

Tel: The Manageress, Hawkshead (096 66) 334

Directions: 3 miles S. of Hawkshead on the B5285, in the village of Near Sawry

There is nothing very unusual about the house at Hill Top. It is a small 17th century farmhouse with a pretty garden. But for many people, both the house and the rooms inside will seem familiar. Beatrix Potter lived at Hill Top in the early years of this century and many of her children's books are illustrated with delightful drawings of the house and its furniture. Although she married and moved to another house in the village in 1913, Hill Top was not sold or altered. On the ground floor are the slate-floored kitchen and the parlour; upstairs are three small bedrooms and a gallery containing many of the original drawings. The house is small and has many visitors. In high summer there are sometimes long delays, but those waiting can refresh themselves at the pub next door, which is also owned by the National Trust. There is no electric light in the house so dark days are perhaps best avoided.

Opening times: April to end Oct, daily except Fri, 10–5.30, Sun 2–5.30.

Entrance charges: £1.50; children 60p.

Parking: There is parking space for about five cars opposite the entrance to the house.

Wheelchair access: Possible to ground floor (two rooms) only; apply at the ticket office about access, best to avoid weekends.

Guidebook: A miniature booklet containing a room-by-room guide.

Catering: None.

WCs: None in the house.

Shop: A fairly large shop at the entrance selling the books and other Beatrix Potter material.

HOLKER HALL   Cark in Cartmel (Hugh Cavendish Esq)
Tel: Flookburgh (044 853) 328
Directions: 4 miles W. of Grange over Sands on the B5278

Holker Hall is a sprawling house. The oldest part of the building is the cement-faced range called the old wing, built in the 17th century but altered in 1840. This is not open to the public. In 1871 a large part of the house burnt down and was replaced by a grand new wing designed by Paley & Austin, probably the best architects in north west England at this time. The new wing is built of red sandstone in the Elizabethan style, with tall gables and a tower poking up above the roof. The interior is spacious and comfortable. The woodwork and the marble for the chimneypieces came from the estate or nearby, and is finished to a high standard. On the ground floor is a large hall and four large rooms which look out on the garden. They are filled with a mixture of fine furniture and deep armchairs, as most great houses were at the time of World War I. A very elaborate carved staircase leads to the upper hall and the bedrooms opening off it. There is the same mixture of Georgian and later furniture and some sketches by Gainsborough hang behind one of the bedroom doors. Visitors proceed under their own steam without ropes to keep them to the edge of the rooms. There are guides in some rooms but no feeling of being watched like a potential criminal. The large garden is a mixture of formal and informal planting and contains the oldest monkey-puzzle tree in England, and other rare trees and shrubs.

Opening times: Easter Sun to 3 Oct, daily except Sat, 10.30–6. Last admission to hall, 5.15.
Entrance charges: £2.00; children £1.30; OAPs £1.60. 'All-in' ticket £2.75; children £1.85. (HHA)
Parking: Free car park about 50 yards from the house.
Wheelchair access: Possible to all ground floor rooms, ramps in the garden.
Guidebook: Large and glossy with many illustrations. A well-written account of the family and a room-by-room guide, no plan but a bird's eye view instead.
Catering: Excellent and spotless cafeteria serving morning coffee, lunch and tea; seats outside in good weather.
WCs: Next to the shop, free and clean but rather small; there are ramps but the cubicles are too small for wheelchairs.
Shop: A large shop with a good range of novelties. There is also a shop in the Motor Museum.
Extras: The Motor Museum houses about 60 old cars and motorcycles, a reconstructed garage of the 1920s and a full-size replica of Sir Malcolm Campbell's *Bluebird*. No extra charge is made for the Countryside Museum, Lakeland Craft Museum, model railway or adventure playground.

HUTTON IN THE FOREST   nr Penrith (Lord and Lady Inglewood)
Tel: Skelton (085 34) 207
Directions: 6 miles N.W. of Penrith on the B5305 (M6 exit 41)

An untidy but attractive mixture of buildings. The oldest part of Hutton is the 14th century tower over the main entrance. To the north of the tower is a wing of 1641–5, to the east is a square Baroque front of about 1685 and beyond this front is a heavy tower in the mediaeval style, added in 1826 and enlarged in the 1870s, which is taller than the rest of the house. Most of the different parts are by local architects and each has its own fascination. The north wing by Alexander Pogmire contains the long gallery. The ground floor of the wing was once open and has curious columns which might have been copied from a building of 1340. The Baroque centre of the main front was designed by Edward Addison and is one of the earliest examples of this style in the north. It is built in a lighter stone than the rest of the houe and the busy decoration stands out well. Thomas Webster of Kendal built the larger tower and was helped by Anthony Salvin, who returned in 1871 to improve the inside of the house. For the most part, the interior rooms are disappointing. Salvin swept away the old decorations and replaced them with his own rather dreary ones. The rooms are filled with a mixed collection of paintings and furniture which is carefully described on the handboards available in every room. One survival from the 1680s decoration is the staircase in the hall, carved with fat jolly cherubs. Visitors can make their own through the rooms, with the minimum of restriction.

Opening times: Bank Holiday Mon April to August; 20 May to 14 Oct, Thurs 2–5; also Sun 15, 22, 29 Aug, 2–5. Parties by arrangement any weekday May to Oct.
Entrance charges: £1.00p; children 50p; no dogs. Reduced rates for parties. (HHA)
Parking: Free parking on grass about 50 yards from front of house.
Wheelchair access: Possible to hall, dining room, cafeteria and gardens.
Guidebook: A long history of house and family, brief room-by-room guide (supplemented with handboards in each room) and many black and white illustrations. No plan, but otherwise excellent.
Catering: Tea and coffee by the cup and excellent home-made cakes served in the grond floor of the north wing.
WCs: Small but adequate and clean; unsuitable for the disabled.
Shop: A small shop under the north wing sells souvenirs and postcards.

LEVENS HALL Kendal (O.R. Bagot Esq)
Tel: Sedgwick (0448) 60321
Directions: 5 miles S. of Kendal on the A6, immediately S. of the junction with the A590

Like many houses in the north, Levens began as a mediaeval pele tower. The tower still stands just to the right of the main entrance but the rest of the house is the product of rebuilding carried out between 1570 and 1590 by the Bellinghams, who were also responsible for the splendid decoration of the rooms. The final touches were added by Col. James Grahme who made the garden and filled the rooms with furniture of high quality. The house, built of rough stone, is tall and irregular in appearance. The entrance leads straight into the great hall with its panelled walls and plaster ceiling. The frieze above the panelling is decorated with the coat of arms of Queen Elizabeth I and those of various Bellingham alliances. Of the other rooms on the ground floor, the drawing room, small drawing room and the dining room all have fine ceilings and carved chimneypieces; the walls of the first two are panelled but in the dining room the wall covering is Spanish leather. Each one of these rooms, and indeed every room in the house, is filled with fine furniture, much of it made for Col. Grahme in about 1700. There is also a respectable collection of Dutch paintings. In one of the bedrooms on the first floor is a patchwork quilt, said to be the first in England, made of chintz from India by one of Col. Grahme's daughters. Visitors take themselves around the house with a minimum of restriction and there are guides in every room. The topiary gardens are probably better known than the house iself; they were laid out by Monseigneur Beaumont, a pupil of Le Nôtre, in 1692 and have been little altered since then.

Opening times: House Easter Sun to 30 Sept, Tues, Wed, Thurs, Sun and Bank Holiday Mon 11–5. Gardens and plant centre Easter Sun to end Sept, daily 11–5.

Entrance charges: House and Steam Collection £1.60; children 80p. Gardens and Steam Collection 90p; children 45p. Gardens only 80p; children 40p. Reduced rates for parties. (HHA)

Paring: Free car park about 50 yards from the house.

Wheelchair access: Not possible to the house; garden and tea room both accessible.

Guidebook: A detailed room-by-room guide with a brief history of the gardens and of the family. Many pictures but no plan and not a great deal of information about the building itself.

Catering: The small but pleasant tea room (tablecloths and plastic cups) serves tea by the cup and good cakes. Bar lunches 12–2, served in a panelled room with an Elizabethan fireplace.

WCs: In the rear courtyard, newly built and free. The cubicle for wheelchair users looks rather cramped.

Shop: In the basement sells tea towels, postcards and other souvenirs but nothing special. The prices of plants in the Garden Centre seem very reasonable.

Extras: In the Steam Collection is a fascinating display of small 'table engines', all working. There are also a full size and a miniature traction engine which steam occasionally. Open 2–5. Another extra is the garden centre offering plants for sale.

MUNCASTER CASTLE Ravenglass (Sir William Pennington-Ramsden Bart)

Tel: Ravenglass (065 77) 614

Directions: 1 mile S.E. of Ravenglass village on the A595

The long but pleasant walk from the main gate to the house makes a good introduction to the beautiful park and gardens of Muncaster. The rhododendrons are famous and the view of the Lakeland hills from the Terrace Walk is spectacular. The house incorporates a mediaeval tower, but most of this pink granite castle is the work of the architect Anthony Salvin and was built between 1862 and 1866. The rooms within are solidly Victorian, but recently painted in bright colours. Most of the rooms shown are on the ground floor. The hall, dining room and the large octagonal library contain some good 17th century furniture and fine paintings and sculpture, much of it brought into the house during this century. Upstairs are two bedrooms with elaborate Tudor fireplaces brought from another house and furnishings of about the same date. The last room on the ground floor is the dining room, much the pleasantest room on show, with its curved plaster ceiling, fine carpets, Italian furniture and, most of all, the excellent collection of English portraits. Unfortunately a rope prevents close inspection of the pictures.

Opening times: Good Friday to 4 Oct. Gardens daily except Fri 12–5; Castle Tues, Wed, Thurs, Sun and Bank Holidays 2–5.
Entrance charges: (1981) Castle and grounds £1.00; children 75p. Grounds only 50p. (HHA)
Parking: Free car park by the main road, about a third of a mile from the house.
Wheelchair access: Possible to main ground floor rooms.
Guidebook: Brief history of the family and castle with a room-by-room guide. Many illustrations, including a colour picture of every room, but no plan.
Catering: A cafeteria in the outbuildings serves fried meals, sandwiches, teas and cakes, but the surroundings are not very pleasant nor is the food appetizing.
WCs: In the outbuildings, and in the rhododendrons near the main entrance; both offer very basic facilities.
Shop: Near the cafeteria; sells some locally made pottery, which is enterprising, but otherwise a dreary selection of souvenirs.
Extras: In the grounds there are several enclosures for exotic birds, wallabies, bush-babies and a bear pit with Himalayan bears. Near the castle is an adventure playground which seems very popular.

RUSLAND HALL nr Newby Bridge
Tel: Satterthwaite (022 984) 276
Directions: 2½ miles N.W. of Newby Bridge in the village of Rusland. The roads hereabout are unclassified but the house is signed from Newby Bridge

No one seems to know very much about the history of Rusland Hall, except that it was built by the Rawlinson family in about 1720 and extended by the Archibald family in about 1845. The three-storey central block with its handsome door-surround is the earliest part; the wings and the buildings at the rear came later. The rooms inside are not elaborately decorated and contain mainly 19th century furniture. The greatest interest lies in the collections of early photographic equipment and mechanical musical instruments on the ground floor. Several of the pianos can actually be played by putting money in the slot. The four acre garden is simply planted, not to say bare; perhaps the peacocks are responsible.

Opening times: April to Sept, daily, except Sat 11–5.30.
Entrance charges: £1.00; children 50p; OAPs 80p.
Parking: Free parking in the drive of the house.
Wheelchair access: Possible to the ground floor of the house.
Guidebook: None. A free leaflet containing two paragraphs of information is given free to each visitor.
Catering: None.
WCs: None for public use.
Shop: None.

RYDAL MOUNT   Rydal, Ambleside (Mary Henderson)
Tel: Ambleside (096 63) 3002
Directions: 3 miles N. of Ambleside on the A591

Rydal Mount is an ample Lakeland house dating partly from the 16th century but principally from the late 18th and 19th centuries. It is built of stone, whitewashed, and makes no claim to architectural distinction. William Wordsworth lived here during the greater part of his adult life from 1813 to 1850. Rydal was purchased by one of Wordsworth's descendants and opened to the public only a few years ago. Much of the original contents have gone but there is still a respectable quantity of the furniture, portraits and relics usual in literary shrines. Visitors make their own way round, guided by information leaflets (which are available in 18 languages as well as in braille). Wordsworth was a keen gardener and the four-and-a-half acres of garden at Rydal were laid out by him to make the most of the view of the country around.

Opening times: March to Oct, daily, 10–5.30; Nov to mid-Jan, 10–12.30 and 2–4.
Entrance charges: House and gardens 70p; pensioners and students 60p; children 40p. (HHA)
Parking: A small (15 cars) steeply-sloping car park near the house.
Wheelchair access: Wheelchair users are admitted free and can see all ground floor rooms.
Guidebook: A history of the house and a room-by-room guide, full of anecdotes about the Wordsworths and their friends.
Catering: None.
WCs: There are public toilets.
Shop: A small shop sells mostly books about or by Wordsworth, as well as the smaller sort of souvenirs.

SIZERGH CASTLE   nr Kendal (The National Trust)
Tel: Sedgwick (0448) 60285
Directions: 3½ miles S. of Kendal, 1 mile N. of junction of A6 and A65

The Strickland family have owned Sizergh since 1239 although no buildings of this date are standing. The main part of the house is a large square tower of about 1350 and a smaller block next to it which started life in about 1450 as the Great Hall. From the main house stretch two long wings, built in the 16th century as servants' quarters and barracks for the armed men needed in this wild part of of the north of England. Both the great hall and the wings have been altered inside and later windows have been put in. The main entrance leads directly into the lower hall through a carved wooden screen dated 1558; this is a taste of what is in store. Broad stairs lead up to the rooms on the first floor which contain some of the best early Elizabethan woodwork to be found in any house in England. Five rooms have spectacular carved chimneypieces of various dates, from 1563 in the Elizabethan dining room to 1575 in the Boynton room. The walls of the rooms are panelled and the ceilings have wooden ornament of the same date as the chimneypieces. Unfortunately, the most elaborate woodwork, from the inlaid room, was sold to the Victoria and Albert Museum in London in 1896 and is no longer in the house. The house has good furnishings of Elizabethan and of later dates and there are a number of relics of the Stuart Royal Family in the museum on the top floor of the tower. To the north east of the house is a notable rock garden which was laid out in the 1920s.

Opening times: April to Sept, Wed and Sun and Bank Holiday Mon, also Thurs in July and Aug, 2–5.45. Garden only April to end June and Sept, Thurs 2–5.45; Oct, Wed and Thurs 2–5.45.

Entrance charges: £1.10; children 55p. Garden only 40p and 20p.

Parking: Large free car park near house.

Wheelchair access: Not practicable to the house but possible to the garden.

Guidebook: Written by a former owner of the house and very full in its account of the family and the building; there is a room-by-room guide and an excellent plan of the building – for which full marks.

Catering: None.

WCs: Inside the house and near coach park free, well-maintained.

Shop: Next to the barn and near the car park; a good standard National Trust shop with the usual range of tea towels, educational toys, pot pourri, etc.

SWARTHMOOR HALL nr Ulverston (The Society of Friends)
Tel: Ulverston (0229) 53204
Directions: ¾ mile S. of Ulverston off the A590 (turn at the Miners' Arms public house)

To the majority of its visitors, Swarthmoor is famous as the cradle of the Quaker set. The Fell family of Swarthmoor were strong supporters of George Fox and it was partly because of their support that he was able to build up a following. The hall was built in the early 17th century by George Fell. From the outside it does not look impressive; the front is irregular and the walls are covered with grey cement rendering. The inside comes as a pleasant surprise with its panelled rooms, some of the panelling replaced in the 1930s and some original. One very unusual feature is the staircase which has a heavily timbered open well in the centre; this is worth a visit on its own account. Most of the rooms shown to the public are not occupied but have sturdy 17th century furniture. There is a small garden.

Opening times: Mid-March to mid-Oct, Mon, Tues, Wed, Sat, 10–12 and 2–5. Other times by arrangement.

Entrance charges: Free, donations welcomed.

Parking: Free car park next to the house.

Guidebook: A small pamphlet, mostly concerned with the Quaker connections, but with a brief list of 'points of interest' about the house.

Catering: None.

WCs: In the house.

Shop: None.

TOWNEND   Troutbeck (The National Trust)
Tel: Ambleside (096 63) 2628
Directions: 3 miles S.E. of Ambleside on the edge of Troutbeck village near
   Windermere; signposted from the A591 and A592

When George Browne of Townend married Susannah Rawlinson in 1623 it
was a condition of the marriage that he should rebuild the old family house.
His new house is the present Townend, a small building with roughcast
walls, mullioned windows and the large circular chimneys found on many
houses in the Lake District. The Brownes continued to live here until 1943.
They were mostly wealthy farmers and took an active part in public life, but
the long winters gave them time for home improvements. Woodcarving
seems to have been a favourite pastime, and the rooms of Townend, particularly the kitchen and 'firehouse' or hall downstairs, are crammed full of cup-
boads, drawers and tables made and decorated by the Brownes. In one place
a grandfather clock has been completely enclosed by a set of drawers. The
third downstairs room is the library, whose books show that the family read
widely. Upstairs the riot of carving continues and it is strange to see how the
fireplace in the main bedroom (dated 1881) differs little from the work done
two hundred years before. All the odds and ends of the domestic life of the
family have been left untouched; there is not even electric light, which limits
the visiting hours. Visitors make their own way round after a brief introduction from the National Trust resident. The dairy next to the main house is
laid out with equipment borrowed from the Lakeland Life Museum at Kendal.

Opening times: April to end Oct daily, except Sat and Mon and Good Friday (open Bank Holi-
   day Mon) 2–6, or dusk if earlier.
Entrance charges: 80p; children 40p.
Parking: A free car park with access to the house by footpath; no parking outside the house.
Wheelchair access: Not possible.
Guidebook: A short and well-written history of the family and their house and a room-by-
   room guide; illustrated with drawings and a plan.
Catering: None.
WCs: Yes.
Shop: None.

WORDSWORTH HOUSE High Street, Cockermouth (The National
   Trust)
Tel: Cockermouth (0900) 824805
Directions: In the centre of the town at the west end of the main street

Cockermouth is a pretty little town whose principal buildings are stretched
along the tree-lined High street. One of the best buildings in the town is this
substantial mid-18th century house where William Wordsworth was born.
The house was built in 1745, according to an inscription over the back door.
It has a long whitewashed stone front and is set back from the street behind

Townend, Cumbria

tall gates. Almost all the rooms inside the house are open to the public. As a contrast to the plain exterior, they have elaborate cornices and overdoors. The drawing room especially is elegant and serves as a reminder that Wordworth's father, as agent to Sir James Lowther, was a man of importance in local life. Most of the furniture in the room dates from the lifetime of the poet, and some pieces are associated with him. Information boards in each room provide full information. A charming garden at the back of the house runs down to a terrace on the bank of the River Derwent. The way out lies through an audio-visual exhibit about Wordsworth and Cockermouth.

Opening times: April to end Oct, daily except Thurs and Good Friday 11–5, Sun 2–5.
Entrance charges: £1.00p; children 50p
Parking: No visitor's car park, but plenty of on-street parking available.
Wheelchair access: Not possible.
Guidebook: A short literary essay on Wordsworth and Cockermouth and a room-by-room guide; several illustrations, three poems, no plan.
Catering: Coffee, lunch and tea served in the old kitchen and housekeeper's room. The food is enterprising. There is a lunch-time licence and a fire in cold weather.
WCs: Modern block in the courtyard behind the house.
Shop: In the building adjacent to the house; visitors pass through the shop on the way out, but it also has a street entrance. All the usual National Trust stock but with more than usually pleasant staff.

Derbyshire

BAKEWELL: THE OLD HOUSE MUSEUM (Bakewell Historical Society)
Tel: For party bookings only, Bakewell (062 981) 3647
Directions: In Bakewell, above the church, signposted from the roundabout in the town centre

The grey limestone building of the Old House lies on a steep hill above the town centre and is now surrounded by Victorian villas. The main part of the house is a single storey hall with a parlour and service room at one end and bedrooms above. The house was built in the 1530s, by Ralph Gell, probably to house his bailiff. Some alterations were made in the 1620s when the house was extended and a porch was added. In about 1780 the building was divided up into small dwellings for workers from Sir Richard Arkwright's cotton mill. In 1954 the whole building was declared unfit for human habitation, but was saved by a local society who have now restored it. Among the surviving features are the chamfered ceiling beams and an original first floor garderobe. The small rooms are set out with museum displays of old household objects old toys, lacework, and things to do with local history. There is no formal tour, but the staff are eager to explain house and contents.

Opening times: Easter to end Oct, daily, 2.30–5.
Entrance charges: 40p; children 20p.
Parking: Parking in nearby streets is not difficult.
Wheelchair access: Not practicable.
Guidebook: A history of the house and detailed description of the features of each room, with a plan showing the development.
Catering: None.
WCs: None.
Shop: None.

BOLSOVER CASTLE Bolsover (Ancient Monument)

Tel: (0246) 823349
Directions: In Bolsover, 6 miles E. of Chesterfield, 2 miles E. of the M1 on the A632

Bolsover lies a few miles north of Hardwick hall, on the edge of the same ridge, overlooking a landscape of coal mines and farmland. There was a mediaeval castle here, but it was destroyed to make way for the fantastic house of the Cavendish family, and all the surviving buildings date from the 17th century. Inside the massive rusticated gates is a huge grassy court, enclosed by gutted or empty buildings. The oldest is the Little Keep, a pretend castle in mediaeval style built by Robert Smythson for Sir Charles Cavendish between 1612 and 1620. The rooms inside are small and mysterious, with vaulted ceilings, ornamental panelling and extraordinary fireplaces. A roofless but impressive range stretching from the keep along the crest of the ridge contains the hall, long gallery and other main rooms. It was built by John Smythson, son of Robert, between about 1620 and 1640. The carved stone ornament is wildly out of the ordinary, especially the curious buttresses, which look like giant vertical cannons. The remaining range of buildings fronting the great courtyard still has a roof. It contains a 17th century riding school which is still used for its original purpose, and its splendid ornamental timber roof can be inspected at close quarters from the gallery at one end. The riding school range and that section of the main apartments which adjoins it may not have been built until the 1660s. Bolsover is an attractive place, despite its industrial surroundings, and an impressive example of what is known as the 'Artisan Mannerist' style.

Opening times: Standard hours (SM), see page xii.
Entrance charges: 50p; children and OAPs 25p.
Parking: Free car park by main entrance, about 300 yards from the castle.
Wheelchair access: It would be possible to see all the exterior, the most interesting part; the keep would not be accessible.
Guidebook: Either a very brief leaflet, with a plan, or a very detailed description in the Official Handbook. There is some dispute about the date of 1620 given to the main apartments in the Handbook.
Catering: None.
WCs: Near the gates, free; unsuitable for wheelchairs.
Shop: Only postcards and slides.

CHATSWORTH   nr Bakewell (Trustees of the Chatsworth Settlement)
Tel: Baslow (024 688) 2204
Directions: 10 miles W. of Chesterfield, 3 miles E. of Bakewell, 2 miles S. of Baslow on the B6012

The grounds of Chatsworth are enormous, the great classical house is impressive and its contents are outstanding. These attractions bring crowds of visitors, but there seems to be room for all of them. The first Chatsworth was an Elizabethan house planned round a courtyard. The court still remains but each side of the house was rebuilt in turn between 1687 and 1707 by William Cavendish, First Duke of Devonshire. The south and east sides were designed by William Talman. The architect of the pedimented west side is unknown, but it was probably Thomas Archer, whose curving north front completed the building. The massive and ugly north wing was added a century later by the Sixth Duke, whose architect was Jeffry Wyatville. Many of the rooms in the main house still have their early Georgian character, with ceilings painted by Verrio and Laguerre and first-rate carved decoration by Samuel Watson and others. Visitors follow a set route, starting in a gloomy entrance hall in the north front and leading through the painted hall, the oak room with its woodwork from a German monastery, and the chapel, finished in 1694. Its alabaster altarpiece is excellently carved, the upper walls and ceiling were painted by Laguerre and the air is perfumed by the cedarwood panelling. The State Apartment on the second floor is a series of rooms of overpowering splendour which occupies the whole south front. The route through the rooms is defined by low kerbs, which are less obtrusive than the usual ropes. After the State Apartment the Queen of Scots and Leicester Apartments may be seen, for an extra charge. They are mainly bedrooms and small sitting rooms with decoration and furniture of the 1830s. The route then proceeds by way of the great staircase, painted hall and oak stairs to the long library, formed from the old long gallery, which maybe seen but not entered. The last rooms on the tour are the dining room, sculpture gallery and orangery, which also date from the 1830s. Chatsworth has exceptionally good collections of paintings and furniture, augmented by the contents of Devonshire House and Chiswick House in London and every room contains things of interest and beauty. A small part of the gardens to the south of the house is private, but the spectacular cascade, the camellia houses and a number of lawns and formal gardens are accessible. If the crowds prove too much the vast park offers instant solitude.

Opening times: 28 March to 31 Oct, daily; house 11.30–4.30, grounds 11.30–5; farmyard 28 March to 3 Oct, Mon to Fri 10.30–4.30, Sat and Sun 11.30–4.30.
Entrance charges: (1981) House and garden £1.90; children 90p. Garden only 90p; children 40p. Farmyard 60p; children 30p. Family ticket £5.
Parking: Next to the house; a charge is made.
Wheelchair access: Not possible to house, possible but not easy to gardens.
Guidebook: Available in English, French and German; a souvenir guide with many pictures,

Chatsworth, Derbyshire

descriptions of each room, but no plan.

Catering: In the splendid stable block, designed by James Paine and built 1758–63, the tables are placed in the original stalls. The food (salads and snacks) does not live up to its surroundings. There are also ice cream kiosks near the car park and the garden.

WCs: By the car park, adequate but over-used; one for wheelchairs.

Shop: A large pleasant shop in the orangery (available only to those who pay for admission to house or garden). Large selection of high-class commercial products.

Extras: The Farmyard behind the stables has been arranged in an attempt to explain farming with the help of real machinery and live animals.

HADDON HALL   nr Bakewell (The Duke of Rutland)
Tel: Bakewell (062 981) 2855
Directions: 2 miles S.E. of Bakewell, 6½ miles N. of Matlock on the A6

Haddon is a grey stone house of the Middle Ages, a jumble of battlemented walls, towers and chimneys, standing on a wooded slope above the River Wye. It was abandoned by the Manners family in 1700 and, apart from some careful restoration in the 1920s, everything remains as they left it. The house originally had one large central courtyard, but in about 1370 a range containing great hall, kitchen and parlour was built across the middle, forming two smaller courts. A steep path leads to the gatehouse and so into the lower court. The little museum to the left of the gatehouse which contains finds made during the restoration work and the chapel on the far side of the court should be visited first. the walls of the chapel have mediaeval paintings and the roof and other woodwork date from 1624. Visitors then make their way back across the court to the house entrance. The great hall roof dates from the 1920s but the screen is of 1450. The kitchens at one end of the hall still have their meal arks, salting troughs and other Tudor fittings. There is also a good collection of early bread cupboards. The parlours beyond the hall has a decorated ceiling of about 1500 and panelling of the 1540s. Both are rare examples of English interior decoration of this period. Upstairs are the great chamber, some smaller rooms and the long gallery with its beautifully carved panelling of about 1600. This room is made doubly attractive by the light streaming in through the large bay windows. Although the rooms at Haddon are not occupied they are furnished and hung with tapestries. The furniture is mostly of the 16th and 17th centuries. Visitors are free to wander at their own speed with a minimum of restriction. Information about decoration and furniture is given on boards in each room. The garden was laid out in the 17th century in a series of terraces and is now planted with roses. Although crowded at week-ends, the place is often marvellously empty during the week.

Opening times: 1 April to 30 Sept, Tues to Sat and Bank Holiday Mon 11–6, Bank Holiday Sun 2–6.

Entrance charges: House and garden £1.50; children 80p; no dogs or push chairs. (HHA)

Parking: Free car park across the main road from the entrance gate, about 500 yards and a

steep climb from the house.
Wheelchair access: Not practicable to house or garden.
Guidebook: A fully illustrated room-by-room guide with notes on the Vernon and Manners families. There are information boards in each room.
Catering: On the upper floor of the old stables, at the foot of the approach to the house; waitress service, unremarkable salads and teas.
WCs: Underneath the tea room, passable.
Shop: The Orpheus Room (the last room seen in the house) has a selection of souvenirs ranging from bookmarks to lace and Crown Derby china.

HARDWICK HALL nr Chesterfield (The National Trust)

Tel: Chesterfield (0246) 850430
Directions: 6½ miles N.W. of Mansfield, 9½ miles S.E. of Chesterfield, 2 miles S. of the A617

Elizabeth, Countess of Shrewsbury, better known as Bess of Hardwick, married four times and rose further up the social ladder with each marriage. When she parted from her last husband and left his house at Chatsworth she set about enlarging her family manor house at Hardwick. After his death in 1590, she began a new mansion house next door to the old one. It was finished in seven years. Her architect was probably Robert Smythson, the best man of his day. The house is very tall. Its plan is an H with a tower at each end and two towers on either side. The buff stone walls are pierced by huge mullioned windows, which gave rise to the rhyme 'Hardwick Hall, more window than wall'. Few Elizabethan houses look as crisp and modern. The central entrance door leads into the hall, which is unusual in its plan as it runs from front to back, not across the width of the house. The rest of the ground floor was used mainly by the servants. The family living rooms are on the first floor and the state rooms, which were used only on great occasions, are on the top floor. Many of these rooms still have their original furniture and hangings. Visitors follow a set route, starting in the hall, which has some unusual panels of 16th century appliqué work. At the back of the hall, the great staircase rises past the private drawing room, which has 18th and 19th century furniture belonging to the late Duchess of Devonshire, as well as Flemish tapestries belonging to Bess of Hardwick. The stairs are also hung with tapestry. At the top of the stairs is the High Great Chamber, the main state room, with a huge painted plaster frieze by Abraham Smith, who did a lot of the decorative work at Hardwick. The room was designed to fit the tapestry which still lines the walls. Behind the chamber is the long gallery running the full width of the house, its tapestry-lined walls hung with pictures and lit by the enormous bay windows. The two huge fireplaces here were carved by Thomas Accres. The other rooms on the top floor are smaller, but with rich decoration and important furniture, often with its original upholstery. A back staircase, hung with examples of the embroidery for which the house is famous, leads to the family living rooms and chapel on the first floor and so down to the kitchen, now the tea room, with a fine display of copper cooking pots. Outside the house, the original garden walls and lodges survive, but the garden itself has been replanted with herbaceous borders and clipped hedges. Across from the house are the large ruins of the old manor house, which is under repair and not open. Hardwick attracts many visitors.

Opening times: Park all year daily. April to end Oct, House Wed, Thurs, Sat, Sun and Bank Holiday Mon 1–5.30 or sunset, last admission 5. Garden daily 12–5.30.

Entrance charges: Park (parking charge) 25p. House and garden £1.60; children 80p. Garden only 80p; children 40p.

Parking: Free car park next to house for visitors to house and garden.

Wheelchair access: Not practicable to the house; possible to the garden.

Guidebook: A selection: i) the ordinary guide, adequate for most purposes, with history, description of rooms and furniture, plans, black and white illustrations; ii) 'Look at Hardwick Hall', a simpler cheaper booklet for children with jolly drawings; iii) a very expensive history and guide by Mark Girouard with a detailed history of the house and details of the pictures and other items.

Catering: In the old kitchen; lunches and teas throughout the season, waitress service.

WCs: Next to the shop and tea room, adequate, but not suitable for wheelchairs.

Shop: Near the exit from the house, though accessible from outside, with a good selection of the National Trust standard items.

KEDLESTON HALL　nr Derby (Viscount Scarsdale)

Tel: Derby (0332) 842191

Directions: 4½ miles N.W. of Derby, 1½ miles N. of the A52, signposted locally

At Kedleston the parkland sweeps up from the lake to the long main front of the house. The great pedimented central block is flanked by pavilions each the size of a decent country mansion. The house was built for Sir Nathaniel Curzon between 1759 and 1765. His first architect was Matthew Brettingham, who provided the basic plan; in 1760 James Paine took over, but almost at once Robert Adam replaced him. Adam modified Paine's Palladian design for the entrance front but designed a completely new and original south front based on a Roman triumphal arch. Visitors climb to the great portico and enter the marble hall, a grand stately and sombre room with alabaster columns, and plasterwork by Adam's favourite plasterer, Joseph Rose. The other rooms in the house were all decorated to Adam's designs. Many of the ceilings have been repainted in what are said to be the original colours. The three rooms to the left of the hall have rich Adam ceilings and good furnishings. The Italian and Dutch 17th century paintings were mostly bought by Sir Nathaniel and are hung in the positions he chose for them. At the centre of the house is the rotunda, a huge circular room based on the Pantheon at Rome and intended for the display of sculpture. On the other side of the building are four more state rooms, including the boudoir, bedroom and dining room. All have good pictures and furniture specially designed for them by Adam; the most striking item is the state bed whose cedarwood posts are carved to resemble palm trees. The corridors which link the main house to its pavilions contain tapestry, and furniture, and a display of family portraits. The pavilions themselves are not shown. Visitors follow a prescribed route through the building, but large areas of each room are roped off, limiting circulation space. The basement houses a museum of Indran objects collected by Marquess Curzon of Kedleston, who was Viceroy. The garden is not large, but the park is enormous and it contains a great variety of garden buildings designed by Adam. Among the best are the bridge over the lake and the charming fishing house and boathouse nearby.

Opening times: Easter Sun, Mon and Tues, then Sun from 25 April to 26 Sept; also Bank Holiday Mon and Tues. Park 12.30 6; house and museum 2 6.

Entrance charges: House and grounds £1.50; children 70p. Gardens only 70p, no reductions. (HHA)

Parking: Free parking on grass about 50 yards from the house.

Wheelchair access: Park accessible; entrance to house not forbidden, but it can only be reached by ascending 30 shallow steps.

Guidebook: Illustrated souvenir guide describing each room; no plan.

Catering: In the old kitchen, housed in one of the pavilions; long tables, gingham table cloths, self-service, home-made cakes.

WCs: In the stable block near the car park; free and clean but not for wheelchairs.

Shop: A tiny kiosk near the car park sells honey, sweets and souvenirs.

Extras: Not really an extra since there is no extra charge for admission to the mediaeval parish church next to the house, with the Curzon family monuments.

MELBOURNE HALL Melbourne (The Marquess of Lothian)

Tel: Melbourne (033 16) 2502

Directions: 8 miles S. of Derby on the A514 in the town of Melbourne

Melbourne is a pleasant little town with a fine Norman church. The house is close to the church and part of the mediaeval parsonage may be hidden in this mainly 17th and 18th century building. The only coherent front is the garden side of the east wing. The wing itself was built in 1725 by Francis Smith, but the plain grey Palladian front was added by his son William Smith in 1744. Inside, the rooms are as mixed in style and date as the outside. Visitors enter by the original forecourt, converted by the Victorians into a conservatory. The dark panelled dining room was once the great hall. Most of the other rooms have plain 18th century decoration. There is a mixture of good and ordinary furniture and some good paintings, including portraits of the Stuart courtiers who were friends of Thomas Coke, owner of Melbourne in the early 1700s. There is also an enchanting portrait of the Leventhorpe family, who married into the Cokes. Visitors make their own way round. The pleasant upstairs bedrooms contain mementos of Lord Melbourne, the political tutor and friend of the young Queen Victoria. The gardens are splendid. They were laid out in 1704 by Thomas Coke in the formal French style and remain more or less unchanged, a rare survival. The great lawn slopes down to a formal pond. Beyond the water, the focal point is a small wrought iron arbour or summer house made by the famous smith Robert Bakewell. Tall clipped view hedges enclose the path leading from the arbour to the rest of the formally arranged garden.

Opening times: 6 June to 3 Oct, Sun 2–5.
Entrance charges: House and garden £2.00; children £1.00. Garden only £1.00 and 50p. (HHA)
Parking: Free car park across the road from the entrance to the house and garden.
Wheelchair access: Possible to the ground floor of the house; the garden lends itself well to wheelchairs.
Guidebook: A chatty souvenir guide with many pictures but a irritating place to look for information; no plan.
Catering: In the stable yard; self-service tea room below and a waitress service above; not very exciting.
WCs: In the stable yard; unsuitable for wheelchairs.
Shop: Next to the tea shop, a fairly wide selection of souvenirs and novelties in cramped surroundings.

SUDBURY HALL Sudbury (The National Trust)
Tel: Sudbury (028 378) 305
Directions: 12 miles W. of Derby, 6 miles E. of Uttoxeter, off the A50 in Sudbury

Sudbury Hall is a comfortable red brick house whose rooms have the richest Charles II decoration in England. Building started in about 1662 and finished by 1700. The architect may have been George Vernon, the owner. The exterior is an odd mixture. It combines Jacobean features (mullioned windows and a two-storey porch) with the hipped roof and tall cupola more typical of Restoration houses. The rooms follow the familiar Jacobean arrangement, with a great hall, several parlours, and a first-floor long gallery, but the plasterwork and carved woodwork is typical of the 1670s and 80s: ceilings and walls drip with fruit and foliage. The first craftsmen to work here were local men, but in about 1675 they were replaced by the London carvers Edward Pierce and Grinling Gibbons, and the plasterers Bradbury and Pettifer. Detailed information about who worked in which rooms is given in the guide book. Best of all is the staircase carved by Pierce, although the long gallery comes a close second in magnificence. All the rooms have been repainted by the National Trust in 'authentic' pastel shades. There is very little furniture in the house but there are many paintings, mostly English portraits. Visitors make their own way round and can see most rooms on both floors. One of the upstairs rooms is thoughtfully set aside as a sitting-out place for visitors. The lawns surrounding the house are accessible but the 18th century landscaped park is now farmed privately. A 19th century wing has been turned into a Museum of Childhood run by Derbyshire County Council (small charge). It seems rather small and cramped but is very popular with its young visitors, who were especially keen on climbing the artificial chimney.

Opening times: April to end Oct, Wed, Thurs, Fri, Sat, Sun and Bank Holiday Mon, 1–5.30. Closed Good Friday.

Entrance charges: House and grounds £1.50; children 75p; dogs in grounds only.

Parking: Free parking in the stable yard, a short distance from the house.

Wheelchair access: The National Trust decrees the house unsuitable for wheelchairs, but there is only a shallow flight of steps to the front door and two internal steps in the main ground floor rooms. The Museum of Childhood and the grounds are accessible.

Guidebook: The main guidebook is a good detailed account of the house, full of information and with plans and illustrations. There is a childrens' guide which is bigger, with lively drawings, but the text is no simpler than the main guide. There is also a fold-out sheet about the Museum.

Catering: Tea room in stable yard, which serves light lunches and teas.

WCs: In the stable yard, free; wheelchair access to WC in the Museum.

Shop: At the end of the tour of the house, a good range of National Trust souvenirs; there is a smaller shop in the Museum entrance.

Devon

A LA RONDE Summer Lane, nr Exmouth (Mrs U.R. Tudor Perkins)
Tel: Exmouth (039 52) 5514
Directions: 8 miles S.E. of Exeter, 2 miles N. of Exmouth off the A377

A la Ronde is a curious polygonal house built in 1795 for two artistic ladies who designed the building and filled it with their handicrafts. Jane Parminter and her orphan cousin Mary spent ten years travelling the continent before returning to settle at Exmouth. The house they built has 16 sides and a steep conical roof, which was originally thatched. The interior is much more spacious than one might imagine and full of ingenious space-saving devices. The main rooms on the first floor are built round a octagonal central hall 60 feet high, said to have been based on the Byzantine church of San Vitale in Ravenna. But instead of Byzantine mosaics the upper parts of the hall are encrusted with shells and pictures of birds done in featherwork. The drawing room has an unusual featherwork cornice, shells and grottoes fill fireplaces, and the furnishings include sand and seaweed pictures, rows of family silhouettes and other belongings of the Parminter ladies. Guided tours lasting about an hour are conducted by one of the family. The odd-shaped windows have views over the river Exe and the pleasant garden outside.

Opening times: 1 April to end Oct, weekdays 10–6, Sun 2–7.

Entrance charges: 90p; children 40p. Reduced rates for parties. Evenings by arrangement. (HHA)

Parking: Free parking beside the house.
Wheelchair access: Possible to ground floor (not the best part of the house) and to the garden.
Guidebook: A brief and jolly history of the house and the Parminter spinsters; little on the contents, no plan.
Catering: Teas in the kitchen at the end of the tour. Evening parties include wine, cheese, coffee, etc.
WCs: Inside the house, left of the entrance; accessible to wheelchairs.
Shop: Some souvenirs on sale in the tea room.

ARLINGTON COURT nr Barnstaple (The National Trust)
Tel: Shirwell (027 182) 296
Directions: 8 miles N.E. of Barnstaple, signposted off the A39

Arlington had belonged to the Chichester family for 500 years when it was given to the National Trust by Miss Rosalie Chichester (aunt of Sir Francis Chichester) in 1949. The house itself is a plain white-painted neo-classical box designed by Thomas Lee of Barnstaple in 1820. It looks small, but the kitchens and servants' quarters are hidden away in a basement, leaving the whole ground floor for living rooms. Most of the important rooms in the house are shown. They are grouped round a surprisingly grand central staircase, which was formed in 1865 by removing rooms on the north side. The appearance of the living rooms has probably changed little since the 1860s. Three rooms along the south front open into each other, forming one long, elegant apartment divided only by scagliola columns. The first of them, the Morning Room, retains its original wallpaper. The furniture here and elsewhere is mostly Regency and Victorian. The paintings are portraits and local views, apart from one valuable water colour by William Blake. Miss Chichester herself collected pewter, shells, musical instruments and, best of all, model ships. Her collections are displayed in the house, which is very pleasant to visit. There is a guide in each room but restrictions are minimal. The stables at Arlington, which were built in 1864, now contain an above-average museum of horse-drawn carriages and the large park contains Shetland ponies, Jacob sheep and quantities of wildlife.

Opening times: April to end Oct, house and carriage collection, every day except Sat, including Good Friday and Bank Holiday Mon 11–6, last admission 5.30; Nov to end March, gardens and park only open during daylight.
Entrance charges: £2.00; children £1.00. Stables, garden and grounds only £1.10; children 55p.
Parking: Free parking 300 yards from house.
Wheelchair access: Gravel path from car park; steps to entrance but ground floor level; six rooms and staircase hall can be seen, resturant accessible.
Guidebook: Two guides to the house, both with the same information, but one has more pictures; neither have a plan of the house. The free leaflet contains more information. The separate guide to the carriage museum seems a bit short; there is also a fold-out guide sheet to the park and woods, for those who want to tell a bogbean from a pennywort.
Catering: Quite expensive licensed restaurant serving lunches and teas 11–5.30 daily.

WCs: Next to the restaurant; facilities for wheelchairs.
Shop: Sells National Trust standard range.

BERRY POMEROY CASTLE nr Totnes (Ancient Monument)
Tel: Totnes (0803) 863397
Directions: 2 miles N.E. of Totnes off the A385 on minor roads; badly
  signposted

Dense woods surround the ruins of the castle. The north and west fronts
rise sheer above the Gatcombe valley with its little stream. The Pomeroy
family built a stone castle here in about 1300 to replace an earlier wooden
building. The grim gatehouse and a stretch of wall linking it to St Magaret's
tower are of this date. In 1547 the Pomeroys sold their castle to the
Seymours and between 1548 and 1613 Sir Edward Seymour built a splendid
mansion house with a large amount of carved ornament inside the castle
walls. All that now remains of the mansion is a ruined three-storey block of
living rooms round a small courtyard. The great hall on the north side of the
castle and the kitchen block are less well preserved. The ruins are
picturesque and as the guide book says 'a surprising number of plants gain
sustenance and support from the thick walls'. As well as the ruins, Berry
Pomeroy offers good woodland walks.

Opening times: Summer, daily 9.30–5.30; Nov to Feb, except Christmas, Mon to Fri 10–4.
Entrance charges: Free.
Parking: Free parking in front of the castle.
Wheelchair access: Access to castle presents no difficulty, but there is some rough grass.
Guidebook: Small, fairly chatty, many illustrations and a plan but it is a little confused about
  the dates of the different Edward Seymours.
Catering: Café serving tea and cake, very reasonable.
WCs: Next to the café; not adapted for wheelchairs.
Shop: The café sells guide books and souvenirs.

BICKLEIGH CASTLE nr Tiverton (Mr and Mrs O.N. Boxall)
Tel: Bickleigh (088 45) 363
Directions: 11 miles N. of Exeter, 4 miles S. of Tiverton; turn off the A396
  at Bickleigh Bridge onto the A3072 and follow signs

A broad tree-hung stretch of the river Exe divides the village and church
from the castle, which consists of a pink stone gatehouse, a 17th century
farmhouse and a tiny thatched chapel. The restored chapel dates from about
1100 and is the earliest building on the site. The gatehouse is a survivor of a
small castle built by the Courtenay family, the great Devon landlords, who
acquired Bickleigh by 1410. The castle was later given to the Carews. In the
Civil War the north and west wings were destroyed and the east wing
damaged by parliamentary troops when Sir Henry Carew held Bickleigh for
the King. After the war Sir Henry rebuilt the north wing, but in mud and

timber, not in stone. In the 19th century the buildings decayed, but have been restored by a series of owners in the present century. The guided tours conducted by the present owners take about half an hour. The interior has some fine oak furniture, a varied collection of weapons and armour and a very large and curious carved overmantel rescued from the great hall of the castle. A thatched barn nearby has been turned into a 'Museum of Past and Present' where modern objects are juxtaposed with their earlier equivalents. The old moat has been turned into a garden and there is an extremely pretty pair of 18th century Italian wrought-iron gates at the entrance.

Opening times: Easter to end May, Wed, Sun and Bank Holiday Mon; June to 10 Oct, daily, except Sat 2–5.
Entrance charges: (1981) £1.10; children under 16 50p. (HHA)
Parking: Free parking next to house.
Wheelchair access: Possible to chapel and ground floors of gatehouse and cottage wing.
Guidebook: A souvenir guide, with several colour pictures.
Catering: Tea and biscuits in the barn, accessible to wheelchairs.
WCs: In the barn.
Shop: In the barn, selling booklets and souvenirs.

BRADLEY MANOR   Newton Abbot (The National Trust)
Tel: Enquiries to National Trust HQ, Hele (039 288) 345
Directions: On the W. edge of Newton Abbot, on the W. side of the A381 to Totnes; the drive gate is about 100 yds inside the 30 mph limit. The gates are too narrow for coaches

The mediaeval manor house lies secretly in the wooded valley of the River Lemon. It has an irregular front, roughcast and limewashed, with big gables and four oriel windows. The building history is complicated and is best unravelled with the guide book. There are remains of a 13th century house in the south wing, but the principal range is a house of about 1420, with a great hall and the usual rooms to either side. A projecting chapel was added in 1427, and in about 1490 the present gabled front was built alongside the hall, incorporating the earlier porch. Although the gatehouse and some lesser buildings have been destroyed, the house is remarkably well-preserved. Some of the original windows and a certain amount of interior decoration dating from the 15th and 16th centuries still survives. One later addition is some very attractive plasterwork in an upstairs room, which was probably done by the Abbot family of Frithelstock in the late 17th century. Visitors are issued with information boards and left to wander round on their own through the greater part of the house. Bradley Major is occupied by National Trust tenants whose furniture fills the rooms. Woods and meadows near the house are open at all times, free of charge, to those on foot.

Opening times: April to end Sept, Wed 2–5; also Thurs 29 April, 27 May, 26 Aug and 30 Sept 2–5.

Entrance chages: 70p; children under 16 35p; parties must book in writing.
Parking: Free car park near the house, during opening hours only.
Wheelchair access: No.
Guidebook: A good guide of the old-fashioned sort with a very large amount of information on the building and the owners with several illustrations and plans.
Catering: None.
WCs: Public convenience in the municipal Baker's Park nearby; unsuitable for wheelchairs.
Shop: None.

BUCKLAND ABBEY nr Yelverton (The National Trust and Plymouth Corporation)

Tel. Yelverton (082 285) 3607
Directions: 11 miles N. of Plymouth, 6 miles S. of Tavistock, 3 miles W. of Yelverton between the A386 and the river Tavy

Buckland Abbey is famous as the home of Sir Francis Drake, who bought the house in 1581 with the proceeds from his voyage round the world. But, as its name suggests, the building is older than Drake and consists of the nave and chancel of a great Benedictine Abbey church. The abbey buildings were purchased by Sir Richard Grenville in 1541 and his grandson, also Sir Richard, converted the church into a three-storey mansion house in the 1570s. The result is a rather ungainly stone building with a fat square tower in the middle. Although Sir Francis Drake made no alterations, a few of the rooms were re-done in the 1770s and others were rebuilt after a fire in 1937. The house is now a museum, containing relics of both Grenville and Drake. Two of its rooms have fine panelling and the banqueting hall, in the original nave, has a decorated plaster ceiling and an allegorical frieze. Several of the rooms are furnished in 16th or 18th century style, but naval exhibits and folk art predominate. Probably the most famous object in the house is Drake's drum, which is supposed to sound by itself to warn England of danger. The house is surrounded by lawns and flower beds and a short distance away is an immense tithe barn, with a number of horse-drawn carriages displayed inside.

Opening times: Good Friday to end Sept, weekdays including Bank Holidays 11–6, Sun 2–6, last admission 5.30. Oct to Wed before Easter, Wed, Sat and Sun 2–5, last admission 4.30.
Entrance charges: £1.20; children under 16 60p (subject to alteration).
Parking: Free parking, 150 yards from the house.
Wheelchair access: Would only be possible to a small part of the ground floor, besides the tithe barn and the gardens.
Guidebook: ·'Buckland Abbey' by Crispin Gill is cheaper and has more information than 'Buckland Abbey' by A. Cumming; the latter has colour plates. Neither has a plan of the house.
Catering: Light lunches and teas in the old kitchen, Good Friday to end Sept 2–5, July and Aug 11–6.
WCs: In the basement of the house and in the car park; not for wheelchairs.
Shop: There is a National Trust shop at the W. end of the Abbey.

CADHAY Ottery St Mary (Lady William-Powlett)
Tel: Ottery St May (040 481) 2432
Directions: 11 miles E. of Exeter on the A30, 1 mile N. of Ottery St Mary;
    leave the A30 at Fairmile

The 18th century front of Cadhay conceals one of the most attractive and interesting Tudor houses in Devon. The original house was built in about 1550 for John Haydon, a lawyer who had made a small fortune out of his dealings in confiscated church lands. He acquired stone from the College of Priests in Ottery St Mary to build his new house. It was arranged round three sides of an oblong court, with the south side left open. In 1587 Cadhay passed to a great nephew, Robert Haydon, who closed the south side of the court with a range containing a long gallery. He also faced the courtyard walls with flint and stone in a chequer pattern and added four primitive statues of Tudor monarchs, one of which is dated 1617. In 1736 the house was sold by the Haydons to Peere Williams, who attempted to modernise it by adding the new entrance front. In the 19th century Cadhay went downhill, and was only rescued at the last minute by Mr Dampier Whetham. It now has an amiable and lived-in atmosphere. The guided tour of the principal rooms lasts about an hour. The great hall in the north wing was divided into two storeys by Peere Williams as part of his improvements, but the massive Tudor fireplace survives downstairs, and the curved chestnut braces of the mutilated hammer-beam roof can be seen in the Roof Chamber above. Several of the rooms have plain panelling of the mid-18th century. There are some interesting marine paintings and a collection of pewter in the very narrow long gallery. The gardens are not elaborate, but the bright flowerbeds and the fish ponds make a good setting for the house.

Opening times: Spring and Summer Bank Holiday Sun and Mon, also 21 July to 2 Aug, Wed
    and Thurs 2–6.
Entrance charges: £1.00; children under 14 50p. (HHA)
Parking: Free parking in a field in front of the house.
Wheelchair access: Possible to ground floor rooms and to the courtyard and garden.
Guidebook: A very good guide to the house and its owners, with illustrations and plans; could
    do with more about the furniture.
Catering: None.
WCs: By the garden entrance; unsuitable for wheelchairs.
Shop: None.

CASTLE DROGO Drewsteignton (The National Trust)
Tel: Chagford (064 73) 3306
Directions: 12 miles W. of Exeter, 3 mile S. of the A30 at Crockernwell; a
    more scenic approach is by the A382, turning off at Sandy Park

Castle Drogo was designed by Edwin Lutyens in 1910–13 for Mr Julius Drewe, founder of the Home and Colonial Stores, who made his fortune

Castle Drogo, Devon

early and retired at the age of 33. Drewe decided to build himself a castle in this sublime setting above the gorge of the river Teign because a genealogist had traced his ancestry back to a Norman Baron called Drogo who owned land in Devonshire. It is among the last English houses planned on the grand scale. The original designs were for a bigger building and there are fascinating photographs on display of the full-sized wood and canvas mock-ups that Lutyens made to demonstrate the intended effect. Even in reduced form the castle took twenty years to build and was not completed until 1930. The Drewes still occupy the upper floor but the rest of the Castle is open to visitors, who make their own way round. The interior is cold and austere, with high unplastered walls (both Julius Drewe and Lutyens loved naked granite). Full advantage was taken of the sloping site to make theatrical effects by changes of level and in many ways the dramatic great staircase and passages are the most memorable parts of the house. The living rooms are furnished principally with the tapestries and other things which Drewe bought wholesale from a bankrupt Spanish financier. Among the more attractive items are the 20th century portraits of the family. Besides the living rooms, visitors also see the basement kitchen and other service rooms which still have their original fitments and the whole house offers a valuable insight into early 20th century country-house life. The gardens, laid out by George Dillingstone of Tunbridge Wells, are surrounded by massive square-cut yew hedges which contrast with the wild bracken-covered slopes of the rest of the estate.

Opening times: April to end Oct, daily 11–6, last admission 5.30.
Entrance charges: £1.80; children under 16 80p. Grounds only £1.00 and 50p.
Parking: Free parking 500 yards from the house; disabled visitors can be driven to the entrance.
Wheelchair access: Only part of the ground floor (2 rooms) can be seen without tackling stairs; the terraces and gardens are only partly accessible.
Guidebook: A good recent guide book on the building and the family with a full plan of the house; the contents are covered by the admirable free leaflet.
Catering: In the basement and not accessible to wheelchairs; two rooms serving good teas and light lunches 11–6.
WCs: By the car park and also in the house; neither adapted for wheelchairs.
Shop: In the car park with a wide range of National Trust products; the building won a Civic Trust award.

CHAMBERCOMBE MANOR   Ilfracombe (The Chambercombe Trust)
Tel: Ilfracombe (0271) 62624
Directions: 1 mile S.E. of Ilfracombe, between the A399 and B3230

The small house is hidden in a deep valley running down to the sea. The manor takes its name from the Champernon family who owned it from the 12th to the 15th century. Many of the later occupants were farmers, some of whom were wreckers and smugglers in their spare time. The whitewashed buildings huddle round a cobbled courtyard. There are probably remains of the 15th century house but most of what is visible dates from the 16th and 17th centuries. The hall and seven rooms shown to visitors have some good furniture, again mostly 17th century. In summer the house can get crowded, but the tours (which last nearly an hour) are sensibly oganised to minimise crush. The small garden contains a pond populated with wildfowl.

Opening times: Easter Sun to end Sept, Mon to Fri 10.30–1, 2–5, Sun 2–5. Closed Sat.
Entrance charges: 80p; children under 15 40p. (HHA)
Parking: Free car parks.
Wheelchair access: Not practicable.
Guidebook: A souvenir booklet, of little real use.
Catering: Good value teas and light lunches in the front courtyard; there is a children's menu.
WCs: Next to the shop; not for wheelchairs.
Shop: None.

COMPTON CASTLE nr Paignton (The National Trust)
Tel: Kingskerwell (08047) 2112
Directions: 4 miles W. of Torquay, 1 mile N. of Marldon, between the A3022 and A381

The long, lively facade of Compton, with its towers, battlements and buttresses, always captivates visitors and film directors looking for locations. For the last 600 years the castle has mostly been in the hands of the Gilbert family, among them Sir Walter Raleigh's half-brother Sir Humphrey Gilbert and his son Raleigh Gilbert who were both active in opening up North America. The spectacular front wall is in fact a screen which was added to a small 14th century house in 1530 by John Gilbert, as part of a programme of rebuilding and fortification against French raiders. The original great hall has gone but the main living room to the west and the chapel, added in about 1450, remain. None of the present living rooms is shown to the public. Of the four rooms that are open, the great hall dates entirely from the 1950s. It is the most conspicuous part of an extensive restoration and rebuilding carried out by Commander and Mrs Gilbert since 1937. Other rooms on view include the chapel and the kitchen which dates from the 1520s. A series of information boards are issued to help visitors guide themselves round. There is not a great deal to see inside, apart from some Elizabethan portraits in the hall, but the castle is certainly worth a visit for its own sake, and for its setting in the steep-sided combe.

Opening times: April to end Oct, Mon, Wed, Thurs 10–12, 2–5.
Entrance chages: 90p, children under 16 45p.
Parking: Free parking in front of the castle.
Wheelchair access: Possible to all rooms shown and to the whole of the exterior.
Guidebook: A good account of the house with a plan, and an extraordinary photo of the castle in 1900, completely overgrown with creepers; about half the guide is concerned with family history.
Catering: None.

WCs: In the house, enquire at the desk; not for wheelchairs.
Shop: No shop to speak of.

DARTINGTON HALL   nr Totnes (The Dartington Hall Trust)
Tel: Totnes (0803) 862271
Directions: 2 miles N.W. of Totnes, signposted off the A384 as 'School of
   Art'

The name 'Dartington' has many connotations; a progressive school, a
sociological experiment in pursuit of the fuller life, music and Dartington
glassware. But the starting point for all these things is a large mediaeval
house of some importance. The Hall was built in 1388–1400 by John
Holand, half-brother of Richard II, and it was on a kingly scale. Of the two
original courtyards the smaller, with the state apartments, has vanished, but
the much larger outer court, where the retainers lived, has survived more or
less intact. It is most attractive. On the south side of the court is the great
hall, the only room which is open to visitors (when not in use for functions).
Although the hammer-beam roof and the windows date from 1931, the hall
is among the best of its date in England. The fortunes of Dartington
changed in 1925 when Leonard and Dorothy Elmhirst bought the semi-
derelict house and estate. Their aim was (broadly) to regenerate the
agriculture and commerce of the district and provide a full life for everyone
involved with Dartington, whether artists, farmers or schoolchildren. The
success of their project is clear rom the number of later buildings which have
sprung up near the house to cater for the various activities. Much attention
was also given to the gardens on their splendid sloping site. There are tall
yews and other trees planted by former occupants of the Hall, and later
planting and terracing by Dorthy Elmhirst, Beatrix Farrand and Percy
Fane.

Opening times: All year, every day at reasonable times.
Entrance charges: Free (donated of 50p suggested); no coaches or dogs.
Parking: Free car park by hall; when full there is more space by the Cider Press Centre, but
   this is some distance from the house.
Wheelchair access: Possible to Hall and a part of the garden.
Guidebook: Deals with the history of the house in fairly general terms, as well as the work of
   the Dartington Hall Trust.
Catering: All sorts of adventurous vegetarian food and drink at the restaurant in the Cider
   Press Centre and 'mainstream' lunches and teas at 'Muggins'.
WCs: At the Hall, on the left before the gatehouse, or in the Cider Press Centre.
Shops: A number of craft shops in the Centre selling attractive and expensive goods; the
   pottery seconds shop is cheaper, and there is also top quality home-made edible produce for
   sale.

DARTMOUTH CASTLE (Ancient Monument)
Directions: 1 mile S.E. of Dartmouth by the B3205; signposted from the
   town centre

The estuary at Dartmouth is one of the loveliest in England, but the castle has seen plenty of action, even in World War II when heavy guns were installed and camouflaged as ruins. The town became prosperous in the 14th century and the earliest fortifications date from that time. The main castle was begun in 1481. It was the first in England to have guns as the main armament (strapped down to a bed, not mounted on carriages) and for extra defence a chain which could be stretched across the estuary from Dartmouth to Kingswear castle on the other side. The buildings at Dartmouth now contain armour from the Civil War and two guns from the 1870s. On the headland is the old gun-battery of the 1860s, now a restaurant, and on the landward side is the Maiden Fort built in 1749. Oddly enough, the castle is dominated not by fortifications, but by the tower of the church of St Petroc, a mid-16th century building which stands inside the walls. Before returning to the town, visitors should follow the cliff road above the castle for a short distance; the reward is a magnificent view down the coast.

Opening times: Standard hours (SM), see page xii.
Entrance charges: 60p; OAPs and children under 16 30p.
Parking: Opposite the castle; steep steps down.
Wheelchair access: Too many steep steps everywhere.
Guidebook: A thorough Official Handbook with plans and illustrations.
Catering: Self-service café overlooking the sea, also the Old Battery Café and Restaurant; neither produce gastronomic delights.
WCs: Left of the castle, signposted.
Shop: Some souvenirs and leaflets for sale.

FLETE Ermington, nr Plymouth (Mutual Households Association)
Tel: Holbeton (075 530) 308
Directions: 11 miles E. of Plymouth, signposted off the A379 between Yealmpton and Modbury

The luxuriantly winding drive leads to what seems an unmistakably Victorian mansion, but part of Flete is an old house that was rebuilt in about 1620 and a Jacobean wing with its five gables can still be seen on one side. The great Victorian rebuilding was the work of the architect Richard Norman Shaw. His client was H.B. Mildmay, a director of Barings Bank who had married Georgina Bulteel, the Flete heiress. Shaw was forced to work piecemeal, designing a bit at a time, and the result is a shambling granite house, with few bold accents to give it character. It is now cut up into flats, but the three main reception rooms shared by the residents are open to visitors in a conducted tour which lasts perhaps half an hour. There are various architectural surprises, like the intimate and richly-decorated staircase, the lively plasterwork in the drawing rooms and the impressive long gallery (now the communal dining room) but the contents of the house are not of great interest. The house stands on the side of a slope, laid out with smooth lawns. The more formal parts of the gardens are beautifully maintained by the residents and Lady Mildmay's Italian Garden is presently being restored.

Opening times: May to end Sept, Wed and Thurs 2–4.
Entrance charges: 40p; children 25p.
Parking: Free parking in front of the house.
Wheelchair access: Possible to all rooms shown and most of the garden.
Guidebook: A decent account of the house and its owner, with black and white photos but no plan; there is an interesting section on the nuts and bolts of running a house like Flete in is heyday.
Catering: None.
WCs: In the house; not for wheelchairs.
Shop: None.

KILLERTON HOUSE nr Exeter (The National Trust)
Tel: Hele (039 288) 345
Directions: 7 miles N.E. of Exeter, signposted off the B3181 (the old A38) at Budlake

Killerton has a beautiful setting, with rolling parkland in front and a wooded hill behind. The house is a low and reticent Georgian building, plain to the point of dullness. It was designed by John Johnson for Sir Thomas Acland and built in 1778–9. The interior was altered in the 1890s and further alterations were made by the Arts and Crafts architect Randall Wells after a fire in 1924. The Aclands left in 1939 and for the next forty years Killerton housed various institutions. The National Trust has now brought in furniture from elsewhere and combined it with family pictures and mementoes to give the appearance of an occupied house. In one sense the rooms *are* occupied, for the dining room, the drawing room, and the rooms upstairs are used to display the very good collection of period costumes given to the Trust by Paulise de Bush. As always, the dummies have a grisly life of their own. Visitors can spend as long as they like in the house. The gardens at Killerton are both attractive and important. They were first laid out in the late 18th and early 19th century by John Veitch, a famous nurseryman who planted many rare trees and new species brought from abroad. In the 1890s William Robinson (author of *The English Flower Garden*) was called in and the terrace border and rockery which he devised still exist. At the eastern edge of the park is the family chapel, a neo-Norman building, designed by C.R. Cockerell in 1840 and based on the chapel of St Joseph of Arimathea at Glastonbury.

Opening times: House, April to end Oct, daily 11–6, last admission 5.30. Garden all year every day in daylight hours.
Entrance charges: House and garden £1.60; children 80p. Garden only £1.20 and 60p.
Parking: Free car park about 300 yards from the house.
Wheelchair access: Disabled visitors may be driven to entrance; easy steps to front door, and the ground floor is level; but the bulk of the costume collection is upstairs and cannot be reached.

Guidebook: History of the house and garden with all necessary information and a garden plan; a free information sheet describes thecontents of each room; there is a plan of the gardens but not of the house.

Catering: An excellent licensed restaurant serving lunches and teas 11–5.30; English dishes a speciality.

WCs: Behind the house, extremely decorative; suitable for whelchairs.

Shop: A large National Trust shop in the entrance hall.

KNIGHTSHAYES COURT   nr Tiverton (The National Trust)

Tel: Tiverton (0884) 254665

Directions: 2 miles N. of Tiverton, signposted off the A396

This High Victorian house arouses strong emotions among its visitors, sometimes hostile ones. It was built between 1868 and 1874 for Sir John Heathcoat-Amory MP, whose maternal grandfather had invented a lace-making machine and founded the family's fortunes. The architect was William Burges, best remembered for his fantastic Gothic work at Cardiff Castle. Knightshayes is built of red sandstone with yellow stone dressings, in a muscular High Gothic style. Burges could produce spectacular decoration, as the drawings in the entrance hall show, but he was dismissed from this job early on and replaced by Crace and Co., a distingushed but less exciting firm of decorators. Their work in turn was later removed or covered up, but the Trust is salvaging as much as possible of the highly-coloured Burges and Crace interiors. The furniture fills the rooms pleasantly enough but there are not many objects of special interest, except Sir John Amory's collection of minor paintings by major artists, which is hung in the drawing room. Visitors follow a set route through the main rooms, and there is a guide in each one. Many people visit Knightshayes for the gardens which were created after World War II by the late Sir John and Lady Heathcoat-Amory. They simplified the Victorian terraces below the house, underplanted the woodland with a variety of bulbs and flowers and created the paved and pool gardens where statues are set against green and silver foliage. In all parts of the garden there are fine mature trees.

Opening times: April to end Oct, daily; garden 11–6; house 1.30–6.

Entrance charges: House and garden £1.60; children 80p. Garden only £1.20 and 60p.

Parking: Free parking about 500 yards from the house.

Wheelchair access: Cars may stop at the house entrace; one shallow step to front door then ground floor (5 main rooms and main stair) on one level; restaurant and shop also accessible.

Guidebook: No guide book, merely a large fold-out plan of the garden with some information about the house on the back; there is also a free leaflet on the contents.

Catering: Rather expensive lunches and teas in the licensed restaurant (open 12.30–6). The room itself (once the billiard room) has carved decoration by Burges and contains the only piece of furniture in the house by him, a large sideboard.

WCs: Next to the restaurant; there is a lavatory for the disabled near the house.

Shop: Large shop selling plants and National Trust approved souvenirs.

LYDFORD CASTLE Lydford, nr Okehampton (Ancient Monument)
Directions: 7 miles N.N.E. of Tavistock, 8 miles S.W. of Okehampton, signposted off the A386

All that remains of Lydford Castle is a stern square keep on a high mound. Lydford was an important Anglo-Saxon town and the castle was built on the site of a ancient British hill-fort, with the deep gorge of the river Lyd on three sides. The present keep dates from 1195 and is of two storeys with two rooms on each floor. Until the last century it continued in use as the seat of the Stannary Court of Devon, with the courtroom on the first floor and the prison below. A local poet wrote in the 17th century:
'I oft have heard of Lydford Law
How in the morn they hang and draw
And sit in judgement after'
It is possible to walk down the gorge to the White Lady Waterfall and mediaeval bridge (National Trust – admission charge).

Opening times: Open at all reasonable times.
Entrance charges: Free.
Parking: Opposite the castle entrance, free.
Wheelchair access: Not practicable.
Guidebook: Inexpensive leaflet usually available from Lydford Post Office.
Catering: None.
WCs: None.
Shop: None.

OKEHAMPTON CASTLE Okehampton (Ancient Monument)
Tel: Okehampton (0837) 2844
Directions: Signposted from the centre of Okehampton

The castle is a gaunt and eerie ruin on a spur of land above the Oakment river with the moor beyond. There is something sinister about the slivers of the keep wall which brood over the ruined domestic buildings in the bailey. The Normans selected Okehampton as the centre of their administration in Devon and soon replaced the original wooden buildings with a square stone keep. In 1172 the castle came into the possession of the powerful Courtenay family. It was probably Hugh Courtenay, Earl of Devon, who added another block to the keep and built more comfortable living quarters in the bailey in the early 14th century. A later Courtenay Earl was beheaded in 1538 for plotting against King Henry VIII and the castle was dismantled and never occupied again. The hall, kitchens and other buildings in the bailey are roofless and damaged but they can be identified and plaques giving descriptions of their original functions are attached to the walls. Excavations are in progress to discover more about the castle.

Opening times: Standard hours (S), see page xii.
Entrance charges: 40p; OAPs and children under 16 20p.

Parking: Free parking next to castle.
Wheelchair access: Steep slopes and uneven ground make access difficult.
Guidebook: A cheap leaflet with a brief history, desription and plan.
Catering: None.
WCs: To the right of the entrance, sometimes locked; not for wheelchairs.
Shop: Some publications and postcards at the ticket kiosk.

PAIGNTON: KIRKHAM HOUSE   Kirkham Street (Ancient Monument)

Directions: In the town centre, near the parish church, signposted

This small late 14th century stone house probably belonged to a prosperous trader or a priest from the nearby Kirkham chantry. It has an unusual plan for its date, with the main living rooms on either side of the screens passage instead of all at one end. Beyond the hall is a small room with its own door from the street (now blocked) which may have been a shop. A timber-framed gallery at the back contains the stairs to the upper rooms, one of which borrows space from the upper part of the hall. The stonework and the roof have been extensively restored. The house contains a collection of furniture made by local craftsmen and is clean and well looked after. The foundations of the original kitchen can be seen at the back of the building and a tiny garden has been laid out among them.

Opening times: Standard hours (S, April to Sept only), see page xii.
Entrance charges: 30p; OAPs and children under 16 15p.
Parking: Difficult; probably best to use the municipal car park.
Wheelchair access: Possible to the three ground floor rooms and the garden.
Guidebook. A very good cheap leaflet with a photo and plan.
Catering: None.
WCs: None.
Shop: None.

PAIGNTON: OLDWAY MANSION   (Torbay Borough Council)

Tel: Paignton (0803) 550711

Directions: In Paignton, signposted off the A379 between Paignton and Torquay

Oldway was the home of a family of American millionaires — Singer of Singer sewing machines. Isaac Singer bought the estate in 1871 and employed a local architect, George Bridgeman, to design him a house ('I want a big wigwam' he told Bridgeman) and also a riding pavilion. The pavilion still stands but in 1904 Paris Eugene Singer rebuilt his father's wigwam in the grand French manner. He seems to have been his own architect and borrowed his designs wholesale from French examples. The south front is based on a small music pavilion in the grounds of the Petit Trianon and the columned east front was inspired by the Place de la

Concorde. The interior is of overpowering splendour. Both the staircase and its painted ceilings are copied from Le Brun's designs for Versailles. The large ugly brown curtain on the main landing covers the space once occupied by J.L. David's painting of *Napoleon Crowning Josephine*, now in the Louvre. The ballroom on the east front has rich white and gold Louis Seize decoration and several of the smaller rooms are in the same vein. The house is now used as Council offices and beautifully maintained, although incongruous signs among the coloured marble and potted palms point the way to rent rebates and refuse disposal. The main rooms are open to visitors when not in use and there are few restrictions. The designs for the 'wigwam' and an early Singer sewing machine are displayed in the hall. The elaborate gardens were laid out by Achille Duchesne (who did the water garden at Blenheim Palace) and they still preserve much of their turn-of-the-century formality.

Opening times: May to Sept, Mon to Thurs, 9–1, 2–5, Fri 9–1, 2–4.15, Sat and Sun 2–5. Oct to April, Mon to Fri 9–1, 2.15–5.15; closed Sat and Sun.

Entrance charges: Free.

Parking: Free car park opposite house.

Wheelchair access: Possible to ground floor only, enough to get the flavour of the house; the gardens are also accessible.

Guidebook: A decent little guide with most of the relevant information and a few illustrations but no plan.

Catering: A surly service cafe provides lunches and teas.

WCs: On the ground floor; not for wheelchairs.

Shop: None.

PLYMOUTH: ELIZABETHAN HOUSE 32 New Street (Plymouth Corporation)

Tel: Plymouth (0752) 668000, ext. 4380

Directions: In the centre of Plymouth; follow signs to Barbican; New Street leads off the quay

This late 16th century merchant's house with its jettied timber front and wide windows is the most interesting of the three houses open in Plymouth. It was restored in 1926 and is kept in excellent repair by the Corporation; the rear wall has been re-hung with moorstone slates. The whole of the interior is open from cellar to attic, by way of the pole staircase built round an old ship's mast. There is some very good 16th century furniture, both English and French, which goes well with the house. At the time of writing there is no electric light and the dim light filtering through the small-paned windows onto the dark oak panelling and furniture makes one realise why the Elizabethans were so fond of brightly-coloured clothes and hangings. Altogether a pleasant place, with a fig tree flourishing in the sunny little garden behind.

Opening times: All year, weekdays 10–1 and 2.15–6 (dusk in winter), also April to Sept, Sun 3–5.
Entrance charges: 20p; children 10p.
Parking: Free parking on quay but space is scarce; municipal car park in Exchange Street.
Wheelchair access: Not practicable.
Guidebook: A small leaflet written in a jolly style which contains a lot of information.
WCs: None.
Shop: None.

PLYMOUTH: MERCHANT'S HOUSE MUSEUM 33 St Andrew's Street (Plymouth Corporation)
Tel: Plymouth (0752) 668000, ext. 4381
Directions: In the centre of Plymouth, near the Guildhall

In the late 16th century Plymouth was a boom town and the New Quay (now the Barbican) was built in 1572 to cater for the needs of adventurers like Drake and Hawkins. The well-to-do of Plymouth lived in the area north east of the Barbican and the Merchant's House is a survivor of that time. The massive limestone walls and a few details inside suggest that it was built in the early 16th century, but the timber street-front, with its long bands of windows, is one of the improvements made in about 1600. At this time the house was occupied by William Parker, a trader and sea-captain who was Mayor of Plymouth in 1601 and later died on a voyage to Java. The house is now a local history museum and renovation has deprived the interior of its original atmosphere. The rooms are carpeted throughout and contain well-organised local history displays with plenty of photographs.

Opening times: All year, Mon to Sat 10–6, Sun 3–5.
Entrance charges: 20p; children 10p.
Parking: Difficult in the street outside, municipal car parks in St Andrew's Street or Whimple Street nearby.
Wheelchair access: Possible to the two ground floor rooms.
Guidebook: A history of the house with some account of the restoration work.
Catering: None.
WCs: None.
Shop: Some local history publications on sale.

PLYMOUTH: PRYSTEN HOUSE Finewell Street (St Andrew's Vestry)
Tel: Plymouth (0752) 661414, Mon to Fri 9.30–1.
Directions: In the centre of Plymouth near St Andrew's church

This fine mediaeval house was built about 1500 for Thomas Yogge, a prosperous Cornish merchant. It is of limestone with granite dressings and is built round a courtyard. The court was originally open on one side but the opening has since been filled by the Abbey Hall. A timber gallery runs round the court at first floor level, now hung with colourful baskets of geraniums. For many yeas it was thought that the house was used by chantry priests who served in St Andrew's church but it has recently been shown that the prysten (or priesten) house was a smaller building which was demolished some time ago. Apart from the courtyard, there is not a great deal to see. The walls of all the rooms have been scraped back to the stone and they are now used for parish activities. There is no furniture of interest apart from a remarkable carved settle and a large model of Plymouth at the time of the Pilgrim Fathers, which can be made to light up. Visitors are allowed to wander freely but some rooms are occasionally closed.

Opening times: All year, daily except Sun 10–4.
Entrance charges: 40p; OAPs and children 5–15 20p; students in parties 15p each.
Wheelchair access: Not practicable.
Guidebook: Contains a plan but its account of the house is totally wrong and outdated. A more accurate history, written by Jennifer Barber and printed in Transactions of the Devonshire Association 1973 is on sale in the Merchant's House in St Andrew's Street.
Catering: None.
WCs: None.
Shop: None.

POWDERHAM CASTLE   nr Exeter (The Earl and Countess of Devon)
Tel: Starcross (0626) 890243
Directions: 8 miles S.W. of Exeter off the A379

This sprawling and iregular stone mansion has been the seat of the Courtenays since the 14th century. The main branch of the family was snuffed out by Henry VIII and the Earldom of Devon which they held was not revived until the 19th century. The house originally stood on an island of firm ground in the marshes of the river Exe, but the land was drained in the 18th century and turned into rich parkland. At the core of the building is a fortified house of 1390–1420, which was altered by several piecemeal improvements in the 18th century. In a 19th century building campaign, after the revival of the Earldom, the architect Charles Fowler created the present entrance courtyard and the banqueting hall by which visitors enter the house. Fowler's work dates from about 1840 and his hall is in the Gothic style with much heraldic paraphernalia relating to the Courtenays but the majority of the main rooms still have an 18th century appearance. By far the most spectacular is the great staircase with its elaborately carved balustrade and its walls covered with plaster vegetation and animals. It was made in 1754 by James Garrett and John Jenkins, the local joiner and plasterer. In the 1790s the very handsome domed music room was added by James Wyatt; the medallions on the walls were painted by the Third Viscount Courtenay and some of his 13 sisters. Visitors make their own way through nearly a dozen main rooms. The furniture is generally of high quality and includes a number of paintings by the local artist Thomas Hudson, master of Sir Joshua Reynolds, and a pair of Baroque English bookcases in the ante-

Powderham Castle, Devon

room which are dated 1740. The mixture of building of many different periods makes Powderham an exciting house, both outside and in. The grounds are mostly parkland with a lovely view of the river estuary.

Opening times: Easter Sun and Mon, then Sun only until 23 May; 24 May to 24 Sept daily, except Fri and Sat 2–6, last admission 5.30.
Entrance charges: £1.50; OAPs and children 6–18 80p. (HHA)
Parking: Free parking on gravel 500 yards from the house.
Wheelchair access: Possible to a part of the ground floor.
Guidebook: A thorough and well-illustrated booklet, which would be greatly improved by the addition of a plan of the house. A new edition is planned for 1982.
Catering: Home-made teas served in a new tea room.
WCs: In the courtyard and also next to the tea room; not for wheelchairs.
Shop: A shop in the courtyard sells souvenirs.
Extras: Several of the private rooms are shown on Thursdays 2–5; admission 25p. From 23 May to 23 Sept there will be an exhibition on Maritime England, with a retrospective on The Life and Times of Captain Bligh. Admission 25p; catalogue £1.50.

SALTRAM   Plympton (The National Trust)
Tel: Plymouth (0752) 336546
Directions: 3½ miles E. of Plymouth, 2 miles W. of Plympton between the A38 and the A379

Saltram is a large square house painted pink. The exterior is unimpressive but inside are sumptuous rooms by Robert Adam and a fine collection of paintings and china. The original small Tudor house was greatly enlarged in the 1740s by John Parker and his wife Lady Catherine who built the main south front and made the west front regular. Robert Adam was employed to complete the east side in 1768. There were a number of minor changes in later years of which the front porch of 1818 is the most obvious. The National Trust acquired the house with all its contents so the furniture and paintings properly belong here. The first few rooms, on the south side, are excellent mid-Georgian work with plaster decoration attributed to Vassali. The little morning room has hardly changed since Sir Joshua Reynolds was a regular visitor. The grand saloon and dining room were completely designed by Adam, from the delicately painted plaster ceilings to the carpets, furniture and fittings. The Trust ensures that their colours are preserved by showing these rooms in darkened conditions, which can be trying for the visitor. Several rooms on the first floor are shown, including a delightful Chinese Chippendale bedroom and dressing room. At the end of the route is a spacious library, formed in 1819, and the Mirror Room, which is hung with 18th century Chinese mirror paintings. The great kitchen (in use until 1963) has a separate entrance. The park has been mutilated by the Plympton by-pass and seems almost to belong to the suburbs of Plymouth but what remains is still spacious, with lawns and trees. There are several garden buildings, including an elegant 18th century orangery, and the chapel, built in 1776, has recently been renovated.

Opening times: April to end Oct, garden daily 11–6; house Tues to Sun and Bank Holiday Mon 12.30–6; kitchen and art gallery in chapel 11–6; last admission 5.30. Nov to end March, garden every day during daylight.

Entrance charges: House, kitchen and garden £2.00; children under 16 £1.00. Garden only 70p and 35p.

Parking: Free parking near the simple stable block, through which house and grounds are reached.

Wheelchair access: Gravel path from car park, but arrangements can be made *in advance* to drive to front door; two steps up to ground floor which is more or less level, lift access to first floor. Both restaurant and shop are accessible.

Guidebook: The ordinary guide is an excellent account of the history of the house and the Parker family with illustrations and a plan of the house; a free leaflet describes the contents of each room. There is also *The Saltram Collection* which describes the contents of the house in scholarly detail. The separate leaflet on the kitchen is superfluous.

Catering: Very good licensed restaurant in the centre of the house; waitress service lunches and teas, English specialities, last orders 5.30.

WCs: In the house near the restaurant; unsuitable for wheelchairs. There is a separate lavatory in the house with space for a wheelchair which may be used on application to the staff.

Shop: National Trust standard shop in the stables.

Extras: Small Industrial Museum in one room of the stable block, mainly railway objects. The chapel has an exhibition of the work of local artists; the work is for sale.

TAPELEY PARK Instow, Nr. Bideford (Miss Rosamund Christie)
Tel: Instow (0271) 860528
Directions: 1½ miles W. of Instow, on the A39 between Barnstaple and Bideford

Tapeley occupies a magnificent hilltop position with views across the estuaries of the Taw and Torridge and interesting furniture and a very fine garden. An earlier house was rebuilt for the Cleveland family in 1702. It was gothicised in the 1880s by Ewan Christian, a boring architect, and altered again by John Belcher in 1901. The house passed to the Christie family in the 19th century. They also owned Glyndebourne estate in Sussex and in 1931 John Christie started the famous opera house. His daughter still lives at Tapeley. The guided tours start only when enough people have assembled and this can mean a long wait. The tours last about 40 minutes. Some of the rooms on the west front have early 18th century interiors and the contents include William Morris furniture, Minton *pâte-sur-pâte* china and a fine 17th century Flemish chest. The Italian terraced gardens below the house were also designed by John Belcher and are planted with sub-tropical plants; there are a number of other less formal gardens, all extremely attractive.

Opening times: House and garden Easter to Oct, daily except Mon and Sat (but including Bank Holiday Mons and Sat in August) 10–6; Nov to April garden only during daylight hours.

Entrance charges: (1981) House and garden £1.50; chilren 80p. Gardens only 80p and 40p.

Parking: Free parking beside the house.

Wheelchair access: All rooms shown in the house are accessible, but only a small part of the garden.
Guidebook: None.
Catering: Interesting and reasonably-priced light linches and teas in the rose-festooned dairy, an attractive setting.
WCs: Next to the tea room; suitable for wheelchairs.
Shop: Plants on sale outside the house.

TIVERTON CASTLE   Tiverton (Mr and Mrs Ivar Campbell)
Tel: Tiverton (0884) 253200
Directions: On the outskirts of Tiverton, beside St Peter's church

Tiverton Castle began as a Norman stronghold, built in 1106 by Richard de Redvers. At the end of the 13th century it came into the hands of the Courtenays who seem to have owned almost every major house in Devon at some time or another. Tiverton was their chief residence until the family disgrace in the 16th century. There have been several owners since then, notably the Carews, another major West Country family. The castle was partly taken down in the Civil War, but the 14th century gatehouse and two towers have survived intact, while the ruined walls bound the garden. They are grouped round a small courtyard, with an Elizabethan wing dated 1588 and a long two-storey range of uncertain date; it looks 17th century but is not shown on a 1730 print of the castle. All the buildings of the castle are of pink sandstone or faced in pink cement. The interior is a little disappointing. Many of the small rooms shown have been restored and shorn of original features. Besides Persian rugs and Continental furniture, there are a large number of modern copies of earlier paintings. Many of them are set out in the Joan of Arc Gallery in the gatehouse to illustrate some unusual theories about the life of the French heroine. The castle also houses a modern chapel dedicated to St Francis of Assisi and an impressive collection of clocks is displayed in the mediaeval lavatory tower.

Opening times: Easter Holiday (23–18 April) then 17 May–24 Sept, daily except Fri and Sat 2.30–5.30.
Entrance charges: (1981) £1.00; OAPs and children 5–14 50p. (HHA)
Parking: Free parking in the castle grounds.
Wheelchair access: Not practicable to the interior.
Guidebook: An illustrated history and room-by-room guide, no plan.
Catering: None.
WCs: On application to the guide.
Shop: None.

TORQUAY: TORRE ABBEY   King's Drive (Torbay Borough Council)
Tel: Torbay (0803) 23593
Directions: In Torbay, near the sea front, signposted.

The Abbey was founded in 1196 as a thank-offering for the safe return of the son of William de Brewer from Austria, where he had been a hostage. Generous endowments were given and the Abbey buildings were on a large scale. After the dissolution of the monasteries in 1539 the great church was left to decay, but the west and south sides of the cloister court were converted into a house. In the 18th century the south side facing the sea was enlarged by the addition of a top floor and two small wings. The rooms in this part of the house now house the municipal art gallery. The rooms themselves are dull, but the collection contains several unexpected delights and is strong in early 19th century works: de Loutherbourg, William Blake and John Martin are all well-represented. There is also the Meres collection of English drinking glasses. A substantial number of the Abbey buildings have survived, including a very spectacular tithe barn and the Mohun gatehouse which dates from 1330. Little remains of the church itself but there are several well-preserved mediaeval doorways.

Opening times: March to end Oct, every day 10–1, 2–5; parties in winter by appointment.
Entrance charges: (1981) 25p; OAPs free.
Parking: Limited parking in the grounds near the 'Spanish Barn'. On-street parking for up to one hour or the municipal car park to the east by the tennis courts.
Wheelchair access: Not to the house, since most of the collection is on the first floor.
Guidebook: A very useful leaflet 'Torre Abbey Guided Tour' with a plan and a bird's-eye view of the buildings; 'The Story of Torre Abbey' has a history of the mediaeval buildings and a plan; 'Torre Abbey' is a brief history of the ruins and a brief guide to the collection in the gallery. There is also a scholarly guide to the collection of drinking glasses.
Catering: Café behind the tennis courts; economical but uninspiring salads and teas.
WCs: On the east side of the Abbey; unpleasant,
Shop: None.

TOTNES CASTLE   Totnes (Ancient Monument)
Directions: In central Totnes, signposted

Totnes is a delightful old town, away from the main tourist routes, which commands the head of the river Dart. The castle is a fine, straightforward example of the motte and bailey (or mound and enclosure) type of fort. The ditches round the bailey can still be seen, although they are covered by modern gardens. The motte is crowned by what is known as a shell keep — a circular sandstone wall built in the early 14th century to replace a wooden palisade. All other buildings have disappeared.

Opening times: Standard hours (SM), see page xii.
Entrance charges: 40p; OAPs and children under 16 20p.
Parking: Municipal car park 5 mins walk away.
Wheelchair access: Not practicable.
Guidebook: A good informative leaflet with a plan.
Catering: None.
WCs: None.
Shop: None.

UGBROOKE   nr Chudleigh (Lord and Lady Clifford)
Tel: Chudleigh (0626) 852179
Directions: 9 miles S.W. of Exeter; turn off main A38 into Chudleigh
   village, house is signposted from village centre (about 3 miles).

In the Middle Ages the house at Ugbrooke belonged to the Precentor of
Exeter Cathedral, but it was acquired by the Duke of Somerset in the 16th
century and passed from him to the Courtenays and then by marriage to the
Cliffords. The old house was very largely rebuilt between 1763 and 1771 for
the 4th Lord Clifford. The architect was Robert Adam and it was one of his
first designs in the castle style, with corner towers and battlements. The
Cliffords were Roman Catholics and Adam provided a private chapel which
was later decorated in Italianate style. The chapel, which is claimed to be the
earliest Roman Catholic church in the south of England, is separate from the
house and should be visited first. About half of the house is open to visitors
and the family live in the other half, but there are many signs of recent
occupation in the elegant interiors. Visitors take themselves round and there
are friendly guides in each room. The morning room showpieces are an 18th
century walnut secretaire and a breakfront bookcase made for the house by
Gillow of Lancaster. The drawing room contains portraits by Lely and the
dining room is laid out for a ceremonial meal. The main stair, like the
rooms, is much plainer than Adam's usual work but it has a domed ceiling
and in the staircase hall is displayed the elaborate silver-gilt basin and ewer
given to Charles Clifford by his Godfather, King Charles II. The remaining
rooms have some interesting tapestry and embroidery and there are some
guest bedrooms to peer into, while the elegant library houses a collection of
uniforms. The park may be explored, but what would 'Capability' Brown
think if he knew that his trees were inhabited by budgerigars?

Opening times: May, Sun and Bank Holidays 2–5; June to Sept, daily except Fri and Sat 2–5.
Entrance charges: £1.50; children 80p. (HHA)
Parking: Large free car park about 2 mins walk from the house.
Wheelchair access: Possible but complicated; the second half of the tour would have to be
   made against the flow; it would be best to ring beforehand, and to avoid times when there
   are large parties of visitors.
Guidebook: Chatty, many illustrations, better on the history of the family and the contents of
   the rooms than on the house itself, no plan.
Catering: Teas and snacks in the old stable block near the car park.
WCs: Portaloos opposite the car park (i.e. some distance from the house), clean, but
   sometimes short of water; facilities for wheelchairs.
Shop: Last room in the house on the tour, trinkets and many plastic souvenirs, also honey,
   clotted cream, toffee. The Mini Market, opposite the tea room in the stable block, sells
   plants and needlecraft.

Dorset

ATHELHAMPTON Nr. Puddletown (Sir Robert Cooke)
Tel: Puddletown (030 584) 363
Directions: ½ mile E. of Puddletown on the A35

This is Thomas Hardy's Athelhall and suitably romantic. The main part of the house, with its tall oriel window lighting the Great Hall, was built in the 1480s for Sir William Martyn, Lord Mayor of London. The taller wing next to it was added about 50 years later. Both parts of the house were the best that money could buy, but they are built of different stone and make odd companions. The finest of the rooms inside the house is undoubtedly the Great Hall, which is still full height and has a very ornate timber roof. Other rooms in the house have panelled walls and plaster ceilings. Much of this decoration dates from the 1890s, when Athelhampton was extensively restored or was brought in at that time. The rooms are furnished with a catholic mixture of Tudor, Georgian and neo-Tudor pieces. Visitors make their own way around but some of the rooms have ropes across the doorways. The chained ape, which was the crest of the Martyns, appears in many places at Athelhampton in stained glass and carved stone. Their motto was 'He who looks at Martyn's ape, Martyn's ape shall look at him'. The charming formal gardens to the south east of the house were laid out in the 1890s and are in the architectural manner which was just then becoming fashionable.

Opening times: Good Friday to 11 Oct, Wed, Thurs and Sun, also Bank Holiday Mon and Tues and Fri in August 2–6.
Entrance charges: House and garden, £1.50; children 75p.
Parking: Free parking next to the house.
Wheelchair access: Possible to ground floor rooms and garden.
Guidebook: A history of occupants and a room-by-room guide which is coy about the extensive restorations of the last 100 years.
Catering: Afternoon tea with the waitress service is to be found in a thatched stable building near the entrance to the gardens. The pots of tea are generous.
WCs: Adjacent to the garden entrance, spacious and free; facilities suitable for wheelchair-users.
Shop: The shop in the house sells postcards and tasteful items like scented soap in floral packages and beeswax candles. There is another shop selling bric-a-brac near the garden entrance.

CHETTLE HOUSE Blandford Forum
Tel: Tarrant Hinton (025889) 209
Directions: 6 miles N.E. of Blandford Forum off the A354

Chettle is a fine example of the English Baroque style. It was probably designed in about 1710 by Thomas Archer, whose other work includes the Church of St John, Smith Square in London. Archer had travelled abroad to Italy and it is the tricks of style which he borrowed from the Italians which make his buildings interesting. In this case the house is a two-storey red brick box, with rounded ends and a tall rounded bow on one side, which rises above the roofline. On what used to be the entrance front, the centre has two tiers of round windows and bands of stone ornament to make it stand out from the rest. Although a substantial part of Chettle has been converted into flats, the great staircase survives. It is like a set for grand opera: two flights of steps rise from the hall, join, disappear through a door on the first floor and re-emerge as balconies on each side. The only other main room on show is the drawing room, which was decorated in the 1840s; enthusiasts of building construction can take a spiral staircase to the basement which is vaulted. The house stands in a formal terraced garden.

Opening times: Exterior daily 10.30–sunset; interior usually open.
Entrance charges: Free.
Parking: Limited parking space next to the house.
Wheelchair access: There is a flight of seven steps to the entrance.
Guidebook: A small booklet with a brief history and colour illustrations.
Catering: None.
WCs: None.
Shop: None.

COMPTON HOUSE   Over Compton, nr Sherbourne (Worldwide Butterflies Ltd)
Tel: Yeovil (0935) 4608
Directions: 4 miles W. of Sherbourne off the A30; signposted locally 'Worldwide Butterflies'

In essence, this is a large early Victorian house full of butterflies. The previous house, of which the 17th century outbuildings still survive, was completely rebuilt in 1839 under the direction of the architect John Pinch of Bath. He created a romantic pile with tall gables and chimneystacks in imitation of more famous houses such as Montacute. Since 1746, Compton has been owned by the Gooden family and in the the 1970s Robert Gooden turned the house into a showplace for his butterfly business. Several of the ground floor rooms are used to display these colourful creatures and the Lullingstone Silk Farm has recently removed from Hampshire and is housed in pre-fabs a short distance from the house. In them can be seen live silk worms and demonstrations of silk-making. Across the lawn from the house is the parish church, which is partly mediaeval.

Opening times: 1 April to 31 Oct, daily 10–5.
Entrance charges: (1981) £1.65; children 85p. (HHA)
Parking: Free parking adjacent to the house.
Wheelchair access: Possible to house and also to silk farm (steep ramp).
Guidebook: A choice between very cheap or very expensive; both have colour illustrations and are intended to sell butterflies.
Catering: There is pop and ice-cream in the shop by the car park and a 'Little Chef' restaurant

at the entrance gate.
WCs: At the house and also at the silk farm, clean and spacious.
Shop: There are several in both house and farm offering mounted butterflies, butterfly cages, silk scarves and everything else for the lepidopterist.

CORFE CASTLE Corfe, nr Wareham (The Bankes Estate)
Tel: Corfe Castle (0929) 480442
Directions: Between Wareham and Swanage on the A351, in the village of Corfe

Corfe was one of the strongest castles in the country, but is now a ruin. Like many other English castles it was thoroughly blown up after the Civil War. The setting is unforgettable for the castle stands on a steep mound in the middle of a narrow gap between taller hills, with excellent views of Wareham and the Isle of Purbeck. There is no wonder that Corfe was King John's favourite castle. On the peak of the hill is what remains of the keep, built in about 1100, and near it are the ruins of a stone building with elegant pointed arches which was the 'gloriette', an unfortified house round a courtyard built for King John in 1202. Broadly speaking, the earliest buildings are at the top of the mound, near the keep, while the walls enclosing the lower ward come later. By 1285 all that stands today had been built.

Opening times: March to Oct, daily 10–dusk; Nov to Feb, Sat and Sun 2–4.
Entrance charges: 50p; children 30p.
Parking: There is no official car park. A limited amount of free parking is available in the village at the gate.
Wheelchair access: Not really practicable because of steep slopes and uneven ground.
Guidebook: A full history of the castle and its owners but rather out of date. More is known about the buildings than the book admits. There is a plan showing the castle layout before its destruction.
Catering: None.
WCs: None.
Shop: The ticket office sells postcards and a small selection of souvenirs and ice cream.

DEWLISH HOUSE Dewlish (Mr J. Anthony Boyden)
Tel: Milbourne St. Andrew (025 887) 224
Directions: 3 miles N. of Puddletown off the A354 on the edge of Dewlish village. The house is not signposted and the main gate says 'no admittance'

The main attraction of Dewlish is the entrance front, built of Purbeck limestone, long, low and comfortable-looking, with a touch of elegance in the curved pediment over the three centre windows. This front dates from 1702 and was built for Thomas Skinner, whose father had been a merchant in London and whose coat of arms is carved over the front door. When the house changed hands in 1756 alterations were made. The garden front was rebuilt in brick and a number of the rooms inside were given elaborate carved chimney pieces. A fine new staircase was also installed. These are now the principal features of the interior, which has been completely redecorated by the present owner. Visitors are conducted round the house by a member of the staff and are shown all the principal ground floor rooms and several bedrooms upstairs. The garden has been newly laid-out and the house sits in its valley on an expanse of perfect lawn.

Opening times: May to Sept, Thurs (except Bank Holidays) 2–5.
Entrance charges: £1.00; children 50p.
Parking: Free parking in front of the house.
Wheelchair access: Two steps up to the front door, after that all the ground floor rooms are accessible.
Guidebook: None.
Catering: None.

FORDE ABBEY   nr Chard (M. Roper Esq)
Tel: South Chard (0460) 20231
Directions: 4 miles S.E. of Chard between the B3162 and the B3167; well-signposted locally

It should be remembered that Forde was a large and important Abbey for 400 years, before it was closed by King Henry VIII. The Abbey Church stood on what is now the front lawn. The house was made by converting some of the other buildings of the Abbey and combining them with new work. The result is a long front, built of beautiful stone but made up of unrelated parts. In the years just before the closure of the Abbey, the last Abbot, Thomas Chard, spent enormous sums of money on new buildings. The tower over the main entrance and the Great Hall next to it were built by him in the 1520s and 1530s; both are decorated with carved stonework of high quality. In 1549 Forde was bought by Sir Edmund Prideaux, Oliver Cromwell's Attorney General, and it was he who turned the Abbey buildings into a grand private house. Part of the Great Hall was chopped off to make a dining room and drawing room. A large and splendid saloon was built next to the entrance tower and also some smaller rooms over Thomas Chard's cloister. These alterations were finished by about 1660 and little has been altered since that time. Visitors see the inside of the Great Hall, the saloon, the mediaeval refectory, and the smaller rooms over the cloister. All of these have been furnished in a style suitable to the house. The last room shown is a delightful conservatory made out of the surviving cloister range. At one end of the house, but entered separately, is the Norman chapter house, a last reminder of the original Abbey, now converted into a chapel. The large informal garden fits the house perfectly.

Opening times: May to Sept, Wed and Sun 2–6, also Easter Sunday and Summer Bank Holidays 2–6. Garden only, March, April and Oct, Sun 2–4.30.
Entrance charges: (1981) House and garden £1.40; children 70p. Garden only 85p. (HHA)
Parking: A large free car park next to the house.

Forde Abbey, Dorset

Wheelchair access: Only possible to Great Hall, but the outside of this house is as good as the inside. Tea room accessible if entered by exit.

Guidebook: A brief history, a tour of the house and many colour illustrations. A plan of the gardens but not of the house.

Catering: An elegant setting in the undercroft of the 13th century dormitory. Self service; food unmemorable.

WCs: In the house, free; suitable for wheelchair-users.

Shop: At the back of the house, by the visitors' exit; the usual range of a large gift shop but with a bit more flair than usual. Forde Abbey marmalade and local honey are sold.

Extras: At the right season there is a 'pick your own' fruit farm on the estate which is open daily.

MILTON ABBEY nr Blandford Forum (The Governors of Milton Abbey School)

Tel: Milton Abbas (0258) 880484

Directions: 9 miles S.W. of Blandford Forum off the A354 on the edge of Milton Abbas village

The name Milton Abbey now applies equally to the house and the church which stands next to it, but the church has the prior claim. It was built in the 14th century to replace an earlier church which had been burnt in 1309. Only the choir, transepts and tower were ever built. Next to the church stood the domestic buildings of the Abbey and a small market town, but between 1770 and 1790 Lord Milton removed everything except the Abbot's Great Hall, built in 1498, which he made into part of a new house for himself. The hall forms one side of a courtyard. The three other sides are enclosed by an elegant Georgian house of 1771–5. The new house is in the Gothic style, perhaps out of respect for the Abbot's hall, but Sir William Chambers, who was the architect, detested Gothic. The result is a house with two symmetrical main fronts dressed up in half-hearted Gothic ornament. The stone is of the highest quality and the ornament is as crisp as the day it was cut. The house is now a school and the grounds about it, which were laid out by 'Capability' Brown, are covered with goal posts or cricket pitches according to the time of year. The Abbot's hall serves as the school dining room, and the elaborate roof and the original screen can still be admired. In the main house several rooms are open on both the ground and first floors where the decoration was designed by James Wyatt, who took over from Chambers in 1775. All the rooms have utilitarian furniture and have suffered at schoolboy hands (and feet).

Opening times: House 1–12 April and 18 July to 30 Aug, 10–7.30 or dusk; the Abbey church is open at all times.

Entrance charges: 40p; children free.

Parking: Free parking in school outbuildings.

Wheelchair access: Possible to church, Great Hall and ground floor of house (up 3 steps).

Guidebook: Deals mainly with the church — in fact there is only one paragraph about the house.

Catering: A modern tea-cum-tuck shop near the north front of the house, serves tea, scones,

sandwiches in a functional setting.
WCs: Near the car park, pretty grim and not suitable for wheelchairs.
Shop: There is a small gift shop.

PARNHAM HOUSE Beaminster (Mr John Makepeace)
Tel: Beaminster (0308) 862204
Directions: 1 mile S. of Beaminster on the A3066

The main front of Parnham has all the things a Tudor house should have, large windows, gables and pinnacles built of Ham Hill stone which has mellowed a rich golden brown, but not everything is of the same date. The half to the left of the porch was built in about 1540, the half to the right about 1600 by two different members of the Strode family. The pinnacles and battlements, together with the other two sides of the house, were added in 1807–10 in a campaign of improvements by the architect John Nash. The inside of the house was completely overhauled and the large formal gardens laid out in 1910 as part of another campaign of the same kind. Parnham is now the home of the John Makepeace Furniture Workshop and the John Makepeace School for Craftsmen in Wood. The main rooms of the old house are used to display the finest modern furniture. The rooms on show are the great hall, drawing room, library, Oak Room and Strode bedroom.

Opening times: 4 April to 31 Oct, Wed, Sun and Bank Holidays 10–5.
Entrance charges: £1.20; children under 16 60p. (HHA)
Parking: Free and adjacent to the house.
Wheelchair access: Possible to all rooms on ground floor; not the Strode bedroom.
Guidebook: Includes general information about the house, the Furniture Workshop and the school. There is a block plan of the house and grounds but no detailed plan of the interior. Display boards in each room contain more detailed information.
Catering: Lunches and teas in the Oak Room; modern Italian furniture and waitress service, cream teas or coffee by the cup and tea by the pot. The room has associations with both Sir Walter Raleigh and General Eisenhower.
WCs: In the house and near the car parks.
Shop: In the Minstrel's Gallery; sells postcards, books and small items made in the Workshop.
Extras: There are usually exhibitions in the drawing room and one of the workshops is open to the public.

PURSE CAUNDLE MANOR Purse Caundle (R.E. Wincklemann Esq)
Tel: Milbourne Port (0963) 250400
Directions: 4 miles E. of Sherbourne, just off the A30 in the village of Purse Caundle

This modest grey stone manor house is set back from the road behind a high wall, all except one wing, whose oriel window looks out over the village. At the centre of the house is the great hall which was built in the late 15th century. The rooms on either side, including the wing with the oriel, are of the same date. In about 1550 William Hanham enlarged the house and the long south front looking out over the bowling green is mainly his work. He also made some changes inside the building and no one is quite sure how the rooms on either side of the hall were first arranged. The conducted tour of the house takes in the hall, with its rich timber roof, the winter parlour, the great chamber, which is the room behind the oriel window, and several bedrooms. Much was restored at the beginning of this century by Lady Victoria Herbert, and not all the panelling, for example, is original to the house. Purse Caundle is still occupied and the furniture is a comfortable mixture of the old and not so old.

Opening times: April to end Oct, Wed, Thur, Sun and Bank Holiday Mon 2–5.
Entrance charges: 80p; children 30p.
Parking: Free and close to house.
Wheelchair access: Only possible to the hall and adjacent rooms.
Guidebook: Cheap and useful history of owners with a few words about the house itself.
Catering: None.
WCs: None for public use.
Shop: None.

RUSSELL-COTES ART GALLERY AND MUSEUM (Bournemouth Corporation)
Tel: Bournemouth (0202) 21009
Directions: In Russell-Cotes Road, on the East Cliff, near the centre of Bournemouth

Sir Merton Russell-Cotes was the man who put Bournemouth on the map. He owned the Royal Bath Hotel and poured his energy into developing the town around it. As a symbol of his success, he employed J.F. Fogerty to design him a house in the centre of town combining the Italianate and Scottish Baronial styles, overlooking both the sea and the hotel. Little of the outside can be seen because of the steeply sloping ground and the trees, but glimpses of the three rounded verandahs with their red-tiled roofs can be caught from the cliff paths. Steps lead down from the entrance to the main hall, with its tinkling fountain and vaguely erotic sculptures. Opening off the main hall on the sea side are lace-curtained rooms with overblown furniture, oriental curios and rather unexciting 19th century landscape paintings. The gallery round the hall on the first floor leads to the bedrooms which now house such diverse objects as oriental costumes and relics of the actor Henry Irving. Although this is a museum, with a large picture gallery of late 19th and 20th century paintings attached, it vividly conjures up the life of this self-made man and his formidable wife.

Opening times: All year, Mon to Sat, 10.30–5.30 (last tickets 5pm) (except Good Friday, Christmas and Boxing Day).
Entrance charges: 20p; children 5p.
Parking: There is no car park for visitors. On-street parking is possible nearby but not always easily found in summer.
Wheelchair access: Not possible.

Guidebook: There is a small guide to the museum.
Catering: A surprising and delightful little tea room down some stairs off the main gallery.
WCs: In the museum, free.
Shop: At the entrance, selling postcards, booklets and souvenirs.

SHERBORNE CASTLE Sherborne (Simon Wingfield Digby Esq)
Tel: Sherborne (093 581) 3182
Directions: 5 miles E. of Yeovil, just S. of Sherborne off the A30

There are two castles at Sherborne. The older castle lies across the valley. In 1592 Queen Elizabeth leased it to Sir Walter Raleigh who began to carry out repairs but quickly gave up and in 1594 built himself a new house close by. The new house was tall and square but not very large and Raleigh called it 'The Lodge'. By the time Raleigh lost his head on Tower Hill in 1618 his property at Sherborne had been given to Sir John Digby. Digby also fell from favour because of his failure to secure a royal Spanish marriage. He retired to his country estate in 1625 and set about enlarging the Lodge. He added two wings on each side, with towers to match those of the older house. The result is something like a castle in outline, but with many more windows. All the walls are rendered and their yellow ochre colour blends with the ornaments of brown Ham Hill stone. After the weird exterior, the inside is a little disappointing. A vast amount of redecoration was done by 1859 by the architect P.C. Hardwick and some of the plaster ceilings are his work. There are some survivals of an earlier period including the Gothic plasterwork of 1760 in the library, and the oak room which has not changed much since the 1620s. Most of the most rooms are on show and they contain good Georgian furniture and some excellent portraits. The park was landscaped by 'Capability' Brown and is open to the public at the same time as the house.

Opening times: Easter Sat to end May, Thurs, Sat, Sun and Bank Holiday Mon, 1 June to end Sept daily 2–6 (last admission 5.30).
Entrance charges: (1981) £1.50; children 70p. (HHA)
Parking: Free parking next to the house.
Wheelchair access: Would be possible to the ground floor of the house but the narrow doors and other obstacles might still prove difficult; best to telephone in advance.
Guidebook: A rather expensive, heavyweight guide which is fulsome about the Raleigh and Digby families, briefer about the building; room-by-room guide, many illustrations, no plan. There is no cheap guide but the ladies in each room are helpful. Tour translations available in French, German and Dutch.
Catering: New self-service tea room.
WCs: Adequate, but not suitable for wheelchair users.
Shop: A small shop selling honey, smocks, ties and the usual postcards.
Extras: Sherborne Old Castle, across the valley, is worth a visit.

SMEDMORE HOUSE　Kimmeridge (Major and Mrs John Mansel)
Tel:　Corfe Castle (0929) 480717
Directions:　7 miles S. of Wareham; turn off the A351 at Corfe Castle for
　Kimmeridge

Behind Smedmore are the Purbeck Hills and in front of it lies the sea. The beach nearby has a greyish colour because of the oil contained in the shale and Sir William Clavell built himself a small house in the 1620s with the idea of using the oil for fuelling a glass factory. His plan came to nothing and his house is now concealed in later buildings. The first addition was the early 18th century south west front, only five windows wide and two storeys high, but with elegant carved stone ornament. One end of this front was lost when a new north range with large bow windows was added in the 1760s. The house has four main rooms on the ground floor and all are open to the public. The cedar room has early 18th century panelling. The other three rooms were decorated in 1765 by the Bastards of Blandford, a well-known family of Dorset architects. A great deal of the furniture and many of the paintings at Smedmore are Dutch. There is good marquetry work and pictures by Mierveld and Van Huysum, as well as the usual country house mixture of dates and styles.

Opening times:　June, July and Aug, Wed; first two Weds in Sept, 2.15–5.30; last admission
　5.00.
Entrance charges:　(1981) 80p; children 40p. (HHA)
Parking:　Free parking to one side of the house.
Wheelchair access:　Possible to all rooms; apply at the house for entry by the front door, which
　avoids the tortuous back route.
Guidebook:　A small but very adequate booklet with a brief history, tour of the house and
　grounds, and a useful plan of the building.
Catering:　None.
WCs:　In the outbuildings behind the house, three steps to the door, but otherwise suitable for
　wheelchairs.
Shop:　Some garden produce only.
Extras:　In the old kitchen at the back of the house is a museum with a display of dolls and also
　photographs and documents about the house, free.

WOLVETON HOUSE　Charminster (Capt N.T.L. Thimbleby)
Tel:　Dorchester (0305) 63500
Directions:　1½ miles N.W. of Dorchester on the A37

Thomas Hardy described Wolveton as 'an ivied manor house, flanked by battlemented towers, more than usually distinguished by the size of its mullioned windows'; this is still apt, though there is less ivy. The lopsided gatehouse, one of whose chimney breasts has an inscription dating construction to 1534, once led into the centre of a neat little courtyard house, built in about 1530 by Sir Thomas Trenchard. Most of this building was demolished in the late 19th century, leaving only the gatehouse and a fragment of one side. Next to the fragment is a taller range added in about 1600, with large mullioned windows which remind one of Longleat, only 35 miles away. The house has suffered from all the demolition and re-arrangement, but still contains some rich fireplaces and a magnificent stone staircase which may be the work of one of the Longleat carvers. Restoration work is in progress, but the comfortable feel of the house in no way appears to be threatened. The grounds are far from the neatly-trimmed norm, with sheep on the lawn and nettles in the flower beds; romantically unspoilt or ruinously run-down, according to your point of view.

Opening times: 1 May to 30 Sept, Tues, Thurs, Sun and Bank Holiday Mon; August, daily except Sat 2–6.
Entrance charges: £1.00; children 55p.
Parking: Free and next to house.
Wheelchair access: Possible to ground floor rooms.
Guidebook: Short, clear and informative with a good plan and black and white illustrations. There are printed guides in each room.
Catering: Only by prior arrangement, but a glass of excellent cider is given to all on leaving.
WCs: None.
Shop: None, but home-produced cider is sold in the hall.
Extras: The large barn to the north of the house is the earliest surviving riding school in England; it was built in about 1610, but it is not open to the public. The Cider House in the outbuildings is open to view and the ancient presses are still in use.

Durham

BARNARD CASTLE (Ancient Monument)
Directions: Barnard Castle stands in the town of the same name, 15 miles W. of Darlington at the junction of the A67 and A688

Barnard Castle was an important military centre during the Middle Ages. It was originally owned by the Baliol family, one of the most powerful families in Britain. John Baliol became King of Scotland in 1292 and went to war against Edward I of England. After his defeat the family lost the castle and its estates, which passed to the Beauchamps, then the Nevilles and finally reverted to the Crown. In 1569 the castle had a final moment of glory when the King's Steward held out for 11 days against the Earls of Westmoreland and Northumberland during the 'Rising of the North'. The castle stands in a naturally strong positin above the River Tees with sheer cliffs on two sides. The inner ward, containing the principal buildings, was perched at their edge and was cut off from the rest of the castle by a ditch. The buildings were altered so often that their dating is still incomplete. Mostly they date from between about 1250 and 1350. The Baliol Tower at the north corner of the ward is the one building that is almost intact and dominates the site. the outer and town wards, which had no stone constructions apart from the walls, are now just pleasant grassy areas embellished by a small private orchard.

Opening times: Standard times (SM), see page xii.
Entrance charges: 40p; OAPs and children 20p.
Parking: Free parking in the town nearby.
Wheelchair access: Possible.
Guidebook: Inexpensive and scholarly, with an outline plan but no illustrations.
Catering: In the town.
WCs: None.
Shop: None.
Extras: At the other end of the town is the excellent Bowes Museum.

DURHAM CASTLE Cathedral Close (University College, Durham)
Tel: Durham (0385) 65481
Directions: In the centre of the city, follow signs to the Cathedral

The Cathedral and castle stand together on high ground in a loop of the River Wear and completely dominate the town. The castle was begun at the same time as the Cathedral and very soon became the palace of the Prince-Bishops. It was converted to its present use as an undergraduate college when Durham University was founded in the 1830s. The present buildings still follow the 'motte and bailey' plan of a typical Norman fortress, with the octagonal keep on top of its grassed mound and the main residential buildings grouped round a courtyard next to it. The keep was much restored in the 1830s and is not open to visitors. The other buildings were constantly being altered and improved by the Bishops and are a confusing mixture. A porch in the courtyard dating from Bishop Cosin's reign in the 1660s leads to a screens passage with the great kitchen (still in use) on one side and the great hall on the other. The hall is an impressive room, first built in the 14th century but with panelling and stained glass of the 1830s and solemn portraits of University dignitaries. The main chapel also has much 19th century work, although there are some amusing mediaeval carvings on the stalls against the walls. The high points of the visit are Bishop Cosin's 'Black Staircase' with its carved side panels of delicate wooden tracery, a small Norman chapel on the lower ground floor which has a fine series of Romanesque capitals and the Norman doorway in Bishop Tunstall's gallery. This used to be the main entrance to the Bishops' Palace and the door surround is very richly carved. The building of the gallery protected the carving from the weather and it is unusually crisp. A number of State Rooms, richly decorated in various styles, appear fascinating in the guide book but do not figure in the tour.

Opening times: 27 Sept to 12 July, Mon, Wed, Sat 2–4 (first 3 weeks in April, daily 2–4); 12 July to 30 Sept, Mon to Sat 10–12, 2–4.30; Sun 2–5. May be closed for University functions.

Entrance charges: (1981) 80p; children and OAPs 30p. (HHA)
Parking: Limited stay parking in the Cathedral Close, or there are pay car parks in the city centre about ¼ mile away.
Wheelchair access: Not practicable.
Guidebook: A plan, short history, room-by-room guide and many illustrations.
Catering: Excellent cream teas are available in the Cathedral buttery nearby. Lunches are also served.

RABY CASTLE Staindrop (Lord Barnard)
Tel: Staindrop (083 3) 60202
Directions: 11 miles W. of Darlington on the A688, between Bishop Auckland and Barnard Castle

One of the best things about Raby is its long battlemented silhouette seen across the deer park. The oldest parts of the castle date from the 12th century, but it was used as a residence until recently and is consequently well-maintained and heavily restored. The basic layout and apearance is that of a 14th century castle, but later additions and alterations have transformed the buildings into a vast and comfortable country house. The most spectacular of the surviving mediaeval buildings is the Nevill gateway, two slanted towers guarding a long deep passageway leading to the central courtyard. Inside the house the entrance hall, with its tall dark red columns and vaulted roof, is Gothic revival work of 1783 by John Carr of York, who usually preferred the Classical style. Many of the other rooms which are open to visitors owe their appearance to the architect William Burn, who was working at Raby in the 1840s. His octagon room, with its heavy gilded ceiling in French 17th century style, silk-lined walls and ornate mirrors, is the centrepiece of the ground floor. The most impressive room in the castle is the Barons' Hall on the first floor, which Burn lengthened by 52 feet and re-roofed. It was in this room that the 'Rising of the North' against Queen Elizabeth was planned in 1569. The failure of this revolt destroyed the power of the Nevill family and in 1626 Raby Castle passed into the hands of Sir Henry Vane, whose descendants still own it. The castle has a large collection of paintings, including good portraits by Sir Peter Lely and Sir Joshua Reynolds, and an interesting 'Artist's Studio' by David Teniers the younger. In addition, there is much French 19th century furniture and porcelain and Hiram Power's popular statue of a chained naked slave girl.

Opening times: Easter to end Sept; April to June, Wed and Sun; July to end Sept, daily except Sat, also Bank Holiday Sat, Sun, Mon and Tues; Park and gardens 1–5.30. Castle 2–5.
Entrance charges: (1981) £1.00; children and OAPs 60p. (HHA)
Parking: Free parking in the grounds.
Wheelchair access: No special facilities but part of the house is accessible.
Guidebook: New guide planned for 1982.
Catering: A tea room has been formed out of the old stables where rather basic teas may be had.

WCs: Adequate; facilities for wheelchairs in tea room.
Shop: The usual souvenirs.
Extras: There is an impressive display of coaching equipment in the stables. A visit to the large walled garden is recommended.

Essex

AUDLEY END   Saffron Walden (Department of the Environment)
   Directions: 1 mile W. of Saffron Walden, off the A11, signposted locally

The impressive Jacobean house with its many turrets and great mullioned windows is only a third part of the palace built by Thomas Howard, 1st Earl of Suffolk, between 1603 and 1616. There was originally a great outer courtyard, and a complete inner courtyard behind the existing hall. The design for the house was made by a Dutch sculptor called Bernhard Janssen and the two very elaborate front porches are good examples of the Anglo-Flemish style. The Third Earl sold the house to Charles II as a Royal Palace but William III returned it to the Fifth Earl. He pulled down the outer court in 1721 on the advice of the architect Sir John Vanbrugh, who also designed the stone screen in the hall. In the 1760s the principal living rooms were redecorated by Robert Adam and more redecoration was carried out in the 1820s but every effort was made to keep in the style of the older work. The house is now in the care of the State, but much of the furniture and many paintings belonging to Lord Braybrooke, the last private owner, are still here. The ground floor contains the original hall, with its huge and barbarous carved screen, and several rooms which have recently been redecorated in the Adam style, the lower gallery with its host of stuffed animals and the two secondary stairs. On the first floor is a very pretty Gothick chapel designed by John Hobcraft in 1768 and the main state rooms comprising the dining room, libraries, drawing room and saloon. These have splendid fireplaces and much 18th and early 19th century furniture and fittings. The south library is particularly memorable for the bindings of all the books in a red and gold chequer pattern. The great saloon was once known as the Fish Room from the number of sea creatures in its elaborate Jacobean ceiling. There are rope barriers and attendants in some rooms, but otherwise visitors are left to themselves. The large park was landscaped by 'Capability' Brown in the 1760s. It contains a number of elegant garden buildings (some of which can only be inspected by prior arrangement) and there is also a Jacobean red brick stable block.

Opening times: April to Sept, daily ercept Mon (open Bank Holiday Mon except May Day) 1–6.30. Grounds open at 12.
Entrance charges: £1.80; children 90p.

Parking: Free parking near the house.
Wheelchair access: The great hall, the newly redecorated Adam rooms and the lower gallery containing the stuffed animal collection would all be easily accessible.
Guidebook: The present guide book contains the history of the house and its owners, with many illustrations and a plan; however, a new guide book is in preparation.
Catering: There is a fairly small self-service restaurant near the entrance to the house; tea and coffee, biscuits and hot meals; adequate food but uninspiring surroundings.
WCs: Near the restaurant, adequate; but no facilities for wheelchair users.
Shop: Small bookstall in entrance hall.
Extras: Near the stables is a garden centre selling fruit, vegetables and plants grown on the estate; they have a better-than-average selection of herbs. Just outside the main gate is a miniature railway; this is a separate concern, for which a separate charge is made.

CASTLE HOUSE Dedham (Castle House Trust)
Tel: Colchester (0206) 322127
Directions: 7 miles N.E. of Colchester, 2 miles E. of the A12, on th edge of Dedham, on an unclassified road

Castle House is open to the public because it was the home of Sir Alfred Munnings, who became famous in the first half of this century as a painter of horses. Munnings came to Dedham in 1919 and died here in 1959. The building itself is a confused mixture of Georgian and earlier work, all washed over with pink cement. The rooms inside are more like an art gallery with furniture than living rooms, and there is total absence of the usual painter's clutter. Visitors make their own way round and there are no ropes or barriers. The paintings are surprisingly varied. Horses are certainly in the majority, but there are landscapes, paintings of gypsies, portraits, and some attractive studies done by Munnings when he was in Paris. A group of outbuildings has been converted into a gallery to display some of the larger canvases. Outside in the garden is Munnings' studio which contains many of the vigorous drawings he did in his youth for posters to advertise chocolates. Here also can be found his palette, racing silks and a rather loud tweed suit with velvet collar and cuffs. The garden is quite small; over the fence can be seen the stables where the painter and his wife kept their own horses.

Opening times: 9 May to 10 Oct, Wed, Sun and Bank Holiday Mon, also Thurs and Sat in Aug, 2–5.
Entrance charges: 50p; children 15. (HHA)
Parking: Free parking on grass near the house.
Wheelchair access: Possible to the ground floor rooms, which contain the bulk of the collection, and to the studio.
Guidebook: A biography of Munnings with many illustrations of the rooms in the house, and of some of his paintings.
Catering: None.
Wcs: In the garden, next to the studio; no facilities for wheelchairs.
Shop: Prints and cards sold in the entrance lobby.
Extras: The lane by Castle House leads appropriately to the Heavy Horse Centre, which is open to the public.

GOSFIELD HALL Halstead (Mutual Households Association)
Tel: Halstead (078 74) 2914
Directions: 4 miles N. of Braintree, 2 miles W. of Halstead off the A1017;
turn off in the village by red brick lodge, not signposted

The entrance front of Gosfield Hall looks quite extraordinary. The lower part is clearly of the early 18th century, but above it rises a great clerestory in a revived Tudor style. The rest of the building is equally mixed. Gosfield was originally built in about 1545 for Sir John Wentworth and the west front and central courtyard of his house still exist with only a few alterations. The east or entrance front was rebuilt in the early 18th century and the north and south sides were also very much altered in the 18th century, but there seems to be no sure information about the dates of the various parts. The house has now been converted into a number of apartments, although the main rooms have been preserved and are shown to visitors in a guided tour conducted by one of the residents. The tour begins in the grand early 18th century hall or saloon and next to it is the principal staircase of the same date. The library in the south wing is a pleasant dark-grained room and a passage leads from it to the north wing, whose first floor is largely taken up by a splendid 18th century ballroom with a good fireplace and grained panelling. The first floor of the west wing is the 16th century Long Gallery, completely lined with linenfold panelling, which now serves as the residents' dining room. The furniture in the rooms mostly belongs to the residents. The tours end with a detour to the outbuildings to see the well, with its pump which was driven by a horse, and a circuit of the outside to see the garden.

Opening times: 1 May to 30 Sept, Wed and Thurs 2–4.
Entrance charges: 40p; children 20p; entrance charges includes cost of guide book.
Parking: Next to the house.
Wheelchair access: Would be possible to entrance hall and library, but not to ballroom or long gallery; the whole of the outside and the inner courtyard is accessible.
Guidebook: Given free with each entrance charge; a useful history of the various owners of Gosfield, but the information about the building iself is vague and sometimes of doubtful accuracy.
Catering: None.
WCs: None for public use.
Shop: None.

HEDINGHAM CASTLE Castle Hedingham (Dr Margery Blackie)
Tel: Hedingham (0787) 60435
Directions: 8 miles N. of Braintree, off the A604 in Castle Hedingham; the entrance to the castle is in Bayley Street at the edge of the village

This massive square stone tower is a spectacular relic of the mighty castle of the de Vere family. It was built in about 1130 and is similar to the keep at

Rochester in Kent, which is of the same date and may be by the same builder. The keep now stands by itself in a level grassy enclosure which was orignally the inner bailey containing the great hall, chapel and other principal buildings of the castle. The outer bailey is occupied by a red brick Georgian house which is not open to visitors. All the exterior walls of the keep still stand, but two of the four small corner towers have gone and also the forebuilding protecting the steps leading to the main entrance at first floor level. The entrance opens into a large room filling the whole first floor. Stone stairs in the north west tower lead up to the great hall filling the second floor. The hall has a gallery running all the way round in the thickness of the walls and its roof is supported on a spectacular stone arch, supposed to be the best of its kind and date in the country. There is a further room above the hall but there is no public access to the roof, which seems a pity since the keep commands the surrounding countryside for several miles. The rooms inside the keep have no furniture, but some old prints and other material are laid out in the great hall. The greensward surrounding the castle makes an excellent place for picnics.

Opening times: 1 May to 30 Sept Tues to Sat 1–5; also Spring and Summer Bank Holidays 11–5.
Entrance charges: 50p; children 20p, payable inside the keep.
Parking: On the grass round the castle; there is an entrance charge for cars of 50p.
Wheelchair acces: Totally impracticable to the interior of the keep, but all of the outside can be seen.
Guidebook: Better than nothing; it makes colourful reading.
Catering: None.
WCs: At the edge of the castle enclosure, fairly recent, small; not for wheelchairs.
Shop: None.

LAYER MARNEY TOWER nr Colchester (Major and Mrs Gerald Charrington)
Tel: Colchester (0206) 330202
Directions: 7 miles of S.W. of Colchester, 3 miles N.E. of Tiptree; signed off the B1022 at Smythe's Green

Henry Marney rose from decent obscurity to wealth and influence under Henry VII; he was made a Privy Councillor and given a title by Henry VIII but died early in 1523. His son's death in 1525 brought the line to an end, but between 1520 and 1525 the family began to build a huge new brick house, with Italianate terra cotta decoration in the very latest fashion. The house was never finished but the magnificent gatehouse intended as its showpiece still survives. It is three storeys high, but the pairs of towers which flank the entrance door have seven or eight tiers of windows and rise clear above the roofline to finish in elaborate terra cotta crests. There is no larger or more impressive gatehouse of its date in England. The present owners live in the range adjoining the tower, which is not open to the public (except by prior arrangement). Visitors are admitted to the inside of the tower and may ascend through its bare and unplastered rooms to the roof, where there is a fine view of the flat Essex country and an opportunity to see the Tudor decoration at close quarters. The garden was originally the forecourt of the house and the stair towers on this side are polygonal, for extra effect. On one side of the garden is the parish church containing the Marney tombs. On the other is a long brick range, originally stables with lodgings over, which was converted into a long gallery in the present century. This range has a good 16th century timber roof. A small part of another outbuilding is also accessible. Visitors make their own way round all these buildings.

Opening times: 1 April to 1 Oct, Thurs and Sun, also Tues in July and Aug 2–6. Easter, Spring and Autumn Bank Holidays, Sat, Sun and Mon 11–6.
Entrance charges: 70p; children 20p. (HHA)
Parking: In front of the gatehouse.
Wheelchair access: The upper part of the tower would not be accessible, but both sides of the tower could be viewed without difficulty, also the long gallery.
Guidebook: A useful booklet with a history of house and occupants and several photographs of the buildings.
Catering: Only by prior arrangement for groups.
WCs: One of each.
Shop: None, though a few souvenirs are sold at the ticket desk in the tower.

PAYCOCKE'S West Street, Great Coggeshall (The National Trust)
   Directions: 5½ miles E. of Braintree, in Great Coggeshall, on the S. side of West Street (the A120)

In the 15th and 16th centuries Coggeshall was well-known for the production of cloth. One of the leading clothiers was Thomas Paycocke, who died in 1505 leaving three houes, of which Paycocke's was one. The house is a timber-framed building two storeys high fronting directly onto the road. Brick infilling between the timbers has replaced the original plaster and the whole of the building has been extensively restored in the present century, but the carved decoration for which Paycocke's is famous has survived very well. On the left hand side of the front is a carriage-way whose double doors have fine linenfold carving and the bressumer at the base of the jettied upper story has more elaborate carved decoration, which includes the trade marks and initials of Thomas Paycocke. The small rooms inside all have decorative carving on the wooden uprights and ceiling joists and there is also some panelling. The house is let to tenants of the National Trust and some of the furniture is theirs, but most of the larger pieces of 16th and 17th century oak furniture have been lent to the house. At the back is an attractive small garden running down to a tributary of the river Blackwater. From the garden can be seen the clutter of smaller buildings at the back of the house, some of which are in fact earlier in date than the main range.

Opening times: April to end Sept, Wed, Thurs, Sun and Bank Holiday Mon 2–5.30.
Entrance charges: 80p; children 40p, but must be accompanied by an adult; parties of more than six must make arrangements prior to visit.
Parking: By the roadside in front of the house, no parking restrictions.
Wheelchair access: The roadside front is easily visible, there is a step up to the entrance hall, but this should present no difficulties.
Guidebook: A small booklet with a history of the owners and an acount of the house with a diagram to show the structure; more might be said about the original use and arrangement of the rooms. There is no information about the furniture.
Catering: None.
WCs: None.
Shop: None.

ST OSYTH'S PRIORY St Osyth (Somerset and Lady Juliet de Chair)
Tel: St Osyth (0255) 820492
Directions: 12 miles S.E. of Colchester, 4 miles W. of Clacton, off the B1027 in St Osyth village

The most handsome building at St Osyth is the late 15th century gatehouse belonging to the mediaeval Priory. Its outer face is elaborately decorated with 'flushwork', of white stone tracery set into black knapped flints. Beyond the gate is a beautiful landscaped garden containing the remains of the other Priory buildings and some later additions. The Abbey Church iself has completely disappeared. Directly across from the gatehouse is another gateway with a great oriel window above it belonging to the splendid Lodgings built by Abbot John Vintoner in the 1520s. To the left is a red brick Georgian house part of which is open to the public in August. A fragment of the fine 13th century architecture of the original Priory can be seen in the little building which is now the chapel. It lies near the ruins of a range of domestic buildings erected for Lord Darcy in the late 16th century after the Priory had become his private house. The chequered tower of the lodgings is still intact and may be climbed for a good general view and a close-up of a very fine 16th century chimney stack. Flanking the gatehouse are two-storey ranges which contain the living rooms of the present owners. The rooms in the east wing are open to the public and contain a varied mixture of antique furniture and modern paintings, as well as works by Van Dyck and Stubbs.

Opening times: Easter weekend, then 1 May to 30 Sept, daily 10.30–12.30; 2.30–4.30. Gardens and monuments 10–5.
Entrance charges: 80p; children 40p. (HHA)
Parking: Large, free car park outside the gatehouse.
Wheelchair access: The best architectural features and the garden are easily accessible.
Guidebook: An adequate historical account with many illustrations and a layout plan of the Priory grounds.
Catering: None.
WCs: Ladies only.
Shop: None.
Extras: Art Gallery; admission 30p.

Gloucestershire

BERKELEY CASTLE   Berkeley (Mr and Mrs R.J. Berkeley)
Tel: Berkeley (0453) 810 332
Directions: 10 miles S.W. of Stroud, mid way between Bristol and Gloucester, on the B4509 at the S. end of Berkeley

Berkeley is a large and irregular castle built of the local pinkish-grey stone. There was a castle here soon after the Norman Conquest and parts of the circular keep and the thick walls of the inner bailey date from the 12th century but most of the buildings packed tightly round the smaller inner courtyard were rebuilt by Thomas, Lord Berkeley between 1340 and 1350. Visitors may either take themselves round or wait for one of the regular guided tours. After a special foray to see the room where King Edward II was brutally murdered the route threads through a series of smaller rooms to reach the service end of the mediaeval house, notably the great kitchen with its massive timber roof and a fine array of cooking utensils. The doors into the great hall have very unusual five-sided arches, of a type known as 'Berkeley Arches' because they are only found here and in a few other places in the West Country. The hall still has its impressive original timber roof but the 16th century painted screen and the mediaeval fireplace were both brought to Berkeley in the present century by the Eighth Earl, who restored the castle and also re-used several mediaeval French doors and windows which can be seen in the courtyard. The principal staircase beyond the hall, which is hung with scarlet 17th century cloth, leads to the 14th century chapel and great chamber which are now the principal living rooms. The morning room, which was once the chapel, has its mediaeval fireplace and coloured ceiling, but the chapel gallery has been moved to the long drawing room next door. The furniture in these rooms belongs to the 17th and 18th centuries, and the windows overlook the terraced gardens falling away from the castle down to the water meadows. The walls of the castle on this side are covered with cascades of wistaria and other climbing plants.

Opening times: April and Sept, daily except Mon, 2–5; May to Aug, weekdays except Mon, 11–5, Sun 2–5; Oct, Sun only 2–4.30, also Bank Holiday Mon 11–5.
Entrance charges: House and garden £1.40; OAPs £1.20, children 70p. (HHA)
Parking: Free car park about 100 yards from the castle.
Wheelchair access: Possible to see much of the outside, but the interior has too many steps and access is not practicable.
Guidebook: A slightly sentimental tour through the house and a history of the family; rather vague about the building itself, and especially about those things that were imported by the 8th Earl; no plan but many illustrations.
Catering: Tea room in a pretty little outbuilding beside the castle with tables outside; self-service, tea by the cup and home made cake.
WCs: Near the tea room, adequate, but not for wheelchair users.
Shop: A small souvenir shop near the tea room.

BUCKLAND RECTORY   nr Broadway (The Rector)
Directions: 2 miles S.W. of Broadway (Worcs) off the A434

Buckland is a peaceful small village with the oldest parsonage house in Gloucestershire still used for its original purpose. The stone-faced parsonage looks like any farmhouse, except for the mullioned windows of the great hall in the centre. It seems that this hall was built between 1466 and 1483 as an addition to an existing small house. The small wing projecting at one end of the front is a 17th century addition, and there were a number of fairly minor alterations in the 19th century as well. The Rector is an informed and amusing guide to his own house. Many of the small rooms have had their more interesting features defaced or removed in the past, but the hall has a good hammer-beam roof and some mediaeval window-glass which helps to date the building work. There is also a mediaeval stone stair. The building itself is of more interest than either the furniture or the garden, though the Rector's heroic attempts to level himelf a croquet lawn inspire admiration.

Opening times: May to end Sept, Mon, also Fri in Aug, 11–4.
Entrance charges: Free, but donations welcomed.
Parking: In the village by the roadside.
Wheelchair access: Possible to the great hall, which is the principal room.
Guidebook: None.
Catering: None.
WCs: None for public use.
Shop: None.

CHAVENAGE   Tetbury (Mr David Lowsley-Williams)
Tel: Tetbury (0666) 52329
Directions: 2 miles N.W. of Tetbury; a small turning off the A4135, difficult to find

The first view of Chavenage is the best and most beautiful, with the grey stone Tudor front framed by tall gate piers and dark spreading trees. The core of the house may be mediaeval but the date of 1576 carved on the porch looks about right for the existing building. Chavenage was built for the Stephens family who were wealthy sheep farmers. It has the common Tudor E-plan with two projecting wings and a central porch. The windows of the hall to the left of the porch are unusually tall and stately. There have been many later additions to the house and the garden front is a pleasant conglomeration, with bits from every century since the 16th. The back part of the house was enlarged by John Micklethwaite in 1905, shortly after the present family came here. The guided tours include most of the principal rooms. The great hall is a fine room, with part of its original screen, a good fireplace of about 1680, and some mediaeval and later glass in the great windows which may have come from the old ruined Horsley Priory. Upstairs are two bedrooms with tapestry-lined walls and dark oak furniture which create a pleasantly 17th century atmosphere. They are called Cromwell and Ireton after the Parliamentary generals who slept here. There is a rather grand billiard room which looks as if it might have been intended for a formal dining room, but perhaps the best room in the house is the small drawing room off the hall lined with barbarous carved and painted panelling. There is evidence of patching and alteration but the carved date of 1627 is acceptable for most of the work. This room also contains some good pieces of porcelain. The way out lies through the 1905 part of the house. A short distance away is the chapel, really a small church, ornamented with carved figures set into the 17th century stonework.

Opening times: April to Sept, Thurs, Sun and Bank Holidays 2–5.
Entrance charges: £1.00, children 50p. (HHA)
Parking: On the gravel sweep in front of the house.
Wheelchair access: Would be possible to hall and dining room, but there are narrow twisting passages to some of the other rooms.
Guidebook: None.
Catering: None.
WCs: The basic facilities are available.
Shop: None.

CLEARWELL CASTLE   nr Coleford (Mr Bernard Yeates)
Tel: Dean (0594) 32320
Directions: 20 miles W. of Gloucester, 5 miles S.E. of Monmouth on the B4231

The approach is gracious enough, but the first sight of the house is faintly depressing; it rears up over the stable courtyard in a dark stone mass. But this is only a side view and from the front lawn Clearwell is revealed as a compact and rather chunky stone house in the castle style, with pointed Gothic windows to the ground floor rooms and spindly battlements with carved crests. In fact, Clearwell was one of the very first 18th century houses in this style. The main range was built for Thomas Wyndham in 1728 and designed by Roger Morris, a Gothic pioneer. The interior is an advertisement for modern do-it-yourself. The house suffered very badly in the first 50 years of this century; it was burnt out in 1929, rebuilt, but then stripped and left to rot after the last war. Mr Frank Yeates from Blackpool, whose father had once been a gardener at Clearwell, came to the rescue. From the mid-1950s his family have made the house habitable and gradually repaired it with what funds and materials they could find. Visitors are given free run of the main rooms. Entrance is by way of the Long Library, once a chapel, at the back of the house. Behind the main facade is a large central hall and two smaller rooms and upstairs there are a number of bedrooms opening off a gallery. In most of these rooms furniture is scarce and the pictures unremarkable. The decorative ceilings are modern reconstructions but the good baroque fireplaces are original. The garden has taken second place to the house and there is little to see beyond a number of different species of birds in the menagerie.

Opening times: Good Friday to 1 Nov, Tues to Fri 1–5.30; Sun and Bank Holiays 11–5.30; July and Aug, daily 11–5.30.

Entrance charges: (1980) £1.00; children and OAPs 60p. (HHA)

Parking: In the Gothic stable court, next to the house.

Wheelchair access: Not easy since the car park is at basement level; might be possible to the ground floor, but special arrangements should be made.

Guidebook: A brief history, but largely concerned with the decline and revival of the house over the last 20 years; some illustrations and a diagrammatic plan.

Catering: The 'restaurant and tea room' in the basement of the house seems to serve only snacks of the lightest kind. 'Historic Banquets' are held on some evenings — advance booking essential.

WCs: In the basement also, adequate.

Shop: A tiny shop in the basement sells commercial souvenirs.

PAINSWICK HOUSE Painswick (Baroncino Nicholas de Piro)

Tel: Painswick (0452) 813646

Directions: 6 miles S. of Gloucester, 10 miles S.W. of Cheltenham, on the outskirts of Painswick off the B4073

The elegant little town of Painswick has an outer ring of 18th century villas, of which Painswick House, originally known as Buenos Ayres, is one. The small central block with its five window front was built in the 1730s for Charles Hyett and was probably designed by one of the local men, John Strahan or William Halfpenny. In 1827 the house was enlarged by George Basevi who added a small wing on each side and gave his wings the same boldly rusticated window surrounds as the older house. He also formed a new main entrance on the east side and his east wing contains a grand entrance hall. The west wing is entirely given up to an enormous dining room. The guided tours begin with a rather ordinary upstairs bedroom, reached by the mid-18th century staircase which was made much grander in 1843 by the addition of a spacious landing with two Corinthian columns from St John's College, Oxford. The principal rooms of the old house are surprisingly tall and elegant and the drawing room has a lively 18th century Chinese wallpaper. There are few outstanding pieces of furniture, although the book cases in the library were designed by Basevi and the portable 18th century chapel in the drawing room is a curiosity. There are also a considerable number of small paintings and drawings by respectable 20th century artists but no mention is made of them in the tour. There is no garden to speak of, but it is possible to walk round the whole of the outside of the house.

Opening times: 1 July to end Sept, Sat and Sun and Bank Holiday. Mon 2–6.

Entrance charges: £1.00; OAPs 50p; children 30p. (HHA)

Parking: Free parking next to house.

Wheelchair access: Three broad shallow steps to reach the main rooms, which are otherwise on the level; the tea room is also accessible.

Guidebook: A brief history of house and family with a room-by-room guide, a few illustrations, no plan.

Catering: The exit from the house lies through a large tea room; tea by the cup, and cakes or scones ready-filled with jam and fresh cream.

WCs: Several scattered about the house; none suitable for wheelchair users.

Shop: In the tea room; there are also a couple of basement rooms hung with many works by local painters which are for sale.

SNOWSHILL MANOR nr Broadway (The National Trust)

Tel: Broadway (0386) 852410

Directions: 3 miles S. of Broadway, 7 miles W. of Moreton in Marsh, 4 miles W. of the junction of the A424 and A44; well signposted

Early 18th century gate piers frame the front of this modest Cotswold manor house. The stonework is of two colours and two dates; the left half with its sash windows is of about 1700, the right half with mullion and transom windows is a hundred years earlier. Behind it is a long tall range with some traces of the original mid-16th century house. In 1919 Snowshill was bought by Charles Paget Wade, who had trained as an architect but inherited a large fortune and gave himself up entirely to his passion for collecting. Nostalgia for sailing ships and for the England swept away by World War I guided his collecting, but many other things attracted his magpie interest and were brought back to his nest at Snowshill. The rooms were first lined with Tudor panelling or painted in 'artistic' colours, then filled with Jacobean furniture, or Japanese armour, or penny-farthings, or ship models, or cuckoo clocks, or musical instruments. There was no room for Mr Wade himself, who lived in an outbuilding; even here he was penned into a corner by old farm implements and roasting spits. The house, its collections and the garden created by Wade were given to the Trust in 1951, and are a perfect magnet. At weekends the narrow spaces and twisting stairs are jammed with visitors and the lane outside is jammed with cars. At quieter times it might be possible to appreciate some of the thousands of assorted objects displayed.

Opening times: April and Oct, Sat and Sun and Bank Holiday Mon 11–1, 2–6; May to end Sept, Wed to Sun and Bank Holiday Mon 11–1, 2–6 or sunset.

Entrance charges: £1.50; children 75p.

Parking: Free park near the main gate; when it overflows parking becomes difficult.

Wheelchair access: Possible to most of the ground floor (about one third of the building) but the terraced garden is only partly accessible.

Guidebook: Mainly a descriptive list of the contents of each room with brief notes on the house itself and on Mr Wade; diagrammatic plan of the house. There are separate leaflets about the spinning wheel collection, about bicyles, the Japanese Samurai and about Mr Wade.

Catering: None.

WCs: In the car park, small but clean; not for wheelchairs.

Shop: There is a small shop by the entrance gates with an abbreviated National Trust range.

SUDELEY CASTLE Winchcombe (Mrs Elizabeth Dent-Brocklehurst)
Tel: Winchcombe (0242) 602308
Directions: 6 miles N.E. of Cheltenham on the A46

The layout of Sudeley was determined by Ralph Boteler, who owned the castle from 1398 until 1469. It is ranged round two large courtyards, with a separate chapel to the east, and a great barn a little distance to the west. From Boteler Sudeley passed to Richard of Gloucester, later King Richard III, who rebuilt the east side of the inner court as a splendid state apartment. In 1547 the castle was given to Admiral Seymour who married Henry VIII's ex-wife, Katherine Parr. She died at Sudeley in 1548 and was buried in the chapel, but her husband was beheaded in the Tower of London. His castle was given to the first Lord Chandos who had the outer courtyard largely rebuilt with the wide, mullioned windows typical of Tudor work. The sixth Lord Chandos held the castle for King Charles in the Civil War, and although he later changed sides, his house was 'slighted' and most of the inner courtyard demolished. For nearly two hundred years it remained a ruin, growing gradually more neglected, but in 1837 it was bought by the Dent brothers, prosperous glove makers. Sir George Gilbert Scott restored the chapel for them and he and J.D. Wyatt restored part of the house to contain their collection of art objects. The rooms open to visitors occupy one side of the outer courtyard. The interior decoration is almost entirely 19th century and not outstanding but the contents include a collection of lace in the first floor corridor, a rare Sheldon tapestry of the late 16th century and paintings by Rubens, Van Dyck, Constable and Turner. Visitors follow a set route defined by rope barriers. The probable site of the great hall, dividing the two courtyards, is now occupied by a Victorian corridor in which Emma Dent's collection of autographs of eminent men is displayed. The great Dungeon tower in the inner courtyard, a survival from Ralph Boteler's building, is used for exhibitions and contains the largest private collection of toys and dolls on view in Europe. The 19th century gardens are superbly maintained and very attractive.

Opening times: March to Oct, daily including Bank Holidays 12–5.30; grounds open from 11.
Entrance charges: £2.25; OAPs £1.75; children £1.00 (all inclusive). (HHA)
Parking: On grass about 200 yards from the house.
Wheelchair access: Possible to the chapel, gardens and exterior without difficulty, also to the ground floor rooms and the restaurant.
Guidebook: Very glossy, many colour pictures but a thin text with only a brief account of the history of Sudeley. No information about the contents of the rooms but the exemplary back page has both a plan and a bird's eye view of the castle.
Catering: Licensed restaurant in the outer courtyard, serves lunches, snacks, high teas, cream teas in any combination and in pleasant surroundings.
WCs: In the house, very adequate but not suitable for wheelchairs.
Shop: A souvenir shop in the old gatehouse to the outer courtyard, kitchen shop in the old kitchen selling both foods and utensils.
Extras: There is a very good adventure playground half way between the car park and the house — no charge for this.

UPPER SLAUGHTER MANOR HOUSE Upper Slaughter (Eric Turrell Esq)
Tel: Bourton on the Water (0451) 20927
Directions: 2½ miles S.W. of Stow on the Wold, between the A429 and A436; from both these roads follow signs to 'The Slaughters'

The pretty villages of the Cotswolds attract many tourists, but there are surprisingly few houses in the area which are open to the public. Upper Slaughter is among the larger villages and its manor house is a typical Cotswold building of local stone with steep gables and mullion and transom windows. In the Middle Ages, the manor belonged to the Abbey of Fécamp, but in 1539 it was acquired by the Slaughter family who built a new house on top of the existing one. Their house was L-shaped, with three gables on each of the two main fronts. In the early 17th century an elegant two-storey porch was added to the entrance front. The Slaughter family emigrated to America in the mid-18th century and the manor house became the centre of a farm, but at the end of the last century it was thoroughly restored and in 1913 a fourth gable was added to the entrance front to make it look more or less symmetrical. The house is built on a steeply sloping site and an attractive terrace garden has been formed to the south. Visitors usually have plenty of time to look at the outside while waiting for their tour. It covers the hall and one other room on the ground floor, both plain comfortable rooms with simple 16th century fireplaces. A restored 17th century stair leads down to the basement where there are two more rooms, one with a heavy 15th century stone vaulted roof which must belong to the late mediaeval house.

Opening times: 1 May to 30 Sept, Fri 2–5.30, guided tours every half hour.
Entrance charges: 50p; no reductions.
Parking: Free parking in front of the house.
Wheelchair access: The front of the building can be seen without difficulty but the sloping site makes the garden difficult for access and the stairs inside the house are steep.
Guidebook: Free leaflet given with each entrance fee; it is mostly concerned with the history of ownership since the Norman Conquest, very little with the present house.
Catering: None.
WCs: One; not for wheelchair users.
Shop: None.

Hampshire

AVINGTON PARK nr Winchester (J.B. Hickson Esq)
Tel: Itchen Abbas (096278) 202
Directions: 5 miles N.E. of Winchester, just S. of the B3047 near Itchen
  Abbas

The main front of Avington was built in about 1700 for George Brydges as
an improvement to an older house. High quality brickwork and a portico
rather like that of Chelsea Hospital in London suggest that the architect was
a follower of Sir Christopher Wren. Later in the 18th century the Duke of
Chandos began a campaign of improvement which brought the small
pediments on the side walls and also the very fine lime avenue which was
meant to lead from the main gates to a new entrance front. In recent years
Avington has been divided into flats and visitors are conducted round part
of the owner's flat, which includes the entrance hall, staircase, two upstairs
rooms and the library. The walls of these three rooms have painted
decoration; trellis work of about 1800 in the hall, early 18th century ceiling
paintings in the ballroom or saloon, and romantic figures of the 1840s in the
Red Drawing Room. The library also has painted figures, this time in
Pompeian style. From here a door leads to the large Victorian conservatory,
whose curving glass walls make a pleasant contrast to the rest of the house,
and an exotic setting for tea.

Opening times: May to Sept; Sat, Sun, Bank Holiday Mon 2.30–5.30. Occasionally closed on
  Sat.
Entrance charges: 80p; children under 10 40p. (HHA)
Parking: Free parking directly in front of the house.
Wheelchair access: Only the ground floor rooms (hall and library) are accessible.
Guidebook: Cheap or not so cheap, but both have similar contents, i.e. a brief history of the
  house and owners and a description of the rooms shown.
Catering: Tea and cakes in the conservatory or orangery on Sundays and Bank Holidays only.
WCs: Fairly new, behind the orangery, rather small and not suitable for wheelchairs.
Shop: None.

BEAULIEU ABBEY Palace House, Beaulieu (The Lord Montagu)
Tel: Beaulieu (0590) 612345
Directions: 14 miles W. of Southampton, off the B3056 in Beaulieu village

Most people go to Beaulieu for the cars in the Motor Museum. With all the
other attractions, it is easy to forget about the house, sitting quietly on its
lawn well away from the sharp end of the business. Palace House began as
the gatehouse of the mediaeval abbey, and the outline of the main entrance
can still be seen on the south side. In 1870 the architect Arthur Blomfield
restored the 14th century gatehouse and added to it, making a comfortable-

Palace House, Beaulieu Abbey, Hampshire

sized house with a rather Scottish flavour. The rooms which are open to the public are those in the old gatehouse. The decoration is mostly Victorian; the furniture is good but not outstanding. Although Lord Montagu still lives in the house, the rooms which are open to the public are rather like a museum, peopled by wax figures in period costume.

Opening times: All year daily, open at 10. Closing times, Jan to mid-March 5pm, Sun 5.30; mid-March to mid-April, Palace House and Abbey 6pm, Motor Museum 6.30; mid-April to mid-May 5.30 and 6pm; mid-May to mid-July 6pm and 6.30; mid-July to mid-Sept 6.30 and 7pm; mid-Sept to mid-Oct 5.30 and 6pm; Oct to Dec 5pm.

Entrance charges: (1981) £2.50 (including House, Motor Museum and Abbey ruins); children and OAPs £1.25. (HHA)

Parking: Enormous free car park outside the main entrance, about ¼ mile from Palace House.

Wheelchair access: Possible to ground floor of house (4 steps); Abbey ruins, Motor Museum and restaurants also accessible. Wheelchairs available at main entrance.

Guidebook: A glossy production; half on the house, half on the abbey ruins. The room-by-room guide keeps breaking off with snippets of history, which is confusing. More use as a souvenir than a guide.

Catering: Cafeteria (also restaurant and bar in summer) near the Motor Museum; modern, clean and functional but can get very crowded.

WCs: Free, modern facilities in the abbey ruins and the catering block; the latter are suitable for wheelchairs.

Shop: There are shops everywhere. Besides the souvenir supermarket at the main gate there is a plant shop, herb shop, kitchen shop and two ordinary gift shops.

Extras: In this case the extras dominate the house. The huge and excellent Motor Museum, and the ruins of the Abbey, which house a display of monastic life, are covered by the entrance fee. For the monorail, the veteran bus, model railway exhibition and the rest, you pay more.

BREAMORE HOUSE nr Fordingbridge (Sir Westrow Hulse Bart)
Tel: Downton (0725) 22233
Directions: 8 miles S. of Salisbury, 3 miles N. of Fordingbridge off the A338, well-signed locally

Breamore is a large and unusually plain Elizabethan house of red brick. The main front (which can only be seen from a distance) is 'E'-shaped, with five gables and large mullioned and transomed windows. The brickwork of the entrance front looks fairly modern. The answer is that Breamore was first built in 1583, burnt in 1856, and rebuilt soon afterwards. The guided tour covers most of the main rooms on the ground floor of the house, including the Long Hall on the principal front. The decoration dates from after the fire, but two good chimneypieces survived, as did most of the furniture, which is more interesting than the house. At the top of the staircase is a series of paintings showing fourteen different kinds of mixed race marriages possible in late 17th century Mexico. The tour also covers the east wing which was not damaged in the fire. One of the bedrooms here contains an Elizabethan fireplace and is furnished accordingly. On the ground floor the great kitchen is complete with all its fittings and was in full use until a short time ago.

Opening times: April to Sept, Tues, Wed, Thurs, Sat, Sun and all public holidays 2–5.30.
Entrance charges: House £1.30; children 70p. Inclusive ticket to house, Carriage Museum and Countryside Museum £1.60, children 80p. (HHA)
Parking: Free car park a short walk from the house. The disabled may park next to the house.
Wheelchair access: Possible to ground floor of house and to the museum in the stables.
Guidebook: A brief history and a room-by-room guide describing the contents; colour illustrations, no plan.
Catering: Rather small tea room near the car park. Reasonable cakes but slow service.
WCs: In outbuildings near the car park, fairly new and clean; not suitable for wheelchairs.
Shop: Souvenir shop near the car park.
Extras: Several carriages on display in the stable block near the house, entrance 70p; children 35p. Countryside museum near car park £1.00; children 50p.

BROADLANDS Romsey (Lord Romsey)
Tel: Romsey (0794) 516878
Directions: On the S. side of Romsey, off the A31 Romsey by-pass (Map 6,

In 1981 Broadlands has been chiefly associated with the Prince and Princess of Wales, who spent their wedding night here. Its previous owners have included Lord Palmerston, the most popular Prime Minister the country has ever had, and Lord Mountbatten. The house predates them both and dates originally from the 16th century. In 1766 the second Viscount Palmerston employed 'Capability' Brown to lay out the garden and also to improve the old house. Brown gave the building a skin of greyish-yellow bricks which were then fashionable and a grand new portico facing the river. Further improvements were made in the 1780s by Henry Holland, who enlarged the house on the entrance side, partly filling in the previous open courtyard. The main entrance leads to the Octagon Room, an entrance hall with some impressive antique sculpture. From here visitors follow a set route through the main rooms on the ground floor. Most of them are decorated in the Adam style and much has been restored in recent years. The house is very much 'lived-in' and comfortable artristocratic furniture is mixed with finer, mainly late 18th and 19th century pieces and some good paintings, including four Van Dycks. Several upstairs bedrooms are shown, whose interest is enhanced by their association with royalty, and also the private house cinema. There is a mural display of warships commanded by Lord Mountbatten, and also a room devoted to Palmerston, containing the tall desk where he stood up to work.

Opening times: 1 April to 30 Sept, Tues to Sun, also Mon in Aug and Sept and Bank Holiday Mon 10–6.
Entrance charges: (1981) £1.60; children 80p; OAPs £1.10. (HHA)
Parking: Free parking, on grass, some way from the house.
Wheelchair access: Possible to ground floor of house, Mountbatten exhibition and to all facilities.
Guidebook: Glossy and expensive but a bit vague about the history of the building. Room-by-room guide and much information about the Mountbattens. Many illustrations but no plan.

There is a separate guide to the exhibition.

Catering: New, clean and functional cafeteria; self service; salads, coffee, teas. No smoking allowed inside; seats outside; open as house.

WCs: Portakabins are adequate, but a bit smelly; facilities for wheelchair users.

Shop: Part of the ticket office sells Wedgewood china, small glass objects and other fairly expensive souvenirs.

Extras: Not really an 'extra' since there is no extra charge. A converted red brick stable building houses a very interesting exhibition on the lives of the Mountbattens, with much original material; well laid out, but circulation space is limited.

CHAWTON: JANE AUSTEN'S HOUSE (The Jane Austen Memorial Trust)

Tel: Alton (0420) 83262

Directions: 1 mile S.W. of Alton, off the A31 in the village of Chawton

Jane Austen lived in this house from 1809 until 1817 and it was here she wrote *Emma*, *Mansfield Park*, *Persuasion*, and finished *Pride and Prejudice*. The two-storey red brick building is nothing out of the ordinary for Hampshire and it comes as no surprise to discover it was built as an inn. The rooms are furnished with objects which belonged to the Austens or which date from the same period and the small-patterned wallpapers give the rooms the right early 19th century appearance. Catalogues in each room give details of each object. There is plenty of material here to breathe life into a GCE English course.

Opening times: All year; April to Oct, daily 11–4.30; Nov to March, Wed to Sun 11–4.30. Closed Christmas Day and Boxing Day.

Entrance charges: 60p; children 10p.

Parking: There is a small free car park next to the house and a larger one across the road from the house.

Wheelchair access: Possible to ground floor, which means that Jane's bedroom with its patchwork quilt has to be missed.

Guidebook: The story of what Jane did in the house, not of the house itself, but it brings most of the exhibits to life.

Catering: None.

Shop: Postcards, pamphlets, Jane Austen's novels, and various trinkets.

GROVE PLACE Nursling (The Northcliffe School Trust Ltd)

Tel: (0703) 732406

Directions: 5 miles N.W. of Southampton centre, off the A3057 on the N. side of the M27; Motorway Exit 3

A fine avenue of old lime trees leads up to the main front of Grove Place. The house is said to have been built in about 1565 and follows a fairly common Elizabethan type, with a central range, long wings on each side and stair-turrets in the angle between the wings and the centre. The walls are of red brick. There have been many alterations and many of the original windows have been replaced by sashes, but the north front still has an impressive array of Tudor chimneys. The house is now a prep. school and visitors are shown round by one of the children, who seem to enjoy their job. The rooms contain the usual school furniture and the long gallery serves as a dormitory with a fine show of teddy-bears, but there is some original plasterwork in the dining room and in the long gallery on the top floor. The staff room and the room which serves as a chapel have good quality mid-Georgian woodwork. The best thing in the house is the massive spiral staircase with its curving handrail in the east tower.

Opening times: Sundays, 24 Jan; 7, 14, 28 Feb; 7 March; 2, 9, 16, 23 May; 6, 13 June; 26 Sept; 3, 10, 17 Oct; 7, 14, 28 Nov; 5 Dec.
Entrance charges: Free.
Parking: Free parking in front of the house.
Wheelchair access: Would be possible to most of the ground floor, which contains all the best rooms.
Guidebook: Two duplicated leaflets, both with much the same information.
Catering: None.
WCs: None for public use.
Shop: None.

MOTTISFONT ABBEY Mottisfont (The National Trust)
Tel: Lockerly (0794) 40278
Directions: 4½ miles N.W. of Romsey off the A3507 in Mottisfont village

Something rather amazing; a mediaeval church with a house built into the nave. The man responsible was the first Lord Sandys, builder of The Vyne near Basingstoke, who acquired Mottisfont in 1536. The north front is still obviously a church, with a squat tower at one end. The south front was Georgianised and given a central pediment in 1745 by an unknown architect. This is just the kind of house which one would like to see inside, but very little of the interior is open. The remains of the Abbey are given pride of place and visitors are shown the vaulted cellar of the Prior's lodgings and some odd fragments of carved stone embedded in later walls. After that come one small room, and one large room painted by Rex Whistler in 1938 with false columns, curtains and other tricks. It is fun, though not as jolly or as witty as the Tate Gallery restaurant by the same artist. The guided tours operate every half hour and the size of each party is limited. This seems ludicrous as only three rooms are shown and the delays can cause understandable hostility on busy days. The very fine park by the side of the River Test has huge trees and is some compensation. Rose enthusiasts will find a collection of species and old-fashioned flowers in the walled garden near the car park.

Opening times: April to end Sept: grounds, daily except Sun, Mon and Good Friday 2.30–6; house, Wed and Sat 2.30–6; last admission 5.

Entrance charges: House and gardens £1.10; children 60p. Gardens only 80p; children 40p.
Parking: Free car park in part of the old kitchen garden, 500 yards from the house.
Wheelchair access: Not possible to house, gravel drive to the park, but the rose garden is easily accessible.
Guidebook: There are sections on the Priory, the previous owners, and the buildings, but nothing about the greater part of the house which is not open. The plan shows features of the Priory, with the present house only in outline.
Catering: None.
WCs: Excellent new facilities in the car park, which are suitable for wheelchairs.
Shop: The ticket booth in the car park sells a limited number of souvenirs.

PORTCHESTER CASTLE Portchester (Ancient Monument)
Directions: Between Portsmouth and Fareham off the A27, at the S. end of Portchester village

Portchester is not like other English castles; both the site and the building are unusual. The site is a flat piece of land jutting out into Portsmouth Harbour, and on it is a large enclosure, more than 200 yards across, with walls 20 feet high. These walls were built by the Romans in 321 and Portchester is the only Roman fort in northern Europe whose walls are still full height. In one corner is a mediaeval castle. The square keep was built in about 1120. It has been given modern floors and a new roof and makes an excellent vantage point for looking at the castle and harbour beyond. All the other mediaeval buildings are more or less ruined but between the keep and the gatehouse there are two ranges which were built between 1396 and 1399 as a small palace for King Richard II. The main rooms were all on the first floor, with the great hall on the gatehouse wall and the great chamber next to the keep. The remainder of the space inside the Roman walls is grassed and makes a good picnic place.

Opening times: Standard hours (SM), see page xii.
Entrance charges: Main enclosure free; mediaeval castle 50p; children and OAPs 25p.
Parking: Smallish free car park near the castle gate, larger pay car park nearby.
Wheelchair access: Possible to inside of castle on ground level.
Guidebook: The official handbook is expensive and rather old, but it contains a full account of the castle and two plans. There are also cheaper 'card guides', which are available in French and German as well as English.
Catering: None.
WCs: None in the castle.
Shop: Only postcards and guides sold.

PORTSMOUTH: CHARLES DICKENS BIRTHPLACE MUSEUM
393 Old Commerical Road (Portsmouth City Museums)
Tel: Portsmouth (0705) 827261
Directions: On the N. side of Portsmouth, signed off Mile End Road (A3)

The house, which was built in about 1800, is an ordinary two-storey red brick terraced house. Charles Dickens was born here in February 1812, but only a few months later his family moved to another house in the town which no longer exists. On the strength of this connection, Portsmouth Corporation bought the building as long ago as 1903. Now that the Dickens Library has been moved elsewhere the rooms have been furnished as they might have looked at the time of his birth, using plain late 18th and early 19th century pieces. This works well, although it is a pity that one cannot actually go into the rooms but is forced to peer from the doorways. There are a few items connected with Dickens, including the couch upon which he died.

Opening times: All year, daily except 25 and 26 Dec, 10.30–5.30.
Entrance charges: (1981) 30p; children and OAPs 12p.
Parking: Limited parking in Victoria Street, adjacent to Commercial Road.
Wheelchair access: Not possible.
Guidebook: A small glossy booklet about the house and contents; the illustrations have captions in English, French and German.
Catering: None.
WCs: One each, small but clean.
Shop: Sells postcards and material about Dickens.

STRATFIELD SAYE HOUSE (The Duke of Wellington)
Tel: Basingstoke (0256) 882882
Directions: Between Reading and Basingstoke, off the A33

A long, low house, built between 1630 and 1640 by Sir William Pitt with some later additions. The most important alterations were those made for the First Duke of Wellington, to whom it was presented by a grateful nation in 1817, by his architect Benjamin Dean Wyatt during the years 1830–40. The projecting wings are distinguished by curvilinear gables with small pediments. The old brick work was stuccoed in the 18th century by Lord Rivers, and is washed over in pale apricot colour. There is a fine large entrance hall, with a colonnade and gallery along the back wall and some Roman mosaics brought from a villa at Silchester. Otherwise the rooms are small and cosy, with some very pretty plaster ceilings, and are full of pictures, some of which were brought back from Spain by the First Duke as spoils of war. The house feels very much like a home, but large numbers of visitors can clog up the narrow doorways and passages. There are guides at strategic points to assist the visitor to make his own way through the house. Detailed information on the furniture is available in publications on sale in the Reception Centre. The First Duke, who won the battle of Waterloo, and his horse Copenhagen, whose tombstone is in the grounds, are featured in the house, and the general impression is that it is little changed since the Great Duke's time. The gardens have been recently restored, apart from the pleasure grounds on each side of the house which have some superb fully-grown trees.

Stratfield Saye House, Hampshire

Opening times: 4 April to 26 Sept, daily except Fri 11.30–5.00.
Entrance charges: Adults £1.90; children 95p; OAPs and disabled £1.35 (Tues only). (HHA)
Parking: Free parking fairly near the house.
Wheelchair access: All rooms shown are directly accessible.
Guidebook: A glossy production with many large colour plates and a room-by-room guide.
Catering: Teas, snacks and meals in the old stables in front of the house. Some home produce sold here too.
WCs: By the recently built Reception Centre and in the stables block; suitable for wheelchairs.
Shop: A pleasant roomy shop in the Reception Centre with middle-range souvenirs.
Extras: There is a permanent exhibition about the First Duke in the stable block, including his funeral carriage made from Napoleon's melted down cannons — recently removed from St Paul's Cathedral. There is also a 20-acre Wildfowl Sanctuary, with exotic wildfowl and deer.

TITCHFIELD ABBEY   Titchfield (Ancient Monument)
Directions: 2 miles W. of Fareham, off the A27, ½ mile N. of Titchfield village

The original Abbey was founded in 1232 and led a peaceful existence for three hundred years before it was closed in 1537. The land and buildings were then acquired by Thomas Wriothesley and by 1542 the nave of the Abbey church had been transformed into a mansion called Palace House. Much the same thing was done at Mottisfont Abbey on the other side of Southampton. The master mason in charge of the alterations at Titchfield was Thomas Bertie of Winchester. He removed the centre of the nave and built a great stone gatehouse which was the main feature of the mansion. Thomas Wriothesley was later made Earl of Southampton and he and his descendants were host to many English monarchs at Titchfield, which was a convenient stopping place near Portsmouth. In 1781 the greater part of the house was destroyed, leaving only the tall gatehouse and fragments of other walls. The ruins have been tidied up to reveal the outlines of the Abbey buildings, and a large number of mediaeval floor tiles have been uncovered.

Opening times: Standard hours, see page xii.
Entrance charges: 30p; children and OAPs 15p.
Parking: Free parking by the ticket office next to the ruin.
Wheelchair access: All of the ruin is on level ground, but some of the paths have a gravel surface.
Guidebook: A fairly recent Official Handbook, which is mostly concerned with the Abbey buildings and the Earls of Southampton. There is little about the house as it stood for over 200 years.
Catering: None.
WCs: None.
Shop: Only postcards.

THE VYNE   nr Basingstoke (The National Trust)
Tel: Basingstoke (0256) 881337
Directions: 4 miles N. of Basingstoke, off the A340 near the village of Sherborne St John. Well sign-posted locally

The Vyne is one of the best advertisements for the National Trust, a good house in a beautiful setting with first rate furniture. There are no ropes or barriers inside and no set route for visitors, so it is possible to see everything with ease. Like many Tudor houses, The Vyne is set in a hollow. The house was built for Lord Sandys in about 1520 and the long red brick entrance front dates from that time. But all the windows of this front and the portico on the other side, overlooking the lake, date from about 1654, when Chaloner Chute employed John Webb to improve the old house. The portico is the first of its kind on an English house. Webb also provided several of the chimneypieces inside the house, but much of the best work here dates from the 1760s when John Chute made more improvements, which he designed himself. Almost all the rooms on the ground floor are open and they range from the chapel and chapel parlour, which still have woodwork of Lord Sandys time, to the quite extraordinary and magnificent staircase put in by John Chute. Upstairs are three more rooms, including the long gallery, with its early 16th century panelling. All the rooms are fully-furnished, with information boards and guides at intervals.

Opening times: April to end Oct, Tues, Wed, Thurs, Sat and Sun, 2–6 (closes 5.30 in Oct). Bank Holiday Mon 11–6, closed Tues following; closed Good Friday.
Entrance charges: House and gardens £1.30; children 65p. Gardens only 60p; children 30p; no dogs.
Parking: Free car park about 30 yards from the house.
Wheelchair access: All the ground floor rooms are accessible (2 steps), the tea room is a long push on gravel paths. Wheelchairs available at the entrance.
Guidebook: A new (1981) guidebook with a history of the building and its owners and a more than usually thorough room-by-room description, many good illustrations and plans.
Catering: A good tea is served from 3 to 5.30 in the Old Brew House.
WCs: Next to the tea room; free and clean but not suitable for wheelchairs.
Shop: A converted Tudor cottage next to the Old Brew House sells the full National Trust range.

WEST GREEN HOUSE Hartley Wintney (The National Trust)
Directions: 10 miles E. of Basingstoke, 1½ miles N. of Hartley Wintney on the edge of West Green village

No one has yet sorted out the building history of this small red brick house. The main problem to solve is which of the two main fronts was built first. Both look like early or mid-18th century work, and the west front, with its row of five busts instead of first floor windows, is unusual. The only information available is that something was done in about 1750 by General Hawley, a keen sportsman and the real butcher of the Scots at Culloden. Visitors are conducted round three rooms on the ground floor only. The panelled dining room is quite small, which makes the impact of the saloon even greater. This one room runs the full length of the west front and takes up about a quarter of the whole house. It would not look at all out of place in one of the grander stately homes. West Green House is occupied by a

National Trust tenant, to whom all the furniture belongs, and the same tenant has carried out extensive improvements to the very pleasant garden.

Opening times: April to Sept, House and garden, Wed 2–6. Garden only, Thurs and Sun 2–6.
Entrance charges: House and garden 80p; children 40p. Garden only 60p; children 30p; no dogs.
Parking: Free car park a short way from the house.
Wheelchair access: Not possible to inside of house (too many steps). The garden is mostly on the level.
Guidebook: A free leaflet contains a brief history and description.
Catering: None.
WCs: None.
Shop: None.

Herefordshire and Worcestershire

BERRINGTON HALL nr Leominster (The National Trust)
Tel: Yarpole (056 885) 253
Directions: 3 miles N. of Leominster; turn W. off A49 Leominster-Ludlow road, two entrances, both clearly marked

Thomas Harley, Lord Mayor of London at the age of 37, employed the architect Henry Holland to design him a new house on a site chosen with the advice of 'Capability' Brown. The house was built between 1778 and 1781, a neat rectangle of reddish sandstone with a tall and wide portico. Holland skilfully manipulated the window and door openings of the front to provide unusual variety. The stables, kitchen and other necessary buildings are tucked into a courtyard at the back. The exquisite interior contains some fine chimney pieces and many delicately-painted plaster friezes and ceilings. Much of the paintwork is original as are some of the fittings, including the original curtain-boxes in the drawing room. The rooms are enhanced by immaculate furnishings, including Aubusson-Felletin tapestries woven in about 1901. One of the most exciting rooms is the staircase hall in the centre of the house where Holland took the opportunity to show his skill in the handling of spaces. Berrington was occupied by the Dowager Lady Cawley until 1978. A great deal of the original external stonework of the house was replaced between 1966 and 1970, but the interior has hardly been altered since the time it was built. The whole of the ground floor and part of the first floor is open to the public; visitors make their own way round. The Victorian Laundry and the original Dairy may be seen in the outbuildings and the garden is also open.

Opening times: April and Oct, Sat, Sun and Easter Mon 2–5 or sunset; May to end Sept, Wed to Sun and Bank Holiday Mon 2–6.
Entrance charges: £1.20; children 60p. Joint ticket with Croft Castle £1.75; children 85p.
Parking: In front of house.
Wheelchair access: Steps up to front door, but all rooms open to the public are on the flat.
Guidebook: A well-written pamphlet by James Lees-Milne with a short history and room-by-room guide, some illustrations and a map of the estate.
Catering: Teas with home-made cakes served on Sat, Sun and Bank Holiday Mon only 3–5.30 in the stable block.
WCs: Spotless facilities in the stable block
Shop: None.

BURTON COURT Eardisland (Lt Cdr and Mrs R.M. Simpson)
Tel: Pembridge (054 47) 231
Directions: 6 miles W. of Leominster on the S. side of the A44 at Eardisland; signposted from the main road

Burton Court is a moderate sized house, mainly of the late 18th century, and is now the centre of a soft fruit farm. From outside it looks like a 19th century building as the result of the alterations made in 1865 by the Victorian architect Kempson, and the jolly stone porch in a free Tudor style which was added in 1912 by Clough Williams Ellis, architect of Portmeirion. The large gaunt rooms have been redecorated in recent years and the furniture they contain is mostly Victorian. But at the centre of the house is the surprising survival of a 14th century great hall with an elaborate timber roof made of sweet chestnut wood and a rich carved overmantel dated 1654. The roof has been heavily restored and the animal heads on the walls recall Osbert Lancaster's Scottish Baronial interior. Beyond the hall is a room containing a collection of models of fairground amusements. Six rooms are shown altogether and each of them contains several examples of period costume from the owner's collection. All the costumes are displayed on female shop models, which gives the military uniforms a bizarre effect. There are few restrictions in the rooms and the owner is usually on hand to answer questions.

Opening times: 23 May to mid Sept, Wed, Thurs, Sat, Sun and Bank Holiday Mon 2.30–6.
Entrance charges: 75p; children 35p. (HHA)
Parking: In front of the house.
Wheelchair access: Entrance at the rear of the house with no steps involved; all rooms shown are on the ground floor.
Guidebook: An inexpensive account of the house written by the present owner and as good as many more expensive guide books.
Catering: Teas are served in the house in a cheerful room with check tablecloths; home-made cakes and scones, cream and strawberries from the farm.
WCs: In the house, old fashioned and spacious; accessible to wheelchairs.
Shop: None.
Extras: Soft fruit picking in season in the fields near the house.

CROFT CASTLE   nr Leominster (The National Trust)
Tel: Yarpole (056 885) 246
Directions: 5 miles N.W. of Leominster. Turn W. off A49 or E. off A4410
on to B4362, house is well signed locally

The property belonged to the Crofts at the time of The Domesday Book and members of the same family still live at the castle. Many of the tombs of their ancestors can be seen in the church which stands next to the house. The walls of the main building and the round towers at each corner were built in the 14th and 15th centuries. By the 16th century Croft Castle had become a house rather than a stronghold and the park was laid out with avenues of trees, some of which survive and have grown to enormous size. The Crofts were forced to sell in 1746 and they did not return until 1923. The new owners were the Knights, who drew their money from the local iron industry. They were leaders of the fashionable taste for the 'Picturesque' and for the irregular appearance of Gothic buildings. In 1765 the castle was 'improved'; part of the open courtyard in the centre was built over and what had been an opening in the eastern side was filled in with a new Gothick centrepiece, containing the main entrance. A new great staircase in the Gothick style was provided at the same time and most of the chief rooms were redecorated. The architect for this was Thomas Pritchard, who is probably best known for his bridge at Ironbridge. Most of the interior decoration is his work although some Jacobean panelling still remains. There are fine ceilings, wall decorations, tiles and chimneypieces in both Rococo and Gothick styles. Among the many family portraits are Gainsboroughs and Lawrences; the furniture includes pieces by Chippendale. Visitors may examine the rooms at their own pace. The grounds of the castle are extensive and the trees magnificent.

Opening times: April and Oct, Sat, Sun and Easter Mon 2–5 or sunset; May to end Sept, Wed
to Sun and Bank Holiday Mon 2–6.
Entrance charges: £1.00; children 50p. Joint ticket with nearby Berrington Hall £1.75;
children 85p.
Parking: In a field off the drive, 100 yards from the house.
Wheelchair access: Possible to house (all rooms shown are on ground floor); the garden is also
accessible.
Guidebook: Brief history of owners and building and a room-by-room guide; illustrations but
no plan. There are brief printed guides in each room.
Catering: None.
WCs: Inside the house, free, adequate.
Shop: None.

DINMORE MANOR   nr Hereford (Gordon Howard Murray Esq)
Tel: 061 941 2313
Directions: 6 miles N. of Hereford, 1½ miles W. of A49 Leominster-
Hereford Road

The situation of Dinmore is delightful, above a secluded and wooded valley, and the elaborate rockery garden is unusual. The house itself is largely a 20th century fantasy in mediaeval style. From the 12th to the 16th centuries Dinmore was an important property of the semi-military Order of the Knights of St John of Jerusalem. The chapel, which stands on its own next to the house, is part of a larger building which was built for the Knights in the 14th century, but the house itself gives little sign of antiquity. The east wing dates from about 1600 and the range next to it from the 17th century; both are overwhelmed by the huge additions made between 1932 and 1936 by the local architects Messrs Bettington for Richard Hollis Murray. They built the Great Hall (now the Music Room) and the cloisters, which are the only parts of Dinmore open to the public apart from the chapel.

Opening times: All year, daily except Christmas Day and Boxing Day, 10–6.
Entrance charges: 50p; children and OAPs 25p.
Parking: Free parking in drive about 50 yards from the house.
Wheelchair access: All parts of the house which are open to the public are accessible.
Guidebook: Fairly expensive, concerned very largely with the mediaeval history of the manor and not so helpful about the present building. Contains illustrations and a plan, but the plan is of a building in Northumberland.
Catering: None.
WCs: Two.
Shop: None.

EASTNOR CASTLE   nr Ledbury (The Hon. Mrs Hervey-Bathurst)
Tel: Ledbury (0531) 2304
Directions: 2 miles E. of Ledbury off the A438 Hereford-Tewkesbury road in Eastnor Village

The dramatic stone pile of Eastnor Castle was built for the first Lord Somers between 1812 and 1815. It is an early work of the architect Robert Smirke who is probably best known as the designer of the British Museum. Smirke later became hugely successful (and very wealthy) because he was reliable and usually kept to the well-tried Classical style. Here, as a young man, he tried his hand with Gothic and experimented with a cast-iron roof structure which is still in place. The castle is a great stone mass with a tower at each corner. The rooms inside are on the same massive scale. A few of them are as Smirke left them, but the elaborate plasterwork of the drawing room was richly decorated by Augustus Pugin in 1849 and the Great Hall and Long Library were done by George Fox in the 1860s. At the same time, the third Lord Somers brought in many of the Italian bits and pieces with which the rooms are filled and also the 17th century Italian panelling in the Little Library. All the rooms shown to the public are on the ground floor of the castle. There is a collection of suits of armour, 17th century and earlier tapestries, and also some good English portraits. The Staircase Hall is now dominated by a series of fresco paintings by G.F. Watts, which were brought from Carlton House Terrace in London and installed at Eastnor in 1976.

Opening times: 23 May to end Sept, Sun, also Spring and Summer Bank Holiday Sun and Mon, and Wed and Thurs in July and Aug, 2.15–6.
Entrance charges: House and grounds 80p; children and OAPs 40p. Grounds only 30p. (HHA)
Parking: Free parking in front of the house.
Wheelchair access: Not easy; there are a large number of steps
Guidebook: A brief history of the house, room-by-room guide in the list style, notes on the families and a few small illustrations, no plan.
Catering: Tea is dispensed from an urn by local ladies in the old kitchen; there are also home-made cakes.
WCs: Both inside the house and near the tea room, adequate but not suitable for wheelchairs.
Shop: Some souvenirs on sale.

ELGAR'S BIRTHPLACE Lower Broadheath, nr Worcester (The Elgar Foundation)
Tel: Cotheridge (090 566) 224
Directions: 3 miles W. of Worcester off the A44 Worcester-Leominster road in Lower Broadheath village. Elgar's Birthplace is a small cottage on the outskirts of the village, near the pub

Sir Edward Elgar was born and lived the first two years of his life in this pleasant, ordinary Victorian cottage. The house is now a museum, or rather a shrine, devoted to the composer. The contents include letters, photographs, personal possessions and musical scores. The main appeal is to the Elgar enthusiast, but there is something for devotees of pokerwork as well. The cottage has a pleasant small garden with views over the countryside which inspired much of Elgar's music.

Opening times: 1 May to end Sept, daily except Wed 1.30–6.30; 1 Oct to end April, daily except Wed 1.30–4.30. Bank Holidays, 10.30–12.30 plus afternoons as above.
Entrance charges: 50p; children 20p; students 30p.
Parking: At the Plough Inn, 70 yards away.
Wheelchair access: Restricted space makes this difficult.
Guidebook: Anecdotes of Elgar and remarks on some of the objects displayed.
Catering: None, but refreshments at the Plough Inn.
WCs: Salubrious and historic, in a block built by Elgar's father and uncle.
Shop: Books, records, cassettes, busts, bookmarks and postcards on sale.

EYE MANOR nr Leominster (Mr and Mrs Christopher Sandford)
Tel: Yarpole (056 885) 244
Directions: 4 miles N. of Leominster, signposted off the A49 Leominster-Ludlow Road

Eye Manor is a fairly small house of red brick which stands near the village church. Its plain exterior gives no hint of the rich interior decoration. The house was built in 1680 for a retired slave trader and sugar merchant called

Ferdinando Gorges, whose Godfather of the same name has been called 'The Father of Colonisation in America'. The younger Ferdinando must have spent a considerable sum of money on his new house. All the main rooms have rich plaster ceilings, decorated with garlands of leaves, flowers and fruit. Most of the other fittings have also survived and the panelling of the walls, the fireplaces and the staircase with its barleysugar balusters all date from the late 17th century. Eye is still very much the home of its owners, but visitors may wander over the whole house. There is a quantity of Irish furniture and other attractions include private-press books, china, needlework, costumes and a large collection of corn dollies. Outside is an old herb garden and a horse-drawn caravan.

Opening times: 1 April to 30 June, daily except Fri 2.30–5.30; 1 July to 30 Sept, daily 2.30–5.30.
Entrance charges: £1.00; OAPs 80p; children 14–18 50p; under 14 25p. (HHA)
Parking: Free parking in front of house.
Wheelchair access: Possible to four rooms on ground floor.
Guidebook: A room-by-room guide with a history of the family, several illustrations but no plan.
Catering: By arrangement only.
WCs: Clean but basic facilities in an outbuilding; not suitable for wheelchairs.
Shop: Corn dollies, craftwork and postcards on sale in the entrance hall.

GOODRICH CASTLE   nr Ross-on-Wye (Ancient Monument)
Directions: 6 miles N.E. of Monmouth, 3 miles S. of Ross-on-Wye on the E. side of the A40

Goodrich is a real castle, ruined but still majestic, standing on an outcrop of red sandstone and built of the same material. Nearly square, with a great round tower at each corner, it is the cousin of Welsh castles like Harlech and Beaumaris. The small rectangular keep is the oldest part of the building and dates from the middle of the 13th century; the walls and towers which surround it were probably built in the 1280s. The castle is approached by a well-preserved barbican which defended the entrance. From the barbican, a causeway leads through the vaulted gatehouse into the central courtyard which is completely surrounded by the buildings which contained the living rooms of the castle. These include the Great Hall (65 feet long), the buttery and pantry in the south west tower with the kitchen beyond, the solar, the chapel, and the garderobe block with privies emptying into the moat below. Not the least of the attractions of Goodrich is its setting in the deepest English countryside.

Opening times: Standard hours (S), see page xii
Entrance charges: 50p; children and OAPs 25p.
Parking: Large car park with automatic barrier 150 yards from the castle (entrance fee).
Wheelchair access: The interior of the castle is not accessible.
Guidebook: The Official Handbook contains a brief history and a description of each part; it is well-written, brief, and contains a plan of the building.

Catering: None at the castle.
WCs: In the car park, adequate, free; not suitable for wheelchairs.
Shop: Postcards etc. are on sale at the ticket office.

HANBURY HALL   nr Droitwich (The National Trust)
Tel: Hanbury (052 784) 214
Directions: 2½ miles E. of Droitwich. Turn N. off B4090 Droitwich-Alcester road, entrance to house after 1 mile

Hanbury is in the Queen Anne style which everyone associates with Sir Christopher Wren. It has red brick walls, a hipped roof with wide eaves and a jolly pediment in the centre of the main front. Over the door is the date 1701. The house was built for Thomas Vernon but the name of his architect is still unknown. Vernon seems to have copied the front of his house from Ragley Hall, eight miles away. The hall and staircase at another nearby house called Stoke Edith were painted by James Thornhill, and Vernon borrowed this idea as well. The front door of Hanbury leads directly into the hall which fills the whole of the centre of the house. The staircase rises at one end and its walls and ceiling are covered with Thornhill's paintings. His signature appears on a scroll held by a cherub. The Long Room has ceiling panels by Thornhill, but here they are surrounded by rich plasterwork of about 1710. The other rooms have decoration and fittings from later in the century. Most of the furnishings in the house have been brought in by the National Trust and belong to the first half of the 18th century. They include a fine bed of about 1725 in one upstairs room which still has its original blue hangings. The Long Room houses the Watney collection of English porcelain figures and of flower paintings. Most of the ground floor is open, and three rooms upstairs. Visitors make their own way round the house. The orangery and the Long Gallery in the garden should not be missed.

Opening times: April and Oct, Sat, Sun, Easter Mon and following Tues 2–5; May to end Sept, Wed to Sun and Bank Holiday Mon and Tues 2–6.
Entrance charges: £1.10; children 55p.
Parking: Roomy car park next to stable block at side of house.
Wheelchair access: All rooms on the ground floor are easily accessible.
Guidebook: Recently revised and containing a brief history of the house, a plan, a room-by-room guide and an account of the gardens. There is printed information about the contents in every room. A separate duplicated leaflet guides the visitor around the grounds. Braille guide available.
Catering: High quality cream teas with a choice of cakes served in a pleasant room in the house overlooking the terrace.
WCs: One small cubicle next to the tea room or near the car park; facilities for wheelchairs.
Shop: The National Trust shop beyond the tea room sells tea towels, jams, books, tablemats and the usual items; it is very much a quart in a pint pot.

HARVINGTON HALL nr Kidderminster (The Roman Catholic Archdiocese of Birmingham)
Tel: Chaddesley Corbett (056 283) 267

Directions: 4 miles S.E. of Kidderminster, off A440 Kidderminster-Bromsgrove road, signposted locally

Harvington Hall looks like a typical large Elizabethan manor house, with rich red brick walls and tall gables and chimneys reflected in the water of a moat, but the main part of the house is pre-Elizabethan and is timber-framed. The old house was given a new skin of brickwork as part of the alterations and additions made by John Pakington in the 1570s. Further alterations were made by the Throckmorton family in about 1700. New rooms for the servants were added on top of the great hall in the south wing, making a great arch over the hall windows. The Throckmortons also removed the drawbridge and took the original main staircase to Coughton Court in Warwickshire, leaving a replica in its place. For almost 200 years after 1700 the interior of Harvington was left untouched and in this century the Roman Catholic Diocesan owners have carefully restored the house, removing nothing. There is much original panelling and woodwork, but the principal attractions for visitors must be the priest holes and the wall-paintings. There are no less than seven priest holes concealed in various parts of the house, a reflection of the Pakingtons' Catholic sympathies. Another Catholic reminder is the small upstairs room once used as a chapel, whose walls are decorated with large painted drops of blood. Most of the surviving paintings can be found on the walls of passages; these are delicate arabesques of nude figures and animals interwoven with foliage and a series depicting the Nine Worthies. This is work of the highest quality which must have been common enough in large Elizabethan houses but is now very rare.

Opening times: 1 Feb to Easter, daily except Mon 2–6; also Easter to Sept 11.30–1; Oct and Nov 2–6 closed Dec and Jan and every Mon but open Bank Holiday Mon and closed following Fri.
Entrance charges: 65p; children 35p (must be accompanied).
Parking: In driveway 30 yards from the house.
Wheelchair access: Possible to ground floor, but the wall-paintings are all upstairs.
Guidebook: A useful historical account with many illustrations and a plan, but it cannot be purchased before the end of the tour of the house. There are printed guides in each room and handboards to carry round.
Catering: The Tudor Tea Room in the house serves tea, coffee, biscuits and scones; all commercial produce.
WCs: In an outbuilding, adequate.
Shop: In the grounds, sells postcards, guide books and souvenirs.

HELLEN'S Much Marcle, nr Ledbury (Major Malcolm Munthe MC)
Directions: 4 miles S.W. of Ledbury. In Much Marcle village turn E. off the A449 Ledbury-Ross road and then left before church

This Jacobean manor house now sits at the end of a rough track. The buildings are the remains of a large brick courtyard house. Their predominant character is the result of the modernisation carried out by Fulke Walwyn in 1641. He improved the main part of the house by providing it with new ceilings, a new staircase and new windows. Among the surviving parts of the older house are the hall or court room and the Queen's Room, where the initials of Mary Tudor in the overmantel are a reminder that the Walwyns were Roman Catholics. Several of the rooms have 17th century fittings, notably the Cordova Room, whose walls are lined with Spanish leather; the fireplace in this room is said to be the work of John Abel, a famous local carpenter. Slightly dilapidated, quiet and unspoilt, Hellen's has much charm and is still occupied by its owners. Chatty guided tours are conducted every hour and take about 40 minutes. Visitors are free to wander in the grounds. There is a dovecote of the 1640s and a collection of cider presses and 19th century coaches in the barns of the courtyard.

Opening times: Easter to end Oct, Wed, Sat and Sun 2–6; guided tours on the hour.
Entrance charges: £1.00; children accompanied by an adult 50p.
Parking: In small courtyard at side of house, or in the drive.
Wheelchair access: Not really possible; too many changes of level inside.
Guidebook: A little pamphlet with a room-by-room guide and a pedigree of occupants. No illustrations, no plan.
Catering: None.
WCs: In the garden room.
Shop: Postcards and books by Major Munthe on sale in the court room.
Extras: The collection of mediaeval tombs in the parish church nearby is a good one and repays a visit.

HEREFORD: THE OLD HOUSE   High Town (Hereford City Museums)
Tel: Hereford (0432) 68121 ext. 225
Directions: High Town and High Street now form the main pedestrian shopping precinct in the centre of Hereford. The Old House stands on its own at one end

The Old House was built in 1621. Carved angels on the roof gables carry this date on their shields. The house formed part of a row of timber-framed buildings known as The Butchery, leading to the Guild Hall, which was the most fantastic timber building in England before its demolition in 1862. Now The Old House stands alone, prominent against the modern shop fronts. No one is sure whether the building was intended as a house or a Guild Hall for the Butchers. For the first three decades of this century it served as a bank, and much of the building, especially the ground floor, was restored and adapted to fit the new use. The Old House has now been furnished by the City Museum as a private house of the early 17th century, with kitchen, dining room, bedroom etc. There is a good collection of oak furniture. This is a good example of how well this kind of thing can be done by museums; the bareness of some of the rooms is perfectly authentic.

Opening times: All year, weekdays 10–1, 2–5.30; closed Monday afternoons.

Entrance charges: 20p; children 10p; free on Monday. Children accompanied by adults free at all times.
Parking: There are pay car parks within 100 yards of the house.
Wheelchair access: Possible to ground floor.
Guidebook: A brief history of the building and a room-by-room guide, many illustrations.
Catering: None.
WCs: None.
Shop: Booklets, postcards and a small selection of souvenirs.

LITTLE MALVERN COURT Little Malvern (M.T.P. Berrington)
Tel: Hanley Swan (06843) 202
Directions: 3 miles S. of Great Malvern, near the junction of the A4104 and A449

One of the best things about Little Malvern Court is its setting at the foot of the Malvern Hills. The Priory of Little Malvern was founded in 1171 and the chancel and tower of the mediaeval priory church still survive, though now used as the parish church. The only other surviving part of the Priory buildings is the 14th century Prior's Hall which forms the east side of the house. Other parts of the house are Elizabethan and Victorian, but only the Prior's Hall is open to the public. It is a fine tall room with a perfect early 14th century timber roof. The roof has two tiers of decorated wind-braces and still shows some signs of blackening from the open fire which was the original means of heating the hall.

Opening times: May to Sept, Wed 2.30–5.30.
Entrance charges: 40p. (HHA)
Parking: There is no car park and visitors must park on the road outside opposite the entrance.
Wheelchair access: The hall is raised on an undercroft and only accessible by means of the outside staircase.
Guidebook: There is a free leaflet containing the basic information about both church and hall.
Catering: None.
WCs: None.
Shop: None.

LOWER BROCKHAMPTON HOUSE Brockhampton, nr Bromyard
(The National Trust)
Tel: Bromyard (088 52) 2258
Directions: 2 miles E. of Bromyard off A44 Leominster-Worcester road; follow signposted drive for 1½ miles past Brockhampton House to Lower Brockhampton

The countryside around Lower Brockhampton consists of farmland interspersed with orchards and the house itself is part of a working farm. The drive leads first to a miniature timber-framed gatehouse built in the 15th century with just one room over the entrance passage. Of the main house, the central range and one of the two wings survive; both date from the 14th century. They are timber-framed with a mixture of close-set vertical timbers and the square panels which are usual in the West Country. The only part of the house which is open to the public is the hall, which has a good timber roof. The buildings are surrounded on three sides by a moat, in a setting which could hardly be more peaceful.

Opening times: April to end Oct, Wed to Sat and Bank Holiday Mon 10–1 and 2–6, Sun 10–1. Closed Good Friday.
Entrance charges: 75p; children 35p.
Parking: Free parking in the driveway and orchard near the house.
Wheelchair access: No difficulties.
Guidebook: None, but there are handboards with printed information.
Catering: None.
WCs: Clean, next to cows.
Shop: None.

MOCCAS COURT   Moccas (Mr Richard Chester-Master)
Tel: Moccas (098 17) 381
Directions: 13 miles W. of Hereford, off B4352 Hereford-Hay road in Moccas village; the drive of the house is signposted

This is the sort of house that 18th century writers called 'a neat brick edifice'. It is a red brick box, seven windows wide in front and three storeys high, set in a fold of wooded country on the banks of the River Wye which conceals the house until the last minute. The house was built between 1775 and 1781 for Sir George Cornewall by a local architect called Anthony Keck. The much more famous and fashionable architects Robert and James Adam also made a design for the house, which was not used, and several drawings for chimneypieces and a ceiling, which were. Only the ground floor of the house is open to the public but the rooms here boast refined decoration and good furniture. Inside the porch, two flights of steps curve round a pedestal into the entrance hall. The prescribed route runs through the Library and South Drawing Room, which both have notable fireplaces and ornamental ceilings, and thence into the Circular Drawing Room. The windows of this elegant room look down to the river and the walls are decorated with unusual French ornamental paper panels. Opening off this room in the centre of the house is an oval staircase hall. The setting of Moccas owes much to 'Capability' Brown, who made a plan for the park in 1778. A great deal has been done in recent years to restore both house and park.

Opening times: April to Sept, Thurs 2–6.
Entrance charges: 70p; children 35p.
Wheelchair access: There is a short flight of curving steps inside the front door, but all rooms are on the level.
Guidebook: A leaflet with the basic details.
Catering: None at the house.
WCs: Inside the house, one cubicle, well-maintained; unsuitable for wheelchairs.
Shop: Postcards only.

PEMBRIDGE CASTLE Welsh Newton (Mr R.A. Cooke)
Directions: 4 miles N. of Monmouth. Turn W. off A466 Monmouth-
Hereford road in village of Welsh Newton at signpost to Broad Oak,
Garway and Pontrilas; continue along hilly road for about 2 miles

Pembridge is a small moated Border castle with an impressive gatehouse. It
dates essentially from the 13th century and is relatively well preserved. The
oldest part is probably the round northwest corner tower, which may have
been started before 1200. The castle was first lived in by Ralph de
Pembridge, *c* 1135. Much later it suffered severely in the Civil Wars as an
outpost to the Royalist garrison in Monmouth. Subsequently repaired by
George Kemble, it had strong Catholic associations in the 17th century. The
entrance towers, chapel and some curtain walls were restored by the
antiquarian, Dr Hedley Bartlett, who bought the castle in 1912. Today the
castle is lived in as a farmhouse and the lawns and flower beds of the central
courtyard give it a delightful intimate atmosphere, in the midst of the wild
and remote Marches. Only the chapel and hall are shown to visitors.

Opening times: May to Sept, Thurs 10–7.
Entrance charges: 10p.
Parking: There is no car park; it is possible to park by the roadside 100 yards from the castle.
Wheelchair access: Not suitable.
Guidebook: None, but brief history on a printed board in the chapel.
Catering: None.
WCs: None.
Shop: None.

WITLEY COURT Great Witley (Department of the Environment)
Directions: 5 miles W. of Stourport-on-Severn. Turn S. off A443
Droitwich-Tenbury road down a track which is signed from the main
road

Witley Court stands as a sad but splendid monument to a vanished age of
garden parties, shooting expeditions and royal house guests, all held
together by an army of servants. A wing of the house was burnt out in 1937
and the whole structure fell into decay, helped by vandals. The inside is now
unsafe and out of bounds but the empty shell covered in rusty scaffolding
still makes one gasp at its size and magnificence. The man responsible was
the architect Samuel Dawkes, who altered and modernised an older house
for Lord Ward in the 1860s. The entrance front has a huge portico flanked
by towers and long wings; on the garden side is another giant portico and a
curved wall leading to a pavilion and the orangery. The west portico is the
work of John Nash and dates from 1805, but it fits well with Dawkes' work.
The terraces and gardens surrounding the house were laid out by W.E.
Nesfield in the 19th century. The most striking feature is the Perseus
Fountain by James Forsyth — a prancing horse 26 feet above the water. The

chapel, now Great Witley parish church, is quite as rich as the house. It was made in the 1730s for the first Lord Foley, to the designs of an unknown architect. The ceiling is covered with three large and twenty small paintings by Antonio Belluci, set in what appears to be stucco but is in fact papier-mâché. The paintings and the stained glass windows were purchased by the second Lord Foley in 1747 at the sale of Canons, the palace of the Duke of Chandos near Edgware. The woodwork in the Italian Baroque style was designed by Dawkes.

Opening times: Open at all reasonable times.
Entrance charges: Free.
Parking: On a track, about 50 yards from the house.
Wheelchair access: Possible to the chapel; most of the outside could be seen.
Guidebook: A leaflet about the church is on sale in the building. There is a display of illustrations and information about the house at the back of the church.
Catering: None.
WCs: None.
Shop: None.

WORCESTER: THE COMMANDERY   Sidbury (Worcester City Museum Service)

Tel: Worcester (0905) 344071
Directions: In the centre of Worcester; Sidbury is the extension of College Street, which runs past the E. end of the Cathedral

The Commandery began life as the Hospital of St Wulstan and was founded at least as early as 1200 for sheltering the aged poor. In 1540 it became a private house. The present buildings, tucked away from the main street down an alleyway next to the Worcester and Birmingham Canal, partly date from about 1450. They are all timber-framed and consist of a great hall in the centre with long wings on either side, making the shape of an H. In the last few years the Commandery has been restored by the City Council for use as a museum. The great hall has a very impressive open timber roof with ornamental tracery and the oriel window contains late 15th century glass. Some of the small panes have very charming paintings of birds on them. In many of the other rooms the timbers have carved and moulded decoration and the first floor Painted Chamber has a well-preserved painted ceiling of the late 15th century. A few of the rooms are furnished in 17th century style, others contain museum displays about the Battle of Worcester and the English Civil War, the story of Worcester and local crafts. Visitors have complete freedom to wander through the building.

Opening times: All year, Tues to Sat 10.30–5; April to Sept, Sun 2.30–5; open Bank Holiday Mon.
Entrance charges: Summer months only 35p; OAPs and children 10p; rest of year free.
Parking: No car parking facilities; the best plan is probably to use the 'Cathedral Visitors' car park on the opposite side of Sidbury.
Wheelchair access: There is car access for the disabled to the rear of the building. Both the

garden and the great hall, easily the most impressive room, would be accessible without difficulty.
Guidebook: Either the full guide with a history, room-by-room tour and a plan, or just the plan.
Catering: A fairly simple tea room in the ground floor of the west wing, serves tea, coffee, cakes, salads etc; the room opens onto the towpath of the canal and one can sit outside and watch boats going through the lock.
WCs: In the house near the tea room; clean and new but no facilities for wheelchairs.
Shop: Postcards and local museum publications sold at the ticket desk.

WORCESTER: TUDOR HOUSE   Friar Street (Worcester City Museum Service)

Tel: Worcester (0905) 25371
Directions: Friar Street lies N. of the cathedral between the outer city walls road and the inner ring road

The Tudor House is a timber-framed building of the 16th century whose first floor overhangs the street. In 1614 and for some time afterwards the building was the Cross Keys Inn, but is now an excellent museum of local life, with period rooms including a schoolroom and Victorian bathroom. There are also displays of farming implements. One of the ground floor rooms contains two large stone fireplaces, while the Tudor and Stuart Room has a good plaster ceiling and part of the wall-covering has been removed to show the wattle and daub underneath.

Opening times: All year, Mon to Sat except Thurs 10.30–5; closed 25 and 26 Dec and 1 Jan.
Entrance charges: Free.
Parking: On-street parking for up to an hour or one of the town car parks within 200 yards.
Wheelchair access: Not suitable for wheelchairs.
Guidebook: Free leaflets in each room giving description of the contents.
Catering: None.
WCs: None.
Shop: None.

Hertfordshire

GORHAMBURY   nr St Albans (The Earl of Verulam)

Tel: St Albans 54051
Directions: 2½ miles N.W. of St Albans off the A414 near its junction with the A5

Gorhambury is a name with Elizabethan associations and it comes as a surprise to find this large 18th century mansion at the end of the drive. The house Sir Nicholas Bacon and his son Sir Francis knew is now a ruin in the park; its successor was built in the 1780s to the designs of Robert Taylor for

Viscount Grimston. The house is staring white, having been completely refaced in Portland stone in the last few years. Taylor is best known for small convenient villas but everything at Gorhambury is on a large scale. A massive stair leads to a giant Corinthian portico, behind which is an enormous cubical entrance hall. Visitors are shown the hall and four main rooms, all with contents of the highest quality. When Sir Harbottle Grimston bought the old house and estate in 1651 he also acquired the furniture belonging to the Bacon family and it is still here. The hall has two large panels of unusual enamelled glass from the Tudor house and a highly important carpet woven in Ipswich in 1570, as well as portraits of the later Grimstons. The dining room has portraits of Sir Francis Bacon, Sir Harbottle Grimston and of the latter's Royalist friends. In the ballroom are four rare and beautiful paintings by Sir Nathaniel Bacon, portraits and still lifes, which show him to have been among the best of English 16th century artists. The Yellow Drawing Room represents the 18th century, with Reynolds and Ramsey portraits and one of two fireplaces in the house by Piranesi. The library has another Piranesi fireplace and three very unusual life-size terra cotta busts of Sir Nicholas Bacon, his wife and son. In this library were found some of the earliest printed editions of Shakespeare's plays; the originals are now loaned to the Bodleian Library, but there are photocopies on display. All the rooms shown are occupied by the family, the guides seem unusually well-informed and everything can be seen in comfort.

Opening times: May to Sept, Thurs 2–5.
Entrance charges: £1.00p; children and OAPs 60p. (HHA)
Parking: Free parking in front of the house.
Wheelchair access: Not practicable, there is a long flight of steps to the entrance.
Guidebook: Consists principally of a room-by-room guide with the history of the house and occupants worked in; no plan, no illustration of the main front.
Catering: None.
WCs: None.
Shop: None.

HATFIELD HOUSE Hatfield (The Marquess of Salisbury)
Tel: Hatfield 62823, Catering 62055
Directions: In Hatfield, opposite the railway station

Hatfield is one of the foremost Jacobean houses in England and its rooms still give a powerful impression of the early 17th century. King James I persuaded Robert Cecil, First Earl of Salisbury, to trade his house at Theobalds for the old Bishop's Palace at Hatfield. The exchange was made in 1607 and Cecil at once pulled down most of the old palace and re-used the bricks in his new house. The design was probably by his carpenter Robert Liminge and the work was supervised by the King's Surveyor, Simon Basil. The clock tower may be by Basil's successor, Inigo Jones. Hatfield is a very

Hatfield House, Hertfordshire

large house in a U-shape with the state rooms in the centre and a separate apartment in each of the wings. The main entrance was originally on the south, between the wings, and this side of the house is elaborately decorated. The present entrance is from the north, very bare and forbidding because its original ornament has been removed. The guided tour takes about an hour and begins in the great hall which is richly panelled and has a screen at each end which is most unusual. On the walls are two fine and famous portraits of Queen Elizabeth, a reminder that Robert Cecil's father was the Queen's close adviser. Beyond the hall is the main staircase, elaborately carved by John Bucke with cupids and dragons on the main posts. It leads to the main reception room, now called King James' Drawing Room from the life-size statue of the King in Maximilien Colt's chimneypiece. The room has gilded 18th century furniture and a selection of fine portraits, including one of the Third Marquess of Salisbury, three times Prime Minister in the hey-day of the British Empire. The Long Gallery beyond is dark from its panelled walls and rich from its 19th century gilded ceiling. The modern sofas are hardly noticed beside the walnut and lacquer furniture of the 17th century and the Tudor treasures, like the exquisite gold and glass posset set given to Queen Mary and Philip of Spain, or the embroidered hat and silk stockings and gloves worn by Queen Elizabeth. The Winter Dining Room and the Library were both altered in the 19th century, but the atmosphere produced by their panelled walls and elaborate 16th century chimneypieces is similar to that of the Long Gallery. At the end of the tour is the chapel and the armoury, formed out of what was an open loggia on the south front. The gardens are extremely pleasant and visitors should also seek out the separate enclosure from which the old entrance front may be viewed. The surviving part of the Old Bishops Palace, with brickwork of the 1490s and a very fine timber roof should also be visited.

Opening times: House and West gardens, 25 March to 10 Oct, daily, except Mon and Good Friday but open Bank Holiday Mon; weekdays 12–5, Sun 2–5.30, Bank Holidays 11–5. No guided tours on Sun or Bank Holidays. East and West gardens also open Mon 2–5. Park daily 10.30–8.

Entrance charges: House, park and gardens £1.70; children £1.10. Park and gardens only 65p and 45p.

Parking: Free parking in front of the house.

Wheelchair access: Wheelchairs are allowed into the hall, but all the other rooms shown are on the first floor and accessible only by the stairs.

Guidebook: An adequate history and room-by-room guide with colour pictures and a plan of the house and of the old palace, but there is not much information about the furniture.

Catering: Cafeteria in the stableyard near the Old Palace, self-service, hot meals or tea and coffee, fairly pleasant.

WCs: In the stableyard, new and well looked after; facilities for wheelchairs.

Shop: One souvenir shop in the house and another in the stableyard.

Extras: Mediaeval banquets are held in the Old Palace; telephone Hatfield 62055 for details. Double exhibition of Scenes from Shakespeare and Model Soldiers in the stableyard, open one hour before the house. Admission charge 35p; children 30p.

KNEBWORTH HOUSE nr Stevenage (The Hon David Lytton Cobbold)
Tel: Stevenage (0438) 812661, Catering 813825
Directions: 1 mile S. of Stevenage, off the A1 (M)

The drive leads towards a romantic silhouette of pinnacles and towers of the kind which produced a *frisson* in Victorian breasts. On closer inspection it appears that the outside of the house is indeed Victorian Gothic work of the coarsest kind, but the Lytton family are of ancient descent and under the cement skin is one wing of a large Tudor brick house; the rest was pulled down in 1811 by Elizabeth Bulwer Lytton and made Gothic for her by J.B. Rebecca. In the 1840s Edward Bulwer Lytton, a famous Victorian novelist, employed Henry Kendall to embroider the simple Gothic of his mother's time and improve the interior. The rooms inside the house which are shown on the guided tour are a curious mixture. The original great hall of the Tudor house is now entirely 17th century, with a very fine Jacobean screen, and elegant panelled walls of about 1700. Some of its seat furniture is covered with material from King James I's bed hangings. The drawing room has plain white 20th century panelling and family portraits but the library conjures up Edward Bulwer Lytton, whose many-volume novels fill the shelves. The Jacobean style staircase is entirely of the 1840s and it leads to Bulwer Lytton's study (where he entertained Charles Dickens and other literary friends) and to the State Drawing Room. Originally the presence chamber leading to the demolished long gallery, it is now one of the best surviving examples of High Victorian Gothic decoration. John Crace, the decorator, was the leader in his field; walls and ceiling are painted with heraldry in red, white and green, and there is Gothic furniture to match. The appropriate furnishings include Daniel Maclise's painting of Caxton — a subject taken from one of Bulwer Lytton's novels. At the end of the tour are several small bedrooms, one in Tudor style, the rest with late 18th century decoration and furniture. The architect Edwin Lutyens married into the family and besides re-arranging some of the rooms he also simplified the layout of the garden, which is an immaculate enclave in the rather shaggy park. Most of the park is open to visitors.

Opening times: April to end Sept, daily except Mon but open Bank Holiday Mon and Sun in Oct. House 11.30–5.30; park 11–6.

Entrance charges: House, Durbar Hall and park £1.80. Park only £1.40; no reductions for children. Bank Holidays, House and park £2.00. Park only £1.60. Mon to Fri outside school holidays £1.60 and £1.20.

Parking: Free parking on grass about 200 yards from the house.

Wheelchair access: Could see ground floor without difficulty.

Guidebook: Room-by-room guide with many colour pictures, followed by a useful account of the house with drawings of the Tudor buildings; no plan.

Catering: Between the car park and house is a cafeteria and restaurant in two timber-framed barns, brought from elsewhere on the estate; self-service, rather uninspiring food, tables outside overlooking the childrens' amusements.

WCs: In the restaurant/amusement area, alright in themselves, but inadequate for the numbers of visitors; no wheelchair facilities.

Shop: The old souvenir shop has been 'completely modernised'.
Extras: Visitors to the house have the option of seeing the Durbar exhibition which contains mementoes of India (The First Earl was Viceroy, the Second Earl acting Viceroy and Governor of Bengal). There is also a narrow gauge railway, an adventure playground, a skate park and various other amusements.

MOOR PARK   nr Rickmansworth (Three Rivers District Council)
Tel: Rickmansworth 76611
Directions: 1 mile S.E. of Rickmansworth off the B4145 near its junction with the A404; follow signs to 'Public and Moor Park Golf Course

The grandest 18th century mansion in Hertfordshire is now a golf club-house. A brick house was built here in the 1680s for the Duke of Monmouth and was much admired. In 1720 the estate was bought by Benjamin Styles, one of the lucky few who made a great deal of money from the ill-fated South Sea Company. He spent part of his fortune on rebuilding the house to the designs of Sir James Thornhill, better known as a painter. Thornhill's huge house is of Portland stone, two and a half storeys high with a massive Corinthian portico; it used to have pavilions on each side but they were demolished in 1785. In the centre of the building is the entrance hall, an enormous cube room with painted decoration by Amigoni, Sleter and Thornhill himself. The elaborate plaster decoration on the walls and door surrounds is probably by Artari and Bagutti. A door to one side leads to the stairs whose painted walls (now in shocking condition) are signed by Sleter and dated 1737; the stairs lead to a gallery which runs round the hall. Of the other main rooms on the ground floor the saloon has mediocre paintings by Verrio, which must have belonged to the Duke of Monmouth's house; the present lounge bar has a good mid-18th century coved ceiling and the dining roon has a coffered ceiling of 1769 with decoration by Cipriani. Apart from the Amigoni paintings in the hall the furniture is best ignored. A small part of the Italianate garden laid out in the 1830s for the Duke of Westminster still survives, but most of the surrounding landscape is the smooth turf of the golf course. Visitors should report to the desk in the entrance hall and are then free to wander round.

Opening times: All year, Mon except Bank Holiday Mon 9–4.30.
Entrance charges: Free.
Parking: In front of the house, free.
Wheelchair access: The main rooms are on the ground floor; the main entrance has a revolving door, but it would be possible to enter from the garden side by way of the saloon.
Guidebook: Choice of two: i) *Moor Park Golf Club* is cheaper and has a brief history of the house and description of the pictures; ii) *A History of Moor Park* is expensive, more thorough and begins 3,000 years before the birth of Christ; it has some interesting photos of the rooms at the turn of the century. Sadly, both guides contain information which is out of date.
Catering: None.

WCs: None.
Shop: None.

68 PICCOTT'S END nr Hemel Hempstead (A.C. Lindley Esq)
Tel: Hemel Hempstead (0442) 56729
Directions: ¾ mile N. of Hemel Hempstead, off the A4146

There is nothing extraordinary about the outside of this row of brick and timber cottages, but inside is a very well-preserved religious wall-painting of about 1500. It covers the whole of one wall of the house, and the floor of the upstairs room has been partly cut away so that the painting can be seen entire. The probable explanation is that the cottages were originally a hostel for pilgrims and the painting ornamented the upper end of the great hall. Some time after its discovery in 1953 another wall-painting dating from about 1600 was found in one of the upstairs rooms. In the early 19th century the cottages served as the first cottage hospital in England, and there is a gruesome display of early medical instruments, as well as some 16th and 17th century country furniture. But the painting is the main attraction and the custodian of the house is most eager to explain the symbols, which are apparently heretical.

Opening times: March to Nov, daily 10–6.
Entrance charges: 70p; children 35p.
Parking: Free parking by the roadside in front of the house.
Wheelchair access: Not very easy, because of the steps up from the road, but it might be possible with energetic helpers.
Guidebook: A sheet of information about the painting, but very little on the other things in the house.
Catering: None.
WCs: None.
Shop: None.

SHAW'S CORNER Ayot St Lawrence (The National Trust)
Tel: Stevenage (0438) 820307
Directions: 2 miles N.E. of Wheathampstead, at the S.W. end of Ayot St Lawrence village

This ordinary little red brick house was built in 1902. George Bernard Shaw moved here in 1906 when he was 50 and already a very successful playwright. He remained here contentedly until his death in 1950. Shaw's living rooms are kept as he left them, although they are now a little dried-up. His large collection of hats hangs in the hall and his study contains his desk and filing cabinet as well as photos of his heroes. The drawing room and dining room are filled with other mementoes, also a fine bust of Shaw by Rodin, and a fine painting of him by Augustus John. For those who already know a little about the man, his house is illuminating. The garden is large and sloping, not particularly elegant, but it provides a good walk to the bottom, where Shaw had a summer house as a quiet refuge.

Opening times: March and Nov, Sat and Sun; April to end Oct, Wed to Sun and Bank Holiday Mon 11–1, 2–6; closed Good Friday.
Entrance charges: £1.10; children 55p.
Parking: Small free car park.
Wheelchair access: Not practicable, the spaces are too small.
Guidebook: The slim National Trust guide gives a very adequate account of the house and the main contents of each room. There is also a rhyming picture guide to the village, written and illustrated by Shaw himself. His doggerel is excruciating.
Catering: None.
WCs: At the house.
Shop: None.
Extras: Plays by Shaw are staged in the garden during the summer — telephone for details. Visitors might also like to visit the church at Ayot St Lawrence, built in 1778–9 to the designs of Nicholas Revett, and one of the first neo-classical churches in England.

Humberside

BEVERLEY: LAIRGATE HALL Lairgate (Beverley Council)
Tel: Hull (0482) 882255
Directions: In Lairgate, which runs south from the centre of Beverley, the Hall is a large detached house set back from the road

Lairgate Hall is one of the principal houses in Beverley and stands a little apart from the main market area in its own grounds. The large asphalted car park in front proclaims that the house is now municipal offices. It was built for the Pennyman family in about 1700. A stone centrepiece and porch were added to the red brick front in about 1780 and the interior was redecorated at the same time. On application to the enquiry desk, visitors are shown one of the rooms, which must have been a drawing room but now serves as the council meeting room. The elegant plaster ceiling is decorated in the manner of Joseph Rose and the walls are covered with 18th century Chinese wallpaper. The adjoining room also has an ornamental ceiling, which can be glimpsed over the partitions of the rent-collection office.

Opening times: All year, Mon to Thurs 8.45–5.30, Fri 9–4.
Entrance charges: Free.
Parking: Free car park in front of house.
Wheelchair access: Steps up to front door, otherwise all flat.
Guidebook: None.
Catering: None.
WCs: None for public use.
Shop: None.

BURTON AGNES HALL Burton Agnes (Burton Agnes Hall Preservation Trust)
Tel: Burton Agnes (026 289) 324 (Estate Office)
Directions: 5 miles S.W. of Bridlington on the A166 Bridlington-Driffield road in Burton Agnes village

The entrance to Burton Agnes Hall is a broad brick gatehouse of 1610 with the arms of King James I and allegorical figures carved over the central archway. Behind the arch a broad gravel path slopes up to the main front. There are plenty of red brick Jacobean houses in England, but the careful symmetry of this front tells of a talented architect. It comes as no surprise to find that Burton Agnes is the work of Robert Smythson, the architect of Hardwick Hall in Derbyshire and several other first-rate houses. He designed Burton Agnes for Sir Henry Griffiths and it was built between 1601 and 1610. The main entrance, (turned sideways so as not to upset the symmetry of the front) opens into the screens passage, and so into the Hall, which contains an astonishing carved stone screen and a chimney piece of the same kind. The wood carving is continued in the drawing room, where a 'Dance of Death' over the fireplace is the climax of the panelling which covers the walls. The other rooms shown on the ground floor and those on the first floor were renovated in the 1730s, probably by the local architect William Etty, but the original staircase with its elaborate carved newel posts, was left untouched. Visitors can wander as they please. All of the rooms are in use and, since the Boynton family has been in residence since 1654, there is an accumulation of good furniture, happily mixed with less noble but more comforting pieces. The two highlights are probably the 16th century Nonsuch cabinet in the Hall and the satinwood commode in the Upper Drawing Room. But best of all are the early 20th century French and English paintings collected by the present owner, which combine very well with the Jacobean house. Many of them are hung on the walls of the great Long Gallery at the top of the house, which has been recently restored with a splendid new barrel ceiling. The grounds are simply laid out with lawns and bushes which set off the old red brick of the house.

Opening times: 1 April to 31 Oct, Mon to Fri 1.45–5, Sun 1.45–6.
Entrance charges: Hall and gardens 80p; children and OAPs 60p. Gardens only 60p. (HHA)
Parking: Free parking outside gatehouse, 50 yards from house.
Wheelchair access: Cars can be driven to the front door. There is a special entrance for wheelchairs and the ground floor rooms (the best carving) are all on the flat. Tea room accessible.
Guidebook: Excellent value, a well-written guide to the contents with many colour illustrations, though more could be said about the building; the lack of a plan is a glaring omission in a house of this complexity but a new edition with a plan is intended.
Catering: Tea room in outbuildings, gingham cloths, tea by cup or pot, good quality commercial cake — full meals by arrangement.
WCs: Near the tea room, small and clean, but not suitable for wheelchairs.
Shop: No shop as such, but a few souvenirs are sold in the tea room and some postcards in the house.

BURTON AGNES OLD HALL Burton Agnes (Ancient Monument)
Tel: Burton Agnes (026 289) 324
Directions: 5 miles S.W. of Bridlington on the A166, in the village of
  Burton Agnes

Most visitors come to Burton Agnes to see the great Jacobean house and
may neglect this small red brick building next door, but the brickwork is
only a skin, put on in the 18th century. Underneath is the first hall, which
was built in about 1170. The ground floor room is a stone-vaulted store
room, from which a spiral stair leads to the hall above. The original roof of
the hall has gone and the present roof dates from the 15th century. The bare
walls show the scars of the many alterations made when the building was
converted for use, first as servants' quarters, and later as the laundry for the
big house. Behind the house is a shed containing the well and the 17th
century donkey-wheel used to raise the water.

Opening times: Standard Hours (S): see page xii.
Entrance charges: Free.
Parking: Free parking in front of the big house.
Wheelchair access: Only possible to ground floor room.
Guidebook: The cheap and excellent old Ministry of Works leaflet, containing a full
  description and plan, can be obtained from the big house, when open.
Catering: As for the big house.
WCs: As for the big house.

BURTON CONSTABLE HALL   Sproatley, nr Hull (Mr John Chi-
  chester-Constable)
Tel: The Controller, Skirlaugh (0401) 62400
Directions: 7½ miles N.E. of Hull, 2 miles E. of A165 Hull–Bridlington
  road, well-signed locally

Burton Constable is a large Tudor house in a large park — a suitable home
for the 46th Lord Paramount of the Seigniory of Holderness. Most of the
house was built in about 1600, using the common formula of red brick walls
and a grid of large windows on the two main fronts, while leaving the other
haphazard. By comparing the main front with a painting in the house it may
be seen that a new top storey has been added and the main door moved into
the centre. A painting in another room shows that the whole of the outside
was once covered in yellow stucco. The public are shown most of the main
rooms and follow a prescribed route through the house. A number of
architects and craftsmen worked at Burton Constable during the 18th
century, replacing the original decoration with their work. The unusual
Rococo-Jacobean plasterwork in the Great Hall was designed by Timothy
Lightoler, who also formed the staircase hall in a former courtyard, added
the new top storey of the house and designed the stable block. The Long
Gallery was formed in after 1740 and its plasterwork was copied from the
Bodleian Library in Oxford. There are also rooms by James Wyatt and

Thomas Atkinson. A last twist in the string of contrasting rooms is given by the 1830s Chinese Room, which might have escaped from the Brighton Pavilion. The furniture matches the rooms in diversity and richness. Two rooms especially stick in the memory, the Long Gallery with its outrageously gilded Jacobean furniture, and the Blue Drawing Room, which was formed by Thomas Atkinson inside the great Tudor bay window and now overpowers with the richness of its Victorian velvet upholstery. The garden consists mostly of lawns and dark bushes, enlivened by decaying statues.

Opening times: Good Friday to last Sun in Sept, Sat, Sun and Bank Holiday Mon, also Tues, Wed and Fri in Aug 12–5.

Entrance charges: (1981) House and gardens £1.20; children 50p. (HHA)

Parking: Free parking in a grassed enclosure about 100 yards from the house.

Wheelchair access: Possible to all ground floor rooms, but only by going against the usual flow; weekdays and Saturdays would be most convenient.

Guidebook: New guide in preparation for 1982.

Catering: Large self-service cafeteria in the stable block, mass catering rolls, cakes and tea by the cup.

WCs: In the stable block; not suitable for wheelchairs.

Shop: In the stables, craft shop with souvenirs which run from peaches in brandy, through soft toys to tea-towels and ashtrays.

Extras: The price of the ticket covers a museum of coaches and one of farm implements, besides the menagerie. The model railway display has a separate entrance charge. There is also a country park with a separate entrance.

EPWORTH OLD RECTORY Epworth (Trustees of the World Methodist Council)

Tel: Epworth (0427) 268

Directions: On the outskirts of Epworth, not signed, take the road for Owston Ferry

Epworth is a large, sleepy village with a pleasant little square. The Old Rectory, which stands on the edge of the village, was built in 1709, after the previous rectory had burnt down. It is a good-sized house with a seven-window front built of the local brown brick and a roof of the local pantiles. The Rector at the time of building was Samuel Wesley and his more famous sons John and Charles grew up here. When the Church of England had no further use for the building it was acquired by the Methodists and restored by them as a memorial to their founder. The house was opened in 1957. The restoration was thorough, although much of the old fabric remains, including a reed and plaster floor which will excite vernacular architecture enthusiasts. The period furniture has for the most part been donated by individual Methodists, many of them Americans. Some items have associations with the Wesley family and it is to Wesley enthusiasts that the house will appeal.

Opening times: March to Oct, Mon to Sat 10–12 and 2–4; Sun 2–4.

Entrance charges: Free (but donations welcomed).
Parking: Unrestricted on-street parking in front of house.
Wheelchair access: Apart from hall and kitchen, all rooms shown are on the upper floors.
Guidebook: Free leaflet with basic details or more expensive guide with little more about the house but a great deal about the Wesleys and Epworth generally.
Catering: Only by appointment. It is also possible to book overnight accommodation for up to four people.
WCs: None for public use.
Shop: Books about the Wesleys, pottery and a few other souvenirs on sale.

HULL: MAISTER HOUSE 160 High Street (The National Trust)
Directions: In the High Street, opposite the Museum of Transport and Archaeology

The narrow High Street of Hull runs close to the river and many of the richest merchants lived here to be close to their wharves. The setting is hardly glamorous but there was plenty of money about, and when Henry Maister's old house burnt down in 1743 he at once rebuilt it in grand style. The five bay brick front is plain enough, but inside, at the back of the house, is the best staircase in Hull. The ironwork is by the famous blacksmith Robert Bakewell of Derby and the plasterwork by a local man called Joseph Page, who also designed the rest of the house with some advice from Lord Burlington. Only the entrance hall and staircase are on public view; the rest of the house is used as offices.

Opening times: All year, Mon to Fri 10–4; closed Good Friday and Bank Holidays.
Entrance charges: 30p, which includes the cost of a guide book.
Parking: There is no car park; some restricted on-street parking nearby.
Wheelchair access: Eight steps to front door; once inside much of the staircase can be seen from ground floor level.
Guidebook: Included in entrance fee. Eight pages of information and three photographs, excellent value for money.
Catering: None.
WCs: None.
Shop: None.

HULL: WILBERFORCE HOUSE 25 High Street with 24 and 23 High Street (Hull City Council)
Tel: Hull (0482) 223111 ext. 2737
Directions: At the N. end of High Street

Wilberforce House was built by two families, the Listers and the Wilberforces. Sir John Lister, twice Mayor of Hull, had a house here by 1639, in which year he entertained King Charles I, but the present red brick front probably dates from the 1660s. The brickwork is cut to look like stone and the curious ornaments on the gate piers and porch towers seem to fit the later date much better. The Wilberforces acquired the building in about 1732 and made several improvements inside. Although the house is now a museum a great deal of the decoration of the house survives. The best rooms are the staircase with mid-18th century rococo plasterwork and the panelled great chamber on the first floor, which is probably a survivor from Sir John Lister's house and is furnished accordingly. There are also two downstairs rooms with 18th century decoration, some of which was brought from other houses in the High Street. Among the exhibits is a life-like effigy of William Wilberforce in his study and many horrifying relics of the slave trade against which he was a vigorous campaigner. A corridor on the first floor leads into Nos. 23 and 24 High Street, two mid-18th century houses which have been converted to provide more functional exhibition rooms. The ground between the back of the house and the river has been laid out as a very pleasant enclosed garden, recently extended by the addition of a herb garden.

Opening times: All year, Mon to Sat 10–5, Sun 2.30–4.30. Closed Good Friday, Christmas Day and Boxing Day.
Entrance charges: Free.
Parking: Free car park next to museum (street parking is restricted).
Wheelchair access: Possible to ground floor only.
Guidebook: A good cheap guide with a history of the house and a full description of all the rooms and their contents.
Catering: None.
WCs: Available on request; not for wheelchair users.
Shop: Books and postcards on sale.

NORMANBY HALL nr Scunthorpe (Scunthorpe Borough Council)
Tel: Scunthorpe (0724) 720215
Directions: 4 miles N. of Scunthorpe on B1430, well signposted

Scunthorpe is not the most attractive English town, but Normanby Hall is screened from the steelworks by 170 acres of gardens and parkland. There was a grand Tudor house here and a rather ordinary mid-Georgian house, both built by the Sheffield family but these have disappeared. The present house was built in 1820 to the designs of Sir Robert Smirke. He was a serious-minded architect and Normanby was one of his attempts to introduce a 'cubical' style. The house is designed as a series of intersecting stone cubes. This does not make for elegance and the rear wing, which is in the Baroque style, and was added by Walter Brierly in 1906, is more instantly attractive. The Sheffields left Normanby in 1963 and the property was leased to Scunthorpe Corporation. The house, which was left empty, has been refurnished in the style of the 1820s. There are no ropes or barriers and few attendants. To all intents, the house might still be lived in. The rooms are large and they are furnished with a dull richness which is not at all like a museum. Only the upstairs rooms, occupied by wax people, have a museum-like atmosphere.

Opening times: Grounds open during daylight hours. House, Nov to March, Mon to Fri 10–12.30 and 2.5, Sun 2–5; April to Oct, Mon to Sat (except Thurs) 10–5.30, Sun 2–5.30. Saturday openings liable to fluctuation.

Entrance charges: 30p; children and OAPs 15p.

Parking: Free car park about 100 yards from the house.

Wheelchair access: Four steps to front door, but all ground floor rooms on the flat.

Guidebook: Very good value, well-written, well-illustrated; the only thing missing is a plan of the house as it is now.

Catering: The cafeteria in the park has erratic opening hours and probably serves tea and commercial snacks.

WCs: Excellent grand facilities inside the house and less grand ones in the park; neither suitable for wheelchairs.

Shop: Pottery and crafts for sale in stable yard.

Extras: Pony rides, putting green and joy rides through the park at weekends.

SEWERBY HALL Bridlington (Borough of East Yorkshire)

Tel: Enquiries to Director of Parks and Recreation, Bridlington (0262) 78255

Directions: 2 miles N.E. of Bridlington off the B1255 Bridlington–Flamborough road; also accessible from cliff path

Sewerby and its 50-acre park are is just along the cliffs from the more commercial amusements of Bridlington. The house at the centre of the park was built by several generations of the Greame family. The old manor house was replaced, in about 1715, by a tall square building, seven windows wide with a central pediment. Bow-fronted wings were added in 1808 and more improvements made in the 1820s and 1940s. The final result is quite a large white-painted front with stone window surrounds, which looks more Scottish than English. Inside the Oak Room has its early Georgian panelling and the 1715 staircase still survives. The rest of the rooms are a mixture of early and late Georgian decoration: those on the ground floor contain a museum of local history. Upstairs there is the Amy Johnson room, which contains relics of Bridlington's famous daughter, and a small art gallery.

Opening times: Grounds open all year, 9–dusk. House open Easter to end Sept, Sun to Fri 10–12.30 and 1.30–6, Sat 1.30–6.

Entrance charges: Grounds and house 35p; children 20p (subject to revision).

Parking: Free parking about 100 yards from the house.

Wheelchair access: Six steps up the ground floor.

Guidebook: Covers both house and grounds; excellent in many ways, with a plan of the house and sketches to show the various alterations but with so much information that it is difficult to take it all in.

Catering: Municipal self-service cafeteria in the old conservatory opens 12.00. Licensed bar in the stable block.

WCs: In the old laundry next to the stable yard, large and municipal with pay cubicles, none adapted for wheelchair users.

Shop: There is a souvenir shop.

Extras: Zoo, archery, kiddies' corner, putting course, bowling green, croquet lawn.

SLEDMERE HOUSE Sledmere (Sir Tatton Sykes, Bart)
Tel: Driffield (0377) 86208
Directions: 24 miles E.N.E. of York, 4 miles N. off the A166, in Sledmere village at the junction of the B1251 and B1253

The house is large and stands at the head of a great landscaped park that makes one think at once of 'Capability' Brown. He was brought here in 1777 by Sir Charles Sykes, who also changed the countryside round about from a neglected wilderness into farms. A little later Sir Christopher made designs for improving the house, which had been built by his uncle in 1751. He refaced the old house, gave it a new pediment and added a large wing on each side, using a quiet grey stone from Nottinghamshire. The outside was finished by 1786 and in 1787 the rooms were decorated with plaster ornament by Joseph Rose. All the decoration was destroyed by fire in 1911, but excellently restored to its former appearance by the architect Walter Brierley. At the centre of the house is the great staircase hall, and the drawing room, music room and dining room are on the same grand scale. The plasterwork is matched by first class 18th century paintings and furniture, much of it made for the house. Among the other rooms on the ground floor is the Turkish Room with blue tiled walls. The best room of all is the library on the first floor of the wing overlooking the park, which was intended to house Sir Christopher's valuable collection of books. Many of these have been sold, but enough remain to preserve appearances. The great arched ceiling is in the Roman manner with rich plaster decoration; it is matched by the parquet floor of 1911, which replaces a specially-woven carpet. Visitors can see most of the rooms on both main floors with the minimum of interference. The guides in the rooms are friendly but not expert. Next to the house is the Italian garden, ornamented with classical statues. The park is open for walks.

Opening times: 9–13 April and following Suns till 2 May; then 4 May to 26 Sept daily except Mon and Fri; open Bank Holiday Mon.
Entrance charges: House £1.20; OAPs 80p; children 65p. Grounds only 50p; children 30p.
Parking: Free parking under trees near the house.
Wheelchair access: Three steps to entrance, ground floor on the level; upper floor accessible by lift (best to telephone about lift beforehand).
Guidebook: A new (1981) edition of the old test, but much improved in layout. Exemplary in most respects, lacking only a plan to make it so.
Catering: A good tea room, with tea by the cup and home-made cakes. Seating both inside and outside. There is also a restaurant for booked parties only.
WCs: In the stable block, free and well-maintained but not suitable for wheelchairs.
Shop: In the outbuildings.

Isle of Wight

APPULDURCOMBE HOUSE   Wroxall (Ancient Monument)
Directions: 3 miles north of Ventor on the B3327 on the edge of Wroxall village; signposted in village centre

It is a pity that the grandest house on the island should be in ruins. The walls still stand to their full height, but the roof has gone and the interior has been gutted. The Worsley family owned Appuldurcombe from the reign of Henry VIII until 1806. Sir Robert Worsley started to replace the old house with a new one in 1701. The family moved into it 12 years later, when the work was still only half finished. Their presence does not seem to have speeded up the building works, which dragged on until 1782. The design is unusual. It consists of a central block with a pedimented pavilion at each corner, giving four very similar fronts with a porch in the one to be used as the main entrance. The screen wall to the rear elevation is a later addition. The architect was probably John James, who worked with Sir Christopher Wren on St Paul's Cathedral and the Greenwich Hospital. The most striking thing about Appuldurcombe is the beauty of the local stone and the high quality of the carving on the pavilions and, more particularly, on the porch to the main entrance, where the carved drapery has hardly weathered at all. It is quite safe to visit the interior, though there is not a great deal left of it, but it is very instructive to see the familiar 'Ancient Monument' treatment in what is still recognisably an eighteenth century house. The house is set in a park that was landscaped by 'Capability' Brown in 1781; it must be one of the only parks by him that does not have a lake.

Opening times: Standard hours (S) see page xii.
Entrance charges: 40p; children and OAPs 20p; no horses.
Parking: Free car park for visitors in Wroxall, about ¼ mile from the entrance. There is no car park at the house.
Wheelchair access: Would be possible; drive to entrance, then asphalt path downhill to house (about 100 yards).
Guidebook: The official handbook is fairly recent, covers the history of owner and building and contains illustrations and plans; good value.
Catering: None.
WCs: Free but rather primitive; not suitable for wheelchairs.
Shop: Postcards only.
Extras: There is a small, free exhibition about the house, past and present in the superintendent's lodge. It includes some photographs of the rooms before they were gutted and some documentation of the famous (and scandalous) divorce of one of its owners.

ARRETON MANOR   Arreton (Count and Countess Slade de Pomeroy)
Tel: Newport (0983) 528134
Directions: 2 miles S.E. of Newport on A3056 Newport–Sandown road

Appuldurcombe House, Isle of Wight

Arreton is a small manor house of the local stone with central porch and two cross-wings. The porch is dated 1639, which seems about right for the rest of the house. The hall and dining room on the ground floor are panelled rooms furnished with mainly 17th century furniture. The panelling is probably of the same date as the house and has carved ornament. The first floor rooms are a bedroom furnished in the same style as the downstairs rooms and the Long Room with a collection of exhibits, some to do with lace-making. The top floor houses a museum of childhood. The stairs are narrow and the rooms cluttered, with the result that traffic-jams can occur. But there is a pleasant atmosphere and the exhibits in the childhood museum are all too irresistible to some younger visitors. There is a small garden, and Arreton Down is just behind the house for serious walkers.

Opening times: Week before Easter to 31 Oct, Mon to Sat 10–6, Sun 2–6.

Entrance charges: House and Wireless Museum 80p; child 40p. Museum only 20p; child 10p.(HHA)

Parking: Free car park, signed from A3056, a short walk from the house.

Wheelchair access: Seven steps give access to the ground floor only; no admission charge for wheelchair users.

Guidebook: A chatty history with a room-by-room guide and illustrations; no plan.

Catering: Light lunches and tea served either in the tea room or outdoors on the lawn; pots of tea and home-made cakes; better than the other houses on the Island.

WCs: Basic and inadequate for the number of visitors; not suitable for wheelchairs.

Shop: There are two shops; the Pomeroy shop in the museum sells herbs, spices, corn dollies and second-hand books; the Old Dairy shop near the tea room sells more conventional souvenirs.

Extras: The Pomeroy Museum contans a large dolls' house, whose occupants tremble as visitors walk across the springy floor towards them. Next to it is the Wireless Museum, containing receivers dating back to the First World War.

CARISBROOKE CASTLE   Newport (Ancient Monument)

Directions: On the south side of Newport, off the B3401, Newport–Freshwater road

Carisbrooke was the strongest castle on the Island, though it does not dominate the countryside like many other castles. There are traces of a Roman fort underneath the later buildings. The main curtain wall and the circular keep on its tall mound were finished by 1136. The keep is reached up 71 steps; the reward is a fine view. In the centre of the castle enclosure are the domstic buildings; these are mostly of the 13th century, with upper parts of the 16th. Some are in ruins but the main rooms were the official residence of the Governor of the Isle of Wight until the 1940s and they are still in good repair. The Great Hall, Great Chamber and several smaller rooms are open to the public and an upper room contains the Isle of Wight Museum. Most rooms are partly furnished, but on the whole it is the fireplaces, and other features of the rooms themselves which are most interesting. One of the main subjects of the Museum is King Charles I, who was imprisoned at Carisbrooke. He tried to escape in 1648, but couldn't get through the bars of his window. Near the domstic buildings is the well–house with its donkey wheel. As it is still operated by donkeys, the wheel is a great attraction. Next to the main gate is the chapel which was rebuilt on old foundations in 1905. Surrounding the whole castle are large earthworks, designed by an Italian called Federigo Gianibelli and begun in the year before the Spanish Armada. They were finished in the 1590s; the outer gate has the date 1598 and the arms of Queen Elizabeth I. Carisbrooke is a popular attraction and gets very crowded in summer.

Opening times: Castle open standard hours (SM), see page xii. Museum open Easter to end Sept.

Entrance charges: Summer £1.20; child and OAPs 60p; winter 65p; child and OAPs 30p.

Parking: Large car park at castle entrance, charge made in summer only.

Guidebook: A choice between the Official Handbook with a serious description and history with good plans or the souvenir guide with more pictures but less text.

Catering: The refreshment room is a shack in the dry moat, serving coffee and tea with cling-film wrapped cakes and snacks. Improvements are promised for 1982.

WCs: Free, well-maintained; not suitable for wheelchairs.

Shop: Books, slides, postcards and a few other souvenirs on sale.

HASELEY MANOR Hazely Combe, Arreton (R. J. Young Esq)
Tel: Arreton 420
Directions: 3 miles S. of Newport, just off the A3056 Newport–Sandown road

Haseley is essentially a Tudor house, extensively remodelled in 1787, but still retaining a very picturesque appearance by reason of its irregular chimneys and mixture of building materials. A taped 'guided tour' of each room inside the house is triggered off when the door is opened. Mediaeval music and anecdotes are used to illuminate the (sometimes rather tenuous) connections between the house and a number of famous people. The tour starts in the study, a low-ceilinged room with restored oak panelling and a modern plaster ceiling. In the high and airy drawing room a panel set into one wall reveals beams with the dates 1567 and 1787 carved into them. The main feature of the dining room is a fireplace believed to date from 1538 and there are also models in period costume representing former inhabitants. The tour continues through the old hall, with its wide kitchen fireplace and reproductions of parts of the Bayeux Tapestry and also takes in a large bedroom and three servants' bedrooms upstairs. the house has been extensively repaired by its owners since the mid-1970s and some photographs of the house before restoration and some curious objects found during the work are displayed on the way out.

Opening times: Daily 10–6.

Entrance charges: (1981) 75p; OAPs 60p; children 35p.

Parking: Free parking just off the main road.

Wheelchair access: Might be possible to downstairs rooms, but there is a long uneven gravel drive from the car park to the ticket office.

Guidebook: Concentrates on the history of the past owners and occupants of the house, but includes a good plan of the building.

Catering: Salads, ploughman's lunches and teas with home-made cakes or rolls are served in the former kitchen, or in the garden.

WCs: Two unisex cubicles in the yard outside the kitchen; not for wheelchairs.

Shop: A pottery studio selling the work of local potters.

Extras: Childrens' play area in the garden, also a small Museum of Rural Life in one wing of the house.

MORTON MANOR   Brading (Mr and Mrs Trzebinski)

Tel: Sandown (0983) 406168

Directions: Just south of Brading off the A3055 Brading–Sandown road

Morton Manor is a fairly ordinary small house, perhaps dating back to the 17th century but with many later alterations. The few ground floor rooms shown in the tour are filled with mainly 19th century furniture. It is, however, a pleasant place to have tea.

Opening times: Easter Sunday to Whitsun, 11–6; Whitsun to end Sept, 11–6; closed Sat.

Entrance charges: 75p; OAPs 60p; children 30p.

Parking: Free parking but limited space.

Wheelchair access: Possible.

Guidebook: Salads, tea and coffee and home-made cakes served in the thatched tea room on the lawn.

Catering: Salads, tea and coffee and home-made cakes served in the thatched tea room on the lawn.

WCs: Those in the house serve the public.

Shop: Sells hand made children's clothes and local crafts.

NORRIS CASTLE   East Cowes (Mr R.W.B. Lacon)

Tel: Cowes (0983) 293434

Directions: On the coast, ½ mile east of East Cowes; signposted from the A3021

Norris Castle was designed in 1799 by James Wyatt as a seaside house for Lord Henry Seymour. Queen Victoria lived here for a time when she was a girl and liked the place so much that later she built Osborne House nearby. The castle stands at the top of a rough grass slope leading straight down to the sea and commands a view of the Solent and Southampton Water. It is strongly built, with thick walls of rough grey stone, the mortar joints strengthened with flint chips, a practice known as galletting. The main rooms of the castle are grouped round a tall round tower which, rather unexpectedly, contains the ballroom. Stretching out to one side is a long symmetrical wing, which conains the service rooms and the stables. The main drive passes the estate farmbuildings and the kitchen garden, which are also decked out with battlements and towers. The three main rooms on the ground floor and the bedrooms upstairs are furnished in the same style, in which late 18th and 19th century furniture and paintings are mixed with press cuttings and souvenirs of the Prince and Princess of Wales, and bizarre curios and oddments including life-size models of people in period costume. The route through some of the rooms is marked off by ropes and most of the contents appear to be wired down.

Opening times: Good Friday to Easter Mon, then 22 May to 20 Sept, Sat, Sun and Mon, also daily during Cowes Week, 11–5.
Entrance charges: £1.00; child 25p. (HHA)
Parking: Free car park about 300 yards from the house.
Wheelchair access: Several steps up to the main entrance, but all principal ground floor rooms one one level. The cafeteria is also accessible.
Guidebook: A stencilled booklet with a brief history of the house and a list of contents of each room; several drawings but no plan.
Catering: Tea bar in the roofed-over kitchen courtyard sells tea and coffee, sandwiches and cakes. Average food and a seedy setting.
WCs: In the kitchen court, free, old and spacious but full of junk; not specially adapted for wheelchairs but might be suitable.
Shop: None; postcards and a few souvenirs on sale at main entrance.

OSBORNE HOUSE East Cowes (Department of the Environment)
Directions: 1 mile south east of East Cowes on the A3021

A visit to Osborne should be compulsory for anyone who uses the word 'Victorian' as an insult. The young Queen Victoria bought the estate in 1845. Over the next three years the architect Thomas Cubitt built a house in which the royal couple could live a private life with their children. The marvellous view over the Solent reminded Albert of the Bay of Naples and he chose an Italianate style for the new house, with tall towers and balconies overlooking the sea. When he died in 1861, the interior of the house was kept exactly as he had left it and time has stood still ever since. Next to the house was built a large wing for the rest of the Royal household, which now serves as a convalescent home. The terraced gardens facing the sea belong to the home and are not open; visitors are confined to the courtyard in front of the main entrance. On the left side of the courtyard is the Durbar room which was added in 1890. This great room is decorated with quite extraordinary plasterwork in the Indian style, in honour of the Queen's possessions in that country, and contains many Indian objects and items presented to the Queen at her two Jubilees. The Grand Corridor lined with portraits of Indian Princes leads past the Horn Room, with its grisly array of deer antlers, to the three principal rooms which fill most of the ground floor of the royal house. Although the decoration is rich and heavy and the furniture entirely Victorian, they are pleasant roms, especially on sunny days when the Solent really might be the Bay of Naples. The Private Suite on the first floor is a complete contrast. In these rooms Victoria and Albert lived their private lives with ordinary furniture, sentimental paintings and marble replicas of their children's hands and feet, and it was here that the old Queen chose to die. The park surrounding Osborne is not open to the public.

Opening times   Easter Monday to June, Mon to Sat 11–5; July and Aug, Mon to Sat 10–5; Sept and early Oct, Mon to Sat 11–5.

Entrance charges: £1.80; children 90p.

Parking: Large car park by the ticket office; coaches 20p; cars 10p; M/C 5p.

Wheelchair access: Possible to ground floor of house. The minibus serving the Swiss Cottage will transport wheelchairs and their occupants but wheelchairs are not allowed inside the cottage.

Guidebook: A model guidebook, well written and well arranged with illustrations and a plan. There is also a catalogue of exhibits and leaflets in French and German.

Catering: Rather seedy cafeteria next to the ticket office, stewed tea in plastic cups and commercially produced snacks.

WCs: New facilities in the ticket office; suitable for wheelchairs.

Shop: Slides, books and souvenirs on sale at ticket office.

Extras: Half a mile from the house, at the end of a tree lined avenue, is a genuine Swiss Chalet where the royal children learnt carpentry and cookery (in a miniature kitchen). A shed near the chalet contains the miniature garden tools which they used and a second building houses a museum of natural curiosities, collected by the children on their father's instructions There is a model fort, laid out to teach the little Princes about military matters, and also the royal bathing machine, from which Queen Victoria modestly entered the sea. There is no extra charge for these exhibits but the minibus service from the ticket office costs 10p (1981).

Kent

ALLINGTON CASTLE   nr Maidstone (The Order of Carmelites)

Tel: Maidstone (0622) 54080

Directions: 2 miles N. of Maidstone off the A20, take the turning opposite the Tudor Garage

Allington is hidden away down a very unpromising road: a small stone castle wth a moat, surrounded by trees. It was built by Stephen de Penchester in 1281. Sir Henry Wyatt repaired the castle in the early 16th century and divided the inner courtyard into two by building a new range of buildings. By 1905 the castle had become a ruin, but in that year it was bought by Martin Conway (later Lord Conway). Over the next 20 years he restored the buildings, with the help of the two architects W.D. Caroe and Philip Tilden. Most of the upper parts of the castle are modern, but on the whole the restoration was well done. The Carmelites use the castle as a conference and retreat centre. Visitors are shown the chapel, formed in a room next to the gatehouse, the Great Hall, which is entirely by W.D. Caroe, a modern bedroom in one of the towers and the first floor library. With the exception of the hall, all of these rooms have modern furniture, enlivened by icons and 17th and 18th century religious paintings. At the height of the tourist season, the often multi-national conducted parties can be much too large for the rooms. The brown pigeons which are kept at the castle are supposed to be the descendants of a breed that was brought from Italy by Sir Henry Wyatt.

Opening times All year, daily 2–4.
Entrance charges: 60p; children (under 12) 30p.
Parking: Free car parking about 100 yards from the castle.
Wheelchair access: Possible to internal courtyard, chapel and Great Hall, also to the barn where tea is served.
Guidebook: A choice of two: 'An Introduction to Allington Castle' in which 'the castle speaks of its history' (with a plan) or 'Allington Castle, The Mediaeval Phase' tracing the history of the building until 1492. Neither can be purchased before the end of the guided tour. An information leaflet in French can be borrowed for use during the tour.
Catering: Refreshments (tea, coffee and Penguins) are served in an old barn near the car park.
WCs: Excellent facilities, free and clean; suitable for wheelchairs.
Shop: At the end of the guided tour selling books, postcards and souvenirs.

BOUGHTON MONCHELSEA PLACE nr Maidstone (M.B. Winch Esq)

Tel: Maidstone (0622) 43120
Directions: 5 miles S. of Maidstone off the A229 in the village of Boughton Monchelsea

Dramatically sited on the edge of a ridge, the house looks down across its deer park into the heart of Kent. The original house of the 1570s was built round a courtyard and two sides remain, forming the present L-shaped building. The entrance door and the dormer windows are 16th century survivals, but the battlements and the other windows date from 1819, when the Gothic style had become fashionable again. The entrance hall is also mock-Gothic but the main staircase and the first floor landing are good examples of late 17th century woodwork. Most of the rooms shown are in the east range. The furniture is mostly of the 18th century with a few earlier pieces. Visitors are conducted around in parties. The gardens are open to the public but access to the park is not permitted.

Opening times: Good Friday to 4 Oct, Sat, Sun and Bank Holidays (also Wed during Aug) 2.15–6.
Entrance charges: House and garden 90p; children (under 14) 40p. Gardens only 50p; children 20p. (HHA)
Parking: In a field near the house, good for picnics.
Wheelchair access: Possible to the ground floor rooms, which are the most interesting.
Guidebook: A general account of the occupants of the house with some mention of the buildings; no plan but plenty of illustrations.
Catering: Tea room in the house serving pots of tea and home-made cakes.
WCs: In an outbuilding off the courtyard, primitive and cramped; not suitable for wheelchairs.
Shop: A booth outside the house sells tickets and a few souvenirs.
Extras: Some old carriages and farm implements are on display in the farmyard behind the

house and it is worth visiting the parish church nearby, if only to see the mediaeval wooden lych-gate.

CHARTWELL   Westerham (The National Trust)
Tel: Crockham Hill (073 278) 368
Directions: 2 miles S. of Westerham off the B2026. The house is well signed

From 1924 until his death, Chartwell was the home of Sir Winston Churchill and the house is a shrine to his memory. The building itself is an old farmhouse, much altered and enlarged. The east wing was added and the entrance front altered for Churchill by Philip Tilden, a fashionable architect of the 1920s. He did not make a good job of the house and it is a formless red brick pile whose only redeeming feature is a very pretty 18th century wooden doorway which Tilden brought in from somewhere else. The interior is a curious mixture. The drawing room, dining room, library, Churchill's study and Lady Churchill's bedroom have been kept as they were with books, paintings and comfortable furniture, but several upstairs rooms have ben converted into a museum of Churchill's life, with his uniforms, medals and other mementos. Unless you are interested in Churchill and his time the house offers little except the view across the Weald of Kent from many of the rooms. Visitors can take their own time going round, but this is a popular house and can get very crowded. A timed ticket system is in operation which at least minimises queues to enter the builing.

Opening times: March to end Nov, Tues, Wed, Thurs 2–6, closed Tues after Bank Holidays. Sat and Sun and Bank Holiday Mon 11–6; also July and Aug, Wed and Thurs mornings from 11. Studio and garden: April to mid Oct, same times as house.

Entrance charges: House and garden £1.70; children 80p. Garden only 70p. Studio 40p extra; no reduction for children.

Parking: Large free car park next to restaurant and lavatories, a few minutes walk from the house.

Wheelchair access: Wheelchairs are admitted to the house and there is lift access to upper floors; it is best to telephone in advance.

Guidebook: A full historical account of the house and its present contents, few pictures and no plan. There is also a more basic information sheet.

Catering: A modern cafeteria/restaurant in the car park area serves teas or full meals. Decent food but the place can get full.

WCs: New lavatories, free. There is a disabled persons lavatory near the restaurant, which has ramp access.

Shop: The main emphasis is on Churchill and his works but there are many of the standard National Trust goods.

Extras: In the summer the park is open for walks and picnics. Sir Winston's garden studio containing many of his paintings is also open, entrance 30p.

CHIDDINGSTONE CASTLE nr Edenbridge (Executors of the late Denys E. Bower)
Tel: Penshurst (0892) 870347
Directions: 5 miles E. of Edenbridge off the B2027

Chiddingstone was originally a large red brick house of about 1680 which was transformed during the 50 years after 1800 by the architects William Atkinson and Henry Kendall into a stone castle with battlements and towers. Inside, the great hall comes as a surprise after the other rooms of normal size. The main interest lies in the collections of the late owner: downstairs orientalia, including Japanese laquer and ironwork and mementos of the Royal House of Stuart; upstairs a collection of Egyptian antiquities displayed in old-fashioned showcases. Visitors may wander at will through the house. There is no garden in the accepted sense, but 30 acres of lake and parkland.

Opening times: 28 March to 31 Oct, Tues to Fri 2–5.30, Sat, Sun and Bank Holidays 11.30–5.30 (Fishing 7–7).
Entrance charges: 75p; children 35p. Fishing £4. (HHA)
Parking: Free car park near the house.
Wheelchair access: Possible to all ground floor rooms.
Guidebook: A brief account of the building and its owners and a brief room-by-room guide to the collections; no plan.
Catering: By arrangement only.
WCs: In the house, free; not suitable for wheelchairs.
Shop: Postcards and souvenirs.

COBHAM HALL Cobham (The Westwood Educational Trust)
Tel: Shorne (047 482) 3371
Directions: 4 miles W. of Rochester, off the A2 and B2009

Cobham is a large and splendid red brick house. The two wings were built by Lord Cobham between 1580 and 1602, but in 1603 he was sent to the Tower for treason and his house was left unfinished. The central part dates from the 1660s, when the architect Peter Mills was called in to finish the building. After the last war the house was taken over and restored by the Ministry of Works and then sold again. It has been in use as a private girls' school since 1962. Visitors are shown round the most important rooms. The furniture is largely utilitarian and many of the paintings on the walls are copies, but there are some extremely fine things to be seen, especially the lively Elizabethan fireplaces and the Gilt Hall in the centre of the house, which is an amazing piece of 17th century English decoration. The landscaped garden was once enormous, but has ben much reduced. Some of the trees which Humphrey Repton planted near the house still survive and, despite the new school buildings, there is still an air of grandeur.

Opening times: 9 to 12 April, daily; 28 July to 2 Sept, Mon, Wed, Thurs and Sun, 2–6. Last admission 5.30.

Entrance charges: 60p; children and OAPs 30p. (HHA)

Parking: Limited parking next to the house.

Wheelchair access: The best rooms are on the ground floor, but the upstairs rooms are shown first; it might be advisable to telephone in advance.

Guidebook: A brief history and a room-by-room guide; the history names John Webb as the architect of the central portion, although it is now establishd that Peter Mills was responsible.

Catering: Tea is served in the school dining room (which has a good fireplace); both food and service remind one of school meals.

WCs: Near the dining room, free, adequate; not suitable for wheelchairs.

DEAL CASTLE   Deal (Ancient Monument)
Directions: On the sea front at Deal

Deal is one of the three castles built by King Henry VIII in 1539. They were intended to guard the sea along this part of the Kent coast, which provided a valuable safe anchorage for sailing ships. The forts were very up-to-date and looked vastly different from the usual English castle. From the air Deal looks like a six-petalled flower and at ground level it appears as a series of low curving walls with openings for guns. The castle was converted into an official residence in the 18th century, but a World War II bomb destroyed the later additions and the seaward side of the castle has been rebuilt to match the original landward side. There are no furnishings to speak of except a few guns and an exhibition about King Henry's other castles.

Opening times: Standard hours (SM), see page xii.

Entrance charges: 50p; children and OAPs 25p.

Parking: There is no car park, but on-street parking is available nearby.

Wheelchair access: It would be possible to get into the inner ring of the fort, but not inside the buildings nor on to the ramparts.

Guidebook: A joint guide to Deal Castle and to Walmer Castle nearby, with a history, description and plan of both buildings.

Catering: None.

WCs: Free but minimal, inside the castle.

Shop: None.

DOVER CASTLE   Dover (Ancient Monument)
Directions: On the east side of the town, clearly visible and signposted from the centre and the ring road

Dover Castle is one of the largest and most impressive castles in the country and also one of the best-preserved. The great keep and the curtain wall which surrounds it were built between 1180 and 1188, but there have been continuous alterations and improvements ever since that time. The last army detachments only left the castle in 1958. Most of the castle is open to the public free of charge, including the Roman lighthouse, the Saxon church and the outer and inner wards. A charge is made to visit the inside of the keep and it must be said that the interior is not very exciting. There are two bare rooms on the ground floor (one of which contains a model of the battle of Waterloo) and two large rooms on the floor above, with some suits of armour and weapons. Each floor has its chapel and several other small rooms within the thickness of the wall. This is fine for castle enthusiasts, but for most people the greatest attraction is the climb up the two big spiral staircases to the roof of the keep and the view of Dover and (sometimes) France.

Opening times: Keep and grounds standard hours (SM), see page xii. Underground works standard hours (S).

Entrance charges: Keep: summer £1.00; children and OAPs 50p; winter 60p, and 30p. Underground Works: 50p; children and OAPs 25p.

Parking: Car park in the centre of the castle, 10p.

Wheelchair access: The castle enclosure is accessible by paths and road, the keep is not accessible.

Guidebook: A choice between the Official Handbook, with a full history and description with the plans, and the Souvenir Guide, which has more pictures. The latter also comes in French and German.

Catering: A large cheerful self-service cafeteria in the inner ward, open during the summer only. Food of the tea, biscuits and filled rolls variety.

WCs: In both the inner and outer wards, free and clean, but not suitable for wheelchairs.

Shop: A bare shop in the inner ward sells slides, postcards and a few books.

Extras: The Underground Works, a long dark tunnel under the walls, begun in the 13th century but improved in the Napoleonic Wars (extra charge).

EYHORNE MANOR Hillingbourne (Mr and Mrs Derek Simmons)
Directions: 5 miles E. of Maidstone, N. of the A20 on the B2613

Eyhorne makes an interesting contrast to the more commercial Leeds Castle a mile to the south. It is a timber-framed 'Wealden' house, of which hundreds were built in Kent in the 15th and 16th centuries for prosperous yeomen. The hall in the centre must have been quite small even when it was open to the roof-timbers and in the 17th century it was sub-divided to make several smaller and more comfortable rooms. The present owners have lovingly restored the house themselves and produced a great deal of the furniture inside it, making Eyhorne something of a latter-day arts and crafts temple. Visitors may see virtually every room in the building, even the gallery inside the great chimney where bacon flitches were smoked. The rooms are in daily occupaton by the owners. Visitors are given a printed sheet to guide them round, which supplements the guidebook, and there are diagrams in each room showing its location within the timber frame of the building. The lower part of the smoking bay houses a curious and interesting display of laundry equipment, including a primitive iron of 19th century type still supplied to tribes in Polynesia. The garden is densely planted with herbs and plants which could be found in England in the 17th century; it makes very suitable surroundings for the house with its picturesque red-tiled roof.

Opening times: Good Friday to 30 Sept, Sat and Sun and Bank Holiday Mon; also Tues, Wed and Thurs in Aug 2–6.

Entrance charges: (1981) 70p; children 35p.

Parking: Limited parking (for up to 6 cars) outside the house.

Wheelchair access: Not practicable.

Guidebook: A well-produced book, with vivid drawings of the rooms in mediaeval times and transparent overlays which make a good job of the difficult task of explaining how the building grew.

Catering: Teas of various kinds and home-made cakes in the little garden house or at one of the tables dotted about the garden.

WCs: Inside the house.

Shop: There is a permanent sales table with postcards, pots and other items, as well as plants from the garden.

Extras: The garden house contains an exhibition of photographs taken by the architect C.F.A. Voysey, one of the heroes of the Arts and Crafts Movement.

FINCHCOCKS nr Goudhurst (Mr and Mrs Richard Burnett)
Tel: Goudhurst (0580) 211702
Directions: 10 miles E. of Tunbridge Wells, 1½ miles W. of Goudhurst, off the A262, signposted locally

Finchcocks was built in 1725 for Edward Bathurst. It is a compact little house of beautiful red brick, with small wings to make the entrance front seem grander. The unknown designer was clearly aware of what the more famous architects of the time, like Sir John Vanbrugh or Sir Christopher Wren, were doing. The house is now run as a museum of historical keyboard instruments, with particular emphasis on early pianos. The rooms are full of instruments, which are demonstrated on open days. There is little other furniture, but the interior is extremely pleasant and it is not difficult to imagine how the panelled rooms must have looked when they contained sturdy early 18th century furnishings. All the ground floor rooms, the fine staircase and most of the rooms on the upstairs landing are open for visitors to wander around. There is a garden, but it is neither large nor elaborate and obviously takes second place to the harpsichords.

Opening times: 11 April to 26 Sept, Sun; Aug, Wed to Sun 2–6.

Entrance charges: £1.50; children £1.00. Private visits, day £2.00, evening £2.50 by prior arrangement. (HHA)

Parking: In front of the house.

Wheelchair access: Possible to major ground floor rooms only. Tea room inaccessible, but tea can be bought upstairs.

Guidebook: None.

Catering: Tea room in the cheerfully-painted cellars; tea by the pot and home-made cakes.

WCs: On the first floor or in a garden portakabin.

Shop: Postcards, beeswax candles and other minor art and craft products but the main emphasis is on musical items.

GODINTON PARK Nr. Ashford (Mr A. Wyndham Green)
Tel: Ashford (0233) 20773
Directions: 1½ miles north west of Ashford on the south side of the A20,
reached from a minor road

Godinton nestles comfortably in its park, half hidden behind clipped yew
hedges. The main front of mellowed red brick with its two great bay
windows dates from the 1620s, but there is an earlier timber-framed house
behind. The two outstanding rooms are the 15th century great hall and the
great chamber on the first floor. The hall is lined with 17th century carved
woodwork brought to Godinton in about 1800. The great chamber, which
occupies the centre of the main front, has original carved oak panelling of
1630 with a frieze of pikemen. After the great chamber comes the staircase,
almost as good as the staircase at Knole and with yet more carved
decoration. The rooms contain excellent furniture, china, carpets and
paintings about which the guides are informative. The tour lasts about 50
minutes, takes in all the principal rooms, and is a model of how such tours
should be conducted. Some alterations were made to the house in 1902 by
the architect Reginald Blomfield, who also designed the formal garden
inside the great hedges.

Opening times: Easter Sat, Sun and Mon, then June to Sept, Sun 2–5.
Entrance charges: 80p; children (under 16) 40p; no dogs. (HHA)
Parking: On the side of the drive near the house.
Wheelchair access: About half the rooms shown are on the ground floor.
Guidebook: Very little information about the building, rather more about the owners and a
   room-by-room guide to the contents, no plan.
Catering: None.
WCs: In the servants' wing, small; not suitable for wheelchairs.
Shop: None.

GREAT MAYTHAM HALL Rolvenden (The Mutual Households
   Association)
Tel: Rolvenden (058 084) 346
Directions: 12 miles south west of Ashford off the A28, on the outskirts of
   Rolvenden village

An avenue of stately trees leads to this large house built of grey and red brick
in a stripped-down version of the Georgian style. Great Maytham was
designed in 1909 by Sir Edwin Lutyens, the most famous English architect
of this century. A smaller house of 1721 which already stood on the site was
incorporated into the central block, but there is no sign of this earlier
building, except in the basement. Lutyens turned Great Maytham into a
luxurious house for the Tennant family, but the house was abandoned after
World War II and suffered dismally. It was only rescued at the last minute
by the MHA. The greater part of the house has now been converted into flats
and only the entrance hall, drawing room and dining room are shown to

visitors. They are pleasant Edwardian rooms which serve as common rooms for the present occupants. All the furniture is modern. The grounds include a walled garden which is supposed to have given Frances Hodgson Burnett the idea for her book, *The Secret Garden*.

Opening times: May to Sept, Wed and Thurs 2–5.
Entrance charges: 40p.
Parking: In front of the house.
Wheelchair access: Gravel round the house and a steep flight of steps to the front door.
Guidebook: A home-made product but none the worse for that, with a brief history, sketches and a plan of the house.
Catering: None.
WCs: Inside the house, on the ground floor.
Shop: None.

HEVER CASTLE   nr Edenbridge (Lord Astor of Hever)
Tel: Edenbridge (0732) 862205
Directions: 7 miles south of Sevenoaks, 2 miles east of Edenbridge, signed off the B2026

Hever is a small stone castle, like a toy fort, in a rectangular moat. The castle was begun in the 1380s by Sir John de Cobham and improved in the 15th and 16th centuries by the Bullen family. Anne Bullen, later Boleyn, married King Henry VIII and was the mother of the future Queen Elizabeth I. For a time the castle played host to royalty, but the fortunes of Hever fell with Anne's head on Tower Hill. By the end of the last century the castle had become a farmhouse. It was saved by the American millionaire, William Waldorf Astor, who bought Hever in 1903 and made it his country house. His architect, F.L. Pearson, carefully restored the outside walls and largely rebuilt the house inside the walls in 16th century style. The guest rooms and servants' quarters were housed in a straggle of stone and tile-roofed buildings, which were intended to look like a mediaeval village huddled against the walls of the castle, and are linked to it by a bridge across the moat. The rooms in the castle were enriched with carved woodwork; there is still some original panelling in the morning room and in the long gallery, but the 20th century work is much more elaborate. The panelling sets off the contents of Hever, collected by Mr Astor from every country in Europe, always with an eye for historical association and the best quality. The suits of armour, tapestries and silver chairs combine with comfortable upholstered sofas and a very opulent Edwardian interior. Visitors follow a set route through the house, with restricted access to some of the rooms. Near to the castle is a very large formal garden in the Italian style whose clipped hedges make a good setting for a collection of Roman and Italian marbles.

Opening times: 4 April to 31 Oct daily except Mon and Thurs 11.30–6, last entry 5.00. Closed Good Friday and 23 May, open Bank Holidays. Connoisseurs Day Thurs throughout the year at 11.00 for pre-booked parties.

Hever Castle, Kent

Entrance charges: Garden £1.00; children 50p. Castle £1.50; chilren 70p. (HHA)

Parking: On grass about 50 yards from the house.

Wheelchair access: Possible to gardens and ground floor of house; the garden paths have a gravel surface.

Guidebook: Expensive but worth it; a full history of the castle and its owners, many illustrations, plan of castle and grounds, insert with room-by-room guide.

Catering: Large modern cafeteria south of the Italian garden; the tea room in the loggia overlooking the lake serves tea in plastic cups and quick snacks — what a waste of a beautiful setting!

WCs: Next to the cafeteria and in the car park; clean and free; suitable for wheelchairs.

Shop: The shop near the car park sells postcards and slides, as well as souvenirs. There is also a shop selling farm produce and plants.

IGHTHAM MOTE Ivy Hatch (C.H. Robinson Esq)

Tel: Sevenoaks (0732) 62235

Directions: 6 miles E. of Sevenoaks off the A25 and 2½miles S. of Ightham off A227 (signposted)

The main entrance to Ightham Mote was once through the gateway in the row of cottages which fronts the road. This entrance is now closed and visitors approach from the side. Although it is surrounded by a moat, the house does not look the least forbidding. The exterior is an irregular domestic mixture of creamy-yellow rag-stone, timber framing and red tile roofs. The timber framing is mainly 16th century work, while the stone is earlier; part of the house dates back to the 14th century. One of the best things about Ightham is the cobbled courtyard, surrounded by two-storey ranges of domestic buildings with an 'Olde Englishe' dog kennel at one side. Opposite the main gateway is the great hall, built in the 14th century, with a large window added in about 1500. The hall is the best of the small number of rooms which are open to the public. Its only rival is the Tudor chapel (built in the 1520s and rebuilt in the 1890s), whose wooden ceiling is covered with painted decoration in the Tudor royal colours, with the royal badges superimposed. The paint is a little faded after 400 years. By contrast, the 18th century Chinese wallpaper in the drawing room is in excellent condition. The decorations are the more noticeable because the rooms are sparsely furnished. Visitors make their own way around and there are guides in the rooms.

Opening times: March to Oct, Fri 2–5; Nov to Feb, Fri 2–4; also April to Sept, Sun 2–5.

Entrance charges: £1.00; children 60p. (HHA)

Parking: Free car park about 100 yards from the house.

Wheelchair access: Of the rooms, only the hall is accessible, but the exterior of the house is more rewarding than the interior.

Guidebook: A brief history, room-by-room guide, and a plan of those parts of the house which are open.

Catering: None.

WCs: Inside the house, free, very adequate.

Shop: None.

KNOLE Sevenoaks (The National Trust)
Tel: The Administrator, Sevenoaks (0732) 53006 and 50608
Directions: On the south east edge of Sevenoaks off the A225

The great park with its ancient trees and herds of deer make a moving introduction. Knole is a vast house arranged round seven courtyards of varying size. Its building history is complicated, but may be simplified as follows: Thomas Bourchier, Archbishop of Canterbury, bought the property in 1456 and over the next 30 years built himself a palace. King Henry VIII acquired the building and greatly enlarged it in the 1540s by adding a great outer courtyard which is now called The Green Court. Between 1630 and 1608 Thomas Sackville, First Earl of Dorset, altered and improved the house, renewed all the roofs and created a series of grand state rooms on the first floor of Archbishop Bourchier's old palace. The grey rag-stone exterior has changed little since then and Knole looks much the same now as it did when Thomas Sackville died in 1608. The long east front with the central gatehouse is part of Henry VIII's additions. Visitors pass through it into The Green Court and thence through Bourchier's gatehouse into the Stone Court. Most of one side of the court is occupied by the 15th century great hall, which was redecorated in the early 17th century. Next to the hall is the great staircase, painted all over with allegorical figures and other ornaments. On the first floor the visitors see first a series of small rooms and passages with simple 17th century panelling and finally the four great state rooms fitted out by Thomas Sackville with plasterwork, panelling and fireplaces of the highest quality. The rooms are filled with furniture acquired by the Sixth Earl of Dorset. It is probably the largest and best collection of late 17th century furniture in England; many of the chairs still have their original coverings. The King's room contains a state bed with gold tissue hangings and a suite of silver furniture. All the furniture at Knole has been carefully conserved; nearly half a million pounds of public money has been spent on the house and its contents over the last twenty years.

Opening times: Park open all year daily to pedestrians; house, April to end Sept, Wed to Sat, Bank Holiday Mon and Good Friday 11–5, Sun 2–5; Oct and Nov, Wed to Sat 11–4, Sun 2–4. Conoisseurs' Day Fri. House closed Dec to end March. Garden open May to Sept, first Wed in each month; last admission 1 hour before closing. N.B. The great hall will be closed for repair during 1982.

Entrance charges: £1.70; children 80p; Fri (extra rooms shown) £2.20, no reductions. Garden 50p.

Parking: Near the house, £1.00 for non-members of the National Trust.

Wheelchair access: Exterior visible but most rooms shown are on the first floor.

Guidebook: A large and recent guide with a fairly brief description of the buildings, a very detailed description of the rooms and their contents and a history of Knole and its owners by Vita Sackville-West. Many illustrations and a plan of the main part of the house.

Catering: None.

WCs: In The Green Court, free and well maintained but not suitable for wheelchairs.

Shop: In The Green Court, a large shop stocking all the usual National Trust wares (ties, tea-towels, pot-pourri, etc.).

Extras: The garden is open May to Sept on the first Wed of the month. These are the only times that the south and west fronts may be inspected from close-to.

LEEDS CASTLE   nr Maidstone (The Leeds Castle Foundation)
Tel: Maidstone (0622) 65400
Directions: 6 miles south east of Maidstone off the A20 and on the B2163 near Leeds village, signposted locally

Leeds Castle is romantically sited in the middle of a large moat and looks splendid from a distance. Some parts of the castle are genuinely mediaeval, but much dates from the 1820s, when the main house was rebuilt (in the castle style) and the encircling walls cut down to give a view over the moat. A bridge connects the main castle to its gloriette, which is the name given to a small island keep. The walls of the gloriette are mediaeval, but the interior was reconstructed and made habitable in the 1920s by Owen Little. He also imported genuine mediaeval fireplaces and panelling. The rooms of the gloriette are furnished with tapestries and heavy carved wooden furniture in keeping with the bare walls and heavy-beamed ceilings. Visitors follow the route through these rooms and then mount spiral stairs to smaller rooms which contain some notable treasures, including two paintings by the Impressionist Pisarro. The route then leads back across the bridge into the main house where, as a conrast, there are two elegant rooms, one of which has extremely fine mid-17th century panelling from Thorpe Hall in Cambridgeshire. The house is popular and there are usually large numbers of visitors. Much of the park surrounding the house is used as a golf course, but the pedestrian route from the car park passes through the duckery. There is also a herb garden next to the group of outbuildings now containing the restaurant and shop.

Opening times: April to end Oct, Tues, Wed, Thurs, Sun and Bank Holidays 12–5.30; July, Aug and Sept, daily.
Entrance charges: Adults £2.50; OAPs £1.80; children under 16 £1.30.
Parking: A very large car park, in reality a substantial piece of parkland with many trees. The disadvantage is that it lies 15 minutes walk from the castle. An open trailer carries OAPs and the disabled to the castle free of charge.
Wheelchair access: Possible to the rooms in the main house.
Guidebook: A lavish guide with many beautiful colour photographs and a respectable text, but the 19th and 20th century work on the building is glossed over. There is also a cheaper illustrated history.
Catering: A large barn has been converted into a restaurant serving cooked meals and teas; the food is of pub standard.
WCs: Several; facilities for wheelchair users.
Shop: A room in the converted outbuildings with a respectable collection of souvenirs.
Extras: Sloping ground on one side of the outbuildings has been laid out as an aviary.

Leeds Castle, Kent

LONG BARN Sevenoaks Weald (W.S. Martin Esq)
Tel: Weald (073 277) 282
Directions: 2 miles S. of Sevenoaks off the A21; take the exit for Weald and
   pass village green on left. Long Barn is the last house on the left in Long
   Barn Road

William Caxton was born in about 1420; there is a dubious tradition that he
was born at Long Barn. Modern owners have made a more positive
contribution to the house. In 1915 Harold Nicolson and Vita Sackville-West
purchased this timber-framed building of the 15th and 16th centuries.
During their residence they made alterations to the building and enlarged it
by re-erecting a old barn from the bottom of the garden as a new wing. In
1930 the Nicolsons acquired Sissinghurst Castle and moved away. The
rooms which once saw all the Bloomsbury Group are now filled with the
furniture of the present owners but some Nicolson features remain. Most
startling is the entrance hall with its Turkish panelling painted bright blue.
The garden also retains the elements of the layout designed by the Nicolsons
with the help of Edwin Lutyens, but parts of it have been replanted. Visitors
are conducted round the house but have free run of the garden.

Opening times: April to end Sept, Wed 2–6.
Entrance charges: £1.00; children 50p.
Parking: Free parking outside the Catholic church about 50 yards uphill from the house.
Wheelchair access: Very difficult because of the sloping site and many steps inside and
   outside the house.
Guidebook: A good account of the recent history of Long Barn with several drawings and a
   plan.
Catering: None.
WCs: Yes.
Shop: None.

LULLINGSTONE CASTLE Eynsford (Guy Hart-Dyke Esq)
Tel: Farningham (0322) 862114
Directions: 6 miles N. of Sevenoaks on the A225. Turn off in Eynsford
   village following signs to Lullingstone Roman Villa; the house is beyond
   the villa

The introduction to Lullingstone Castle is a brick gatehouse built in about
1497, an early example of its kind. Between the gateway and the house itself
lies a vast lawn with the small church to one side. The red brick front of the
house is curiously irregular, a central block flanked by taller wings of
different sizes. The brickwork dates from the early 18th century but it is
merely a skin enclosing a Tudor house and there is a painting in the Great
Hall which shows the appearance of Lullingstone before these alterations.
The internal arrangements of the Tudor house were not altered, but several
of the rooms were richly panelled in the early 18th century. The main
entrance opens directly into the Great Hall. Both the hall and the state

dining room next to it have panelled decoration. An 18th century staircase leads to the Tudor great chamber on the first floor which is known as the State Drawing Room. The decoration combines a barrel-vaulted Tudor ceiling with plaster strapwork ornament and early 18th century oak panelling of the highest quality. This panelling, like the rest of the 18th century refurbishing, was carried out for Percival Hart. The principal rooms and a number of minor rooms open to the public are filled with the furniture collected by the Peche, Hart and Dyke families over the last 500 years. The family still live in the house, but visitors are allowed to wander pretty freely through the rooms. The park was landscaped in the 1760s and the large lake to one side of the house dates from this time.

Opening times: House and grounds, April to Sept, Sat, Sun and Bank Holiday Mon 2–6. Grounds only open Wed, Thurs and Fri at reduced rates.
Entrance charges: £1.25p; children 50p; OAPs 75p.
Parking: Free parking outside the gatehouse, about 100 yards from the front door.
Wheelchair access: Possible to Great Hall, dining room, library and foot of staircase.
Guidebook: A small, fold-out leaflet with a history of the family and a description of each room. More material on the house itself would be welcome, but perhaps nothing more is known than is told; no plan.
Catering: None.
WCs: Yes.
Shop: None.
Extras: The church on the front lawn is a 14th century building with some 18th century plaster ceilings and fine family tombs. The Roman Villa at Lullingstone (separate entrance fee and car park fee) is one of the few such villas in the counry to have been scentifically excavated and attractively displayed for public inspecton.

LYMPNE CASTLE nr Hythe (Harry Margary Esq)
Tel: Hythe (0303) 67571
Directions: 8 miles W. of Folkestone, off the B2067 in Lympne village

A small castle with a large hall in the centre and a tower at each end. The tower nearest the church was built in the 13th century, the hall in the 14th and the west tower in the 15th. In 1906 the old buildings were repaired and turned into part of a larger house with stables and outbuildings designed by Sir Robert Lorimer. Only the mediaeval buildings are open to the public. There is little furniture in the rooms which is the result of a deliberate policy to give the flavour of mediaeval life. The hall is impressive, but the smaller rooms are less interesting. The dark twisting stairs too easily get clogged with people. There is a small toy museum in two upstairs rooms in the west tower. The setting of the castle is spectacular; it stands in a terraced garden on the edge of a ridge looking out over the Romney marshes to the sea. The best view is from the World War II observation post on top of the east tower.

Opening times: Bank Holidays and June to Sept, daily 10.30–6.
Entrance charges: 60p; children 15p. (HHA)

Parking: Parking space near the castle.
Wheelchair access: Possible to the hall but not much else.
Guidebook: Includes a history of Lympne, a history of the buildings and a plan; good value.
Catering: Teas on Sundays only.
*WCs:*In the castle with modern fittings.
Shop: None, but a few small souvenirs on sale in the hall.

MARGATE: TUDOR HOUSE   King Street (Margate Council)
Tel: Thanet (0843) 21348
Directions: King Street leads inland from the old town centre

Margate is a curious mixture of 18th century houses and modern amusement arcades but the Tudor House belongs to a time before the seaside holiday had become an institution. It is a timber-framed building, probably dating from the first half of the 16th century. The house stands on a flint base and the upper storey overhangs the lower at the front and sides. In about 1815 the old house was converted into three cottages and a number of alterations were made. In 1951 it was restored as nearly as possible to its original appearance. The restoration was well done and it is possible to appreciate that Tudor House is a timber building of high quality. The three ground floor rooms contain a collection of foreign sea shells and local souvenirs. The central hall is particuarly interesting because of its 17th century plaster ceiling. The upstairs rooms are empty and the timber frame can be seen to good advantage.

Opening times: Mid-May to mid-Sept, Mon to Sat 10–12.30 and 2–4.30.
Entrance charges: 20p; children 10p.
Parking: There is a very large pay car park opposite the house which is entered from Hawley Street.
Wheelchair access: The outside is easily visible from the road, the inside has a number of steps and narrow doorways.
Guidebook: There is no separate guide book; 'Historic Margate' by G.E. Clarke, on sale in the house, contains four pages of information about the building and its owners.
Catering: None.
WCs: None.
Shop: None, but postcards, etc. on sale.

OLD SOAR MANOR   Plaxtol (The National Trust and Department of the Environment)
Directions: 2 miles S. of Borough Green approached via A227 and Plaxtol village, difficult to find and not well signposted

At Old Soar Manor can be seen the living rooms of a wealthy family of about 1290. The most important room, the Great Hall, has been replaced by a red brick Georgian house which is not open to the public. What remains of the mediaeval house is the solar on the first floor with a garderobe and a chapel-cum-study opening off it and a vaulted undercroft. The building still has its roof but is completely empty.

Opening times: March to 15 Oct, daily 9.30–1, 2–6.30.
Entrance charges: 30p; children and OAPs 15p.
Parking: Parking space for about three cars in the lane in front of the entrance.
Wheelchair access: Only the exterior can conveniently be seen.
Guidebook: A leaflet containing history, description and plan.
Catering: None.
WCs: None.
Shop: None.

OSPRINGE: MAISON DIEU (Ancient Monument)
Directions: 1 mile S.W. of Faversham in the centre of Ospringe, at the junction of the main A2 and Water Lane

Maison Dieu was a mediaeval hospital for pilgrims and other travellers on the north side of the main Dover road. All that remains are two buildings on the south side of the road, which may have been priests' houses. One of these buildings is open to the public. The stone ground floor dates from about 1300; it was always an undercroft, intended to support a hall or chamber above. The present timber-framed upper floor, with its unusually low-set curved braces, is probably the result of rebuilding shortly after 1516. The stone undercroft has been extensively rebuilt in recent times, but 16th century timber framing survives in both the hall on the ground floor and the great chamber above. The rooms are empty of furniture, but there is a small museum of Roman remains in the two upstairs rooms.

Opening times: April to Sept, Sat 9.30–6.30, Sun 2–6.30.
Entrance charges: 40p; children 20p.
Parking: Free parking in the street outside the house.
Wheelchair access: Not possible, too many steps.
Guidebook: The Official Handbook contains a section on the building and one on the museum. There is a plan of the house.
Catering: None.
WCs: One immaculate lavatory.
Shop: None.

OWLETTS Cobham (The National Trust)
Tel: Meopham (0474) 814260
Directions: 4 miles N.W. of Rochester, 1 mile S. of A2 at W. end of Cobham village; the house fronts the B2009

The chimneystacks of Owletts are dated 1683 and the ceiling of the staircase is dated 1684. The house was built for a wealthy farmer named Bonham Hayes; its elegant red brick seven window front, with a slight projection at each end, is fully abreast of the London fashions of the late 17th century. The parapet, which is of a different brick, was added in 1754. The most striking feature of the interior is the plaster ceiling of the staircase, decorated all over with leaves, fruit and flowers. The only other parts of the house which are open to the public are the two ground floor rooms which owe their present appearance to the architect Sir Herbert Baker, who came to live at Owletts in 1917. He added an 18th century porch to the front of the house, stripped the paint from the doors and dado in the dining room, renewed the ceiling of the living room and panelled its walls in cedar wood. He also installed the elaborate clock over the fireplace, which tells the time in different parts of the British Empire. Sir Herbert's family still live in the house and the rooms contain a number of very attractive sketches by him. Across the road from the house, but belonging to it, is a spring-time garden.

Opening times: April to end Sept, Wed and Thurs 2–5.
Entrance charges: 50p; no reductions; no photography in the house.
Parking: Limited parking in the drive.
Wheelchair access: Would be possible to the ground floor rooms despite steps up to front door.
Guidebook: None.
Catering: None.
WCs: None.
Shop: None.

PATTYNDENNE MANOR Goudhurst (D.C. Spearing Esq)
Tel: Goudhurst (0580) 211361
Directions: 8 miles W. of Tunbridge Wells, 1 mile S. of Goudhurst off the B2079

Pattyndenne is a fine example of what is known as a 'Wealden' or 'Recessed Front' house, with the central hall and two slightly projecting wings all under one deep roof. Houses of this kind were built all over Kent and Sussex between 1450 and 1550, and there are still many of them in existence. At Pattyndenne, the great timbers which make up the main structure can be clearly seen and many of them are richly ornamented. The central hall was floored over in the 17th century but it is not difficult to imagine how it must have looked when it was open to the roof. There are some nice pieces of furniture, but the main thing here is the building itself. Visitors can go into every room, even into the roof for a close look at the main beams. The outside is prettily black and white.

Opening times: Spring Bank Holiday Sun and Mon, then Sun, from second in July to third in Sept, 2–5.30.
Entrance charges: £1.00; children 50p.
Parking: On grass, next to the house.
Wheelchair access: There are too many steps to the front door to make a visit easy.
Guidebook: Sensibly concentrates on explaining the building, without making up bogus history for what is a fairly common type of house.
Catering: None.
WCs: At owner's discretion.
Shop: None.

PENSHURST PLACE Penshurst (The Lord De L'Isle)
Tel: Penshurst (0892) 870307
Directions: 7 miles S. of Sevenoaks, off the B2176 and B2188 in Penshurst
village

Penshurst is one of the best surviving examples of a large mediaeval house.
The oldest part of the building dates from the 1340s when Sir John de
Pulteney, Lord Mayor of London, built himself a grand country residence.
His cream-coloured stone house survives more or less intact, but there have
been many additions since his time. The approach for visitors lies through a
very English garden, a pleasant mixture of herbaceous borders, formal beds
and orchards, to the original main entrance. Sir John's great hall is marked
out by its large windows, tall roof and staircase tower leading to the solar.
Stretching away to the left is the Buckingham Building, added in the 1430s,
and an Elizabethan wing at right angles to it added in the 1570s. The hall still
looks very much as it must have done when new, with its fine chestnut roof
and the open hearth in the middle of the floor, but the solar is now the state
dining room. Beyond it are two cavernous state rooms in the Buckingham
Building, and a pleasant long gallery in the Elizabethan wing with a
decorative plaster ceiling and oak panelling. From the gallery a turret stair
leads down to another panelled room with a late 17th century four-poster
bed and red lacquer furniture of the same period, and the Nether Gallery.
All the rooms at Penshurst contain interesting furniture of the 16th, 17th
and 18th centuries, but it is the portraits which are most memorable,
especially those of the Elizabethan period when Penshurst belonged to the
famous Sidney family. The northern half of the house is still occupied by the
owner and not open to visitors, though the exterior can be seen from the
road nearby and from the park, most of which is open to visitors throughout
the year.

Opening times: 1 April to 3 Oct, daily except Mon but including Easter, Spring and Summer
Bank Holidays, 12.30–6. (Bank Holidays 11.30–6).
Entrance charges: House and grounds £2.00; OAPs £1.50; children £1.00. Grounds only
£1.00 and 50p. Toy Museum 25p. (HHA)
Parking: Free parking just outside the gardens, about 200 yards from the house.
Wheelchair access: Only the garden is easily accessible; there are steps up to the great hall and
the other rooms shown are on the first floor.
Guidebook: There are a number of different guidebooks covering the history and architecture
of Penshurst. The basic guide is good value and contains a brief history of the occupants and
a plan of the house, with a room-by-room guide as an insert.
Catering: A cafeteria has been formed in an old building next to the house; self-service,
average food.
WCs: In an outbuilding, not very large and not very clean.
Shop: A souvenir shop in the old kitchen on the way out of the house sells a wide variety of
novelties, slides and postcards.
Extras: Small Toy Museum, with an interesting collection; too many of the exhibits are above
the eye-level of child visitors. There is also an adventure playground in the park, about 200
yards from the house.

PORT LYMPNE   Lympne, nr Hythe (John Aspinall Esq)
Tel: Hythe (0303) 60618/9
Directions: 8 miles W. of Folkestone on the B2067

The admission charge covers both the Zoo Park and the house. The latter was built in 1912 for Sir Philip Sassoon, a millionaire who knew all the top people. His architect was Sir Herbert Baker, whose best work was done in South Africa and India. The house is built in the same Dutch style as many South African houses. The outside is red brick; inside were several expensively decorated rooms. Much of the decoration was destroyed when the house was used by the army during World War II but the amusing painted room decorated by Rex Whistler has survived, and also the extraordinary Moorish courtyard in the centre of the house. The rooms are unfurnished and contain exhibitions about wild animals. Not much atmosphere remains, although it is still possible to get a whiff of the former opulence. The gardens are laid out on a steep hillside behind the house. There are many terraces and a giant staircase like something from Imperial Rome. Until recently the garden was much overgrown, but it is being restored gradually.

Opening times: All year, daily except Christmas Day 10–5.30 (or sunset if earlier).
Entrance charges: Adults £2.50; children and OAPs £1.50. (HHA)
Parking: The car park is in a field well away from the house, which is reached by a bridge over the main road. The walk to the house is about ¼ mile and includes a steep flight of steps; there is an alternative but longer route without steps.
Wheelchair access: Wheelchair users can reach most of the park; they should go directly to the main entance (not to the car park) and apply for admission. Most of the rooms shown in the house are on the ground floor.
Guidebook: More about the animals than the house, but there is a brief history of the building and its owners.
Catering: The cafeteria in the stableyard next to the house serves tea and sandwiches; it is geared to handle large numbers.
WCs: Free and well maintained, in the stable courtyard.
Extras: The large wildlife park covers nearly 300 acres and specialises in rare and endangered species.

QUEBEC HOUSE   Westerham (The National Trust)
Tel: Westerham (0959) 62206
Directions: 5 miles W. of Sevenoaks, on the edge of Westerham, fronting the A25

This neat little red brick house stands close to a dangerous corner on the main road. It is square in plan, with three tall gables on each front. The outer walls date from the 17th century but there are remains of an older building inside. Quebec House was the childhood home of General Wolfe, who captured Quebec for the British in 1759. He lived here from his birth in 1727 until 1738. On this account the house is now a museum in his memory. The entrance hall and the two downstairs rooms which are open to the public contain mostly paintings and prints of Wolfe and his exploits in Canada, and some dining room furniture. A sturdy 17th century oak staircase leads to the principal room on the first floor, pleasantly furnished as a mid-18th century drawing room. There is a small garden and the Tudor coach house contains an exhibition about the Battle of Quebec.

Opening times: March, Sun only 2–6; April to end Oct, Mon, Tues, Wed, Fri and Sun (incl. Good Friday) 2–6, last admission 5.30.
Entrance charges: 90p; children 45p.
Parking: In Westerham village.
Guidebook: Brief history of house and brief biography of Wolfe with a guide to the contents. It would be helpful to have more on the house itself; no plan.
Catering: None.
WCs: Yes.
Shop: Only slides and postcards.

QUEX PARK (The Powell-Cotton Museum) Birchington (Trustees of the Powell-Cotton Museum)
Tel: The Curator, Thanet (0843) 42168
Directions: 3 miles W. of Margate on the B2048, ½ mile from the centre of Birchington

Major Percy Powell-Cotton spent much of his time between 1887 and 1938 in the wilder parts of Africa. The museum contains the spoils of his visits. There are several large dioramas with a wide variety of stuffed animals and an endless array of antlers, weapons and costumes brought from all parts of Africa and Asia. The dioramas are very good of their kind and the other displays are well-mounted but a very large number of animals were killed to provide the exhibits for this collection. The museum is attached to Major Powell-Cotton's family house. It is a large and probably ugly building almost completely covered with creeper. The earliest part dates from 1808, wings were added in 1883 and internal alterations made early this century. Most of the decoration seems to belong to the late 19th or early 20th centuries. The rooms are fully furnished with an English country house mixture, which includes some pleasant Chippendale and Sheraton style chairs and cabinets. Visitors make their own way round the six rooms which are open. The house has a pleasant garden, which is open to the public, and a park which is not, although one may, with permisson, walk to the extraordinary bell tower built in 1818.

Opening times: Museum only: Jan, Feb, Nov and Dec Thurs 2.30–6; March and Oct, Thurs, Sun 2.15–6. Museum, house and gardens: April and May, Thurs, Sun and Bank Holidays 2.15–6; June and July, Wed, Thurs, Sun 2.15–6; Aug, Wed, Thurs, Fri, Sun and Bank Holidays 2.15–6; Sept, Wed, Thurs, Sun 2.15–6.
Entrance charges: Jan, Feb, March, Oct, 20p; children and OAPs 10p. April, May, June, July, Aug, Sept, 60p; children and OAPs 40p. Nov and Dec, 30p; children and OAPs 20p.
Parking: Free parking under the trees, 50 yards from the house.
Wheelchair access: Ground floor rooms and museum only suitable for the disabled.

Guidebook: An admirably cheap guide to the collections and to the house with several illustrations.
Catering: None.
WCs: Next to the museum, free, adequate; not suitable for wheelchairs.
Shop: None, but postcards etc. on sale at entrance.

ROCHESTER CASTLE   Rochester (Ancient Monument)
Directions: In the centre of Rochester, next to the Cathedral

The great keep of Rochester Castle dominates the town. Although ruined inside, it still stands to its full height. The outer ward is now a grassy open space, accessible at all times. The walls of the outer ward are partly broken down but still impressive, especially on the side facing the cathedral. The first stone castle was built here by Bishop Gundulf soon after 1088. The rectangular keep was added by William of Corbeuil, Archbishop of Canterbury, between 1127 and 1139. Apart from the South East Tower, which was rebuilt in 1226, the keep has altered very little. It is one of the largest keeps in England and must also have been one of the most luxurious. The second and third floors, which are marked on the outside by large windows, were thrown together to make one splendid great hall, divided by a central arcade. The rich details of the hall can still be seen, although the floors have all gone. There are a number of small rooms in the thickness of the walls, as well as staircases which enable visitors to reach the roof. The climb is an exciting experience when a stiff wind is blowing through the window openings.

Opening times: Standard hours (SM), see page xii.
Entrance charges: 50p; children 25p.
Parking: There is no visitors' car park but parking space is available in the cathedral close or in nearby streets.
Wheelchair access: Not possible to keep.
Guidebook: The Official Handbook, first published in 1969, is full of information, perhaps too full for some people; several illustrations and plans and sections of the castle and keep.
WCs: Sordid municipal lavatories in the outer ward; not suitable for wheelchairs.
Shop: None.

ROYDON HALL   nr Maidstone (The World Government of the Age of Enlightenment)
Tel: Maidstone (0622) 813243
Directions: 10 miles S.W. of Maidstone on the E. side of the B2016, 1 mile S. of the junction with the A26; a small unsigned turning leads to the house

Roydon has a lovely setting in a valley overlooking the Weald, but the house itself is a little disappointing. The original Tudor house was damaged by fire in the 1870s and very extensively rebuilt; only the west side still has some original brickwork. Visitors enter by way of a courtyard of the 16th century, and a porch of about 1600. The house was originally a hollow square with a central courtyard, which was roofed over in the 1870s and made into a staircase hall. The rooms opening off the hall have mostly 19th century decoration, although there is some 16th century panelling in two rooms on the east side. The house is now occupied by the disciples of the Maharishi Mahesh Yogi (who also owns Mentmore in Bucks) and the guided tours are part history and part information about Transcendental Meditation. The furniture is modern, and includes mattresses to soften the rigours of levitation. The tours also include the pretty stables built in the 1850s and the garden terraces which have some 16th century walling.

Opening times: All year, Sun 1.30–4.30; 25 March to Oct Wed 1.30–4.30.
Entrance charges: (1981) House and gardens £1.00; children and OAPs 50p. (HHA) N.B. The right is reserved to close without prior notice.
Parking: Free parking next to the house.
Wheelchair access: There are a number of steps which would have to be negotiated.
Guidebook: None.
Catering: Tea is served as part of the tour, sometimes in the company of the guide; the tea and cakes are made on the premises.
WCs: In the house; not for wheelchairs.
Shop: A great deal of literature is available about Transcendental Meditation.

SALTWOOD CASTLE (The Hon. Alan Clark MP)
Tel: Hythe (0303) 67190
Directions: 5 miles W. of Folkestone, 2 miles N.W. of Hythe, follow local signs to Saltwood

There has probably been a castle on the present site since the 11th century. The inner ward of the castle was protected on three sides by a lake moat and on the fourth by an outer ward, whose ruined walls still survive. During most of the Middle Ages, the property was owned by the Archbishops of Canterbury and Archbishop Courtenay made several additions, including the massive gatehouse which was built in about 1830. An earthquake damaged the castle in 1580 but in 1885 the gatehouse was made into a house. During the 1930s the architect Philip Tilden supervised another major restoration. The public are seldom admitted to the house itself. Visitors can walk the circle of the walls and enjoy the pleasant garden in the inner ward, but the inhabited rooms are only open by appointment for parties of 12 or more. This seems a pity, since many visitors may be interested in the castle chiefly as the former home of Lord Clark. The gardens round the castle are pleasant, though not large, and are filled with peacocks, bantams and other fowl.

Opening times: Whit Sunday to end Aug, Sun and Bank Holiday Mon, also Tues to Fri in Aug, 2–5.30.
Entrance charges: 70p; children 25p. (HHA)
Parking: Free parking in a field about 100 yards from the castle.
Wheelchair access: Everything except the wall-walk is accessible.

Guidebook: A brief, chatty history with a simple plan and many pictures.
Catering: Cups of tea and good home-made cakes served in the outbuildings near the gatehouse.
WCs: Gothic facilities inside the castle.
Shop: Souvenirs, postcards, china, oddments.
Extras: The owner's collection of vintage cars can be inspected free.

SISSINGHURST CASTLE   Sissinghurst (The National Trust)
Tel: Cranbrook (058 04) 712850
Directions: 14 miles E. of Tunbridge Wells off the A262

Most people visit Sissinghurst to see the marvellous garden created by Vita Sackville-West and Harold Nicolson. The shape of the garden was dictated by the remains of a great Tudor mansion, which the Nicolsons converted into a picturesque but inconvenient house. The long red brick entrance range belongs to a house which was built by the Baker family in about 1500. The tower behind was the entrance to the courtyard of a much grander house, built by Sir Richard Baker between 1560 and 1570 and demolished by Sir Horace Mann in about 1800. Visitors may climb the tower and look into the first floor room which is still furnished as Vita Sackville-West's sitting room. They may also look into the library in the long entrance range. Both rooms are furnished with a rich mixture of polished oak, books, Persian carpets and objets d'art.

Opening times: April to 15 Oct, Tues to Fri 1–6.30, Sat, Sun and Good Friday 10–6.30.
Entrance charges: £1.70; children 90p; no dogs.
Parking: Free car park in front of the entrance.
Wheelchair access: Most of the garden is accessible but not the tower; only two wheelchairs allowed in at any one time.
Guidebook: Written by Nigel Nicolson; a brief history of the house with an account of how it was restored and the garden laid out after 1930. There are several illustrations of the old house and a garden by garden guide.
Catering: The excellent oast house restaurant is open at Easter and weekends only in April, then daily May to Sept, 12.00–6. Salads, first class coffee, home-made cakes etc. The restaurant is on the first floor, but food can be carried out.
WCs: Near the restaurant, clean and free; facilities for wheelchair users.
Shop: The shop stocks the usual National Trust lines, patterned tins, tea towels, Olde English sweets as well as local crafts and books and there is often a very interesting selection of plants for sale.

SMALLHYTHE PLACE   Smallhythe, Tenterden (The National Trust)
Tel: Tenterden (058 06) 2334
Directions: 2 miles S. of Tenterden on the B2082 to Rye

Smallhythe is a tiny, lonely hamlet which was once a small shipbuilding port. The channel which brought barges up from Rye has now silted-up. In 1516 a fire destroyed most of the village and both the small red brick church and the two large timber-framed houses next to it were probably built soon

Smallhythe Place, Kent

afterwards. In 1899 one of these houses was bought by the great actress Ellen Terry. It was her country home until her death in 1928 and is now her memorial. The house itself is a long two-storey building with a jettied upper floor and a roof of old red tiles. Together with the huddle of outbuildings it makes an attractive group. The Ellen Terry memorial fills the greater part of both floors of the house. The rooms contain a treasure house of theatrical souvenirs, costumes and portraits of both Ellen Terry and Sir Henry Irving. Only her bedroom, kept as she left it, excludes the theatre. Visitors make their own way round the house, which is one of the best of the many shrines in England to great people. The house is popular and visits are best made out of the peak tourist season.

Opening times: March to end Oct, Sun, Mon, Wed, Thurs, Sat 2–6, or dusk if earlier; last admission ½ hour before closing.
Entrance charges: 80p; children 40p.
Parking: There is parking space for about 15 cars off the road near the house.
Wheelchair access: The house is considered unsuitable; access to the garden is possible.
Guidebook: Concerned almost wholly with Ellen Terry, brief biography and a room-by-room guide to the contents. The house is worth a bit more description than it gets.
Catering: None.
WCs: None.
Shop: None, but some postcards etc. on sale.

SQUERRYES COURT   Westerham (Mr J. St A. Warde)
Tel: Westerham 62345
Directions: On the W. side of Westerham, off the A25

Squerryes is a modest house of the 1680s. It is built of red brick, seven windows wide with a small pediment in the centre. The wings on either side, which gave the house more consequence, were demolished long ago. The rooms are well-proportioned but as plain as the outside; there have been several alterations but a few original fireplaces remain. The three principal downstairs rooms and the large staircase hall on the upper floor contain a remarkably good collection of Dutch and Flemish paintings, as well as other furnishings. In addition, one of the upstairs rooms contains a collection of objects associated with General Wolfe, the captor of Quebec who came from Westerham, and one room downstairs contains the regimental museum of the Kent and Sharpshooters yeomanry. The house has a pleasant setting in a small park; the grass in front of the entrance slopes down to a lake.

Opening times: March and Oct, Sat, Sun and Bank Holidays, May to Aug, Wed, Thurs, Sat, Sun and Bank Holidays 2–6; last admission 5.30.
Entrance charges: House and gardens £1.00; children 50p. Gardens only 50p; children 25p. No dogs. (HHA)
Parking: On the gravel sweep in front of the house.
Wheelchair access: Not allowed.
Guidebook: A brief history and room-by-room guide, no plan.
Catering: None.

WCs: In the gardens, free, adequate.
Shop: None.

STONEACRE Otham, nr Maidstone (The National Trust)
Directions: 3 miles S.E. of Maidstone, 1 mile S. of the A20; the lane to
  Stoneacre leads off the village green at Otham, not well signposted

Stoneacre is a timber framed house of medium size, the north end partly
rebuilt in stone in the 16th century to prevent it sliding down the hill. The
good condition of the external woodwork and the suspiciously correct
windows suggest that the house has been restored. At the centre is the Great
Hall, which was probably built in about 1480, but the building owes its
present appearance to Mr Aymer Vallance. Between 1920 and 1926 he
supervised a complete restoration of Stoneacre, according to his own idea of
how it had one been. He also built a new north wing with timbers brought
from North Bore Place at Chiddingstone. His restoration was, on the whole,
better than many others of the time. Visitors are conducted round in a tour
which takes about 40 minutes. Undoubtedly the best room is the Great Hall,
which has a splendid crown-post roof. The dining room contains the blue
and white china collected by Aymer Vallance. The other rooms shown are in
the east wing and on the first floor of the west wing. There is a modest
needlework exhibition and also a pleasant garden.

Opening times: April to end Sept, Wed and Sat 2–6.
Entrance charges: 70p; children 35p.
Parking: Car park in lower paddock.
Wheelchair access: Not practicable.
Guidebook: A cheap little guide written in 1949, adequate, no plan.
Catering: None.
WCs: Two in the house.
Shop: None.

TEMPLE MANOR Knight Road, Strood, Rochester (Ancient Monument)
Directions: ½ mile W. of Strood High Street; Knight Road is a turning off
  the A2

A grim site in the middle of an industrial estate makes this small building a
surprising find. The older stone part, with its cellar and first floor hall, was
built in about 1240 as an overnight stopping-place for high ranking officials
of the Knights Templar. The brick additions were made in the 17th
century; they consist of a three-storey wing at the west end and a smaller
wing at the east end with a large bay window which must have had a fine
view over the river to Rochester Castle before the railway embankment
arrived. By the end of World War I the house had become a wreck, but it has

been rescued. All the rooms are empty, but in the hall lurks a huge brick chimney-stack, put in to replace the open fire, which was the original method of heating. Well worth a short visit.

Opening times: Standard hours (S) April to Sept only, see page xii.
Entrance charges: 30p; children and OAPs 15p.
Parking: Free parking for about four cars, probably adequate.
Wheelchair access: Not really possible to any of the interior.
Guidebook: The Official Handbook is reliable, if somewhat stodgy, with illustrations and a plan.
Catering: None.
WCs: None.

WALMER CASTLE Walmer (Department of the Environment)
Directions: On the sea front at Walmer, 6 miles N.E. of Dover on the B2057, off the A258

Deal, Walmer and Sandown Castles were all built in 1539–40 as part of the same system of coastal defence. Walmer was built in the shape of a quatrefoil with a circular keep in the middle. Since the beginning of the 18th century the castle has been the official residence of the Lord Warden of the Cinque Ports and alterations were made to the Tudor keep in the 1730s and the 1860s to make this grim fort into a more comfortable place to live. The very pleasant garden with its windswept hedges is another 19th century improvement. The Duke of Wellington, in particular, found Walmer very much to his taste during his time as Lord Warden (1829–52); he frequently stayed here and it was here that he died. Guns are still mounted on the outer walls but the rooms on the first floor of the keep, which are open to the public, are furnished as domestic living rooms of the time of the Duke of Wellington. His own room has been returned to something like its original appearance and next to it is a small room housing a collection of Wellingtoniana. The other rooms, which contain some interesting furniture, are arranged as though they were inhabited.

Entrance charges: Standard hours (SM), see page xii, but closed on Good Friday and also Mon, Oct to March, except Easter Monday; may be closed at short notice for Government functions. Gardens closed in winter.
Entrance charges: Summer 90p; children 50p. Winter 50p; children 25p.
Parking: Free parking in front of entrance.
Wheelchair access: Not possible, all internal rooms shown are on the first floor.
Guidebook: A joint guide to Walmer and Deal Castles, with a history and descripton of both and several plans.
Catering: None.
WCs: Inside the castle.
Shop: None.

Lancashire

ASTLEY HALL Chorley (Chorley Borough Council)
Tel: Chorley (025 72) 2166
Directions: 1 mile N.W. of Chorley town centre, off the A6, well
   signposted

Astley Hall is a compact house built in about 1630, set in front of an earlier
timber-framed house. It must be counted a remarkable survival,
surrounded as it is by a large housing estate not far from Chorley centre.
The main front seen from across the lake seems all windows. Two great bay
windows rise the full height of the house and a continuous strip of glazing on
the upper floor lights the long gallery. Sadly, the 17th century brickwork
has been covered with rendering. The main door, flanked by clumsy
columns, gives a foretaste of the rooms inside. All the main ground floor
rooms, the hall, drawing room and morning room, have very elaborate
moulded plasterwork of the 1660s. It is unbelievably barbaric, but very
spectacular. The walls of the hall have painted panels of 17th century heroes
let into the wainscot and there is a vigorously carved main staircase. These
rooms are rather sparsely furnished. The hall contains a chair brought from
Hoghton Tower, from which King James I allegedly knighted a loin of beef
— Sir Loin. Of the upstairs rooms, the Cromwell room in the west wing has
an excellent 17th century interior and another room has a magnificent four-
poster bed which bears Cromwell's name, but the others are a little dreary.
This cannot be said of the long gallery on the second floor; it runs the full
width of the house and provides a magnificent setting for an enormous and
solid shovel-board table with 20 legs. Visitors make their own way round
the house. The extensive grounds have a rather municipal character.

Opening times: Open all year daily; April to Sept 12–6; Oct to March Mon to Fri 12–3.30, Sat
   10–3.30, Sun 11–3.30.
Entrance charges: House 45p; accompanied children 11p (unaccompanied 25p); to be
   revised March 1981.
Parking: Large free car park behind house.
Wheelchair access: Possible to the ground floor rooms, which have the best plasterwork.
Guidebook: i) The official guide: good value, with a brief history, a descripton of each room
   and a few anecdotes, but no plan. ii) The illustrated guide: better photographs than the
   other, but the text is laid out like a tabloid newspaper with headings like 'FIVE WIVES',
   'GOT LOST'. It is probably less useful than the first.
Catering: Teas and snacks in the cafe in part of the 18th century stable block; both food and
   decor ordinary.
WCs: Adequate; facilities for wheelchair users.
Shop: Postcards and slides sold in entrance hall.
Extras: Bowling green, tennis courts, playgrounds, etc. A nature trail has been set up in the
   wood.

BROWSHOLME HALL nr Clitheroe (Robert Parker Esq)
Tel: Stonyhurst (025 486) 330
Directions: 11 miles N. of Blackburn, 4 miles N.W. of Clitheroe; from
Clitheroe take the road to Whitewell via Mitton

Browsholme is basically a Tudor and Jacobean house, with some 18th
century alterations. The main front is of red sandstone and quite plain,
apart from the 'Tower of the Orders' which forms its centrepiece. The
house is particularly noted for its contents. The Parker family have lived
here since the house was built and have hoarded a remarkable collection of
objects which rival any museum of comparable size. They range in date
from the Stone Age to the 20th century. The house is still lived in and the
guided tour is very well conducted by a member of the family. The rooms
owe much of their character to the antiquarian bent of Thomas Lister
Parker who, like his friend Charles Towneley of Towneley Hall near
Burnley, was among the first to appreciate the exciting possibilities of the
Elizabethan and Jacobean objects which could be bought cheaply in the
early 19th century. Like Towneley, he employed Sir Jeffry Wyattville to
modify his house. The drawing room was remodelled and the dining room
added and furnished in the Regency manner under Wyattville's direction.
Among the treasures of the house are several fine family portraits and other
paintings by Reynolds, Romney, Lely, Kneller, Gerald van Honthorst, and
two charming portraits by Arthur Devis. The landscaped grounds on which
Thomas Lister Parker lavished much money are also open to visitors.
Restoration work is going on in both house and grounds, where the lake has
been dredged and re-filled.

Opening times: 10–18 April, 29 May to 6 June, 21 Aug to 5 Sept, daily 2–5.
Entrance charges: £1.00; children 50p. (HHA)
Parking: Free parking in stable courtyard, 75 yards from the house.
Wheelchair access: Possible to ground floor rooms, more than half the rooms shown.
Guidebook: A new (1980) guide with a solidly informative text and many illustrations; a
room-by-room tour is followed by a brief history of the Parker family.
Catering: None.
WCs: In the house; wheelchairs can be accommodated in the private parts of house on
request.
Shop: A small selection of items.

CHINGLE HALL Goosnargh, nr Preston (Executors of the late Miss
Strickland)
Tel: Goosnargh (077 476) 216
Directions: 5 miles N. of Preston, ½ mile S.W. of Goosnargh on the B5269
(Map 1, B6)

Chingle is said to be the most haunted house in Britain. It is a small plain
manor house on a cruciform plan with whitewashed stone walls,
surrounded by the remains of a moat. The building is said to date from 1260

(this is difficult to believe) but it does have a splendid 13th century front door of tarred oak. There are plenty of old beams inside and a great deal is made of the various ghosts and apparitions which have been seen. Most of the house is open, including various secret rooms.

Opening times: All year, daily except Mon and Fri, but including Bank Holidays 2–6.
Entrance charges: 60p; children 30p.
Parking: Very limited parking by the roadside.
Wheelchair access: Possible to the ground floor.
Guidebook: Rather disappointing, poorly illustrated and containing little except ghost stories.
Catering: None.
WCs: One available, in the house bathroom; not for wheelchairs.
Shop: None.

CLITHEROE CASTLE Clitheroe (Clitheroe Borough Council)
Tel: Clitheroe (0200) 24635 (Museum), or 25111 (Council offices)
Directions: Clitheroe is 16 miles N.W. of Preston off the A59, the castle is in the town centre

Clitheroe is a ruined Norman castle, probably built in the late 11th century, with one of the smallest keeps in the country, only 35 feet square. It has lost all its floors, but the keep still dominates the town from its position on an outcrop. The other parts of the original castle were mostly destroyed in the Civil War. The present buildings in the outer bailey are thought to have been designed in the 1740s by the Duke of Montagu, who owned Clitheroe at the time, and are an early example of the revival of interest in mediaeval architecture. Since 1981 these buildings have housed a Heritage Centre and the Castle Museum, whose exhibits about local archaeology and history are being steadily expanded. The grounds serve as the town park.

Opening times: Keep open at all times. Museum and Heritage Centre Easter to end Sept, Tues, Thurs, Sat and Sun 2–4.30; also Bank Holidays, last two weeks of July and all of Aug, daily 2–4.30.
Entrance charges: (1981) Keep free. Museum 15p; Heritage Centre 10p; accompanied children free.
Parking: It is usually possble to find parking space nearby in the town.
Wheelchair access: Difficult, but a steep road does wind up to the museum.
Guidebook: A reasonably full historical account of the castle, the museum is not covered.
Catering: Snacks and ice creams available in the castle grounds.
WCs: Opposite the museum, only fair.
Shop: None.
Extras: Municipal bowling green, tennis courts and playground in the castle grounds.

GAWTHORPE HALL Padiham, nr Burnley (The National Trust)
Tel: Padiham (0282) 78511
Directions: 3 miles N.W. of Burnley centre, on the eastern outskirts of Padiham off the A671

Gawthorpe was built between 1600 and 1605 for the Rev Lawrence Shuttleworth. It has been suggested that Robert Smythson may have designed the original house, but it is certain that Sir Charles Barry, architect of the Houses of Parliament, restored it rather thoroughly in the early 1850s for James Kay-Shuttleworth. Yet Gawthorpe remains an important Jacobean house. It is very tall and compact and is built round a square tower, which may be older than the rest of the building, although the top of the tower was added by Barry. The plan of the house is unusual because the servants' rooms are in the basement and the great hall is at the back rather than the front. The building is now used as an educational centre and some rooms are occasionally closed to visitors. The drawing room has a good original plaster ceiling and panelling, and the hall has original woodwork although the ceiling is an imitation by Barry. The best room is the long gallery which runs the full width of the second floor and has not only the original ceiling but a massive overmantel dated 1603. The main rooms are furnished with items which are approximately contemporary with the house, but there is also the Rachael Kay-Shuttleworth Collection of textiles, mainly 19th and 20th century work of considerable interest. There are no guided tours and visitors may take their time in the house.

Opening times: 17 March to end Oct, Wed, Sat and Sun and Bank Holiday Mon, also Tues in July and Aug 2–6. Craft Gallery open daily except Mon 2–5.
Entrance charges: 80p; children 40p. Craft Gallery free.
Parking: Free parking in stable courtyard.
Wheelchair access: Possible to ground floor (i.e. the main rooms but not the Kay-Shuttleworth collection); also to the basement by arrangement.
Guidebook: Reasonably informative about the house and the Shuttleworth family, but short on information about the furniture; black and white illustrations and full plans of the house.
Catering: Teas served Sat and Sun only 3–5 in the old basement kitchen; pleasant food in interesting surroundings.
WCs: Well-maintained; facilities for wheelchairs.
Shop: In the coach house, a fairly large National Trust shop with an emphasis on the Crafts.
Extras: Next to the shop is the Craft Gallery with displays of lace, embroidery, woven and printed shawls and other aspects of the textile craft from all over the world.

HOGHTON TOWER   Hoghton, nr Preston (Sir Bernard de Hoghton Bt)
Tel: Hoghton (025 485) 2986
Directions: 6 miles E. of Preston, 4 miles W. of Blackburn

Hoghton is a fortified house in a splendid position on top of a hill, and it looks very dramatic from the steep main drive. Thomas Hoghton began building his new house in the 1560s, but it was probably not finished until the following century. The main living rooms are built round an inner courtyard, while the service buildings, stables, wellhouse and gatehouse, form an outer court. Between the two courts there was originally a great tower, which gave the house its name, but this was burnt down in the Civil

War. The de Hoghton family still own the house, but abandoned it for a time in the last century. The buildings needed major restoration in the later 19th century to make them habitable and the interior is now less evocative of the 17th century heyday of Hoghton than the guides and guidebook claim. The furniture and paintings are also slightly disappointing because many of the best things were destroyed in a 19th century fire. But there is still plenty to see. Most of the main rooms of the inner courtyard are open to visitors and many of them have excellent 19th century woodwork. The largest is the great hall where King James I knighted a piece of beef in 1617 — hence Sirloin. There is also Jacobean and later 17th century furniture and a good collection of dolls and dolls' houses. The walled gardens beside the house and the park are also open.

Opening times: Easter Sat, Sun and Mon, then Sun thereafter until end Oct, also Sat and Sun in July and Aug and all Bank Holidays, 2–5.
Entrance charges: £1.00; children under 14 25p. (HHA)
Parking: In front of house, 20p.
Wheelchair access: Only possible to the gardens.
Guidebook: A history of the house and family, very small print, good plans of the building, some colour pictures, nothing about the furniture.
Catering: Passable teas in the south wing of the house tea and coffee by the pot or cup, scones, fresh cream, pies etc.
WCs: In the outer courtyard, over-used; access possible for wheelchairs.
Shop: Craft and souvenir shop in the house; pottery, baskets and knick-knacks.

LANCASTER CASTLE Lancaster
Tel: Lancaster (0524) 64998
Directions: In the centre of Lancaster, the entrance is opposite the Priory

The castle at Lancaster occupies an impressive position by the river. There was a Roman fort here and the site still contains the prison and Crown Courts. The prison is, of course, not accessible to visitors, and the court rooms are only open to view when the courts are not in session. Of the mediaeval castle, the most impressive remains are the Norman keep, built in about 1100 and the great gatehouse of 1400; there are also several smaller towers, but most of the original walls have ben demolished. In 1788 the architect Thomas Harrison made a scheme for adapting the castle to serve as the Shire Hall. Harrison's buildings were begun soon after, but they were finished in the early 19th century by another architect, Joseph Gandy. The Shire Hall and Crown Court both have fine 18th century Gothic interiors and the walls are hung with colourful coats of arms. Among the more grisly sights are the holdfast (to hold criminals' hands steady for branding), the dungeons, and also the Drop-Room, where prisoners were pinioned before being executed. The guided tour takes between half and one hour.

Opening times: Easter Holiday, then Whitsun to end Sept, 10.30–4.30. It is essential to telephone beforehand to discover whether the Courts are in session, when only a shortened tour is available.

Entrance charges: (1981) Full tour 50p; children 25p. Half-tour 35p; children 20p; no photographs.

Parking: Roadside parking outside castle, sometimes difficult.

Wheelchair access: Not practicable.

Guidebook: A fairly thorough and inexpensive guide to the existing buildings. There is pre-recorded commentary in each room, but it is often inaudible.

Catering: None.

WCs: Public lavatory on the first floor.

Shop: Postcards and slides in the shop at the end of the tour.

LEIGHTON HALL Yealand Conyers, nr Carnforth (Mr and Mrs R.G. Reynolds)

Tel: Carnforth (0524) 734474

Directions: 8 miles N. of Lancaster, off the A6, to the W. of Yealand Conyers

Leighton Hall has a setting as fine as any in Lancashire; the brilliant white limestone house looks startling against a background of wooded hills and the mountains of the Lake District. An older house was largely rebuilt in 1765 for George Townley by a carpenter named John Hird in a chaste classical style. Harrison of Chester made the house Gothick by adding battlements and pinnacles and giving the stables in the wing a tall pointed chapel window. Another small wing, consisting of a tower in early 17th century style, was added in 1870 by the local architects Paley & Austin. Visitors are conducted round the principal rooms on both floors. The main entrance hall is Gothick and is divided from the elegant curving stair by a delicate arched screen. The drawing room has good paintings and furniture but is chiefly memorable for its view across the gardens to the mountains. The dining room was originally a billiard room and still has its central skylight. Much of the furniture in these two rooms and in one of the principal bedrooms is early work by the famous firm of Gillow of Lancaster, one of the leading English furniture makers in the 18th and early 19th century. Leighton was purchased in 1822 by Richard Gillow, the son of the firm's founder, and it is still occupied by the same family. The gardens and grounds are open to visitors. Eagles and other raptors are flown in the park most afternoons if the weather is right and sometimes the guided tours of the house wait on the return of the birds.

Opening times: House and grounds, May to Sept, Sun, Tues, Wed, Thurs 2–5, last tour 4.30.

Entrance charges: House and grounds £1.00; children 70p. Grounds only 70p and 60p. (HHA)

Parking: Free parking, ample space about 75 yards from the house.

Wheelchair access: The usual pedestrian approach is by way of a cattle grid and a gravel drive, but if wheelchair users are driven to the front door the ground floor rooms would be accessible; the garden can also be reached.

Guidebook: Well-produced booklet which gives the basic information about the house, furniture and owners, no plan, but some early drawings of the house.
Catering: Home-made teas in ground floor kitchen area; in good weather one can sit outside in the sheltered courtyard which is very pleasant.
WCs: Adequate and clean.
Shop: In the music room at the end of the tour of the house, a small selection of gifts.
Extras: The birds of prey are included in the entrance fee. There is also a large American dolls' house on temporary loan, admission charge 30p, children 20p.

RUFFORD OLD HALL Rufford (The National Trust)
Tel: Rufford (0704) 821254
Directions: 5 miles W. of the M6, 6 miles N.N.E. of Ormskirk on the A59

Until 1936 Rufford was the home of the Hesketh family. The most ancient part of the house is the timber-framed great hall, a fine example of the richly ornamented 'black and white' buildings of the north west. The two original wings of the hall have disappeared, but on one side is a brick wing of 1662 and the angle between the hall and wing was built up in 1821. Visitors enter by the 1662 wing and make their own way through to the hall. It is one of the most impressive mediaeval halls in England. The massive timber roof has carved decoration, the walls have quatrefoil panels and at the 'high' end of the room is a coved canopy, behind which a priest's hole was found during restoration work in 1949. But the most famous feature of the hall is the screen, said to be the only moveable screen still surviving complete. It is a massive object with three barbaric carved pinnacles unlike any other English decoration. The hall, together with the dining room and the drawing room on the first floor, are furnished with 17th century wood furniture and arms and armour from Lord Hesketh's collection, which was given to the Trust with the house. Several rooms in the 1662 wing are filled with the Rufford Village Museum, a collection of everyday objects to be found in rural Lancashire from the Stone Age until the middle of the last century. The house has extensive gardens which are well planted and tended.

Opening times: March to 22 Dec, Tues to Sun and Bank Holiday Mon 1–6; also closed Wed in March, Oct, Nov and Dec.
Entrance charges: £1.10; children 55p. Gardens only 40p and 20p.
Parking: Free parking 30 yards from the entrance.
Wheelchair access: The ground floor, including the hall, can be reached if a few stairs can be negotiated. Possible to garden.
Guidebook: Good on the history of the house and contains a plan, but details of the contents are lacking; black and white illustrations. there is also a guide and 'discovery sheets' for children.
Catering: Good teas on the ground floor of the 1662 wing, either full afternoon tea, or the separate components (tea, scones, jam).
WCs: At the back of the house in the courtyard; wheelchair access possible.
Shop: Next to the tea shop, small, but up to the usual National Trust standards.

Rufford Old Hall, Lancashire

SAMLESBURY HALL Samlesbury, nr Preston (Samlesbury Hall Trust)
Tel: Mellor (025 481) 2010 or 2229
Directions: 4 miles E. of Preston centre on the A677, just E. of the junction
with the A59, M6 junction 31

The Hall stands close to the main road. It is first cousin to Rufford Old Hall,
a 15th century timber-framed house with a 'black and white' exterior, in this
case much more black than white. Of the original house a part of the great
hall survives, and the whole of the long south wing which contained
apartments. The buildings were heavily restored in 1835, when the entire
western side of the wing was rebuilt in brick, and there are also 19th century
outbuildings which form a pleasant courtyard behind the great hall
Samlesbury is now an exhibition centre and antique shop run by the Council
for the Preservation of Rural England. Visitors have access to the hall and
the rooms on both floors of the south wing, including the chapel and a first
floor long gallery formed out of several smaller rooms. There is no furniture
of special interest, although the hall contains the remains of a fantastic
screen like that at Rufford, which is dated 1532. The grounds are pleasantly
neat and tidy; they include an archery field and a old water garden which is
now a nature reserve with a nature trail.

Opening times: All year, daily except Mon, 9 Feb to 28 March and 26 Oct to 31 Dec 11.30–
4.40; March to 24 Oct 11.30–5. Open Bank Holiday Mon.
Entrance charges: 60p; children under 16 30p.
Parking: Free parking near the house.
Wheelchair access: Possible to the ground floor rooms (the most interesting part of the
building) and to the restaurant.
Guidebook: A free leaflet with a brief history of the buildings and plans.
Catering: Home-made soup, savouries and teas; good quality, reasonably-priced food in
pleasant surroundings; open 11.30 for tea and coffee, 12 noon for meals, closes 4.30.
WCs: Very good; accessible to wheelchairs.
Shop: Antiques for sale in most rooms, also special exhibitions which sometimes have items
for sale.
Extras: The nature trail, mainly for children, has a descriptive leaflet.

THURNHAM HALL Thurnham, nr Lancaster (Mr and Mrs S.H.
Crabtree)
Tel: Galgate (0524) 751766
Directions: 6 miles S. of Lancaster on the A588 Lancaster–Cockerham
road; from M6 junction 33 follow signs for Glasson Dock

The stone front of the house with its battlements and turrets dates from
1823, and the small chapel to one side from 1845, but behind the front is a
building of the 16th century or even earlier. Sadly, Thurnham was allowed
to decay for many years before the present owner set about a complete
restoration in 1973 and the work is still not finished. At the start of the
guided tour, which is conducted by the owners, visitors are shown

photographs of the repair work which has been carried out. The tour covers the hall, with its simple 16th century ceiling and panelling of the same period brought from another house, a sturdy 17th century staircase, a gallery and one bedroom. At the back of the bedroom fireplace is a priest's hole, a reminder that the Dalton family of Thurnham were Roman Catholics. The Victorian chapel has a small private gallery which now contains a permanent exhibition about the Turin shroud (for which an extra charge is made).

Opening times: April (from Good Friday), May, Sept, Oct, Mon to Thurs 2–5, Sun 11–5; June, July, Aug, Mon to Fri 2–5, Sun 11–5.
Entrance charges: 90p; OAPs 80p; children 40p. (HHA)
Parking: Free parking in front of the house.
Wheelchair access: Very limited.
Guidebook: Good illustrations but short on information about the building.
Catering: Home-made teas in the old kitchen of the house with its splendid dresser; pleasant surroundings and a good tea.
WCs: Only one for all visitors, next to the shop.
Shop: Selection of souvenirs, gifts, brasses etc. in office entrance.
Extras: The exhibition on the Turin shroud costs 50p (1980).

TOWNELEY HALL ART GALLERY AND MUSEUMS Burnley
(Burnley Borough Council)
Tel: Burnley (0282) 24213
Directions: ½ mile S.E. of Burnley centre on the A646 Burnley–Todmorden road

The house stands in large grounds. It is a sombre grey stone building with towers and spindly battlements typical of the early 19th century, but these are only the last of a series of additions to the mediaeval house of the Towneley family. The house originally had a central courtyard, but the eastern side was demolished in about 1700. In 1725 Richard Towneley made improvements to the great hall in the centre of the house and gave the west side of the hall its present heavy-looking front with massively rusticated door and windows. More extensive alterations were made for Peregrine Towneley between 1814 and 1820 under the direction of the architect Jeffry Wyatt. It was during this period that the towers were added and the large windows made in the south east wing. The house now serves as Burnley's Art Gallery. The most impressive room is the great hall with very fine early Georgian stucco decoration by the Italian Andrea Vassalli. From the hall an 18th century cantilevered stair leads to the long gallery, a fine early 17th century room, although lacking the painted portraits which were once set into its panelling. The furniture in these and other main rooms has been collected by the gallery since 1901 and is arranged in a domestic way and not like a museum. But the upper floor of the north west wing is purely a picture gallery and has several good 19th century paintings and also a painting by

Zoffany of Charles Towneley, whose collection of antique sculpture forms the basis of the collection now in the British Museum. The chapel in the house has a very fine 16th century carved reredos from the Netherlands. The museum collections are extensive and there is a great deal to see. An old brew house in the grounds to the east of the main hall has been converted into a museum of local crafts and industries, and there is also an ice-house, which can be inspected by prior arrangement.

Opening times: All year, Mon to Fri 10–5.30 (winter 5.15), Sun 12–5; closed Sat, Christmas Day, Boxing Day and New Year's Day.
Entrance charges: Free.
Parking: Free parking near the house.
Wheelchair access: Level access can be provided through a back door on request, thereafter most of the ground floor can be seen.
Guidebook: i) The official guidebook has poor illustrations and a rambling text, but an improved edition is in preparation. ii) The guide to the museum of local crafts is better on both counts. iii) An Introduction to the Architecture of Towneley Hall; lots of plans and other information about the house, but expensive at £1.50.
Catering: In the stable block; the interior and the food are both uninspired, but it is possible to sit outside with one's plastic cup of tea.
WCs: To the east of the house, adequate; wheelchair access possible.
Shop: Postcards and booklets sold in entrance hall.
Extras: The usual municipal amusements in the park (pitch and putt, tennis, bowls).

TURTON TOWER
Tel: Turton (0204) 852203
Directions: Off the B6391 just S. of Turton village

Turton Tower stands on the edge of a wood between Blackburn and Bolton. The core of the house is a 15th century stone tower, which peers over the top of a sprawl of later additions, partly stone and partly timber, and of various dates. There are three large rooms in the tower and a number of smaller ones furnished with a mixture of old English oak furniture and some heavy Victorian pieces. The top floor of the tower is a museum of armour and other bits and pieces. Visitors can wander at will, but the narrow and steep staircases could easily clog up if the house was at all crowded.

Opening times: All year, Sat to Wed 12–6.
Entrance charges: (1981) 25p; children 10p.
Parking: Free parking a few yards from the house.
Wheelchair access: Not a practicable proposition as there are steps between most rooms.
Guidebook: The text is mainly concerned with the various owners of the building, and there is little about the building itself; good plan and coloured and black and white illustrations. Nothing at all about the contents.
Catering: None.
WCs: Inside the house, small, free.
Shop: None.

Leicestershire

BELGRAVE HALL Thurcaston Road, Leicester (Leicestershire Museums Service)
Tel: Leicester (0533) 554100
Directions: 2 miles N. of the centre of Leicester, off the A6 near the ring road

The house stands in a peaceful leafy turning on the fringes of Leicester's tedious suburbs. It was built for Edmund and Anne Cradock, whose initials appear on the rainwater heads, together with the dates 1709 and 1713. Next to the road is a fine iron gateway, but the house itself is rather bald and every side looks like the back. The museum has furnished the rooms on the ground and first floors to illustrate life in a moderately well-to-do 18th century English house. The interior decoration is appropriate, with plain painted panelling and a handsome staircase with twisted balusters. The drawing room and dining room contain some fine furniture notably the red lacquer bureau and the set of early 18th century mahogany chairs with embroidered covers in the drawing room. The other rooms include a large kitchen, a work room, a music room, several bedrooms and a nursery. The arrangements are well done but in the main rooms visitors are restricted to a small area near the door. The original front garden has become a separate park, but the garden at the rear still belongs to the house and is pleasantly laid out in a series of small enclosures. The stables have a collection of horse harnesses, farm implements and a very fine example of a mid 18th century coach.

Opening times: All year daily except Fri and 25–26 Dec and Good Friday 10–5.30, Sun 2–5.30.
Entrance charges: Free (but no unaccompanied children in garden at weekends).
Parking: Free parking in front of the house.
Wheelchair access: Possible to the ground floor (which has the best furniture) and also to the large garden at the back, which is entered through the house.
Guidebook: New guidebook in preparation.
Catering: None.
WCs: None in the house.
Shop: Only a few publications.

BELVOIR CASTLE nr Grantham (The Duke of Rutland)
Tel: Knipton (047 682) 262
Directions: 7 miles W.S.W. of Grantham between the A52 and A607

It is easy to see how Belvoir Castle got its name for it stands on the top of a ridge with magnificent views across the Belvoir Vale. The mediaeval castle has gone and there is nothing to be seen of the great classical house of the

Belvoir Castle, Leicestershire

1650s designed by John Webb for the Eighth Earl of Rutland, except a wooden model in the ballroom. The present castle is a Gothic fantasy of the early 19th century built for the Fifth Duke just after his coming of age. James Wyatt was employed as architect, but he died in 1813 and much of his work was destroyed by fire three years later. The castle was completed for the second time under the supervision of the Duke's friend Sir John Thoroton, who employed Wyatt's son Benjamin to design the interiors. The work was finished in 1830. Visitors take themselves round a set route through the main rooms. The first of these, the guard room, entrance hall, great staircase and ballroom, are all in a cold and cavernous Gothic which Sir John copied from Lincoln Cathedral. They are decorated with arms and armour and there is more of this in the 17th/21st Lancers Museum at the top of the stairs. After a bedroom and dressing room in the Chinese style comes the immensely opulent Elizabeth Saloon, with its gilded and painted ceiling, French gilt wall carvings and French furniture and carpet. The room was named after Elizabeth, Duchess of Rutland, whose white marble statue stands in the room. The dining room is cavernous and cold, but the picture gallery beyond it has a fine vaulted ceiling and contains several great treasures. There are paintings by Poussin, Holbein and Gainsborough, miniatures by Hilliard and Oliver and also a great 17th century state bed with its original hangings of Venetian velvet. After the King's Rooms, fitted out for George IV when Prince Regent, comes the Regent's Gallery, the principal surviving room from James Wyatt's house. The room is over 130 feet long with a great bow in the centre. Its decoration is slightly less ornate than the later rooms, but the ceiling beams are carved and gilded and the walls are hung with tapestry. There are yet more rooms after this, including the chapel, the kitchen and the cellars, for those who have the stamina. Only a part of the garden is open and it is not possible to see the whole exterior of the building.

Opening times: 31 March to 2 Oct, Wed, Thurs and Sat 12–6, Sun 2–7; Sun in June, July and Aug 12–7, Bank Holiday Mon 11–7, Bank Holiday Tues and Good Friday 12–6, also Sun in Oct 2–6.

Entrance charges: £1.50; children 80p; no dogs. (HHA)

Parking: Free car park at the bottom of the hill, there is a very steep climb up to the castle but elderly or disabled may be driven closer; ask at ticket office or telephone.

Wheelchair access: Difficult; although wheelchair users can be driven to the door there are steps inside the castle.

Guidebook: A brief history at the back, otherwise a fully illustrated room-by-room tour describing the decoration and contents of the rooms; no plan but there is an aerial view of the castle.

Catering: A large, low tea room in the basement (which can only be reached through the house). Self-service, salads, snacks, filled rolls, tea in plastic cups, commercial cakes.

WCs: Inside the house near the tea room, free, old fashioned and well-kept. There are more lavatories on the terrace outside.

Shop: In the basement at the end of the route through the house there are two souvenir shops selling dolls trimmed with Nottinghamshire lace and a large range of cheap souvenirs.

DONNINGTON-LE-HEATH MANOR HOUSE nr Coalville
(Leicestershire Museums Service)
Tel: Coalville (0530) 31259
Directions: 13 miles N.W. of Leicester, 1 mile S.W, of Coalville off the
A50

This small stone building dates from about 1280 and is probably the oldest
house in Leicestershire. It has been fully restored by the County Council in
recent years. The house is a small rectangular block with the hall on the first
floor and the great kitchen below. There are two small wings at the back. A
few alterations have been made; the outside staircase to the hall no longer
exists and some mullioned windows were inserted in the 17th century, but
despite its present over-tidy appearance it is not difficult to visualise the
building in its original state. Visitors make their own way round. The
kitchen is convincingly furnished, but the other rooms contain little except
a few pieces of 16th and 17th century oak furniture and photographs of the
restoration work in progress. The house itself is the main exhibit. There is a
pleasant garden of flat lawns and rosebeds, and an old barn which has also
been restored to serve as a hall and tea room.

Opening times: Wed before Easter to 1 Oct, Wed, Thurs, Fri, Sat, Sun, Bank Holiday Mon
and Tues 2–6.
Entrance charges: Free.
Parking: Car park in grounds.
Wheelchair access: There are shallow steps from the road to the garden and only a small part
of the inside of the house would be accessible.
Guidebook: A fairly thorough description of the house and its restoration, with illustrations
and a plan.
Catering: Self-service tea room in the barn, dispensing tea by the pot, toasted tea cakes, crisps,
etc.; there is a very pleasant garden terrace outside accessible to wheelchairs.
WCs: In the barn, new; not for wheelchair users.
Shop: Inside the house selling mainly literature about Leicestershire history.

KIRBY MUXLOE CASTLE Kirby Muxloe, nr Leicester (Ancient
Monument)
Directions: 4 miles W. of Leicester midway between the A47 and A50,
signposted

The castle is a attractive ruin on the edge of the village. Within the moat one
corner tower and the gatehouse still stand, but the walls and the other towers
are merely stumps. Kirby had a sad and short life. It was begun in 1480 for
William, Lord Hastings, a rich and respected nobleman and supporter of
the Yorkist King Edward IV. Three years later he was suddenly executed by
Richard III for suspected treason and his new castle was never finished. It
was a typical late 15th century castle, with a rectangular curtain wall,
defended by towers at regular intervals and surrounded by a moat. The
main living rooms were built against the inner side of the walls. The outer

face of the walls has brick patterning, including a curious mediaeval shape which was the badge of Lord Hastings. The accounts for the building work have survived and it is possible to trace every step of the process. The chief masons were John Cowper and Robert Staynforth and a Dutchman called Antony Yzebrond was employed to supervise the making of the bricks of which the castle was built. There are also references to 'murder holes', probably meaning the key-hole openings for cannon which can be seen in the gatehouse walls.

Opening times: Standard hours (S), see page xii.
Entrance charges: 40p; children 20p.
Parking: Free car park by entrance gate.
Wheelchair access: Level access across the moat bridge to the castle site is not difficult; the site itself is mostly grassed.
Guidebook: A good Official Handbook with a history, description and plan of the castle; there are large extracts from the building accounts to show how a building of this kind was constructed.
Catering: None.
WCs: None.
Shop: Postcards and guidebooks only.

LANGTON HALL West Langton, nr Market Harborough
  (G.R. Spencer Esq)
Tel: East Langton (085 884) 240
Directions: 4½ miles N.N.W. of Market Harborough, off the A6

Langton is a fairly small country house. The north wing was built in 1550 but the central part of the building dates from the 1660s. A new south front, two and a half storeys high, was added towards the end of the 18th century and in the early 19th century battlements and gothic windows were added to make the house more picturesque. The entrance hall inside is also Gothic in style but the other main rooms have simple 18th century cornices and plain ceilings. The furnishings are an unexpected mixture of French and Oriental. There are heavy French chimney pieces, and 17th and 18th century French furniture in the Large Drawing Room. The small drawing room has more Louis XV furniture and its walls are completely covered with Venetian lace, which was applied in the late 18th century. There is also a large Coromandel screen which gives a foretaste of the best furniture in the house. This is in the dining room and consists of some extremely rare and beautiful Chinese rosewood chests and altar tables. Visitors are guided round the house. It is surrounded by some of the finest fox-hunting country in the world; indeed Hugo Meynell, founder of the famous Quorn Hunt, lived at Langton. It is appropriate that the outbuildings at Langton should have become a 'raptor centre' for the breeding and care of birds of prey. The birds can be seen in their mews and spectacular flying demonstrations are given on the lawn.

Opening times: Good Friday to 3 Oct, Thurs, Sat, Sun and Bank Holiday Mon and Tues 2–5.
Entrance charges: £1.20; children and OAPs 60p. (HHA)
Parking: Free parking in a field 100 yards from the house.
Wheelchair access: Possible to ground floor of house (which contains the best furniture), gardens and also to the raptor centre.
Guidebook: A new guide has just been printed.
Catering: Refreshments are available.
WCs: In the outbuildings.
Shop: A small souvenir and trinket shop inside the house.

LEICESTER: WYGSTON'S HOUSE Applegate
(Leicestershire Museums Service)
Tel: Leicester (0533) 554100
Directions: On the W. side of the city centre, fronting a pedestrian way adjacent to St Nicholas' Circle, a busy traffic system

The brick front of the house, facing a very busy street, dates from 1796. It is an elegant three-storey composition with giant pilasters at the corners. Behind the front range and at right angles to it is a timber framed building of the late 15th or early 16th century which is probably the oldest surviving house in the city. It may have been the home of Roger Wygston, a wool merchant, and it is now a museum. The whole of the ground floor front of the old house is occupied by a row of windows, once filled with painted glass. The glass has been preserved elsewhere. The upper floor is jettied out on ornamental brackets. There is not very much to see in the old part of the building except the structure of walls and roof, which is carefully exposed, but the 18th century part of the house contains a series of period rooms (18th, 19th and 20th centuries) and a display of garments from the Museum's costume collection. Tucked away in a back extension is a delightful part of the museum which consists of a complete shoe shop and a haberdasher's shop of the early years of this century.

Opening times: Daily except Fri 10–5.30, Sun 2–5.30; closed Good Friday and 25–26 Dec.
Entrance charges: Free.
Parking: No museum car park, but there is a pay car park in the centre of St Nicholas' Circle next to the museum; otherwise parking is difficult. Parking for the disabled in Carey's Close at rear of building.
Wheelchair access: Would be possible to the ground floor.
Catering: None.
WCs: Inside the house, well-maintained; no wheelchair access.
Shop: Postcards, literature and things to do with Leicestershire museums on sale; also leaflets on the costumes displayed in the museum.
Extras: Visitors to Wygston's House should not miss the very fine mediaeval Guildhall in Guildhall Lane opposite.

LYDDINGTON BEDE HOUSE Lyddington (Ancient Monument)
Directions: 7 miles S. of Oakham, 5 miles N. of Corby, ½ mile E. of the
 A6003

The Bede house, like many other houses in this quiet village, is built of the
local ironstone. It stands on the edge of the churchyard, a long building with
large mullioned windows and a steep roof. The house was built in the mid
15th century as a palace for the Bishop of Lincoln, and was probably much
larger than it is now. In 1602 it became a bedehouse or almshouse for old
men, and was divided up with wooden partitions, some of which have now
been removed. On the principal floor are two large rooms, the audience
chamber and private chamber of the bishop; they have 15th century painted
glass in the windows and very beautiful early 16th century wooden ceilings
with a delicate carved coving round the edge. Opening off the private
chamber is an inner chamber with a garderobe and a stone sink for the
bishop's private use. None of the rooms has any furniture, but the building
is well cared for and extremely attractive.

Opening times: Standard hours (S) April to Sept, see page xii.
Entrance charges: 40p; children and OAPs 20p.
Parking: Free parking in the village street.
Wheelchair access: Possible to see the outside, but not the main rooms.
Catering: None.
WCs: None.
Shop: Slides and postcards.

OAKHAM CASTLE Oakham (Leicestershire Museums Service)
Tel: Oakham (0572) 3654
Directions: Oakham is 18 miles E. of Leicester; the castle is in the town
 centre

Oakham Castle consists of only one building, the great hall. Everything else
is now hidden under the turf. The hall was probably built in about 1180 and
is historically very important as a well-preserved 12th century hall. It looks
rather like a towerless church, with nave and aisles. Inside there are two
stone arcades with elaborate stone capitals. The carving of these capitals and
of other features in the hall is very like that of the chancel of Canterbury
Cathedral, which dates from 1175, and this is the reason for dating the hall
to 1180. The building was restored in the last century and the main entrance
has been moved from its original position at one end to the centre of the
front, but inside the hall the triple doorways originally leading to the kichen,
pantry and buttery still survive. The walls of the hall are covered with horse-
shoes of many different sizes, because of a old custom that demanded that
any peer passing through Oakham should forfeit a horse-shoe to the Lord of
the Manor. To judge by the shoes some of the horses must have been larger
than elephants.

Opening times: April to Oct, Sun and Mon 2–5.30, Tues to Sat and Bank Holiday Mon 10–1, 2–5.30. Nov to March as above but closes at 4 every day. The hall may be closed for magistrates' court hearings usually held on Mon.
Entrance charges: Free.
Parking: In the town, not usually difficult.
Wheelchair access: No difficulty.
Guidebook: A free and very brief leaflet about the building; also publications on the horse-shoes and sculpture.
Catering: None.
WCs: None.
Shop: A small sales desk for publications and souvenirs.

QUENBY HALL Hungarton (The Squire de Lisle)
Tel: Hungarton (053 750) 224
Directions: 7 miles N.E. on minor roads, signposted from the A47

Quenby has a large and well-kept park which makes a suitable setting for the best Jacobean house in Leicestershire. It was built in about 1620 for George Ashby and it has been suggested that the designer may have been one of the famous Smythson family. Everything looks typically Jacobean; the three tall storeys are of red brick with diaper ornament and stone for the quoins and the mullion and transom windows. The plan is an H, with a three storey porch in the centre of the main front. From the outside nothing looks altered. Some rather drastic 18th century 'improvements' to the interior were tidied away by the great Victorian church architect G.F. Bodley, so the rooms also look Jacobean. The library has a fireplace brought from Garendon Hall, the former home of the present owner, and some 17th century oak furniture. The panelled dining room has an excellent original fireplace and is hung with family portraits. The best room on the ground floor is the Brown Parlour in the cross-wing which has very fine original carved panelling, a good plaster ceiling and furnishings which include pastel portraits by Rosalba Carriera, a leading practitioner of this art. The 17th century staircase leads to the ballroom, originally the great chamber, which has a 19th century ceiling copied from Knole in Kent and the massive carved chimneypiece which properly belongs to the hall below. There are a number of bedrooms, with interesting panelling and plasterwork, as well as modern embroidered hangings to the beds. The William and Mary Bedroom has an early 18th century state bed from St Donat's Castle, Wales. Visitors make their own way round and there are guides in each room. Circulation to some rooms is restricted by rope barriers. It is said that Stilton cheese was invented in the Quenby kitchen, to be sold, through a complex series of family connections, to the Landlord of The Bell at Stilton.

Opening times: 1 June to 30 Sept, Sun 2–6; also Bank Holiday Sun and Mon, April to Aug 2–6.
Entrance charges: £1; children 50p. (HHA)

Parking: Free parking on grass in front of the house.
Wheelchair access: There is a flight of steps to the entrance, but three rooms would be accessible thereafter.
Guidebook: A room-by-room guide and brief history of the families who have lived here, several illustrations, no plan.
Catering: Self-service teas in an outbuilding; tea by the pot, scones, cake etc. Pleasant surroundings.
WCs: Near the tea room, but unsuitable for wheelchairs.
Shop: At the entrance to the tea-room; souvenirs, some Stilton cheese, local pottery and toys; more original than many shops, desite its small size.

STANFORD HALL   Lutterworth (Lord and Lady Braye)
Tel: Swinford (078 885) 250
Directions: 7½ miles N.E. of Rugby, off the B5414; 3½ miles E. of the A5 (M1 exits 18 and 20; M6 exit 1)

Stanford is a large and gracious William and Mary house in an ample park next to the river Avon. The main front is of grey stone, with two storeys of tall sash windows and a deep hipped roof; the other sides are built of more homely brick. The house was begun in 1697 by Sir Roger Cave, as a replacement for the old family home close to the river. It was designed by William Smith of Warwick; William's brother Francis was responsible for many of the interiors and also designed the elegant red brick stable block next to the house. The guided tours take in most of the main ground floor rooms and two upstairs bedrooms. All are well-proportioned and most have their original panelling, fireplaces, doors and plaster ceilings. The great staircase has elegant turned balusters of three different patterns. The family furniture has never been dispersed, and there is a great feeling of continuity about the rooms, which are still in use. Noteworthy items include a collection of Stuart portraits and religious objects belonging to Cardinal Henry Stuart (King Henry IX to Jacobites) which was purchased by Baroness Braye in 1842 and is now displayed in the Ballroom. The Green Drawing Room has good 17th century English portraits and a collection of family portraits are hung on the stairs. In the Old Dining Room, towards the end of the tour, are several pieces of furniture brought from the previous house, including a mediaeval refectory table and several Charles I chairs. There is a great deal to see and the guides appear to be very well acquainted with the rooms on view. Percy Pilcher, the first man in England to fly, was tragically killed when his machine crashed at Stanford. In the stable block is a replica of his plane 'The Hawk' and some early photos of the first English flight. The large park is open to visitors and a nature trail has been devised round its edge.

Opening times: Easter Sun to end Sept, Thurs, Sat and Sun 2.30–6, also Bank Holiday Mon; grounds 12–6, house 2.30–6.
Entrance charges: House and grounds £1.20; children 55p. Grounds only 50p and 20p, payable at gate. (HHA)

Parking: Free parking on grass near the house.

Wheelchair access: Not practicable to interior of house, and it would be difficult to see all of the exterior.

Guidebook: A very adequate booklet with a general history and room-by-room guide, illustrations, but no plan. There is a charming story about ferrets being used to run the electricity wires under the floorboards in the 1890s. There is also a handbook to the nature trail in the grounds.

Catering: In the stable block, upstairs; amiable ladies serve tea and home-made cakes.

WCs: In the stable block, adequate but unsuitable for wheelchairs.

Shop: There is a souvenir shop in the basement of the house which can be reached without going on the tour; there are also several craft studios in the stables (pottery and knitted tea-cosies) whose products may be bought.

Extras. The stables house a motorcycle museum with a good collection of racing motorcycles; entrance charge.

STAPLEFORD PARK nr Melton Mowbray (Lord Gretton)
Tel: Wymondham (057 284) 245 and 229
Directions: 5 miles E. of Melton Mowbray, 1 mile S. of the B676, well-signposted

The usual way of approaching the house is by the miniature railway which runs from the car park and both railway and house are fine specimens. Stapleford was the home of the Sherard family from 1402 until 1885. The oldest surviving part is the small wing nearest the station which dates from 1500. It was repaired in 1633 by Lady Abigail Sherard, a lover of antiquities who covered the ouside with small statues and ornaments taken from other buildings. The main house dates from about 1680 and has the generous proportions and large hipped roofs typical of that time. The exception is the Jacobean-style south front of 1894, which was added for Mr Gretton shortly after he had bought the house. The guided tours take in most of the ground floor rooms and last about three quarters of an hour. The anteroom and the dining room (which was originally on the first floor) both have very heavy carved decoration of the 1680s, but several of the other rooms were re-done in the later 18th century and the drawing room is in an elegant late Victorian French manner. The furniture and carpet in this room are also French while the paintings include two Guardi's and a de Hooch. The Old Kitchen is a survivor from an earlier house and has a massive central pier with a table built round it. On the walls are portraits of Lady Abigail Sherard and her husband. The last room in the tour is the first floor long gallery in the 1894 part of the house. It was never finished, but the rough plaster of the walls makes a surprisingly good background for Dutch farmhouse furniture and Mortlake tapestries. As well as the house, visitors should make the effort to find the church, hidden by trees a short distance away. It was built in 1783 for the Fourth Earl of Harborough by George Richardson and is an impressive Gothick building with some good family tombs. Other parts of the grounds can be seen from the miniature railway, the fare for which and for the passenger boats on the lake, is included in the entrance charge.

Opening times: 11–15, 18 and 25 April, Sun and Bank Holiday Mon in May; June to Aug, Tues, Wed, Thurs, Sun and Bank Holiday Mon; Sept, Sun, Wed and Thurs, 1.30–6.30.

Entrance charges: (1981) £1.40; children 70p; includes entrance to house and rides on miniature train and boats. (HHA)

Parking: Free car park, about ¼ mile from house, but served by miniature railway.

Wheelchair access: Possible to all rooms shown except the first floor gallery. Disabled visitors can drive to the house and there is a ramp at the entrance.

Guidebook: A room-by-room guide with lists of the pictures, and a brief history of the family; it is a good read, and well illustrated, but lacks a plan of the house.

Catering: Sit-down teas in the former riding school. The same food can be had from a self-service hatch and eaten at tables in the garden. There is also a licensed snack bar in the car park.

WCs: In the house and in the car park; both fairly basic and neither suitable for wheelchair users.

Shop: Two small kiosks near the house sell souvenirs and a few pot plants.

Extras: The fare for the miniature transport system is included in the entrance fee. The Balston collection of Staffordshire figures, housed in one room of the house, is free to National Trust members but a small contribution is requested from others. 'Animal Land' and other amusements in the car park have separate charges.

Lincolnshire

ALFORD MANOR HOUSE FOLK MUSEUM   West Street, Alford
Tel: Alford (052 12) 2278
Directions: Alford is 25 miles N.E. of Boston. West Street leads out of the market square

The Manor house is an attractive three-storey thatched building, set back a little from the street. The original house was timber-framed, with a central hall and a cross-wing on each side, built in about 1540. Shortly after 1703 it was smartened up with a new brick front. The Manor House acts as a local folk museum and the rooms contain a variety of displays including a chemist's shop, a cobbler's, a railway ticket office and a veterinary surgery. there is a room devoted to Alford school founded in 1566, and a display about the history and travels of Captain John Smith, born at Willoughby, near Alford in 1580. Above and around these exhibits parts of the original structure can be seen. The museum overflows into the outhouses; there are local farm implements in the barn and early farm machinery, including a man-driven lathe in the scout house.

Opening times: May to Sept, Mon, Tues, Wed, Fri 10.30–1.00, 2–4.30.

Entrance charges: 25p; children 15p.

Parking: Free parking in town centre car park, ¼ mile from the house.

Wheelchair access: Possible to part of the house only.

Guidebook: A simple, informative, home-produced booklet which includes a plan.

Catering: Tea and biscuits on the lawn on Tuesdays and Fridays.

WCs: Behind the hall, reasonable; not suitable for wheelchairs.
Shop: Postcards, etc. sold in the entrance hall. The first floor of the house is used by the Lincolnshire and South Humberside Trust for Nature Conservation. Their wildlife gift shop is open all year during office hours.

ALLINGTON MANOR HOUSE Allington (Mr J.H. Palin)
Tel: Long Bennington (040 05) 358)
Directions: 5 miles N.W. of Grantham, off the A1 in Allington village, take the No Through Road by the pub

This Dutch-gabled house of local yellow ironstone dates from about 1660. It was unoccupied from the 1860s until the 1940s. The present owner, who uses the outhouses to make furniture and restore antiques, has rescued the building single-handed. There has been only one alteration to the house since the 17th century and that was on a small scale. The woodwork is in excellent condition from the cellar, which until recently housed an open drainage system, to the roof timbers. Visitors are shown over the whole house by the owner. Particular points of interest are the stone fireplaces and the 17th century staircase. The fascinating tour of the house ends with a stroll along the valley between the ridges of the roof.

Opening times: Normal business hours.
Entrance charges: Free; dogs allowed only if they do not fight with resident dog.
Parking: Free parking in drive.
Wheelchair access: Permitted, but only part of the house is accessible.
Guidebook: None.
Catering: None.
WCs: Behind the house, clean; unsuitable for wheelchairs.

BELTON HOUSE nr Grantham (Lord Brownlow)
Tel: The Administration Office, Grantham (0476) 66116
Directions: 2 miles N.E. of Grantham on the E. side of the A607

Belton, built for Sir John Brownlow between 1685 and 1688, is a magnificent example of a gentleman's house of the late 17th century. For many years Christopher Wren was thought to be the architect, but Captain William Winde now seems a more likely designer. The walls are of grey-gold Ancaster stone and the plan of the house is an H, the centre of the house, or cross-bar of the H, being two rooms deep. Both the main fronts are 11 windows wide with a pediment in the centre rising in front of the steeply-pitched roof. From outside Belton looks much as it did in the 1680s, apart from the surround of the front door, which was added by James Wyatt in 1777. A great deal of the original interior decoration has also survived. There are particularly splendid plaster ceilings by Edward Goudge in the Saloon, the Little Marble Hall, and the Chapel (his best work). The Library and Boudoir have ceilings by James Wyatt, who was responsible for giving the house a face-lift in the 1770s. Many of the rooms have panelled walls; in the Chapel Drawing Room the panels are painted dark green and gold in imitation of marble, making a rich background for the late 17th century English tapestries. In the Chapel and Marble Hall there is also some excellent woodcarving, probably by Edward Carpenter and well up to Grinling Gibbons's standard. The house contains an enormous amount of fine furniture, much of it of the same period as the house. The Blue Bedroom contains a 17th century bed with its original hangings and an early 18th century walnut bureau of the finest craftsmanship. The Tyrconnel room has a very unusual painted floor. The paintings in the house are a mixture of English portraits and Old Masters attributed to famous painters. There are guides in most of the rooms, but it would be helpful if more individual items were labelled. The park was laid out in the 18th century by William Eames. Its ornamental gardens have now been supplemented by a woodland playground for children.

Opening times: 9 April to 3 Oct, Tues to Sun and Bank Holiday Mons, grounds 12–5.30; house 2–5; museum 12–5.
Entrance charges: £1.50; OAPs and children 90p. (HHA)
Parking: Free parking in field 100 yards from the house.
Wheelchair access: Wheelchair users have free entry, and are given every assistance to see about half of the house.
Guidebook: Strong on family history, weaker on architectural history. Many illustrations, little about individual items, no plan of the house.
Catering: Licensed bar (normal licensing hours), snacks and meals (hot meals 12–2.30) all served in the Orangery or on tables outside. The cakes are home-made; hot meals of the plaice and chips variety. There is also a snack kiosk at the entrance to 'Jungleland'.
WCs: Excellent, old-fashioned, clean, free facilities in the Blue Bathroom near the end of the tour of the house. Not suitable for wheelchairs. More modern facilities at the rear of the house (entrance through garden).
Shop: At the end of the tour of the house, selling literature, trinkets, and confectionery. The garden shop next to the orangery sells plants, baskets etc.
Extras: Boat trips on the river, miniature steam railway trips, the Museum of the Horse, the National Cycle Museum and the Chilren's Adventure Jungleland (which is free).

BOURNE: THE RED HALL   (Bourne United Charities)
Tel: Bourne (077 82) 2387
Directions: 14 miles N. of Peterborough on the southern edge of Bourne; leaving Bourne on the A15 Peterborough road, turn right at the first double bend, by the library

The Red Hall has lost its status as the grand house of the town, and now has a warehouse on one side and a screen of modern buildings in front. The rectangular red brick house was built at the beginning of the 17th century for the Fisher family, perhaps to the designs of John Thorpe. It is not a large building; the main front has three steep gables of differing sizes, with a two-storey porch more or less in the centre. A large amount of restoration has been done in recent years to make the house suitable for use by the local community. The interior is somewhat bare, but at least it is cared for. Among the rooms open to visitors are the great chamber on the first floor and the gallery above it in which the roof timbers can be seen. The original staircase has turned balusters and tall newels. The few items of furniture include a 17th century chest on the ground floor and a carved 17th century screen in the gallery.

Opening times: All year, Mon to Fri 9–12.
Entrance charges: Free.
Parking: Free parking in the drive.
Wheelchair access: Only possible to the ground floor, where there is not a great deal to see.
Guidebook: A small pamphlet gives some history, but there is very little hard information about the building and its architecture.
Catering: None.
WCs: Downstairs, clean, free; not suitable for wheelchairs.
Shop: None.

DODDINGTON HALL Doddington (Mr and Mrs Antony Jarvis)
Tel: Doddington (052 274) 227
Directions: 5 miles W. of Lincoln on the B1190 in Doddington village

Like many Elizabethan great houses, Doddington stands in the centre of the village, close to the church and other lesser buildings. Behind the small gatehouse stretches a long red brick entrance front, three storeys high with projecting wings on each side. The front is symmetrical and without ornament, except for the carved porch and the three domed cupolas on the flat roof. The perfect balance of the front suggests a good architect and Doddington is probably the work of Robert Smythson, the designer of several major houses in the East Midlands, including Hardwick Hall in Derbyshire and Burton Agnes in Humberside. While the exterior has hardly changed since the time it was finished in 1600 none of the original decoration remains in any of the main rooms. The Brown Parlour has early 18th century panelling, but most of the other rooms are the work of a Lincoln carpenter called Thomas Lumby who refurbished the house in 1760–5 for Sir John Hussey Delaval. His are the simple plaster ceilings and the rich overmantels and doorcases. He also blocked the windows on one side of the long gallery on the top floor. There are a number of notable furnishings. In the White Hall is a set of Cromwellian bobbin-turned chairs and two large 16th century Venetian chests. The Holly Room is hung with 17th century Flemish tapestries and the long gallery has a diverse collection of 17th and 18th century porcelain. The house has never been sold since it was built and besides the accumulated furniture contains a continuous sequence of family potraits, many of good quality. Visitors may take their own time in the rooms and in the pleasant gardens outside.

Opening times: May to Sept, Sun, Wed and Bank Holiday Mon 2–6.
Entrance charges: £1.10; children (under 14) 55p. Gardens half price. (HHA)
Parking: Free parking in a field over the road from the house.
Wheelchair access: Possible to downstairs rooms only (about one third of the rooms on view).
Guidebook: A recent (1980) guide with a room-by-room description and a brief history of the family. Many colour illustrations, no plan, but a useful bird's eye view of house and gardens.
Catering: Small tea room in a converted 17th century building with its own garden; acceptable tea, scones and cakes.
WCs: Small, temporary-style facilities near garden exit; not suitable for wheelchairs.
Shop: In the entrance lodge, sells literature and souvenirs and ice cream.

FYDELL HOUSE South Street, Boston (The Boston Preservation Trust)
Tel: Boston (0205) 51520
Directions: South Street leads out of the Market Place, Fydell House is next to the Guildhall

This substantial town house stands back a little from the business of South Street behind an ironwork screen and gateway. The front is six bays wide, with a giant order of pilasters and a heavy parapet. The pedimented front door is squashed between two small round-headed windows. The house was built in 1726 for William Fydell; a plaque in front says the architect was Henry Bell of King's Lynn, but he died in 1713. It is more likely that the designer was a local man such as William Sands of Spalding. The house is now used by a college of further education. Inside, the main attractions are some fine original panelling, interesting Rococo plasterwork and a superb mahogany staircase with carved balusters of three different types.

Opening times: All year during term time, Mon to Fri 11.30–4.30 or by appointment with the Boston Preservation Trust. Rooms in use for teaching are not shown to visitors.
Entrance charges: Free.
Parking: Cheap on-street parking in South Street, 100 yards from the house.
Wheelchair access: Not practicable.
Guidebook: None.
Catering: None.
WCs: Under the stairs, free, adequate.
Shop: None.

GAINSBOROUGH: THE OLD HALL (Lincolnshire County Museums Service)
Tel: Gainsborough (0427) 2669
Directions: In the centre of Gainsborough, well-signposted

The Old Hall rises up grandly out of dreary urban surroundings, proclaiming itself to be a late mediaeval house of the first importance. Sir Thomas Burgh's mansion was burnt down in 1470, but had been sufficiently rebuilt by 1484 for him to entertain King Richard III there. It was originally a courtyard house; the north range of buildings containing the great hall and the kitchen still survives, the east and west sides were built in the 1590s by William Kickman, and the south side has completely disappeared. The exterior is a confusion of stone, brick and timber-framed walls. The west side of the west wing, with its four tall projections housing chimneys and lavatories for the lodgings inside, is a dramatic sight. The chief glory of the interior is the great hall, of enormous size, with its original arch-braced roof and the bay window at the high end. Even more unusual is the survival of the mediaeval catering facilities; the buttery, servery, cellar and kitchen on the west side of the hall are all more or less intact. The kitchen is possibly the most complete mediaeval kitchen in England. Besides the hall and kitchen, the guided tour takes in a number of other rooms in the north and east wings, including the main living rooms which were altered in the 1840s. Several of the rooms house displays of local archaeology and similar subjects, but otherwise the building is scantily furnished.

Opening times: All year, Mon to Sat 10–5; Easter to Oct Sun 2–5.
Entrance charges: 50p; children and OAPs 20p; dogs on leads and cameras allowed.
Parking: Free parking for up to two hours next to the Hall.
Wheelchair access: Ramps for all downstairs rooms, which includes the best parts of the tour.
Guidebook: A cheap room-by-room guide and history, with a good plan of the ground floor; adequate, but would be better with more precise information about the structure of the building.
Catering: Light refreshments on Tues afternoons only.
WCs: Free and clean, at end of entrance corridor; no wheelchair access.
Shop: Cards and prints sold at entrance.

GUNBY HALL Burgh le Marsh (The National Trust)
Directions: 2½ miles N.W. of Burgh le Marsh, 7 miles W. of Skegness on the S. side of the A158

The red brick front of Gunby is quite plain, except for the doorcase which has an elaborate pediment and a keystone dated 1700. To the north is a lower two-storey wing added in 1873, but in the style of the older building. Entrance to the house is now from the stable courtyard by way of the wing. Since the beginning of the 18th century Gunby has been the home of the Massingberds, although the property has many times descended through the female line to Langton-Massingberds and Montgomery-Massingberds, and the contents of the main rooms have been gathered by the family over the last 300 years. Only four ground floor rooms and the main staircase are shown. In the old house, the library and the dining room have been formed in fairly recent times by combining smaller rooms. The fine staircase with its twisted balusters is probably original but the staircase window is somewhat later. Prominent in the library is the large scrapwork screen made by Field Marshall Sir Archibald Montgomery-Massingberd, who died in 1947, and the walls of the staircase are hung with family portraits, including Emily Caroline Massingberd a celebrated campaigner for women's rights. But the greatest treasures are to be found in the large panelled drawing room in the north wing. Here is some fine Jacobean furniture, two good portraits by Sir Joshua Reynolds and miniatures of members of the royal house of Stuart. The excellent guided tours which start every hour (sometimes more frequently) allow plenty of time to look at everything and there are no barriers. There is a large garden, including a luxuriant walled garden with vegetables, fruit trees and herbaceous flowers in vigorous profusion.

Opening times: April to end Sept, Thurs 2–6.
Entrance charges: 90p; children 45p. Garden only 65p and 30p.
Parking: Free parking near the house.
Wheelchair access: Not practicable to house, there is a steep flight of steps to the entrance; the gardens are easily accessible.
Guidebook: An elegant account which is much better on the family than the house; indeed the description of the interior is scanty; no plan.
Catering: None.
WCs: In the coutyard, adequate, but not for wheelchairs.
Shop: None.

HARRINGTON HALL　Harrington, nr Spilsby (Lady Maitland)
Directions: 5 miles E. of Horncastle on the A158 on the Lincoln–Skegness road, turn left after Hagworthingham, follow signs to Harrington

The Copledyke family rebuilt the house at Harrington on older foundations in about 1535. In 1673 the Tudor building was purchased by Vincent Amcott and the main part of the house was again rebuilt leaving only the thin Tudor entrance tower projecting from the new west front. Since that time the long brick house has been altered very little, although a small courtyard at the back was filled in during the 18th century. Only ground floor rooms are shown in the guided tour. The hall of the Tudor house remains, but owes its present appearance to a remodelling of the 1720s when the Doric panelling and the low arch on the line of the hall screen were brought in. The staircase is also of the 1720s, but was reconstructed in 1951. Most of the other rooms are also panelled; the panelling in the dining room has recently been painted Indian Red, while the panelling in the morning room dates from the 1930s. The contents are an attractive mixture of 17th and 18th century furniture and paintings. The semi-formal walled garden is full of colour and is said to have been the 'High Hall Garden' in Tennyson's poem *Maud*.

Opening times: Easter to end of Sept, Thurs 2–5; also Easter, May and Spring Bank Holiday Sun 11–12 April; 2, 16, 30 May; 6, 20 June; 4, 25 July 2–6. Garden and garden centre, 11 April to 28 Oct, Wed and Thurs, also Easter Sun and Mon 12–8 or dusk.
Entrance charges: House £1.00; OAPs 75p; children 50p. Gardens and garden centre free. (HHA)
Parking: Free parking in car park under terrace wall.
Wheelchair access: The path to the house is gravel, but all rooms open to the public are accessible.

Guidebook: A stencilled information sheet with a very brief history and room-by-room guide.
Catering: On Charity Sundays only.
WCs: Yes.
Shop Souvenirs tee-shirts, and small china dishes are sold in the entrance hall.

LINCOLN: THE OLD BISHOP'S PALACE (Department of the Environment)

Directions: The entrance is about 100 yards downhill from the S.E. corner of the cathedral

From Lincoln Cathedral the land slopes steeply down to the south. Built into the slope are the complicated remains of the Old Palace, which was begun by St Hugh in the early 13th century, on the site of a earlier palace. More buildings were added by Bishop Alnwick in the mid-15th century, but by the 17th century all was in ruins. Bishop King converted part of the palace into a chapel in 1898 with the help of the architects Bodley & Garner; the remainder is still ruinous. At the north end of the mediaeval ranges is Alnwick Tower, here there is a plan showing the original layout of the palace. Parts of the outer walls of the enormous West Hall still survive. The East, or Lesser, Hall, has all but disappeared, although it is still possible to enter the vaulted chamber beneath. The site is being excavated.

Opening times: Standard hours (S) April to Sept only, see page xii.
Entrance charges: 40p, OAPs and children 20p.
Parking: Free parking for two hours in Minster Yard, 150 yards from the Old Palace along the S. side of the cathedral.
Wheelchair access: Possible to all parts of the ruin.
Guidebook: None, but there is a plan at the entrance and a free leaflet with the basic information.
Catering: None.
WCs: None.
Shop: None.

TATTERSHALL CASTLE Tattershall (The National Trust)

Tel: Coningsby (0526) 4253
Directions: 13 miles N.E of Sleaford on the A153 Louth road, at the western end of Tattershall village

The great brick keep of Tattershall Castle dominates the surrounding country. The first castle here was built in 1231 and consisted of a wall, strengthened at intervals by round towers and enclosed by a moat. Between 1430 and 1450 Ralph Cromwell, Lord Treasurer of England, extended the area of the castle, constructed a new outer moat and added many new buildings of brick, of which the most notable was the great tower. He kept the hall and other buildings of the earlier castle. The new tower contained the private state rooms and was linked to the hall by a first floor passage. Now all these buildings have gone except the tower, a small gatehouse and a few ruins in the outer ward. The tower itself was only saved from demolition at the last minute by Lord Curzon in 1911, who restored the top two storeys and built new floors to replace those that had collapsed. The ground, first, second and third storeys each have one large chamber, with smaller rooms and passages in the corner turrets and within the thickness of the walls. The fourth floor is open to the sky, with an arcade which carries the wall walk inside the battlements. There are a few scraps of furniture, but the most impressive features of the great rooms are the fireplaces which Lord Curzon rescued from being shipped to America. Ralph Cromwell also built almshouses, a college for priests and a new church at Tattershall.

Opening times: All year, daily (except Christmas and Boxing Day) weekdays 11–6.30 or sunset, Sun 1–6.30 or sunset. Oct to end March closed 1–2.
Entrance charges: 90p; children 45p; dogs on leads allowed in grounds.
Parking: Free parking by the outer moat.
Wheelchair access: Gravel paths and access only to ground floor of keep, but that is worth seeing.
Guidebook: An excellent, recent and well-written guide with illustrations and plans; also a very good young person's guide, slightly cheaper.
Catering: None.
WCs: At the end of the car park, free; suitable for wheelchairs.
Shop: National Trust literature and gifts on sale in the guardhouse.
Extras: There are collections of archaeological finds, plans, and a model of the castle upstairs in the guardhouse.

THORPE TILNEY HALL   nr Lincoln (F.M. Stockdale)
Tel: Martin (052 67) 231
Directions: 12 miles S.E. of Lincoln on the B1189 between Metheringham and Billinghay

This is a small red brick mansion, about the right size for a country rectory or a dower house with a small stable block. It is apparently built on the cellars of an earlier house which was struck by lightning and destroyed in 1709. Visitors may see the principal downstairs rooms and one bedroom upstairs. They contain a miscellany of furniture from European and Oriental countries dating from every century since the 17th. There are information boards in each room which supplement the guidebook. The large garden surrounding the house has been re-planted fairly recently and so is a little bare in places. To one side of the front lawn stands a large new garden pavilion in the Palladian style designed by Francis Johnson. It is principally intended for musical events but also serves as a tea room for visitors.

Opening times: 18 July to 12 Sept, some Sun and Bank Holiday Mon 2–5.
Entrance charges: £1.
Parking: Near the stable block a short distance from the house.
Wheelchair access: Possible to garden and to the ground floor of the house.
Guidebook: A brief account of the house and its furniture.

Catering: Tea can be obtained from the kitchen in the new pavilion, and consumed inside or out.
WCs: In the pavilion; not for wheelchair users.
Shop: None.

WOOLSTHORPE MANOR Colsterworth (The National Trust)
Directions: 7 miles S. of Grantham on the W. side of the A1. In Woolsthorpe village turn down Newton Way

Woolsthorpe Manor is a small limestone house, probably built about 1620. Isaac Newton was born here in 1642. Whilst staying here to avoid the plague in 1665 he discovered the principles of differential calculus, one of his major contributions to mathematics. Several furnished rooms on both floors are open to visitors, including the old kitchen which contains some graffiti said to be by Newton.

Opening times: April to Oct, Mon, Wed, Fri, Sun 11–12.30 and 2–6; closed Good Friday.
Entrance charges: 90p; children 45p; no dogs.
Parking: Free parking.
Wheelchair access: Wheelchair users could see about half the rooms.
Guidebook: A small but adequate guidebook.
Catering: None.
WCs: At the back of the house, approached from outside, spotless.
Shop: None.

London

APSLEY HOUSE MUSEUM Hyde Park Corner (Victoria & Albert Museum)
Tel: 01 499 5676
Directions: At Hyde Park Corner, completely surrounded by roadway and best approached by the pedestrian subways

Apsley House is one of the 18th century noblemen's houses which once lined the north side of Piccadilly, but road improvements in the 1960s cut the house off from the rest of the street. The house is famous as the home of the Duke of Wellington, but it was built for Lord Bathurst in 1768 to the designs of Robert Adam. The house was originally faced with red brick and it took its name from the owner's subsidiary title of Viscount Apsley. The Duke of Wellington purchased the house in 1817 and in 1828 it was enlarged for him and re-faced in stone by Benjamin Wyatt. In 1947 the house was given to the state and is now the Wellington Museum. An attempt has been made to restore the main rooms as they were in the Duke's time, but the atmosphere is that of a museum, with personal mementoes of the Duke and the excellent collection of paintings which he bought, or was given by grateful monarchs. The Waterloo Gallery, added in 1828, was the scene of the banquets held to commemorate the famous battle and in the centre of the table is a huge silver centrepiece, 26 feet long, presented to the Duke in 1816 by the Prince Regent of Portugal. Most of the rooms shown are on the first floor, although there is some material on the ground floor and in the basement.

Opening times: All year Tues, Wed, Thus and Sat 10–6, Sun 2.30–6.
Entrance charges: Free.
Parking: No parking facilities, and parking nearby is difficult.
Wheelchair access: Possible to all main rooms; the subways leading to the house have ramps and there is a lift in the house serving the first floor.
Guidebook: A thorough guidebook on the house and its contents, containing much information about the Duke of Wellington.
Catering: None.
WCs: In the basement, adequate but no facilities for wheelchair users.
Shop: Postcards and museum publications.

CARLYLE'S HOUSE 24 Cheyne Row, Chelsea (The National Trust)
Tel: 01 352 7087
Directions: Near the river, just off the Chelsea embankment close to the Albert Bridge; nearest tube station Sloane Square (1 mile)

Thomas Carlyle's works are not much read nowadays, but he was very much admired in the last century as a philosopher and historian. He and his temperamental wife Jane lived in this solid early 18th century terrace house from 1834 until Carlyle's death in 1881. The Carlyles were not wealthy and they filled their house with an undistinguished but solid and comfortable mixture of furniture, either brought from their own home in Scotland or purchased secondhand in London. The rooms have been brought back to something very like their original appearance and now look much as they did when Dickens, Tennyson and Browning came to call. The only additions are a few showcases in the attic room containing small personal possessions and other things relating to the family. There are no ropes or barriers and visitors have the run of the three principal floors and the little garden at the back. Wintertime visitors should take heed that some rooms have no artificial light.

Opening times: April to end Oct, Wed to Sat 11–5, Sun 2–5; closed Good Friday; last admisson ½ hour before closing.
Entrance charges: 90p; children 45p.
Parking: There is some metered parking space in the street outside.
Wheelchair access: Not practicable; there are steps to the main entrance and space on the groundfloor is very restricted.
Guidebook: A thorough guide with details of the contents of each room and lively quotations from the letters of Thomas and Jane Carlyle.
Catering: None.
WCs: In the garden.
Shop: None.

Chiswick House, London

CHISWICK HOUSE Burlington Lane, Chiswick (Department of the Environment)
Directions: In Chiswick, just off the A4 at the Hogarth Roundabout; nearest station Chiswick

In the early years of the 18th century one of the most influential men of taste and patrons of the Arts was Lord Burlington. He was also a very capable architect and favoured the Palladian style against the Baroque of Sir Christopher Wren and Sir John Vanbrugh. In 1723 he designed himself a villa, based loosely on Palladio's Villa Capra in northern Italy, which was built in the grounds of his house at Chiswick. It was intended as a Temple of the Arts rather than a place to live and the domed central saloon with several small and richly-decorated rooms around it were used for displaying sculpture, paintings and other objects of value. The main house has since been demolished and the villa now stands alone. It has been restored and the exterior is very impressive, with plenty of crisp carved ornament. The rooms inside, many of them decorated by William Kent, are less impressive; the flock wallpaper is a cheap substitute for the original velvet and is rubbed and shabby-looking; there is very little furniture. Kent also designed the garden which is in many ways as important as the house. It was one of the first gardens to break away from the old tradition of straight lines and clipped hedges in favour of a slightly more natural appearance, though there are still avenues which lead the eye to little temples or groups of sculpture.

Opening times: 16 Oct to 14 March, Wed to Sun 9.30–4; 15 March to 15 Oct, daily 9.30–6.30.
Entrance charges: 50p; OAPs and children 25p.
Parking: No car park, but it is usually possible to park in the side roads near the house.
Wheelchair access: The outside and the ground floor rooms can be seen without difficulty, but the principal rooms are on the first floor and reached by a spiral stair.
Guidebook: Rather elderly, but full of information, with drawings and plans of the house and garden.
Catering: Very basic tea room near the house, usually closed.
WCs: Next to the tea room, best avoide1.
Shop: Postcards and publications.

THE DICKENS HOUSE MUSEUM 48 Doughty Street, Bloomsbury (Trustees of the Dickens House)
Tel: 01 405 2127
Directions: Doughty Street is parallel to Gray's Inn Road; nearest tube stations Holborn and Russell Square

Doughty Street is wide and spacious. It was originally a private road, laid out at the end of the 18th century and lined with terraces of tall brick houses. In April 1837 Charles Dickens and his wife took up residence at No. 4, where they lived until late 1839. During these three years Dickens wrote part of *The Pickwick Papers*, *Oliver Twist*, *Nicholas Nickleby* and *Barnaby*

Rudge. The house was saved from demolition in 1922 by The Dickens Fellowship and has become a museum and library, with books by Dickens, books about him, many portraits and a host of objects which he owned, or which were connected with him. Many of the exhibits are in showcases but some rooms are arranged as if occupied and Dickens' drawing room is being reconstructed. For Dickens enthusiasts there is a very great deal to see. Four floors, including the basement, are open to visitors and most things are labelled and explained.

Opening times: All year, weekdays 10–5; closed Sun, Bank Holidays and Public Holidays.
Entrance charges: 75p; students 50p; children 25p.
Parking: Restricted parking in Doughty Street.
Wheelchair access: Only the two ground floor rooms can be seen; a reduced entry fee is charged.
Guidebook: A brief account of Dickens' life at the time he lived in the house; also a tour of the rooms.
Catering: None.
WCs: None.
Shop: Small shop on the ground floor selling an assortment of books about Dickens and a few commercial souvenirs.

DOCTOR JOHNSON'S HOUSE 17 Gough Square (The Trustees of Dr Johnson's House)
Tel: 01 353 3745
Directions: Gough Square is a small pedestrian square between Fleet Street and Fetter Lane; from Fleet Street it is best reached by way of Dr Johnson's Court

The great Dr Samuel Johnson lived in this comfortable late 17th century house from 1748 until 1759 and he prepared his famous English Dictionary in the large attic. Despite long periods of neglect and bomb damage in the last war, the house still has enough of its original features to evoke mid-18th century London. There is not a great deal of furniture, but the walls are hung with paintings and prints of Dr Johnson and his various friends and enemies. There are also showcases containing letters and other mementoes, including of course a copy of the first edition of the Dictionary. All the rooms in the house are open to visitors and in every one is a pile of information boards which carry full details of the things on show.

Opening times: Daily except Sun, May to Sept, 11–5.30; Oct to April, 11–5.
Entrance charges: 70p; OAPs, students and children 50p.
Parking: The house is only directly accessible on foot; parking in the vicinity is difficult.
Wheelchair access: Not practicable.
Guidebook: Gives biographical details of Johnson and his associates.
Catering: None.
WCs: None.
Shop: There are postcards and publicatons for sale.

DOWN HOUSE   Downe, nr Bromley (The Royal College of Surgeons)
Tel: Farnborough (0689) 59119
Directions: On the southern edge of London, 5½ miles S. of Bromley, off
the A233 in Downe village

Life at Down is delightfully describd in Gwen Raverat's book *Period Piece*.
The house is remarkable chiefly for having been the home of Charles
Darwin, who lived here from 1842 until 1882 and wrote his *Origin of
Species* here. The tall front of the building is slightly forbidding, but the
back facing the garden is pleasant enough. The main house dates from the
late 18th or early 19th century and a number of additions were made to it by
the Darwin family. All the rooms on the ground floor are open to visitors.
Two of them, the old study and the drawing room, are furnished as they
were in Charles Darwin's day; the others are now museum rooms which
display items relating to the family and attempt to explain the theory of
evolution in pictures. Visitors may take their time in each room. The garden
is large enough to provide a pleasant walk and it contains the sinister-
sounding 'Worm Stone', a device invented by Darwin for measuring the
activity of worms in the earth.

Opening times: All year except the Christmas period and Feb, daily except Mon and Fri
1–5.30.
Entrance charges: 70p; children 20p.
Parking: Some space in front of the house, otherwise parking is difficult in the narrow lanes.
Wheelchair access: Possible to all rooms shown without difficulty.
Guidebook: A very adequate guide with a plan of the house, a room-by-room tour and a short
biograhy of Darwin.
Catering: None.
WCs: In the house; the ladies is suitable for wheelchair users.
Shop: A small bookstall.

ELTHAM PALACE   Eltham (Department of the Environment)
Tel: 01 859 2112
Directions: About 9 miles S.E. of central London, off the main A20 and
A208; the approach road to the Palace is called Tilt-Yard

The impressive remains of this moated royal palace are hidden away at the
end of a leafy suburban street. The first notable owner was Bishop Bek, who
built himself a house here in about 1300, but it soon passed into the
ownership of the crown. Edward II, Edward III, Henry VII and Henry VIII
all stayed at the palace and each made improvements to the buildings, but
under Queen Elizabeth the palace was neglected and it fell into decay. In
1931 the ruins were leased by Stephen Courtauld. He built himself a new
house inside the moat and repaired the great hall, which was by then the
only part of the old palace still standing. The main approach passes some
timber-framed buildings which are the remains of a large outer courtyard
and crosses the moat by a mediaeval bridge. Mr Courtauld's 20th century

house (not open to visitors) is immediately on the left and beyond it is the great Hall built by Edward IV in 1479. The hall is 100 feet long and built of brick faced with stone, with pairs of large windows between the wall-buttresses and a large projecting oriel window at the east end. The hall is entered in the usual way through a screens passage, in this case a modern restoration. The best feature of the interior is the splendid hammerbeam roof; its main timbers have heavy moulded ornament and in the centre can be seen the smoke louver, which allowed the smoke from the open hearth to escape. There is little furniture in the hall, except a massive oak table at the dais end. The other royal apartments are completely ruinous; some of them can be explored but the majority are not accessible to the public.

Opening times: Thurs and Sun 10.30–12.15, 2.15–6 (2.15–4 Nov to March).
Entrance charges: Free.
Parking: Free parking outside the palace.
Wheelchair access: No difficulty about access.
Guidebook: A thorough Official Handbook, which includes a note on recent archaeological excavations.
Catering: None.
WCs: None.
Shop: None.

FENTON HOUSE Hampstead Grove, Hampstead (The National Trust)
Tel: 01 435 3471
Directions: 300 yards from Hampstead underground station on the W. side of Hampstead Grove

Fenton House is a substantial William and Mary building of excellent red brick which was built in 1693, probably for a wealthy London merchant. It stands in what is now an exclusive suburb, close to the road, but with a pleasant secluded garden on either side. The external appearance of the house is not much altered, although the entrance has been moved from the south to the east front, but several of the original rooms inside have been thrown together to make larger living spaces. Most of these rooms were redecorated for the National Trust by the late John Fowler in lush tones of pink and apricot. The house contains Lady Binning's collecton of 18th century porcelain and Major Benton Fletcher's celebrated collection of keyboard musical instruments. Pieces from the two collectons are distributed throughout the building and mingled with other 18th century furniture, giving a setting which is more attractive than many museums. An added bonus is that it is often possible to hear one of the instruments being played. The only drawback is that the house is fairly small and quickly becomes overcrowded, especially at weekends.

Opening times: Feb, March, and Nov, Sat and Sun; April to end Oct, Mon to Wed and Sat 11–5, Sun 2–5, or sunset if earlier; last admission ½ hour before closing.
Entrance charges: House, £1.40; children 70p. Garden free.

Parking: There is no car park, and the street parking is restricted.
Wheelchair access: Not practicable.
Guidebook: Brief description of the collections, brief history of the house, room-by-room tour, several illustrations and plans.
Catering: None.
WCs: Inside the house, on the first floor, one of each; no wheelchair access.
Shop: None.

FORTY HALL   Forty Hill, Enfield (London Borough of Enfield)
Tel: 01 363 8196
Directions: 1 mile N. of the centre of Enfield; nearest station Enfield Town

The well-wooded park is a pleasant surprise after driving through the dreary waste of industrial north London. Forty Hall was built in 1629 for a wealthy city trader named Sir Nicholas Raynton. It is a tall square red brick building in the fashionable style of the day, looking like a Dutch house in general appearance, but with ornamental details borrowed from Italy. The rooms inside had rather wild and Jacobean-looking plaster decoration. This decoration still survives in the hall and drawing room but the rest of the interior was made more elegant in the 18th century. The house is not lived in, but serves the borough as an art gallery and furniture museum. On the north side of the house is an enclosed courtyard with an elaborate brick gateway leading to the outbuildings, now converted for other uses. In front of the house is a lake and an avenue which leads away downhill into the park.

Opening times: Easter to Sept, Tues to Fri 10–6, Sat and Sun 10–8; Oct to Easter, daily except Mon 10–5.
Entrance charges: Free.
Parking: Free car park 50 yards from the house.
Wheelchair access: The whole of the exterior and all the ground floor can be seen.
Guidebook: An adequate guide.
Catering: During the summer tea and biscuits can be had in the outbuildings; they may be taken into the very pleasant walled garden.
WCs: In the outbuildings; no facilities for wheelchair-users.
Shop: None.

HALL PLACE   Bexley (London Borough of Bexley)
Directions: About 13 miles S.E. of central London, just off the A2 near its junction with the A23, not signposted

Hall Place is a substantial and venerable mansion, a reminder of the days before Bexley was a suburb of London and bisected by dual carriageways. Part of the house dates from the 16th century and part from the 17th; the two parts are easily distinguishd because the older house is of black and white chequerwork and the addition is of red brick. The great hall and parts of the two wings enclosing the older front courtyard were built in the 1530s for Sir John Champneys. Forty years later his son, Sir Justinian, extended the wings and added a second bay window to make the front of the hall look symmetrical. In 1649 the house was bought by Sir Richard Austen and during the next ten years, even though the country was in the middle of a civil war, he added the new red brick courtyard behind the front range. The house is now owned by the local authority. It has been heavily restored and is used for a variety of exhibitions. Visitors to the house may see the inside of the great hall, the staircase which dates from 1653, and two upstairs rooms, one of which has a lively plaster ceiling. The central part of this ceiling probably dates from the 1660s but the edges may be a survival from a earlier time. There is no furniture of interest in the house. The 17th century part of the building is not open, nor is it possible to get into the front courtyard, though this can be seen through the front gates. The gardens are some compensation. They slope gently down to the river Cray and combine topiary with elaborate displays of bedding plants. The greenhouses are open in the summer months and contain very spectacular fuchsias.

Opening times: Gardens open all year during daylight hours. House open all year weekdays 10–5, also April to Sept, Sun 2–6.
Entrance charges: Free.
Parking: Free car park near house.
Wheelchair access: Possible to see all the outside and also the inside of the great hall.
Guidebook: Starts with prehistoric finds, ends with ghost stories; in between is a fairly brief account of the various stages of building, biographies of the various owners and an excellent plan of the house.
Catering: Snack bar facing the car park, adequate for a quick cup of tea.
WCs: In the car park, adequate.
Shop: Postcards and pamphlets.

HAM HOUSE Richmond (The National Trust and The Victoria and Albert Museum)
Tel: 01 940 1950
Directions: 8 miles S.W. of central London, 1 mile S.W. of Richmond off the A307

Ham began as an H-shaped Jacobean house which was built for Sir Thomas Vavasour in 1610. Some alterations were made in the 1630s by the First Earl of Dysart, but the house as it appears today is largely the creation of his daughter Elizabeth and her husband, the Duke of Lauderdale. During the 1670s they employed the gentleman-architect William Samwell to enlarge the house and then furnished the interior in an unusually lavish manner. By some miracle the house and its contents have survived almost untouched and the series of 17th century rooms has few equals in England. The great entrance hall and the private apartments are on the ground floor, most of them panelled or hung with leather and containing 17th or early 18th century furniture. A great staircase with elaborately carved and grained decoration leads to the state rooms on the first floor which are even more richly decorated. In recent years the paintwork and fabrics in some rooms have been renewed in order to show the kind of brilliant colours which the original decorations would have had. Some may find the restoration unwelcome but the work of renewal has been carefully done and one room on the first floor is set aside to display some of the best preserved examples of the original fabrics which were copied. Visitors follow a set route through the house, but it is perfectly possible to double back and have a second look at any of the rooms. To complete the 17th century appearance of Ham, the garden has been laid out in the formal 17th century fashion. As yet the planting has not matured and the garden still looks rather bare.

Opening times: All year, daily except Mon 2–6; Oct to March 12–4, open all Bank Holiday Mon except May Day; closed Good Friday and Christmas.

Entrance charges: Garden free. House 50p; OAPs and children 20p; children under 12 must be accompanied.

Parking: Free parking near the house, about 200 yards away.

Wheelchair access: Two flights of shallow steps to entrance, ground floor rooms are all on one level.

Guidebook: An excellent guide, thorough and informative with plans of both floors and a room-by-room guide which is easy to use on a visit.

Catering: Tea room overlooking the walled garden with tables outside; a very pleasant setting and the cakes are good.

WCs: In the yard behind the house, free and immaculate; facilities for wheelchair users.

Shop: There is a small National Trust shop in the house with the usual souvenirs and unmistakeable smell of pot-pourri.

HAMPTON COURT PALACE Hampton (Department of the Environment)

Directions: On the N. bank of the Thames at Hampton Court; nearest station Hampton Court

Cardinal Wolsey's enormous red brick manor house was built here on the bank of the river between 1514 and 1520. The house originally had two courtyards, a large outer court and a smaller inner court around which the main rooms were grouped. King Henry VIII took the house for himself, enlarged and enriched it and turned it into a palace. When William and Mary came to the throne in 1688 they determined to rival Louis XIV at Versailles and commanded Sir Christopher Wren to rebuild the whole palace in the classical style, and on a much larger scale, but the work was left half-completed after Queen Mary's death in 1694. Wolsey's buildings and Wren's buildings co-exist quite happily since they are both built of red brick. Wren provided two complete suites of state rooms for William and Mary, each with its own grand staircase and these are the rooms open to the public. Most of them contain very few pieces of furniture, but a large number of paintings from the Royal collection are on display, including Sir Peter Lely's 'Hampton Court Beauties', and also some tapestries. The rooms themselves, with their dark panelling, are sombre and stately. Only a very small part of the interior of the Tudor buildings can be seen, but visitors should not miss the Chapel Royal with its magnificent 16th century ceiling, nor the even larger Great Hall.

Hampton Court still has a very large park, whose layout has not changed a great deal since the beginning of the 18th century, with formal canals and avenues of trees radiating from the house. Next to the buildings are the Privy Garden, the Great Fountain Garden and the Wilderness; the trees and flowers are set off by the superb ironwork screens by Tijou and stone ornaments.

Opening times: Standard hours (SM), see page xii.

Entrance charges: It costs nothing to walk through the courtyards of the house but the charges for the State Apartments are: summer £1.80; OAPs and children 90p; winter 90p and 50p.

Parking: Car park about 200 yards from the main entrance; charge 20p.

Wheelchair access: It is possible to wheel through the courtyards, but there is no access to the State Apartments.

Guidebook: Reliable and well-written guide to the house and another guide to the gardens and park; also available in French and German.

Catering: Tiltyard Restaurant and the Cafeteria are in the garden on the north side of the house. The restaurant does lunches and set teas; the cafe is cheaper and more basic, though pleasant to sit outside.

WCs: Near the ticket office between the Base Court and the Clock Court; facilities for wheelchair users.

Shop: Guide books, postcards and souvenirs at the east entrance and in the State Apartments.

Extras: The admission charge covers a number of things beside the house, including the King's private apartments, Mantegna's newly restored paintings of the *Triumph of Caesar*. The Great Vine, Henry VIII's Tennis Court and the Cellars can be visited free of charge. A small charge is made for admission to the Maze and to the display of carriages and royal children's pedal cars in the Orangery.

HOGARTH'S HOUSE Chiswick (London Borough of Hounslow)

Tel: 01 994 6757

Directions: Just off the main A4 (The Great West Road) by Hogarth Roundabout

The great 18th century satirical artist William Hogarth lived in this house from 1749–64 and he and his family are buried in the churchyard nearby. The house itself is an early 18th century brick building of three storeys with a large first floor bay window overlooking the quiet walled garden with its old mulberry tree. But Hogarth's 'little country box by the Thames' is now surrounded by factories, houses, flats and a very busy road. His wooden studio, which stood in the garden, collapsed in 1868. Since 1904 the house has been a Hogarth Museum. The small white-painted rooms are hung with his famous prints, some single and some in series like *The Rake's Progress* and *Marriage à la Mode*. There is very little else to see, except a few sticks of 18th century furniture.

Opening times: April to Sept, daily 11–6, Sun 2–6; Oct to March daily except Tues 11–4, Sun 2–4.

Entrance charges: Free at present; a charge may be imposed in April 1982.

Parking: In the road outside the house, no parking restrictions.

Wheelchair access: Two steps down to the ground floor.

Guidebook: A good account of the house and of Hogarth and his work.

Catering: None.

WCs: None.

Shop: Some prints for sale.

Extras: A short distance away is Chiswick House (q.v.).

KENSINGTON PALACE Kensington (Department of the Environment)

Tel: 01 937 9561 ext. 2

Directions: On the W. side of Kensington Gardens, nearest tube station High Street, Kensington

The Palace of Kensington is an attractive sprawl of old red brick buildings on the edge of the park. Much of the Palace is still occupied by various members of the Royal Family, but the State Apartments have been open to the public since 1899. Kensington first became a palace in the 1690s, when William III decided to live here and Sir Christopher Wren made additions to the old house. More additions were made for George I in 1718–21, when many of the rooms were decorated by William Kent, better known as an architect. His painted decorations have been restored in recent years and the State Apartments returned to something like their original 18th century appearance. The rooms contain furniture and paintings of the appropriate period from the Royal Collection. Visitors make their own way round, following a set route. Halfway through the tour one comes suddenly upon a suite of rooms furnished in the Victorian taste. They are a reminder that Queen Victoria was born at Kensington Palace in 1819. It is largely because of her affection for her childhood home that it was not pulled down. The last room to be seen is the Cupola Room, part of the 1720 additions and intended to be the principal state room in the palace; its walls are ornamented with pilasters, gilded statues of Roman Gods and gilded busts of Roman emperors. Near the palace is the Orangery, built in 1704, which has a very fine interior. There is also a sunken garden, laid out in Edwardian times but intended to recall the great formal layout of early Georgian days.

Opening times: All year, weekdays 9–5, Sun 1–5. Closed New Year's Day, Good Friday, Christmas Eve, Christmas Day and Boxing Day.

Entrance charges: Summer 80p; OAPs and children 40p. Winter 40p and 20p.

Parking: There is no car park; the palace must be reached on foot by way of the park.

Wheelchair access: Not practicable; all rooms shown are on the first floor.

Guidebook: A well-written and thorough guide and history, with many illustrations and a plan of the State Apartments.

Catering: None at the palace.

WCs: None.

Shop: A small shop selling postcards and publications.

KENWOOD HOUSE (THE IVEAGH BEQUEST) (Greater London Council)

Tel: 01 348 1286

Directions: On the N. side of Hampstead Heath, off Hampstead Lane, nearest tube station Hampstead (1 mile)

Kenwood House lies on the northern edge of the great expanse of Hampstead Heath. It is an elegant mansion, now used to display the Iveagh Bequest of paintings. At the core of the building is a plain house of about 1700, but this was much altered in the mid-1760s when Robert Adam carried out extensive improvements for Lord Mansfield, a distinguished lawyer who was both Attorney General and Lord Chief Justice. Adam designed the grand entrance portico and the garden front overlooking the Heath. He also built a library on the east side to balance the orangery on the west and redecorated most of the main rooms. There have been several additions to the house since then, including the two wings flanking the entrance portico which were added in 1793 by George Saunders. In 1927 Kenwood was bequeathed to the nation by the Earl of Iveagh, together with his celebrated collection of paintings. There are outstanding works by Rembrandt, Vermeer and Hals and delightful examples of the work of the great 18th century English portraitists. Although the rooms contain some fine furniture as well as the paintings they are arranged like gallery rooms. The only exception is Adam's delicate library, which is one of his very best interiors. The arrangement of the downstairs rooms is unvarying, but there are often temporary exhibitions of paintings upstairs.

Opening times: All year daily except Christmas Eve, Christmas Day and Good Friday, April to Sept, 10–7; Oct, Feb, Mar 10–5; Nov to Jan 10–4.
Entrance charges: Free.
Parking: Free parking in front of the house.
Wheelchair access: Possible to the ground floor rooms which contain the main collection.
Guidebook: A very satisfactory guide by Sir John Summerson, with several illustrations and a plan of the building.
Catering: There is a restaurant and also a self-service cafeteria in the outbuildings to one side of the house; the latter becomes very crowded at weekends.
WCs: In the outbuildings near the tea room, adequate; no wheelchair facilities.
Shop: Postcards and publications on sale in the house.
Extras: None.

KEW PALACE (THE DUTCH HOUSE) Kew Gardens (Department of the Environment)

Directions: In the Botanical Garden at Kew, on the S. bank of the river Thames; nearest tube and railway station Kew Gardens

Long before the Botanical Gardens existed a London merchant called Samuel Fortrey built himself a small country house by the river at Kew. It was finished in 1631, a tall Dutch-looking building of red brick with a great deal of brick ornament and large shaped gables. By the end of the 18th century the Dutch House, as it was called, had become part of the royal estate at Kew and stood near a house called White Lodge, which was then the main royal residence. When White Lodge was pulled down in 1802 to make way for a new palace, King George III and Queen Charlotte took up temporary residence in the Dutch House. The new palace was never finished. George III died and his wife continued to live on at the Dutch House until her own death in 1818. The rooms inside have been restored to something like their appearance in late Georgian times. All the rooms on the ground and first floors are open to visitors; they are small and intimate and as a result are often overcrowded at summer weekends. Very little of the original 17th century decoration survives, though there is some plasterwork of this period in the Queen's Boudoir. Most of the furniture and paintings are of the late 18th century. Visitors follow a set route and there are rope barriers in some rooms. One ground floor room has a permanent collection of royal bygones and family playthings. The little garden between the house and the river has been laid out to give some idea of a typical mid-17th century garden, although it looks more like a survivor from the Festival of Britain.

Opening times: April to mid-Oct, Mon to Sat 11–5.30, Sun 2–6; closed Maundy Thursday and Good Friday.
Entrance charges: Entrance charge to Kew Gardens 10p. Entrance to house 60p; OAPs and children 30p. The house can only be reached through the gardens.
Parking: In the streets outside the gardens, fairly easy.
Wheelchair access: Easy access to Kew Gardens, three steps to the floor of the house, after which all five ground floor rooms could be seen; there is a wheelchair entrance to the garden behind the house.
Guidebook: A small cheap leaflet with a very brief history, room-by-room guide and an exploded plan.
Catering: None in the house, there is a cafeteria in Kew Gardens.
WCs: None in the house.
Shop: None.
Extras: At the extreme opposite end of Kew Gardens (about a mile from the Dutch House) lies The Queen's Cottage, a pretty ornamental thatched cottage built for Queen Charlotte in about 1772 and used by the Royal Family in the 18th century for summer meals. The cottage is open on Sat and Sun and Bank Holidays 11–5.30; admission 30p; OAPs and children 15p.

LANCASTER HOUSE Stable Yard, St James' (Department of the Environment)
Tel: 01-839 3488
Directions: Lancaster House faces the Mall, near Buckingham Palace; it lies between St James' Park and St James' Palace

Lancaster House began as a royal mansion. It was built for the Duke of York in 1825 to designs by Benjamin Wyatt. Two years later it passed to the enormously wealthy Marquis of Stafford, later Duke of Sutherland, and the name of the building was changed from York House to Stafford House. In 1913 it was bought by Lord Leverhulme, the soap millionaire, who re-named it Lancaster House after his native county. In the last century Stafford House was one of the greatest aristocratic and political centres of London. It was so richly decorated and fabulously furnished that Queen Victoria used to joke with the Duchess about 'coming from my house to your palace'. Lord Leverhulme left the house to the nation and it is now used as a government 'Hospitality Centre' — which means that receptions and conferences are held there. There are both paintings and furniture, but they are generally of less interest than the splendid rooms themselves, which visitors may wander round with a minimuim of restriction. On the ground floor the series of rooms includes two fine dining rooms with heavily gilded decoration and furnishings. At the centre of the house is the magnificent staircase hall, one of the most impressive rooms in London. Its walls are painted a sombre red and yellow to imitate marble, on three sides is a deep gallery behind giant columns and the ceiling is coved and gilded. The best of the first floor rooms is the Great Gallery which occupies one whole side of the house; its walls are white and gold and in the central section of the room is one of the richest of Victorian fireplaces, with allegorical figures of Architecture and Painting.

Opening times: Easter Eve to mid Dec, Sat, Sun and Bank Holidays 2–6; may be closed at short notice for official functions.
Entrance charges: 60p, OAPs and children under 16 30p.
Parking: There is no car park, but there are parking meters very near the house.
Wheelchair access: Possible to ground floor rooms and staircase hall.
Guidebook: A good and cheap little guidebook with illustrations and plans.
Catering: None.
WCs: None.
Shop: None.

MARBLE HILL HOUSE Twickenham (Greater London Council)
Tel: 01 892 5115
Directions: 11 miles S.W. of central London on the banks of the river Thames; nearest railway station St Margarets

Marble Hill is a small and very perfect villa in the English Palladian style, which has been restored to something aproaching its original condition. The house was built as a country retreat for Henrietta Howard, Countess of Suffolk, a charming but unhappy woman who was for many years the mistress of the Prince of Wales, later George II. The design of the building seems to have a combined effort involving the architects Colen Campbell and Roger Morris as well as the noble conoisseur Lord Herbert. Building started in 1724 and the house was completed in 1729. The exterior now looks very much as it did when just finished. The small and convenient rooms inside have been redecorated in an 18th century manner. The centre of the river front on the first floor is occupied by the Great Room, which has elaborate carved and gilded ornament and a high coved ceiling. There is a certain amount of 18th century furniture and some early Georgian paintings, most of which have been purchased in recent years. There are often temporary exhibitions of paintings or drawings in one or more of the ground floor rooms. Visitors may wander through the buildings at their leisure. The large riverside park belonging to the house is now a public park.

Opening times: All year, daily except Fri 10–5, closes 4pm Nov to March.
Entrance charges: Free.
Parking: In Montpelier Row or Orleans Road, off the main Richmond Road; the house is then a short walk away.
Wheelchair access: The exterior of the house and the ground floor rooms can be seen without difficulty.
Guidebook: A good little history of the house and description of each room with illustrations and a plan, but better still is *Marble Hill and its Owners*, published in 1970, a very full history of the house and its restoration and outstanding value for money at £1.60.
Catering: There is a cafeteria near the house serving tea, coffee, sandwiches and snacks; fairly basic but it is possible to sit outside overlooking the park.
WCs: Next to the house, adequate but not suitable for wheelchair users.
Shop: None.
Extras: The boathouse near Marble Hill operates a passenger ferry across the river at weekends, making it possible to reach Ham House.

OSTERLEY PARK HOUSE Osterley (The National Trust and The Victoria and Albert Museum)

Tel: 01 560 3918
Directions: ½ miles N. of the Great West road (A4); turn off at the traffic lights near Osterley tube station

Osterley was built in the late 1570s for Sir Thomas Gresham and although most of his building survives none of it can be seen, for it was completely refaced in the 18th century. Sir Thomas's house was arranged round three sides of a square courtyard; there may have been a fourth range but no trace of it remains. Major changes took place in the late 1750s, when the Tudor house was refaced in red brick and the long gallery was added across the whole of the west front. Some of the rooms were also remodelled. Sir Francis Child may have employed Sir William Chambers as the architect for this work. About ten years later Robert Adam took over as architect. He filled the open side of the courtyard with a very grand pedimented screen and supervised the complete redecoration of most of the major rooms. Many of these rooms are still as Adam left them, with furniture designed by him and paintings of the period. The dignified entrance hall and the four rooms which make up the Great Apartment in the south wing are very fine but some of the other rooms, the eating room and library for example, seem rather gaunt. Visitors make their own way through the rooms, some of which are partly roped-off. The last room on the tour and the south passage leading from it back to the hall contain a very interesting display of photographs of Adam's drawings of the decorations and for the furniture. Osterley is set in a large park, but that portion of it between the house and the car park is less attractive than the rest. The original manor house which stood here before Sir Thomas's building is thought to survive as the west wing of the stable block.

Opening times: House daily except Mon, April to Sept 2–6; Oct to March 12–4; also open all Bank Holiday Mon; closed Good Friday and May Day. Garden open all year.

Entrance charges: 50p; OAPs and children under 16 20p; children under 12 must be accompanied. No admission charge for the garden and park.

Parking: Car park inside the park about 200 yards from the house, charge 20p.

Wheelchair access: There is a daunting flight of steps to the main portico, but if this could be conquered all rooms shown would be accessible.

Guidebook: A good thorough history and guide, with a room-by-room description, illustrations and a plan of the house and of the park.

Catering: On the stable block, open from April to Sept except Mon, self service tea and cakes, it is possible to sit outside in the stable yard.

WCs: Near the stables; facilities for wheelchair users.

Shop: Postcards only.

THE QUEEN'S HOUSE Greenwich (National Maritime Museum)
Tel: 01 858 4422
Directions: In Greenwich, at the bottom of Greenwich Park, off Romney Road (A206)

The Queen's House is now part of the National Maritime Museum and is linked by colonnades to large wings on either side which contain the bulk of the exhibits; but this elegant classical villa was originally intended as a quiet retreat for the Queen of James I. It is historically important because it was the first major work by Inigo Jones, England's first classical architect. The house was begun in 1616 but not finally completed until 1637. When first built it consisted of two oblong ranges; one facing downhill over the royal gardens and the other facing uphill over the royal park. Between them ran the busy Dover Road and the two halves of the house were connected by a 20 foot wide 'bridge room' at first floor level. Two extra bridges were added in 1662 by John Webb, giving the house its present form, but in the 1690s the road was diverted to run between the house and the river. In its later years the house had a chequered history but the rooms inside have now been restored as closely as possible to their original 17th century appearance. The most impressive room is the hall, a grand vestibule in the shape of a 40 foot cube with a fine marble floor whose design echoes that of the painted ceiling. Opening off it are a number of smaller rooms and also the elegant 'Tulip Staircase', so called from the design of the iron balustrade. The first floor contains the Queen's principal living rooms, some of which have elaborate decoration. They are used to display 17th century portraits, marine paintings and other objects of the period belonging to the museum. The network of rooms on this floor can be confusing because of the three bridges, but there is a great deal to see. Besides the Queen's House there is the remainder of the large museum, which relates to all aspects of ships and the sea.

Opening times: Easter to Oct, daily except Mon 10–6, Sun 2–5.30; Nov to Easter, Tues to Fri 10–5, Sat 10–6, Sun 2–5.
Entrance charges: Free.
Parking: Free parking in the streets near the museum.
Wheelchair access: Possible to ground floor rooms.
Guidebook: A good and recent guide with several illustrations and plans.
Catering: In the museum.
WCs: None in the Queen's House, facilities in the museum.
Shop: The museum has quite large bookstalls with a wide collection of publications about ships.

RANGER'S HOUSE Blackheath (Greater London Council)
Tel: 01 853 0035
Directions: On the S. side of Blackheath, just off the main A2; the house backs onto Greenwich Park and may be entered from the park

Ranger's House is one of the most distinguished buildings on the edge of Blackheath. It dates from the 1690s and is built of red brick, with stone ornament in the recessed central section containing the main entrance. In 1748 the house was inherited by Lord Chesterfield, who added a gallery on the north side. A matching gallery was built on the south side in the 1780s to make the front symmetrical. The house is now owned by the Greater London Council and has been restored to serve as a picture gallery. The great majority of the paintings are portraits from the Countess of Suffolk's collection and by far the most important is the series of early 17th century full-length portraits by Phillip Larkin, which now hangs in Lord Chesterfield's gallery.

Opening times: All year, daily except Christmas Eve, Christmas Day and Good Friday 10–5; Nov to Jan closes at 4.
Entrance charges: Free.
Parking: Free parking in front of the house.
Wheelchair access: There is a steep flight of steps to the front door, but once inside all rooms shown are on the ground floor.
Guidebook: No guide to the house, but there is a catalogue of the Suffolk Collection of paintings.
Catering: None, although there is a tea room in Greenwich Park nearby.
WCs: In the house, very adequate; no facilities for the disabled.
Shop: Postcards only.

SIR JOHN SOANE'S MUSEUM 13 Lincoln's Inn Fields, WC2
Tel: 01 405 2107
Directions: On the N. side of Lincoln's Inn Fields; nearest tube station
Holborn

This was the home of Sir John Soane, one of England's most original
architects. When he died in 1837 his house and its contents passed to the
nation as a museum. Among the buildings designed by Soane were the old
Bank of England, the Art Gallery at Dulwich and many country houses. His
own house, both inside and out, gives a good idea of the unusual character of
his style. Soane was a collector of antiquities and works of art. Besides the
fragments of classical buildings useful to an architect he accumulated
antique sculpture, pottery and more modern paintings, including major
works by Hogarth (The Rake's Progress series) and Canaletto. There are
also many paintings and drawings of his own architectural schemes. As the
collection grew Soane was forced to spread into the next-door house and into
the gardens behind. He connected them all together and the result is a
spectacular maze in a small space, filled with objects of interest and value
and quite unlike anything else in England. The guided tours on Saturday
afternoons make a good introduction but on other days visitors may absorb
the rooms at their leisure.

Opening times: Tues to Sat 10–5; closed Sun, Mon and Bank Holidays.
Entrance charges: Free.
Parking: No car park; there is limited parking in busy Lincoln's Inn Fields.
Wheelchair access: Not practicable; there are steps to the door and narrow spaces inside.
Guidebook: A short cheap description or a more elaborate illustrated version; both excellent.
Catering: None.
WCs: None.
Shop: None

SYON HOUSE Brentford (The Duke of Northumberland)
Tel: 01 560 0881/2
Directions: 7 miles S.W. of central London, on the N. bank of the river
Thames

It is strange to find a grand nobleman's house, complete with its park,
surviving in the London suburbs. The Garden Centre in the park attracts
crowds of visitors, but few of them seem to bother with the house. Syon
takes its name from a nunnery founded here in 1415 by Henry V. The
nunnery lands were given to the Duke of Somerset in 1547 and he built
himself a large courtyard house, incorporating parts of the nunnery
buildings. This house forms the shell of the present mansion, although the
Bath stone facing and sash windows give the building an 18th century
appearance. King James I granted Syon to the Ninth Earl of
Northumberland, ancestor of the present owner. In 1762 the architect

Syon House, London

Robert Adam was commissioned by the First Duke to remodel the old house and he formed a splendid series of rooms which is among his best work. Visitors follow the route through the rooms which Adam intended. The solemn entrance hall in Roman style with its marble floor and antique statues contrasts dramatically with the ante-room next to it, which glows with coloured marble, scagliola and gilding. The dining room is mainly ivory and gold, while the drawing room has its original red silk wall coverings and a very fine Moorfields carpet with the makers name and the date 1769 woven into one corner. The ceiling of this room is coved and gilded and has decorative red and blue roundels. The pictures here are all 17th century English portraits of good quality; the furniture, like that of the other rooms, is ornate 18th century work. The last room in this splendid series is the long gallery, a survival from the Jacobean house, but redecorated by Adam, who attempted to increase the apparent width of the room, which is 136 feet long but only 14 feet wide. The last part of the route is through oak-panelled passages, whose walls are closely hung with portraits of lesser importance. Although the gardens are open to visitors, those parts of the gardens nearest the house are still private and as a result it is only possible to see one side of the house.

Opening times: House, Good Friday to 26 Sept, daily except Fri and Sat 12–5; last admission 4.15; also Sun in Oct 12–5. Gardens open all year, March to Oct 10–6; Nov to Feb daily 10–dusk; last admission 1 hour before closing.

Entrance charges: House 75p; children and OAP's 40p. Gardens, summer, 70p; children and OAPs 40p; reduced rates in winter. (HHA)

Parking: Large free car park midway between house and gardens.

Wheelchair access: Not possible to house, too many steps, but access is possible to the gardens, the Garden Centre, the Heritage Motor Museum and the Butterfly House.

Guidebook: i) *Syon House,* a brief history, good and cheap, contains all the basic information and also Adam's plan for the improvement of the house. ii) *Syon,* more or less the same text as i) but with many colour photographs; it is confusingly arranged and lacks the plan but has a bird's-eye view of house and park as a loose-leaf addition.

Catering: Near the car park, a large and basic cafeteria, self-service, piped music, ordinary food. There is also a more formal and more expensive restaurant.

WCs: Next to the house, or near the car park, both adequate; facilities for wheelchair users on the road to the Motor Museum.

Shop: An enormous Garden Centre and shop by the car park; it has far more visitors than the house.

Extras: The number of extras increases annually. At present they are a small toy museum near the garden centre; the attractive botanical garden with its famous Great Conservatory housing an aviary and aquarium; the British Leyland Heritage Motor Museum with over 70 vehicles and the Butterfly House, where one can walk among clouds of free-flying exotic butterflies. All of these have their own entrance charges.

THE TOWER OF LONDON Tower Hill (Department of the Environment)
Tel: 01 709 0765
Directions: On the N. bank of the Thames, above Tower Bridge, nearest tube station Tower Hill

The most famous castle in England and among the most visited. Every day thousands flock into these forbidding buildings to pick up the atmosphere of imprisonings and beheadings. The Tower stands by the river, guarding the eastern side of the old City of London. The layout of the buildings is fairly straightforward; in the centre is the White Tower built by William the Conqueror in about 1080 to keep the Saxons in order. Around it are barracks and domestic buildings, encircled by two rings of massive walls with towers at intervals. The inner wall was largely built by Richard I (1189–99) and Henry II (1216–72), the outer wall by Edward I (1272–1307). The walls have been rebuilt and repaired many times but the basic arrangement has not changed. After gaining admission visitors can either wait for one of the free regular tours conducted by the Beefeaters or make their own way round. Some of the towers are open and there are several exhibitions in the buildings facing Tower Green, the central area of the castle. The White Tower is wholly given over to the very large collection of arms and armour, though the simple Norman chapel is kept as a chapel. Among the smaller towers are the Bloody Tower, where Richard III murdered the little princes and Sir Walter Raleigh was imprisoned; the Beauchamp Tower, whose walls inside are covered with the carvings made by prisoners awaiting trial or execution and The Bowyer Tower, which contains the block, the axe, and instruments of torture. Waterloo barracks, a large Victorian building facing the White Tower, houses an exhibition of oriental weapons, including a splendid suit of elephant armour and there is also a small exhibition on Royal Heralds. All these are covered by the admission charge but the Crown Jewels are an extra. Despite all the crowds the Tower still manages to keep something of its atmosphere.

Opening times: All year, March to Oct, weekdays 9.30–5, Sun 2–5; Nov to Feb, weekdays 9.30–4, closed Sun. Jewel Tower closed Feb 1982.

Entrance charges: Nov to Feb £2.00; children £1.00: Mar to June and Sept to Oct £2.50 and £1.20: July and Aug £2.00 and £1.50.

Parking: There is a visitor's car park at the top of Tower Hill.

Wheelchair access: It would be possible to see most of the castle, although the distances involved are large and many of the roads are cobbled. The exhibitions of Oriental Armour and Heraldry would be accessible, but access would not be possible to the White Tower, the Bloody, Beauchamp or Bowyer Towers, or to the Jewel House.

Guidebook: The basic guide is very adequate, with illustrations and a plan; it also comes in French, German, Italian, Spanish and Japanese. A separate guide to the Crown Jewels comes also in French and German. There are a number of other guide books on armour, instruments of torture etc.

Catering: None, though there are any number of snack bars outside the castle gates.

WCs: Several within the castle all well maintained, but none suitable for wheelchairs.
Shop: One shop inside the main entrance selling guide books and souvenirs, others in the various exhibition rooms.
Extras: The principal extra is the Crown Jewels for which the entrance charge is 60p. The collection is very well worth seeing but visitors should be warned that there are often long queues to get into the Jewel House. Another extra is the Royal Fusiliers Regimental Museum, for which the charge is 10p.

WHITE LODGE Richmond Park (Governors of the Royal Ballet School)
Tel: 01 748 1236
Directions: In the middle of Richmond Park; the house can be reached by car or on foot; drivers should follow signs to the Royal Ballet School and disregard *No Unauthorised Vehicles* signs

White Lodge was built in 1717 as a hunting lodge for King George I and is hidden away in the middle of the park. It is a small square Palladian house with a bold portico on the west side overlooking the Queen's Ride. Two flanking pavilions were added to the house in the 1750s. In the early 19th century James Wyatt linked these pavilions to the house by curving corridors meeting in the middle of the east side, where he provided a new entrance portico. After serving as the home of many minor royalties the house became the Royal Ballet School in 1955 and a number of new buildings have been added to serve the needs of the young dancers. On arrival, visitors are invited to browse over a display of ballet souvenirs in Wyatt's front corridor and then shown three ground floor rooms. These are the old dining room, now a common room, the old library, now the headmistress's study, and the Great Saloon, now an exercise room. All have at least some of their original fitments. The walls are hung with examples from the Ballet School Museum's collection of stage designs, including work by Rex Whistler and Leslie Hurry. A grand staircase leads down from the saloon to the garden, from where it is possible to see the original main front of the house. There is also a small rose garden.

Opening times: August, daily 2–6.
Entrance charges: £1.00.
Parking: In front of the house.
Wheelchair access: Would be possible to all rooms shown.
Guidebook: A very full guide to the house and ballet exhibits on duplicated sheets, no illustrations or plan.
Catering: None.
WCs: None.
Shop: None.

Greater Manchester

DUNHAM MASSEY HALL   nr Altrincham (The National Trust)
Tel: 061 941 1025
Directions: 3 miles S.W. of Altrincham, signposted off the A56; M6 exit 19

The house and its splendid park were left to the National Trust by the Tenth Earl of Stamford as recently as 1976. The present red brick house was built in 1732 for George Booth, Second Earl of Warrington, by an obscure architect called John Norris. The size of some of the rooms and the general arrangement of the house, which has an open courtyard in the centre, were dictated by a Tudor house already on the site. The east side was given a bow front in 1822 and the original stone centrepieces of the north and south fronts were made more elaborate in 1905 by the architect J.C. Hall. The principal attractions of the interior are the excellent early Georgian paintings and furniture and the Huguenot silver collected by the Second Earl for his new house. Most of the state rooms were redecorated in the early years of this century under the supervision of Percy Macquoid, a furniture historian who took particular care to provide decorations in keeping with the furniture. Visitors make their own way through the rooms, some of which have restricting rope barriers. On the ground floor are the Green Saloon and Great Hall (with a ceiling in 17th century style dating from 1905) and also the chapel, which was furnished in about 1710. Most of the other rooms shown are on the first floor. They include the gallery, which has been repainted and contains an unusual collection of 17th and 18th century paintings of the house. Beyond it is Queen Anne's Room, now fitted out to display the silver collection, the Stamford Gallery, which contains many excellent pieces of walnut furniture, and a series of bedrooms. The ground floor library contains the famous relief of the Crucifixion by Grinling Gibbons, probably the one which he was carving when he was 'discovered' by John Evelyn. Next to the house is a handsome range of stables, which contain the visitors' facilities; there is a pleasant garden and the deer park is also open.

Opening times: April to end Oct, every day except Fri, 12–5.30. Because of the large number of visitors a timed ticket system is in operation.
Entrance charges: House £1.60; garden and outbuildings 60p; car park 40p.
Parking: Large car park about five minutes walk from the house. 40p for non-members of the National Trust.
Wheelchair access: Possible to kitchens, outbuildings garden and park; access to the house presents problems because there are steps even on the ground floor.
Guidebook: A thorough new guide with a history and room-by-room description of the house with plans and illustrations as well as a history of the Booth and Grey families who lived here.
Catering: An excellent range of food in the attractively furnished restaurant on the first floor

of the stable block (built in 1721).

WCs: Very good; in the stable block with facilities for wheelchair users.

Shop: A pleasant room in the stable block with the usual National Trust range.

Extras: A special exhibition of Post Office stamps in the stable block, covered by the entrance fee.

FLETCHER MOSS ART GALLERY The Old Parsonage, Didsbury (Manchester City Art Galleries)

Tel: (061) 236 9422 ext. 226

Directions: 5 miles S. of Manchester centre on the A5145, next to Didsbury Church

Fletcher Moss is a rather ordinary-looking rambling early 19th century vicarage, though there may be bits of an older house hidden underneath the rendering. The building was left to Manchester Corporation by Mr Fletcher Moss, who died in 1919. He hoped that it might be retained with all its contents as a typical example of a middle-class home. Sadly, the Corporaton did not feel able to comply with his wishes, and the building has been converted to serve as a local heritage and teaching centre. Mr Moss's 'Olde Englishe' garden remains, slightly municipalised.

Opening times: April to Sept, Mon to Sat 10–6, Sun 12–6 (April and Sept 2–6), closed Oct to March.

Entrance charges: Free.

Parking: No car park, but on-street car parking available nearby.

Wheelchair access: Single step at entrance, three ground floor rooms only accessible.

Guidebook: 15p. A saddening account of Mr Fletcher Moss's unsuccessful attempts to benefit Didsbury, hardly any specific information about the house.

Catering: None.

WCs: One.

Shop: None.

FOXDENTON HOUSE Foxdenton Park, Chadderton (Oldham District Council)

Tel: (Assembly Halls Manager) Royton (061 620) 3505

Directions: 5 miles N.E. of Manchester centre on the B6189 (Foxdenton Lane)

Foxdenton is a small early 18th century mansion, built by Alexander Radclyffe between 1710 and 1730. The house is of red brick, but has a stone basement which may be part of an earlier building on the same site. In 1960 the local council acquired the house and have restored it to something approaching its original appearance, putting back glazing bars of the correct thickness in the windows and restoring the panelling of the rooms inside. Visitors see one room on each floor, and the handsome staircase with its twisted balusters. The furniture is all modern.

Opening times: Tues, Sun, Bank Holidays 2–dusk.

266   *The Historic Houses Handbook*

Entrance charges: Free.
Parking: There is a free car park opposite the entrance to the grounds, about 50 yards from the house.
Wheelchair access: Permitted but difficult; there is a flight of steps to the front door.
Guidebook: A free leaflet gives a short history and description of the house; better than nothing.
Catering: None.
WCs: Modern, inside the house.
Shop: None.

HALL ITH WOOD Crompton Way, Bolton (Bolton Metropolitan Borough)
Tel: Bolton (0204) 51159
Directions: On the north side of Bolton; the house is reached by a turning off Crompton Way (A58), part of the by-pass road

It is a little difficult to find Hall ith Wood, tucked away at the back of a housing estate, but worth the effort. Part of this small manor house is a highly ornamental timber-framed structure of the late 15th century, with stone-built additions of 1591 and 1639. Nothing has been added since and although the house fell on bad times it was lovingly restored by Lord Leverhulme, the soap millionaire. The interior is a delight. Lord Leverhulme furnished the house as a typical 17th century yeoman's dwelling, but it contains far more fine oak furniture than the typical yeoman would have had. Some rooms also have panelling brought from other houses, and all the woodwork glows with polish. There is a small collection of objects connected with Samuel Crompton, who invented his 'Mule' cotton-spinning machine here. The only drawback is that the house is sometimes crowded with school parties.

Opening times; Oct to end March, Mon, Tues, Wed, Fri, Sat 10–5; April to end Sept, daily except Thurs 10–6, also Sun 2–6.
Entrance charges: 30p; OAPs and children 20p.
Parking: Limited parking adjacent to the house.
Wheelchair access: Difficult. There are many changes of level inside the house, even on the ground floor.
Guidebook: Gives a very brief history of the house, but mostly consists of coloured and black and white photographs. No plan.
Catering: None.
WCs: Behind the house, key obtainable on request. Rather primitive; not suitable for wheelchairs.
Shop: None, but postcards on sale.

HEATON HALL Heaton Park, Prestwich (Manchester City Art Galleries)
Tel: 061 773 1231
Directions: 4 miles N. of Manchester centre, off the A576

The house stands in a large and rather bare park. The main block is a plain building of about 1750, enlarged and altered in 1772 by James Wyatt, one of the great architects of the 18th century. His client was Sir Thomas Egerton, later First Earl of Wilton. Wyatt was just becoming fashionable on account of his simple neo-classical style, and the garden front at Heaton is one of the best examples of this style in the country, with some tricks like the Coade stone capitals to the columns. The house was acquired by Manchester Corporation in 1902 and is now used as a museum. Many of the rooms are decorated in what are said to be the original colours and contain good 18th century furniture and pictures, which visitors can examine at their leisure, but only from the walkways. There is a grand central staircase and, on the first floor, a bow-ended room prettily decorated in the Etruscan style by Biagio Rebecca. The house is undergoing considerable restoration and refurbishing. More rooms will be opened when this is complete.

Opening times: House, April to Sept, Mon to Sat 10–6, Sun 12–6 (April and Sept 2–6). Park open all year.
Entrance charges: Free.
Parking: There is a large free car park about 5 mins. walk from the house.
Wheelchair access: Easy access to ground floor; all main rooms can be seen, except Pompeian room on first floor.
Guidebook: A small pamphlet.
Catering: Tea and snacks are available in summer from a kiosk next to the house; no pretensions.
WCs: Free, in the car park, not suitable for wheelchairs.
Shop: None, some postcards for sale.

NEWTON HALL Dukinfield Road (W. Kenyon & Sons)
Tel: 061–308–2721
Directions: 7 miles W. of Manchester centre

A late 14th century timber-framed hall-house, simply one large room in the middle of a cleared grassed area. The house has been restored recently and looks spanking new, with a new floor, new furniture, and a curious new window let into one side of the building for its full height. This is a house for the timber-frame enthusiast only.

Opening times: All year, Mon to Fri 10–4; Key obtainable from the adjacent offices of W. Kenyon & Sons.
Entrance charges: Free.
Parking: Free car park adjacent to house.
Wheelchair access: Would be possible with help.
Guidebook: None.
Catering: None.
WCs: None.
Shop: None.

ORDSALL HALL Taylorson Street, Salford (City of Salford)
Tel: Manchester (061) 872 0251
Directions: 2 miles S.W. of Manchester centre, on the S. side of the A57,
  signposted but still rather difficult to find

Ordsall Hall is worth hunting for among the new buildings of this
'development area'; the house is a museum, restored and opened in 1972 to
provide a sense of history for local people. The first sight from the road is of
the ugly south side, rebuilt in the 1890s, but matters improve on the
entrance side. Here is one of the best ornamental timber houses near
Manchester. The front probably dates from the 1520s, though there was a
house standing before then. The brick wing to the right of the entrance was
added in 1639. By far the best room inside is the Great Hall, rising the full
height of the house and with most of its woodwork intact; there are a few
pieces of early oak furniture but the building itself is the main thing. Other
rooms on the ground floor include the 'Star Chamber' and a kitchen fully
fitted up with 19th century equipment. The upstairs space is used for local
history material and for a display of long-forgotten everyday things.

Opening times: All year, except 1 Jan, Good Friday, 24, 25 and 26 Dec, Mon to Fri 10–5,
  Sun, 2–5.
Entrance charges: Free.
Parking: No car park, but on-street parking in front of house.
Wheelchair access: Possible to Great Hall and most of ground floor.
Guidebook: Cheap and contains only some information about the owners of Ordsall,
  practically nothing on the building.
Catering: None.
WCs: Inside the museum, free, well-maintained; not suitable for wheelchairs.
Shop: Postcards, guidebooks and a few other bits and pieces.

PLATT HALL Platt Fields, Rusholme (Manchester City Art Galleries)
Tel: Manchester (061) 224 5217
Directions: 2 miles S. of Manchester centre on the A6010

Platt Hall was completed in 1764 for John and Deborah Lees. The architect
was probably Timothy Lightoler, who was also a carver, and drawings by
him are on view. The house is of red brick with little external ornament. It
is a modest building, with a seven-bay main block, linked to lower wings.
There have been some unfortunate internal alterations in the past, but the
staircase and first floor dining room are intact and have pretty mid-18th
century plaster decoration. The staircase has been restored and conservation
of the dining room decoration is in progress. Richard Wilson's painting 'A
Summer Evening' hangs over the fireplace, for which it was commissioned
in 1764. This charming house, which stands in what is now a municipal
park, contains a very important costume collection and library.

Opening times: April to Sept, Mon to Sat 10–6, Sun 12–6 (April and Sept 2–6), closed Oct to
  March.

Entrance charges: Free.
Parking: At the back of the house; disabled visitors may park in front of the house.
Wheelchair access: Ground floor galleries, hall and staircase accessible; attendants will assist up two front steps.
Guidebook: In preparation.
Catering: None at the house; tea shop in park during summer.
WCs: Inside the house; key on application; not suitable for the disabled.
Shop: Small sales desk selling postcards and book on costume.

SMITHILLS HALL Smithills Dean Road, Bolton (Bolton Metropolitan Borough)

Tel: Bolton (0204) 41265
Directions: Smithills Dean Road is a part of the A6099, just north of its junction with the A58; the house stands in a large park

The first impression is of an entirely Victorian house, but the 19th century buildings are only additions to one of the oldest surviving houses in the area. The mediaeval house is best seen from the garden; it is made up of three ranges round an open courtyard. Inside the house visitors can make their own way through the great hall of 1400–50, with its huge exposed timbers and small doorways which originally led to the pantry and the buttery. The small east wing contains some fine oak furniture. The larger wing next to it, which was built in the 1530s, includes the drawing room or parlour with carved wooden panelling of the highest quality. The west wing of the house is an old people's home and is not open to the public.

Opening times: All year except 25 and 26 Dec, 1 Jan and 9 April; 1 April to 30 Sept, weekdays except Thurs 10–5.15, Sun 2–5; 1 Oct to 31 March 10 4.15.
Entrance charges: 30p; children 20p.
Parking: Free, next to house.
Wheelchair access: Direct access to hall and parlour.
Guidebook: A brief history and description of the older parts of the house, with many illustrations and a plan of that part of the ground floor which is open to the public.
Catering: None.
WCs: At the house; free, small but well-maintained. Not suitable for wheelchairs.
Shop: None.

Merseyside

CROXTETH HALL   Liverpool (Merseyside County Museums)
Tel: Liverpool (051) 228 5311
Directions: 5 miles N.E. of Liverpool centre signposted from the A580 and
   A5088

This 530 acre country estate inside the city boundary is being organised as
a country park. Cars are kept to the outside edge, and the home farm and
walled garden are being continued for public enjoyment. Until very
recently Croxteth belonged to the Molyneaux family, Earls of Sefton, and
the oldest part of the house was built for Richard Molyneaux in 1575. It has
since been swamped by several large additions. The first of these was the
spectacular red brick south front, added in 1702. The long two-storey block
sits on a raised terrace and is busy with carved ornament. The other
additions are Victorian. The north range dates from the 1870s and the west
side with the principal entrance from 1902. It is at present only possible to
see a limited amount of the interior. The ground floor of the north side has
been arranged as the 'Croxteth Heritage' exhibition, with large numbers of
stuffed animals and big glossy photographs. Of the original
accommodation, visitors may see the 1874 kitchens and some of the
principal first floor rooms. They are large, but much of their original
decoration was destroyed by fire in the 1950s and has been replaced by
modern reproductions. Each room is furnished in the style of an Edwardian
country house and populated by dummies in historical costume. There are
some good Victorian and Edwardian paintings, but in many cases rope
barriers prevent close scrutiny. Presumably more rooms will be opened as
restoration progresses. The most impressive interior is the fine and grand
staircase by which visitors descend to the ground floor again.

Opening times: Outer park open daily throughout the year 9–dusk; inner park including hall,
    farm and gardens open Good Friday to end Sept, daily 11–5.
Entrance charges: (1981) House 50p; walled garden 30; home farm 60p; inclusive ticket
    £1.20. Children and OAPs half price. Free entrance to park.
Parking: Free car parks at the vehicle entrance off Muirhead Avenue East (A5049).
Wheelchair access: Possible to the park, farm and gardens but only to the Heritage
    Exhibition, courtyard and kitchen in the house.
Guidebook: A selection of leaflets with basic information. A fuller guidebook is in
    preparation.
Catering: Ice creams, crisps etc. from a booth by the entrance to the house; there is a tea room
    at the south end of the west terrace, pleasant surroundings and it is possible to sit outside.
WCs: Near the car park and near the home farm; neither suitable for wheelchairs.
Shop: Some pamphlets and country park souvenirs on sale at the house.
Extras: Extra charges for the home farm and the walled garden.

SPEKE HALL The Walk, Liverpool (The National Trust and Merseyside District Council)
Tel: Liverpool (051) 427 7231
Directions: 8 miles S.E. of central Liverpool, off the A561, very near Speke Airport

Speke Hall is a large timber-framed house built round an open courtyard which contains two large yew trees. Various parts of the house were built at different times by various members of the Norris family. No one is quite sure of the age of the great hall, which is the oldest part, but most of the house was built between 1500 and 1600. The outside is picturesque, with gables, leaded windows and ornamental timberwork picked out in black and white like many of the other big houses in this part of England. The guided tours of the inside show most of the main rooms, including the great hall with its splendid Flemish panelling and the parlour, which has a good plaster ceiling and a very odd carved overmantel. There are also a number of 'secret' rooms. Most of the rooms are full of oak furniture, much of it made up from bits and pieces by the Watt family who took over the house in 1796. The guides, who are used to parties of schoolchildren, have a good line in patter, which is alright if you like that kind of thing. Speke is one of the few houses open to the public near Liverpool and can get very crowded, especially in summer. Although it is rather too close to Liverpool airport, the good-sized park is full of trees and very pleasant.

Opening times: April to Sept, weekdays 10–5, Bank Holiday 10–7, Sun 2–7; Oct to end March, Mon to Sat 10–5, Sun 2–5, last admission one hour before closing. In the winter visitors are sometimes asked to wait outside until the start of the tour.
Entrance charges: 60p; OAPs and children 30p; subject to revision.
Parking: Free car park 50 yards from the house.
Wheelchair access: The great hall, parlour, kitchen and several downstairs rooms are accessible; there is no access to the first floor. A wheelchair is available at the house.
Guidebook: Glossy and well-illustrated; rather vague on the dating of the house but better on the furniture and the various owners. A full plan of the house is very welcome.
Catering: Tea room in the summer months.
WCs: In the car park; unsuitable for wheelchairs and unpleasant for everyone else. There are additional (and preferable) facilities by the tea room.
Shop: None, but slides and postcards are on sale in the house.

West Midlands

ASBURY COTTAGE Newton Road, Great Barr (Metropolitan Borough of Sandwell)
Tel: The Curator, Birmingham (021) 566 0683
Directions: 3 miles E. of the centre of West Bromwich on the A4041
   3, C3)

This tiny early 18th century brick house, perched on the side of the Newton Road dual carriageway, was once the home of Francis Asbury, first Bishop of the American Methodist church. He lived here with his parents until the age of 26, when he answered Wesley's call for missionaries to America. It is difficult to imagine the place in Asbury's time because the district is now built up and the cottage has been heavily restored. Most of the furniture in the four small rooms has been given by American well-wishers and is not of the type that Asbury and his parents would have used, nor is there much information available about the Bishop and his work.

Opening times: All year, Mon to Fri 2–4.
Entrance charges: Free.
Parking: In one of the side streets off Newton Road.
Wheelchair access: Cramped and difficult.
Guidebook: Chiefly concerned to make kind remarks about the Bishop and give an account of
   the restoration of the house by the local council.
Catering: None.
WCs: None.
Shop: None.

ASTON HALL Trinity Road, Aston (Birmingham Corporation)
Tel: Birmingham (021) 327 0062
Directions: 2½ miles N. of Birmingham centre, to the W. of the A38

Aston Hall is an impressive Jacobean mansion, now surrounded by factories and mean streets. Fine views of Spaghetti Junction can be had from many windows and Aston Villa football ground occupies what was once the kitchen gardens. The house consists of a main block with projecting wings and a pair of detached gatehouses, all built in the brownish local brick with stone dressings. The skyline is alive with curved gables, chimneys and towers. It is not known who Sir Thomas Holte employed as his architect at Aston, but it may have been John Thorpe. The house was begun in 1618 and finished by 1638 and there have not been any major alterations. There are some original plaster ceilings, especially those in the great dining room and long gallery, a good strapwork staircase and some contemporary panelling. The furniture accumulated by the Holte family was dispersed in 1819. The present contents are drawn from the City Museum, the Victoria and Albert

Museum in London and from private collectors, and are changed from time to time. Most of the rooms are open and contain 17th and 18th century furniture, tapestries and paintings. In the early 19th century Aston was leased to James Watt, son of the engineer, who worked the family crest into the decoration wherever possible; a number of the upstairs rooms are laid out in the mid-19th century taste. Some rooms are not always shown. There are guided tours, with very amiable guides, which last about an hour. The gardens round the house have a municipal flavour.

Opening times: Easter to end Oct, Mon to Sat 10–1, 2–5, Sun 2–5.
Entrance charges: 40p; OAPs and children under 16 20p. Friends of Birmingham Art Gallery free.
Parking: In front of the house, or in the car park, signposted off Frederick Road, both free.
Wheelchair access: Possible to ground floor only, the staff are most helpful.
Guidebook: A good little guide, well-illustrated and covering the house, its contents and past owners; there are also plans of the building.
Catering: None.
WCs: To the right of the entrance courtyard; not suitable for wheelchairs.
Shop: Postcards and slides in the entrance hall.

BLAKESLEY HALL Blakesley Road, Yardley (Birmingham Corporation)
Tel: Birmingham (021) 783 2193
Directions: Yardley is on the E. side of Birmingham centre. Blakesley Road crosses the ring road (A4040) ⅔ mile N. of its junction with the A45

In 1900 Yardley was a small country village with a few timber-framed farmhouses and a mediaeval church. The growth of Birmingham engulfed the village, leaving only the church, with the 15th century grammar school beside it, and Blakesley Hall, which became a museum in 1935. The immediate surroundings of the house are attractive, with lawns, an apple-walk, a herb garden and an unusual 18th century moon-dial which came from Elford Hall in Staffordshire. Next to the house is a fine barn of 18th century brick (not open to visitors). Richard Smalbroke built the house between 1573 and 1590 and it has the elaborate and decorative timber-framing typical of that time. The original house was L-shaped, with a hall and screens passage in the main part and a parlour wing to the west. The upper floor is jettied out on large, ornate brackets. In the mid-17th century a brick kitchen wing was added behind the hall and, in the 18th century, a still room and boulting house was built on to the east end (boulting is a means of separating flour from bran). In 1684 the Hall was bought by Henry Greswolde, and remained in his family until 1899. His extraordinary monument can be seen in the church. One of the most interesting features of the house is the upstairs painted room, probably decorated in the 1570s, which is now furnished as a 17th century bedroom. The great parlour on the ground floor has an exhibition of photograhs of timber-framed buildings and other rooms have exhibitions on thatching, tanning and other rural crafts, all of them well-arranged.

Opening times: All year, Mon to Sat 1.30–5.30.
Entrance charges: 25p; OAPs and children under 16 15p; no unaccompanied children; no dogs.
Parking: In the road outside.
Wheelchair access: Possible to ground floor rooms.
Guidebook: An inexpensive sheet with reliable information and a plan.
Catering: None.
WCs: Next to the ticket counter; unsuitable for wheelchairs.
Shop: Books and postcards on sale in the house.

DUDLEY CASTLE AND ZOO The Broadway, Dudley (Dudley and W. Midlands Zoological Society)
Tel: Dudley (0384) 52401
Directions: 9 miles W.N.W. of central Birmingham in the centre of Dudley on the A461

The buildings of the castle were partly destroyed in the English Civil War and are now in ruins. The wooded hill at Dudley was fortified before the Norman conquest but the present buildings mostly date from the 14th and 16th centuries. The keep was built by John de Somery in the early 14th century. He also built a wall round the bailey, but this was incorporated into the range of domestic buildings erected in the mid-16th century by John Dudley, Duke of Northumberland. The mason he employed for the work was John Chapman, who had worked at Lacock Abbey in Wiltshire for Sir William Sharington and favoured the new Renaissance style. He built the great hall on the first floor. It was entered by a flight of steps through an Ionic colonnade which has since been destroyed. The hall is flanked by the chapel and kitchens, whose walls still stand to their full height. The Duke of Northumberland was executed in 1553, when his plan to set his daughter Lady Jane Grey on the throne misfired, but one of his younger sons was Queen Elizabeth's favourite, Robert Dudley, Earl of Leicester. The Queen returned the castle to him, but the Earl spent most of his time at Kenilworth. All the main parts of the ruin are clearly labelled with diagrams and helpful descriptions. Limestone quarrying into the hillside in the 19th century created a number of pits, which were attractively landscaped when the site was turned into a zoo in 1937. The architects for the work were Lubetkin and the Tecton group, pioneers of modern architecture, who had already designed the penguin pool at the London Zoo.

Opening times: All year, weekdays 9–4, Sun 10–4; closes 4pm winter and 4.30 summer.
Entrance charges: Winter £1.00; children and OAPs 50p. Summer £1.50; children and OAPs 80p.
Parking: Large pay-car park next to the zoo.

Wheelchair access: Possible to most parts of the castle.
Guidebook: Guide to the zoo and separate guide to the castle with illustrations and a plan.
Catering: Snacks in the moat cafe, lunches in the Queen Mary Ballroom, also the fully-licensed Safari Steak Bar.
WCs: Situated at the gates; not adapted for wheelchairs.
Shop: Souvenir shop, catering for younger members of the public.
Extras: Cable car rides.

HAGLEY HALL nr Stourbridge (Viscount and Viscountess Cobham)
Tel: Hagley (0562) 882408
Directions: 12 miles S.E. of Birmingham centre, 6 miles N.E. of Kidderminster, just off the A456

The house and park at Hagley were created in the 1750s for George, first Lord Lyttelton. The architect was his friend Sanderson Miller, a local gentleman with a reputation for Gothick garden buildings. Lyttelton said he was 'pretty indifferent about the outside' of his house and Miller produced a very plain stone building in the English Palladian style with square towers at the four corners. The principal rooms are on the first floor, where there is lively rococo plaster decoration by Francesco Vassali in both the hall and dining room. The rich festoons of flowers and musical instruments in the dining room are seen to advantage against the turquoise paint. The more delicate plasterwork in the drawing room is complimented by the carving of the overdoors and mirror frames between the beautiful Soho tapestries woven in the 1720s. Although the western half of the house was badly damaged by fire in 1925, all the decorations have been restored with great skill. A quantity of furniture and paintings were destroyed at the same time, but many good portraits survive and the furniture includes a pair of notable pier-glasses in the long gallery, which may be by Thomas Johnson. All the main rooms are shown in the half-hourly tours which last about an hour. The park was begun before the house, and was laid out with advice from the poet-gardener William Shenstone, and contains some famous garden buildings. It takes over an hour to walk the circuit. The high points are Sanderson Miller's sham castle and the temple of Theseus by 'Athenian' Stuart, a smaller version of the original in Athens, but there are several other buildings, obelisks and fine views.

Opening times: April and May, Sat and Sun; also Easter Mon and Tues; June to 5 Sept, daily 12.30–5.
Entrance charges: £1.50; OAPs £1.00; children 75p. (HHA)
parking: Free parking in a field beside the house.
Wheelchair access: The main rooms in the house are on the first floor, but ring in advance and arrangements can be made for access; restaurant and shop are on the ground floor.
Guidebook: A good, well-illustrated guide covering the house and contents in detail, with a description of the church and of the Lyttelton family, but without a plan of the house. There is a separate guide to the park, but this gives no indication of the gradients, which are steep in places.
Catering: Lunches and home-made teas in the basement restaurant.

Hagley Hall, West Midlands

WCs: Near the restaurant; unsuitable for wheelchairs.
Shop: Sells sweets, gifts and craft work.

MOSELY OLD HALL nr Wolverhampton (The National Trust)
Tel: Wolverhampton (0902) 782808
Directions: 4 miles N. of Wolverhampton, between the A449 ad A460 roads (M6 exit 11)

Moseley Old Hall is difficult to find and at first looks a disappointment. The small timber-framed manor house built in about 1600, which gave refuge to King Charles II after his defeat at the Battle of Worcester in 1651, was completely encased in ugly purple bricks in the 1870s, but the original chimneys still survive and the interior has been little altered. The building was acquired by the Trust in 1962, mainly because of its associations with the King. It was empty, but now contains some 17th century furniture, including the bed in which King Charles slept, English china, and a handful of portraits relating to the Whitgrave family who gave Charles hospitality. As the family was Roman Catholic there is a small chapel and a priest's hole. Some related documents are exhibited. The guided tours last about 40 minutes. There is a small knot garden outside the house. Although laid out recently, it is based on a design of the 1640s and only uses plants that would have been available in the 17th century. The trellis walk to one side is hung with vines and clematis and leads, by way of a hornbeam arbour and nut walk, towards the gateway through which Charles entered.

Opening times: March to end Nov. March and Nov, Wed and Sun 2–6 or sunset. April to end Oct, Wed, Thurs, Sat, Sun and Bank Holiday Mon (also Tues following Easter, Spring and late Summer Bank Holiday) 2–6; closed Good Friday.
Entrance charges: £1.00, children 50p; no unaccompanied children under 12.
Parking: Free parking.
Wheelchair access: Possible to the ground floor only.
Guidebook: A description, history, and room-by-room guide with a few illustrations, including one of the house before it was faced in brick, no plan.
Catering: Home-made teas, excellent scones, 3–5.30.
WCs: At the back of the house; unsuitable for wheelchairs.
Shop: The standard National Trust gifts.

OAK HOUSE Oak Road, West Bromwich (Metropolitan Borough of Sandwell)
Tel: Birmingham (021) 553 0759
Directions: ¼ mile W. of West Bromwich centre, near the A41

A spectacular timber framed house of the 16th century, with a gabled front and a timber tower perched on the roof. The original house had a central hall with wings on each side. The porch with its decorative framing, was added in the late 16th century and there were major changes in the 1630s when the back of the house was extended and faced in brick. A cellar was also dug out at this time and it is open to visitors on request. The rooms inside have kept most of their original panelling and there is some fine carved decoration, particularly the overmantel in the main bedroom upstairs. Some restoration work was done by the firm of Wood & Kendrick in 1898, including the opening up of the hall ceiling, but it was done well. The house makes a handsome background for the mainly 16th and 17th century furniture donated by local residents and there is a comfortable and authentic atmosphere. There are rosebeds in front of the house and a well-kept bowling green behind it, but this is a depressing area to visit. The wasteland to the east seems to attract vandals and the windows of Oak House are frequent targets; perhaps the stocks in the garden should be brought back into use as a deterrent.

Opening times: April to Sept, Mon to Sat 10–5, Thurs 10–1, Sun 2.30–5. Oct to March 10–1.
Entrance charges: Free.
Parking: Free parking in the road.
Wheelchair access: Possible to the ground floor, and all the outside is visible.
Guidebook: An informative and generally reliable booklet with illustrations and a plan of the house; there are also information sheets in each room.
Catering: None.
WCs: Public conveniences in the garden, basic.
Extras: Enthusiasts for timber-framed buildings might like to visit the Old Manor House in Hall Green Road, about 2 miles to the north, which is a largely mediaeval courtyard house with an early 14th century great hall and a canopied dais. The moat was re-dug and the building restored in the 1950s; it is now a bar and restaurant.

SELLY MANOR AND MINWORTH GREAVES Maple Road, Bournville (The Bournville Village Trust)

Tel: Curator, Birmingham (021) 472 0199, during opening hours
Directions: Bournville is 5 miles S.W. of Birmingham centre, on the A38. The two houses are near the village green

Selly Manor House is an attractive timber-framed house of the 14th century which originally stood in Bournbrook Road near the University. It was saved from demolition in 1907 by George Cadbury, who bought the house and had it re-erected here in 1912–16. The house had been altered over the years. The chimneys are Tudor, and the brick herringbone infill between the main timbers is a Tudor replacement of the original lath and plaster. The house is furnished with 17th century furniture and domestic utensils collected by the Mr L.J. Cadbury. The curator has tried to give the house an authentic lived-in atmosphere. There are bundles of herbs from the garden drying by the fireplace and real rush lights. Exhibits are clearly labelled and explained. Minworth Greaves was also rescued from demolition. It was re-erected here between 1929 and 1932. The property dated from the 13th or 14th century but was in such a bad state that only the hall could be saved, with the addition of timbers brought from other buildings. It is a good example of the cruck type of construction. Inside the furniture includes a very fine refectory table from Crook Hall in Lancashire and a finely carved oak coffer. There is a small garden.

Opening times: Mid-Jan to mid-Dec Tues, Wed and Fri 2–5, except Easter Tues and Spring Bank Holiday Tues.
Entrance charges: Free; no unaccompanied children.
Parking: Free parking in the road outside.
Wheelchair access: Possible to ground floor of both properties.
Guidebook: A little illustrated booklet with basic facts; there are information boards in the buildings.
Catering: None.
WCs: One lavatory; unsuitable for wheelchairs.

WIGHTWICK MANOR Wightwick Bank, Wolverhampton (The National Trust)
Tel: Wolverhampton (0902) 761108
Directions: 3 miles W. of Wolverhampton off the A454, beside the Mermaid Inn

Wightwick (pronounced Witick) is a late Victorian house with excellent decorations by various members of the Pre-Raphaelite movement. A paint manufacturer named Theodore Mander bought the old manor house and its estate in 1887 and employed the architect Edward Ould to build him a new house near the old one. The design included elements copied from the timber-framed houses of the district, but Ould also used a lot of hard shiny red brick from Ruabon. In 1893 he added an east wing in a similar style, with very elaborate timbering. The interior was decorated by Morris & Co. and most of it is still intact. The wallpapers and fabrics designed by William Morris still survive in almost every room. There is also much stained glass by C.E. Kempe, metalwork by W.A.S. Benson, and tiles by William de Morgan. Against this rich background are hung paintings by Edward Burne-Jones and other Pre-Raphaelites, while the furnishings are a mixture of Victorian pieces, Jacobean oak, and the Persian rugs and blue and white china which were so popular with the 'advanced' taste of the 1890s. The collection belonging to the house has been supplemented by the present Lady Mander, an informed enthusiast for the period. On most days only the ground floor rooms are open to visitors, but on Saturdays five additional rooms upstairs are also shown. These contain more furnishings of the same high quality. The library of the house has an important collection of books on William Morris and his period, which may be consulted by written permission only. The gardens are contemporary with the house and were designed to be in keeping with it. They were laid out by Alfred Parsons and have been little altered.

Opening times: All year (except Feb), Thurs, Sat, Bank Holiday Mon and preceeding Sun 2.30–5.30; also May to end Sept Wed 2.30–5.30. Closed Good Friday, 25–26 Dec, 1–2 Jan.
Entrance charges: £1.00 (Sat £1.50); no children under 10; children half price; students 40p.

Wightwick Manor, West Midlands

Garden only 40p.
Parking: Free parking in front of the house.
Wheelchair access: Possible to ground floor rooms (most of the house).
Guidebook: Principally a room-by-room guide, with a brief account of the house and the Manders; illustrated, but no plan of the building.
Catering: None.
WCs: In the stable block; unsuitable for wheelchairs.
Shop: Sells books and postcards; there is also a small secondhand bookshop and a pottery in the outbuildings.

Norfolk

BACONSTHORPE CASTLE Baconsthorpe (Ancient Monument)
Directions: 6 miles S.W. of Cromer; Baconsthorpe village is 2 miles S. of the A148 near Holt and the castle is signposted from Baconsthorpe village, 1 mile down farm roads (Map 4, A6)

The ruins of the castle stand next to a farm in remote countryside. They are enclosed by a water filled moat on three sides and by a mere on the fourth. The castle was really a fortified manor house, begun by Sir John Heydon in the 1480s and enlarged by later members of his family. About half the walls of the original enclosure still stand, together with the flint-faced gatehouse. There are remains of other buildings, many of them altered or rebuilt in the 17th century when the castle was converted into a factory for the production of cloth. The Elizabethan outer gatehouse was occupied as recently as the 1920s. It is now a pretty ruin with one of the two original little turrets still standing.

Opening times: Open at all reasonable times.
Entrance charges: Free.
Parking: Free parking next to castle.
Wheelchair access: Turnstiles at entrance make this difficult.
Guidebook: Not obtainable at the property.
Catering: None, although this would make a good place for a picnic.
WCs: None.
Shop: Postcards only.

BEESTON HALL nr Wroxham (Sir Richard and Lady Preston)
Tel: Horning (0692) 630771
Directions: 11 miles N.E. of Norwich, 2½ miles N.E. of Wroxham on the S. side of the A1151

Beeston Hall is a trim Gothick box with battlements and spindly corner towers, walls faced with knapped flint and sash windows with pointed tops. Its appearance is marred by an ugly porch added in 1870 and by the red brick wing on one side built to house the servants. Beeston was built for Jacob Preston in 1786; the design is attributed to William Wilkins of Norwich who did a lot of work in the Gothick style. The interior is a carefree mixture of Gothic and Classical. Rooms facing towards the church are Gothick, the rest Classical, and the shapes of doors and windows chop and change to suit each room. The contents include a number of mementoes from Russia, brought back by Sir Thomas Preston, who was Consul in Ekaterinburg in 1918, and pleasant Georgian furniture, like the shield-back hall chairs. The park was landscaped by Mr Richmond, a follower of 'Capability' Brown.

Opening times: 11 April to 12 Sept, Fri, Sun and Bank Holiday 2–5.30.
Entrance charges: 80p; children 40p; OAPs 60p; no dogs or photography in house. (HHA)
Parking: Free.
Wheelchair access: Possible to garden only.
Guidebook: The small guidebook contains a short but adequate history of the house and owners; there is no plan and nothing about the furniture. An information sheet with a room-by-room guide is lent out free at the start of each visit.
Catering: Good home-made cakes and tea in the old orangery.
WCs: Close to the orangery, free, fairly clean; unsuitable for wheelchairs.
Shop: Sales counter in orangery.

BLICKLING HALL Blickling (The National Trust)
Tel: Aylsham (026 373) 3084
Directions: 3 miles N.W. of Aylsham on the B1345 (Aylsham is 15 miles N. of Norwich on the A140)

Blickling is one of the most memorable Jacobean houses in the country. The red brick front is approached by a long forecourt flanked first by giant yew hedges and then by low ranges of gabled outbuildings. Behind the shaped gables and tall corner turrets of the front is an oblong house whose size was determined by the moat of an earlier house on the same site. The Jacobean house was built for Sir Henry Hobart between 1619 and 1627; it was designed by Robert Lyminge, who was also responsible for Hatfield House in Hertfordshire. Although the red brick walls of the exterior look all of a piece, the west front and most of the north front were rebuilt in the 1760s under the direction of the architects Thomas and William Ivory of Norwich. They also moved the original main staircase of the house into the great hall and redecorated several of the rooms. Further alterations were made in the 19th century and much of the interior panelling dates from the 1840s. Most of the principal rooms are open to visitors. The main living rooms are on the first floor and of these the most spectacular are the south drawing room, originally the great chamber, with its elaborate plaster ceiling designed by Robert Lyminge, and the long gallery. The gallery also has an outstanding original plaster ceiling and a good 19th century painted frieze by John Hungerford Pollen who also designed the shelves which hold an extremely valuable private library. The furniture, tapestries and paintings in the rooms have been accumulated by successive owners over three hundred years. The park is probably based on the original 17th century layout but was made less formal by 18th century landscaping. John Adey Repton was responsible for some building work at the house ad his father, Humphrey Repton, may have had a hand in the park.

Opening times: April to 20 May and 5–31 Oct, Tues, Wed, Thurs, Sat, Sun and Bank Holiday Mon 2–6. Closed Good Friday. 22 May to end Sept, Tues, Wed, Thurs, Sat and Bank Holiday Mon 11–6 (closed 12.30–1.30), Sun 2–6. Garden as above and 22 May to 1 Oct, Mon and Fri 2–6.

Entrance charges: £1.40; children 70p. Garden only, Mon and Fri 90p; no dogs; no pushchairs in house.

Parking: Free, next to the house.

Wheelchair access: Possible to ground floor (four rooms), gardens and tea room.

Guidebook: Very full, plans of house and of grounds, excellent value.

Catering: Teas in east wing, morning coffee and light lunches, 26 May to 30 Sept; set lunches, set teas, or tea by the cup and good cakes; closed 1.45–2.30.

WCs: At north end of east wing; modern, clean and free, with facilities for disabled women; lavatory for disabled men in boundary wall to south west of house.

Shop: In the east wing with an extensive selection of National Trust material.

Extras: Fishing permits available for the lake.

CAISTER CASTLE Caister on Sea, Gt Yarmouth (Dr P.R. Hill JP)
Tel: Great Yarmouth (0943) 720267
Directions: 3 miles N. of Gt Yarmouth, 1 mile W. of Caister on Sea, on the S. side of the A1064

The twin attractions of Caister Castle are the spectacular ruins of the castle itself and the motor car museum. The castle was built by Sir John Fastolfe between 1433 and 1448 on the site of an earlier house. The building combined comfortable living rooms with strong defences. It was one of the first brick-built castles in England and had an elaborate system of water defences, like some German castles of the same period. Although both his name and character were twisted by Shakespeare, Sir John Fastolfe was in reality a successful soldier in the European wars and may have copied his new castle from such foreign examples. Only one moat now remains, encircling the ruins. At the western corner rises a great tower, which can be climbed for an excellent view, although with a minimal feeling of security. The motor museum is housed in modern buildings with bits and pieces dotted around some of the older buildings. The collection is one of the best in the country and includes trams and motor bikes as well as cars. The trees round the castle contain the tree walk, a refugee from the Battersea Fun Fair in London.

Opening times: May to end Sept, Sun to Fri 10.30–5.

Entrance charges: (1981) £1.25; children 60p; OAPs 80p; dogs and cameras allowed in grounds but not in museum.

Parking: Free car park 50 yards from the castle.
Wheelchair access: Access to all except tower and tree walk.
Guidebook: Good on the history of the castle, but describes the buildings as they were in the 15th century, not as they are today. It does not point out, for example, that the moat between outer and inner courts no longer exists. The text is almost all about the castle, the illustrations are almost all of old motor vehicles. A plan shows the castle as first built.
Catering: In the kitchen, tea and ordinary cakes.
WCs: At the entrance, free and fairly clean; unsuitable fo wheelchairs.
Shop: Postcards on sale at the end of the motor museum tour.

CASTLE RISING　nr King's Lynn (Ancient Monument)
Directions: 5 miles N.E. of King's Lynn, best approached from the A149 Hunstanton road

The castle stands on the edge of the village. Its great grassy banks and ditches enclose a very large stone keep, rivalling the keep of Norwich Castle in size and splendour. The exterior, especially the forebuilding which contains the main staircase, carries the remains of interlacing arches and other original decoration. The interior was almost entirely filled by two splendid large rooms, the great hall and great chamber, with a chapel and a few other small rooms and basements underneath. The keep was built by William de Albini in about 1138. In this same year he married Queen Alice, widow of King Henry I, and at once became one of the leading members of the aristocracy, with enormous wealth and the new title of Earl of Lincoln. Both Castle Rising and the castle at Buckenham, also in Norfolk, were built by William to show off his new position. The rooms of the keep have lost their roof and their floors but they are still impressive; the forebuilding with its splendid staircase has survived nearly complete. Of the other castle buildings, only the bridge and the Norman gatehouse remain, together with the base of the walls of a Norman church. Visitors have free run of the buildings.

Opening times: Standard hours (S),see page xii.
Entrance charges: 50p; children under 16 and OAPs 20p.
Parking: Next to the castle mound.
Wheelchair access: No access to the inside of the keep, but all the exterior is visible.
Guidebook: The Official Handbook has a full history and description, with plans of the keep; there is also an inexpensive leaflet which gives all the basic information.
Catering: None.
WCs: In the car park; clean, free; suitable for wheelchairs.
Shop: Only DoE literature.

FELBRIGG HALL　nr Cromer (The National Trust)
Tel: West Runton (026 375) 444
Directions: 21 miles N. of Norwich, 3 miles S.W. of Cromer, signposted off the A148 and A140

The approach to the house passes a brick stable block built in the 1820s to the design of William Donthorne and the neat little service wing and clock tower added by James Paine in the 1750s on its way to the south front. This belongs to the attractive red brick Jacobean house, built for Thomas Windham in about 1620 on the site of an older building. There are three projecting bays with large mullion and transom windows and above them the words 'GLORIA IN EXCELSIS DEO' are spelt out in the parapet. Round the corner is the west front which was added in the 1680s following a design by the local gentleman architect William Samwell. The two fronts are the same height, but Samwell's quiet brick front makes a complete contrast to the Jacobean work. The interior owes much to 18th and 19th century alterations. The rooms behind the west front have both original plasterwork (in the drawing room and cabinet) and fruity rococo decoration added by James Paine, who also added a new main staircase, fitted out the library in the Gothick style, and redecorated the bedrooms. The heavy plaster decoration of the great hall is probably Donthorne's work of the 1830s. The excellent furnishings include three English Savonnerie carpets, Chinese Chippendale chairs, and a Louis XIV Buhl chest. The general standard of paintings and furniture throughout the house is high. The same William Windham who added the west side of the house also planted great quantities of trees in the park, and both the woods and the walled gardens at Felbrigg are a source of pleasure.

Opening times: April to 10 Oct, Tues, Wed, Thurs, Sat, Sun and Bank Holiday Mon 2–6.
Entrance charges: £1.40; children 70p; no dogs.
Parking: Free parking in a field 200 yards from the house.
Wheelchair access: All the rooms on the ground floor are accessible, and two wheelchairs are available at the door. The tea room and shop and also accessible.
Guidebook: A straightforward account of the house and its owners with a room-by-room guide, illustrated but without a plan. There are separate fold-out guides to the walled garden and the lakeside walk.
Catering: In the old kitchen of the house; a good setting; tea and reasonable cakes.
WCs: On the ground floor of the house; free, clean and suitable for wheelchairs.
Shop: In the servants' block near the exit; one of the best National Trust shops, with a bookshop adjoining.

GREAT YARMOUTH: ANNA SEWELL'S HOUSE Church Plain (Mr and Mrs Mummery)
Tel: Great Yarmouth (0492) 3372 or 58083
Directions: Church Plain opens off the Market Square

This little house, with its timber-framed gable, was the birthplace of Anna Sewell, author of *Black Beauty*. The book has sold about 38 million copies since it was first published in the 1870s. The front of the house carries the date 1641, which seems about right for the building, though some parts may be earlier. A former owner brought in the front window from one of Yarmouth's 'Row Houses' and a recent restoration has removed layers of paint and wallpaper and uncovered several original fireplaces. It is intended that the house should look as it did in 1820, when Anna Sewell was born. There are no possessions of the Sewell family but instead there are over 100 English editions of *Black Beauty*.

Opening times: All year, Mon to Sat 9.30–6.
Entrance charges: 20p; children 10p.
Parking: Car park in front of house, 20p per hour.
Wheelchair access: Possible to ground floor only.
Guidebook: An eight page booklet with a few scraps of history.
Catering: None.
WCs: None.
Shop: Black Beauty can be purchased at the entrance.

GREAT YARMOUTH: THE OLD MERCHANTS' HOUSE Row 117 with Nos. 7 and 8, Row 111 and The Greyfriars (Department of the Environment)

Tel: Great Yarmouth (0493) 37940
Directions: All three houses are off South Quay

The southern part of Great Yarmouth, next to the sea, was originally laid our rather like a kipper, with Middlegate Street as the backbone and the smaller bones leading from it represented by 145 passages about 3 feet wide known as 'The Rows'. A fire destroyed the greater part of the town in 1571 and the Row houses were rebuilt over the next 50 years in fireproof flint and brick. These houses were built for both wealthy merchants and the less well off and their size varied; many had courtyards and even small gardens. But in the 18th and 19th centuries the courtyards were built over and the Row houses became overpopulated slums. The whole area was badly damaged in the last war but two of the houses have been preserved and they contain a collection of objects salvaged from other houses. Numbers 7 and 8, Row 111 were originally one house, built in about 1600 and extended about 100 years later, although at one time the building was divided into three separate dwellings. The three floors of small rooms have mainly 18th and 19th century fittings. They contain collections of doors, fireplaces and iron firegates from other houses. The walls of the small courtyard have been rebuilt to show the different types of brick and flint walling used in the area. The Old Merchant's House is much grander, with rich plaster ceilings in two of the rooms. These suffered when the size of the rooms was reduced. Several of the rooms and passages are panelled and the attics house a collection of the ornamental wall-anchors, which seem to have been a Yarmouth speciality. The guided tour of these two buildings ends with a visit to the ruins of the 14th century cloister buildings of the Greyfriars monastery.

Opening times: April to Sept, Mon to Fri, guided tours only, lasting about 1 hour 20 minutes, starting at the Row 111 houses and including the two other properties; tours at 9.45, 11.20, 2.15 and 3.45. There is a waiting room but it is closed between 1 and 2.

Entrance charges: 40p; OAPs and children under 16 20p.
Parking: Up to 1½ hours free parking in South Quay, 50 yards away.
Wheelchair access: Only possible to about one third of the houses.
Guidebook: Small free leaflet on the Old Merchant's House or a good inexpensive leaflet on the two Row houses, with plans.
Catering: None.
WCs: None.
Shop: None.

GREAT YARMOUTH: 4 SOUTH QUAY (The National Trust and Norfolk Museum Service)

Tel: Great Yarmouth (0493) 55746
Directions: On South Quay, facing the river

The front of the house promises little; it was faced in white brick soon after 1809 and the only ornaments are the cast iron window balconies and a Doric porch. In fact, the front covers part of a splendid late Elizabethan house, built in 1596 for a merchant named Benjamin Cowper. Both the dining room and the thirty foot long drawing room above it have very richly decorated plaster ceilings with floral and geometrical designs and a mass of pendants. The carved wooden chimneypieces in these rooms and in the south chamber are equally magnificent. Other survivals include the mullioned windows in the kitchen and elsewhere and the painted beam in the north chamber. The building now serves as a museum of local life, but the furniture is better than the description implies. It includes an inlaid chair of about 1650, a rare Italian folding chair of about 1550 and a good mid-18th century long-case clock in the Chinese taste. There are also first class displays of domestic equipment, 18th century china and glass and toys and dolls. Some of the windows have recently been fitted with 16th and 17th century glass; one Flemish roundel of 1612 has a painting of a herring-fishing boat, not so very different from the 'Lydia Eva' moored against the quay outside. There are no official guided tours, but the Curator is extremely helpful and quite willing to take you round.

Opening times: June to Sept, daily except Sat 10–1, 2–5.30; Oct to May, Mon to Fri 10–1, 2–5.30.
Entrance charges: 10p (Spring Bank Holiday to Sept 20p), children 5p.
Parking: Up to 1½ hours free parking on the quayside.
Wheelchair access: Only to downstairs, with a few small steps.
Guidebook: The house is illustrated briefly and described in 'Treasures of Yarmouth Museums' which covers five museums, including the Steam Drifter 'Lydia Eva'.
Catering: None.
WCs: None.
Shop: Some leaflets at the entrance.

HOLKHAM HALL   nr Wells (Viscount Coke)
Tel: Fakenham (0328) 710227
Directions: 2 miles W. of Wells, off the A149 Hunstanton road; Garden
  Centre entrance at weekends off the B1155

Thomas Coke, First Earl of Leicester, was a wealthy and cultivated
nobleman who was a great art collector. He built Holkham Hall between
1734 and 1761 to house his collection. The building was designed by
William Kent, one of the leading architects of the time, and is a good
example of the English Palladian style. The large central block contains the
state apartments, while the everyday living rooms, the chapel and the
kitchen are in the four small pavilions linked to the main block by corridors.
The whole building is of greyish-yellow brick which looks like stone from a
distance. A small entrance door in the north front leads at once into the
famous Marble Hall, with its rich purple, pink and green alabaster walls and
coffered ceiling. Grand stairs lead up between alabaster columns to the
principal floor and so to the State rooms. Of these, the most magnificent are
the Statue Gallery, with its two smaller galleries or tribunes, which occupies
one side of the house, and the saloon which is behind the great portico of the
south front. The walls of the saloon are hung with 18th century red velvet
and the furniture, which was designed for the house by William Kent, is
upholstered in the same material. The smaller rooms contain other furniture
by Kent, but perhaps the paintings deserve pride of place. The Landscape
Room is entirely hung with works by Nicholas Poussin, Claude Lorrain and
Gaspard Poussin, while the saloon contains Rubens' 'Return of the Holy
Family'. The desolate countryside which surrounded the house when it was
first built has been changed into a vast park, which owes much of its
appearance to the landscaping carried out under the direction of the first two
Earls of Leicester. The formal Victorian terraces were added in 1854 by
Nesfield. The park contains an obelisk by Kent erected in 1729 and is
dominated by a tall column erected to Thomas William Coke in 1845; it
shows some of his agricultural improvements and is topped with a
wheatsheaf.

Opening times: Spring and Summer Bank Holiday Mon; June and Sept, Mon, Thjurs, Sun 2–
    5; July and Aug, Mon, Wed, Thurs 11.30–5, Sun 2–5. Garden Centre and Pottery open all
    week; Pottery 2–5; Garden Centre 10–5.
Entrance charges: £1.00; children 50p; OAPs 75p; no dogs; no photography in house. (HHA)
Parking: Near the house, 30p.
Wheelchair access: Very difficult as all rooms shown are on the first floor (20 or more steps)
    and the park has gravel paths. Possible to Bygones Collection.
Guidebook: The principal guide is well written, well illustrated and includes a plan on an
    opening flap which is very convenient, but the information about the furniture is a bit thin.
    There is also a much cheaper guide with a plan, a brief history and a description of the
    house, and a note on each room.
Catering: A tea tent near the house dispenses tea and cake.
WCs: Free but unsuitable for wheelchairs.

Holkham Hall, Norfolk

Shop: Slides and postcards at the house exits; plants near the entrance; pottery at the pottery shop behind the house. There is also a separate Garden Centre.

Extras: The Bygones Collection includes an old coach, traction engines, agricultural, riding, veterinary and other equipment. Open all week 2–5. Admission 50p; children 25p; 110 page Bygones guide £1.50.

HOUGHTON HALL Houghton (The Marquess of Cholmondeley)
Tel: East Rudham (048 522) 569
Directions: 13 miles E. of King's Lynn, 10 miles W. of Fakenham; turn off
   A148 in East Rudham, follows signs to Gt Bircham, then to Houghton

Sir Robert Walpole, who was Prime Minister to both George I and George II, employed the architect Colen Campbell to design him a house. It is a large rectangle, nine windows wide, faced with Aislaby stone of the best quality and linked by curving colonnades to wings on either side. Campbell had to share the honours because Walpole, against every connoisseur's advice, got James Gibbs to add the four domes which enliven the house. For the interior, Walpole turned to yet another architect, William Kent; the result is the most complete and sumptuous Palladian house in England. Entrance is through the lower hall — meant for dogs, drinking bouts and muddy boots — up the great staircase, which winds round a bronze gladiator, to the state apartments which fill the main floor. In the centre of the front is the Stone Hall, a 40 foot cube whose walls and ceiling drip with full-blooded carving; the ceiling is by Artari, the chimneypiece by Rysbrack. The chairs, which were made for the room, retain their original velvet upholstery, as do most others in the house. All the decoration in the hall is on the grand scale and it is the same in the other state rooms. Every one of them has a painted and gilded ceiling. In addition, the Marble Parlour has another Rysbrack chimneypiece, the Cabinet Room has a Chinese wallpaper of the 1790s, the Tapestry Room is lined with a Mortlake tapestry showing the Stuart Kings and Queens, while the Green Velvet Bedchamber has a four-poster, designed by Kent which is still hung with its original green velvet. The climax is the saloon, whose crimson Genoa velvet walls set off the heavy gilt furniture. Everything at Houghton is of the highest quality and so rich there is a danger of visual indigestion. Fortunately visitors can take as long as they like in each room, although circulation space is a little tight in places.

Opening times: 11 April to 26 Sept, Thurs and Bank Holidays 10.30–5.30, Sun 1.30–5.30 (gates and picnic area 12.00), last admission 5.00.
Entrance charges: House and gardens £1.50; OAPs £1.00; children 50p. Park, grounds and stables only £1.00; 80p; and 30p. No photography in house; dogs on leads in grounds only. (HHA)
Parking: Free parking in a field behind the stables, 150 yards from the house. Invalids' car park next to house.
Wheelchair access: Lift to main floor gives almost complete access to all parts of the house,

tea room also accessible.

Guidebook: A good brief illustrated history and a room-by-room guide.

Catering: Tea room in the north wing, with a pleasant tea garden outside; tea, home-made cakes, good shortbread.

WCs: Near the south side of the house, free and clean; suitable for wheelchairs.

Shop: A very classy shop in the south wing.

Extras: No extra charge is made for admission to the stables which house Shire horses, Shetland ponies and a collection of antique riding equipment. A charge is made for the Model Soldier Collection.

NORWICH: NORWICH CASTLE MUSEUM (Norfolk Museums Service)
Tel: Norwich (0603) 611277
Directions: In the centre of Norwich

Norwich Castle dominates the City more convincingly than the low-set cathedral. The only building of the extensive mediaeval castle which survives is the large stone keep which was probably built between 1120 and 1130. The keep is unusual because the outside is decorated with tiers of round arches. From about 1220 until 1887 the castle keep served as the gaol and some of the walls inside are decorated with carvings made by prisoners. The outside walls were completely refaced between 1834 and 1839, under the direction of the architects Francis Stone and Anthony Salvin. They replaced the white Caen stone of the mediaeval castle with much yellower Bath stone. At the end of the 19th century the castle was purchased by the City Corporation and converted into a museum. The partly ruined keep was restored yet again and together with the prison buildings it was converted into museum galleries. The Castle Museum has large and important collections of paintings and silver, as well as a Social History collection. The keep is used mainly to display arms and armour and and other mediaeval material.

Opening times: All year, weekdays 10–5, Sun 2–5.

Entrance charges: 25p; children 10p; students 15p. Spring Bank Holiday to Sept inclusive, adults 50p; students 25p.

Parking: Some limited-stay on-street parking, or the Castle Car Park, 200 yards from the castle.

Wheelchair access: A steep slope and two steps up from street level, ramps within the museum; no access to upper floors but the installation of a lift is planned for 1981–2.

Guidebook: 'Norwich Castle' deals with the history of the castle only and contains a plan of the keep in its original state. 'Norwich Castle Museum' is an account of both the building and the collections in it.

Catering: Cafeteria with a wide selection of commercial snacks and tea by the pot. There is also a Buttery and Bar (no children under 14) with a wide selection of food.

WCs: Books, brass rubbings and other museum material.

Shop: At either end of the North Galleries, free, clean and suitable for wheelchairs; more in the entrance hall.

NORWICH: STRANGERS' HALL   Charing Cross (Norfolk Museum Service)
Tel: Norwich (0603) 611277 Ext 275
Directions: In the centre of Norwich, on the Dereham road

Behind the quiet 17th century street front is a complicated and attractive old house. Despite its name, Strangers' Hall has been, for most of its life, the private home of a succession of rich Norwich merchants. Many of them made additions or improvements to the house so that it now contains work of the 14th, 15th, 16th, 17th and 18th centuries. The most striking room is the great hall, built in about 1450 by William Barley and given a new crown-post roof in the 1530s by Nicholas Sotherton. The rooms are disposed around three small courtyards. There is such variety in the dates and fittings of the rooms that Strangers' Hall is the perfect place for the display of furniture of different dates. The Walnut Room has walnut furniture of 1690–1720, the Georgian Dining Room has mid-18th century furniture, and other rooms have furniture of the Regency and Victorian periods. There are about 20 such rooms all told.

Opening times: All year, weekdays 10–5.
Entrance charges: 15p. Spring Bank Holiday to Sept 30, 30p; children 5p; students 10p (summer 15p).
Parking: Multi-storey car park in Duke Street, 200 yards away.
Wheelchair access: Access is possible only into the main courtyard but not to the interior.
Guidebook: An excellent book, based on original research and with a room-by-room guide and a very useful plan.
Catering: None.
WCs: On the left of the steps to the entrance porch, unmarked, free and clean but unsuitable for wheelchairs.
Shop: None.

OXBURGH HALL Oxborough (The National Trust)
Tel: Gooderstone (036 21) 258
Directions: 18 miles S.E. of King's Lynn, 7 miles S.W. of Swaffham on the S. side of the Swaffham-Stoke Ferry road

Oxburgh was built in the 1480s, when agricultural unrest and scavenging bands of unemployed soldiers threatened security. Sir Edmund Bedingfeld took no chances and surrounded his new house with a square moat wide enough to keep out casual robbers. In the centre of the north front is a great gatehouse with two tall octagonal towers. Elsewhere the old red brick walls rise sheer out of the moat but, in spite of these castle-like features, it is clear from the large windows that Oxburgh was intended as a house. Various members of the Bedingfeld family made alterations to the building; Sir Richard pulled down the great hall in 1778, leaving a gap in the south side of the house, while Sir Henry carried out large scale repairs in the 1830s. The windows, battlements and chimneys date from his time, as does the square stumpy tower at the south east corner. The family still live in part of the house. The rooms open to the public include Sir Richard Bedingfeld's saloon of 1778 and three dark, richly patterned rooms with decorated ceilings, which were formed in the 19th century. The library has a fireplace by A.W.N. Pugin, who may have had a hand in the 19th century restoration. Other attractions are the two staircases, whose walls are hung with embossed Spanish leather dating from the 17th century, and a small room on the first floor which contains embroidery worked by Mary Queen of Scots and Bess of Hardwick in about 1570. The tour ends with two large rooms in the gatehouse furnished in 17th century style and linked by a spiral staircase which is a masterpiece of bricklaying. The stair extends to the roof, which gives a view over the flat countryside and of the formal parterre gardens laid out in about 1845 in the French manner and recently replanted.

Opening times: 1 April to 10 Oct, Mon, Tues, Wed, Sat, Sun incl. Bank Holiday Monday 2–6; last admission 5.30.

Entrance charges: £1.40; children 70p.

Parking: Free car park about 200 yards from the house.

Wheelchair access: Possible to four ground floor rooms, also to shop and tea room.

Guidebook: A history of the house and the Bedingfeld family (who are still in residence), also a room-by-room guide. There is not much information about the 19th century restoration, although there is a plan of the basement made in 1774. There is also a separate guide for young visitors.

Catering: In the old kitchen off the courtyard of the house, tea and good cakes, also set cream teas.

WCs: In the grounds N.E. of the Hall, free and spotless but not adapted for wheelchair users.

Shop: A large shop in the house with the full range of National Trust books, gifts and souvenirs.

SANDRINGHAM HOUSE (Her Majesty the Queen)

Tel: King's Lynn (0553) 2675

Directions: 8 miles N.E. of King's Lynn: well-signposted off the A149 and A148

There is no escaping the fact that Sandringham is an unwieldy and sprawling house, but for most visitors the appearance of the building will matter less than its association with the Royal Family. Sandringham has been in royal hands since 1861, when Queen Victoria bought the estate for her eldest son, later Edward VII, so that he might have a retreat from public life, similar to her own retreats at Osborne and Balmoral. The original house was replaced by the present red brick pile in 1870; the architect was A.J. Humbert who did a great deal of work for the royal family, but is otherwise hardly known. He used the Jacobean style. A ballroom was added in 1883 and the top floor of the main house was rebuilt after a fire in 1891. Visitors may enter the house at the time punched on their ticket to view four main rooms and a number of corridors. The saloon is a 19th century version of a great hall, with a minstrels' gallery at one end and 17th century tapestries on the walls; the small drawing room is a comfy little mid-Victorian sitting room, while the main drawing room is in the French style with richly decorated walls and ceiling. The paintings on the walls are mainly Victorian, with many portraits among them, while the furniture is a catholic mixture of 18th, 19th and 20th century pieces. These are the living rooms which are still used by the present Royal Family, and there are signs of modern occupation, but the atmosphere remains Edwardian. The old stable block close to the house has been converted into a museum which is included in the main entrance charge. There are big game trophies, gifts presented to Her Majesty, some archaeological finds and the royal stable of vintage cars. There is also the horse museum. The layout of the garden has been simplified but there is still a large amount of strong colour, supplied by daffodils, azaleas, camellias and rhododendrons planted among and around the glades and the two lakes. Guided walks of the estate take place every 1½ hours.

Opening times: Easter Sun to 30 Sept, Mon, Tues, Wed, Thurs 10.30–4.45; Sun 11.30–4.45.
   Closed 19 July to 7 Aug. The house and grounds are always closed when the Royal Family
   is in residence.
Entrance charges: £1.10; OAPs 90p; children 60p. No dogs, no picnics, no photography, no
   prams or pushchairs in the house.
Parking: Free and shady, but ¼ mile from the house.
Wheelchair access: Access possible to everything except a small part of the museum. Some
   gravel paths in the grounds.
Guidebook: A lavish souvenir guide with many pictures and a tour of the house, grounds and
   museum as well as a short historical account. There is also a cheap handlist of the pictures
   and works of art on show in the house.
Catering: Self-service snacks and salads, commercial cake and tea in polystyrene mugs in the
   cafeteria near the car park.
WCs: Near the car park and also the south of the house, free.
Shop: Near the car park, sells trinkets, souvenirs associated with Sandringham and the Royal
   Family as well as pottery and books. There is another shop of this kind in the museum.

Northamptonshire

ALTHORP nr Northampton (The Earl Spencer)
Tel: East Haddon (060 125) 209
Directions: 6 miles N.W. of Northampton, off the A428 near the village of
   East Haddon

The first building encountered by visitors is the stable block, a grand rectangle of dark glowing ironstone, built in 1732 to the designs of the architect Roger Morris. It makes a sharp contrast with the main house, which was faced with grey brick-tiles in the late 18th century. Under this skin there is a red brick Elizabethan house, which was remodelled in the

1660s by Anthony Ellis. It was not given its present appearance until the 1780s, when Henry Holland altered and 'improved' both the outside and the interior. The main rooms reflect this complex building history; the entrance hall is a marvellous Palladian room by Roger Morris, the grand staircase dates from 1650 and the huge Picture Gallery on the first floor has 17th century panelling. Many of the other rooms were redecorated under the direction of Henry Holland. There are also a number of fireplaces and other fittings from Spencer House, which was the family's town house in London. The rooms are filled with one of the finest private art collections in England, begun in the later 17th century by Robert, Second Earl of Sunderland, and improved and enlarged by every generation of the Spencer family. The Marlborough room contains some of the best portraits by Reynolds and Gainsborough, the Picture Gallery has excellent Van Dycks and other 17th century portraits. There are also Old Master paintings in abundance. The porcelain and furniture in the rooms is of a quality equal to the paintings, especially some of the 18th century furniture brought from Spencer House. Visitors are guided through the house in parties which, for once, seems very sensible; the knowledgeable guides make it slightly easier to absorb the best things; the tour takes over an hour. Althorp is the family home of Lady Diana Spencer, now Princess of Wales. In 1981 there were crowds of visitors and it was difficult to avoid queuing. It is to be hoped that things will be easier in 1982.

Opening times: Tues, Thurs and Bank Holiday Mon. Also Fri in Aug and Sat all year except June and July. Connoisseurs' Day Wed (extra rooms) except in Aug. Gates open 2.20; House 2.30–5.30; Aug 2.30–6; Bank Holidays 11.30–6.

Entrance charges: £2.00; children £1.00. Wed (Connoisseurs' Day) £3.00. Grounds only 50p; children 25p.

Parking: Free, next to the stable block or further away near the entrance.

Wheelchair access: Wheelchairs not admitted to house but the shop, tea room and grounds are accessible.

Guidebook: A room-by-room guide, and a brief family history.

Catering: A very pleasant self-service tea room in the stables with tea by the cup and home-made cakes and scones.

WCs: In the stable block, modern, small; unsuitable for wheelchairs.

Shop: In the stable block, elegant and expensive objects (price range 99p to £200), silver plate, china and glass, nothing of the usual commercial kind. There is a separate wine shop.

AYNHOE PARK Aynho (The Mutual Households Association)
Tel: Croughton (0869) 810659
Directions: 6 miles S.E. of Banbury on the A41 in the centre of the village

The great house stands right in the village, which is unusual in England. It has a complicated building history. A Jacobean house was partly burned down in 1645 during the Civil War and rebuilt in the 1680s by the King's mason, Edward Marshall, who gave the house a new five bay centre.

Between 1707 and 1714 the main house was refaced and given a big central pediment. Two long, low wings were added and two blocks of outbuildings were put up on either side of a large forecourt. The architect for this work was probably Thomas Archer. Between 1799 and 1804 another remodelling was carried out, this time by Sir John Soane. He joined the outbuildings to the main house by triumphal arches, and altered many of the main rooms. Unfortunately, the exterior of the house has been covered with cement rendering which gives it a gaunt appearance. Soane's light and elegant rooms and the heavier work of Archer can still be enjoyed, but most of the art treasures which once filled the rooms were removed when the Cartwright family sold the house a few years ago. The building now belongs to the Mutual Households Association and is partially converted into flats. The residents act as enthusiastic guides. The gardens are pleasant but not outstanding. Immediately next to the house is the parish church, rebuilt in 1723–5 to the designs of the local architect, Edward Wing.

Opening times: May to Sept, Wed and Thurs 2–5.
Entrance charges: 40p; children 25p; no dogs.
Parking: Free parking in front of house, restricted space.
Wheelchair access: Possible to most of the rooms which are open.
Guidebook: The guide book was compiled before the Cartwrights sold the house and the rooms are shown with their original splendid furniture. There is no plan, but the historical information is reliable and there are many illustrations.
Catering: None.
WCs: Facilities in the house.
Shop: None.

BOUGHTON HOUSE nr Kettering (The Duke of Buccleuch and Queensbury)
Tel: Kettering (0536) 82248
Directions: 3 miles N. of Kettering; turn off the A43 at Geddington; signposted locally

Boughton is a very large house indeed, like a complete Oxford college set down in the middle of an enormous park. What first strikes the eye is the elegant north range, with its arcaded ground floor and mansard roof, which was built for Ralph, First Duke of Montagu in the 1680s. He was twice Ambassador to France and was enthusiastic about French art and architecture. It is possible that he used a French architect at Boughton and the elegant stone facade is certainly French in appearance. Behind the north range is an older house built round three main courtyards. Many of the buildings are Tudor but they were refaced with stone in the late 17th century. The interior of the house remains almost as it was left in 1709 at the death of the First Duke. Most of the subsequent owners of Boughton did not live in the house and it escaped alteration or modernisation. The regular tour of the interior includes all the rooms round the main courtyard, which

Boughton House, Northamptonshire

is known as the Fish Court. Several of the rooms have good, solid 17th century panelling and are richly furnished, while the great hall and the Egyptian Hall have dramatic painted ceilings of the 1680s. Visitors may take their own time through these rooms, which contain much of interest but it would be lunacy not to pay the extra charge for the guided tour of the State Rooms. This grand series of rooms filling the first floor of the north front must have about the best late 17th century interior in England, with the first parquet floor in the country, walls painted in the original drab colour, fine Mortlake tapestries and painted ceilings by Chéron. Much of the furniture was made for the rooms and among the imports are some very fine Persian carpets. The park is largely grassland with a splendid vista from the west front down to the lake; there is also a small flower garden and an adventure playground.

Opening times: 9–18, 25 April, 1, 2, 3, 29, 30, 31 May, 25 July to 26 Sept daily except Fri, also Thurs, Sat & Sun in Oct; gardens 1–5.15; house 2–5.

Entrance charges: House and grounds £1.50; OAPs £1.00; children 50p; State Rooms extra. (HHA)

Parking: Free parking on drive near front of house, disabled can drive closer.

Wheelchair access: Possible to the main circuit of rooms on the ground floor but not the State Rooms; disabled visitors should apply at the entrance, and will be separately admitted.

Guidebook: Could be better; a very brief history of the house, a room-by-room guide and some information about the family. Many illustrations but no plan. A handlist of the furniture in the State Rooms comes free with every admission.

Catering: Teas are served in the clean and pleasant old kitchen; self-service, tea by the cup, the cakes and scones which are made in the house are very good.

WCs: Modern lavatories behind the stables some distance from the house; free, clean and suitable for wheelchairs.

Shop: In the east pavilion of the north front, a part of the house which was left unfinished in 1709. The shop sells souvenirs, recipe books, plants and produce.

CASTLE ASHBY nr Northampton (The Marquess of Northampton)
Tel: Yardley Hastings (0601 29) 234
Directions: 6 miles E. of Northampton, on the N. side of the A428

The park and gardens at Castle Ashby are excellent of their kind. On the north and east sides are formal gardens laid out in the 1860s, the park beyond is mainly the work of 'Capability' Brown and includes two long grassy rides from before his time, one of which leads to the south front of the house. The architectural history of the house is best understood from this front. The original house, which was begun in 1574, enclosed three sides of a courtyard and had two polygonal staircase towers attached to the wings. Some additions were made between 1620 and 1640, including the roof balustrade with its texts from Psalm 127 and the delightful screen which fills the centre of the front. The architect of the screen is unknown, but it is an early example of the Palladian style in England. The other fronts of the house show a similar mixture of Elizabethan and 17th century stonework.

The interior has recently been adapted to serve as a conference centre, but disruption has been minimal. Visitors are conducted through the main living rooms in the east range, the great hall, and the long gallery. The east range was rebuilt after a fire in the 1670s and most of the rooms shown date from that time, with the exception of the plaster ceiling in the great chamber on the first floor, which escaped damage and dates from about 1620. The hall and long gallery were redecorated in the 1880s. The furniture, and the paintings at Castle Ashby are of high quality. The stables next to the house are Jacobean and there are also a large number of garden buildings, many of them designed in the 1860s by Sir Matthew Digby Wyatt.

Opening times: 1 July to 31 Aug, every day 2–6.
Entrance charges: House and garden £1.50; OAPs £1.00; children 75p. (HHA)
Parking: In a field 250 yards from the house.
Wheelchair access: Permitted, but only the ground floor is easily accessible (about half the rooms on view).
Guidebook: A readable account of the house and the owners, with a room-by-room guide and some colour illustrations but no plan.
Catering: Restaurant in the N.W. corner of the house in what used to be the kitchen; self-service, tea and cakes made on the premises.
WCs: New lavatories near the Great Kitchen.
Shop: At the end of the guided tour, sells slides of the house as well as souvenirs.

DELAPRÉ ABBEY Northampton, Northamptonshire County Record Office (Northamptonshire County Council)
Tel: Northampton (0604) 62297
Directions: One mile S. of the centre of Northampton on the A508 London road

The Abbey began life as a Cluniac nunnery in about 1145. It was closed in 1538, served as private house for the next 400 years and is now a Record Office. The buildings are grouped around a rectangular courtyard which was probably the cloister of the nunnery. Many of the buildings were removed or rebuilt between 1617 and 1650 by the owner Zouch Hall, who also added the ironstone entrance front with its battlements, projecting porch and shaped gables (of which only one remains). In the 1750s a member of the Tate family rebuilt the south side of the house which contained the main rooms and built the stable block of glowing red ironstone which was completed by 1756. The last addition was the unpleasant little chapel at the south west corner, dating from about 1830, which spoils the appearance of both fronts. Visitors are shown the passage round the internal courtyard, with brief glimpses into several store rooms, and finish in the chapel, which is now a library. Very little can be seen of the main rooms, but they appear to have mid-19th century decoration. The house is surrounded by a pleasant park, from which all the best of the exterior can be seen.

Opening times: House, all year, Thurs 2.30–5.00 (4.30 Oct to April), Park open every day.
Entrance charges: House and park both free.
Parking: Free parking next to the house.
Wheelchair access: Only the passage round the court is accessible without ascending steps.
Guidebook: A reliable history of the house and its owners with two plans and a reproduction of a drawing showing the house in 1818 before the chapel.
Catering: None.
WCs: Inside the house, off the main staircase, free and well-maintained.
Shop: None.

KELMARSH HALL   nr Market Harborough (Miss V.C. Lancaster)
Directions: 5 miles S. of Market Harborough, 13 miles N. of Northampton on the A508 in Kelmarsh village

Kelmarsh Hall is a plain but elegantly-proportioned red brick house built for William Hanbury between 1728 and 1732. His architect was James Gibbs. The rectangular main block is seven windows wide and has a pediment on each of the two main fronts. On the entrance side curving walls link the house with two large square pavilions. A number of Victorian additions were removed in the 1950s and Kelmarsh was restored to the appearance shown in the architect's original drawings. Visitors are shown the main rooms on the principal floor. At the centre of the house are the entrance hall and saloon, both tall and impressive with extremely elegant plasterwork. The hall plasterwork is probably original, but that in the drawing room may be by James Wyatt and date from the 1770s. The whole interior was redecorated in the 1920s, and it is not quite clear how much of the decoration dates from that time. The furniture is mainly English Georgian work and fits well with the rooms. The garden layout probably dates from this century and mixes plain lawns sloping down to the lake with topiary work and parterres. There is also a herd of English Park Cattle to add to the authentic 18th century appearance.

Opening times: April to end Aug Sat and Sun 2–6.
Entrance charges: £1.00; no reductions.
Parking: Free parking in the stableyard near the house.
Wheelchair access: There is a long flight of steps to the front door, but thereafter all the main rooms are on the level.
Guidebook: None.
Catering: There is a clean little tea room in one of the pavilions, which serves tea, cakes and scones.
WCs: Modern facilities.
Shop: Only postcards.

KIRBY HALL   Gretton, nr Corby (Ancient Monument)
Directions: 4 miles N.E. of Corby, near Gretton village

The house lies in a lonely hollow, the buildings are empty and only part of the roof is left, but Kirby is still a marvellous Elizabethan house. Most of it was built for Sir Humphrey Stafford between 1570 and 1575. Additions and improvements were made between 1580 and 1640, but these did not alter the main features of the building. From the car park in the north forecourt, visitors pass through the altered north range into the inner court; directly in front is the main range containing the great hall, while on either side are ranges which contained 'lodgings' or guest rooms. The lodgings to the left are gutted and part of the main range is roofless, but the fronts are still intact. They are decorated with a giant order of pilasters, probably the first use of a giant order in England. An elaborate two-storey porch leads into the great hall, which still has its original timber roof and late 17th century gallery but is otherwise empty. Most of the main rooms of the house are still intact, in that they have floors, roofs, fireplaces and glass in the windows, but are otherwise derelict. The long gallery still survives on the first floor of the west lodgings. The west front of the house overlooks a large formal garden, which is a reconstruction of the garden made here in 1685 for Christopher Hatton. At one end of this front is a wing which was added to the main house in about 1600, whose twin bow windows are among the earliest in the country. Ruins can be depressing and it is best to visit Kirby on a sunny day when the richly carved stonework shows up well.

Opening times: Standard hours (S) see page xii.
Entrance charges: 40p; children and OAPS 20p.
Parking: Free parking in the forecourt next the the house.
Wheelchair access: Possible to the garden, the courtyard, the great hall and some of the rooms.
Guidebook: The Official Handbook contains a brief history, a description and two plans; excellent so far but most of the guide was written in 1937 and the information about the architects of Kirby is open to question.
Catering: Catering.
WCs: Modern and fairly clean; not suitable for wheelchairs.
Shop: None.

LAMPORT HALL Lamport (Lamport Hall Preservation Trust)
Tel: Maidwell (060 128) 653
Directions: 8 miles N. of Northampton, near the junction of the A508 and B576

Very little remains of the Elizabethan house built here by the Isham family. The oldest part of the exterior is the little Italianate villa, designed by John Webb and built for Sir Justinian Isham in 1655, which now forms the centre of the main south front. Between 1732 and 1738 the villa was extended by the addition of two wings in a similar style; these were designed by Francis Smith of Warwick. Some improvements were made inside the house at the same time. During the first half of the 19th century there were a whole series of alterations and rebuildings in the course of which most of the last remains of the Elizabethan house were removed. The present north front was built in 1861 to the designs of William Burn. Visitors are free to wander round the interior, which is an odd mixture of rather small and surprisingly large rooms. Among the latter is the Music Hall, part of Webb's original house, but with an ornamental plaster ceiling that was added in 1738. The additions and alterations to the rooms are all carefully set down in the guide book. Among the furnishings are a fine collection of family portraits, an 'Adoration of the Shepherds' by Guido Reni, two very large 17th century Venetian cabinets with paint on glass and some remarkable 17th and 18th century Chinese porcelain. The gardens were first laid out in 1677, but owe most to Sir Charles Isham, who lived at Lamport from 1847 until 1898. He planted the Irish Yews and had the Italian garden laid out, but his most original contribution was the rockery, in which alpine plants were mixed the the earliest garden gnomes in England. Only one gnome survives, inside the house.

Opening times: Easter to end Sept, Sun and Bank Holiday Mon; also 22 July to 28 Aug, Wed, Thurs and Fri 2.15–5.15.
Entrance charges: £1.00; children 50p; OAPs £1.00 including guidebook. (HHA)
Parking: Ample free parking close to hall.
Wheelchair access: Gravel paths and some steps to the interior, but all the main rooms are on the level.
Guidebook: One of the best for its detailed and accurate information; it includes the history of the house and family with a room-by-room guide and some colour illustrations but no plan.
Catering: Light refreshments in the old dining room; rather ordinary tea and cake.
WCs: Free and clean, outside the hall; unsuitable for wheelchairs.
Shop: Only postcards, on sale at the entrance.

LYVEDEN NEW BIELD nr Oundle (The National Trust)
Directions: 3 miles S.W. of Oundle, 8 miles N.E. of Kettering, between the A427 and A6116 on a minor road; the house can be reached only by a half mile walk along a rough track

It takes faith to abandon the car and walk the rough field to this ruined house. The reward is a roofless building of excellent stone built on the plan of a cross and ornamented with mystical Christian symbols and texts from the Roman Catholic Mass. Lyveden was one of the homes of Sir Thomas Tresham, a strong Catholic, whose son was one of the conspirators in the Gunpowder Plot. The New Bield was intended as a lodging or summer retreat from his main house, Lyveden Old Bield, which was further down the hill, and has now largely been demolished. The design for the New Bield was made by Robert Stickells. Work began in 1595 and elaborate gardens were laid out between the Old and New Bields, but the building was unfinished at the time of Sir Thomas's death, and it was never completed. The gardens have now also disappeared and the lodge stands alone — a monument to Tresham's religious convictions.

Opening times: All year, daily.
Entrance charges: Free, but there is a box for 20p contribution to upkeep.

Parking: There is a lay-by on the road for about five cars.
Wheelchair access: Virtually impossible.
Guidebook: Obtainable from the cottage near the New Bield, a good and inexpensive booklet.
Catering: None.
WCs: None.
Shop: None.
Extras: Further examples of Tresham's symbolic buildings can be seen in the district; the Triangular Lodge at Rushton (DoE) was a gamekeeper's cottage symbolising the Holy Trinity and the Market House at Rothwell symbolises the friendship between the leading families of the area.

ROCKINGHAM CASTLE Rockingham, nr Corby (Commander Michael Saunders Watson)
Tel: Rockingham (0536) 770240
Directions: 2 miles N. of Corby near the junction of the A670 and A6116

Rockingham Castle was used by Charles Dickens as the model for Chesney Wold in *Bleak House*. It occupies a position with dramatic views over the Welland Valley. William the Conqueror built a castle here, which was enlarged and strengthened by later English Kings, but then allowed to decay. In 1553 the castle was taken on lease by Edward Watson, ancestor of the present owner. Under the Watsons, the castle buildings, including the 13th century great hall, were converted into a pleasant, rambling and untidy looking house. The only parts of the mediaeval castle left are the gatehouse which was given its round towers by King Edward in about 1280, some stretches of wall, and the tall mound on which the keep once stood. The rebuilding of Rockingham continued slowly and piecemeal until the 1630s and recommenced after the Civil War. The final touches were given by the architect Anthony Salvin, who made some alterations in 1850 and added a tower. The visitors' route threads through the servants' hall and kitchen to the great hall, so called, although the original great hall was twice as long and twice as high until it was divided up by Edward Watson. Among the furniture is a portrait of Francis I of France by Joos Van Cleve, a number of Elizabethan portraits and some furniture of the same period. The other half of the hall is now the Panel Room, whose walls are hung with Post-Impressionist paintings. The elegant 17th century Long Gallery contains a number of pieces of 18th century French furniture and contains several paintings by Ben Marshall, as well as a charming Zoffany of Lord Sondes' children playing cricket. There are guides in each room and plans of the house are displayed.

Opening times: Easter Sun to 30 Sept, Thurs, Sun and Bank Holiday Mon and Tues 2–6.
Entrance charges: House and grounds £1.20; children 60p; OAPs £1.00. Cameras not allowed in the house, dogs must be carried. (HHA)
Parking: Free parking close to the main entrance.
Wheelchair access: Wheelchairs are allowed in the house but there are no special provisions;

there are gravel paths and steps to negotiate. Most of the rooms on view are on the ground floor.

Guidebook: Mainly a room-by-room guide, with a brief history, illustrations and a plan of the castle; there is also a leaflet about walks in the grounds and a leaflet for children with questions to answer and pictures to colour.

Catering: Tea room in Walker's House, a 16th century building next to the main gate which was rebuilt in 1655. Tea and cakes (the cakes come in pairs) or a cream tea; the cakes are of average quality.

WCs: Within the gatehouse, free, clean; facilities for the disabled inside the castle.

Shop: Off the courtyard, nothing out of the ordinary except for the display of Rockingham china.

Extras: There is a small charge for admission to Salvin's tower, which gives a good view of the surrounding countryside.

RUSHTON HALL Ruston, nr Kettering (Royal National Institute for the Blind)

Tel: Kettering (0536) 710506

Directions: 4 miles N.W. of Kettering, off the A6003 on the outskirts of Rushton village

The Gothic entrance lodges make a pretty introduction to the house, which now serves as a school for blind children. Rushton Hall is a Tudor and Jacobean house, of three main ranges round a courtyard, with a stone screen closing the fourth side. Most of the house dates from the middle of the 16th century, when the property belonged to the Tresham family, but the screen and the ends of the wings on either side were added after 1619, when the house was sold to Sir William Cockayne, Lord Mayor of London. The exterior was heavily restored in about 1848, and almost every one of the gables seems to bear a different date, so that it is difficult to be certain how the house evolved. The great hall is in the south wing and its original 16th century bow window can be seen from the charming courtyard. The three other bow windows were added in the 19th century. Visitors can sometimes be shown round the most important rooms, namely the drawing room, great hall, library, staircase, and a small oratory which was presumably built for Sir Thomas Tresham, a mystical Roman Catholic of the late 16th century. None of the rooms has any furniture of note and there is a large amount of 19th century decoration masquerading as 16th century work.

Opening times: Easter and August, daily, grounds 10–4; telephone to arrange access to house.

Entrance charges: Free.

Parking: Parking space about 200 yards from the house; cars are allowed no closer in order to safeguard the children.

Wheelchair access: Possible to most of the rooms shown, all paths are asphalt.

Guidebook: In preparation.

Catering: None.

WCs: None.

Shop: None.

Extras: In one corner of the park at Rushton, some distance from the house, is the famous Triangular Lodge built for Sir Thomas Tresham between 1594 and 1597 to symbolise the

Holy Trinity and the Mass. Everything about the lodge is based on the number three (three sides, three storeys, three windows in each side, etc.). It is under the care of the Department of the Environment and is open to visitors throughout the year).

SULGRAVE MANOR Sulgrave, nr Brackley (The Sulgrave Manor Board)
Tel: Sulgrave (029 576) 205
Directions: 7 miles N.W. of Brackley, 8 miles N.E. of Banbury off the B4524 in the village of Sulgrave

Lawrence Washington bought Sulgrave Manor in 1539 and built himself a new manor house here in about 1560. The house passed out of the family in 1659, but one of Lawrence Washington's descendants was George Washington, first President of the United States of America and in 1914 the house was purchased by subscription and restored as a memorial to Anglo-American friendship. Sulgrave is a modest little manor house, built of local stone. It has suffered several alterations; the rear wing dates from about 1700 and one end of the main range was entirely rebuilt to match the original work in 1921 and now serves as the private house of the Curator. Visitors are conducted through the older parts of the house, which are furnished in the styles of different periods. Most of the furniture is good but not outstanding, and of course there is a quantity of material relating to the Washingtons. The old kitchen has many curious household implements. The Resident Director is an informative guide. There is a pleasant, small garden and the village itself is attractive.

Opening times: All year except Jan, daily except Wed; April to Sept 10.30–1, 2–5.30; Oct to March 10.30–1, 2–4.
Entrance charges: 50p.
Parking: Free car park next to the house.
Wheelchair access: Possible to the great hall, oak parlour and kitchen.
Guidebook: A brief but adequate history of Sulgrave, with many illustrations.
Catering: None (pub opposite).
WCs: In the car park, free and very well maintained; unsuitable for wheelchairs.
Shop: None.

Northumberland

ALNWICK CASTLE Alnwick (The Duke of Northumberland)
Tel: Alnwick (0665) 2456
Directions: The castle stands on the north west edge of Alnwick

Alnwick was one of the principal residences of the Percy family, from whom the present owners are descended. The castle was a vital military stronghold throughout the Middle Ages. It then suffered a long period of neglect but was restored as a country seat by the First Duke of Northumberland in the 1750s. The present appearance of the castle is largely due to a second restoration begun 100 years later under the direction of the architect Anthony Salvin. He re-established the mediaeval character of the exterior while the interior was transformed into a re-creation of an Italian Renaissance palace. The plan of the castle is 14th century and numerous parts of the original structure remain, the most interesting of these being the barbican at the main entrance. The principal rooms open to the public are the hall, the library, the music room, the drawing room and the dining room. Each of these is sumptuously decorated and furnished. The most striking features are the ceilings, particularly the carved wood ceiling of the dining room, based on that of San Lorenzo in Rome, and the delicate painted friezes in the music room and the drawing room. The paintings on display include two Titians, two interesting pieces of fresco by Sebastiano del Piombo, a portrait of Queen Henrietta Maria by Van Dyck and a charming view of Alnwick in the 18th century by Canaletto. The castle is placed at the top of the little town in a picturesque situation overlooking the river; the walk along the river bank, with a distant view of the battlements, is one of the supplementary pleasures open to the visitor.

Opening times: 16 May to 8 Oct, daily except Sat 1–5; last admission 4.30.
Entrance charges: £1.00; OAPs and children 50p. (HHA)
Parking: Free car park.
Wheelchair access: There are no special facilities, but the exterior is accessible and the staff are helpful.
Guidebook: An extensive history of the family and a room-by-room guide with colour illustrations.
Catering: None.
WCs: In the castle; unsuitable for wheelchairs.
Shop: None.
Extras: The fine State Coach built for the Third Duke of Northumberland in the early 19th century is on view in the coachyard.

BAMBURGH CASTLE Bamburgh (Lord Armstrong)
Tel: Bamburgh (066 84) 208
Directions: Bamburgh lies on the coast 5 miles east of the main A1 (turn off at Belford)

Bamburgh Castle occupies a large and dramatic site, high on a rocky coastal outcrop a few miles south of Holy Island. The castle was an important military holding of the Crown between the 11th and 15th centuries and its basic layout dates from this period. However, the present fabric is largely the result of restoration carried out for the first Lord Armstrong in the late 19th century. The interior is a monument to Victorian historicism, with large convenient rooms dressed up in the style of the Middle Ages. This is especially true of the centrepiece of the castle, the King's Hall, a long airy

Bamburgh Castle, Northumberland

room leading into a raised cross hall at one end. This follows the plan of the original hall, and has a fine 'false hammer-beam' roof, while the luxurious wooden panelling is in the classical style and the furniture is 'English Country House'. The other major attraction of the guided tour is the guard room at the foot of the square keep, where a large miscellany of objects is on display, including some fine china, tapestries and an important collection of armour and weapons. The keep is the least altered part of the buildings but its upper floors are occupied by Lord Armstrong and are not open to the public. For Anthony Powell readers, the castle has a definite flavour of Sir Magnus Donners.

Opening times: 25 March to end Oct, daily: March, April, May, June, Sept 1–5; July and Aug 1–6; Oct 1–4.30.
Entrance charges: £1.30; children 60p. (HHA)
Parking: At the foot of the castle.
Wheelchair access: Not practicable.
Guidebook: Lavishly illustrated but rather short on useful text. The guide himself probably provides slightly more information in an engaging fashion.
Catering: Teas at the Castle.
WCs: Adequate.
Shop: A small souvenir shop.
Extras: The magnificent beach on the sea side is a good place for a picnic.

BRINKBURN PRIORY   nr Rothbury (Ancient Monument)
Directions: 5 miles E. of Rothbury, 1 mile W. of the A697 on the B6344

Brinkburn Priory is a beautiful example of a small scale monastic church from early in the period of monastic expansion in England. The Priory was founded during the 1130s and the architecture is transitional, showing characteristics of both Romanesque and Gothic styles. The church building is simple, a long, tall, square-ended block with a transept and only one aisle. The principal windows have pointed arches, but the upper windows are rounded and the north doorway is finely decorated in the Romanesque manner. None of the other buildings survive; they were pillaged to provide the building materials for the house which later owners constructed on the site. Part of this house dates from about 1810 and part from the 1830s, when it was Gothicised by the local architect John Dobson. At present the house is being restored, but when the work is complete the shell of the building will be open to the public. It is not surprising that a private residence was built here. The monks had chosen a splendid position on a bend of the river Coquet, surrounded by high, tree-covered banks.

Opening times: Standard hours (S) see page xii.
Entrance charges: 40p; OAPs and children 20p.
Parking: Free parking at the entrance.
Wheelchair access: Everything is visible from ground level.
Guidebook: Short but adequate, and costs only 1p.

Catering: None.
WCs: None.
Shop: None.

CALLALY CASTLE Whittingham (Major A.J.C. Browne)
Tel: Whittingham (066 574) 663
Directions: 8 miles W. of Alnwick, 5 miles N. of Rothbury, 2 miles W. of
   the A697

Callaly Castle is a substantial country house in a remote part of the county
surrounded by old and beautiful woods. The Clavering family held the
estate from the 13th century until 1877, when it was sold to the grandfather
of the present owner, who is a descendant of the Claverings through the
female line. The whole house has a fairly uniform classical appearance but
this is deceptive as the stone facings cover a patchwork of buildings
constructed over five hundred years. One wing of the south front is a 14th
century tower, the centre dates from 1676 and the other wing from 1707.
Even the large Victorian additions harmonise with the older work. The tour
of the house takes in most of the principal ground floor rooms. The
showpiece is the drawing room which occupies two storeys of the south
front. The room was created in about 1750 and has plasterwork of fabulous
richness, with chinoiserie galleries at either end. This room also contains
two fine Italian scagiola tables. The other main state room is the ballroom. It
is two storeys high and was originally designed as a chapel, and was fitted out
with good panelling in the 1890s. It is now hung with tapestries, including
four 18th century Gobelins panels depicting a romance of Henri IV of
France. Among the paintings, some of the most interesting are the panels
which used to decorate the private boxes at the Vauxhall pleasure gardens in
18th century London; three of the panels are by Hayman, while the fourth
is said to be by William Hogarth. There is also a collection of Victoriana.
One of the major characteristics of the house which contributes a special
atmosphere is that it is privately owned and still in use; for a little while the
visitor may share in the leisured way of life of the country gentry of 50 years
ago. The owner loves his home dearly and is very glad to talk about it with
sympathetic visitors.

Opening times: 1 May to 26 Sept, Sat, Sun and Bank Holiday Mon 2.15–5.30.
Entrance charges: £1.00; children 50p; no dogs. (HHA)
Parking: Free parking.
Wheelchair access: Not practicable.
Guidebook: Thorough if unexciting and not lavishly illustrated. Most of the furniture is listed
   and there is an outline plan of the buildings to show what was built when.
Catering: Sun and Bank Holiday Mon only.
WCs: Magnificent.
Shop: None.

CRAGSIDE   Rothbury (The National Trust)
Tel: Rothbury (0669) 20333
Directions: 1 mile E. of Rothbury on the B6344

Cragside combines three exceptional attractions, a spectacular site, rare architectural qualities, and an insight into the social history of the Victorian period. The house was built for the first Lord Armstrong, the inventor and industrialist, who amassed a vast fortune as a result of the late 19th century boom in the armaments industry. It is set on a steep and rocky hillside, surrounded by splendid trees and acres of rhododendrons and overlooks a valley which is crossed by an elegant iron bridge. In its present form, the house is largely the work of the architect Norman Shaw, whom Lord Armstrong employed to expand his small country retreat. Shaw produced a masterpiece of elegant eclecticism, combining Tudor and mediaeval stylistic elements in a controlled sprawl which provided a perfect shell for the idealized domesticity of the interior, and also made it possible to add new rooms without disturbing the design. All the main rooms of the house, and most of the bedrooms, are open to visitors. They include several productions of the William Morris firm and a large number of Pre-Raphaelite paintings by Evelyn de Morgan. The most attractive of all the rooms is probably the library, with its gothicised wall and ceiling, huge marble fireplace and bay window overlooking the valley. This room contains the original light fittings by J. Swan. Cragside was one of the first private houses in the world to have electric light. Lord Armstrong's technological interests are evident throughout the building, including the spacious kitchen, which was equipped with a hydraulic spit.

Opening times: Grounds, April to end Sept, daily 10.30–6; Oct, daily 10.30–5; Nov to March, Sat and Sun 10.30–4. House April to end Sept, daily except Mon 1–6, but open Bank Holiday Mon; Oct, Wed, Sat and Sun 2–5; last admission half hour before closing.
Entrance charges: House and grounds £1.60; grounds only 60p; children and OAPs half price.
Parking: Free car park about 200 yards from the house.
Wheelchair access: Possible to much of the house; there is a lift to the first floor.
Guidebook: A good guide with plans, a tour of the house and a biography of Lord Armstrong.
Catering: Planned.
WCs: Portaloos in the car park, barely adequate on crowded days.
Shop: National Trust information office with a few books and postcards in the car park.
Extras: The grounds at Cragside are large and splendid, particularly if you like rhododendrons.

DUNSTANBURGH CASTLE   nr Craster (Ancient Monument)
Directions: On the coast, 1 mile N. of Craster and 10 miles N. of Alnwick. No direct access by car

Dunstanburgh Castle is a ruin, and a very spectacular one. Its leaning tower, perched on a cliff, dominates the entire coastline between Craster and

Newton. Like the castles to the north and south, Dunstanburgh was an important stronghold throughout the Middle Ages. The main construction was finished by 1314 and refinements were made to the defences at the end of the 14th century by the building of the barbican with its deep entrance passage. The south side of the castle is quite well-preserved. A long wall leads up from the sea to the keep, which is really an exceptionally strong gatehouse with two imposing towers. The castle used to be virtually an island. A ditch was cut round it from Embleton bay on the north to the south side where there was an inlet used as a harbour. A lot of fighting took place here, both because of the border wars with Scotland and because of the rivalries within the English ruling class, which reached a climax in the Wars of the Roses when Dunstanburgh was besieged by an army ten thousand strong. Dunstanburgh is now a remote spot which can only be reached after a respectable walk of about a mile.

Opening times: Standard hours (SM) see page xii.
Entrance charges: 40p; OAPs and children 20p.
Parking: There is some parking space in both Craster and Embleton, where footpaths lead to the castle (approx. 1 mile away).
Wheelchair access: Not practicable.
Guidebook: A scholarly and thorough official handbook with a measured plan of the castle.
Catering: None.
WCs: In the car park at Craster; facilities for the disabled.
Shop: None.
Extras: The coast around Dunstanburgh is some of the most beautiful in the region. Golfing enthusiasts can play on Embleton links. Gourmets should purchase a box of Craster kippers, which are said to be the best in Britain.

LINDISFARNE CASTLE Holy Island (The National Trust)
Tel: Holy Island (0289) 89244
Directions: Holy Island lies off the Northumbrian coast about 9 miles S. of Berwick and 6 miles E. of the A1. The island is only accessible when the tide allows — telephone the house during opening hours for information about the tides

Built on a rock on the seaward side of Holy Island, directly across the bay from Bamburgh Castle, Lindisfarne Castle occupies the ideal position for a 20th century weekend home, and this is what it became. The existing 16th century fort was purchased in 1901 by the founder of *Country Life* magazine, who set about converting it into a comfortable and charming small country house. He employed as his architect Edwin Lutyens, who was particularly skilful at adapting traditional materials and styles to modern needs. The interior of the house is a series of small oddly-shaped rooms in which stone and brick surfaces predominate. The overall flavour is a mixture of the mediaeval and the vaguely nautical with the cosiness of the Home Counties. The furnishings are mainly those approved by Lutyens; they include a curved high back bench in the kitchen, an oval dining table designed by the architect himself and two 17th century Flemish beds. Full advantage has been taken of the pretty views afforded by the site across the bay and across the harbour to the ruined priory. A short distance from the castle, in strange isolation due to the fact that other schemes for the grounds never materialised, there is a walled garden laid out by Gertrude Jekyll. Looking back from here to the castle one notices Lutyens' red tiled domestic roof perched on the castle walls; this oddly successful contrast sums up the spirit of the building.

Opening times: April to end Sept, daily except Fri but open Good Friday 11–5, Oct, Sat and Sun 11–5; last admission 4.30.
Entrance charges: £1.10; children 55p.
Parking: ¼ mile from castle; there is a charge.
Wheelchair access: Not practicable.
Guidebook: A glossy history and room-by-room guide, plan on the inside cover.
Catering: None.
WCs: None.
Shop: None.

NORHAM CASTLE   Norham (Ancient Monument)
Directions: Norham lies on the River Tweed 8 miles S.W. of Berwick and 7 miles N.E. of Coldstream, off the A698

Norham, overlooks the Tweed and dominates the quiet border village at its foot. The castle is built out of the grey-pink stone of the region. Half of its tall keep is still intact and there are substantial remains of the stone walls enclosing the inner and outer wards. The ruins are picturesque and it is not surprising that the castle was one of Turner's favourite subjects. Its past was violent and dramatic. Norham belonged to the Prince Bishops of Durham, but because of its highly strategic position in the border country, it was 'lent' to the King in war time. The keep, which is the earliest part of the castle, was built early in the 12th century by the tough royal chancellor Ranulf Flambard and for the next 400 years its garrison was repeatedly in action against the Scots. At the time of a siege in 1318. Norham was considered the most dangerous place in Britain. Because of this turbulent existence, the walls were frequently strengthened or rebuilt. There are traces of early work but most of what is now standing dates from the 15th and 16th centuries.

Opening times: Standard hours (S), see page xii.
Entrance charges: 50p; OAPs and children 25p.
Parking: By the roadside or in the village ¼ mile away.
Wheelchair access: The site slopes steeply in places and is not really suitable for wheelchairs.
Guidebook: An excellent Official Handbook with a full history, and architectural description and an accurate plan.
Catering: None, but there are two pubs in the village.
WCs: None.
Shop: None.
Extras: The village church also has some good Norman work and is well worth visiting.

Seaton Delaval Hall, Northumberland

SEATON DELAVAL HALL (Lord Hastings)
Tel: Seaton Delaval (0632) 481759
Directions: 12 miles N.E. of Newcastle on the A190, between Seaton
  Delaval and Seaton Sluice

Georgian houses are often as alike as peas in a pod, but there is no forgetting
Seaton Delaval. The landscape here is sour, with cold sea winds, and the
house faces north to the dreary industrial skyline of Blyth. Admiral Delaval
asked Sir John Vanbrugh to design him a house 'for the entertainment of our
old age'; it was begun in 1720 and finished in 1728. The plan is that of a small
Palladian villa, with a large forecourt enclosed by wings. These are
straightforward buildings with arcades on the ground floor and pediments
over the centre. Beyond them the dark stone mass of the house rears up.
Vanbrugh had a passion for castles and at Seaton he took the standard
elements of classical architecture and used them to produce a house with the
heaviness of a castle and the skyline of an Elizabethan mansion. This is best
seen on the north front where the hall pushes up in the centre of the house,
lifting its pediment far above the massive pairs of columns which should
support it. The south front has a more conventional portico and is altogether
quieter and less theatrical. It comes as no surprise to learn that few of the
Delaval family ever died in their beds. Something of the same curse may
have touched the building for in 1822 the main house was gutted by fire and
is still empty and only partly restored. Apart from the hall itself, visitors
may see part of the kitchen wing which is now the home of the owner and the
magnificent classical stables in the other wing. The flower gardens to the
south of the house are relatively modern.

Opening times: 1 May to 30 Sept, Wed and Sun 2–6.
Entrance charges: 50p; OAPs and children 25p. (HHA)
Parking: Free parking near the house.
Wheelchair access: Access to the house is only by way of a broad but long flight of steps.
Guidebook: Apparently written by the owner, with predictable faults and virtues. It is good
  on the facts of the restoration, adequate on the history of the building and anecdotal about
  the family. Few illustrations and no plan.
Catering: None (but see below).
WCs: Free and clean but unsuitable for wheelchairs.
Shop: None.
Extras: 'Mediaeval' banquets are held here in the evenings.

WALLINGTON Cambo (The National Trust)
Tel: Scots Gap (067 074) 673
Directions: 20 miles N.W. of Newcastle, off the A696 on the B6342

There are mediaeval cellars at Wallington but the present house was built
for Sir William Blackett in about 1688. The external walls were refronted
with honey coloured stone in the 1740s for Sir William Blackett by his

architect Daniel Garrett. There exteriors are in the simplest classical style of the period, but the interior was treated in a much more elaborate way. The main rooms were redecorated with plasterwork by the Francini brothers and marble chimneypieces by the best English craftsmen; at the same time the house was made more convenient by building a passage round all four sides of the internal courtyard. It was roofed over 100 years later to make a large central room. This was done by Sir Walter and Lady Trevelyan who followed Ruskin's advice and employed William Bell Scott and a number of other painters to decorate the walls of the hall with mural paintings. The house makes a good setting for the rich mixture of furnishings collected by successive generations of inhabitants, and visitors may take their time going round. 'Capability' Brown laid out the park here in the 1760s and created his usual lake (although he left some unusual trees from a former layout). The flower gardens owe more to the 19th and 20th centuries, and especially to Lady Trevelyan's work of the 1930s. There is also a fine walled garden.

Opening times: Walled garden and grounds open all year. House, April to end Sept, daily except Tues 1–6; Oct, Wed, Sat and Sun 2–5; evening opening last Sat in June, July and Aug, 7–9.30pm.
Entrance charges: House and grounds £1.70; grounds only 60p; children half price.
Parking: Free parking.
Wheelchair access: Ramps give access to the ground floor, seven rooms are accessible, as well as the collection of dolls' houses. The gardens are accessible, but ring Scots Gap 274 to arrange about tea.
Guidebook: Sensible and informative, only a few illustrations. There are separate booklets on the gardens and the dolls' houses.
Catering: Lunches and teas are available in the Clock Tower restaurant and are good value for money. If you are lucky, the lady who runs it will play the Northumbrian bagpipes.
WCs: In the courtyard; suitable for wheelchairs.
Shop: The shop attached to the restaurant provides a comprehensive collection of booklets, and sells excellent jam made by the Women's Institute.
Extras: The house has various mementoes of people associated with the Trevelyan family, including the desk at which Lord Macaulay wrote his famous history of England.

WARKWORTH CASTLE Warkworth (Ancient Monument)
Directions: Warkworth is on the coast 6 miles S.E. of Alnwick on the A1068

Warkworth is in many ways the most interesting of all the Northumbrian castles and its site is spectacular. The castle was an important military base from the 12th century onwards and the basic layout was established during this period. The walls, gatehouse, great hall and chapel (only traces of the last two remain) date from before 1215. In 1332 the castle passed into the hands of Lord Percy, later Earl of Northumberland and he and his son Harry 'Hotspur' made Warkworth their principal residence. Many alterations and improvements were carried out. The hall was refurbished and a tower built at one end, decorated with the lion emblem of the new owners, while the keep was transformed into a small palace on three floors.

The ground floor consists of store rooms with the principal living rooms on the two floors above. The keep is very well preserved and, although some small alterations were made in the 1850s, the rooms still convey a powerful impression of late mediaeval living conditions. The keep stands on the northern end of the castle mound, which rears up above the high street of the small town below. The river Coquet runs past one side of the mound and it is possible to walk along the river from the castle to the mediaeval Hermitage, half-a-mile upstream.

Opening times: Standard hours (SM) April to Sept only, see page xii.
Entrance charges: 50p; children and OAPs 25p.
Parking: Free parking by the castle entrance.
Wheelchair access: Possible to the outer parts of the castle which are grassed.
Guidebook: A very thorough Official Handbook with history and description, a plan of the castle and a more detailed plan of the keep.
Catering: None at the castle, but plenty of choice in the town.
WCs: Free, adequate; unsuitable for wheelchairs.
Shop: None.

Nottinghamshire

HOLME PIERREPONT HALL Radcliffe on Trent, nr Nottingham (Mr and Mrs Robin Brackenbury)
Tel: Radcliffe on Trent (060 73) 2371
Directions: 3½ miles W. of Nottingham centre, off the A52. Follow signs to the National Water Sports Centre and continue past the Centre to the house

It takes perseverance to find the house, which is hidden away behind the Water Sports Centre. Holme Pierrepont is the surviving part of an early 16th century courtyard house which was one of the first brick buildings in Nottinghamshire. It was greatly enlarged in Jacobean times, but most of the Jacobean building was demolished in the 1730s. The present house consists of the red brick front range of the Tudor building, one surviving range of the Jacobean house and a Victorian range of the 1870s grouped round three sides of a courtyard garden, which is laid out as it was in 1875. The buildings were allowed to get into a bad state, but are now being repaired gradually by the present owners, who are descended from the Pierrepont family. Visitors make their own way round the building. The rooms on the first floor of the east range are reached by a good 17th century staircase brought from elsewhere in the house. One of these rooms will eventually have an elaborate plaster ceiling of the 1660s brought from a house in Nottingham. The early 16th century front range has been fully restored. The ornamental timber roof has been exposed and the rooms on the ground floor have been left with bare brick walls. The rooms were originally used as lodgings and still retain their mediaeval garderobes, but are now furnished with the collection accumulated by the owner's family over the last 250 years. There are no Van Dycks or pieces by Chippendale, but many lesser items of interest.

Opening times: Easter Sun, Mon and Tues, May Day, Spring and Summer Bank Holiday, Sun, Mon and Tues; then June to Aug, Tues, Thurs, Fri and Sun; also Sun in Sept; all 2–6.
Entrance charges: Not decided. (HHA)
Parking: Free parking on the approach to the house (50 yards away).
Wheelchair access: Permitted, but most of the best things are on the first floor, which can only be reached by stairs.
Guidebook: A small leaflet contains a brief history and a description of the furniture in each room.
Catering: Tea in the house.
WCs: In the house; facilities for wheelchair users.
Shop: A few souvenirs are sold at the entrance.

NEWSTEAD ABBEY Linby (Nottingham City Council)
Tel: Bidworth (062 34) 3557, during office hours
Directions: 11 miles N. of Nottingham

The long drive twists past the rhododendrons and heathland of the large park and stops before the late 13th century west front of the original Abbey Church. The front is all that remains of the church, but the other buildings of the Abbey were turned into a large house by the Byron family, who acquired Newstead in 1540. By the time that the Sixth Lord Byron (the poet) inherited in 1798, the house was in poor condition; one of his friends described Newstead as 'a heap of rubbish', and there was no money for repairs. In 1818 it was sold to a Colonel Wildman, who restored the house with the help of the architect John Shaw. Almost all of the outside of the present house is Shaw's work. The inside is more diverse. The Byrons built their house around the cloister of the Abbey and at the heart of the building there is the original cloister courtyard with a grotesque fountain in the middle and stone vaulted mediaeval rooms on all sides. Above these rooms are the main apartments, linked by galleries built over the cloister walk in the 17th century. The galleries themselves contain many mementoes of Lord Byron and the rooms opening off them are very varied; one has an early 18th century painted ceiling, another is decorated with Japanese screens and all are furnished with a mixture of things belonging to the 19th century owners of the house and more recently purchased objects. The grandest room is the saloon with its unusual plaster ceiling, part of which dates from 1631–3; but it is rivalled by the great hall, which is entirely the work of John Shaw. Visitors follow a set route through the rooms and a short conducted tour of the poet's bedroom starts from the North Gallery at hourly intervals (presently on the half hour). The house is surrounded by large and elaborate gardens; in front of it is a lake overlooked by mock 18th century forts and on all sides is the large and splendid park.

Opening times: Park and gardens Jan to end Nov, daily 10 to dusk. House, Good Friday to 30 Sept, daily 2–6; last admission 5.15.
Entrance charges: Grounds and gardens 60p; children 20p. House 50p extra; children 10p extra.
Parking: Free car park about 200 yards from the house.
Wheelchair access: Possible to ground floor (cloister and crypt chapel); entry by side door.
Guidebook: A tour of the house and a brief history of the occupiers; many illustrations, but no plan; a plan is available separately.
Catering: In the front wing of the house; tea or coffee, sandwiches, biscuits; open when the park is open.
WCs: Next to the car park, fairly new, rustic style; also on the west side of the house; neither are suitable for wheelchairs.
Shop: In the Prior's kitchen of the Abbey, postcards and guidebooks.

NOTTINGHAM CASTLE MUSEUM Nottingham (Nottingham City Council)
Tel: Nottingham (0602) 411881
Directions: In the centre of Nottingham, off Castle Road

The mediaeval Nottingham Castle, once one of the strongest fortresses in the country, was allowed to decay and was finally blown up after the Civil War. The only remains of the castle still above ground today are the gatehouse, first built in 1252 but much restored, a stretch of the outer curtain wall and a stone bridge. In the late 17th century the demolition of the castle was completed by the first Duke of Newcastle, who built himself a new and splendid house on the site of the upper ward. His architect was probably a local man named Samuel Marsh. The new house was an Italianate style and its principal front is decorated with extravagant carving. The interior must have been equally rich but was almost completely destroyed in 1831, when the house was set on fire by a mob who resented the Duke of Newcastle's opposition to the reform of Parliament. After the fire, the house was left derelict for 40 years until 1878 when it was restored as the City Museum and Art Gallery.

Opening times: All year, daily except Christmas Day; April to Sept 10–5.45 (Sun 4.45); Oct to March 10–4.45.
Entrance charges: 15p.
Parking: There is no visitors' car park but limited on-street parking is available at the foot of the castle rock. There are two multi-storey car parks fairly close by.
Wheelchair access: Possible to the ground floor of the castle. Entrance to the small park surrounding the castle is by turnstile, but there is a gate next to it which is open to admit wheelchairs and pushchairs.
Guidebook: 'Notthingham Castle' on sale in the museum is a basic history but with little information about the building. 'Nottingham's Royal Castle' on sale in the gatehouse is better and cheaper.
Catering: The licensed Buttery Bar in the museum serves drinks, tea, coffee and commercial snacks.
WCs: In the castle building, free and clean and with facilities for the disabled; there are also

lavatories in the park with facilities for wheelchair users, but the key must be sought from the park keepers.

Shop: The Nottingham Civil Society runs a good little souvenir shop in the gatehouse which sells, among other things, full-size replicas of swords and armour.

Extras: Below the castle rock is the Brewhouse Yard museum and in nearby Castle Gate is the Costume Museum and Lace Centre.

THORESBY HALL Ollerton (Countess Manvers)

Tel: Mansfield (0623) 823210

Directions: 20 miles N. of Nottingham on the W. side of the A614 near Ollerton

There have been three great houses in Thoresby Park in the last three hundred years. The first was built in the 1650s and burnt down in 1745. The second was built in the 1760s and was replaced in its turn by the present large Victorian house, designed by Anthony Salvin and built between 1865 and 1871. Salvin's house is a pompous stone building in the Elizabethan style with a spiky skyline. The five storey entrance front looks rather like a grand hotel, with its rows of small bedroom windows. The interior was meant to impress and the low stone entrance hall and staircase lead to a vast Great Hall, whose stone walls are decorated with suits of armour and stags' heads and pierced by balconies looking down from the bedroom floor. The state bedrooms still look Victorian, even though much of the furniture is Georgian; brown and cream are the predominant colours. The series of state rooms along the garden front has ornate plaster ceilings in the Elizabethan style and heavy French and English furniture. There is a Victorian carved overmantel in the library with a carving showing the Major Oak, a reminder that the trees on the edge of Thoresby Park belong to Sherwood Forest. Visitors follow a set route through the house and are usually kept to the edges of the rooms.

Opening times: Easter Sun and Mon, then Bank Holidays 2–3 and 30–31 May, 29–30 Aug; also June to Aug, Sun. Bank Holidays: Park 11–6; House 2–5. Other Suns, Park 12–6; House 2–5.

Entrance charges: £1.20; children 60p. (HHA)

Parking: Free parking on grass about 100 yards from the house.

Wheelchair access: Not possible to the inside of the house.

Guidebook: A glossy souvenir guide with plenty of illustrations; the text is a room-by-room guide, mixed up with the history of the Pierrepont family and information about how the estate is run; the book is difficult to use although it is well written. There is no plan of the house or park.

Catering: A rather gaunt self-service tea room in the outbuildings with adequate cups of tea and cakes. There is also a kiosk near the car park.

WCs: Near the tea room, free and clean; unsuitable for wheelchairs.

Shop: Near the tea room.

Extras: There is a miniature model railway in the park, fairly near the house, for which an extra charge is made.

WOLLATON HALL Wollaton, Nottingham (City of Nottingham
  Museums)
Tel: Nottingham (0602) 281333
Directions: 2½ miles W. of Nottingham centre off the A609 in a large park

It seems strange that one of the most spectacular Elizabethan houses in
England should now be filled with stuffed animals, but this is the fate of
Wollaton. From the outside nothing has changed. Most of the enormous
park is still intact and the full grown trees hide that part of it which has been
built up. The house stands on a hill in the centre of the park. It was built
between 1580 and 1588 for Sir Francis Willoughby and was paid for from a
fortune swelled by profits from the family coal mines. Sir Francis wanted to
show off his wealth and his architect, Robert Smythson, designed a highly
unusual house which groans under the weight of carved ornament. It is a
rectangular building with a great square tower at each corner. In the centre
is the great hall with the tower room above it which soars up, taller than the
all the rest. The interior serves as a natural history museum and it is fair to
say that most visitors come to look at the exhibits, not the house.
Nevertheless the great hall with its fine carved screen is an odd setting for a
threadbare giraffe. In the park below the house is the massive early 18th
century stable block, which is being converted into an industrial museum.
Another attraction close by is an early 19th century camellia house of iron
and glass.

Opening times: April to Sept, weekdays 10–7, Sun 2–5; Oct to March, weekdays 10–dusk,
  Sun 1.30–4.30. Closed Christmas Day.
Entrance charges: 35p; 10p.
Parking: Free car park below the house.
Wheelchair access: The house stands at the top of a slope and there are seven steps up to the
  entrance, but entry is not forbidden.
Guidebook: A history and description of the building and a history of the Willoughby family
  who built it, several illustrations but no plan, nevertheless good value.
Catering: There is a rather sordid snack bar behind the stable block, with a good view over the
  park.
WCs: Free, clean and fairly new facilities in the stable court near the industrial museum;
  suitable for wheelchairs. More WCs at one side of the house, best avoided.
Shop: Sales counter selling postcards and booklets.
Extras: The industrial museum is worth a visit; there is a beam engine which is sometimes in
  steam.

Oxfordshire

ASHDOWN HOUSE Ashbury, nr Swindon (The National Trust)
Directions: 3½ miles N. of Lambourn, 2½ miles S. of Ashbury on the W.
side of the B4000.

Ashdown has a lonely setting, high on the Downs. It was built for Lord
Craven in about 1660 and like many houses built after the Civil War has a
rather Dutch appearance. The main block is only five bays wide but very
tall, with a steep roof topped by a balustrade and cupola. On each side are
little lodge buildings and the total effect is that of a doll's house. Craven's
architect was probably William Winde, who had built other houses for him
and was well-acquainted with Holland. It comes as a disappointment to find
that only the staircase is on view inside the house. This is a sturdy piece of
carpentry, hung with a quantity of Craven portraits, many of which are by
Gerard van Honthorst. The staircase leads out onto the roof, where there
are views of the Downs somewhat obscured by trees. The house was
probably intended as a hunting box, giving grandstand views of the sport,
but there is another tradition that the Earl of Craven intended it as a plague
refuge for Elizabeth of Bohemia, the Winter Queen.

Opening times: April, Wed only; May to end Sept, first and third Sat in the month 2–6;
   conducted tours of staircase and roof at 2.30, 3.30, 4.30 and 5.30.
Entrance charges: House and grounds 60p. Grounds only 40p. Children half price.
Parking: Next to the house, free.
Wheelchair access: Access to the interior not practicable.
Guidebook: History and description of the house and a detailed list of the paintings, but these
   have been rehung since the book was written; no plan of the interior, some black and white
   illustrations.
Catering: None.
WCs: Inside the house, enquire at the ticket desk.
Shop: None.

BLENHEIM PALACE Woodstock (The Duke of Marlborough)
Tel: Woodstock (0993) 811325 (24 hours)
Directions: 8 miles N.W. of Oxford on the A34; the main entrance is in
   Woodstock

Blenheim in its parkland setting is one of the finest sights in England. The
view from the Woodstock gate of the house itself and of the lake with its
great bridge is magnificent, a continuing pleasure through the changing
seasons. The Palace was the gift of Queen Anne to the First Duke of
Marlborough as a reward for his military services and it is named after one
of his victories. Sir John Vanbrugh began the building in 1705, but after
bitter quarrels with the Duchess he was dismissed as architect in 1716 and
replaced by his associate Nicholas Hawksmoor. Blenheim is one of the

Blenheim Palace, Oxfordshire

masterpieces of the English Baroque style, combining massiveness with vigorous ornament. The walls are of golden stone. The main house is attached by curving colonnades to the kitchen courtyard on one side and the stables on the other, forming a grand open court in front. This is where visitors queue for entry and it is a good place from which to admire the romantic silhouette of the main front. The hall inside is massive and overpowering, but Hawksmoor's dining room and library, and the other ground floor state rooms are handsomely decorated and richly furnished. There are excellent tapestries, paintings and furniture, including some Boulle, as well as an exhibition about Sir Winston Churchill, who was born at Blenheim. The guided tours take about an hour; they can get a bit crowded on summer weekends and weekdays are more comfortable. The gardens next to the house were made in the present century for the Ninth Duke by Achille Duchêne; the Italian garden on the east front is private, but the water garden stepping down to the lake on the west is open to visitors. The lake itself, which encloses the house on two sides, was made by 'Capability' Brown in the 1760s, and the park as a whole is one of his best creations. Most of the park is open to visitors.

Opening times: House, 15 March to 31 Oct, daily 11.30 5. Park all year 9–5.

Entrance charges: House and grounds £2.25; children 16–18 and OAPs £1.60; children 5–15 £1.10. Grounds only, car and occupants £1.50; pedestrians 10p. (HHA)

Parking: Beside the house, about 150 yards from the front door; charge 10p.

Wheelchair access: Best to telephone in advance, no special arrangements but it should be easy.

Guidebook: A glossy souvenir guide with many colour illustrations; history of the building and room-by-room guide, bird's eye view of the house and a plan of the park; separate guide to the garden. Some foreign language guides would be a good idea.

Catering: Visitors to grounds only have access to a self-service machine. Visitors to the house have self-service cafeteria on the west terrace 11.30–5.30, or may take lunch 12–2, or tea 3.30–5 in the attractive India Room; neither are cheap. Picnics are allowed in the park.

WCs: Several; either in the kitchen courtyard near the car park, or on the west terrace near the cafeteria; none is suitable for wheelchairs.

Shop: By the entrance court: one well-filled and expensive giftshop, also a sweets and comestibles shop.

Extras: The garden centre in the park is open all year. Tour of the Duke's Private Apartment every half hour, nothing special. Motor launch trips on the lake. Narrow gauge railway rides. All charged extra.

BROUGHTON CASTLE nr Banbury (Lord Saye and Sele)
Tel: Banbury (0295) 62624
Directions: 2 miles S.W. of Banbury, off the B4035

The wide moat surrounding Broughton probably belongs to the house built by Sir John de Broughton in about 1300. Between about 1530 and 1600 Richard Fiennes and his son Richard enlarged the house, nearly doubling its size; two new storeys were added, new state rooms west of the great hall, two bay windows at the front and two stair towers at the back. In the mid-

18th century the long gallery was formed and the ceilings in the hall and elsewhere re-done and the house was restored in the 1860s and 70s by G.G. Scott Junior. Visitors follow a set route through the house and there are guides in each room. The hall is large and bare, its walls decorated with armour from the Civil War, when the family fought against King Charles I. To the east are the vaulted dining room, a 14th century private chapel and Queen Anne's Room, with a grand fireplace of the 1540s. The long gallery upstairs is Gothick but the Star Chamber next to it has a magnificent 16th century overmantel in the French style. The state rooms at the west end have good 16th century ceilings, and one is panelled, with an unusual internal porch. There are several good portraits and pieces of furniture, mixed with modern comforts and the house has a mellow and expansive atmosphere. Outside is a little garden, concealed from the courtyard by a high wall and easily missed. It contains a delightful knot garden, with lavender and roses planted between the box hedges.

Opening times: 18 May to 12 Sept, Wed and Sun, also Thurs in July and Aug and Bank Holiday Sun and Mon 2–5.
Entrance charges: £1.20; children 70p. (HHA)
Parking: Free parking beside the church, or in the park overlooking the moat.
Wheelchair access: Possible to part of the ground floor and the grounds.
Guidebook: An illustrated room-by-room guide, not very detailed but accurate as far as it goes, no plan. There are information boards in each room. A synopsis of the contents of each room in French, German, Dutch, Spanish and Italian is available on request.
Catering: Good home-made teas on Sun and Bank Holidays in the old stables.
WCs: In the car park; unsuitable for wheelchairs.
Shop: None.

BUSCOT PARK nr Faringdon (The National Trust)
Tel: Faringdon (0367) 20786
Directions: 3 miles N.W. of Faringdon on the A417

Buscot is a simple classical house of about 1780 built for, and probably designed by, its owner William Townsend. In 1889 it was purchased by Arthur Henderson MP, art collector and agricultural reformer, who was made Lord Faringdon in 1916. His grandson, the Second Lord Faringdon, employed the architect Geddes Hyslop just before World War II to remove some Victorian additions and restore the house to something like its original appearance. The interest of Buscot lies partly in this neo-Georgian work of the 1930s, both inside and out, but more in the very fine art collection of the First Lord Faringdon, and in the water garden made for him by Harold Peto early this century. Nearly all the main rooms are open to visitors and contain paintings and fine furniture. Upstairs are Victorian paintings bought by Arthur Henderson, downstairs are English 18th century paintings and old masters. Among the highlights are the Egyptian style furnishings of the entrance hall designed by Thomas Hope, the Rembrandt portrait of Clement de Jongh in the Music Room, and four paintings of the 'Briar Rose' series by Edward Burne-Jones, which form the wall decoration of the saloon. The walls of the dining room have charming chinoiserie murals of 1953 by L.R. Hobdell but the ceiling, like those of the other rooms, is in the Adam style. There are fine views from the house across the park with its lakes and on the east side is the Italianate water garden created in 1905–10 by Harold Peto.

Opening times: April to end Sept, Wed, Thurs, Fri (including Good Friday) also second and fourth Sat and Sun in each month 2–6; last admission to house 5.30.
Entrance charges: House and grounds £1.20. Grounds only 60p. Children half price.
Parking: Free parking in front of the house.
Wheelchair access: Difficult to house; possible to part of garden.
Guidebook: A very brief history of the building, but with very detailed information about the paintings and adequate coverage of the furniture. Guidebooks can be hired. There are information boards in each room.
Catering: Tea and biscuits available in July and August and at weekends.
WCs: In the stable block at some distance from the house, rather primitive.
Shop: None.

CHASTLETON HOUSE nr Moreton in Marsh (Mrs Clutton-Brock)
Tel: Barton on the Heath (060 874) 355
Directions: 22 miles N.W. of Oxford, 5 miles N.W. of Chipping Norton, 1 mile S. of the A44

Few houses conjure up the past as vividly as Chastleton, which was built soon after 1602 for Walter Jones, a wool merchant from Witney. He died in 1632 and it looks as though little has changed since then. The tall front of golden Cotswold stone steps back regularly from the centre to the tall staircase towers on each side. It is an accomplished design, recalling Burton Agnes in Yorkshire, Hardwick in Derbyshire and other houses designed by Robert Smythson. Chastleton is built round a small courtyard and is much bigger than it looks from the front. The front door, set sideways, leads into a screens passage and so into the great hall with its long oak table and heavy carved chimneypiece. This room is the assembly point for the guided tours which thread their way through the main rooms. The most spectacular of these is the great chamber on the first floor with elaborate panelling and a vigorous, if rather coarse, plaster ceiling. There are several other rooms with similar plasterwork and fireplaces of the early 17th century. The end of the tour is a climb to the long gallery which runs right across the top of the building. The barrel-vaulted ceiling is decorated with interlacing ribs and flowers and the ancient timber floor is splendid. A great deal of the furniture was already in the house in the 1630s and the later additions blend well. The family portraits of the Joneses are crude provincial work but they reinforce the feeling that Chastleton is a family home. The tours last about an hour, but one can join a tour already started. In front of the house is a forecourt with 17th century stable buildings on one side and there is also a large topiary garden in a state of pleasing neglect.

Chasleton House, Oxfordshire

Opening times: All year, Mon, Tues, Thurs and Fri, 10.30–1, 2–5.30; Sat and Sun 2–5 (dusk in winter).
Entrance charges: £1.20; children 60p.
Parking: Free parking on the grass verge by the forecourt wall.
Wheelchair access: Possible to the ground floor only, about a third of the house and not the best rooms.
Guidebook: A fairly short guide with information and anecdotes about each room and some illustrations. A plan would be useful because it is very easy to lose one's bearings.
Catering: The Brewhouse tea room provides an excellent home-made tea, but only at weekends. Closed in winter.
WCs: Beside the tea room and only accessible when the tea room is open; unsuitable for wheelchairs.
Shop: None.

GREYS COURT Rotherfield Greys, nr Henley (The National Trust)
Tel: Rotherfield Greys (049 17) 529
Directions: 3 miles N.W. of Henley on Thames on a minor road signed to Rotherfield Greys and Rotherfield Peppard

Greys Court is a very attractive group of small buildings in a pretty garden setting. The earliest of these buildings are the survivors of a mid-14th century manor house built for Sir John de Greys after 1347. His house consisted of a rectangular walled enclosure with a tower at each corner and a small square keep. Only the keep and three of the towers remain. In 1518 the Knollys family acquired the manor and some time later in the century built a small house whose walls are a mixture of brick, flint and stone. They also built some outbuildings, including the stable block, the Bachelor's Hall (so called because of the inscription over the door which says 'Nothing is better than the celibate life'), and the well house. The house has a 17th century oriel window on the south front and a mid-18th century bow window. Four rooms are shown inside the house, but there is not a great deal of interest apart from the beautiful rococo plaster ceiling in the drawing room. The garden itself has been created in fairly recent times, but incorporates some splendid old trees, including a tulip tree.

Opening times: House, April to end Sept, Mon, Wed, Fri; garden, April to Sept, Mon to Sat; 2.15–6; closed Good Friday.
Entrance charges: Garden 80p; house 40p extra. Children half price to garden. No dogs in gardens.
Parking: 200 yards from the house.
Wheelchair access: Access to the house by the west door at the back, by prior arrangement with the custodian; all rooms except the kitchen can be seen; the tea room in the stable is up three steps.
Guidebook: Slender but adequate. There are information boards in the rooms of the house.
Catering: Teas and biscuits available April to June, Wed and Sat; July to Sept, Mon, Wed, Fri and Sat.
WCs: Beside the donkey wheel; facilities for the disabled.
Shop: There is a small souvenir shop on the first floor of the stables.

KINGSTON HOUSE Kingston Bagpuize (Lord and Lady Tweedsmuir)
Tel: Longworth (0865) 820259
Directions: In the village of Kingston Bagpuize, 5½miles W. of Abingdon, at the junction of the A415 and A420

This is a compact red brick house, with dressings and window surrounds of the local stone. The two longer fronts are similar in appearance; both are two storeys high and seven windows wide, with the centre rising up to support a pediment. The architect is unknown and there is some controversy over the date. The architectural ornament looks typical of the decades after 1700, but the family maintain that the house was standing in 1670. The original entrance front now faces the lawn and the present front door leads directly into the staircase-hall, which is the starting point for the tours conducted by members of the family. The four rooms shown on the ground floor and the three on the first floor are all of similar character; not too large, well-proportioned, with simple Queen Anne fireplaces and sometimes panelled walls. The furniture is predominantly a comfortable mixture of French and English 18th century pieces, with some minor paintings. The very pleasant English garden at Kingston was laid out by Miss Raphael, the previous owner, and is kept up by her niece. There is a pretty 18th century gazebo.

Opening times: House and garden, Easter to June, Sat, Sun and Bank Holiday Mon, also August Bank Holiday weekend, 2–5.30.
Entrance charges: House and garden 70p; garden only 50p and 30p.
Parking: Free parking outside the entrance gate, near the main road.
Wheelchair access: Possible to the garden; there is a flight of steps to the front door of the house.
Guidebook: A slim guide with the basic information and some colour illustrations.
Catering: Light afternoon teas available.
WCs: Inside the house, for visitors to the house.
Shop: None.

MAPLEDURHAM HOUSE Mapledurham, nr Reading (J.J. Eyston Esq)
Tel: Kidmore End (0734) 723350
Directions: 4 miles N.W. of Reading on the N. side of the River Thames, off the A4074 or B4526

The house and its little village are tucked away on the bank of the Thames at the end of a narrow country lane. Mapledurham was built between 1581 and 1612 by Sir Michael Blount, and his descendants still live here. It is an attractive building of patterned red brick with a tall central range containing the main rooms and lower wings to front and rear making an H-plan. Both the main front and the inside have been altered. In the late 18th century the roof gables were replaced by battlements, and the old windows by sashes. The great hall on the ground floor was divided up and a small chapel in the

Gothick style was added at the back of the house. In the 1830s the front was restored to something like its original appearance, a porch was added and the dining room redecorated. Visitors make their own way round the main rooms on both floors. The present entrance hall contains a fascinating collection of carved animal heads of the 17th and 18th centuries symbolising vices and virtues, with a curious wolf in sheep's clothing. Despite the alterations, there is still some 17th century plaster decoration and the elaborate main staircase of the original house. The rooms contain a good collection of English 17th and 18th century furniture and paintings. The portrait of Lady St John in the dining room, dating from about 1615, is a very early example of a landscape background. The poet Alexander Pope was a frequent visitor to Mapledurham in the mid-18th century; he advised on the garden and left all his possessions to Martha Blount. Near to the house is part of the earlier manor house and further afield in the village is a working water mill, recently restored.

Opening times: Easter Sun to end Sept, Sat, Sun and Bank Holidays, 2.30–5.30.
Entrance charges: £1.20; children 5–16 60p. (HHA)
Parking: Free car park 200 yards from the house; there is a small car park beside the tea room for the disabled.
Wheelchair access: Ground floor rooms only.
Guidebook: A room-by-room guide with many colour illustrations.
Catering: Two tea rooms, one waitress service, serving cream teas and home-made cakes.
WCs: Next to the tea room.
Shop: The shop sells an attractive selection of gifts and craftwork.
Extras: The water mill is open as the house, extra charge made. Water trips to the house leave Caversham Bridge at 2.15 on days when house is open.

MILTON MANOR Milton, nr Abingdon (Surgeon Capt and Mrs E.J. Mockler)

Tel: Abingdon (0235) 831287/831871
Directions: 4 miles S. of Abingdon, off the B4016 in Milton village

This pleasant red brick house of modest size stands at the end of a short drive off the village street. The tall central block was completed in about 1663 for Paul Carlton, a local landowner who had just married an heiress. The small wings on either side were added in the late 1760s by Stephen Wright, who was Master Mason of the Royal Works, for a new owner of the house called Bryant Barrett who was a Roman Catholic. Barrett's descendants still live in the house. Visitors are guided round most of the main rooms by members of the family in tours which last about 40 minutes. The ground floor drawing room has a heavy plaster ceiling which must date from the 1660s and the chimneypiece in the hall with hearty ladies holding cornucopias is of the same date. The south wing has a first floor chapel in the Gothick style with windows containing 14th century English and 16th century Netherlandish glass, but the best room is undoubtedly the library on the ground floor of the wing. This is also in the Gothick style and has not been altered since the 1760s, except that the walls have been repainted in what may be the original colours of mushroom and white. The garden consists of lawns, with a pond in front of the house and some majestic trees. The walled garden to the north is planted partly with vegetables and partly with flowers. There are swings and a climbing frame at the back of the house.

Opening times: Easter weekend to 12 Oct, Sat, Sun and Bank Holidays 2–5.30.
Entrance charges: 80p; children under 14 40p.
Parking: Free parking in a field by the entrance gate.
Wheelchair access: A flight of six shallow steps to the door, then all the ground floor rooms (the best part of the house) are accessible.
Guidebook: A pleasant illustrated booklet with a text by the owner; room-by-room tour and a history of ownership.
Catering: Tea rooms to the right of the main block; remarkably good value.
WCs: Beside the tea room; unsuitable for wheelchairs.
Shop: Shop.

MINSTER LOVELL HALL   Minster Lovell, nr Witney (Ancient Monument)
Directions: 15 miles W. of Oxford, 5 miles E. of Burford on the N. side of the A40. The ruins are approached through the churchyard at the E. end of the village

The ruins at Minster Lovell are those of a manor house rebuilt, probably between 1431 and 1442, by William, Seventh Baron Lovell. They stand on the bank of the little river Windrush in a setting which is romantically beautiful, even in the depths of winter. The buildings were arranged round three sides of a courtyard. The great hall, solar and chapel were on the north side, where the visitor now enters; the east wing contained the kitchen and stables, the west wing contained living rooms. The south side of the courtyard was open and only a wall separated the house from the river. Of the east and west wings only foundations remain together with the roofless hall and its entrance porch. The house was confiscated from the Lovells by King Henry VII after the battle of Bosworth in 1485 and passed eventually to the Coke family. Thomas Coke, who became First Earl of Leicester, lived here for a while, but left to live in his new house at Holkham in Norfolk. Minster Lovell was abandoned and in about 1747 the buildings were partly dismantled. Near to the ruins are the 15th century church of St Kenelm, which was rebuilt by the same Baron Lovell who built the manor house, and a 15th century dovecote.

Opening times: Standard hours (S), see page xii, but accessible at all reasonable times.
Entrance charges: 40p; OAPs and children 20p.
Parking: The free car park is about 500 yards from the ruins, but it is possible to set down about 50 yards away.
Wheelchair access: Difficult.

Guidebook: Out of print at present.
Catering: None, but picnics allowed.
WCs: Portakabin facilities, often closed.
Shop: None.

ROUSHAM PARK Steeple Aston (C. Cottrell-Dormer Esq)
Tel: Steeple Aston (0869) 47110
Directions: 12 miles N. of Oxford on the E. side of the A423 Banbury road;
turn off at Hopcrofts Holt Hotel

The grey stone house was built in about 1635 for Sir Robert Dormer. It has the usual E-shaped 17th century plan and is three storeys high. In 1738 General James Dormer employed the architect William Kent to improve the house and lay out the garden. Kent replaced the original gables of the roof with battlements and enlarged the house by building a pavilion on either side. Internally, Kent left the original staircases and one small panelled room, but improved other rooms by bringing in new doors and fireplaces. Two of his rooms are especially fine. The Painted Parlour on the ground floor of the east wing is a very grand room in miniature. The ceiling is painted and the chimneypiece, doors and every other architectural feature richly carved. Kent also supplied some of the furniture and chose the pictures. The Great Parlour in one of the pavilions is more imposing and has a very curious vaulted ceiling. The room was originally the library, but the bookshelves have been replaced by portraits in pretty rococo frames carved by Thomas Roberts of Oxford. The house has a pleasant lived-in atmosphere and contains some interesting family portraits as well as the furniture attributed to Kent. There are guided tours every half hour which last about an hour. The garden, laid out by Kent in 25 acres of ground sloping down to the river Cherwell, has hardly been altered. It is one of the earliest examples of a picturesque garden, intended to give the visitor a series of pleasant and unexpected views. For this reason it is a good idea to walk around the garden in the direction which Kent intended so that the temples, arches and vistas catch the eye as they were meant to.

Opening times: Gardens all year, daily 10.30–5.30. House April to Sept, Wed, Sun and Bank Holidays 2–5.30.
Entrance charges: House and garden £1.50; OAPs and children 70p. House only £1.00. Garden only 50p. Reductions for OAPs and children. (HHA)
Parking: Free parking in the stableyard next to the house.
Wheelchair access: There are six steep steps to the front door, but then all the ground floor (with the two best rooms) are on the level. The garden is mostly grass.
Guidebook: An attractive souvenir with colour plates and a plan showing the garden layout.
Catering: None, picnics allowed in the park.
WCs: New facilities in the stable block.
Shop: No permanent shop, though plants from the estate are sometimes on sale.

STONOR PARK   nr Henley on Thames (Lord and Lady Camoys)
Tel: Turville Heath (049 163) 587
Directions: 4 miles N. of Henley on Thames, 5 miles S.E. of Watlington,
off the B480

The house is set into a remote wooded hillside in the Chilterns and has a long
low red brick front, largely 18th century in appearance, but hinting at
something earlier. In fact, the greater part of a large mediaeval house lies
behind the facade. The Stonor family have lived here since the 12th century.
They have always been Roman Catholics and the heavy fines they had to pay
for their religion after the Reformation prevented them spending much on
new building. The core of the house is the great hall of about 1280, whose
stone arches can still be seen on one side of a small courtyard. Over the next
200 years more buildings were added, including the chapel. In about 1600
Sir Francis Stonor hid the jumble of buildings behind a red brick front with
many gables; all but the central gable was removed when the house was
altered again in the 1750s by the architect John Aitkins. He put in the sash
windows and added the hipped roof with its heavy cornice which gives the
building its 18th century look. He also redecorated the hall inside in a
Gothick style, and another architect used the same style for the redecoration
of the chapel in the late 1790s. Not surprisingly, the inside of Stonor Park is
like a rabbit warren, but there are some pleasant rooms, especially the
dining room with its panoramic wall-paper showing the buildings of Paris.
Some of the other rooms have been redecorated recently. Much of the
original furniture was sold in 1938 and 1975 but the rooms are still decently
furnished, partly with the help of furniture lent from Sawston Hall near
Cambridge. There are good tapestries and important Renaissance bronzes
(placed too far away to see properly) and a splendid bedroom with bed and
chairs in the shape of sea-shells. There is also a quantity of material relating
to secret Roman Catholicism, and especially to the English martyr St
Edmund Campion. Visitors may wander round in their own time and there
are guides in each room. There is a terrace garden, recently restored,
otherwise the estate is parkland with herds of deer.

Opening times: 11 April; May, June, Wed, Thurs, Sun; July, Wed, Thurs, Sun and Sats 17,
24, 31 ; Aug, Wed, Thurs, Sun and Sats 7, 14, 21, 28; Sept, Wed, Thurs, Sun and first Sat
— 2–5.30. Also Bank Holiday Mons 11–5.30.
Entrance charges: £1.30; OAPs £1.10; children 80p. (HHA)
Parking: Free parking near the house, gets muddy in wet weather.
Wheelchair access: Not practicable to inside of house.
Guidebook: A list of the contents is essential because nothing is labelled. There is also a glossy
souvenir history with many pictures and much genealogy. It has no plan, but instead a very
helpful series of diagrams to explain how the house grew.
Catering: An airy ample room with food from a good tea shop in Watlington.
WCs: New, clean and functional.
Shop: In the other half of the tea room: a good selection of books, toys and souvenirs and also
a few Roman Catholic items.

Shropshire

ACTON BURNELL CASTLE Acton Burnell (Ancient Monument)
Directions: 7 miles S.S.E. of Shrewsbury between the A49 and A458, on
minor roads; the castle is near the church, on the edge of the village

The village lies in deep country and the ruined castle stands in the grounds
of an 18th century house. It was built between 1284 and 1293 for Bishop
Robert Burnell, Lord Chancellor of England and a close friend of King
Edward I. 'Castle' is a misleading name because Acton Burnell was
intended principally as a house; its red sandstone walls still have
battlements and square corner towers but there was an ordinary front door
on the ground floor and the main rooms on the first floor had large windows
to the outside world. In fact, this is one of the earliest examples of a semi-
fortified manor house in England. The building fell out of use in the 15th
century and later became a barn, but three of the four sides and all four
corner towers survive, as well as much of the window tracery. Seen from the
nearby churchyard, the castle looks almost habitable. A short distance away
are two large stone gables, the relics of a large barn built by Robert Burnell
at the same time as the house. The church is also the Bishop's work and the
chancel, in particular, is 13th century architecture of the best quality.

Opening times: Open at all reasonable times.
Entrance charges: 10p (contribution box).
Parking: Free parking a short distance from the castle.
Wheelchair access: No problems, the whole of the ruin can be inspected.
Guidebook: A leaflet may be obtained from the keeper of the monument, during the daytime.
Catering: None, but this would make an excellent picnic place.
WCs: None.
Shop: None.

ACTON ROUND HALL nr Bridgnorth (H.L. Kennedy Esq)
Directions: 6 miles W.N.W. of Bridgnorth, off the A5; the house is close to
Acton Round church and is not signposted

This early 18th century house was built as a dower house by Sir Whitmore
Acton of nearby Aldenham Park. It is a beautiful little building of red brick,
seven generous bays wide and two storeys high, with a tall hipped roof. The
interior has hardly been altered and most of the rooms still have their
original panelling and fireplaces. The furniture of the present owners is a
catholic mixture, introduced by a stuffed baboon on the hall chandelier.
There are many items from India, including several oil paintings of
dignified Rajahs and an array of ugly looking knives on the elegant staircase.
Among the finer English items are two side tables in the style of William
Kent which came from Wroxton Abbey in Oxfordshire. One bedroom

contains a trap for the connoisseur in the shape of a good reproduction 18th century table made recently in Italy; the hand-painted Chinese wallpaper is also new. Visitors are conducted round the house by the owners themselves. After visiting the house it is worth making the short detour to the church in order to see the excellent Gothick monument to Sir Whitmore Acton by Thomas Farnolls Pritchard.

Opening times: Mid May to mid Sept, Thurs 2.30–5.30.
Entrance charges: 50p; children 25p.
Parking: On the gravel sweep next to the house.
Wheelchair access: Steps up to the front door; it would be wise to ring beforehand.
Guidebook: None.
Catering: None.
WCs: None for public use.
Shop: None.

ADCOTE   Little Ness, nr Shrewsbury (Adcote School Educational Trust)
Tel: Baschurch (0939) 260202
Directions: 7 miles N.W. of Shrewsbury off the A5 (take the turning for Great Ness or Little Ness)

Adcote is a mid-Victorian mansion by Norman Shaw, the most successful and accomplished of Victorian architects. It was built between 1876 and 1881 for Mrs Rebecca Darby, whose wealth was drawn from the iron and textile industries. Shaw designed the house in a powerful version of the 16th century style, with walls of excellent local limestone, large mullion and transom windows and a varied skyline of gables and tall brick chimneys. The south front, facing the garden, is particularly impressive. The house has become a school and its large rooms are very well fitted for the purpose, especially the enormous great hall with its high roof carried on four stone arches. The lack of furniture in the hall does not really matter but the other main rooms are less impressive on their own, and would look better filled with Victorian clutter. There is a very fine stone stair which leads to the gallery of the hall, but the first floor bedrooms opening off it are also too empty. The redeeming features are the excellent William de Morgan tile decorations to most of the fireplaces. Visitors should report to the school office on arrival (the office entrance is at the side of the house). The tours of the house are conducted by a member of staff. The gardens of Adcote are still excellently kept up with plenty of dark hedges to make a foil for the stonework of the house.

Opening times: 20 April to 9 July (except 28–2 June), then 10 Sept to 30 Sept, daily 2–5.
Entrance charges: Free, visitors should report to school office on arrival.
Parking: Free parking next to the house.
Wheelchair access: Not practicable to the interior, there are too many steps; most of the exterior could be seen without difficulty.
Guidebook: None.
Catering: None.

WCs: No public lavatories.
Shop: None.

ATTINGHAM PARK Atcham, nr Shrewsbury (The National Trust)
Tel: Upton Magna (074 377) 203
Directions: 4 miles S.E. of Shrewsbury on the N. side of the A5 at Atcham, signposted

Attingham looks very impressive seen across the park from the A5. The massive three-storey main block with its tall and spindly portico, the colonnades and pavilions to each side and the rear courtyard were all built in 1782 for Noel Hill, later First Lord Berwick. His architect was George Steuart, who also designed the round church of St Chad at Shrewsbury. In 1805 John Nash incorporated a picture gallery and a new staircase at the centre of the house for the Second Lord Berwick. The interior is uncommonly fine. The rooms were arranged in two apartments; those for Lord Berwick (Dining Room, Libraries and study), on the left, those for Lady Berwick (Drawing Room and three small rooms including a boudoir) on the right of the entrance hall. The large rooms have good plasterwork and of the smaller rooms the circular boudoir has very pretty painted wall decoration in the French manner. Most of the original contents were sold in 1827 but the rooms now have excellent furniture, much of it Neapolitan, collected by the Third Lord Berwick in the mid-19th century. Nash's picture gallery behind the main hall is an extraordinary room. Its walls are painted the original dark red colour, the Italian and Dutch paintings are closely hung, in the approved manner of the 19th century, and the light comes from one of the first ceilings to be made of iron and glass. Behind the gallery is Nash's staircase, also dark red, with reeded wooden walls meant to look like drapery. Visitors make their own way through the house and there are guides in the main rooms. Some of the trees in the park were planted in the 1770s but re-landscaping was undertaken in the 1790s following the advice of Humphrey Repton. It is possible to walk in much of the park.

Opening times: April to end Sept, Mon, Wed, Sat, Sun and Bank Holiday Mon 2–5.30; Oct Sat and Sun only 2–5.30 or sunset; closed Good Friday.
Entrance charges: £1.20; children 60p.
Parking: Free car parking near to the house (about 100 yards away).
Wheelchair access: There is a flight of twelve steps to the main entrance; thereafter all the rooms are on the ground floor.
Guidebook: A good thorough account, with room-by-room tour, histories of house and occupants, a diagrammatic plan and several illustrations. Lists of the pictures can be found in the picture rooms. There is also a braille guidebook.
Catering: Tea room in the outer library, which forms one of the pavilions beside the house; waitress service teas in pleasant surroundings.
WCs: In the basement near the tea room; inaccessible to wheelchair users.
Shop: A very small shop in the tea room with a few souvenirs.

BENTHALL HALL　Much Wenlock (The National Trust)

Tel: Telford (0952) 882254

Directions: 4 miles N.E. of Much Wenlock, 6 miles S. of Wellington, 1 mile N.W. of Broseley, off the B4375

Although it is so close to the old industrial centre of Ironbridge Gorge, Benthall has managed to remain peacefully isolated. The house probably dates from the 1580s. It is a grey sandstone building of moderate size with a very haphazard front in which the two large bay windows and the porch are placed with no regard to the roof gables above. On two sides of the porch are stone tablets arranged in a quincunx, which may have been intended as a sign that the Benthall family were Roman Catholics. Visitors are shown three ground floor rooms and the great chamber above, all of which are still used by the present members of the Benthall family. The hall is a plain room, but the dining room has 16th century panelling and the parlour has both panelling (painted white) and good plaster decoration to the walls and ceiling. Much of the best furniture dates from the 17th century and includes a chest of drawers in the parlour inlaid with mother of pearl and other materials. The oak staircase is an excellent example of vigorous strapwork carving and is believed to have been built in 1618. The great chamber is a pleasant panelled room which now serves as a library. Opening off it is a chamber over the entrance porch which has a secret hiding place in the floor. In several of the rooms are examples of the rare Caughley porcelain made between 1775 and 1799. The part of the garden to which visitors are admitted contains some interesting plants and there is also the small 17th century church to see.

Opening times: Easter Sat to end Sept; Tues, Wed and Sat 2–6, also Bank Holiday Mon (ground floor only) 2–6.

Entrance charges: £1.00; children 50p. Garden only 50p.

Parking: Free parking in the lane leading to the house.

Wheelchair access: Would be possible to the three ground floor rooms.

Guidebook: A very readable history of the family, and an acceptable room-by-room description, but rather undecided and slightly confusing about the date of the house, of which there is no plan. The garden and the church are also described.

Catering: None.

WCs: In the garden, an old fashioned but comfortable lavatory, not easily accessible to wheelchairs; paying a visit to it is the only excuse allowed for looking at the back of the house.

Shop: None.

BOSCOBEL HOUSE　nr Shifnal (Department of the Environment)

Directions: 12 miles E. of Wellington, 3 miles E. of Tong on minor roads between the A5 and A41; signposted

Boscobel is a small timber-framed house of the 17th century whose claim to fame is that the young King Charles II hid there in 1651 after his defeat at the Battle of Worcester. In later years the building was enlarged and became a farmhouse. The later parts are still privately occupied but the original two-storey house is now an historic monument. Its small rooms have some 17th and 18th century wall panelling but are almost completely empty of furniture. There are also two 'secret rooms' which may have been used by the King. The garden is laid out in the 17th century manner, with formal flower beds edged with box hedges. A short distance away, in the middle of a field, is a large oak tree, growing on the site of the famous 'Royal Oak' in which the King hid for a day of his time at Boscobel. The original tree was carried away piecemeal by souvenir hunters. On one side of the house is the farmyard, whose sheds still contain a few animals, and a peaceful duckpond. Visitors are allowed to wander pretty much as they please.

Opening times: Standard hours (S), see page xii.
Entrance charges: 50p; children and OAPs 25p.
Parking: Free car park a short distance from the house.
Wheelchair access: There are some steps inside the house, and the garden has to be reached by this route.
Guidebook: A very full guide, with full details of King Charles' time at Boscobel; also a description of the house, with plans, and a brief description of the ruined mediaeval Whiteladies Priory nearby.
Catering: None.
WCs: In the farmyard, newly built; unsuitable for wheelchairs.
Shop: Slides and postcards only.

DUDMASTON   Quatt, nr Bridgnorth (The National Trust)
Directions: 4 miles S.E. of Bridgnorth on the A442

Dudmaston was only given to the National Trust in 1978 and opened for the first time last year. The approach across a plain park gives no clue to the character of the estate, which has belonged to various members of the Wolryche family for the last 850 years. The house is a substantial mansion of red brick, built in about 1700 for Sir Thomas Wolryche and perhaps designed by Smith of Warwick. Minor alterations were made to the outside in the 19th century and the servants' wing was partly rebuilt. The large extrance hall still keeps its early 18th century character, with panelled walls and an impressive set of late 17th century chairs with embroidered upholstery. The delicate main staircase is part of the improvements made in the 1820s and the library, made by throwing two smaller rooms into one, is also light and airy thanks to its white paint. The small oak room is perhaps the most charming and personal on show. Its panelled walls set off some fine 16th century family portraits, as well as more modern works by such as Guillaumin and Barbara Hepworth. These give a foretaste of the rest of the house, for most of the servants' wing has been converted into gallery rooms to display collections of modern painting and sculpture, modern Spanish pictures, topographical watercolours and Botanical art. These can also be entered separately. But perhaps the most memorable thing about this property is the garden to the south of the house, where the ground falls in a steep dingle down to a large lake. In due course this garden will be brought back to something like its original 1780s layout, with pavilions, paths and cascades.

Opening times: April to end Sept, Wed and Sun 2.30–5.30.
Entrance charges: House £1.20; garden 60p.
Parking: Free parking in the grassed walled area of the former orchard.
Wheelchair access: Possible to the ground floor.
Guidebook: To the house and contents, with a plan; separate guides to both the contemporary art and the botanical drawings.
Catering A newly formed tea room in the outbuildings next to the car park; nice, brown and woody inside, with the best scones of the year.
WCs: In the same range of outbuildings and the tea room, next to the car park, new; facilities for wheelchairs.
Shop: A small souvenir shop in the servants' wing, also some plants for sale.
Extras: In Quatt church, just down the road, are the excellent late mediaeval tombs of the Wolryche family.

MORETON CORBET CASTLE   (Ancient Monument)
Directions: 8 miles N.N.E. of Shrewsbury, between the A53 and A49 off the B5063

At Moreton Corbet visitors will find the ruins of a small castle keep of about 1200 and the remains of a splendid Elizabethan house standing together in flat countryside. The house was built in 1579 for Sir Andrew Corbet, and must have been as fine as Longleat. Some of the outer walls still stand to full height and they have carved stone decoration of excellent quality, still looking crisp. The interior is completely gutted.

Opening times: Open at all reasonable times.
Entrance charges: Free.
Parking: In the lane beside the castle.
Wheelchair access: The normal entrance gate is not suitable for wheelchairs.
Guidebook: None for sale at the castle.
Catering: None.
WCs: None.
Shop: None.

SHIPTON HALL   Much Wenlock (J.N.R.N. Bishop Esq)
Tel: Brickton (074 636) 225
Directions: 6 miles S.W. of Much Wenlock, in Shipton Village on the B4378

The Hall is set back from the road at the top of a long slope which begins as open grass but turns into a formal garden in front of the house. The approach is flanked on one side by a solid 18th century stable block and on the other by the parish church in the trees. Shipton was built in about 1587 by Richard Lutwyche as dowry for his daughter and is first cousin to

Wilderhope Manor nearby. Both houses are of the same grey stone with tall brick chimneys and both have three wide gables and a tall porch; but at Shipton the porch rises clear above the roofline as a four-storey tower. The interior was partly modernised in the 1760s by the architect Thomas Pritchard who also designed the stable block. The hall at the centre of the house is Pritchard's work and probably the staircase and the elegant first floor library. Some of the other rooms have their Elizabethan panelling, much of it painted, but the panelling in the dining room is Victorian. The guided tours cover three ground floor and four first floor rooms and are well-informed and interesting.

Opening times. May to Sept, Thurs and Bank Holidays, also Sun in July and Aug 2.30 5.30.
Entrance charges: 85p; children 50p. (HHA)
Parking: In a field across the road from the house, a distance of about 100 yards.
Wheelchair access: Not practicable without some very energetic help; the approach is steep and there are two flights of steps before the entrance.
Guidebook: Only a leaflet with some basic information which is given free with each admission.
Catering: Only by prior arrangement.
WCs: One outside.
Shop: Home-made jams and marmalade and some postcards sold in the house.

SHREWSBURY: ROWLEY'S HOUSE Hill's Lane (Borough of Shrewsbury and Atcham)
Tel: Shrewsbury (0743) 61196
Directions: In the centre of Shrewsbury; ask for the bus station

Drastic clearances in the 1930s left the great house of Shrewsbury's richest Tudor merchant standing isolated in the middle of the bus station. Roger Rowley came to Shrewsbury in 1594 and made a fortune in the cloth trade. He lived in a very large timber-framed house which was then fairly new, and it soon became known as 'Rowley's House'. In 1618 his son built a large brick addition known as 'Rowley's Mansion' which was probably the first brick house in Shrewsbury. The two parts together are impressive, despite their dismal position. The earlier house was restored in the 1930s with timber and window glass from neighbouring buildings which were being demolished, and one end of it now serves as a small museum of local history. The heavily-timbered rooms contain much Roman material from nearby Viroconium as well as prehistoric and mediaeval objects. The principal parts of the timber house and 'Rowley's Mansion' are not open.

Opening times: All year, Mon to Sat 10–1, 2–5.
Entrance charges: Free.
Parking: No car park; there is a small pay car park next to the house, and a multi-storey car park across the street.
Wheelchair access: Not practicable.
Guidebook: A brief account of the building with a description of the restoration and some early photos.

Catering: None.
WCs: None.
Shop: Postcards, pamphlets and other museum literature can be bought from the custodian.

STOKESAY CASTLE nr Craven Arms (Sir Philip and Lady Magnus-Allcroft)

Directions: 8 miles N.W. of Ludlow, just off the A49 and clearly visible from the main road

This romantic fortified manor house was built when the English were just turning from castles to houses. The main buildings form a compact group inside a partly dry moat in the peaceful valley of the river Onny. At the north end is a small stone tower with an overhanging upper storey of timber, which is part of a 12th century tower house belonging to the Say family. Next to it is the great hall built for Laurence de Ludlow, a rich cloth merchant who purchased Stokesay in 1281. Ten years later he was given leave to fortify his house and added the prominent south tower and the solar with its outside staircase. In the 700 years since then the only addition has been the fancifully decorated timber gatehouse, which dates from 1590. The gatehouse is the curator's cottage, but the main house is unoccupied and the rooms empty. It is very easy to imagine life here in the Middle Ages, especially in the great hall with its wooden shuttered windows and open hearth in the centre of the floor. There has been some careful restoration work; the hall roof is partly original and partly later patching and the solar now has 17th century panelling and a little furniture of the same period, but for the most part Stokesay has survived intact. Visitors are left to wander through the house without restriction.

Opening times: April to Sept, daily except Mon and Tues (but open Mon in July and Aug and Bank Holiday Mon) 10–6; last admission 5.30; March and Oct 10–5, last admission 4.30; closed Nov to Feb.
Entrance charges: 60p; children 25p; no dogs, no sketching and no picnics inside the castle.
Parking: Free car park a short distance from the house.
Wheelchair access: Wheelchairs and prams are not allowed in the castle.
Guidebook: A recent guide with an interesting text, several illustrations and a plan.
Catering: None.
WCs: Just outside the entrance to the castle, adequate, not for wheelchairs.
Shop: Guidebooks, maps and cards sold in the gatehouse.

TYN-Y-RHOS HALL Weston Rhyn, nr Oswestry (Chevalier Thompson-Butler-Lloyd)

Tel: Chirk (069 186) 7898

Directions: 19 miles N.W. of Shrewsbury, 4½ miles N. of Oswestry; turn off the A5 for Weston Rhyn and follow signs in village

The hall has a pleasant front with four gables of assorted sizes. The date of 1711 carved on a stone in the wall is probably correct for the oldest part of the house, although there have been many later additions and alterations. The rooms inside are low and dark, like those of a farmhouse. The furniture mainly dates from the later 18th and 19th centuries. Visitors are graciously conducted through the building by the Chevalier himself.

Opening times: 1 May to 15 Sept, Wed, Thurs, Sat and Sun and Bank Holiday Mon 2.30–6.
Entrance charges: 60p; children 40p.
Parking: In front of the house.
Wheelchair access: Possible to the ground floor.
Guidebook: A leaflet with a description of each room; it is written with aplomb and contains a very mixed bag of information.
Catering: Tea is served at the end of the tour in a small back room; excellent value for money with a large pot of tea, scones, cake and biscuits.
WCs: The house facilities, which are not for wheelchairs.
Shop: None.

UPTON CRESSETT HALL nr Bridgnorth (William Cash Esq)

Tel: Morville (074 631) 307
Directions: 4 miles W. of Bridgnorth, 2 miles S. of the A458 down a narrow twisting lane

The lane leading to Upton gets narrower and narrower but ends at last beside a red brick Tudor gatehouse and the larger more irregular building with massive brick chimneys which is the manor house itself. The brick walls are only a skin stretched over a timber-framed house which may date back to the 14th century. The present owners purchased the property in 1971 and have restored the building and turned it into a very comfortable residence. On the ground floor visitors are shown the dining room, drawing room and kitchen, all of which have some early features and some good pieces of Jacobean furniture, but the most striking room is undoubtedly the upstairs bedroom, half filled with the enormous timber truss of the roof of the original great hall. After seeing the manor house it is possible to explore the gatehouse, whose rooms have elegant plaster ceilings and were obviously intended as principal living rooms. A little way down the valley from the house is the Norman church of St Michael, which is now in the care of the Redundant Churches Fund. The key of the church is kept at the house (it unlocks the side door, not the main door).

Opening times: May to end Sept, Thurs 2.30–5.30.
Entrance charges: 75p; children 35p. (HHA)
Parking: Free parking next to the house.
Wheelchair access: Not practicable to any part of the house or the church.
Guidebook: An illustrated leaflet with an historical account of the house and its various owners; one difficulty is that very little is known about the house.
Catering: By arrangement only.
WCs: In the house.
Shop: None.

THE WHITE HOUSE Aston Munslow (Miss J.C. Purser)
Tel: All enquiries by letter please.
Directions: 14 miles S.W. of Bridgnorth, 9½ miles N. of Ludlow off the
B4368 by the White Swan public house

This small farmhouse, the home of the Stedman family for over three
hundred years, has little in common with the American White House. The
long low wing to one side is a timber-framed hall house of the early 14th
century which was later faced in stone. The timber cross-wing at the rear
dates from the 16th century and the plain square house in front of it from the
late 18th century. Mixtures of this kind are not uncommon in English
houses but the serious guided tours explain the process of development in a
thoroughly fascinating way. It is possible to see how each successive
alteration was made and why. The small rooms are furnished in a timeless
'farmhouse' style with simple furniture. The farm outbuildings shelter an
excellent collection of farm implements from hay-wains to billhooks and the
amiable owner is adept at explaining their purposes. There is a pleasant
small garden, which contains a ruined dovecote built in 1326.

Opening times: House and farm museum Easter to 30 Oct, Sat 11–5 and Wed 2–5.30; Good
    Friday 2–5.30, Bank Holiday weeks daily except Fri and Sun 11–5.30; may also be open at
    other times in the mid-summer months.
Entrance charges: (1981) £1.00; children 50p. (HHA)
Parking: In the yard, but family cars can drive into the orchard to picnic there.
Wheelchair access: Not practicable to the house, but most of the contents of the farm
    museum would be visible.
Guidebook: A scholarly account of the evolution of the house with plans and sections of the
    building; no information about the contents.
Catering: None.
WCs: Rustic.
Shop: Several pamphlets about country buildings and history are on sale at the ticket desk
    along with a selection of sweets — which serve as a warning that visitors may encounter
    school parties.

WILDERHOPE MANOR Easthope, Much Wenlock (The National
    Trust)
Tel: Longville (069 43) 363
Directions: 7 miles S.W. of Much Wenlock, 7 miles E. of Church Streeton,
    ½ mile S. of the B4371 on a minor road

This grey stone Tudor house is hidden in the Corvedale valley, miles from
anywhere. The first sight is of the tall brick chimneys and the staircase tower
at the back of the building. At the front, the two short wings, bay window
and porch all rise the full height of the house to finish in gables. A very
similar front can be found at Shipton Hall a few miles away and the same
masons were probably employed. Wilderhope was built in the 1580s for
Francis Smallman and his wife Ellen, whose initials can be seen in the
plasterwork inside. After falling into decay, the house was repaired in the

1930s and again in the 1970s. It now serves as a Youth Hostel. The principal rooms of the ground and first floors still have their original decorated plaster ceilings; the most elaborate decoration is in the first floor parlour over the hall. The original spiral staircase has also survived, each tread a solid block of wood. Visitors are free to range over most of the house, whose rooms are either common rooms or dormitories with the appropriate modern furniture. There is no garden to speak of, but this increases the romantic isolation of the setting.

Opening times: April to Sept, Wed and Sat 2–4.30; Oct to March, Sat only 2–4.30.
Entrance charges: 70p; children 35p.
Parking: In a yard near the house.
Wheelchair access: Would be possible to the ground floor with athletic assistance, as there are several steps inside and the approach is uneven.
Guidebook: A slim booklet with all the necessary information; a plan would be useful.
Catering: None.
WCs: In the outbuildings next to the house, well-maintained; not for wheelchairs.
Shop: No souvenir shop, but the Youth Hostel shop sells the basics of life, from chocolate to bootlaces and baked beans.

Somerset

AXBRIDGE: KING JOHN'S HUNTING LODGE Market Place (The National Trust)
Tel: Axbridge (0934) 732012
Directions: In Axbridge, 8 miles E.S.E. of Weston Super Mare

Axbridge is a charming little town with its main buildings clustered round the square; mining made the place important in Anglo-Saxon times and wool in the Middle Ages, but later events have passed it by. On one corner of the square is King John's Hunting Lodge, a picturesque timber-framed building with jettied first and second storeys. It was built in about 1500 as a merchant's house and has nothing to do with King John or with hunting. The name probably survives from the time when the building was the King's Head alehouse during the 17th and 18th centuries. When first built, the ground floor front was occupied by small shops, with living rooms behind and above. The house is now a museum of local history, well laid out and with clear explanations of how the house was constructed and restored. The museum also deals with the history of the area from prehistoric times onwards. All three floors are accessible.

Opening times: April to end Sept, daily 2–5.
Entrance charges: Free.
Parking: Car parks in Moorland Street on the south side of the town square and Meadow Street to the west.

Wheelchair access: Possible to ground floor only.
Guidebook: An interesting leaflet about the history of the building and its construction. The
    contents of the house are not mentioned.
Catering: None.
WCs: None in the house, public conveniences in the car park nearby.
Shop: Field guides and archaeological reports of regional interest on sale at the entrance.

AXBRIDGE: THE OLD MANOR HOUSE   High Street (C. Luter Esq)
Tel: Axbridge (0934) 732585
Directions: In Axbridge, 8 miles E.S.E. of Weston Super Mare

In many English towns dull fronts mask interesting interiors and the Old
Manor House is a case in point. Under the 18th century rendering is a house
of about 1500. It was of only two storeys at first with an entrance through
the centre of the front onto an open courtyard. Today the entrance is on the
eastern side by way of a Jacobean doorway, which suggests a date for the
alterations. A further storey was added in about 1690 and a massive
staircase installed. In 1752 it was topped by a belvedere which gives a good
view over the rooftops of the town and the unfortunate car park. The best
feature of the interior is the lively plasterwork of the first floor front room;
four swags hang from the central rose which is decorated with ribbons and
set in an oval frame of flowers and corn. In the 1850s this ceiling was painted
with geometric designs in shades of lavender, green and yellow, and most of
the other ceilings were treated in the same way. The guided tours conducted
by the owner of the house last about 20 minutes.

Opening times: May to end Sept, Wed 2–4, or by appointment.
Entrance charges: Donations to Cancer Relief welcomed.
Parking: Municipal car park in Morland Street, off the town square.
Wheelchair access: Possible to ground floor.
Guidebook: None.
Catering: None.
WCs: None for public use.
Shop: None.

BARFORD PARK   nr Enmore (Mr and and Mrs Michael Stancomb)
Tel: Spaxton (027 867) 269
Directions: 5 miles W.S.W. of Bridgwater; it is easiest to approach via the
    road from Bridgwater to Enmore, then right at the top of the hill to
    Spaxton; Barford lies in the park where the road branches left; it is not
    signposted

Barford is a small red brick mansion of early Georgian date linked by
curving arcades to pedimented pavilions with little bell turrets. Its charm
comes from its miniature scale, which contrasts nicely with the giant cedar
next to the house. The entrance front looks all of the 1720s or '30s, but once

abreast of the house it can be seen that the front hides an earlier building with rubble walls. The rough sandstone garden front may be as early as the 16th century, though the two-storey bow is an 18th century addition. It is not known who designed the house, but the elegant front may be the work of a local man from Bridgwater, and was probably added to mark the marriage of the heiress of the estate to Andrew Guy. The original family continued to live here until 1957 when the house was purchased in poor condition by the present owners. It has been well restored and the interior is simply but tastefully furnished. Six rooms are shown on the conducted tour, which lasts about half an hour. A walled garden has been laid out to the north and the Victorian pleasure ground with its archery glade and water garden has been reclaimed from the wild.

Opening times: May to Sept, Wed, Thurs and Bank Holiday weekends 2–6, or by appointment.
Entrance charges: Voluntary contributions to charity welcomed. (HHA)
Parking: Beside the house.
Wheelchair access: Possible to all the rooms, entrance by way of the front door.
Guidebook: None.
Catering: None.
WCs: On demand, but not for wheelchairs.
Shop: None.

BARRINGTON COURT nr Ilminster (The National Trust)
Tel: Ilminster (046 05) 2242
Directions: 3 miles N.E. of Ilminster, signposted off the B3168 at the E. end of Barrington village

This fine big mansion dates from the 16th century and the exterior appears hardly altered. It is E-shaped and built of Ham Hill stone. The walls are bare, apart from the mullion and transom windows, but above the gables of the roof the skyline erupts in spiral chimney pots and finials. The date of the house is uncertain, but it is now thought to have been built by William Clifton, a Norfolk merchant who bought the estate in 1552. By the end of the last century Barrington had become derelict. It was given to the National Trust in 1907 and leased in 1920 by Col. A. Lyle, who had built up a good collection of panelling and other woodwork and was looking for a house to put it in. He carefully restored the building and kept the original layout of the rooms, but virtually all the woodwork comes from the Colonel's collection. The roof of the staircase is from Hereford, the screen in the small dining room from King's Lynn. The only original features in the house are two overmantels. The house is still leased by the Lyle family and the rooms are furnished, but they have a slightly empty feel. The guided tour covers the whole ground floor and a long gallery in the roof. Besides restoring the house Colonel Lyle employed the famous designer Gertrude Jekyll to advise on the garden, which lies to the west of the house, next to a red brick stable block of the 1670s. Like many of her other gardens it consists of a series of formal enclosures with planting of subtle colour and varied textures. Although not exactly to her design, it is very much in her style.

Opening times: Garden, 11 April to 29 Sept, Sun, Mon, Tues, Wed 2–5.30; house 14 April to 29 Sept, Wed 2–5.30.
Entrance charges: Garden £1.00. House 50p.
Parking: Free parking in front of the house.
Wheelchair access: Possible to garden, discouraged from the house.
Guidebook: A recent guide with brief history of house and family and a plan. The furniture is not described, nor are the various items of woodwork introduced by Col. Lyle.
Catering: None, and no picnics.
WCs: None.
Shop: None.

BRYMPTON D'EVERCY nr Yeovil (Charles Clive-Ponsonby-Fane Esq J.P.)
Tel: West Coker (093 586) 2528
Directions: 2 miles W. of Yeovil, signposted off the A30 and A3088

The first sight of Brympton is a Tudor house of beautiful golden Ham Hill stone, flanked on one side by a mediaeval church and dower house and on the other by the Queen Anne stables, all of the same material. The church and dower house date from about 1450. The first floor hall and solar of the dower house is now used for a museum of West Country life, where cider making and other crafts are explained. The main house was built by the Sydenham family and the left hand side of the front dates from about 1520. The plainer central section is 50 years younger while the porch was made up out of old stonework in 1722. The garden front is on a much grander scale. It was built in the 1670s for Sir John Posthumous Sydenham and is one of the most famous examples of the slightly clumsy classical style of that time. The family were already in financial straits and the building of this range finally bankrupted them. In the 1730s the house was bought by Francis Fane, whose descendants still live here. Seven main ground floor rooms are open to visitors, including the hall, the enormous staircase and the series of rooms behind the garden front which make up the Great Apartment. Most of these rooms have 18th century panelling and contain attractive furniture and paintings. There is a good collection of English water colours and also a display of family wedding dresses. Visitors can wander freely and there is a relaxed and informal atmosphere. The gardens are largely the creation of Lady Georgiana Fane, who nearly married the Duke of Wellington. Instead she formed the lake and the terrace and planted many of the trees in the park.

Opening times: Easter Fri to Mon, then 1 May to 30 Sept, daily except Thurs and Fri 2–6.

Brympton D'Evercy, Somerset

Entrance charges: £1.40; children under 15 70p; discounts for OAPs and National Trust members on Wednesdays; no dogs. (HHA)
Parking: Free parking on grass, near the house.
Wheelchair access: All the rooms shown in the main house are on the ground floor and access is easy.
Guidebook: A cheerful account of the families at Brympton, with some vague words about the house and nothing on the contents; there is a layout plan of the house and gardens.
Catering: Teas served in the Queen Anne stable block; it is possible to sit outside.
WCs: On the E. side of the house; not suitable for wheelchairs.
Shop: Sells a wide range from sweets to pottery; there is also wine and cider produced and bottled on the estate.

COLERIDGE'S COTTAGE   Lime Street, Nether Stowey (The National Trust)
Tel: Nether Stowey (0278) 732662
Directions: 8 miles W. of Bridgwater on the A39, at the W. end of Nether Stowey

Samuel Taylor Coleridge lived in Nether Stowey for three years from December 1796. During that time he wrote *The Rime of the Ancient Mariner*, *Kubla Khan*, and *Christabel*. The house rented by the poet and his young family was a low thatched building with four rooms, rather damp, but with a large garden. In the 19th century it was much enlarged and became an inn. Only the parlour of the old house is now on view and contains various documents relating to Coleridge's time in the village. Coleridge drew on his surroundings; his ancient mariner set out from nearby Watchet and his drugs-inspired composition of *Kubla Khan* was interrupted by knocking at this very front door.

Opening times: April to end Sept, every day except Fri and Sat 2–5; in winter by written appointment.
Entrance charges: 40p; no reductions.
Parking: In the village street.
Wheelchair access: Not practicable, steep steps and narrow spaces.
Guidebook: A leaflet describing Coleridge's time at Nether Stowey, very little about the house, not even a picture.
Catering: None.
WCs: None.
Shop: None, but some of Coleridge's works are on sale.

COMBE SYDENHAM HALL   Monksilver (Mr and Mrs W. Theed)
Tel: Stogumber (098 46) 284
Directions: 3 miles S. of Watchet and 5 miles N. of Wiveliscombe on the B3188

The house is secluded in a wooded valley. The entrance for visitors lies through the farmyard and a range of buildings including a late mediaeval gatehouse which has recently been restored. Combe Sydenham was built by various members of the Sydenham family, who lived here from the 1360s until 1693. The house was originally built round four sides of a courtyard with towers in each angle; now only two sides and a single tower remain. Most of what can be seen is Elizabethan, though there are traces of earlier work, as well as some later alterations. The porch dates from 1580 and bears the initials of George Sydenham. Visitors make their own way through part of the ground floor by way of the hall, once open to the roof but now divided, and the staircase with its late Georgian decoration. Two other rooms, the study and library, may be peered into. These are all in daily use but in the west wing are two further rooms awaiting restoration. The Court Room is floored with 15th century tiles, perhaps from Cleeve Abbey; the Restoration Chamber above has enormous Elizabethan windows. Beyond the garden is a water mill containing some old machinery, but not yet working, while the fish ponds of the old house are most suitably used for trout farming. In the buildings of the farmyard can be found a display of wood-burning stoves and the studio of a local potter.

Opening times: 2 May to 1 Oct, Tues, Wed, Thurs, Fri 1.30–5; last admission 4.30.
Entrance charges: House and fishery £1.20; children 50p.
Parking: In the farmyard, about 100 yards from the house.
Wheelchair access: No special arrangements, but would be possible.
Guidebook: A brief description of the house and its history; not much is known about the building it seems.
Catering: A pleasant small-scale tea room in the gatehouse range, with tables in a small garden outside; serves tea, cakes and pasties.
WCs: In the farmyard, adequate; not suitable for wheelchair users.
Shop: Fish from the fishery, stoves, pots.

DUNSTER CASTLE Dunster, nr Minehead (The National Trust)
Tel: Dunster (064 382) 314
Directions: 3 miles S.E. of Minehead, off the A396 in Dunster village

Dunster Castle has a romantic silhouette of turrets, towers and crenellations rising above the tree tops, all the more convincing for being largely Victorian. The setting is ideal. On one side is the pretty village with its yarn market and fine church, while the south front overlooks a miraculously uninhabited green valley of trees and fields, with the Bristol Channel sparkling in the distance. There has been a castle on the hill since Saxon times and at the Norman Conquest it was given to the Mohun family, who sold it to the Luttrells in 1376. They in turn gave it to the National Trust exactly 600 years later. Little remains of the old castle, apart from a 13th century gateway and the new gatehouse built for Sir Hugh Luttrell in 1420. Between 1589 and 1620 a new house was built in the castle bailey; the mason was William Arnold, who also built Wadham College, Oxford, and Montacute House. The new house had a symmetrical stone front but the south side, incorporating part of the old curtain wall, is irregular. In 1867 Anthony Salvin made some improvements for George Luttrell. He added large towers at front and back and made alterations inside. Visitors follow a set route through the main ground floor rooms and three on the first floor and there are guides in each room. The two halls are mainly Salvin's work but the inner hall contains a most extraordinary painting of Sir John Luttrell by Hans Eworth, dating from 1550. The Luttrell family portraits throughout the house are of a high standard. The dining room, servery and great staircase have very good plasterwork and carving of the 1680s. The carved staircase has cherubs chasing animals through the foliage of the handrail. The upstairs rooms are less elaborate but there is a charming series of leather wall-hangings showing Anthony and Cleopatra, who appears as a jolly-looking girl in 17th century costume. The library by Salvin is unexpectedly delicate, with delightful 19th century plasterwork and wallpaper. Outside, the slopes are terraced to make pleasant, if windy, gardens. On the south terrace is the famous lemon tree, well-established in 1842 and still fruiting.

Opening times: 4 April to end Sept, daily except Fri and Sat 11–5; Oct, Tues, Wed and Sun 2–4.

Entrance charges: House, gardens and park £1.70; children under 16 85p.

Parking: In the park 500 yards from the house, which must be reached by an uphill walk. Free to National Trust members, but for others a charge of £1.00 is made, refundable to house visitors.

Wheelchair access: Would be possible to ground floor rooms, but permission would be needed to drive to the front door and enter by it. Also possible to ground floor of water mill.

Guidebook: A very thorough guide with illustrations and a plan, which is very useful in this complicated building. History of house and family supplemented by descriptions of the main items of interest among the furniture.

Catering: None, but there are plenty of tea shops in the village.

WCs: Near the shop and ticket office.

Shop: A wide variety of National Trust products, books and some gourmet foods on sale in the 17th century stables.

EAST LAMBROOK MANOR nr South Petherton (Mr and Mrs F.H. Boyd-Carpenter)

Tel: South Petherton (0460) 40328

Directions: 8 miles W. of Yeovil, 2 miles N. of South Petherton on the B3165

East Lambrook Manor is known to many through the writings of Margery Fish. She and her husband bought the house and its few acres in 1938 and rescued them from years of neglect. The house is a long low building, partly brick and partly stone, once thatched but now tiled. It was probably built about 1470 and a window of this date has survived in the north east gable. In 1584 (the date carved on a bracket inside) the house was extended by the addition of a wing at the kitchen end. At the same time the hall was divided horizontally and the dining room was panelled. Guided tours of the inside begin when ten or twelve have assembled, and take about half an hour. The whole house is shown. The low-ceilinged rooms have a friendly lived-in atmosphere with plants from the garden much in evidence; the good country furniture was collected in the district. The garden is one of the most attractive in the West Country, planted in a rambling cottage style to provide interest throughout the year, with an emphasis on ground cover and on unusual cottage plants suitable for this clay soil. It was from here that Margery Fish drew the material for her well-known books on gardening. Since her death the garden has been kept up by her sister and brother-in-law.

Opening times: Gardens daily throughout the year 9–5; house March to Oct, Thurs 2–5.
Entrance charges: Garden 15p; children under 10 10p. House 15p and 10p; no dogs. (HHA)
Parking: On the grass verge by the house.
Wheelchair access: Ground floor of the house and part of the garden.
Guidebook: A chatty little guide with some information on each room in the house and also a layout plan of the garden.
Catering: None.
WCs: By the back door; not for wheelchairs.
Shop: In the old Malthouse, sells plants from the garden, books, dried flowers and seeds.

FARLEIGH HUNGERFORD CASTLE nr Trowbridge (Ancient Monument)

Tel: Trowbridge (022 14) 2582
Directions: 3 miles W. of Trowbridge, off the A366 in Farleigh Hungerford

The castle belonged to the Hungerford family from about 1370 until 1686. The 16th and 17th century Hungerfords were rich, ambitious and unscrupulous and their family history is a catalogue of unpleasant crimes. The manor house belonging to the previous owners was rebuilt and fortified by Sir Thomas Hungerford after 1370. He erected a more-or-less regular square curtain wall with a tower at each corner and a gatehouse in the middle of the weakest side. The other sides were defended by ditches or by the natural slope of the grounds. The castle is now a total ruin, with only two corner towers standing to any height. It was not slighted by Cromwell, like so many other castles, but simply fell to pieces. The outer court was added 1420–30 and much of its wall survives. The mid-14th century church of St Leonard was enclosed by the walls and became the castle chapel. It is still intact and has a very fine collection of tombs and some 15th century wall-paintings. The priest's house next to the church has been rebuilt and contains a small museum with documents and other items relating to the castle.

Opening times: Standard hours (S), see page xii.
Entrance charges: 40p; OAPs and children under 16 20p.

Parking: Free parking inside the castle.
Wheelchair access: Possible to part of the ruins.
Guidebook: A good cheap leaflet with a full history, a description and a plan.
Catering: None.
WCs: In the castle.
Shop: None.

GAULDEN MANOR nr Tolland (Mr and Mrs James Le Gendre Starkie)
Tel: Lydeard St Lawrence (098 47) 213
Directions: 9 miles N.W. of Taunton, 1 mile E. of Tolland church, difficult to find

The most notable thing about Gaulden is its marvellous plasterwork, quite unexpected in this ancient farmhouse. There is nothing in the rough stone exterior to suggest the splendour within. The best room is the hall which has a fine mantlepiece with the Turberville arms. Round the top of the wall is an allegorical frieze and the ceiling has three big roundels, the centre one having a pendant. Divided from the hall by a handsome 16th century carved screen is a little room known as the chapel with more plasterwork of the same sort. The two other rooms shown are the dining room in the old kitchen and an upstairs bedroom with a very decorative overmantel whose top has been cut off by a later ceiling. In 1565 the house was let to Bishop Turberville of Exeter, after he had been thrown out of office for refusing to take the oath of supremacy. Some of the wilder plasterwork might be of his time, but most of it looks mid-17th century. The Bishop's great nephew John Turberville bought the house in 1639 and both the hall ceiling and the upstairs fireplace are likely to have been done for him. The guided tour lasts about half an hour. The attractive garden is largely the creation of the present owners, who bought the house in 1966.

Opening times: Easter Sun and Mon; then 2 May to 5 Sept, Sun and Thurs 2–6.
Entrance charges: £1.10p; children under 13 50p. (HHA)
Parking: Free parking 200 yards from the house.
Wheelchair access: Possible to ground floor rooms, which have the best plasterwork.
Guidebook: A conscientious account of the house, which sets out the problem of dating the plasterwork, and ends with a string of ghost stories; several photos but no plan.
Catering: Tea room in the stables, open 3–6.
WCs: In the car park; not suitable for wheelchairs.
Shop: A varied selection of plants, books and home-made preserves.

HALSWAY MANOR Crowcombe (The Halsway Manor Society)
Tel: Crowcombe (098 48) 274
Directions: 10 miles N.W. of Taunton, 6 miles S.E. of Watchet on the A361

The long and picturesque main front of this house on the slopes of the Quantock hills is all in the mediaeval style of the 15th century, but everything to the left of the main porch was added in the 1870s. Both halves are built of the same russet sandstone but the genuine mediaeval work is built of rubble and the later work of smooth ashlar. The Stradling family had the house in the Middle Ages and the Carews in the 18th century. The main responsible for the 19th century additions was William Rowcliffe and he and his successors have largely remodelled the interior. The house is now owned by the Halsway Manor Society which is affiliated to the English Folk Dance Society. The house is used for residential courses and the four public rooms that are shown to visitors are sometimes in use. Visitors should report to the office and may or may not be given a guided tour. The furnishings are of little interest but the rooms themselves have some good fittings. The hall contains a handsomely carved overmantel from Shropshire and 16th century oak panelling from Cocks House, Newcastle. The panelling in the sitting room came from a house in Yorkshire. The Library has a good plaster ceiling and houses a collection of books devoted to folk music. There is a succession of concerts and folk evenings throughout the year, with ceilidhs generally on Saturday night — these functions are normally open to the public.

Opening times: Open at all reasonable times, but please ring in advance.
Entrance charges: Free, but donations gratefully accepted.
Parking: Free parking next to the house.
Wheelchair access: Possible to the main rooms.
Guidebook: Principally a history of the owners of the house, with woodcut illustrations showing the building before alterations and after.
Catering: None.
WCs: Off the hall, signposted.
Shop: Some pottery and preserves are on sale in the hall.

HESTERCOMBE HOUSE nr Taunton (Somerset County Fire Brigade)
Tel: The Communications Officer, Taunton (0823) 87222, ext. 57
Directions: 3 miles N. of Taunton, off the A361 near Cheddon Fitzpaine

By common consent Hestercombe is an ugly building. An 18th century house belonging to the amateur architect and painter Copplestone Warre Bampfylde was grossly enlarged in the 1870s by the Portman family. Their architect was Henry Hall, whose additions are in the free Renaissance style. The house is now the Headquarters of the Somerset Fire Brigade. Visitors should report to the control room on arrival. Hestercombe is famous for its gardens, which were laid out in 1906–10 by Gertrude Jekyll and Sir Edwin Lutyens. The County Council began to restore the gardens in 1973, with the help of original plans found pinned up in a potting shed, and the work is now nearly complete. Below the 19th century terrace Lutyens formed the Great Plat, a rectangular area divided into four by diagonal paths with a pergola all along one side. A round pool at one corner subtly alters the axis of the garden to the east where there is an orangery designed by Lutyens in the Wren style. The garden has a complex hydraulic system to feed the many rills and fountains and the gardeners are very happy to explain its workings.

Opening times: May to Sept, Thurs 12–5; last Sun in May, June and July 2–6.
Entrance charges: Free, but donations accepted.
Parking: Free parking in front of the house.
Wheelchair access: Part of the house and garden would be accessible with help.
Guidebook: Helpful typed information sheets; a layout plan of the garden would be a very welcome addition.
Catering: Light refreshments are served in the main hall on Sundays.
WCs: Outside the house, signposted.
Shop: None.

LYTES CARY nr Ilchester (The National Trust)
Tel: Castle Carey (0963) 50586
Directions: 2½ miles N.E. of Ilchester, 1 mile N. of the Ilchester by-pass

This attractive small stone manor house was built by various members of the Lyte family, who lived here from the 14th to the 18th century. Later additions turned the L-shaped manor house into a courtyard house, but only the older buildings are open to visitors. To the left of the front door is the chapel of about 1343; it was originally detached from the house and has a separate entrance. The woodwork and fittings inside mostly date from the 16th century. The hall of the house probably dates from the 1450s, but the porch and bay window were added later. They may be contemporary with the south side of the house which was added in 1533 for John Lyte. In 1907 the house was acquired by Sir Walter Jenner, who restored the old building and also collected the furniture which it contains. Although the rooms are not lived in, they are pleasantly small and intimate and visitors may wander round on their own. The hall has a fine timber roof and 17th century furniture, including two very fine Delft tulip vases by Adriansz Koax. Arched openings at the upper end lead to the staircase and to a little chamber which may be an early example of a private family dining room. The panelled great parlour has a good selection of 17th and early 18th century furniture and a mirror whose frame was worked by Sir Walter's sister in imitation of 17th century stumpwork. The first floor great chamber is furnished as a 17th century bedroom and has an early example of the typical spidery Elizabethan plaster ceiling. The Little Chamber has first-rate early Georgian bedroom furniture. The fabrics in the house were carefully chosen to evoke the 'antique' and the garden was replanted by Sir Walter with the same purpose. The topiary work of the front lawn and the formal alleys of yew and hornbeam recall the 17th century and the south border has been stocked with plants which would have been known to Henry Lyte, whose *Niewe Herball* was published in 1578.

Opening times: March to end Oct, Wed and Sat 2–6; last admission 5.30.
Entrance charges: £1.00; children under 16 50p.
Parking: Free parking near the house. N.B. Coaches cannot pass between the gate piers at the entrance to the mile-long drive.
Wheelchair access: Possible to the ground floor of house (about half of it) and to most of the garden.
Guidebook: A good guide with a plan, a history of house and owners, and a room-by-room guide. There is a supplementary free leaflet giving more details about the contents of each room.
Catering: None.
WCs: None.
Shop: None.

MIDELNEY MANOR Drayton, nr Langport (Major R.E.F. Cely-Trevilian)

Tel: Langport (0458) 251229
Directions: 10 miles E. of Taunton, signposted off the A378 at Curry Rivel

It is said that the Abbot of Muchelney had his summer retreat at Midelney, where he had a deer park and a pack of hounds. After the dissolution of the monasteries it was occupied by the Trevilian family, who are still in residence. The house dates from the 1540s, when it was rebuilt after a fire. It is a plain stone house with mullioned windows and originally shaped like an H, but two of the wings have been demolished. What makes Midelney unusual is that it was really two houses, built by the brothers Richard and Thomas Trevilian for their separate occupation with separate front doors. The eastern half of the house was remodelled in the 18th century and the rooms have panelling of this period. Among the contents is an intriguing overmantel painting and a beautiful embroidered Queen Anne bedspread. The guided tours last about half an hour, and the house has a very pleasant lived-in atmosphere. To the west of the house is a 17th century barn and beside it is a falcon mews of the same date. Very few examples of this type of building survive, and the Midelney mews is an interesting survival although it is not open to visitors.

Opening times: Bank Holiday Mon, Easter to Oct; also June to mid-Sept, Wed 2–5.30.
Entrance charges: (1981) 75p; children under 16 30p; no dogs.
Parking: Free parking beside the house.
Wheelchair access: Possible to the ground floor rooms and the garden.
Guidebook: None.
Catering: None.
WCs: Yes.
Shop: None.

MONTACUTE HOUSE   Montacute, nr Yeovil (The National Trust)
Tel: Martock (093 582) 3239
Directions: 4 miles W. of Yeovil on the A3088, 3 miles S. of the A303

Elizabethan architecture achieved one of its masterpieces in this beautiful building, erected for Sir Edward Phelips, a West Country lawyer, in 1598. The H-plan with staircases in the angles of the west side, the great height of the three storeys and the vast quantity of windows are hallmarks of the Elizabethan style. The richness contributed by the exquisite forecourt pavilions and balustrades, the shaped gables and the sculptured figures in niches is balanced by the firm clean wall surfaces of Ham Hill stone, now mellowed gold. The architect and builder was probably William Arnold, who also built Wadham College, Oxford, and part of Dunster Castle. In 1786 the main entrance was moved from the east to the west side and the space between the wings filled by a two storey addition ornamented with stonework brought from Clifton Maybank in Dorset, a house of the 1540s. The interior retains much of its original plasterwork and there is a fine carved screen in the great hall, but most of the panelling dates from Lord Curzon's tenancy (1915–25). All the original furniture was dispersed by the time the house was presented to the Trust in 1931, but the state rooms of the ground and first floor have been refurnished with the help of gifts, like the magnificent bequest of tapestries and furniture belonging to Sir Malcolm Stewart. Many of these tapestries are hung on the stairs. The immense long gallery which fills the top floor now contains a large collection of Elizabethan portraits on loan from the National Portrait Gallery. Visitors make their own way round the house. Although the shape of the garden remains much as it has been since the house was built, most of the existing planting dates from the middle of the 19th century.

Opening times: April to end Oct, daily except Tues 12.30–6; last admission 5.30.
Entrance charges: £1.70; children under 16 85p; dogs must be kept in car park.
Parking: Free car park on grass near the house.
Wheelchair access: Not practicable to house because of many internal steps, part of the garden is accessible, and one could see the outside of the house.
Guidebook: A large selection which supplements the free leaflet which is given to each visitor. *Montacute House* is the standard guide with plans, black and white illustrations, history of the house and the Phelips family and room-by-room guide. Abbreviated information of the same kind in the *Souvenir Guide*, but with colour plates and no plan. *The National Portrait Gallery at Montacute* deals exclusively with the paintings on loan from the Gallery, which are not described in the other guides. There is also a *Guide to the Coats of Arms* and a reprint from the *Victoria County History* on the history of the parish.
Catering: Tea room off the courtyard to the south of the house with waitress service; open 3–5.30 and often crowded.
WCs: Beside the shop in the car park; facilities for the disabled.
Shop: Sells a wide range of National Trust gifts and publications.

NUNNEY CASTLE   Nunney, nr Frome (Ancient Monument)
Directions: In Nunney, 3 miles S.W. of Frome on the A361

The castle lies among the houses of the village at the bottom of a valley, a bad site for a castle but a very attractive one. It is really a tall fortified house, with a pair of fat round towers at either end. The building is surrounded by a moat, and the moat was in turn enclosed by a wall on three sides. Nunney was built in 1373 by Sir John de la Mare, who had made his fortune from the wars in France. The castle must have looked very French when the main block still had its steep pitched roof and the four towers their conical caps. It was beseiged in the Civil War and the north side was weakened by gunfire. Shortly afterwards all the floors were removed. The building was never re-occupied and on Christmas Day 1910 the north wall collapsed. Even so, the ruin is very impressive since the other three sides and the towers stand to full height. The rooms were arranged on four floors with the kitchens on the ground floor, the servants' quarters on the first, the great hall on the second, and two more large rooms on the third.

Opening times: Open at all reasonable times.
Entrance charges: Free, but in high season a charge may be made.
Parking: In the village street, free.
Wheelchair access: No problems.
Guidebook: A good official guide with a plan of the castle.
Catering: None.
WCs: None.
Shop: None.

OAKHILL MANOR   Oakhill, nr Bath (W.W. Harper Esq)
Tel: Oakhill (0749) 840210
Directions: 12 miles S.S.W. of Bath, 4 miles N. of Shepton Mallet, signed off the A37

Oakhill is a Victorian house in the Elizabethan Revival style. It was built about 1852 to the designs of an unknown architect for the Spencer family, local brewers who were the main employers in Oakhill, where their brewery still stands. The house is of rubble masonry with squared stone dressings. Some of the windows and other stonework are said to have come from a demolished 16th century house, but it is difficult to identify them. The rooms inside have Victorian panelling and stained glass, but the interest of the house lies in its contents — a very large collection of models of ships, locomotives and fire engines, with related objects. They are mostly the work of professional model makers and are of excellent workmanship. The house attracts many children and visitors are carried from the car park to the house by a miniature railway. The fare is included in the entrance charge. The garden is mainly trees and lawn, with a pond and a 'railway walk'.

Opening times: 8 April to 1 Nov, daily 12–6.

Entrance charges: (1981) £1.35; OAPs 90p; children 6–16 90p; children 2–6 50p; under 2 free.
Parking: Large free car park, access to house by miniature railway.
Wheelchair access: To part of the house, best to ring in advance to arrange access.
Guidebook: A leaflet with a brief description of the contents of each room.
Catering: Teas and light lunches are available.
WCs: Next to the cafeteria.
Shop: There is a gift shop.

POUNDISFORD PARK Poundisford, nr Taunton (Ralph Vivian-Neal Esq)

Tel: Blagdon Hill (082 342) 244
Directions: 3½ miles S. of Taunton on the Trull-Pitminster road, ½ mile W. of the B3170. N.B. Large coaches cannot cross drive bridge

The house at Poundisford is a compact gabled building on an H-plan, with roughcast walls and stone windows and buttresses stained red by lichen. It dates from about 1546, that is to say from King Henry VIII's time. The entrance door leads into a screens passage running across the house and giving access to the great hall, a fine large room with an elaborate 16th century plaster ceiling, one of several in the house. The upper floor is reached by way of a spiral stair and the gallery over the screen; here are a bedroom and a room in which some 18th and 19th century costumes are displayed. There is also a tiny room, hardly more than a cupboard, fitted out for home medicine-making. The main staircase inserted this century leads downstairs again to a small parlour with 18th century decoration and a stately dining room which was added to the house in 1737. Poundisford is in daily occupation and the rooms are furnished with a pleasing mixture of principally English and Dutch pieces and some lively family portraits. After the guided tour of the house visitors are free to wander in the large, simply-planted garden which includes an unusual 17th century brick summer-house.

Opening times: May to Sept, Sun and Thurs, also Easter, May, Spring and Summer Bank Holidays 2–6.
Entrance charges: 85p; children 50p.
Parking: Car park near the house.
Wheelchair access: Possible to the great hall, parlour, dining room, and garden. Also the restaurant.
Guidebook: None at present. Notes available.
Catering: The Tudor kitchen in the outbuildings has been converted into The Well-House Restaurant, a separate concern from the house (Tel: Blagdon Hill 566); this is to the advantage of house visitors who may enjoy excellent light lunches or cream teas inside or in the garden outside. Also traditional Sunday lunches.
WCs: In the restaurant and in the courtyard. Facilities for wheelchair users.
Shop: None.

TINTINHULL HOUSE Tintinhull, nr Yeovil (The National Trust)
Tel: Martock (093 582) 2509
Directions: 5 miles N.W. of Yeovil, ½ mile S. of the A303, on the edge of
   Tintinhull

The small house at Tintinhull is a pleasing adjunct to the two-acre garden,
which is well-known to horticulturalists. The back parts of the house date
from about 1600 and there is a gabled addition dated 1630, with the initial
N, for the Napper family. In about 1720 Andrew Napper added a new
classical front to the west side of the house which combines elegant
proportions and a slim pediment with cross-windows which were old-
fashioned by the 18th century. This front now faces the garden. Inside the
house four ground floor rooms and two staircases are shown. They contain
interesting furniture, china and paintings belonging to the present tenants
which visitors may examine at their leisure. In 1898 Tintinhull was acquired
by Dr Price, a clergyman and distinguished botanist, who laid out the three
rectangular gardens on the west side of the house. The land is flat, but there
are subtle changes of level between the enclosures. In 1933 the property was
purchased by Captain and Mrs Reiss, who transformed the tennis court on
the north side into another formal garden with a rectangular pool and a
loggia. The borders of the garden are thoughtfully planted and a fine cedar
and two holm oaks give distinction.

Opening times: April to end Sept, Wed, Thurs, Sat and Bank Holiday Mon 2 6.
Entrance charges: £1.00; children under 5 free; otherwise no reduction.
Parking: Free parking next to the house.
Wheelchair access: Possible to the garden.
Guidebook: One third on the house, two thirds on the garden; the contents of the rooms are
   not described. A separate inventory of the garden plants gives the latin names only.
Catering: None.
WCs: In the garden, adequate.
Shop: None.

WELLS: THE BISHOP'S PALACE (The Bishop of Bath and Wells)
Tel: Wells (0749) 78691
Directions: In the centre of Wells

Wells has been described as the most memorable Bishop's Palace in the
country, and it is also the best fortified. The buildings are surrounded by a
battlemented wall and a wide moat and are reached through a 14th century
gatehouse. At the centre of the enclosure lie the palace buildings,
surrounded by lawns and spreading trees. Directly opposite the gatehouse is
the great hall built in 1280 by Bishop Burnell. It is now a ruin, but enough
is still standing to give an idea of the large scale and splendour of the
building. Next to the hall is Bishop Burnell's tall chapel with its soaring
interior of great beauty. The tall gabled range which forms the centre of the
palace contains the old palace begun by Bishop Jocelin in about 1230, but its

upper parts and much of the interior are the work of the architect Benjamin Ferrey, who restored the palace for Bishop Bagot in 1846. The ground floor is a vaulted undercroft, now converted to a refectory. The fine staircase to the first floor was inserted in the early 17th century and several of the rooms were thrown together to make a long gallery. Both in the gallery and in the other rooms shown the Victorian plaster decoration and fittings provided by Ferrey are unmistakeable. The rooms are used for conferences and other functions and are hung with portraits of former bishops. There are guides in each room. The present Bishop of Bath and Wells lives in the range of 16th century buildings at right angles to the original palace. This range is not open.

Opening times: Easter, to end Oct, Thurs and Sun and Bank Holiday Mon, also daily in Aug 2–6; last admission 5.30.

Entrance charges: Palace, chapel and grounds 75p; children under 14 25p; OAPs 50p.

Parking: No car park, but it is possible to park in nearby streets.

Wheelchair access: Most of the garden is accessible, also the chapel, but the main rooms in the palace are on the first floor and not accessible.

Guidebook: A leaflet with a useful bird's eye reconstruction of the buildings and anecdotes about various bishops.

Catering: Tea in the refectory.

WCs: By the refectory.

Shop: None.

Staffordshire

ALTON TOWERS   Alton, nr Cheadle

Tel: Oakamoor (0538) 702449

Directions: 5 miles N. of Uttoxeter, 3 miles E. of Cheadle on the B5032m well-signed

The estate at Alton has become a large-scale leisure park (over a million visitors last year), but at its centre is the shell of the vast Gothic house of the Talbots. Most unusually, the gardens were planned before the house. The estate came to the Talbot family by marriage in the 14th century, but it was not until 1812 that Charles Talbot, 15th Earl of Shrewsbury began to lay out an ornamental garden on the rocky hillsides of the Churnet valley. In 1814 he moved into Alveton Lodge, described as a 'comfortable homestead'. Between this time and the death of the 16th Earl in 1852 the homestead was enlarged by a succession of architects and changed its name first to Alton Abbey, then to Alton Towers. The last architect on the scene was Augustus Pugin who supervised the interior decoration between 1837 and 1840 in the grandest Gothic manner. Not much of it remains. Army occupation in the last war and death watch beetle have gutted the interior, which is now like some vast air raid shelter with concrete floors, and rough wooden stairs leading to the different levels and the viewing platforms. Only the painted ceiling and stained glass of the Great Hall give some idea of the richness of Pugin's work. The garden has survived more or less intact. Besides the ornamental trees and the large quantities of rhododendrons there is a vast number of garden buildings all in different styles, ranging from the elaborate conservatory with its seven glass domes to the lovely pagoda fountain in the lake. The garden buildings have to compete with the funfair in the stables, the sea lions, the planetarium and the rest, but the outer edges of the large park are relatively peaceful.

Opening times. 20 March to 1 Nov 9.30 6.
Entrance charges: £3, all inclusive.
Parking: Free parking about 10 mins walks from the ruins of the house.
Wheelchair access: Not to the ruins, but much of the garden is accessible.
Guidebook: A rattling good history of the Talbot family, but little on the house and the garden buildings; diagram of the grounds but no plan of the ruins.
Catering: Two fast food restaurants (The Talbot and the Springfield) and the waitress service Swioo Cottugv.
WCs: Situated in various parts of the grounds and clearly signed; none for wheelchairs.
Shop: The model railway exhibition in the chapel crypt, the camera obscura, motor boats, rowing boats, pony rides, Dinosaur Land, the Aquarium, Planetarium, etc. etc., are covered by the entrance charge.

CHILLINGTON HALL nr Wolverhampton (P.R. de L. Giffard)
Tel: Brewood (0902) 850236
Directions: 8 miles N.W. of Wolverhampton, 4 miles S.W. of the A5 at Gailey, badly signed

Chillington has passed in the direct male line of the Giffard family since the late 12th century. Its enormous landscaped park forms a *cordon sanitaire* between the house and the outskirts of Wolverhampton, now alas to be breached by the M54. The house is effectively an 18th century building, though its layout is dictated by the 16th century courtyard house which formerly stood here. The south side was rebuilt for Peter Giffard in 1724, and the architect of this typically early Georgian red brick range was probably Francis Smith of Warwick. The main front dates from 1786 and is part of a major rebuilding carried out by John Soane for Thomas Giffard. In the centre of his front is a giant pedimented portico on massive drum-columns and the end bays have an extra storey to hide the awkward junction with the taller south range. Visitors are conducted round the house, sometimes by one of the family. Besides the entrance hall there are three tall rooms on the main front, elegantly furnished but rather forbidding. In the dining room is an excellent portrait of Thomas Giffard painted by Pompeo Batoni in 1784. Behind the main front is the saloon, a large rectangular room which Soane formed by putting a domed roof over what had been the hall of the Tudor house. It is much more typical of his usual geometric style than anything else at Chillington. The strange heraldic fireplace probably dates from the 1830s. A small dining room in the 1724 range is shown and a grand staircase of this date, with tread ends carved with the panther crest of the Giffards and plaster decoration in the Italian Baroque manner, leads to an elegant first floor corridor contrived by Soane. The State Bedroom contains a delightful four poster bed, made for a marriage in 1788. Its framework is painted with flowers to match the original chintz hangings and the domed canopy is decorated in the same way. Curtains and chair covers are also made of 18th century chintz. The park at Chillington was landscaped by 'Capability' Brown in the 1770s, but he kept the avenue which runs from the main front for over two miles. It is one of Brown's best parks, with an enormous lake, a winding canal, ornamental bridges and garden buildings.

Opening times: 6 May to 9 Sept, Thurs; also Sun in Aug, Easter Sun and Sun prior to Spring and Summer Bank Holidays 2.30–5.30.
Entrance charges: House and grounds £1.00; grounds only 50p; children half price. (HHA)
Parking: In front of the house, free.
Wheelchair access: There is a broad flight of shallow steps to the main entrance; the main ground floor rooms are level.
Guidebook: A well-written and well-illustrated guide which would be improved by a plan of the house and a map of the grounds.
Catering: None.
WCs: None.
Shop: None.

HANCH HALL   Lichfield (Mr and Mrs D. Milton-Haynes)
Tel: Armitage (0543) 490308
Directions: 4 miles N.W. of Lichfield on the B5014, signposted

The Milton-Haynes family purchased Hanch Hall in 1975; 'from "semi" to stately home in four moves' as one of the family tells visitors in the introduction before the guided tour. The early history of the house is obscure; some 16th century timbers can be seen in one of the rooms. Facing the garden is a splendid early 18th century range, built of red brick, seven windows with a pediment over the centre. The remainder of the exterior seems to date from the 1830s or 1840s. The entrance front has a *porte-cochère* decorated with plaster strapwork and to the east is a 19th century ballroom and an arbor overgrown with wisteria. The downstairs rooms are mostly panelled and there is a sumptuous oak staircase of the 1840s with carved strapwork decoration and heraldic glass in the windows. The furnishings include some Boulle and marquetry-work, but attribution of much of the downstairs furniture to the 18th century seems optimistic! There is an amusing 1920s stool in the ballroom made of four stuffed leopard feet, complete with claws. The upstairs rooms are laid out according to different periods, with collections of needlework, dolls, teapots and christening robes. The public have access to six acres of grounds with varied wildfowl.

Opening times: 11 April to 5 Oct, Sun and Bank Holiday Mon and Tues 2.30–6.
Entrance charges: £1.30; children under 14 75p; no dogs or unaccompanied children.
Parking: Free parking in field next to house.
Wheelchair access: Possible to the ground floor.
Guidebook: In preparation.
Catering: In the stable block; self-service, home-made teas, a bit expensive but very good.
WCs: At the back of the stable block; not for wheelchairs.
Shop: Handicrafts and bric-a-brac in the tack room of the Stable Block.

IZAAK WALTON COTTAGE Shallowfield, nr Gt Bridgeford
   (Staffordshire County Council)
Tel: Stafford (0785) 760278
Directions: 5 miles N.W. of Stafford, off the A5013 between Gt Bridgeford and Yarnfield

This over-restored timber-framed and whitewashed cottage dates from about 1600. It was part of the Halfhead Farm estate given to the town of Stafford for charitable purposes by Izaak Walton, who died in 1683. Walton is best known as the author of *The Compleat Angler*, but he was also a distinguished biographer. He never lived in the cottage himself and his favourite fishing water was the river Dove, some distance further east, but it is sad that the river near the cottage should now be cut off from it by the main railway line. Only two rooms in the cottage are open to the public. They contain a mixture of stuffed fish, old furniture, fishing tackle and notes on Walton's life and works. The cottage was opened as a museum in 1924. It was damaged by fire in 1939 when the original thatched roof was replaced by tiles.

Opening times: All year, Thurs to Sun and Bank Holidays 10–1, 2–5 (under review)
Entrance charges: 15p; children under 16 10p.
Parking: Free parking.
Wheelchair access: Possible to both rooms.
Guidebook: An information sheet about Walton, with a picture of the cottage still thatched.
Catering: None.
WCs: In a small hut in the garden; not for wheelchairs.
Shop: Some postcards and gifts are sold in the cottage.

LICHFIELD: DR JOHNSON'S BIRTHPLACE Breadmarket Street
   (Lichfield Council)
Tel: Lichfield (05432) 24972
Directions: In the centre of Lichfield, signposted

18th century Lichfield produced a number of notable men, among them Dr Johnson, Erasmus Darwin and David Garrick. The Doctor's birthplace at the corner of the market square is now a museum devoted to his memory.

The house dates from 1707 or 1708 and was built by Johnson's father, a bookseller who used part of the ground floor as his shop. The two upper floors are jettied out and supported on Tuscan columns, a curious hangover from an earlier way of building. Visitors may wander through the whole house up to the attics. The rooms contain various mementoes of Johnson and his friends, the Johnson Society has its headquarters here and there is a Johnson Library which may be consulted on application. Although the Doctor spent most of his first 28 years in the house, it needs fairly strong imagination to bring the place to life. The adjoining house is now occupied by the tourist office.

Opening times: All year, weekdays, Oct to April 10–4, May to Sept 2–5 and Sun 2.30–5; closed Christmas holiday, New Year's Day, Good Friday and Spring Bank Holiday.
Entrance charges: 35p; children under 16 15p; under 5 free.
Parking: No car park, there are pay car parks in Gresley Row or Bird Street nearby.
Wheelchair access: Not practicable.
Guidebook: A brief guide with a description of each room's contents.
Catering: None on the premises.
WCs: None.
Shop: Various books about Johnson.

SHUGBOROUGH Milford, nr Stafford (The National Trust and Staffordshire County Council)
    Tel: Little Haywood (0889) 881388
Directions: 5½ miles S.E. of Stafford, signed off the A513 at Milford

Shugborough is famous for its 18th century park and fine collection of garden buildings. The core of the house is a plain building with a seven bay front, erected in 1693 for William Anson. His grandson Thomas added the bow-fronted pavilions on either side. These enlargements were financed by his brother Admiral George Anson, who had made his fortune by capturing the Spanish treasure galleon. After the Admiral's death in 1762 Thomas inherited this fortune and made further improvements to house and park. The house was again enlarged in the 1790s by Samuel Wyatt for the First Lord Anson. Wyatt added the giant colonnade across the main front, formed the great saloon which projects from the garden front and cased the whole house in slate painted to look like stone. The covering was removed in the 1920s but the columns of the portico are still of wood sheathed in slate. The interior decoration is largely the work of Wyatt's plasterer Joseph Rose although the drawing room and dining room on either side of the hall have kept their 1740s decoration, with plasterwork by Vassali. The entire contents of the house were sold in 1842 but the Second Lord Lichfield who succeeded in 1854, gathered an excellent collection of French furniture which is supplemented by family portraits and sporting paintings. There are also many mementoes of Admiral Anson and the Verandah Room is devoted

Shugborough, Staffordshire

to his exploits. Visitors make their own way through the house and should then explore the park and its buildings. A few of these (the Chinese Pavilion, the Shepherds Monument and perhaps the Monument to a Cat) are of the Admiral's time, but more important are those erected by Thomas Anson after his brother's death. The Tower of the Winds, the Doric Temple, the Triumphal Arch and the Lantern of Demosthenes are all by the connoisseur James 'Athenian' Stuart and are among the very first buildings in England in the Greek Revival style. The stables next to the house contain a large museum of Staffordshire Life, which is popular with school parties.

Opening times: 20 March to 24 Oct, Tues to Fri and Bank Holiday Mon (closed Good Friday)10.30–5.30, Sat and Sun 2–5.30. Shugborough Park Farm, Sat and Sun 2–5.30.
Entrance charges: (1981) Entrance to grounds and museum 60p; children under 16 30p. Entrance to house 60p; children 30p. Entrance to farm 25p; children 20p.
Parking: Free parking near the stable block.
Wheelchair access: Disabled visitors may be driven to the front door; there are seven steps to the main entrance but ramps inside; all the main rooms shown are on one floor. The garden and grounds are fairly easily accessible.
Guidebook: A very good guide with a plan of both house and grounds, a history of the house, of the owners, and a room-by-room guide with a detailed list of pictures.
Catering: There is a cafeteria open 12–5.30 (Sat and Sun 2–5.30) snacks and teas.
WCs: In the stableyard; facilities for the disabled.
Shop: The usual National Trust range of souvenirs; the museum sells the wide range of excellent publications by the Staffordshire County Museum.

TAMWORTH CASTLE   Tamworth (Borough of Tamworth)
Tel: Tamworth (0827) 3563
Directions: In the town of Tamworth, 15 miles N.E. of Birmingham

Until recently it was thought that Tamworth castle stood on the site of the palace of Ethelfleda, daughter of King Alfred and Governor of the Kingdom of Mercia in the 9th century. Recent excavations have shown that her palace was elsewhere and that the tall castle mound is Norman work of the 11th century. On top of the mound is a shell keep, and a tower with walls 11 feet thick and 25 feet high. The walls themselves date from the 12th century but the space inside has been gradually filled up by buildings of different periods. The castle managed to escape destruction in the Civil War and has been in more or less continuous occupation since it was built. It was bought by the Borough in 1897 and some of the rooms are now used as a museum of local history. On one side of the small inner courtyard is the great hall, which is largely Jacobean and dates from the time when the castle was owned by the Ferrers family. The first floor has several rooms with fine panelling and carved chimneypieces of the Ferrers' time and furniture of the 16th and 17th centuries. On the floor above are two bedrooms and a long gallery which are used for displays of custome and local history items. There is an excellent collection of Anglo-Saxon coins, many from the Tamworth mint. Visitors make their own way round. The outer parts of the original castle have become a municipal garden.

Opening times: March to Oct, weekdays 10–5.00, Sun 2–5.00; Nov to Feb, weekdays except Fri 10–4.30, Sun 2–4.30; closed Christmas Day but open all Bank Holidays.
Entrance charges: 20p; local residents and OAPs 10p; children under 15 5p (free if accompanied by an adult). Subject to revision.
Parking: Car park at the foot of the castle.
Wheelchair access: Not practicable.
Guidebook: A cheap production, but with a good text and a plan of each floor of the keep.
Catering: None.
WCs: Off the great hall inside the castle.
Shop: Slides, postcards, books, etc.

TUTBURY CASTLE Tutbury (The Duchy of Lancaster)
Tel: Burton on Trent (0283) 812129
Directions: 3 miles N.W. of Burton on Trent on the A50

The ruined walls of the castle surround a grassy D-shaped enclosure on a naturally fortified site with views over the Dove valley to the Derbyshire hills. The castle was owned by the Ferrers family but came to the Earls (later Dukes) of Lancaster in 1265. In later years when the buildings were already in decay Mary Queen of Scots was lodged here several times; she found Tutbury dark, depressing and smelly. The castle was 'slighted' in the Civil War and little remains above ground. The mediaeval keep has gone and its place is occupied by a 'folly' tower of the 1760s. The gatehouse and two 15th century towers of the inner bailey survive in part, and also one wall of the King's Lodgings built in 1631–5 on the site of the old great hall. But the only complete building left in the castle enclosure is a small 18th century house, built of stone poached from the King's Lodgings and from elsewhere; the house is not open to visitors. Jacob sheep graze in the dry moat and the castle is pleasantly peaceful.

Opening times: April to Sept daily 10–6, Oct to March daily 10–4, closed Christmas and Boxing Day.
Entrance charges: 30p; OAPs and children under 14 15p.
Parking: Free parking beside the castle.
Wheelchair access: Most of the ruins are accessible, also the restaurant.
Guidebook: A good historical account with helpful illustrations and plans.
Catering: Teas and light lunches and even mediaeval banquets in the Old Stables outside the castle.
WCs: Beside the restaurant.
Shop: None.

WESTON PARK (The Earl of Bradford)
Tel: Weston-under-Lizard (095 276) 207 or 385
Directions: 4 miles E. of Shifnal, 12 miles N.W. of Wolverhampton; the
main entrance is from the A5

House, church, stables and the impressive buildings of the home farm all
stand together on the edge of the enormous park. The large red brick house
was built in 1671 for Sir Thomas and Lady Wilbraham and was probably
designed by Lady Wilbraham herself. She also designed the stables (in
1688) and perhaps the church (in 1701). Early in the 18th century the estate
came to the Bridgeman family, later Earls of Bradford, who made many
alterations and improvements to both house and park. One of these was the
moving of the main entrance to the east side of the house in 1865. Most of the
rooms inside now have 18th century chimneypieces and plasterwork but
there has also been much re-organisation and re-decoration in recent years.
The dark-grained library and the tapestry room with its walls lined with
rose-coloured Gobelins tapestries are unchanged, but the great dining room
ceiling was finished only in 1968. The furnishings are of a high standard,
especially the paintings. Besides the very fine Van Dyck portraits in the
dining room there is a Stubbs and Jacopo Bassano's important 'Way to
Golgotha' which has a special place in the marble hall. A praiseworthy effort
has been made to display the paintings properly. Visitors can take as long as
they like in each room and there are guides on hand. Most of the main
ground floor rooms are shown and several smaller first floor rooms. The
outbuildings, conservatory and kitchen gardens are open to visitors and the
large park has several attractive garden buildings, especially the Temple of
Diana. The woodland behind the temple hides an extensive adventure
playground.

Opening times: April, May and Sept, Sat and Sun; June, July, Aug, daily except Mon and Fri,
  1–5.30 (last ticket issued at 5).
Entrance charges: £1.70; OAPs and children £1.20. (HHA)
Parking: Free parking on grass about 100 yards from the house.
Wheelchair access: All the rooms shown in the house are easily accessible to wheelchairs.
  There is a lift giving access to the first floor.
Guidebook: An adequate guidebook with many illustrations and a room-by-room guide; a
  plan of the house would be useful.
Catering: Self-service restaurant and tea room in the stable block; food unremarkable and
  setting rather plastic, but it is possible to sit on the grass outside.
WCs: In the outbuildings, rather small but adequate; there are special facilities for wheelchair
  users in the same place.
Shop: Souvenir shop in the outbuildings; there is also a large garden shop selling home grown
  plants.
Extras: The admission charge also covers the various nature trails and the adventure
  playground, Aquarium, the British Wildlife Collection and the Museum of Country
  Bygones. There is an extra charge for the Weston Park miniature railway.

Suffolk

BURY ST EDMUNDS: ANGEL CORNER Angel Hill (The National
Trust and the Borough of St Edmundsbury)
Tel: Bury St Edmunds (0284) 63233 Ext 227
Directions: In the centre of Bury St Edmunds, 100 yards from the Abbey
gate

The rainwater pipes are dated 1702, which seems about right for this
pleasant little house, two storeys high, and four windows wide. In this case
the contents are of more interest than the building because the house
contains a very large and very good collection of clocks (the Gershom-
Parkington Collection). There are clocks of many dates and types, all of
them on the ground floor.

Opening times: All year, Mon to Sat 10–1, 2–5 (Nov to March 2–4); closed Good Friday,
Easter Sat, May Day, 25–26 Dec and 1 Jan.
Entrance charges: Free, but donations expected; no dogs; no photography.
Parking: In the square outside the house; a charge is made.
Wheelchair access: Awkward steps at the front, otherwise all level.
Guidebook: A complete and well-illustrated catalogue of the collection of clocks and watches.
Catering: None.
WCs: None.
Shop: None.

EUSTON HALL nr Thetford (The Duke of Grafton)
Tel: Thetford (0842) 3281
Directions: 3 miles S. of Thetford on the E. side of the A1088

The best thing at Euston Hall is the collection of 17th century English
portraits. The house which contains them is a disappointment. The first
great house at Euston was built for Lord Arlington, a powerful politician,
between 1666 and 1670. It was built round three sides of a courtyard, with
a dome at each corner and a stable block on the north side. In 1750 the old
house and stables were altered by the architect Matthew Brettingham, who
removed the domes, doubled the width of the north wing, and faced the
whole house in red brick. Two thirds of the house was burnt down in 1902,
rebuilt, and taken down once more in 1952. All that is left is the stable block
and the north wing. Five rooms are open to the public and they contain a
first class collection of aristocratic portraits by Van Dyck, Lely, Kneller and
other 17th century painters; there is also the famous painting by Stubbs of
'Mares and Foals'. The furniture is good and the nightdress case belonging
to King Charles II is on display. The grounds were landscaped by William
Kent and later by 'Capability' Brown. In them there are some smaller
buildings of interest; the church built in 1676, like a country version of
Wren's City churches, and the Palladian Temple, designed by William

Kent (now a private house and not open).

Opening times: 3 June to 20 Sept, Thurs 2.30–5.30; last tickets sold 5.00.
Entrance charges: 80p; OAPs and children 40p; no dogs; no photography. (HHA)
Parking: Free parking in a field 100 yards from the house.
Wheelchair access: All except one room is accessible.
Guidebook: A brief but adequate guide containing a history and room-by-room description of the paintings, several black and white photos (including one of the original house) and a plan of the grounds.
Catering: In the old kitchen; extremely good and inexpensive home-made teas.
WCs: Modern facilities available in the courtyard.
Shop: Postcards on sale at the entrance.

FRAMLINGHAM CASTLE Framlingham (Ancient Monument)
Tel: Framlingham (0728) 723330
Directions: 21 miles N.E. of Ipswich on the B1116 and 1119, in Framlingham village

The great curtain wall with its 13 towers is a fine sight. The wall was built between 1190 and 1210 by Roger Bigod, Second Earl of Norfolk, on the site of an older castle. It shows the results of the military lesson learned by the Crusaders in the Holy Land – that the traditional square keep was less effective than a ring of walls with many smaller towers and a strong gatehouse. The castle is approached by a 16th century bridge over a deep ditch where there was once a drawbridge. All the domestic buildings which once stood inside the walls have gone; they were pulled down to make way for a Poorhouse which is still standing. The south wing of the Poorhouse, dated 1636, is where the curator lives; the rest of the building of 1729 is empty and the ground floor is open to the public. By mounting the steps in the westernmost tower the visitors can reach the wall-walk which runs round the whole castle.

Opening times: Standard hours (SM), see page xii.
Entrance charges: 40p; children 20p.
Parking: Free car park 50 yards from the entrance.
Wheelchair access: There are a few steps and some ramps, otherwise access to the castle (except the wall-walk) is straightforward.
Guidebook: The Official Handbook contains a full history and description with a plan, and information about what demolished building have been revealed by excavation. For many the 4p card guide, with plan, potted history and tour will be perfectly adequate.
Catering: None, though the central lawn would make a good picnic place.
WCs: In the north wing of the Poorhouse; clean but difficult for wheelchairs.
Shop: Postcards and guides only.

GAINSBOROUGH'S HOUSE 46 Gainsborough Street, Sudbury
(Gainsborough's House Society)
Tel: Sudbury (0787) 72958
Directions: In the centre of Sudbury on the Chelmsford road out of Market Hill

The painter Thomas Gainsborough was born in this house in 1727. Five years before, his father had bought two old houses in the street and united them by adding the present elegant five-bay red brick front. The old buildings still survive and the 16th and 17th century walling can be seen in several rooms. The back of the house was extended in about 1800. The rooms on view are the entrance room, parlour and one bedroom (which all contain some pleasant 18th century furnishings), as well as modern exhibition rooms formed in the later part of the house. There are only a few original paintings by Gainsborough himself, but several by his contemporaries and two studies by another Suffolk artist, John Constable. Visitors proceed at their own pace.

Opening times: All year, Tues to Sat 10–12.30, 2–5; Sun 2–5.
Entrance charges: 50p; children and OAPs 25p.
Parking: There is no car park, but there is free parking for one hour at the market end of Gainsborough Street, 20 yards from the house.
Wheelchair access: Ground floor only (most of the house); there are a few steps.
Guidebook: A good readable account of both the house itself and the painter, several illustrations.
Catering: None.
WCs: Adequate, but not suitable for wheelchairs.
Shop: Postcards, some Gainsborough reproductions and some souvenirs.

GLEMHAM HALL Little Glemham, nr Woodbridge (Lady Blanche Cobbold)
Tel: Wickham Market (0728) 746219
Directions: 17 miles N.E. of Ipswich, 3 miles N.E. of Wickham Market on the A12

Glemham has a rather plain entrance front of early 18th century red brick. Behind is an Elizabethan house whose irregular gabled roof and mullioned windows can still be seen at the back. Sir Henry Glemham built the earlier house; the additions were made by Dudley North in the 1720s. The house now belongs to the Cobbold family who purchased it in 1923. The generously proportioned rooms inside the house are all Georgian in their appearance, but for one small bedroom. The original great hall has been turned into a panelled entrance hall and the original screen replaced with a screen of grand Corinthian columns. There is a good 1720s staircase, and most of the ground floor rooms have panelling of the same date. Visitors may enter or peer into most of the rooms on the ground and first floors, following a prescribed route through the building. The attractive grounds include a modern rose garden and some stone vases from the Wembley Exhibition on the back lawn.

Opening times: Easter Mon to 29 Sept, Wed and Sun and Bank Holidays 2–5.30.
Entrance charges: House and garden 80p. Garden only 30p. OAPs and children half price. No dogs and no photography. (HHA)
Parking: Free, in a field 200 yards from the house.

Wheelchair access: Possible to garden but not to the house.
Guidebook: A brief history of house and family with a room-by-room guide; several colour illustrations but no plan. There is very little about the original house and more hard information would be welcome, particularly the dates of the furniture.
Catering: In the cellar, tea and good home-made cakes.
WCs: In the house; gents on ground floor at end of tour, ladies on ground or second floors; none are suitable for wheelchairs.
Shop: In the hall; leaflets, postcards and home-produced fruit and vegetables.

HAUGHLEY PARK   nr Wetherden (Mr A.J. Williams)
Tel: Elmswell (0359) 40205
Directions: 4 miles W. of Stowmarket, 1 mile N. of the A45; take turning signposted 'Haughley Park' not 'Haughley'

The red brick front dates from 1620. It has the common E-plan, with projecting end wings and a central porch, in this case with the addition of tall bay windows flanking the porch. The gables are stepped and have pinnacles, while the mullion and transom windows have pediments, a typical Jacobean mixture. The garden front was rebuilt with bow windows in about 1800 and the two dormers above the bay windows on the entrance front are modern replacements of the originals. The right-hand half of the house was severely damaged by fire in 1961 and the whole interior is a modern reconstruction. The restoration work is of the highest quality, especially the new oak staircase. The house is fully occupied; two upstairs and most of the downstairs rooms are shown in the guided tour which lasts about 30 minutes (and only begins when enough people have assembled). There are a number of Dutch 17th century paintings downstairs. There are pleasant grounds with flourishing rhododendrons and a large magnolia tree.

Opening times: May to Sept, Tues 3–6.
Entrance charges: 70p; children 35p; no dogs. (HHA)
Parking: Free, in front of the house.
Wheelchair access: There is a wheelchair available at the house; access to downstairs only, which includes most of the rooms shown to visitors.
Guidebook: A free, duplicated sheet with basic information.
Catering: None.
WCs: Yes.
Shop: None.

ICKWORTH   nr Bury St Edmunds (The National Trust)
Tel: Horringer (028 488) 270
Directions: 3 miles S.W. of Bury St Edmunds; turn off the A143 at Horringer

This extraordinary house was never seen by its creator, Frederick Hervey, Bishop of Derry and Earl of Bristol, a millionaire art collector and traveller after whom all Hotels Bristol are named. Hervey took the idea of a circular house from Belle Isle in Windermere, and built a large elliptical house called Ballyscullion in Ireland, begun in 1787 and dismantled in 1813. Ickworth is an even bigger version of the same idea, with a great domed rotunda in the centre for the living rooms, linked by curving passages to art galleries in the wings. It was half finished at the Bishop's death in 1803, and not completed until 1830. The original design was made by an Italian, Mario Asprucci, but was carried out in Suffolk by Francis Sandys. On the ground floor the rotunda contains three enormous reception rooms, drawing room, library and dining room, grouped round a central entrance and staircase hall lit from above, which owes its present appearance to Sir Reginald Blomfield's alterations of 1907. The enormous principal rooms, with their oddly-curving outer walls, contain good furniture of the 1830s, a collection of excellent family portraits and a few of the Earl Bishop's art treasures, the most notable of which is Flaxman's sculpture of 'The Fury of Athamas' in the hall. There is beautiful porcelain in the east corridor and a large and impressive collection of the Bristol family silver in the west corridor. Each corridor has a room halfway along; on the west side this is the Pompeian Room, decorated by J.D. Crace in 1879, which contains the original papier-mâche architect's model of the house. There are guides in each room, and visitors have free run of the ground floor, except of the east wing which is now the family residence. Ickworth has a splendid park which was largely created for the First Marquess of Bristol in the 1820s.

Opening times: Park open all year daily. House and gardens April to end Oct, Tues, Wed, Thurs, Sat, Sun and Bank Holiday Mon 2–6.

Entrance charges: Park free. House and garden £1.40; accompanied children 70p.

Parking: Car park near house, 50p (free to National Trust members).

Wheelchair access: Two steps to front door, but all rooms open to the public are on one level except the Exhibition Room, shop and tea room (tea may be brought upstairs).

Guidebook: Exceptionally informative and well illustrated, contains a plan of the house. There is also a cheap leaflet available in English, German, Dutch, French, Norwegian and Italian and a free one on the park.

Catering: Reliable National Trust teas on willow-pattern china.

WCs: Clean, free and spacious; disabled visitors may use the staff lavatory down two steps from the hall.

Shop: In the basement kitchen; the National Trust standard package of souvenirs in good taste.

IPSWICH: CHRISTCHURCH MANSION   Christchurch Park
(Borough of Ipswich)

Tel: Ipswich (0473) 53246

Directions: In Christchurch Park, on the N. edge of Ipswich Old Town

The hilly and well-wooded little park makes an agreeable setting for the mansion which is now used as a museum. Christchurch Mansion is a charming building and a fine example of 16th and 17th century brickwork.

The house was built for the Withipoll family between 1548 and 1564. It has the common Tudor layout, with two long wings and a tall porch in the centre of the front, and the walls were originally patterned all over with diaper work. A fire occurred just before 1674 and the upper storey was rebuilt shortly after that with Dutch gables. At the same time the porch was given its two odd giant columns and much of the interior woodwork was renewed. The building has changed little since then, although a few small improvements were made in the 18th century, and a 16th century house from the centre of Ipswich was re-erected at the back of the mansion in 1924. Almost the whole of the interior on both floors is open to the public. Most of the original fittings have survived. The great hall has woodwork of the 1670s and two rooms in the east wing have kept their mid-18th century wallpaper, and grand fireplaces of the same period. Some rooms (for example the great kitchen and the state roooms upstairs) are arranged with the appropriate furnishings; others (like the buttery) are full of museum exhibits like cases of local pottery, or carved fragments rescued from demolished buildings. There is also an art gallery which contains paintings by local artists, including Constable and Gainsborough. Perhaps the most impressive interiors are those of the early Tudor wing behind the great hall where the rooms have good ceilings and panelling, as well as high quality 16th century furniture.

Opening times: All year daily except Good Friday, Christmas Eve and Christmas Day; weekdays 10–5, Sun 2.30–4.30; closes at dusk in winter.
Entrance charges: Free; no dogs in house.
Parking: Up to one hour free parking in Fonnereau Road (about 200 yards away) or in Charles Street car park (¾ mile away).
Wheelchair access: It would be possible to see slightly less than half the rooms on view, but enough to make a visit worthwhile.
Guidebook: An elaborate guide, but with full plan, many black and white illustrations, histories of the house and its owners and room-by-room tour.
Catering: None.
WCs: In the park, uphill from the house, free but vandalised; unsuitable for wheelchairs.
Shop: Pamphlets, postcards, facsimiles of local sketches, etc.

IXWORTH ABBEY Ixworth (Mrs Alan Rowe)
Tel: Pakenham (0359) 30374
Directions: 6 miles N.E. of Bury St Edmunds in Ixworth. The house is not signposted; take the A1088 out of the village towards Thetford, second left into Commister Lane, after ¼ mile turn right and again right

The house at Ixworth has a complicated building history. The oldest part is the south and east cloister ranges of a Priory of Augustinian Canons, which was established here in 1170. The vaulted 13th century undercroft and slype in this part of the building are remarkable for their excellent condition; some of the carved stonework looks almost new. The adjoining Prior's

Lodging formed in 1470 is a timber-framed building of considerable interest and importance with a first-floor screens passage. These original Abbey buildings have been partly overlaid by later additions. The house was extended and improved in the late 17th and early 18th centuries, when the imposing entrance hall was formed, and again in the early 19th century. The present owners, who acquired the property in 1962, are slowly restoring the building and, at the same time, elucidating its development. The guided tours are scholarly.

Opening times: May to Summer Bank Holiday, Tues, Sun, May Day and Spring and Summer Bank Holiday Mon 2.30–5.
Entrance charges: 80p; no reductions.
Parking: Free, in front of the house.
Wheelchair access: Not possible, steps everywhere.
Guidebook: A fold-out leaflet explaining the mediaeval building; more information on the later development of the house would be useful.
Catering: Only by prior arrangement.
WCs: None for public use.
Shop: Postcards on sale.

KENTWELL HALL Long Melford (Mr and Mrs J.P. Phillips)
Tel: Long Melford (078 725) 207
Directions: Long Melford is 3 miles N. of Sudbury on the A134. The entrance to the house is on the W. side of the road to the N. of the green

A lime avenue planted in 1678 makes a fine approach to the house — a red brick Tudor mansion inside a wide water-filled moat. Kentwell Hall was new in 1563 and the exterior is little changed. The house is built on an E-plan with long projecting wings and a turret at the inside corner of each wing. The rooms of the west wing are original but the east wing and the centre of the house were gutted by fire in the 1820s. They were restored by Thomas Hopper, who believed that 'it is an architect's business to understand all styles and to be prejudiced in favour of none', and was equally happy designing Classical, Norman or Jacobean country houses. He used several different styles here at Kentwell. His rooms are good for their date, if a little heavy-handed, and his hall and dining room have been repainted recently as part of an active restoration programme. His library has scagliola columns typical of the 1820s. Of the earlier decoration there is some good 17th century panelling in the servants' hall and a solid oak staircase of about 1680. Notable furnishings include a massive Jacobean-style sideboard and oak canopy bed (both originally from Avening Court), an excellent Georgian bed in the Moat Bedroom, and an extraordinarily horrible hand-carved teak settee. Almost the whole of the building is open to visitors, including the rooms which are being restored. There are fresh flowers everywhere, peacocks in the walled garden, and every effort is made to create a pleasant appearance.

Opening times: Good Friday to Easter Tues, then Easter to end June, Sun, Wed and Thurs; 4–18 July, Historical Re-Creation fortnight, public on Sat and Sun 11–5; 21 July to end Sept, daily except Mon and Tues; also all Bank Holiday Mon and Sat 2–6.
Entrance charges: £1,50; children 75p; OAPs £1.00 (on Thurs only). No dogs or cameras. (HHA)
Parking: On grass verge, 150 yards from the house.
Wheelchair access: Possible to ground floor only which involves some steps; this is about half of the house. There is a gravel drive.
Guidebook: A large folded sheet with a little history, a diagram of the house and a plan of the estate.
Catering: In the old kitchen; genuinely home-made cakes and tea by the cup (the second cup is cheaper).
WCs: Next to the Little Dining Room on the ground floor, free and clean.
Shop: As you enter the house, craftwork and sometimes garden produce for sale.

LAVENHAM: LITTLE HALL Market Place (Suffolk Preservation Society)

Tel: Lavenham (0787) 247179
Directions: Lavenham is 11 miles S.E. of Bury St Edmunds and 18 miles E. of Ipswich; the house is on the E. side of the Market Place

Nothing in Suffolk compares with the timber-framed houses of Lavenham. The streets are full of 15th and 17th century buildings of this type. It is pleasant to record that at least one of the houses is open to the public. Little Hall was built in about 1450, probably for the clothier William Causton. Towards the end of the 16th century the open hearth in the hall was replaced by a fireplace with a brick chimney and the hall itself was divided horizontally into two rooms. Much of the building has been reconstructed in the present century. Although there are one or two interesting pieces of furniture – a 1760 Spanish travelling bureau, a variety of chests and a 17th century Dutch grotesque painting – the best thing in the house is the crown-post roof of the hall, still blackened with smoke from the open hearth, which can be seen in the main upstairs room.

Opening times: Easter to mid-Oct, Sat, Sun and Bank Holiday Mon 2.30–6.
Entrance charges: 40p; children 20p.
Parking: Free parking in the Market Place.e
Wheelchair access: Downstairs only, and even here there are awkward steps.
Guidebook: A stencilled information sheet.
Catering: None.
WCs: None.
Shop: Postcards and guidebooks to Lavenham.

MELFORD HALL Long Melford (The National Trust)

Directions: Long Melford is 12 miles S. of Bury St Edmunds on the A134, Melford Hall is entered from the Green

Melford Hall stands on one side of an emormous sloping green in the centre of this attractive little town. The house was built for Sir William Cordell, Master of the Rolls, in the 1550s or 1560s. It follows a fairly common Tudor arrangement with a main range, which in this case has a rather elegant stone porch, and two long wings enclosing the front courtyard. The wings have stair-turrets on the courtyard side and there are four similar turrets on the back of the main range, facing the Green. The middle pair look something like a mediaeval gatehouse and in fact the house is built on mediaeval cellars (not open to view). The interior now contains little Elizabethan work. The house was redecorated by Sir Cordell Firebrace in the 1740s and major alterations were made in 1813 for Sir William Parker by Thomas Hopper (who also worked at Kentwell nearby). Hopper probably supplied the 18th-century-style doors and fireplace in the Great Hall, but the Blue Drawing Room dates from Sir Cordell's time. This is the sole survivor of a fire in 1942 which gutted the north wing. The rest of the wing has been rebuilt, in plainer style. The very attractive library with its inlaid decoration is Hopper's work and he also formed a very grand and severe staircase leading out of the hall. Visitors may ascend the stairs to reach a series of first floor rooms. The Parker family who purchased Melford Hall in 1786 together with some of the paintings and furniture inside, provided a succession of distinguished naval commanders, and there are a number of nautical paintings. In the 19th century Beatrix Potter was a frequent visitor to the house and two of the upstairs rooms are devoted to her. The walled garden of the house abuts the green, which can be overlooked from an octagonal Elizabethan garden pavilion.

Opening times: April to Sept, Wed, Thurs, Sun and Bank Holiday Mon, 2–6.
Entrance charges: £1.10; children 55p; no dogs.
Parking: Free parking 200 yards from the house.
Wheelchair access: Partly gravel path from car park, one step up into porch, the ground floor rooms and the staircase would be accessible. There is a wheelchair at the house. The gardens are also accessible.
Guidebook: A good average illustrated guide with a plan of the house drawn in the early 17th century which demonstrates how much the building has been altered.
Catering: None.
WCs: At the gatehouse, free and clean. Unsuitable for wheelchairs.
Shop: Postcards and slides only sold in the entrance hall.

ORFORD CASTLE Orford (Ancient Monument)
Directions: 9 miles E. of Woodbridge on the B1084

Orford Castle is just a tall keep overlooking the Suffolk marshes and the sea. The outer walls of the castle are now rough grass banks criss-crossed by footpaths. The keep is impressive and also historically important because it was one of the first in England to abandon the square or oblong shape for something more elaborate — in this case an irregular eighteen-sided cylinder with three square turrets. The man responsible was Alnoth, Keeper of the King's Houses, who built Orford for King Henry II between

1165 and 1172. Some restoration work has been carried out in recent years (see the mauve mortar on the outside) and the internal floors have been replaced. There is a basement, which for once really does contain a dungeon, and two floors of living rooms. On each floor is one large circular room with a number of smaller rooms opening off it, all of them now completely empty, although there are still kitchen fittings and even a urinal built into the walls. Visitors have access to all parts of the keep, including the roof which gives a good view of both land and sea.

Opening times: Standard hours (SM), see page xii.
Entrance charges: 40p; OAPs and children 20p.
Parking: Free parking next to castle.
Wheelchair access: There are many steps and steep slopes, but the exterior can be seen from the car park.
Guidebook: The Official Handbook is a well-written account with plans of Orford and other similar castles and a drawing of Orford made in about 1600.
Catering: None.
WCs: None.
Shop: Postcards and guidebooks only.

SOMERLEYTON HALL   nr Lowestoft (Lord and Lady Somerleyton)
Tel: Lowestoft (0502) 730224
Directions: 5 miles N.W. of Lowestoft off the B1074

A millionaire bricklayer makes a good house builder. Sir Morton Peto made his money by organising the building of such things as Nelson's column, several gentlemen's clubs and railway systems all over the world. In 1844 he employed the sculptor John Thomas to turn the old house at Somerleyton into his idea of a Jacobean mansion. The result is a purely Victorian house of the reddest red brick with lots of stone ornament and a rather Italian-looking tower to one side. The entrance front has a fantastic stone screen across the centre, but this side of the house can only be seen from the exit drive. The garden front is quieter and covered in Virginia creeper, but it does have a powerful central porch in a mixture of styles. The main 'state rooms' on the ground floor are open to visitors. They are an odd mixture because the Oak Parlour, staircase hall and dining room have genuine late 17th century features from the original house (which was not demolished but only swamped), while the decorations in the other three rooms on show are later. The Oak Parlour panelling is enriched with carving in Grinling Gibbons' style, but in other respects the Victorian rooms make a more powerful display especially the dark entrance hall with its painted glass dome and stuffed polar bears. Peto was forced to sell his house with its furniture in 1863 and they were bought by the Crossleys, a family of carpet manufacturers (now Lords of Somerleyton), who still own and occupy the house. Perhaps the outstanding piece of furniture is the Queen Anne silver gilt mirror in the Oak Parlour which Peto bought from Stowe. The gardens are in very much their original condition and make a perfect Victorian

Somerleyton Hall, Suffolk

setting for the house. There is a large maze which was laid out by Nesfield in 1846 and plenty of strong colour from the rhododendrons and roses. All that is missing is the enormous glass Winter Garden which was taken down in 1915. There is also a children's play area and a number of greenhouses are on view.

Opening times: Easter Sun to 3 Oct, Thurs, Sun and Bank Holidays, also Tues and Wed in July and Aug, 2–6.
Entrance charges: (1981) £1.00; children 60p. No dogs, no photography in Hall. (HHA)
Parking: Free parking next to the house.
Wheelchair access: Access possible to all rooms and there are wheelchairs available.
Guidebook: A 'Souvenir' guide, with colour photographs of the house, inside and out, and of the gardens; room-by-room descriptions, describing the best things only; no plan.
Catering: Teas can be taken in the conservatory overlooking a sunken garden, commercial cakes and tea in polystyrene cups.
WCs: Modern lavatories with facilities for the disabled.
Shop: Next to the entrance; pottery, confectionery and assorted gifts.
Extras: Short ride on a pony, short ride in a pony and trap, short ride on a miniature railway; all charged extra.

Surrey

ALBURY PARK   Albury, nr Guildford (Mutual Households Association)
Directions: 4 miles E.S.E. of Guildford, 1½ miles E. of Albury village on the A248

The outside of the house at Albury is entirely Victorian, the work of A.W.N. Pugin and his son Edward; it is a mixture of Gothic and Tudor styles and is only memorable for the fact that each of the 63 chimneys is different. Beneath the red brick and flint skin is a late 17th century house, though much altered by Sir John Soane in 1800 and by Henry Hakewill in 1820. The house has now been converted into flats but the four main rooms have been preserved and are shown to visitors in a tour guided by one of the residents. There is not a great deal of interest to see. The entrance hall has a fine and vigorously-carved chimneypiece of about 1690 and there is another chimneypiece of about the same date in the library. The plain but elegant staircase is by Soane. The furniture in the rooms belongs to the residents and there is no permanent display. The grounds of the house in the steep-sided river valley are attractive and the ancient village church nearby, lovingly cared for by The Redundant Churches Fund, is certainly worth a visit. Across the river from the house are the famous terraced gardens which were laid out by John Evelyn for Henry Howard in 1655–8, but they are separately owned and not open to the public.

Opening times: May to Sept, Wed and Thurs 2–5.
Entrance charges: 40p; children 20p.
Parking: Free parking in the forecourt of the house.
Wheelchair access: Possible to all rooms shown.
Guidebook: An adequate history of the house, grounds and owners, with several illustrations.
Catering: None.
WCs: None.
Shop: None.

CLANDON PARK   West Clandon, nr Guildford (The National Trust)
Tel: Guildford (0483) 222482
Directions: At West Clandon on the A247, 3 miles E. of Guildford; if using A3 follow signs to Ripley to join A247

In about 1730 Thomas, Lord Onslow, decided to rebuild his Elizabethan family home and commissioned the Venetian architect Giacomo Leoni to design a completely new house; the exterior was finished by 1733, the interior some years later. Leoni's house is a large and rather gaunt rectangular block, built of red brick of the highest quality. The entrance front is not improved by the porch which was added in 1876 by the Fourth Lord Onslow. The interior is quite different and contains a series of outstanding Palladian rooms, most of them attractively redecorated in recent years in 'authentic' colours, under the direction of the interior decorator John Fowler. Directly inside the entrance is the magnificent Marble Hall, two storeys high with lavish Baroque plasterwork by Artari and Bagutti and two excellent chimneypieces by the sculptor Rysbrack. Other outstanding rooms are the Palladio Room with French flock wallpaper of about 1780, the Green Drawing Room which takes its name from its original wallpaper of the 1730s and the Saloon, with its blue and biscuit walls and a massive marbled chimneypiece which is one of Fowler's best efforts. Almost the whole of the ground floor and four first floor rooms are open to visitors. They contain an admirable collection of 18th century furniture, paintings and ceramics, much of it from the collection of the late Mrs Gubbay. Visitors make their own way round and some of the rooms are partly roped-off. When first built, Clandon was surrounded by formal gardens, which must have enhanced its appearance. They disappeared when 'Capability' Brown landscaped the park in the 1770s. Most of the park is still privately owned and not open to visitors, but there is a small garden immediately next to the house with a pretty grotto and a Maori House which Lord Onslow brought back from new Zealand in the last century.

Opening times: April to 17 Oct, daily except Mon and Fri, 2–6, last admission 5.30; open Bank Holiday Mon.
Entrance charges: House and garden £1.30; children 75p.
Parking: Free car park about 200 yards from the house.
Wheelchair access: The basement is directly accessible from the back courtyard; the rooms

of the principal floor can be reached by the front entrance where a ramp is kept, the first floor rooms are not accessible.

Guidebook: A very thorough guide to the house and its contents with illustrations and plans of all floors; the book also contains a good account of the Onslow family. Additional guidebooks to the Gubbay collection and the regimental museum are available.

Catering: Spacious self-service licensed restaurant in the basement open 12.30–5.30 for lunches and dependable National Trust teas; the surroundings are attractive.

WCs: In the basement, clean and modern, but no special facilities for wheelchair users.

Shop: An unusually wide range of things sold in cramped basement quarters; besides the usual range of tea-towels, games etc., there are superior food products and the guidebooks to many of the other National Trust properties.

Extras: The basement contains the Museum of the Queen's Royal Surrey Regiment, with uniforms, trophies and other military paraphenalia; a contribution of 10p is invited from each visitor.

CLAREMONT HOUSE Esher (The Claremont Fan Court Foundation Ltd)

Tel: Esher 67841

Directions: ½ mile S.E. of Esher on the A244; turn right through lodge gates opposite Milbourne Lane

The first house at Claremont was a 'very small box' built by Sir John Vanbrugh for himself, but he soon sold the box to his friend Thomas Pelham, later Duke of Newcastle. In 1768 the Claremont estate was bought by Clive of India and Vanbrugh's building was swept away to make room for a new mansion designed by 'Capability' Brown and his partner Henry Holland. It is a dignified house whose front is nine windows wide with a large Corinthian portico. The walls are of pale yellow brick, which was the height of fashion in the 1760s but now seems less attractive. The building is now a school and guided tours of the inside are conducted by relays of pupils who have each learned their piece by heart. By far the most striking room is the entrance hall, where visitors wait for a party to assemble. It was probably designed by Holland's assistant John Soane and has an oval ceiling supported on red scagliola columns and delicate plaster wall decoration. The great drawing room (now the assembly hall) is also impressive, though the plaster wall decoration here is modern. The tour includes all the main rooms on the ground floor; most of them have good ceilings and chimneypieces but are filled with school furniture. The young guides devote less time to the house than to past occupants, especially Princess Charlotte who died in childbed at Claremont in 1817. The tour ends with a visit to the basement to see the plunge bath installed there for Lord Clive as part of the treatment for his nervous disorder. Visitors may explore the grounds, which contain several small buildings by Vanbrugh and his famous Gothic belvedere tower built in 1717. The tower overlooks the major part of the landscaped garden, which is in the care of the National Trust and open to the public, but has a separate entrance.

Opening times: Feb to Nov, first full weekend in each month 2–5.
Entrance charges: 60p; children and OAPs 30p.
Parking: Free parking in front of the house.
Wheelchair access: Not easy because of the long straight flights of steps leading to the main entrance, once inside all rooms are on one level.
Guidebook: A thorough, if expensive, guidebook with plenty of illustrations; it seems odd to have four plans of the gardens and none of the house.
Catering: Teas served in a separate building.
WCs: In the house.
Shop: None.
Extras: The garden at Claremont is one of the earliest English landscape gardens to survive. It was begun by Vanbrugh and Bridgeman before 1720 and extended by William Kent. It is now in the care of the National Trust and open daily April to end Oct 9–7, Nov to end March 9–4, the entrance is on the A307.

DETILLENS Limpsfield (Mr and Mrs D.G. Neville)
Tel: Oxted 3342
Directions: 9 miles E. of Reigate off the A25 in Limpsfield village, opposite the Bull Inn

The name Detillens comes from one of the 18th century owners of the property. The house is of moderate size, with a red brick front of about 1725 which conceals a timber-framed building of the mid-15th century. Originally there was a large open hall in the middle of the house but it was divided in the 16th century to make two storeys and there have been several other minor alterations to the original structure. The guided tours, which take about half an hour, are well-informed and include most of the ground floor rooms and two bedrooms upstairs. The impressive crown-post which was the central support of the hall roof can be seen in one of the bedrooms. Among the more interesting items in the house is a collection of military and sporting guns and a very impressive collection of the stars and coloured ribbons of British and foreign orders of chivalry; these make a dazzling display in the morning room. There is also a walled garden and a display of old farm and domestic implements.

Opening times: May to June, Sat; July to Sept, Wed and Sat 2–5; also Bank Holidays during these periods.
Entrance charges: £1.25; children 60p. (HHA)
Parking: Limited parking next to the house, otherwise it is possible to park by the roadside a short distance away.
Wheelchair access: Not practicable; the house is small and there are many awkward changes of level inside.
Guidebook: Free with each admission, a leaflet with a room-by-room guide; it deals mainly with the house and not at all with the contents.
Catering: None.
WCs: Yes.
Shop: None.

FARNHAM CASTLE   Farnham (Ancient Monument)
Directions: The castle lies on the N. side of the town at the top of Castle Hill

For most of its life Farnham Castle has belonged to the Bishops of Winchester. Henry of Blois, an extremely wealthy bishop, built the first castle in about 1138. It took the usual form of an earth mound with a rectangular stone keep on top. This castle was damaged in 1155 but rebuilt later in the 12th century, when the original mound was tightly enclosed by a hollow shell keep. The space inside the shell was levelled with earth and the older keep completely buried. The best view of the shell is from the car park, but visitors may also go inside to peer down at the partly excavated remains of the first keep and may inspect the 13th century outer walls and the altered 13th century gatehouse which now forms the pedestrian entrance to the castle. Immediately next to the shell are the main living rooms of the castle, grouped round a small triangular courtyard. In many ways they are more interesting than the two keeps; there is much 12th century work, a spectacular brick tower built for Bishop Waynflete in 1470 and the rooms inside have decoration done in the 1670s for Bishop Morley. These buildings are in daily use and are only open to visitors on Wednesdays from 2 until 4.

Opening times: Keep only standard hours (S), see page xii; palace Wed 2–4.
Entrance charges: Keep 30p; children 15p.
Parking: Free parking next to the keep.
Wheelchair access: Not practicable.
Guidebook: The Official Handbook to the castle gives a history of the various bishops who have owned the buildings and describes the keep in detail; it has a plan of both keep and palace.
Catering: None.
WCs: None.
Shop: Postcards only.

GREATHED MANOR   Lingfield (Mutual Households Association)
Tel: Lingfield (0342) 832577
Directions: 15 miles S.S.E. of Croydon, 3 miles S.E. of Lingfield off the B2028; take the unmarked private road by the Plough Inn

The gracious approach through parkland raises expectations which are dashed by the appearance of this large and very ugly house. It looks like a seaside hotel, with its restless mixture of different gables and towers. Greathed was built in 1868 and designed by Robert Kerr, who wrote a very successful book called *The Gentleman's House*, full of advice on how to arrange rooms and how to decorate them. Not much of his own work inside the house can be seen because the building has been divided into flats and only the three principal living rooms are shown on the short guided tour. They have a certain amount of woodwork and plasterwork typical of the

1860s, but the original wallpapers have gone and the furniture is mostly modern. On one side of the house there is a pleasant water garden which was laid out in about 1900 by Harold Peto. The remainder of the garden has been simplified and the park is let to a farmer.

Opening times: May to Sept, Wed and Thurs 2–5.
Entrance charges: 40p; children 25p; no dogs.
Parking: Free parking in front of the house.
Wheelchair access: Possible to all rooms shown.
Guidebook: None, although some information about the history of the house and its owners is available and can be inspected on request.
Catering: None.
WCs: None.
Shop: None.

HATCHLANDS East Clandon (The National Trust)
Tel: Guildford (0483) 222787
Directions: 5 miles E. of Guildford, just E. of East Clandon village on the N. side of the A246

Hatchlands is a compact box of the brightest red brick, built in 1756–7 for Admiral Boscawen. Although the architect is still unknown he was evidently skilful, for the main building is a complex mixture of two, three and four storeys with the different levels connected by convenient staircases. For the interior decoration the Admiral employed young Robert Adam, who had just returned from Italy, but Adam's work at Hatchlands is elegant rather than original. The Admiral died in 1761 and later owners have made a number of small alterations to the building which are best followed with the help of the guidebook. It was written by H.S. Goodhart-Rendel, a leading architect of the inter-war years who owned Hatchlands and gave it to the National Trust in 1945. Sadly, much of the excellent furniture belonging to the house has been dispersed and in recent years the building has been occupied by a finishing school. Only three rooms and the various ground floor halls are open to visitors. They are slightly gloomy, with sparse furnishings and decoration which dates mainly from the 1880s. Of the original Adam decoration there remains the ceiling and chimneypiece in the library and the wall panels in the drawing room. But the most agreeable of the three rooms is the music room which was added in about 1905 to designs of Sir Reginald Blomfield. It is pleasantly light and airy and hung with interesting early 20th century paintings (mostly portraits) by Henry Lamb. Surrounding the house is a simple garden, for the most part laid out by Goodhart-Rendel in the 1920s.

Opening times: April to 17 Oct, Wed, Thurs and Sun 2–6; last admission 5.30.
Entrance charges: 70p; children 35p.
Parking: Free parking in front of the house.
Wheelchair access: All rooms shown are accessible and the whole of the exterior can be seen without difficulty.

Guidebook: A good guide, written by a former owner who was a distinguished architectural historian; he comments at length on the clever planning, which makes the lack of a drawn plan doubly annoying.
Catering: Tea and biscuits in the old kitchen.
WCs: None.
Shop: None.

LOSELY PARK nr Guildford (J.R. More-Molyneux Esq)
Tel: Guildford (0483) 71881/2
Directions: 2½ miles S.W. of Guildford, 1½ miles N. of Godalming off the A3100

Losely is an early Elizabethan house built between 1562 and 1568 for Sir William More, a kinsman of Sir Thomas More. His descendants still live here and run a famous and successful dairy farm on the estate. The house has a grey, gabled front with tall windows whose surrounds are made of the hard white local chalk. A wing containing a long gallery was added in 1600, but it was demolished in about 1835. There have been few other alterations to the outside of the house. The guided tours of the inside last about 40 minutes. The large great hall has some excellent panelling and some painted decoration which is said to have come from Henry VIII's great palace of Nonsuch, long since vanished; there are also good family portraits, including an enormous family group painted by Van Somer in 1739. Beyond the hall is the library, where the panelling is mainly 19th century, but enlivened by some genuine 16th century work. The most impressive room is the drawing room, which has a fairly simple plaster ceiling, panelling of about 1600 and a spectacular chimneypiece carved out of chalk. A bizarre detail of this room is the mullion of the north window, which ends in a large carved animal paw. The furniture includes a 16th century south German wrangelschrank, or marquetry cabinet, inlaid with a design showing a fallen city. The late 17th century staircase leads to the bedrooms which have simple 16th century ceilings and pleasant furniture, mostly dating from the 18th century.

Opening times: June to Sept, Wed, Thurs, Fri and Sat 2–5, also Summer Bank Holidays 2–5.
Entrance charges: £1.00; children 60p. (HHA)
Parking: Free parking, in a field near the house.
Wheelchair access: Small flight of steps to the main entrance, but all the best rooms are on the ground floor and would be accessible.
Guidebook: Adequate; mainly a room-by-room guide with some illustrations, no plan.
Catering: Tea, coffee and home-made cakes available in a little courtyard at the side of the house, all rather cramped and the drinks are served in plastic cups.
WCs: Near the tea place, new, small and not for wheelchairs.
Shop: Sells a limited selection of produce grown on the estate, also bread and the well-known Losely dairy products.

POLESDEN LACEY nr Dorking (The National Trust)
Tel: Bookham 52048
Directions: 3 miles N.W. of Dorking, 1½ miles S. of Gt Bookham off the A246, signposted in Gt Bookham village

In its beautiful downland setting and filled with notable works of art, Polesden Lacy still retains something of the atmosphere of a great Edwardian hostess's country home. At the core of the present house is a small villa built in 1824 on the site of an earlier house which belonged to the playwright Richard Brinsley Sheridan. The villa was greatly enlarged by Ambrose Poynter in 1906 for the Hon. Ronald Greville and his wife. Apart from the pretty portico on the south front, almost all the exterior is Poynter's work. The building was damaged by fire in 1960 but has been carefully restored. In its heyday visitors to the house included Edward VII and George VI. Besides being a notable hostess Mrs Greville was a considerable art collector, as the contents of Polesden Lacey show. Most of the main ground floor rooms are open to visitors, who may wander as they please through the opulent rooms. There is some fine woodwork brought from the old City church of St Matthew Friday Street in the entrance hall. The dining room has British portraits by Richardson, Reynolds and Raeburn but many of the best paintings which include 17th century Dutch works and Flemish and Italian Old Masters are hung in the wide corridor round the internal courtyard. It leads to the cool library and the drawing room, whose walls are encrusted with carved and gilded panelling. The delicate tea room and the masculine billiard room serve as reminders of the sexual segregation in Edwardian houses. The furniture throughout is of high quality; much of it is French and there is also good Chinese porcelain and a collection of majolica. The gardens are very attractive. The long terrace was laid out by Sheridan but most of the planting was done for Mrs Greville in the 1930s. Beyond the garden is farmland and then Ranmore Common, which is popular walking country.

Opening times: Garden open all year daily 11–to sunset. House open March and Nov, Sat and Sun 2–5; April to end Oct daily except Mon and Fri 2–6; open Bank Holiday Mon but closed following Tues; closed Good Friday; last admission ½ hour before closing.

Entrance charges: Park and garden 60p; children 30p. House extra 80p and 40p.

Parking: Free car park about 200 yards from the house.

Wheelchair access: Disabled persons may be driven to the front door and disabled drivers may park there; two steps at entrance, then all rooms accessible.

Guidebook: A good guide with a brief but adequate history of the building and a detailed room-by-room guide to the contents; there are several illustrations, a plan of the house and a useful map of the grounds showing rights of way.

Catering: Restaurant in the stable block, open from 11.00 am on days when house is open; excellent food, home-made soups, good salads, elaborate cakes and pleasant surroundings, but the food is expensive.

WCs: Near the stable block, small and sub-standard compared to the other facilities; not for wheelchair users.

Shop: A fairly elaborate National Trust shop in the stable courtyard, open from 11.00 am on days when house is open, a good range of gifts.

East Sussex

ALFRISTON OLD CLERGY HOUSE (The National Trust)
Tel: Alfriston (0323) 870001
Directions: 7 miles N.W. of Eastbourne, 4 miles N.E. of Seaford in Alfriston village next to the church

The Old Clergy House is of special interest because it was the first house to be saved by The National Trust, who bought it for £10 in 1896. It is a timber framed house of the 'Wealden' or 'recessed front' type and was probably built in about 1350 for the local priest. At the centre is the hall, rising the full height of the house; to the west are the service rooms for storing food and drink with the solar on the floor above. Originally there was a separate two-storey dwelling for the housekeeper of the celibate priest on the east side. These arrangements were altered in later years and the hall was divided to give two storeys, but it has now been restored to its original height. Only the ground floor of the house is open to visitors, who make their own way round. The most impressive room is the hall. The timbers of its crown-post roof are still blackened by the smoke from the open hearth in the centre of the room. The original housekeeper's end is used for small exhibitions and the service rooms now contain a National Trust shop. Part of the original walling can be seen behind perspex in the shop. There is a small and attractive garden.

Opening times: April to end Oct, daily 11–6 or sunset; Nov to 22 Dec (shop only) Wed, Fri, Sat and Sun 11–sunset; last admission ½ hour before closing.
Entrance charges: 50p; accompanied children 25p; Nov and Dec free.
Parking: Limited free parking round village green.
Wheelchair access: Two steps down to entrance, floors uneven, steps to both shops.
Guidebook: An eight page leaflet; adequate but would be improved by a plan or diagram of the building.
Catering: None.
WCs: None.
Shop: None.

BATEMAN'S Burwash (The National Trust)
Tel: Burwash (0435) 882302
Directions: 11 miles S. of Tunbridge Wells, ½ mile S. of the A265; route clearly signposted from W. end of Burwash

A lane which Rudyard Kipling called 'an enlarged rabbit hole' leads to Bateman's, a solid Jacobean stone house with gables and mullioned windows. The house was originally E-shaped with a central porch and a wing on each side, but the right hand wing has disappeared; it was probably demolished in the 18th century when the double oast house was added at the back. Bateman's was built in 1634 for the owner of a local forge. After the collapse of the Sussex iron industry the house was badly neglected. Rudyard Kipling came to the rescue in 1902 and lived at Bateman's until his death in 1936. Three years later the house was left to The National Trust as a memorial to him. It now has many visitors and can get very crowded. The hall, dining and drawing rooms on the ground floor contain furniture and tapestries mostly dating from the 17th century, as well as some mementoes from the Far East. A splendid timber staircase leads to three rooms on the first floor, of which the most interesting is Kipling's study — large, peaceful and lined with books. His chair and table are as he left them, though the table (which he described as ten foot long from north to south and badly congested) must have been tidied up. The guest bedroom is used to exhibit assorted things to do with the writer. Kipling and his wife laid out most of the present garden and his 'Pook's Hill' can be seen from the lawn. A nearby watermill was adapted by Kipling to generate electricity, but the older machinery uses less water than Kipling's turbine, and is now used to grind wholemeal flour.

Opening times: March to end May and Oct, daily except Fri but including Good Friday 2–6; last admission 5.30; June to end Sept, Mon to Thurs 11–6, Sat and Sun 2–6.

Entrance charges: £1.20; children 5–15 60p; no dogs. Special charge during Flower Festival (8–10 July) £1.70 and 80p.

Parking: Free car park in front of house.

Wheelchair access: Wheelchairs not admitted to house in normal hours; shop and tea room accessible.

Guidebook: Fairly basic guidebook, with a room-by-room account but no plan; a separate and highly detailed account of the watermill building comes with the house guide.

Catering: In the outbuildings, soup and salad lunches, tea by the pot, coffee, cake, scones with butter and jam.

WCs: Next to the tea room, adequate, but not really suitable for wheelchairs.

Shop: In the oast house; the usual National Trust range is supplemented by a selection of Kipling's books and some locally made pottery.

Extras: There is no extra admission charge for the water mill which is some distance from the house. Flour ground at the mill is on sale.

BENTLEY nr Halland (Mrs Askew and East Sussex County Council)
Tel: Halland (082 584) 573
Directions: 7½ N.E. of Lewes, off the A22 between Uckfield and Golden Cross; the turning is on a sharpish bend

Bentley was a modest brick farmhouse until the Askews discovered Raymond Erith, and employed him to add a wing on either side and a brand new roof. His additions of the 1960s try hard to be Georgian but their effect is to make the house look like a hugely long bungalow, even though the old centre has three storeys. Each of the wings contains only one large room, with coved ceilings and plasterwork in the neo-Georgian style. Visitors enter by one of these rooms and can see clear through to the exit in the other. All the rooms contain furniture, paintings and other things collected by the Askews, many of them connected with birds in some way. The last room is Erith's 'Chinese Room' hung with 17th century Chinese wallpaper of birds and plants; there can't have been enough to cover the whole room for the paper used between the windows is obviously modern. The house is arranged as occupied by the Askews, but with rope barriers which prevent close inspection of many items. There are information boards in each room, but their information is sketchy. The house very obviously takes second place to the bird garden around it.

Opening times: Wildfowl reserve 14 March to end Oct, daily 11–6; last ticket sold at 4.30. House, June to end Oct, 1–6.

Entrance charges: (1981) Wildfowl reserve only £1.00; OAPs 80p; children 50p; extra charge for admission to house 20p (adults) 15p (children).

Parking: Free parking in a field in front of the entrance.

Wheelchair access: All rooms shown are accessible. The paths in the bird garden are gravel and there are sprung gates at intervals which could be difficult for lone wheelchair users.

Guidebook: Mainly about the wildfowl, but there is a brief section on the house; plan of the grounds only.

Catering: New self-service cafeteria with seats outside.

WCs: In the stables next to the shop; facilities for wheelchairs.

Shop: The route to the ticket counter lies through the shop. Most things for sale are connected with wildfowl (including bags of birdfood).

Extras: It is impossible to reach the house without paying for admission to the wildfowl reserve. The reserve is arranged round a series of lakes and ponds and three different routes are suggested with walking times of 30, 60 and 90 minutes. A new Motor Museum is planned for 1982.

BODIAM CASTLE (The National Trust)
Tel: The Custodian, Staplecross (058 083) 436
Directions: 10 miles N. of Hastings, 4 miles S.E. of Hawkhurst; well signposted locally

Bodiam is a very perfect-looking castle, whose strong high walls and towers are reflected in a wide, still moat. It was built in 1386–8 to defend the countryside against French raiders coming up the river Rother, but as soon as it was finished the English regained control of the Channel and Bodiam became redundant. It fell into ruins, but the outer walls were beautifully restored by Lord Curzon early in this century. Bodiam is a text-book 14th century castle whose defences were copied from continental examples. There is no separate keep — instead a rectangular courtyard is enclosed by a strong wall with a round tower at each corner, a square tower in the middle of each flank, the main gatehouse in front and a small postern gate at the back. The very wide moat was crossed by a stone bridge defended by a barbican half way across, but little remains of the barbican and the present bridge is modern. The castle courtyard is surrounded by the ruins of the main living rooms which were built against the walls. With the help of the plan in the guidebook it is possible to sort out the purpose of the various rooms and this can be supplemented by an audio-visual presentation on 'Life in a Mediaeval Castle'. Three of the towers may be climbed and a short section of the wall-walk is also accessible. Bodiam is an extremely attractive ruin in a lovely setting; it is also much visited and often overcrowded.

Opening times: April to end Oct, daily 10–7; Nov to end March, daily except Sun 10–sunset. Closed 25–27 Dec.

Entrance charges: 80p; children under 17 40p; dogs must be on a lead.

Parking: It is a fairly stiff climb from the car park to the castle; 30p per car, but free to National Trust members.

Wheelchair access: The route from the car park to castle is difficult but the car park attendant will direct car-borne wheelchair users to another entrance giving easier access; the internal courtyard of the castle can be reached.

Guidebook: An excellent guidebook with an essential plan of the castle.

Catering: Fairly basic National Trust cafe in the car park open Easter to Oct 10.30–6. There is an Inn and another tea shop in the village.

WCs: Next to the cafe, recently improved and with facilities for wheelchairs; there are no lavatories at the castle (except the mediaeval garderobes).

Shop: The combined ticket office, National Trust shop and small museum of finds made at the castle is opposite the main gatehouse of the castle.

BRIGHTON: THE ROYAL PAVILION (The Borough of Brighton)
Tel: Brighton (0273) 603005
Directions: In the centre of Brighton, fronting the Old Steine

The Prince of Wales secretly married Mrs Fitzherbert in 1785 and leased a farmhouse in Brighton to be near her. Henry Holland enlarged the house for him by building a new block to match the old and linking the two with a domed saloon. Holland's house was simple and elegant but the Prince wanted something more showy. Between 1815 and 1822 his favourite architect, John Nash, turned the house into a dazzling Indian palace. He added large rooms at either end of the main front and created a roofline of domes, minarets and spires, with some Gothic ornament thrown in for good measure. The interior was fitted out in the Chinese taste by Crace, a famous firm of decorators. The Pavilion is now run by the city corporation. Since the last war it has been restored to something close to its original appearance outside and in, and much of the original furniture has been brought back. No expense was spared in the Prince's house and the main rooms are richly-coloured and gilded in a way which now seems completely overpowering. The dining room with its flying dragon supporting the chandelier and the music room with its glittering dome look like parts of a cinema not a royal palace. Even the great kitchen has a ceiling held up by four iron palm trees. As well as the state rooms, visitors may also see a number of smaller upstairs rooms which have the pretty and elegant interiors we expect of the Regency period. The last rooms to be seen are the Prince's private rooms, coolly

Brighton: The Royal Pavilion, East Sussex

decorated in green, black and gold, with some outstanding furniture by Thomas Hope in the Egyptian taste. There are few guides and it would be sensible to buy a guide book before going round the house. In the holiday season the Pavilion is often uncomfortably crowded.

Opening times: Daily 10–5; July to end Sept 10–6.30; closed Christmas and Boxing Day and one day in June.

Entrance charges: (1981/82) £1.20 or £1.45 according to season; children half price; OAPs 85p–£1. Subject to revision in April 1982.

Parking: There is no car park for visitors, but there is street parking with meters nearby.

Wheelchair access: All the main rooms are on the ground floor and easily accessible.

Guidebook: A lavishly illustrated guide with a brief history of the building, a room-by-room guide and a detailed description of the contents of each room; the only thing missing is a plan of the house.

Catering: There is a tea room in the museum nearby, open 'most days' 10.30–4.30.

WCs: In the house.

Shop: There is a small souvenir shop at the end of the tour.

FIRLE PLACE West Firle, nr Lewes (Viscount Gage KCVO)
Tel: (0323) 843902
Directions: 4 miles S.E. of Lewes on the A27

Although it all looks 18th century, Firle Place is oddly haphazard; this is because it incorporates a large Tudor house built for Sir John Gage. One Tudor gable survives in the south front and a few other traces can be seen inside but it is not clear how much of the older house is concealed under later work. The plan, with its two courtyards, is probably the original one. The house was given its present appearance between 1710 and 1750. It is not known who provided the design, but the Morris family from Lewes are likely candidates; some of the details — the way the front of the great hall has been squashed between the sides of the outer courtyard for example — look like provincial work. The old great hall was divided to form a rather dull entrance hall and a grand Palladian staircase hall with a splendid open stair and robust plaster-work. The old hall roof still survives, hidden above the 18th century ceiling. The normal guided tour takes in the hall and staircase and then follows a route round three sides of the outer courtyard on the first floor, including the 18th century long gallery. The rooms themselves are plain but they contain very good family portraits by many of the best English masters. There is also an outstanding collection of 18th century Sèvres, French 18th century furniture, and some old master paintings. Many of these came to Firle by marriage from Panshanger in Hertfordshire and Fawsley in Northamptonshire. Sadly, it is not possible to see everything from a comfortable distance because of the rope barriers. The best room in the house is the Palladian drawing room on the ground floor, which can only be seen on the first Wednesday of each month, when other extra rooms are shown. The gardens next to the north-west and north-east fronts are open, as is the park, but the south garden and the stable block are out of bounds.

Opening times: June, July, Aug, Sept, Sun, Wed and Thurs, also Easter, Spring and late Summer Bank Holiday Sun and Mon 2.15–5.30.

Entrance charges: £1.20; children 60p; first Wed in month £1.40 and 60p (extra rooms shown in an unguided tour). (HHA)

Parking: Free parking in the park about 50 yards from the house.

Wheelchair access: Permitted, but most rooms shown on normal days are on the first floor; the garden can only be reached by two flights of four or five steps.

Guidebook: The house is well served, with a history and guidebook of the house by Arthur Oswald, with illustrations, plan, and much very interesting historical material; there is a separate booklet with descriptive notes on the paintings, porcelain and furniture.

Catering: Tea in the old kitchen and tea by the cup, biscuits and some home-made cakes.

WCs: Reached through the shop; spacious and modern but with no special facilities for wheelchairs.

Shop: Better than average, with some local produce including pottery, trugs and honey.

Extras: Only visitors to the house may walk in the park.

GLYNDE PLACE nr Lewes (Viscount Hampden)
Tel: Lewes (079 16) 71743 or Glynde (079 159) 337
Directions: 4 miles S.E. of Lewes, on the edge of Glynde village, clearly signed off the A27

After the proud 18th century approach through the pedimented red brick arch of the stables it comes as a surprise to find a Tudor and Jacobean house. The flint-faced front with its shaped gables, twin bows and mullioned windows cannot be much earlier than 1600 but behind it lies a courtyard house built in the 1560s. The original entrance was on the west side with its two massive chimneybreasts and the old doorway still survives, but now opens onto a rose garden (out of bounds to visitors except on Connoisseurs' Day). In the mid-18th century the house was owned by Richard Trevor, Bishop of Lincoln, nicknamed 'The Beauty of Holiness'. He moved the main entrance to the Jacobean east front, 'Georgianised' the great hall and some of the other rooms behind it, and replaced Tudor windows with sash windows on other fronts. The builder employed on the work was John Morris from Lewes, who also put up the grand new stable block. Several of the present 'Tudor' features of the house are 19th century replacements of the features removed by Morris. The interior contains work of several dates. The two most distinguished rooms in the east front are the ground floor hall with a screen of columns at each end and the first floor gallery with heavy panelled walls and a high coved ceiling; both rooms are the work of the Bishop's time. The staircase with its barley sugar balusters looks like 17th century work and was probably brought to Glynde from another house. The little courtyard in the centre of the house is not open to visitors, but it can be glimpsed from a first floor corridor window. The guided tour is much more concerned with the history of the family than with the house and there are many family portraits to back up the narrative. Among items of more general interest is a sketch by Rubens for the ceiling of the Whitehall banqueting house. The small church near the house, built in 1765 to designs of Sir Thomas Robinson as part of the Bishop's improvements, has a pretty interior with a little Flemish and a lot of late Victorian English stained glass.

Opening times: 19 May to 14 Oct, Wed and Thurs; also Spring Bank Holiday Mon; Summer Bank Holiday Sun and Mon, 2.15–5.30. Last Wed of each month Connoisseurs Day.

Entrance charges: £1.00; children 50p Connoisseurs Day £1.30. (HHA)

Parking: Free parking on gravel in front of house.

Wheelchair access: Not really practicable and the principal objects of interest are on the first floor.

Guidebook: An inexpensive room-by-room guide with a large amount of family history.

Catering: Fairly basic tea room in the outbuildings, tea by the cup, home-baked cake by the slice, self-service.

WCs: In the house and also near the tea room; recently modernised.

Shop: Some things for sale in the tea room, including honey and marmalade made at the house.

GREAT DIXTER Northiam (Mr Quentin Lloyd)

Tel: Northiam (079 74) 3160

Directions: 12 miles N. of Hastings, off the A28 in Northiam, signposted locally

Nathaniel Lloyd wrote an important book on English brickwork and it is appropriate that his house should be such a splendid celebration of local building materials. The right half of the main front is a mid-15th century timber-framed house with a gabled two storey wing and a large porch. The quieter tile-hung left half was added in 1910 by Sir Edwin Lutyens, who enlarged the house for Lloyd. At the same time Lutyens carefully restored the old house to its original ornamental splendour and tacked another mediaeval timber house, rescued from Benenden in Kent, onto the back. The guided tour of the house includes the great hall, the parlour and the solar of the original building. Lutyens restored the hall to its original great size and revealed the roof, which has a very unusual combination of crown posts and hammerbeams. The parlour is lit by Tudor windows running the full width of the front wall, while the staircase to the first floor solar is a good example of Lutyens' design in sympathy with, but not imitating, the older work. All the rooms shown have agreeable furniture collected by Lloyd; there is also a quantity of embroidery worked by the Lloyd family and some 18th century samplers. The gardens surrounding the house were also laid out by Lutyens, who incorporated the existing farm buildings in his design. A series of small gardens and terraces is enclosed by clipped hedges and linked by winding paths and flights of steps. The garden is now in the care of the distinguished horticulturalist Christopher Lloyd.

Opening times: April to 10 Oct, daily except Mon but including Bank Holiday Mon, also

16–17 and 23–24 Oct, 2–5.
Entrance charges: House and garden £1.20; children 40p. Garden only 60p and 20p. No dogs in house or garden. (HHA)
Parking: Free parking in a field some distance from the entrance.
Wheelchair access: Two of the three rooms shown are accessible; the garden is full of steps and not suitable.
Guidebook: A brief account of the house on two sides of a single sheet.
Catering: None.
WCs: Between the car park and the entrance, very cramped and not for wheelchairs.
Shop: Home-made furniture sold at the entrance door; books and postcards can be bought in the house during a tour; there is also a nursery in the garden selling plants and specialising in clematis.

LAMB HOUSE West Street, Rye (The National Trust)
Directions: In Rye, on the bend of West Street, which leads out of Church Square

Lamb House is a solid two storey red brick house with a front four bays wide. It was built in 1721–2 for James Lamb, thirteen times Mayor of Rye. The staircase hall with its original stair and the morning room, dining room and study are shown to visitors. The American novelist Henry James lived here from 1897 until 1916 and it is because of his connection with the house that part of it is open, though little remains that is particular to him. The garden room, where he wrote *The Ambassadors*, *The Wings of the Dove*, and *The Golden Bowl*, was destroyed by a bomb in the last war. The room to the right of the hall contains portraits of James and a few of his belongings; the morning room across the hall is furnished as it was in James' time, with some of his own furniture. Both rooms have their original 18th century panelling, but the French windows leading to the beautifully maintained garden are an addition made this century under James' direction. Visitors should be warned that Rye is a very popular tourist town and space at Lamb House is limited.

Opening times: April to end Oct, Wed and Sat 2–6; last entry 5.30.
Entrance charges: 60p; children under 5 free.
Parking: None near the house; on-street parking space is scarce but there are pay car parks in the town.
Wheelchair access: Four steps up to entrance; all three rooms and the garden are level, but it would be sensible to telephone in advance of a visit.
Guidebook: Brief leaflet, which is adequate for most purposes, or an extremely detailed account of Henry James and his house by H. Montgomery Hyde.
Catering: None.
WCs: None.
Shop: Postcards only.

LEWES: ANN OF CLEEVES' HOUSE Southover High Street (Sussex Archaeological Society)
Tel: Lewes (079 16) 4610

Directions: On the S.E. side of the town; Southover High Street is part of the main A275 to Newhaven

Ann of Cleeves' only connection with the house is that it was part of her divorce settlement from King Henry VIII. It is a fairly humble late mediaeval house with a wonderfully varied front of timber, tile, brick and flint and a roof of both tile and stone. The main range facing the street dates from about 1530 but is built over a cellar 200 years older. The small Elizabethan porch dates from 1599 and the rear wing is of the same period. The house is now a museum and most of its rooms are open to visitors. In the centre is the two-storey great hall, with a staircase leading from it to a furnished bedroom; this is the nicest room in the house and has a bay window over the porch. A staircase from the other end of the hall leads to the Furniture Room and to a very small long gallery with collections of children's toys and games and Victorian personalia. Below these rooms is the old kitchen and two galleries devoted to the history of Lewes and the history of the Iron industry in the Sussex Weald. A tiny knot garden has been planted behind the house.

Opening times: 16 Feb to Nov, weekdays 10–5; also April to Oct, Sun 2–5; last admission 5.00.
Entrance charges: 60p; children 30p. Subject to revision.
Parking: No car park, limited street parking, otherwise only pay car parks.
Wheelchair access: Not practicable, except to the hall.
Guidebook: A short leaflet with a room-by-room commentary.
Catering: None.
WCs: On the way to the Wealden Iron gallery.
Shop: Postcards and relevant publications.

MICHELHAM PRIORY Hailsham (Sussex Archaeological Society)
Tel: Hailsham (0323) 844224
Directions: 7 miles N. of Eastbourne, ½ mile E. of Upper Dicker, off the A22 and A27

Michelham has a wide moat which is crossed by a 16th century bridge defended by a 14th century gatehouse. The rich red ironstone house includes part of a Priory of Augustinian canons which was founded here in 1229. The Priory buildings were arranged round a cloister in the usual way and the present house consists of the south-west corner of the cloister and a Tudor wing which was added in the 1590s after the buildings had become a private house. The tallest part of the house contains the two oldest rooms, which are a vaulted undercroft and the Prior's room above it. The Tudor wing was badly damaged by fire in the 1920s and its windows, roof and much of the interior are modern replacements. The original rooms of the Priory are easily recognised by the life-sized models of monks displayed in them. The other rooms have an assortment of 17th century furniture, tapestries, iron-work and stained glass, as well as some modern copies. The rooms are half-heartedly arranged to look as if they might still be occupied, except two first floor rooms which have permanent museum displays; one is concerned with local archaeology, the other contains items from the Alice Mummery collection of 18th century and folk musical instruments. Of the outbuildings, the interior of the gatehouse is accessible and the 16th century barn is used for temporary exhibitions. A small deposit is required for the key of the pillory (a 19th century reproduction). In the stableyard are a forge, a wheelwright's museum and a permanent display of farm wagons and implements. The garden is attractive and there is also a new physic garden.

Opening times: 9 April to 17 Oct, house and grounds daily 11–5.30 but house closed 1–2; last admission 5.00.

Entrance charges: £1.00; children 50p; disabled people 30p. No dogs in house or grounds. (HHA)

Parking: Free car park on the way to the house, about 300 yards from the front door.

Wheelchair access: Possible to grounds and ground floor of house, but most paths are gravel and there are a few steps inside the house.

Guidebook: A small booklet which is mostly colour pictures or an adequate history with a good plan of the buildings.

Catering: Waitress service restaurant in stableyard; salads etc. at lunch time, various set teas (short tea, afternoon tea, Sussex Cream tea).

WCs: In the stableyard, free but donations invited; suitable for wheelchairs.

Shop: Open at same time as house; pottery, books, corn dollies, leatherwork, etc.

Extras: A working water mill, 10p; children 5p; separate explanation sheet 50p. Flour is usually milled on Wednesdays and can be bought from here.

PRESTON MANOR   Brighton (Borough of Brighton)
Tel: Brighton (0273) 55101
Directions: 1 mile N. of Brighton centre, in the suburbs just off the A23 at Preston Park

Compared to the Brighton Pavilion, the five-window front of Preston Manor looks very staid. Parts of a 13th century house survive in the basement but the building was given its present form in 1738 by its owner Thomas Western. Verandahs were built on either side of the main entrance early in this century and a dining room was added at the same time. The interior plan is not regular and a screen of columns was put in the hall to hide the fact. From 1758 until 1938 Preston was occupied by the Stanford family, who bequeathed the house and its contents to Brighton Corporation. Visitors make their own way round. Most of the rooms are shown as they were left by the family, without ropes or barriers and give a vivid impression of a house of the country gentry at the beginning of this century. The only major change has been the clearing of the library to house the Macquoid collection of 16th and 17th century furniture. The library furniture has been arranged in what was an upstairs bedroom. Among the things of special interest are the 18th century staircase, and a curious painting showing a timber mill being dragged through Brighton by 86 oxen in 1797. The gardens have a municipal flavour.

Opening times: All year, Wed to Sat 10–5, Sun 2–5; closed Christmas Day, Boxing Day and Good Friday.
Entrance charges: 65p; OAPs 50p; children 5–15 35p; joint adult ticket with Royal Pavilion £1.60. No dogs or unaccompanied children.
Parking: Limited parking in front of house (no vehicle access from London Road, but from side road immediately before the house).
Wheelchair access: The staff seemed worried by the idea of wheelchairs; advisable to telephone.
Guidebook: A new and very satisfactory guide, with some illustrations and plans of the house.
Catering: None.
WCs: On request.
Shop: Postcards and publications on sale at ticket desk.

SHEFFIELD PARK nr Uckfield (Mr and Mrs P.J. Radford)
Tel: Dane Hill (0825) 790531
Directions: 4½ miles E. of Haywards Heath, 2 miles N. of the junction of the A275 and A272

The house and garden at Sheffield Park parted company in 1972 and are now separately owned. The house is a fairly early example of the revived 18th century Gothic style and was designed by James Wyatt in 1776–7 to replace an older house. His client was James Holroyd, later First Earl of Sheffield. The two best fronts are the east, with its huge Gothic windows, and the south, but visitors to the house are not allowed to walk round the outside and must pay to enter the National Trust gardens in order to see them. The building is covered with cement rendering, which gives a rather dead surface, and there have been a few later additions and alterations both outside and in. The guided tour lasts about an hour and takes in the main rooms on both floors. The best are the tall and light Gothic staircase and the state bedroom on the first floor decorated in white and gold with ceiling paintings of lions, tigers and leopards done by Charles Catton in the 1770s. When the present owners bought Sheffield Park it was empty of furniture and needed repair. Most of the present furnishings are late Georgian or Victorian. The large-patterned wallpapers in some of the rooms also give a rather Victorian look to the place.

Opening times: Easter Sun and Mon, then May to Oct, Wed, Thurs, Sun and Bank Holiday Mon 2–5; last admission 5.00.
Entrance charges: £1.00; no reductions. (HHA)
Parking: On grass near the front of the house.
Wheelchair access: Could see about half the house, including the staircase.
Guidebook: An itinerary, with many pictures; a plan would have been useful.
Catering: None, though there is a tea room nearby.
WCs: In the outbuildings, old but well-maintained; not specially adapted for wheelchairs, but the gents is big enough for access.
Shop: In the outbuildings selling antiques as well as jams and other souvenirs.

Extras: The Sheffield Park Garden (National Trust) offers lakes and shrubs as well as views of the house; open April to 13 Nov, Tues to Sat 11–6, Sun and Bank Holiday Mon 2–6. Last admission ½ hour before closing. Entrance charge £1.40; children 70p. Liable to overcrowding at weekends.

West Sussex

ARUNDEL CASTLE Arundel (The Duke of Norfolk)
Tel: Arundel (0903) 883136
Directions: In Arundel, 10 miles E. of Chichester; the entrance for both cars and visitors is via the lower lodge, at the bottom of the town

Arundel Castle was one of the chief feudal strongholds of the Sussex coast, which it overlooks from the foot of the Downs, but the most impressive-looking parts of this huge castle are fairly recent. The original castle had a central keep with a ward on either side. The circular shell keep of 1180, the gatehouse and the barbican of 1295 still remain, but many of the other mediaeval buildings were destroyed in the Civil War, in which the Howard family played a large part. A partial rebuilding of the inner ward was carried out for the 11th Duke of Norfolk by Robert Abraham between 1795 and 1812. At the end of the 19th century the 15th Duke employed C.A. Buckler to carry out a second rebuilding in a grandiose 13th century style. Visitors may climb the keep, for the splendid view, and then make their own way round, following a prescribed route through the principal rooms. The first of these is the private chapel with its soaring vaulted roof, and excellent stained glass. A low entrance and stair leads onto the huge Baronial hall with its dimly lit collection of family portraits. The hall and the following rooms all date from the late 19th century, but the library is a welcome survival of the 11th Duke's work. It is planned rather like a church with mahogany Gothic decoration of about 1800. The rooms in the east wing are smaller and plainer but have good contents; the billiard room contains a tapestry from designs by Giulio Romano and the breakfast room houses a collection of inlaid furniture. The state robes and family miniatures are displayed in the east drawing room as an optional extra for which a charge is made. As well as the main castle building there is the Fitzalan Chapel (one half of the old parish church) which can only be entered from the castle grounds. It has an outstanding collection of family tombs.

Opening times: April to last Fri in Oct, Sun to Fri 1–5; open at 12 during June, July and Aug and all Bank Holidays; closed Sat.
Entrance charges: £1.70; OAPs and children under 16 £1.00; no dogs. (HHA)
Parking: Car park in castle (cars only); there is a car park opposite the entrance for cars and

Arundel Castle, West Sussex

coaches; charge payable at entry.

Wheelchair access: Possible to both castle and grounds; there is a lift inside the building.

Guidebook: Main guide contains room-by-room description, historical account, a layout plan of castle and grounds and many colour illustrations. The Junior Guide is a lively pictorial guide which is also a cut-out model. There is a separate leaflet on the Fitzalan chapel.

Catering: Light refreshments (cups of tea, sandwiches, ice cream) from a hut just inside the entrance; the open air seating is only for patrons.

WCs: At the entrance (gents only) and also at the very end of the tour route with a cubicle for wheelchair users.

Shop: At the end of the tour; an average gift shop.

Extras: The only extra charge is for the exhibition of state robes inside the castle, but the great park of the castle is one of the most beautiful in the south and is open daily, free.

GOODWOOD HOUSE   nr Chichester (Goodwood Estate Co. Ltd)
Tel: Chichester (0243) 527107
Directions: 3½ miles N.E. of Chichester, between the A285 and A286

Two thirds of the present house at Goodwood were built in the 1790s for the Third Duke of Richmond to the designs of James Wyatt. It was intended to be an enormous octagon round a central courtyard containing the earlier house of 1720, but only three of the eight sides were built. They are two storeys high, with three-storey round towers at the corners. All the walls are faced with knapped flint, but the architectural treatment of each side is different. The rooms shown are those on the ground floor of Wyatt's south east and east fronts and the earlier house, which is reached by means of a modern covered way through the courtyard. Visitors are free to make their own way through these rooms, in which extensive restoration was undertaken in the 1970s. Perhaps the most interesting rooms in the Wyatt ranges are those in the circular towers. In the earlier house the Tapestry Room shows Wyatt's decoration at its best and has a curious fireplace carved by John Bacon. It is treated as a pair of figures parting draperies. The walls of this room are hung with 18th century Gobelins tapestries. The contents of the house include many things of interest and value. Among the paintings are first-rate portraits by Van Dyck and Lely, two views of London by Canaletto and horse paintings by Stubbs and Wootton. There is also a large collection of Sèvres china. The most spectacular curiosity is a huge silver table centrepiece presented to the Fifth Duke by veterans of the Peninsular War. The lawns in front of the east and south east ranges are open to the public, but the other gardens immediately round the house are not. Visitors may walk in the park which contains a number of garden buildings, but none of them is open. The stables, designed by Sir William Chambers and built in 1757–63 are in many ways finer than the house, and more elegant. Next to the stables are some Gothick cottages by Wyatt; his kennels (now a golf club) can be seen from a distance across the park.

Opening times: Easter Sun and Mon; 2 May to 11 Oct, Sun and Mon; and Tues, Wed and

Thurs in Aug, 2–5.
Entrance charges: £1.30; disabled and children 80p. (HHA)
Parking: Free car park about 50 yards from entrance.
Wheelchair access: All rooms open are on the ground floor and there are no steps.
Guidebook: Three in all; a brief leaflet, an illustrated guide with a lot of information about the
    family, a room-by-room guide and many illustrations (the aerial photo is some substitute
    for a plan) and a Young Person's guide, which doubles as a colouring book.
Catering: Set teas (pot of tea, two scones, cake, cream and jam).
WCs: Off the entrance lobby; no special facilities for wheelchairs.
Shop: Several expensive items on sale in the entrance lobby, including bronze animals by
    Edwin Johnson, Goodwood cedar cones in perspex cubes, hand-engraved glassware and
    books about the house and its contents.
Extras: The Goodwood country park is open free of charge every day of the year; there is also
    Goodwood racecourse, which has separate access.

PARHAM PARK nr Pulborough (The Hon Clive and Mrs Gibson and Mr and Mrs P. A. Tritton)

Tel: Storrington (090 66) 2021
Directions: 4 miles S.E. of Pulborough on the A283

Parham lies at the foot of the South Downs in a park which still has a
thriving herd of fallow deer. It is a substantial Elizabethan house of grey
stone, begun in 1577. The foundation stone was laid by a small boy, for
luck. The present drive approaches the east end of the house but the
original main front faces south. It has the common Elizabethan
arrangement of a central porch and shallow gabled wings. The huge
windows of the great hall to the left of the porch are original, the sashes to
the right of the porch are 18th century and the rest are 20th century
restorations in Tudor style by Victor Heal. Visitors enter the house on the
north side, passing an annexe which contains a collection of information
about the house, including some amusing photographs of its wartime
inhabitants. The considerable difference in level between the north and
south fronts is made up by a flight of stairs which lead to the beautiful great
hall, a lofty room flooded with light from its enormous windows. The
elaborate plaster ceiling is probably a 19th century restoration but the
overall effect is still convincingly 16th century. Above the carved oak screen
is a small room for the steward with wood mullioned windows overlooking
the hall. The room contains some magnificent Elizabethan portraits of the
Queen and her more famous courtiers. There is also a good series of portraits
of the Bysshop family who have owned Parham since 1601. Among the other
rooms shown in the guided tour are the saloon dating from about 1790 and
the great parlour and chamber which have very convincing Jacobean style
plasterwork dating from the 1930s. These rooms also contain impressive
portraits and a delightful painting of a kangaroo by George Stubbs, as well as
oriental carpets and tapestries of high quality and a very extensive and
important collection of English embroidery. The tour ends in the long
gallery at the top of the house, an immensely long panelled room with a

modern barrel ceiling painted by Oliver Messel. The gardens are being re-designed by Mr Peter Coats. The greater part of the park is private.

Opening times: 11 April to 3 Oct, Sun, Wed, Thurs and Bank Holiday Mon; gardens 1–6; house 2–6.
Entrance charges: House and garden £1.50; OAPs and children £1.00. Garden only 50p. (HHA)
Parking: Free car park near the house, coaches by arrangement only.
Wheelchair access: The ground floor is accessible by special arrangement with the House Secretary and there is a Silver Jubilee path for wheelchairs in the garden.
Guidebook: A room-by-room guide with many small pictures, some in colour; no plan of the building; there are also separate guides to the needlework and pictures at Parham.
Catering: Set teas only served 3–5.15 in the old kitchen.
WCs: Very civilised facilities, but no special arrangements for wheelchairs.
Shop: Better than average.
Extras: The kitchen garden and greenhouses are open to inspection at no extra charge.

PETWORTH HOUSE Petworth (The National Trust)
Tel: Petworth (0789) 42207
Directions: In the centre of Petworth, 5½ miles E. of Midhurst

Petworth House stands right in the town and it is worth braving the unspeakable traffic on foot to see the fine carved piers of the main gates. Of the old house of the Percy family little can be seen except the 13th century chapel. The present building is largely due to Charles Seymour, Duke of Somerset, who married the Percy heiress in 1682. Rebuilding began in 1686 and the house received a new west front over 300 feet long and very French in appearance; the architect remains unknown. The entrance is through the east front which was partly rebuilt by Anthony Salvin in 1870. Visitors take themselves round the impressive series of rooms on the ground floor whose splendour is matched by their contents — one of the best private art collections in the country. The only room surviving from the 1680s is the marble hall, whose richly carved decoration is unmistakeably French in inspiration. Many of the other rooms were gutted by fire in 1714 and refitted. The square dining room is hung with excellent Van Dyck portraits, notably Sir Robert and Lady Shirley in oriental dress. The Beauty Room has Kneller and Dahl portraits of Queen Anne and her ladies. Laguerre's rather overwhelming mural paintings in the staircase hall are of 1714 but the stair itself was re-arranged in the last century. After this the route doubles back to the Carved Room whose walls were decorated in the 1790s with wood carvings of the highest quality brought from elsewhere in the house. The older work of Grinling Gibbons and John Seldon was made into a consistent scheme by Jonathan Ritson. Considering the amount of time that Turner spent at Petworth, the collection of his paintings in the Turner Room is disappointing, but the collection of ancient sculpture and modern paintings made by his patron the Earl of Egremont is better. The collection is displayed in the bleak North Gallery, and the paintings are still hung in the

19th century fashion, two or three deep. Last of all is the mediaeval chapel, which was finished with carved and painted woodwork in the 17th century. On Tuesdays two extra rooms are shown, both with elaborate mid-18th century decoration and good furnishings. Unlike the other rooms shown these are still occupied. The famous park is one of 'Capability' Brown's triumphs.

Opening times: Park all year, daily 9–sunset. House and gardens April to end Oct, Tues (except after Bank Holidays) Wed, Thurs, Sat, Sun and Bank Holiday Mon 2–6; last admission 5.30; extra rooms shown on Tues.
Entrance charges: Park free. House £1.40: children 70p; Tues £1.60, no reductions for children.
Parking: Free car park within grounds (access by main gates which open at 2.00); there is also a free car park in the town.
Wheelchair access: One low step at entrance, otherwise all rooms are on one level. The shop and restaurant are easily accessible.
Guidebook: i) 'Petworth House' is a thorough guide with small plan, room-by-room commentary, details of the paintings and some illustrations, also brief history of house and family. Two extra pages issued free on Tuesdays describing the two extra rooms shown. ii) A souvenir guide without a plan but with colour illustrations, including some of the paintings.
Catering: In the old service block, all very clean, but not the best of the Trust's tea rooms; tea by pot or cup, scones, cakes etc.
WCs: In the service block, newly made and including a cubicle for wheelchair users.
Shop: The standard National Trust good taste souvenir shop; there should be a larger selection of postcards considering the very large number of important paintings in the house.
Extras: The 700 acre park is a free bonus.

ST MARY'S Bramber (Mr and Mrs P. Smart — The National Butterfly Museum)
Tel: Steyning (0903) 813158
Directions: 1 mile S.E. of Steyning, in Bramber beside the A283

St Mary's is a long two-storey timber-framed building dating from the 15th century. It was probably not built as a house but as the lodging for the wardens of the old Bramber Bridge and there may have been other ranges enclosing a spacious courtyard with galleries on the first floor. There have been many alterations inside, particularly in the 16th century when the chimneys were built. One room of particular interest is on the first floor. Its walls are decorated with late 16th or early 17th century wall-paintings in the form of arched panels in false perspective, framing miniscule landscape views. Everything except the landscapes is grained in imitation of walnut. Most of the rooms contain displays of items of local interest and a collection of early books on butterflies. The Burgess Hall is reached from the half-landing off the stairs. Built in the 19th century, it contains the main butterfly displays which are well laid out and often spectacular. There are small gardens on the east and south sides of the building.

Opening times: All year, daily except Christmas holiday 10–5.
Entrance charges: 85p; children 65p.
Parking: Free car park in front of house.
Wheelchair access: Possible to the ground floor; the butterfly museum is reached by a short flight of stairs for which help is available.
Guidebook: A history of the house with colour illustrations; no plan of the present building but a conjectural reconstruction of the 15th century structure.
Catering: Coffee, tea and light refreshments.
WCs: New WCs in car park; not for wheelchair users.
Shop: Two on the ground floor of the house; most things on sale are to do with butterflies.

STANDEN   East Grinstead (The National Trust)
Tel: East Grinstead (0342) 23029
Directions: On the southern edge of East Grinstead, signposted off the B2110

Standen is a house by Philip Webb, the ablest of the Arts and Crafts architects. It was built between 1892–94 for a wealthy solicitor named James Beale. Webb was a difficult man to deal with, inflexible about altering his designs, but insisting on the highest standards. As a result his output was small. With his friend William Morris he was a co-founder of the Society for the Protection of Ancient Buildings. At Standen he kept the old farmhouse already on the site and added to it a house which borrows its appearance from traditional country buildings. The mixture of brick, stone, tile and weatherboarding seems confused at times, but the garden front with its five-gabled centre is extremely pleasant to look at, and the finish is of the very best quality. Only two generations of the Beale family occupied the house before it passed to the National Trust and it has been possible to restore much of the original character of the interior with some furnishings brought in. The well-lit and comfortable rooms have panelling, painted white or blue-green, combined with lively and colourful fabrics and wallpapers produced by Morris & Co. Most of the contents were made for Standen, or for the Beales other house in London and are by the leading artists, craftsmen or craft firms of the 1890s. There is metal work by W.A.S. Benson, pottery by William de Morgan, furniture by Morris & Co, Heals and Collinson & Lock. All the main rooms on the ground floor are shown and two first floor bedrooms. Visitors make their own way round the rooms, which are partly roped-off. The service wing of the house has been converted into private flats, but its delightful inner courtyard can be seen from the entrance. The steeply-sloping gardens, partly laid out by E.B. Simpson and partly by Philip Webb, are beautifully maintained and offer dramatic views across the Medway valley and the newly-formed reservoir.

Opening times: April to end Oct, Wed, Thurs and Sat 2–5.30. Closed Good Friday and Bank Holidays.

Standen, West Sussex .

Entrance charges: House and garden £1.00; children 5–16 50p. Garden only 40p.

Wheelchair access: Two separate steps into the house, thereafter all ground floor rooms are accessible except the conservatory. It is also possible to see much of the garden, but some of the paths are steep.

Guidebook: i) An excellent guide with plans of ground and first floor and a very informative account of the house and its architect with a room-by-room commentary. ii) A room-by-room guide is loaned at the door but must be returned.

Catering: None.

WCs: In part of the old service wing; no special facilities for wheelchairs.

Shop: Small shop with a few of the usual National Trust items and some extra items relating to William Morris and Victorian arts and crafts.

UPPARK South Harting, nr Petersfield (The National Trust)
Tel: Harting (073 085) 317 and 458
Directions: 5 miles S.E. of Petersfield on the B2146, 1½ miles S. of South Harting

The steepness of the road rising to Uppark quickly explains the name of the house, which has a remote and beautiful setting on the Downs. It was built in the 1690s for Lord Tankerville to designs by William Talman and has the rather Dutch appearance typical of its date. The two storey red brick body of the house is covered by a steep hipped roof with wide over-hanging eaves and a bold cornice. The main entrance was moved from the east to the north side in 1810 by Humphrey Repton, who also designed the Doric colonnade on this front. In 1747 the house was bought by Sir Matthew Featherstonhaugh, who modernised the decoration of the rooms, leaving only the hall, staircase and dining room in their original state. The paintings and furniture are largely those collected by Sir Matthew and his son Sir Harry. English mid-18th century furniture is combined with the Italian and Netherlandish paintings favoured at this time. Visitors follow a set route through the ground floor rooms, ending with a lobby which contains a very fine dolls' house of the 1720s, properly furnished in the early Georgian taste. A number of rooms in the basement have been arranged as they would have been in the 19th century. Sarah Wells (mother of the writer H.G. Wells) was housekeeper here from 1880 to 1893 and he wrote vividly of the life below stairs. Uppark has been called 'The Sleeping Beauty House' because for much of the last century it was owned by two sisters who altered nothing, but the house has also known riotous times and Nelson's Emma Hamilton is said to have danced on the dining room table. One of the memorable features of Uppark is the rough grassland sloping away from the front towards the south, and the magnificent view of the Channel. The park is not open but the garden is accessible, and one of the two 18th century pavilions by James Paine serves as the tea room.

Opening times: April to end Sept, Wed, Thurs, Sun and Bank Holiday Mon 2–6. All visitors guided on Wed except in Aug.

Entrance charges: £1.30; children 75p; no dogs.

Parking: Free car park near the entrance to the garden.
Wheelchair access: Only the ground floor rooms are accessible, these have most of the paintings and furniture.
Guidebook: History and room-by-room guide with plans of both ground floor and basement, but very short on illustrations.
Catering: A huge tea room serving reliable teas.
WCs: In an outbuilding some distance from car park and house; no facilities for wheelchairs.
Shop: One of the basement rooms has a standard National Trust shop with a decent selection of souvenirs.

Tyne and Wear

HYLTON CASTLE (Ancient Monument)
Directions: 3 miles W. of the centre of Sunderland, by the side of the A1290

Hylton Castle stands as a monument to the vicissitudes of the English country residence. The Hyltons were prominent landowners in this area from the mid-12th century and the present castle was built in about 1400 by Sir William Hylton. It is in the form of a hugely enlarged gatehouse and, although there were other buildings on the site, the castle itself contained all the rooms necessary for the Baron's family. The castle was held by the family for the next three and a half centuries and was considerably altered to suit changing tastes. In the early 18th century a large wing was added on either side of the main building and the interior was gutted and refurbished. In 1746 the Hylton line died out, the estate was split up and the buildings were left to deteriorate. They were rescued in the 1860s, at the price of the demolition of both wings and the transformation of the old mediaeval core into a very domesticated castle. The present building represents the Department of the Environment's attempt to salvage as much as possible from the dilapidated remains of this last version of the castle. The outer walls still stand to their full height and the shell of a chapel stands nearby.

Opening times: Open at all reasonable times.
Entrance charges: Free.
Parking: Free parking near the castle.
Wheelchair access: No major problems.
Guidebook: A recent work with plans and photographs; given the state of the building a guidebook is essential.
Catering: None.
WCs: None.
Shop: None.

WASHINGTON OLD HALL Washington Village, Washington New
   Town, District 4 (The National Trust)
Tel: Washington (0632) 466879
Directions: Washington is 6 miles S. of Newcastle; from the A1 take the
   A1231 and follow signs for Washington New Town, District 4

Washington Old Hall is a small stone manor house, rebuilt in the 17th
century, but incorporating some elements of the original mediaeval
structure. Its particular interest lies in its historical associations, as it was
once owned by George Washington's ancestors and gave them their family
name. The house was in a bad way in the 1930s and its present state is due
to careful restoration carried out by the National Trust. Consequently,
although they are very fine, none of the interior fittings properly belongs to
the house. The restored part consists of the entire ground floor, kitchen,
hall and drawing room, and one first floor bedroom. The hall is a long low
room with a stone flagged floor. It is furnished with carved 17th century
pieces and some appropriate paintings on loan from the Bowes Museum.
There are also two 18th century portraits of Washington. The kitchen has a
working spit mechanism and various typical utensils. The most attractive
feature of the house is the drawing room, which has been provided with
17th century oak panelling giving it a quiet, soothing atmosphere. The
furnishings include a 17th century needlework box and an Elizabethan
splay-fronted court cupboard; the fireplace is surrounded by some
outstanding decorative carving.

Opening times: March to end Oct, daily except Wed 1–6; Nov to end Feb, Sat and Sun 2–4.
Entrance charges: 60p; children 30p.
Parking: Car park in grounds.
Wheelchair access: Four steps up to the front door, the ground floor rooms are on the level.
Guidebook: An informative text with black and white illustrations and a plan.
Catering: Tea, coffee and soft drinks in the church next door.
WCs: In the house; unsuitable for wheelchairs.
Shop: A new National Trust shop in the gatekeeper's cottage opened in July 1981.

Warwickshire

ARBURY HALL Windmill Hill, Astley (H. Fitzroy Newdegate Esq)
Tel: Nuneaton (0682) 347478 or Fillongley (0676) 40529
Directions: 2 miles S.W. of Nuneaton, signposted off the B4102

Arbury Hall was built as an Elizabethan courtyard house in 1580 and has
since undergone some spectacular alterations. In the 1670s rather grand

Arbury Hall, Warwickshire

brick stables were added by Sir Richard Newdigate, who consulted Sir Christopher Wren on the design of the stable porch and employed Edward Martin, a plasterer who had worked on Wren's churches in the City of London, to redecorate the chapel in the house. More extensive alterations were made in the 18th century. Sir Roger Newdigate, who was something of a connoisseur, an amateur architect and the founder of the Newdigate Poetry Prize at Oxford, transformed his family home with the assistance of his friend Sanderson Miller and a succession of architects including William Hiorne, Henry Keene and Thomas Couchman. Sir Roger admired the Gothic style and both the exterior and interior were refashioned in a late Perpendicular Gothic copied from such buildings as Henry VII's chapel in Westminster Abbey and the Divinity Schools at Oxford. The work was started in 1748 and continued until Sir Roger's death in 1806. The exterior is a little bleak, especially the entrance front, but the rooms inside have some of the finest 18th century Gothic plasterwork in England. The guided tours, which start every half and hour and last about an hour, take in all the most spectacular rooms, notably the saloon, the dining room, the drawing room and the chapel of 1674. A selection of documents relating to the house is shown in the first-floor long gallery. Among the interesting furniture is a suite embroidered in the 18th century with designs said to show the objects left about by an untidy wife, a very fine cabinet in the saloon with the arms of Archbishop Laud, which may have been made by Adam Browne, and a fine group of 16th century portraits. The grounds were landscaped by Sir Roger with the advice of Sanderson Miller. Two rose gardens and a rock garden have been added since, and two large bay windows from the Elizabethan house have been built into the garden wall to the west of the house, near the lake. The novelist George Eliot was born on the Arbury estate, where her father was the agent, and the house is described in some of her books.

Opening times: Easter Sun to 3 Oct, Sun and Bank Holiday Mon 2.30–6.
Entrance charges: House and gardens £1.00. Gardens and park only 80p; children under 14 40p; no dogs. (HHA)
Parking: In a field outside the entrance gates, free.
Wheelchair access: Possible to the ground floor (most of the best rooms) but not to the tea room, which is on the first floor in the stables.
Guidebook: A scholarly work with black and white and colour illustrations, a room-by-room guide and a family tree, but no plan of the house or the park.
Catering: Good, reasonably priced home-made teas in a snug and cheerful tea room.
WCs: Under the tea room at the east end of the stables; there is another gents at the north west corner and a ladies on the lake front, west of the Tudor remains; none is suitable for wheelchairs.
Shop: Souvenirs on sale in the long gallery, plants from the nursery on sale in the walled garden.
Extras: The Pinkerton cycle collection in the stables is very interesting; there are also typewriters and sewing machines. There is a separate guidebook to the cycle collection.

CHARLECOTE PARK Wellesbourne (The National Trust)
Tel: Stratford upon Avon (0789) 840277
Directions: 5 miles E. of Stratford upon Avon, on the N. side of the B4086

Tradition has it that William Shakespeare was fined for poaching deer at Charlecote and paid back the owner of the house, Sir Thomas Lucy, by satirising him as Justice Shallow. The Lucys have been here since the 12th century and in the 1550s Shakespeare's Sir Thomas built himself a new red brick house. Of this, only the little gatehouse has survived intact; the main building was very much altered in the 1820s and 1850s. The 19th century restorers copied the Elizabethan style of the earlier work, but only the two storey entrance porch is entirely genuine. The 17th century painting of the house reproduced on the cover of the guidebook shows what changes have taken place. Five main rooms inside are shown to visitors, arranged to look as they might have done in the 1860s. The great hall, dining room and library all have rich and highly coloured decorations of about 1830 by William Willement, who is better known as a stained glass designer. There is a good collection of portraits, all numbered, and some interesting furniture. Among the most spectacular are the great table in the hall, which was purchased at the Fonthill sale in 1823, and the monstrous sideboard in the dining room carved by Willcox of Warwick in 1858. It was presented to Queen Victoria, who sensibly declined it. The ebony bedroom and the drawing room in the north wing date from the 1850s and are the work of the architect John Gibson. Visitors make their own way through the house and there are guides in each room. To the south are the outbuildings containing the kitchens, stables and brewhouse, which are all open. The gardens were laid out by 'Capability' Brown in 1760, but there has been some necessary re-planting in recent years. Both house and gardens are encircled by the Rivers Avon and Hele.

Opening times: April and Oct, Sat and Sun also every day in the week after Easter 11–5; May to end Sept, daily except Mon but open Bank Holiday Mon 11–6.
Entrance charges: House and gardens £1.50. Garden, park and kitchen only £1.00; children under 17 half price. Dogs must remain in car park.
Parking: Free parking across the road from the entrance, five mins walk from the house.
Wheelchair access: Easy access, all rooms shown are on ground floor except the Victorian kitchen. Shop and tea room also accessible.
Guidebook: A cheap leaflet with the basic information or the standard guidebook with black and white illustrations; the account of the house itself is rather confusing, but the guide is good and contains a detailed list of paintings and a plan of the grounds. There is also *Charlecote and the Lucys* with colour plates, in some ways a better buy. Leaflets in French and German are available. There is also a braille guide.
Catering: Good coffee, light lunches and teas in the orangery; self service. Picnics allowed in the park but not in the gardens.
WCs: South of the gatehouse; facilities for the disabled near the shop.
Shop: Near the Victorian kitchen, the usual National Trust range.

COUGHTON COURT   nr Alcester (The National Trust)
Tel: Alcester (0789) 762435
Directions: 2 miles N. of Alcester on the E. side of the A435 visible from
the main road

Coughton is the home of the Throckmorton family, whose members have
always been tenacious Roman Catholics. The family acquired Coughton by
marriage in 1409, rebuilt the house on four sides of a courtyard and
defended it with a moat. Of this building, only the splendid gatehouse
remains. The rough stonework of the lower storey may date from the 15th
century, the upper storeys, with corner towers and two tiers of enormous
windows, date from about 1520. The rest of the west range may be 16th
century work, but the present stucco fronts were only added in the 1830s.
The north and south ranges are less impressive than the gatehouse range;
their lower storeys are of stone, with timber-framing above. The great hall
and chapel were in the eastern range, which was destroyed by an anti-
Catholic mob in 1688. The moat was filled in shortly after. Successive
generations have made their mark on the interior. The ground floor of the
gatehouse is now the hall and has a splendid fan-vaulted ceiling. Most of the
other rooms open to visitors are on the upper floor of the house. There are
some charming little rooms within the gatehouse itself, while the dining
room and the Tribune have rich panelling, which is a mixture of 16th and
17th century work. The 16th century staircase in the saloon, was brought
from Harvington Hall near Worcester. As one might expect, there are
several curious objects connected with Roman Catholicism, including the
shift in which Mary Queen of Scots was beheaded. There are also many
family portraits, notably the painting in the drawing room of Sir Robert
Throckmorton by Largillière, the French court painter. The saloon
contains the famous 'Throckmorton Coat', made in a single day in 1811 —
starting with two sheep. Several of the rooms were redecorated in the 1950s,
but this only reinforces the sense of family continuity. Visitors may wander
round and there are guides in each room.

Opening times: April and Oct, Sat and Sun; Easter week every day except Fri; May to Sept,
  Wed,Thurs, Sat, Sun and Bank Holiday Mon and Tues 2–6.
Entrance charges: £1.10; children 55p.
Parking: Free parking in front of the house.
Wheelchair access: Not practicable to the interior, since almost all the rooms shown are on
  the upper floors.
Guidebook: An adequate architectural description, better on the gatehouse than the rest of the
  building; room-by-room guide with a complete list of the pictures and some black and white
  plates, no plan. There is also 'Coughton Court and the Throckmorton Story' which is much
  better illustrated and contains a chatty but well-written account of the family. There is also
  a braille guide.
Catering: A pleasant panelled tea room on the ground floor with waitress service.
WCs: Next to the tea room; not adapted for wheelchairs.
Shop: Sells National Trust products only.

Extras: On Saturdays and Sundays an art gallery in the stable shows contemporary works; a small admission charge is made.

FARNBOROUGH HALL nr Banbury (The National Trust)
Tel: Farnborough (029 589) 202
Directions: 6 miles N. of Banbury, ½ mile W. of the A423

Farnborough is a small and pleasant house of dark honey-coloured ironstone. The west front dates from the late 17th or early 18th century but the rest of the building was remodelled between 1745 and 1755 for William Holbech. The name of his architect is not known, but he may have had advice from Sanderson Miller, a local gentleman and amateur architect who is better known for his Gothick fantasies than his classical buildings. The main interest of the interior lies not in the furnishings but in the very fine plasterwork decoration in the hall and dining room. The work is in the rococo style and was probably carried out by William Perritt, a plasterer from York. The other rooms on view are the staircase (belonging to the earlier part of the house but largely reconstructed after a fire in 1920) and the library which has an early 19th century atmosphere, and was repapered in 1960. There is a splendid walk to be had to the south-east of the house, along the Great Terrace, which was probably made in the 1740s. The east side is lined with beech trees and there are a couple of pavilions set amongst them. To the west is a dramatic drop down the escarpment to the river, with wide views across the Warwickshire plain.

Opening times: April to end Sept, Wed and Sat 2–6.
Entrance charges: House and grounds £1.00. Grounds only 60p; children half price. Dogs in grounds only on leads.
Parking: By the stableyard.
Wheelchair access: Possible to all interior rooms but access is via a gravelled drive.
Guidebook: A temporary booklet with brief history and descriptions on the decorations.
Catering: None, and no picnics.
WCs: Behind a blue door on the W. of the garden front; facilities for wheelchairs.
Shop: None.

HONINGTON HALL nr Shipston on Stour (Major Sir John Wiggin Bt)
Tel: Shipston on Stour (0608) 61434
Directions: 8 miles E. of Stratford upon Avon, 1 mile N. of Shipston on Stour, on the E. side of the A34

After the dreadful A34, Honington is a blessed relief; the village is tranquil and the comfortable red brick house is a gem of late 17th century architecture. It was built in 1682 for the rich London merchant Sir Henry Parker, on the site of an earlier house whose stables and dovecote survive on the north side of the present building. The drive leads to the main east front, seven windows wide, whose broad proportions and tall roof form a copybook example of the English style of the 1680s, enlivened in this case with busts of Roman emperors over the ground floor windows. Visitors enter by the north door, with its fine shell hood, which is known as the Magistrate's Entrance. The interior is a magnificent surprise. In 1737 Honington was bought from the Parkers by Joseph Townsend, who remodelled the house. The entrance hall was given gorgeous stucco decoration, probably by Charles Stanley, and similar decoration appears on the stairway. Under the direction of John Freeman, an amateur architect and friend of Joseph Townsend, the original great staircase of the 1680 house was removed and replaced by a great octagonal saloon with a splendid domed ceiling and richly carved wall decoration. The elaborate plasterwork of the saloon has recently been restored and repainted. Elsewhere on the ground floor the decoration is a mixture of the 1680s and later work. The contents of Honington pale into insignificance beside the decoration. It is very much a lived-in house with wellingtons tucked behind the sofa, but there is an unusual collection of stirrup cups. There are guided tours every half hour, conducted by the owners and lasting about 30 minutes. Much attention is given to the recent restoration work. The garden was also improved for Joseph Townsend in the 1740s and 1750s with the advice of Sanderson Miller, but its elaborate arrangements and garden buildings have mostly gone. The house was originally linked by curved walls to the stables on one side and the parish church on the other; the wall to the church has been demolished but the building itself is a charming work of the 1680s with some good monuments.

Opening times: May to Sept Wed and Bank Holiday Mon 2.30–5.30.
Entrance charges: £1.00; children 50p; no dogs. (HHA)
Parking: In the stableyard beside the house, free.
Wheelchair access: Possible to all ground floor rooms, apply for entrance by the front door.
Guidebook: A very good and inexpensive little leaflet with history, description and plans of the house both before and after the 1750 alterations.
Catering: None, and no picnics allowed.
WCs: Yes.
Shop: None.

KENILWORTH CASTLE   Kenilworth (Ancient Monument)
Tel: Kenilworth (0926) 52078
Directions: Kenilworth is 4 miles N. of Warwick; the castle stands on the N.E. side of the town off the B4103

The spectacular great lake, half a mile wide, which defended the south and west sides of the castle has been dry for 300 years and the buildings are mostly in ruins, but Kenilworth is still one of the grandest castles in the kingdom. It is best to enter from the south, across the causeway which once held back the lake, and through Mortimer's tower. The outer walls mostly date from about 1205, but the impressive group of deep pink sandstone buildings at the centre of the castle are of three different periods. The massive keep, with its square corner turrets and splayed base, was built in about 1180 and is the oldest surviving part, although the windows were modernised in the 16th century. Curving round from the keep is a group of buildings erected for John of Gaunt in 1390. At the centre of the group is the ruined great hall with magnificent traceried windows and moulded panels rising the full height of the building. The floor and roof have both gone, but there is enough left to conjure up one of the finest rooms in 15th century England. In 1563 Kenilworth passed to Robert Dudley, Earl of Leicester and favourite of Queen Elizabeth I. He treated the castle like a great Elizabethan house and built a block of grand apartments for distinguished visitors, now called Leicester's Building, next to John of Gaunt's buildings. He also made a grand new gatehouse on the town side of the castle, which was turned into a private house in the 17th century and is now the custodian's house; near the gatehouse he built a long stable block with a pretty upper storey of brick and ornamental timberwork. Queen Elizabeth came often to Kenilworth and Sir Walter Scott's novel of that name paints a vivid picture of her visit in 1575, when she stayed for 19 days of continuous entertainment.

Opening times: Standard hours (SM), see page xii.
Entrance charges: 50p; children and OAPs 25p.
Parking: Two car parks, one by Leicester's gatehouse on the N., the other to the S.
Wheelchair access: Ramps make most of the castle accessible.
Guidebook: A cheap basic leaflet with a plan; a scholarly Official Handbook with a full history, description and plan, and a souvenir guidebook with the basic information and many photos and drawings and plans which bring the castle vividly to life.
Catering: None, but picnics allowed, and there are tea shops in Castle Hill.
WCs: By Leicester's gatehouse; unsuitable for wheelchairs.
Shop: Some booklets and souvenirs on sale at the two ticket kiosks.

MARY ARDEN'S HOUSE Wilmcote, nr Stratford upon Avon (The Shakespeare Birthplace Trust)
Tel: Stratford upon Avon (0789) 293455
Directions: Wilmcote village is 3 miles N.W. of Stratford upon Avon, off the A34

Shakespeare's mother was a Mary Arden and her family owned this building. It is an attractive timber-framed farmhouse of the early 16th century with herringbone struts on the wing to one side. The plan is the usual one of the time, with a screens passage from front to back, dividing the kitchen from the hall or main living room, which was originally open to the full height of the roof. A floor was later inserted to give two storeys. The rooms are furnished with 16th and 17th century pieces. The farm here was still working in 1930 and there is a fine range of outbuildings of the same age as the house. These now contain a large and fascinating collection of objects connected with farming and rural life; it is a pity that there is not more information about them.

Opening times: Nov to March, weekdays 9–12.45, 2–4, Sun closed; April to Oct, weekdays 9–6, Sun 2–6.
Entrance charges: 50p; children 20p; inclusive ticket to five Shakespeare Trust properties £2.00; children 80p. No dogs.
Parking: Free parking next to the house.
Wheelchair access: Possible to ground floor rooms.
Guidebook: Yes, 30p.
Catering: None.
WCs: In the farmyard; not suitable for wheelchairs.
Shop: Souvenir shop with a rather fuller stock than the other Shakespeare Trust properties, and an emphasis on rural matters.

PACKWOOD HOUSE Hockley Heath (The National Trust)
Tel: Lapworth (056 43) 2024
Directions: 11 miles S.E. of Birmingham centre, 2 miles E. of Hockley Heath, signed from the A34

Packwood is famous for its topiary garden, in which a large number of clipped yews are said to represent the Sermon on the Mount. The house is a tall timber-framed building of about 1560, now rendered and pleasantly overgrown with creeper. On the north side of the entrance court is a range of red brick outbuildings of about 1660 with patterned brickwork. From the 15th century until 1869 the house was owned by the Fetherston family. General Ireton is said to have slept here in the Civil War and King Charles was given refreshment after losing the ba⁺tle of Worcester. The house was considerably altered during the 19th century and had become rundown when it was acquired in 1905 by Mr Alfred Ash, who created the present 'Great Hall' out of a cruck-framed barn. Between 1925 and 1937 his son, Mr Baron Ash, set out to restore the house to as nearly as possible its Tudor form. As part of this work all sash windows were replaced by casements and the hall was given a new floor, screen and gallery. At the same time a new long gallery was made to link the house and Great Hall. The architects for this work were Wood, Kendrick and Reynolds. When the Ash family first acquired Packwood it was empty of furniture and the present contents, all collected by Mr Ash, includes some fine pieces of 17th and 18th century furniture and a notable collection of tapestries and textiles, mostly English. The garden is enclosed by old brick walls; there are bee-boles in its southern side and gazebos at the corners. Contrary to popular opinion, some of the trees forming the 'Sermon on the Mount' were not planted until the 19th century, but the topiary work is nonetheless very impressive.

Opening times: May to Sept, Wed to Sun and Bank Holiday Mon 1–6; Oct to end April, Wed, Sat, Sun and Easter Mon 2–5; closed Christmas Day, 1 Jan and Good Friday.
Entrance charges: House and garden £1.00. Garden only 65p; children half price; no

pushchairs or picnics.

Parking: Free in the stable yard.

Wheelchair access: Chairs can be lifted up three front steps, then all ground floor rooms except Great Hall accessible; part of garden accessible but not topiary garden.

Guidebook: Virtually essential as no guided tours; a decent little book with history, room-by-room description, plans and illustrations.

Catering: None.

WCs: Near the car park and also in the house; not specially adapted for wheelchairs.

Shop: No regular shop.

RAGLEY HALL nr Alcester (The Marquess of Hertford)

Tel: Alcester (0789) 762090

Directions: 8 miles W. of Stratford upon Avon, 2 miles S.W. of Alcester on the A435

Ragley Hall is a large and stately country house, with an elegant park laid out by 'Capability' Brown in 1758. The house itself was built between 1679 and 1683 for Lord Conway. It is built of local white stone with two principal storeys and slightly projecting corner pavilions in the French manner. The design for the house was made by Robert Hooke, an associate of Sir Christopher Wren. It is not clear how quickly the house was finished, and only a fragment of Hooke's decoration survives in the library. In 1750 Lord Conway was made Earl of Hertford and the following year the architect James Gibbs made several improvements to the interior of the house. He refurbished the magnificent entrance hall with elaborate plaster decoration by Giusseppi Artari. The decoration of the study and the Green Drawing Room is also Gibbs' work. Further improvements were made to the house in the 1780s by James Wyatt, who added the stately portico in the centre of the main front and designed the decoration in the Red Saloon, the Mauve Drawing Room and elsewhere. Many of these rooms have been redecorated in recent years, under the direction of Mr John Fowler, and in most cases the colours approximate to the original. Ragley seems to have had two main staircases since it was first built though the present stairs are Victorian. On one hangs an enormous modern painting by Ceri Richards while the other is being enlivened with a mural painting by Graham Rust. There is a good representative collection of paintings and furniture. All of the principal rooms are open to visitors and the guides in each one are helpful and enthusiastic. The present Marquess and his family live permanently at Ragley and the place has the atmosphere of a flourishing estate, not totally dependant on visitors. To the north of the main house is the stable block by James Wyatt and it still houses horses and carriages.

Opening times: 3 April to 3 Oct, Tues, Wed, Thurs, Sat and Sun and Bank Holiday Mon 1.30–5.30. Park opens 11, June to Aug.

Entrance charges: House, park and garden £2.00; children and OAPs £1.00. Park only £1.00; children 50p. (HHA)

Parking: Free parking in front of the house.
Wheelchair access: There is a double flight of shallow steps, thereafter all rooms would be accessible.
Guidebook: Written by the present owner, well laid out with lots of colour plates, but there is not a great deal of text. A plan would be welcome, because the layout of the house is unusual.
Catering: An airy self-service cafeteria in the old basement kitchen with a fine selection of opulent cream cakes. The licensed restaurant is open to casual visitors in July and Aug 12.30–2.30. There is also a picnic area near the lake.
WCs: Next to the cafeteria; facilities for wheelchairs.
Shop: In the basement, selling souvenirs and craft goods.
Extras: The amenities of the park include a nature trail, and a junior assault course, no extra charge for these.

STRATFORD UPON AVON: ANNE HATHAWAY'S COTTAGE
Shottery (The Shakespeare Birthplace Trust)
Tel: Stratford upon Avon (0789) 292100
Directions: Shottery is 1 mile W. of the centre of Stratford, between the A422 and A439

The 'cottage' is a large and picturesque timber-framed farmhouse with a thatched roof, which was the home of Anne Hathaway before her marriage to William Shakespeare in 1582. The core of the building dates back to the 15th century and consists of the original hall and east wing, the western part was added in about 1600. There is some original panelling in the hall, the bread oven is still attached to the kitchen, and a good deal of the furniture has been in the house since the 16th century. But the thousands of people trudging through the building each day can make it difficult to appreciate the items of interest; nothing dampens enthusiasm like a long queue. In front of the cottage is an attractive garden planted in the old style with herbs and summer flowers and there is an orchard on one side.

Opening times: Nov to March, weekdays 9–4.30, Sun 1.30–4.30; April to Oct, weekdays 9–6 (9–7 on Thurs, Sat and on all weekdays, June to Sept), Sun 10–6. Closed 24–26 Dec.
Entrance charges: 80p; children 30p; inclusive ticket to all five Trust properties £2.00; children 80p.
Parking: There is a car park beside the house. Parking is free if you have an inclusive ticket.
Wheelchair access: Not possible; difficult steps.
Guidebook: A decent illustrated booklet.
Catering: None.
WCs: Beside the shop.
Shop: Two souvenir shops selling Shakespeariana.

STRATFORD UPON AVON: HALL'S CROFT Old Town (The Shakespeare Birthplace Trust)
Tel: Stratford upon Avon (0789) 292107

For a time this substantial timber-framed house was the home of

Shakespeare's daughter Susanna and her husband John Hall, a doctor from Bedfordshire. The building probably dates from the end of the 16th century, although the upper parts may be later and there has also been quite a lot of necessary restoration in more recent times. The heavily-beamed parlour and kitchen on the ground floor and several first floor rooms are furnished with appropriate items, mostly of dark oak. In one small first floor room some colourful apothecaries' jars have been assembled to recreate a 16th century dispensary. Certain rooms in the house are used by the Festival Club and are closed to non-members but there is plenty to see. The garden was laid out with lawns and herbaceous borders in the 1950s and there is a fine old mulberry tree.

Opening times: As for Mary Arden's House, Wilmcote.
Entrance charges: 50p; children 20p; inclusive ticket to all five Trust properties £2.00; children 80p.
Parking: Street parking.
Wheelchair access: Access is possible to the ground floor rooms.
Guidebook: A small booklet with many illustrations.
Catering: Coffee and biscuits, which can be consumed in the garden.
WCs: At the back of the house; not suitable for wheelchairs.
Shop: Small souvenir shop.
Extras: Nearby is Holy Trinity church, Shakespeare's burial place.

STRATFORD UPON AVON: HARVARD HOUSE High Street (The Harvard House Memorial Trust)
Tel: Stratford upon Avon (0789) 4507

A narrow-fronted, highly ornate timber-framed house of 1596 with a good deal of carving on its front, like the Garrick Inn next door which is of about the same date. Thomas Rogers, the builder of Harvard House, was a butcher and alderman; his daughter Katherine was the mother of John Harvard, founder of the American college that bears his name. Although he was born in London and educated in Cambridge it seems that John did live in this house for a time before leaving for the New World. Inside everything is clean and bright, with a marvellous smell of polish, though the furnishing is sparse. One of the upstairs rooms contains original pilastered panelling and a crude stucco overmantel. The staircase dates from the mid-17th century. After an introductory talk visitors are left to wander at will. There is no garden.

Opening times: April to Sept, weekdays 9–1, 2–6, Sun 2–6; Oct to March weekdays only 10–1, 2–4. Closed Christmas Eve, Christmas Day, Boxing Day and New Year's Day.
Entrance charges: 40p; children 20p.
Parking: Street parking only.
Wheelchair access: Possible to the ground floor rooms.
Guidebook: A duplicated sheet with the barest facts about the history of the house and its occupants.
Catering: None.

WCs: None.
Shop: None.

STRATFORD UPON AVON: NASH'S HOUSE AND NEW PLACE
Chapel Street (The Shakespeare Birthplace Trust)
Tel: Stratford upon Avon (0789) 292325

Nash's house is a three-storey timber-framed house which belonged to Thomas Nash, the first husband of Shakespeare's grand-daughter. The street front is a modern reconstruction. Original timberwork can be seen on the side wall and in the rooms. Upstairs there is a little museum of Stratford's history, which is interesting and well laid out. Downstairs there is some pottery, pictures and furniture from the 16th and 17th centuries. Shakespeare himself lived next door at New Place, once the largest house in Stratford, and its foundations can be seen in the garden. The house was demolished in 1759 by The Rev Francis Gastrell, who got tired of being pestered by visitors; he obviously didn't have much business sense. The gardens are very attractive. There is a knot garden bordered by a pleached walk, with a topiary garden beyond and the large expanse of lawn is bordered with mature trees.

Opening times: As for Mary Arden's House, Wilmcote.
Entrance charges: 50p; children 20p; inclusive ticket to all five Shakespeare Trust properties £2.00; children 80p.
Parking: No car park, street parking only.
Wheelchair access: Possible to the ground floor rooms and the garden (though this has gravel walks).
Guidebook: A small booklet with colour illustrations, adequate.
Catering: None.
WCs: Behind the house; not suitable for wheelchairs.

STRATFORD UPON AVON: SHAKESPEARE'S BIRTHPLACE
Henley Street (The Shakespeare Birthplace Trust)
Tel: Stratford upon Avon (0789) 4016

The Birthplace consists of two modest timber-framed houses which were once part of a longer row. Shakespeare's father carried on his business as a glover and wool merchant in the eastern house and his son is said to have been born in the western house. Strictly-speaking, there is no proof that the eastern house had been built by 1564 when William Shakespeare was born. In 1858 both houses were restored to their supposed original appearance and there have been other restorations. The rooms inside contain the sort of furniture which might have been found in a 16th century tradesman's house and a museum in the eastern building traces the development of interest in Shakespeare's life and work. The Birthplace is, of course, the centre of the Shakespeare industry and often uncomfortably crowded. Entrance is by way of the large new Shakespeare Centre, where there are usually exhibitions (for which a charge is made). The small Birthplace garden is planted with flowers mentioned in Shakespeare's works.

Opening times: Nov to March weekdays 9–4.30, Sun 1.30–4.30; April to Oct, weekdays 9–6 (9–7 on Thurs and Sat and on all weekdays, June to Sept), Sun 10–6. Closed 24–26 Dec.

Entrance charges: 90p; children 30p; inclusive ticket to all five Shakespeare Trust properties £2.00; children 80p. No dogs.

Parking: Street parking is difficult. There is a multi-storey car park nearby.

Wheelchair access: Not permitted.

Guidebook: An illustrated booklet (which does not actually mention Shakespeare's date of birth) only in English.

Catering: None.

WCs: Near the house. Passable.

Shop: Two shops selling all kinds of Shakespeare souvenirs and his works.

UPTON HOUSE Edge Hill (The National Trust)
Tel: Edge Hill (029 587) 266
Directions: 7 miles N.W. of Banbury on the A422

The contents of Upton are more remarkable than the house. At the core of the building is a house built for Sir Rushout Cullen in 1695 by an unknown architect. In 1927 it was bought by the Second Lord Bearsted, son of the founder of the Shell Corporation and a great art collector. His architect, Percy Morley Horder, greatly extended the house and completely remodelled the interior so that nothing of the 17th century remains except the staircase. The inside of the house has the atmosphere of a grand Bond Street art gallery. There is a set of 16th century Brussels tapestries, some 18th century furniture and a very good collection of English porcelain figures, including Chelsea pieces of the 'gold anchor' period, and much fine continental porcelain. There is also a large collection of Old Master paintings, including works by El Greco, Rembrandt and Bosch, and some very good English pictures by Hogarth, Reynolds, Devis and others. The guided tours start every half hour and last about an hour, but even so there is very little time to look at all the exhibits. The garden contains a delightful surprise; at the end of the lawn the ground suddenly and unexpectedly drops away to reveal a natural coombe. A stone stair leads down through borders and rose gardens to more gardens and a formal pond in the valley.

Opening times: April to end Sept, Mon, Tues, Wed and Thurs and weekends of 8–9, 15–16 May, 31 July–1 Aug, 7–8, 14–15, 21–22 Aug, and all Bank Holiday Mon, 2–6; last admission to house 5.30. No guided tours at weekends or on Bank Holidays.

Entrance charges: House and gardens £1.50; children under 16 70p. Gardens only 70p and 40p. Dogs must be on lead. No photography.

Parking: In front of the house, free.

Wheelchair access: There are five steps to the ground floor; the picture gallery on the lower ground floor is down two flights of stairs.

Guidebook: A history of the house and a guide to the main contents room-by-room, but no

plan. There are separate and more detailed catalogues of both pictures and porcelain.
Catering: None, and no picnics.
WCs: There are facilities for wheelchair users, besides the usual lavatories.
Shop: None, but flowers and plants on sale in nursery garden.

WARWICK CASTLE   Warwick (Madame Tussauds Ltd)
Tel: Warwick (0926) 49421

Warwick Castle is sited on a slope overlooking the River Avon and seen from across the river it is splendidly romantic. The mediaeval fortifications are well-preserved and the landscaped setting is attractive. At one end of the present buildings is the earth mound, made in 1068 for the first wooden castle, but most of the walls and towers are later than this; the greatest building period was the 14th century. The entrance is by the clock tower with its double portcullis and murder-holes. On either side are tall towers, the twelve-sided Guy's Tower and the odd-shaped Caesar's Tower. Guy's Tower may be climbed and makes a good vantage point to see the castle layout. The domestic range on the south side is a mixture of many dates and styles. Most of the basement dates from the 14th century, as do the walls of the great hall, but the state rooms were re-modelled for the Fourth Lord Brooke in the 1670s by William and Roger Hurlbutt. The Great Dining Room was added in the 1760s by Timothy Lightoler and Anthony Salvin made some general alterations in the 1860s; he also rebuilt the roof of the hall after a fire in 1871. These state rooms are massively impressive. When Madame Tussaud's bought the castle from Lord Brooke in 1978 they also acquired most of the paintings, tapestries and other furnishings which have been left as they were. The private apartments have been closed since the sale, but are scheduled to re-open in April 1982 with a re-creation of a house party of the 1890s. Visitors may wander pretty freely in the castle, following a set route in the state apartments, and exploring the various towers which are also open. The armoury has a collection of material from the Middle Ages to the 17th century, there is also a torture museum and various rooms in the clock tower and barbican contain other historical displays about the mediaeval Earls of Warwick. The gardens, landscaped by 'Capability' Brown, afford pretty walks and the conservatory now houses a 'spectacle' entitled 'The Bear's Quest for the Ragged Staff'. Perhaps it should be added that the management sets out to attract large numbers of visitors.

Opening times: 1 March to 31 Oct, daily 10–5.30; 1 Nov to 29 Feb, daily 10–4.30.
Entrance charges: (1981) £2.35; OAPs and children under 15 £1.20; family ticket (2 adults and up to 3 children) £6.95; no dogs in castle or grounds.
Parking: Large free car park with access off the Stratford Road; pay car park in Castle Lane.
Wheelchair access: To the gardens only.
Guidebook: Large and well-illustrated, but not easy to follow, and without any kind of plan. A free leaflet is, however, issued to each visitor with a bird's eye view of the castle layout.

Catering: Licensed restaurant in the servants' hall serving reasonably-priced set lunches 12–2 and snacks and teas 10–12 and 2.30–5.30.
WCs: At the stable entrance, next to the restaurant and next to the conservatory; facilities at stables and conservatory for wheelchair users.
Shop: There are several souvenir shops.

Wiltshire

AVEBURY MANOR Avebury (D. Nevill-Gliddon Esq)
Tel: Avebury (067 23) 203
Directions: 6 miles W. of Marlborough, 10 miles S. of Swindon on the A361, in the village of Avebury

The manor house is on the edge of one of the largest prehistoric stone circles in Europe. It was built on the site of a monastery in about 1550 and has been altered and extended several times. The result is a pleasant and thoroughly domestic building. The south range, which contains the great hall and great chamber, was added in 1601. It has a nearly regular front with mullion and transom windows and a classical entrance porch, which is a 20th century addition. The visitors' entrance is in the east front, with the end of the south range on the left and the rough stone walls and steep gables of the oldest part of the house on the right. The rooms are a mixture of 16th, 17th and 18th century work. The visit starts with the earliest, the Elizabethan Little Parlour. Elsewhere the Great Parlour and the Elizabethan Bedroom are panelled, with original chimneypieces and moulded plaster ceilings. The staircase and the Cavalier Bedroom are both 17th century work. The great hall and the Queen Anne bedroom were redecorated in the 18th century and their heavy classical ornament combines oddly with the mullioned windows of an earlier time. The house contains some good furniture of assorted dates. Visitors are free to wander round the house at their own speed but the larger part of most rooms are roped off and circulation space is restricted. Information about the contents of each room is given on display boards. Outside there is a series of small enclosed gardens, with some topiary work.

Opening times: 1 April to 31 Oct, daily Mon to Fri 11.30–6.30, Sat and Bank Holiday 11.30–7.30, Sun 1.30–6.30.
Entrance charges: £1.00; children under 16 50p; no dogs. (HHA)
Parking: No car park at the house; free car park in the village, but quite a way from the house.
Wheelchair access: Possible to gardens and ground floor only; space is restricted and the house gets crowded, it would be sensible to telephone in advance.
Guidebook: Informative history of the manor and its occupants with a rudimentary room by room guide; there are colour photographs and a plan.
Catering: None at the house, though there is a tea room nearby.
WCs: None at the house; facilities in the village.
Shop: None.

BOWOOD   nr Calne (The Earl of Sherburne)
Tel: Calne (0249) 812102
Directions: Between Chippenham and Calne on the S. side of the A4; take the Derry Hill turning, the house is well-signposted thereafter

It may seem odd to include Bowood since the great house here was demolished in 1955, but the family have always used the 'Little House' along one side of the stable block as an alternative home and there is as much to see as in many other houses. Most of the rooms open to visitors are in the south range, designed by Robert Adam and built as a screen of elegant greenhouses to conceal the outbuildings from the splendid landscaped park. In 1821 the architect C.R. Cockerell added a chapel behind the greenhouses and converted the east end of the range to serve as a library for the Little House; the remainder of the range was converted into a picture gallery. The gallery is a long, light, stone-flagged room with a changing display of Old Master and 19th century paintings. Opening off it are the small room where Dr Joseph Priestly discovered Oxygen in 1774, the chapel, and a new sculpture gallery which has been formed in a building which once housed stables and groom's quarters. New exhibition rooms upstairs contain a rich collection of family heirlooms including the Albanian costume once worn by Lord Byron and a collection of Indian silver caskets. In front of the south range is a formal terraced garden, and beyond it is the superb park, laid out with advice from the Hon C. Hamilton of Pain's Hill, 'Capability' Brown and Humphrey Repton. It was once said that the park at Bowood managed to combine the sublime, the picturesque and the beautiful. At some distance from the house is the stern and noble family mausoleum, designed by Robert Adam and completed in 1765. The part of the garden in which the mausoleum stands is open open to visitors in the early summer, when the rhododendrons are in bloom, and has a separate entrance.

Opening times: Picture gallery, chapel and gardens, Good Friday to 30 Sept, Tues to Sat 2–6, Sun and Bank Holidays 12–6. Rhododendron walks, mid-May to end June.
Entrance charges: Gallery, chapel and gardens £1.30; OAPs and children 70p; no dogs. Rhododendron walks 50p; OAPs and children 25p. (HHA)
Parking: Large free car park on grass, outside the entrance to the gardens.
Wheelchair access: Ramp down to the terrace giving access to the rooms, which are all on the level, but the house is some distance from the car park. The tea room and shop are also accessible by the same route.
Guidebook: Colour photos and a clear commentary about house, grounds and family; there is a plan of the grounds with an outline plan of the house. There is also a separate list giving details of the paintings and one concerned with the landscape planting.
Catering: The 'Bowood Restaurant' in the house serving lunch and tea. The Garden Tea Room in the grounds has an enclosed lawn and 'ranch-style' tables and chairs; self-service.
WCs: Adjacent to both refreshment rooms. There are facilities for wheelchair-users next to the shop.
Shop: Near the tea-room; a fair selection of souvenirs.

*Extras:*Adventure Playground for use of under 14s near the house; small children may be accompanied by an adult, and would need to be as the climbing involved is strenuous.

CHALCOT HOUSE nr Westbury (Mr and Mrs Anthony Rudd)
Tel: Chapmanslade (037 388) 466
Directions: 2 miles W. of Westbury off the A3098, minimal signposting

Romano-British relics have been turned up in the park at Chalcot and the date of the earliest house here is uncertain. The present house has an attractive classical front of red brick and stone which must date from about 1680. The urn above the door and the three panels in the attic storey look rather later in date and it is possible that the front was altered in the 18th century. An extensive restoration of the house was carried out in 1872 by the Cornish architect St Aubyn, who also added a large rear wing. Most of his work was removed in 1971 when the house was completely refurbished by the architect Theo Crosby to make it into a comfortable modern home. Visitors are conducted through the whole house by the owner. The ballroom has elegantly restored plaster decoration; there is some good quality 18th and 19th century furniture and a collection of modern English paintings.

Opening times: Aug, daily 2–5.
Entrance charges: 75p, which includes a leaflet about the building. (HHA)
Parking: Free, next to the house.
Wheelchair access: Only to main rooms on ground floor, but it would be possible to see the south front.
Guidebook: The free leaflet contains an adequate account of the house with the bare historical facts and information about the restoration.
Catering: None.
WCs: None for public use.
Shop: None.

CORSHAM COURT Corsham (Lord Methuen)
Tel: Corsham (0249) 712214
Directions: Corsham lies just S. of the A4, 8 miles N.E. of Bath and 4 miles S.W. of Chippenham

From the entrance gates, the Court looks like a large Elizabethan house of yellow stone with a central tower poking up above the roofline. The central part of the house is indeed of 1582. Paul Methuen bought the house in 1745 and during the 1760s he employed 'Capability' Brown on the house, the gardens and the park. Brown added the outer bay on each side of the entrance front and formed a suite of state rooms in the east wing. Further changes were made in 1800 by the architect John Nash, but little of his work has survived. His gothic entrance hall and north front were completely replaced in 1845 by Thomas Bellamy, who was also responsible for the central tower. All that remains of Nash's work is some decoration on the east front, a dairy and a picturesque cottage on the far side of the lake. Visitors may wander through Bellamy's entrance hall, music room and dining room, and Brown's splendid state rooms. The picture gallery is particularly fine, with its coved and coffered ceiling, with plasterwork by Thomas Stocking and fireplace by Scheemakers. The state rooms were designed to hold Paul Methuen's collection of paintings. The collection, which includes two huge Van Dycks, is still virtually complete and many of the paintings have hung in the same place for over two hundred years. The state room furniture includes some elegant mirrors by the Adam brothers, a commode by John Cobb and other pieces of interest. The Dining Room contains two delightful portraits by Reynolds of Paul Methuen's children. Sadly, 'Capability' Brown and Humphrey Repton's work in the park and gardens has suffered from storms and Dutch Elm disease, but has been re-planted. There is a bath house by Brown and one mile away, by the North Walk, is a rustic dry arch.

Opening times: All year (except 15 Dec–15 Jan) Tues, Wed, Thurs, Sat, Sun and Bank Holiday Mon 2–4 (June, Sept and Bank Holidays 2–6).
Entrance charges: House and gardens £1.20; children 60p. Gardens only 50p and 20p. (HHA)
Parking: Free parking outside the main gate.
Wheelchair access: Four shallow steps to front entrance; all rooms open to the public are on the level.
Guidebook: An expensive and glossy updating of the earlier guidebook with a readable account of the house and family, information about the furniture and a room-by-room guide to some of the pictures. A full catalogue of the paintings and a catalogue of the miniature paintings also on sale. Guidebooks also available in French and German.
Catering: None.
WCs: Next to the ticket desk; unsuitable for wheelchairs.
Shop: None, but postcards and slides are sold at the ticket desk.

GREAT CHALFIELD MANOR   Great Chalfield (The National Trust)
Directions: 2½ miles N.E. of Bradford on Avon on the N. side of the A3053 to Melksham

The manor house and its outbuildings together with the church of All Saints form a very pretty group of mellow stone buildings. Thomas Tropnell acquired the property in 1467 after long legal proceedings. Between 1467 and 1488 he rebuilt the manor house round a courtyard. The south range has disappeared but the north front has probably altered very little in appearance since it was first built. The central hall and the two gabled cross wings with their oriel windows (to the north bedroom and the solar) make a remarkably symmetrical facade for this date, which is enlivened by the carved stone figures perching on the gable-ends. The manor is entered through the original front door, which leads into the screens passage, with a

20th century copy of the original screen. The hall itself is overlooked by three spy windows concealed behind very unusual stone masks. It seems likely that the hall was never used by the family at mealtimes; across the screens passage is a separate eating room which may be the earliest separate dining room in any English house. The staircases to the solar and north bedroom are modern. Most of the roof timbers over the north bedroom are original though the shape of the room itself has been altered. The solar was in such a poor state of repair at the beginning of this century that it was completely rebuilt, apart from the north wall containing the oriel window. Other restoration work was carried out at the same time by Sir Harold Brakespear, who was able to make use of drawings made in 1837 when the building was still unaltered. The guided tours of the house take about 30 minutes. Much of the excellent furniture in the rooms was donated by the present occupiers.

Opening times: 21 April to 29 Sept, Wed 12–1, 2–5; guided tours at 12.15, 2.15, 3.00, 3.45 and 4.30. Historical and other societies can visit on other days by arrangement.
Entrance charges: £1.00; no reductions.
Parking: Free, outside main entrance.
Wheelchair access: No access to the interior.
Guidebook: A new and improved guide which includes a plan of the building.
Catering: None.
WCs: None.
Shop: None.

LACOCK ABBEY Lacock (The National Trust)
Directions: 3 miles S. of Chippenham off the A350 Melksham road on the edge of Lacock

Seen across the park, Lacock Abbey looks like an 18th century Gothick house and the 18th century atmosphere is heightened by the entrance arch and the sweep of the drive, but the building has a much longer history. It was originally an Augustinian nunnery, which was founded in 1229 and flourished until its suppression in 1539. In the following year the estate and the buildings came into the possession of William Sharington, whose descendants have lived here ever since. Sharington demolished the nuns' church, but kept the mediaeval cloister and the buildings round it; his alterations were largely confined to the first floor, where the living accommodation is still, above the original ground floor rooms of the nunnery. Among the most conspicuous of his alterations was the addition of the octagonal tower at the south east corner and the building of the large stable court to the north. In the mid-18th century, the gentleman architect Sanderson Miller was called in by John Ivory Talbot to improve the old house and the splendid Gothick entrance hall is Miller's work. Visitors have the free run of the gardens, the stable court (including the interior of the brewery with its original fittings) the empty rooms round the fine mediaeval cloister and most of the main rooms on the first floor of the house, where information boards about the contents of each room are available. The plans in the guidebook are invaluable for working out how the house and the nunnery fit together. One of the windows on the south front was the subject of one of the first photographs in the world, taken by William Henry Fox Talbot in 1835, and the Fox Talbot Museum of the History of Photography has been established in a converted barn near the entrance to the Abbey. The extremely pretty village of Lacock is wholly owned by the National Trust and attracts very large numbers of visitors in the summer.

Opening times: April to end Oct, daily except Tues and Good Friday 2–6; Nov to March closed.

Entrance charges: House, cloisters and grounds £1.30; children 65p. Grounds and cloisters only 70p.

Parking: Small parking area in front of main gates (about 200 yards from the house), also free public car park immediately opposite.

Wheelchair access: Cars of wheelchair users may park in stable court next to house. 16 steps to hall and further steps inside, but only two steps to the cloisters. There is direct access to part of the photography museum in the village.

Guidebook: An excellent National Trust guide with plans, photographs and a full history of the building and its owners. There is also a leaflet about Fox Talbot's work at Lacock and a guidebook to the village.

Catering: None at the house. There is a reasonable National Trust tea room next to the car park and more expensive set teas can be found in the village.

WCs: At the Abbey or in the car park; both with access for wheelchair users.

Shop: None at the Abbey, but there is a National Trust standard shop in the village.

Extras: For those interested in barns, the tithe barn in the village is usually open free of charge. The Fox Talbot Museum (which is also National Trust) documents the history of photography with exhibits and a slide show; open March to Oct, daily (except Good Friday) 11–6.

LITTLECOTE HOUSE nr Hungerford (D.W. Wills Esq)

Tel: Hungerford (048 86) 2170

Directions: 3 miles W. of Hungerford to the N. of the A4, turn off at Froxfield; M4 exit 14

Littlecote is a large, long house built of brick and flint, both unusual materials for large Wiltshire houses. The outside looks all Elizabethan but at one end of the house are parts of an earlier building. The entrance front is of excellent red brick with a central porch and a regular arrangement of very large windows; those on the left light the great hall, while those on the right were built to match. The rear wall of the house is largely faced with flint and it is here that the great size of the house can best be seen. Littlecote was owned by the Darrell family from 1415 and passed to Sir John Popham in 1589; it was probably Popham who built the present entrance front. His descendants were Puritans and supported Cromwell during the Civil War. The upper walls of the great hall are still decorated with the uniforms and weapons of Cromwellian troops. The hall also has excellent oak panelling and furniture. Among the other rooms on the ground floor are the Brick Hall which has rather good panelling of the mid-17th century and the Dutch Parlour decorated with strange and slightly improper paintings. The chapel is an outstanding example of a puritan religious building; a sober, dark oak gallery runs round three sides of the whitewashed room and the place of the altar is taken by a tall pulpit. In the upstairs bedrooms, said to be haunted by the mother of a baby burnt by William Darrell, there is more panelling some some excellent 17th century crewel embroidery, while the long gallery contains family portraits and good 17th and 18th century furniture. The house is a labyrinth and guided tours are probably the best way of showing it to visitors.

Opening times: April to 30 Sept. April to June, Sat, Sun and Bank Holiday Mon 2–6; also July to Sept weekdays 2–5: last admission ½ hour before closing.
Entrance charges: £1.20; children 70p; no dogs. (HHA)
Parking: Free parking in the stableyard at the side of the house.
Wheelchair access: Possible to grounds and Roman Villa.
Guidebook: A recent well-illustrated room-by-room guide, with a bit of history and a creditable plan of the house.
Catering: The tea shop in the outbuildings is pleasantly set out with long tables; home-made cakes and tea by the cup.
WCs: Free, clean but rather cramped lavatories in the outbuildings and portaloos in the car park; unsuitable for wheelchairs.
Shop: There is a small souvenir shop selling 'local crafts'.
Extras: A short distance from the house is a complete mock Wild West town with costumed cowboys; a sign on the gate advertises 'shoot-outs every hour'; admission 80p; children 60p. In the park is an excavated Roman Villa with the well-known 'Orpheus' mosaic floor; admission 70p; children 50p.

LONGLEAT HOUSE nr Warminster (The Marquess of Bath)
Tel: Maiden Bradley (098 53) 551
Directions: 4 miles S.W. of Warminster off the A362, well-signposted

Longleat is a magnificent Elizabethan house in a park of outstanding beauty, but visitors should be warned that the estate is run as a thoroughly commercial undertaking. The house began as a small mediaeval priory. It was purchased in 1540 by Sir John Thynne, enlarged, burnt down in 1567, rebuilt on a grander scale, then almost at once re-fronted by Robert Smythson. Sir John was directly in touch with the modern architecture of the time and Longleat was one of the first English houses to have all main fronts treated in a uniform way and also one of the first to have a basement (rather than cellars). The long fronts of Bath stone combine large mullioned windows in the English tradition with ornament derived from the Continent. The exterior has changed little since Sir John's death in 1580, although the north front was rebuilt to match the others under the direction of Sir Jeffry Wyatville in about 1810. Of the rooms inside, only the great hall

Longleat House, Wiltshire

has anything like its original appearance; the massive timber hammmberbeam roof has been slightly altered and the fine carved screen dates from about 1600. The other main rooms were redecorated in the 1870s by the firm of Crace & Co, who used the Italian style, with heavy gilded ceilings of almost overpowering splendour and walls covered with richly-patterned paper or embossed leather. The three state rooms on the first floor are the most impressive, especially the dining room and drawing room whose ceilings incorporate full-size 17th century oil paintings. The furniture is of equal opulence, much of it is French 18th century work. There is an impressive collection of paintings and some fine 16th century tapestries in the saloon. There are also signs of recent life in the many large photographs of present members of the Thynne family. The guided tour lasts about three-quarters of an hour and takes in the two main floors of the eastern half of the house; the famous library is not shown. The formal gardens next to the house and a large part of the park laid out by 'Capability' Brown and Humphrey Repton are freely available to visitors. The outbuildings to the west of the house now form part of a large 'entertainment complex'. Longleat is usually crowded on summer weekends.

Opening times: House and grounds all year, daily except Christmas Day, Easter to end Sept 10–6, rest of the year 10–4. Safari Park March to Oct, daily 10–6 or sunset.

Entrance charges: Park, pedestrians free; cars 50p per adult passenger to a maximum of £1.50 per car; m/cs 25p. House £1.50; OAPs and children 60p. Safari Park (hard-topped cars only) £1.60 per person; children £1.00. (Dogs must be left in kennels at entrance). (HHA)

Parking: Large free car park near the house.

Wheelchair access: Steps up to house, but once inside the ground floor rooms are on the level.

Guidebook: A glossy 'souvenir guide' with many colour illustrations and a room-by-room guide, but there is little information about the house itself or about the family.

Catering: There is a large self-service tea room and a salad bar in the basement of the house itself, a prefab pub called the Longleat Arms to the west of the house (no off-sales), a restaurant next to the pub serving a set-price meal, and a café serving fried meals.

WCs: In the basement of the house and in the stable block, where there are facilities for wheelchair users.

Shop: There are several kiosks and souvenir shops on the west side of the house, a 'kitchen shop' in the Victorian kitchens (admission charge) and a wholefood shop.

Extras: There are a number of fairground-style amusements to the west of the house. Visitors may also see the Victorian kitchens, the erotic murals painted by the present Lord Weymouth, the dolls' house, Pets' Corner, the Maze, train rides, boat trips to the gorilla island in the lake, and the famous 'Lions of Longleat' in the Safari Park. All these have their own admission charges. For those who find the attractions irresistable, there is also a caravan site near the house.

LYDIARD PARK Lydiard Tregoze (Borough of Thamesdown)
Tel: Purton (0793) 770401
Directions: 5 miles N. of Swindon, just N. of the A420, signposted locally

The drive leads past the little parish church and the back of the house, which is a mixture of forms and styles of many different dates. The main front of the house is a complete contrast; a long elegant facade of Bath stone with a small central pediment and square corner towers with pyramid roofs. This front and the south east front date from about 1743, when the house was enlarged for Viscount St John. They were added onto a much older building, whose walls were incorporated into the Georgian house. The architect is unknown, but it may have been Roger Morris. All the main rooms on the ground floor of the house are open to visitors, who make their own way round. The rooms on show comprise the main hall, library, dining room, drawing room, bedroom and a small anteroom. All these rooms were formed in the 1740s and have first-class carved and plasterwork decoration of that period, ranging from the rather stern decoration in the entrance hall to the pre-rococo work in the bedchamber. The decoration has been extensively restored since the last war, and much of it is new, but the final result is admirable. When the St John family sold the house to Swindon Corporation it was empty of furniture. The main rooms have been furnished from gifts and loans and they now contain an interesting collection of Georgian furniture. There are also a number of St John family portraits which have been purchased or borrowed for the house. The extensive park around the house is open for public enjoyment, free of charge.

Opening times: All year, daily (except Good Friday, Christmas and Boxing Day). Weekdays 10–1, 2–5.30, Sun 2–5.30.

Entrance charges: Grounds free. House 40p; OAPs and children 20p.

Parking: Free parking in the yard to one side of the house.

Wheelchair access: All rooms shown are on the ground floor and present no problem for wheelchairs.

Guidebook: A history of the St John family, a history of the house and a very readable and reliable guide, a history of the church, with colour illustrations of all three; an accurate plan of the house and a handlist of the paintings are also available at no extra charge.

Catering: A skeleton service on summer weekends.

WCs: In the car park, rather primitive, unsuitable for wheelchairs.

Shop: Souvenirs and publications.

Extras: The church next to the house is a mediaeval building containing the best collection of 17th century funeral monuments in Wiltshire, which are being restored at the present time; other good fittings include 17th century iron communion rails and some early stained glass.

MOMPESSON HOUSE SALISBURY Choristers' Green, Cathedral Close (The National Trust)

Directions: On the N. side of Choristers' Green, which is a small square in one corner of the Close

Mompesson House was built in 1701 by a member of the Mompesson family. It is a pleasant small house with a stone front and a tall hipped roof, separated from the Green by a screen of iron railings. The rooms inside have original panelling with bold mouldings and also some rather good ornamental plaster ceilings which date from the 1740s. The broad staircase also dates from the 1740s and the walls of the staircase compartment have more plaster decoration, which can be examined at extremely close quarters. The work is not as sophisticated as London work of the same period, but shows the excellence of local craftsmanship. In recent years the house and the plasterwork have been cleaned and the walls painted in something like their original colours. The rooms are not 'lived in' but the National Trust has managed to achieve a richness of atmosphere. Among the Georgian furnishings of the rooms are the best of the Turnbull collection of English 18th century drinking glasses. Visitors wander round and there are guides in each room. The attractive garden behind the house is also open to visitors.

Opening times: April to end Oct, Mon, Tues, Wed, Sat and Sun 12.30–6; last admission 5.30.
Entrance charges: 80p; children 40p.
Parking: In the Close if you are lucky, or in one of the many car parks in the town. Parking may be difficult on Saturdays.
Wheelchair access: Possible to ground floor rooms.
Guidebook: A good one, with a tour of the house, a description of the outside, a history of the occupants and a plan of the building. There is also a typed list of the present contents of each room.
Catering: None.
WCs: None.
Shop: None at the house, though there is a National Trust shop in the High Street nearby.

NEWHOUSE Redlynch (Mr and Mrs George Jeffreys)
Tel: Downton (0725) 20055
Directions: 9 miles S. of Salisbury, 3 miles from Downton off the B3080

Newhouse stands without garden or other frivolity on one side of a grassy pasture, as if it had sprung up like a red brick mushroom. It is one of those curious houses built in an odd shape, in this case the shape of a letter Y. The central part of the house was finished by 1619, but two of the arms of the Y were extended in the mid-18th century. Newhouse was probably built as a hunting lodge by Edward Gorges of nearby Longford Castle. He seems to have had a fondness for odd plans, and Longford itself is in the shape of a triangle. Few of the furnishings at Newhouse are of museum quality; they have been acquired over the years by generations of the Eyre and Matcham families, whose descendants are still in residence. Probably the most curious item is the 'Hare' picture painted in about 1640 which shows hares treating humans as humans treat hares. One of the 18th century wings contains a very large drawing room which was lavishly fitted out by Maples in 1906 in late 17th century style; it is now very much in decay, but shows that Newhouse has had its moments of grandeur. Visitors are given free run of most of the main rooms.

Opening times: Easter Mon then 3 May to 30 Aug, Sun and Bank Holidays, also Sat in Aug 2–6.
Entrance charges: £1.00; children 50p. (HHA)

Parking: Free, next to the house.
Wheelchair access: There is a flight of steps to the front door; once in, five rooms and the staircase can be seen on the ground floor.
Guidebook: Free leaflet with each admission giving a brief history of the house and owners, and some guide to the principal contents.
Catering: None.
WCs: None.
Shop: None.

PHILLIPPS HOUSE   Dinton (The National Trust)
Directions: 9 miles W. of Salisbury on the N. (church) side of the B3089

After his marriage to an heiress, William Wyndham employed Sir Jeffrey Wyatville to design him a new house of the local Chilmark stone. It was built between 1814 and 1817 with a very plain nine-bay front with a tall central portico and a curved wing to one side containing the kitchen. Visitors now enter through the former library on the east front and are shown most of the ground floor rooms and the cellars. The rooms have kept their architectural features, though some changes have been made to the fittings. The National Trust have provided some appropriate paintings and furnishings, but most of the furniture belongs to the YWCA (which uses the house as a conference centre), and is of no interest. In a grand room at the centre of the house is the main staircase, which has a certain amount of neo-classical decoration and a circular lantern-light above. The brick cellars are interesting and contain a number of 18th and 19th century wine bottles which were found in the house. Visitors may also examine the boiler and part of a duct of one of the earliest hot air central heating systems. The former kitchen has kept its original sinks, taps and oven, but it has been reduced in size to make way for a niche which is let into its south facing wall to be enjoyed as part of the garden.

Opening times: April to end Sept, Wed only 2.15–5.30, subject to limited viewing during conferences.
Entrance charges: 60p; no reductions.
Parking: Free parking in front of the house.
Wheelchair access: Three shallow steps to entrance door; the ground floor rooms, where there is most to see, are all on the level.
Guidebook: Very clearly written, but without a plan of the building.
Catering: None.
WCs: In the house.
Shop: Yes.

PYT HOUSE   nr Tisbury (Mutual Household Association)
Tel: Tisbury (0747) 870210
Directions: 6 miles N.E. of Shaftesbury, 3 miles S.W. of Tisbury on a minor road near the village of Newtown; rather difficult to find without a good map

Pyt House is an impressive mansion, set against a steep hill and overlooking rolling countryside. Most of what you see was built in about 1805 to the design of Mr John Benett, the owner. He radically altered an earlier house and built the three classical facades to give the building a uniform appearance. The result is very like Phillipps House at Dinton, which is also open to the public. At the back of the house is the Victorian service accommodation. The guided tour lasts about half an hour and includes the principal ground floor rooms, the staircase and the cellars. Mr Benett's main hall and two reception rooms are very tall and the reception rooms have magnificent mid-16th century chimneypieces from North Italy. There are also some family portraits. The staircase was rebuilt with the house; it is lit by an oval lantern and the lowest flight sits on a curious trellis, like that of a verandah. There is not much to see on the first floor except four marble busts of the Benetts and the family portraits. The cellar has a fireplace with a surround of blue and white Dutch tiles. The house is now owned by the Mutual Households Association and all except the principal rooms have been converted into apartments. Most of the furniture is of no special interest. The guide is one of the residents. Visitors can go where they like in the gardens and a good walk can be had by going past the pretty orangery and climbing the hill to the ivy-covered ruined chapel.

Opening times: May to Sept, Wed and Thurs, 2–5.
Entrance charges: 40p; children 25p; no dogs.
Parking: Free in front of the house.
Wheelchair access: 12 steps to main entrance and more inside.
Guidebook: None.
Catering: None.
WCs: Yes.
Shop: None.

SHELDON MANOR nr Chippenham (Major Martin Gibbs)
Tel: Chippenham (0249) 3120
Directions: 1½ miles W. of Chippenham on the S. side of the A420, signposted off A4 and A420

Sheldon is a very attractive small stone manor house. Part of it dates from the 15th century but much was rebuilt in about 1660 and has the tall gables and mullion and transom windows typical of that time. The house possesses an astounding late 13th century porch; it is two storeys high and looks much too large for the present building. The ground floor of the porch has a stone vaulted ceiling and the original stone water cistern fed from the roof. The rooms inside are snug, with plenty of signs of family occupation and a motley but interesting collection of furniture, ranging from early oak pieces to colourful tortoiseshell and marquetry work. Much of the furniture was collected by the grandfather of the present owner, who came from Barrow Court in Somerset, and among the other furniture are several pieces of the rather lumpish Eltonware pottery made at Clevedon Court in Somerset at the end of the last century. Visitors are permitted to wander through most of the house and there are guides (often members of the family) in each room to supplement the information boards provided. The house has a pretty setting with tall old yew trees in front and two 18th century barns to one side.

Opening times: April to end Sept, Thurs, Sun and Bank Holiday Mon 12.30–6.
Entrance charges: 95p; OAPs and children 35p; students 50p. (HHA)
Parking: Free parking near the house.
Wheelchair access: The ground floor rooms are accessible and a word to the lady on the gate will enable drivers to bring their cars to a side door with level entry.
Guidebook: New guide planned for 1982.
Catering: The food is taken seriously at Sheldon; buffet lunches are served from 12.30 on open days, afternoon tea or just tea and good cakes can be had on the lawn; advance notice can provide English food for lunch or supper in the stable barn, while 'not more than 22 visitors' can arrange for breakfast or an elaborate dinner to be served in the dining room of the house.
WCs: Small but comfortable; unsuitable for wheelchairs.
Shop: Between the house and barn; souvenirs, home-made jam, local history books and small gifts for children.

STOURHEAD Stourton, nr Mere (The National Trust)
Tel: Bourton (074 784) 348
Directions: 10 miles S. of Frome, off the B3092 between Maiden Bradley and Mere

Stourhead was one of the first English country houses in the Palladian style. Colen Campbell designed a villa for Sir Henry Hoare (a wealthy banker) which was completed in 1724. This building forms the central part of the present house. Two wings, containing the picture gallery and library, were added in 1793 and the portico on the west side was built in 1840, following a design left by Campbell. The centre of the house was gutted by fire in 1902 and restored to something like its original appearance by Doran and Aston Webb. Visitors have access to most of the ground floor rooms and make their own way round. A short tour leaflet is given to each visitor. The guides are helpful, and there are sepia photographs showing the appearance of the rooms before the fire, when they were filled to overflowing with potted plants. The house contains some very good furniture, notably that designed specially for the building by Thomas Chippendale the younger. Some of the more important paintings collected by the Hoare family have been sold but much still remains and there are many classical landscapes of the kind which inspired the design of the gardens outside. One of the most surprising objects in the house is the library carpet, which is copied from a 19th century design but looks like something from the Festival of Britain. The grounds at Stourhead are justly famous. They were laid out from 1744 onwards and were arranged so that a series of vistas would be revealed in the course of a walk round the lake. At the end of each vista is a little temple or some other building, many of them designed by Henry Flitcroft. Later planting, especially of rhododendrons, has obscured some of the views. The gardens are entered separately from the house and a separate charge is made.

Opening times: Garden open all year, daily 8–7 or sunset. House, April, Sept and Oct, Mon, Wed, Sat, Sun 2–6 or sunset; May to end Aug, daily except Fri, 2–6 or sunset.

Entrance charges: House £1.40; children 70p. Garden £1.00; children 50p; no dogs.

Parking: Car parks next to stable block and in a field a little nearer to the house; a 10p contribution is requested.

Wheelchair access: There are 15 steps to the house, but the rooms inside are on the level. Wheelchair users are allowed to drive up to the house. A complete tour of the gardens can be made, provided the gradients can be managed; some of the garden buildings can only be reached by steps however.

Guidebook: i)The free leaflet given to each visitor. ii) A guide to the house with good informative text and a plan of the main floor showing the dates of the various additions iii) An expensive souvenir booklet with many colour photographs. iv) A map of the grounds, showing the species of trees. v) A guide to the Stourhead landscape with a lot of historical and botanical information.

Catering: Cups of tea and ice creams can be had at the stable block in summer but the Spread Eagle Inn facing the stableyard is much more pleasant and serves morning coffee.

WCs: At the house and also in the stableyard, where there are facilities for the disabled.

Shop: Typical National Trust shop in the stable block selling guidebooks, postcards, books, chutney, honey, tea cloths, beeswax,. candles etc.

WARDOUR CASTLE nr Tisbury (Cranbourne Chase School)
Tel: Tisbury (0747) 870464
Directions: 15 miles W. of Salisbury, 4 miles N.E. of Shaftesbury to the N. of the A30

Wardour Castle, despite its name, is a noble country house, one of the best examples of the English Palladian style with a massive central block containing a group of imposing reception rooms on the first floor and wings on either side containing, in this case, the kitchens and a large Roman Catholic chapel. The entrance front is plain and rather forbidding but the garden front has a majestic central pediment. On both sides of the house the spreading lawns set off the excellent stonework to perfection. James Paine designed the house for the Eighth Lord Arundell and it was built between 1770 and 1776. The Arundells sold the house after the last war and it is now a girls' school. Visitors enter by way of the ground floor hall and pass at once into the magnificent circular staircase hall which fills the centre of the house. The twin arms of the great staircase curve up against the walls to a gallery on the first floor which gives access to the principal rooms. After the staircase, these rooms are an anti-climax. They are well proportioned and contain some elegant plaster decoration and fireplaces as well as some Arundell family portraits, but they also contain large numbers of school desks. The guided tour of the interior lasts about half an hour, but visitors are free to explore the garden at their leisure. They may also see the inside of the chapel, although this is not always open at the same time as the house. The chapel was part of Paine's original design, but it was extended by Sir John

Soane in 1788. The interior is rich and splendid and has been restored recently. There are a number of 18th century paintings and sculptures, most of them Italian.

Opening times: 21 July to 8 Sept, Mon, Wed, Fri and Sat 2.30–6.
Entrance charges: 55p; children 30p.
Parking: Free parking in front of the house.
Wheelchair access: Wheelchair users could see the entrance hall, the staircase hall and the chapel without difficulty; these are much the best rooms.
Guidebook: A decent serious book with sections on the family, house, chapel and grounds, some illustrations, no plan of house.
Catering: Teas are available.
WCs: Off the front hall.
Shop: Postcards and slides.
Extras: It would make sense to visit Wardour Old Castle, just along the valley from the house.

WARDOUR OLD CASTLE (Ancient Monument)
Directions: 14 miles W. of Salisbury, 1½ miles S.W. of Tisbury and 1½ miles N. of the A30

The outer ward of the old castle and the grounds were laid out during the 18th century in the 'Picturesque' style. This has given Wardour the flavour of a romantic ruin which is enhanced by the pretty Gothic banqueting house perched on the outer wall overlooking the lake. But the castle is basically the building which was begun by Lord Lovel in about 1393. It was not a castle in the traditional sense but rather a tower house built for lavish entertainment and domestic comfort. Later alterations, made in the 1570s by the architect Robert Smythson for Sir Matthew Arundell, improved the comforts of the building still further; many of the windows were enlarged and the architectural decoration of the entrance front was brought up to date. The castle was beseiged twice during the Civil War and the south west side was destroyed. The building is now a ruin but with the help of the plan in the back of the guidebook it is possible to gain a good idea of its original layout. On plan, the building is a hexagon with two towers flanking the entrance on the north east side. Within is a central hexagonal courtyard. The grounds around the ruin are very attractive and besides the banqueting house there is also a grotto made in 1792 by Josiah Lane of Tisbury, a famous grotto builder.

Opening times: DOE standard hours (S), see page xii.
Entrance charges: 40; children and OAPs 20p.
Parking: Free parking next to the outer wall of the castle.
Wheelchair access: The area round the castle is flat and grassy; it would be possible to enter the castle itself.
Guidebook: The 'Official Handbook' is a good one, easy to read and with useful plans. It would be an improvement if there were more photographs.
Catering: None.
WCs: None.
Shop: Only postcards and slides.

Extras *:*About a mile away is Wardour Castle, the new house built for the Arundells in the 18th century; it is open to the public.

WESTWOOD MANOR nr Bradford on Avon (The National Trust
Directions: 1½ miles S.W. of Bradford on Avon, off the B3109 in Westwood village; the house is not signposted

A large 15th century stone barn, and a very fine parish church combine with the manor house to form a splendid group of buildings. The house is in the shape of an L with a round turret jammed in at the corner. It is obvious at once that the building history is complicated. A fragment of the house remains from about 1400, but most of what is visible is the work of Thomas Culverhouse in the 1480s, Thomas Horton in the 1520s and John Farewell in the early 17th century. This can best be understood from the plan and text of the guidebook, which should be read before the tour. After a period as a farmhouse in the last century, Westwood Manor was restored to its present condition by E.G. Lister, who left both the house and his collection of furniture to the National Trust in 1957. The most striking feature of the interior is the plaster decoration in the King's Room and great chamber. The latter also have a pair of unusual timber porches inside the room. There are also some attractive wall hangings sewn by Mr Lister himself. The guided tour of the house takes about half an hour. As is often the case with the smaller National Trust houses, there is little information available about the very interesting furniture, some of which belongs to the tenant who lives in the building. The comparatively small modern garden is entered through a topiary hedge cut in the shape of a life-size cottage.

Opening times: April to end Sept, Wed 2.30–6.
Entrance charges: £1.00; no reductions; no photography.
Parking: Free, inside the main gate.
Wheelchair access: Not permitted, and walking sticks may not be taken into the house.
Guidebook: Not a guidebook in the usual sense, but rather an historical account of the house and its owners.
Catering: None.
WCs: None.
Shop: None.

WILTON HOUSE Wilton (The Earl of Pembroke)
Tel: Wilton (0272) 3115; Restaurant Manager: Wilton 3641
Directions: 2½ miles W. of Salisbury, off the A30 in the town of Wilton

Many of the eighteen Earls of Pembroke have been cultivated men; one was Shakespeare's friend and patron, another a talented architect. Their family house is important in the history of English architecture and the contents rank as one of the better private art collections. The building was originally a Tudor courtyard house, built by the First Earl in the 1540s. The south front was rebuilt in the 17th century, the north and west fronts changed by the architect James Wyatt in 1801. The east front however has kept its Tudor centrepiece, and it is here that the range of colours of the Chilmark stone can be admired. The south front gives Wilton its architectural importance. It was designed in about 1636 by Isaac de Caux with the advice of the royal architect Inigo Jones and the corner towers and the Palladian window in the centre of the front were copied many times in English 18th century houses. The state rooms behind the front were burnt out in 1647 and at once rebuilt by Jones' pupil John Webb. They are among the most palatial 17th century rooms left in England. The guided tours of the house start at Wyatt's Gothic hall in the east front and take in two ground floor smoking rooms, one of which contains a large series of paintings of the horses of the Spanish Riding School. After this comes a staircase with a good Ribera and two busts by Roubiliac; then the state rooms on the first floor of the south front, large rooms with rich and heavy decoration and many excellent paintings. The largest and most famous are the Double Cube and Single Cube rooms, with carved and gilded panelling and rich ceilings. The panelling was designed to contain the Van Dyck portraits on the walls and the massive furniture by Kent and Chippendale was also designed for Wilton, but in the 18th century. After the state rooms there is a second sight of the double-decker cloister which Wyatt added round the courtyard. The well-lit upper floor of the cloisters makes a good setting for classical sculptures. A part of the grounds is open, and the Palladian Bridge designed by the Ninth Earl can be seen but not crossed. The Holbein Porch (part of the Tudor House re-erected as a garden folly) and the stables by de Caux may be viewed by appointment.

Opening times: 6 April to 11 Oct, Tues to Sat and Bank Holiday Mon 11–6; Sun 1–6; last admission 5.15.

Entrance charges: £1.50; children under 16 and OAPs 80p. Gardens only 40p and 20p; no dogs. (HHA)

Parking: Free parking outside the gates.

Wheelchair access: Possible to the grounds and to the house.

Guidebook: A history of the house and family with a room-by-room commentary but no plan; many colour photographs. There are also foreign language guides.

Catering: The Wilton Restaurant is large, purpose-built cafeteria inside the grounds open with the house and has a bar which keeps mid-day licensing hours. Pleasant enough, if rather commercialised.

WCs: Next to the restaurant; some have handrails for the disabled but are not wide enough for wheelchair users.

Shop: Fairly standard shop next to the ticket counter.

Extras: There is an exhibition of model soldiers in dioramas, admission charge. Stonehenge is only seven miles away.

Wilton House, Wiltshire

North Yorkshire

BEDALE HALL Bedale (Hambleton District Council)
Tel: Bedale (0677) 23131
Directions: 11 miles N. of Ripon just W. of the main A1 on the A684. The Hall is at the top of the main street of Bedale opposite the church

Bedale Hall stands on one edge of this pleasant little town and the main front faces open country. Until about 1930 this was the home of the de la Poer Beresford-Peirse family; the building now serves as council offices and as the public library. The original house was built of brick but the present main front of stone and stucco dates from about 1740. The exterior is of less interest than the interior, which has some very fine plasterwork, possibly the work of the Italian, Guiseppe Cortese. Visitors see first a pretty staircase and then a room containing a small and fusty collection of local bygones. The outstanding feature of the house is the saloon or ballroom, which fills the centre of the main front. This room is two storeys high and has a richly decorated ceiling, wall panels and swags above the windows as well as a fine chimneypiece. The room is empty of furniture, except for some paintings lent by the Bowes Museum.

Opening times: March to Sept, Tues 2–4.30, or by appointment.
Entrance charges: Free.
Parking: Free parking in the car park next to the Hall, or in the town.
Wheelchair access: Possible to all rooms shown, the only problem is in reaching the 'enquiries' room on the first floor to gain admission.
Guidebook: A free stencilled leaflet containing a small amount of historical information.
Catering: None.
WCs: In the house; no facilities for wheelchair users.
Shop: None.

BENINGBROUGH HALL nr Shipton (The National Trust)
Tel: Beningbrough (0904) 470666
Directions: 8 miles N.W. of York, off the A19, well signposted locally (Map 2, B3)

Beningbrough was built for John Bourchier; the date 1716 inlaid in the staircase landing is probably the date of completion. The man in charge of the building works was a joiner from York named William Thornton, but he may have had advice on the design from more famous architects like Nicholas Hawksmoor and Thomas Archer. The plain, substantial block of the main house is built of unusually small red bricks, with a few stone ornaments which are almost all copied from Italian and French illustrated books of architecture. The house has been repaired and redecorated as a showplace for early 18th century portraits belonging to the National

Portrait Gallery. Those who knew the old interior may have mixed feelings about the new decoration, in which 'authentic' colours are used by a fashionable designer in his own way, but William Thornton's carved woodwork and the contributions of the other original craftsmen are a delight. The best rooms on the ground floor are the great solemn entrance hall and the drawing room, where Thornton's carving is most elaborate. On the first floor, the long and elegant saloon takes first place. All the rooms on the two main floors are hung with portrait paintings which look extremely well in this setting. These rooms are otherwise scantily furnished with 18th century pieces of the highest quality; including two very fine Queen Anne state beds. The attic floor contains some oak panelling from a earlier house and a modern display which provides information about the subjects of the paintings which are on show in the house. Beningbrough is one of the few great houses where visitors can sit down in most of the rooms and this makes it possible to take in each room as it deserves. The pleasant garden on the south side of the house is largely a modern creation.

Opening times: April to end Oct, Tues, Wed, Thurs, Sat and Sun 12–6, Bank Holiday Mon 11–6; garden open from 11; house and garden closed Good Friday.
Entrance charges: £1.40; children 70p. Garden and stable only 90p and 45p; no dogs.
Parking: Free car park near the house.
Wheelchair access: Possible to ground floor of house, garden and all other facilities.
Guidebook: A room-by-room guide, with brief notes on the architecture and a family tree of the Bourchiers; several illustrations and a plan. There is a separate handlist to the portraits, showing their location.
Catering: A very elegant refreshment room for self-service lunches (12–2) and teas.
WCs: In the stable block; suitable for wheelchairs.
Shop: A large shop in the stable block sells the usual selection of National Trust souvenirs and gifts.

BOLTON CASTLE Castle Bolton, nr Leyburn
Tel: Wensleydale (0969) 23408
Directions: 10 miles S.W. of Richmond, 1½ miles N. of the A684

John Lewyn built this castle for Lord Scrope between 1370 and 1399. It was intended to guard the approach to Wensleydale and has a lovely setting on the side of the valley. From a distance the building looks complete; close inspection shows that half is ruined and half is in use as a restaurant. Bolton was intended to be both a fortress and a mansion, with four mighty corner towers and four ranges of living quarters round an enclosed courtyard. One of these ranges contains the restaurant and is only open to its patrons. The two ranges containing the great hall and the main gate are both ruined, and charmingly overgrown with wild flowers and bushes, in a way which the Department of the Environment would never allow. Entrance is gained through the bar of the restaurant; once in, visitors have the run of the courtyard and the ruins, as well as a number of empty chambers. There is more than enough surviving to give a very good idea of living conditions in a castle.

Opening times: All year, daily except Mon, Nov to March 10–4; April to Oct 10–6. Also Bank Holiday Mons.
Entrance charges: 15p; children under 14 10p.
Parking: The restaurant has a car park next to the castle; there is also a free council car park about 100 yards away.
Wheelchair access: All of the outside can be seen, but there is no access to the interior.
Guidebook: A very thorough guide to the building with a plan of each floor and many little sketches.
Catering: The restaurant in the castle serves luncheon, 12.30–2, dinner 7.30–9.30 and tea on Sundays only. The food is quite expensive. There is also a licensed bar.
WCs: In the occupied part of the castle and in the council car park; both are free; neither suitable for wheelchairs.
Shop: The bar sells guide books, postcards and a few souvenirs.

BROUGHTON HALL   nr Skipton (H.R. Tempest Esq)
Tel: Skipton (0756) 2267
Directions: 3½ miles W. of Skipton on the S. side of the A59

Broughton has been the home of the staunchly Roman Catholic Tempest family for several hundred years. The house is a substantial stone mansion with a Italian garden laid out on the slopes behind and to one side of it, and an elegant park. The core of the building is late 16th century but it was re-fronted in about 1750. The stables to one side were added in the 1780s, the elegant pedimented wings in 1810 to designs by William Atkinson and the main portico and clock tower in the 1840s. The hourly guided tours include all the main rooms and, if you are lucky, the guide will be the owner. The hall has mid-18th century decoration and excellent family portraits. The dining room, library and drawing rooms were fitted out between 1809 and 1815 but the slightly faded splendour of their decoration must date from the early years of this century. There is some good furniture by Gillows of Lancaster, the best local makers, and an interesting selection of paintings other than portraits. Two bedrooms upstairs recall the earlier days of the house with their dark woodwork and panelling while the two last rooms on the tour are the study and the living room most used by the family today. The way out lies through the conservatory, a rare survival nowadays, which was added prior to 1855 when W.A. Nesfield laid out the Italian Garden nearby. There is plenty of time to look at everything and no ropes or barriers. To one side of the house is the private chapel; its gay 19th century decoration has recently been renewed.

Opening times: Spring and Summer Bank Holiday Mon 11–5.30, also weekday afternoons in June 2–5.
Entrance charges: £1.50. (HHA)
Parking: Free parking near the house.
Wheelchair access: Not particularly easy steps up to entrance, and the main rooms are on two

levels.
Catering: None.
WCs: At the back of the house, old and spacious but access would be difficult for wheelchair users.
Shop: None.

CARLTON TOWERS nr Goole (The Duke of Norfolk)
Tel: Goole (0405) 860243
Directions: 6 miles W. of Goole, 6 miles S. of Selby on the A1041

Only a few people will find the outside of this house attractive. The long Gothic silhouette of towers and battlements is impressive but the whole building is covered with dreary grey stucco. This is the work of E.W. Pugin and dates from the 1870s; underneath the stucco is a small house of 1614 (to the left of the entrance) and a stable block built in 1777. After re-facing the old buildings Pugin was to have built a great hall and a staircase tower, but he quarrelled with Lord Beaumont and was replaced as architect by J.F. Bentley, the designer of Westminster Cathedral, who was responsible for most of the interior decoration. The state rooms are still as he left them, rich with carving and with gilded and painted plasterwork. The colours have faded a little. Much of the furniture was also designed by Bentley. After the state rooms and some rather ordinary bedrooms, visitors enter the old house. There is a secret hiding place for a priest upstairs, while the downstairs rooms are comfortable living rooms with 18th century decoration and furniture. There is a set route to follow and guides at strategic intervals but visitors are left to themselves to explore this rather sombre house.

Opening times: Easter Sat to Tues, then May to end Sept, Mon, Wed, Sat, Sun; also Bank Holiday Tues. Park 12.15–6. House 1–5; last admission 4.30.
Entrance charges: Park free. House £1.00; OAPs and children 70p; no dogs in house. (HHA)
Parking: Free parking in front of the house.
Wheelchair access: Possible to most of the rooms; there are many steps to the main entrance but the side entrance provides an easier entry.
Guidebook: An expensive production containing a full and well-illustrated room-by-room guide and a short account of the house and family. There is a separate leaflet about the priest's hole.
Catering: There is a small pleasant tea room behind the house.
WCs: Inside the house, well maintained. There will be new lavatories in 1982 with facilities for wheelchair users.
Shop: On the way out of the house; sells silver plate, china and souvenirs.

CASTLE HOWARD   (George Howard Esq)
Tel: Coneysthorpe (065 384) 333
Directions: 15 miles N.E. of York, 6 miles S.W. of Malton on the W. side of the A64

Everything at Castle Howard is on the grand scale. Horace Walpole described the house a 'a palace, a town, a fortified city' and the garden as 'the noblest lawn in the world, fenced by half a horizon'. The great Baroque house was built for the Earl of Carlisle. It was begun in 1699 and was ready for occupation (though not finished) by 1714. The architect was John Vanbrugh, who had never designed a building in his life; he was helped by Nicholas Hawksmoor, a friend and pupil of Sir Christopher Wren. The tall central block with its domed cupola is flanked by lower wings; the west wing was built later than the rest in a different, Palladian, style. It is larger than the east wing, which makes the entrance front lopsided. All the main rooms in the west wing and most of those along the south front are open to the public. A serious fire in 1940 gutted part of the south front and destroyed the dome over the hall; the damage has been only partly repaired but the painted hall is still one of the most impressive rooms in an English house. The best of the furniture and art treasures on show are housed in the long gallery of the west wing, which was added to the house in 1800 by C.H. Tatham. Among the paintings, the two by Holbein of King Henry VIII and Thomas Howard are the most important. Visitors may take their own time through the house and there are guides in each room. Although the rooms contain many fine things, the best things at Castle Howard are the buildings. Besides the house, there are the gates, follies and lodges dotted over the huge park. No one capable of walking should leave without making the pilgrimage from the south front of the house to the Temple of the Four Winds by Vanbrugh, and the great round Mausoleum beyond it which is Hawksmoor's stern but magnificent contribution.

Opening times: Good Friday to end Oct, daily. Gardens 11–5; house and costume gallery 11.30–5.
Entrance charges: (1981) £1.80; children 90p. (HHA)
Parking: Large free car park about 500 yards from the house.
Wheelchair access: The interior is accessible by means of ramps and a stair-lift.
Guidebook: Expensive, fully illustrated, well-written history of both the house and the family; also a room-by-room guide with details of the pictures, a bird's eye view of the grounds and a very very small plan.
Catering: There is a licensed restaurant for booked parties only and a large self-service cafeteria; the latter handles large numbers and the food is unexciting.
WCs: Near the cafe, new, good; suitable for wheelchair users.
Shop: Large shop near the exit from the house which sells wine as well as the usual souvenirs.
Extras: A display of costumes in the stable block near the car park; no extra charge for this.

Castle Howard, North Yorkshire

CONSTABLE BURTON HALL   Leyburn (Mr Charles Wyvill)
Tel: Bedale (0677) 50428
Directions: 6 miles S. of Richmond on the A684 between Leyburn and
   Bedale, in the village of Constable Burton

This neat rectangular stone house was designed by the popular Yorkshire
architect John Carr for Sir Marmaduke Wyvill and built between 1762 and
1768. It is one of the best medium size houses in the Palladian style. The
main front has a recessed portico with a pediment and the double staircase
leading up to it is of a type often used by Palladio himself. The other fronts
have little ornament, relying on the excellence of the stone for their
appearance. Behind the portico is the entrance hall; from here visitors are
taken on a tour of the rooms on one side of the house, returning through the
large staircase hall in the centre. The best items in the rooms are the 18th
century Dutch and Flemish paintings and the furniture by Gillow and
Chippendale; these are mixed with the more modern possessions of the
family. The ground falls away on three sides of the house and is laid out as a
very pleasant garden.

Opening times: House usually open for one summer month; garden 1 April to 1 Aug, daily 9–
   6.
Entrance charges: House 40p, gardens only 30p, children and OAPs 10p. (HHA)
Parking: In front of the house.
Wheelchair access: Very difficult, large flight of steps up to house.
Guidebook: None.
Catering: None.
WCs: None.
Shop: None.

EBBERSTON HALL   Scarborough (Mr and Mrs de Wend Fenton)
Tel: Scarborough (0723) 85516
Directions: 11 miles E. of Scarborough on the N. side of the A170, near
   Ebberston parish church

Ebberston is a miniature stately home; there are only three main rooms but
the broad flight of steps to the entrance and the heavy carved stonework of
the doorway might belong to a much larger house. The explanation is that
the house was built in 1718 as a pavilion in the middle of a large water
garden. The garden was made for William Thompson, MP for
Scarborough, and his architect for the pavilion was Colen Campbell, whose
work includes larger houses like Stourhead in Wiltshire and Houghton in
Norfolk. Campbell usually favoured the Palladian style, but both the
vigorous carved stonework of the exterior and the bold panelling and
woodcarving inside are more like the baroque work at Castle Howard and
Beningbrough. The rooms are filled with the possessions of the present
owners, which include 18th century paintings and furniture. The owners
themselves are also very much in evidence. Of the garden, only the

overgrown canal behind the house remains, the rest has become open fields again.

Opening times: Good Friday to mid-Sept, all week 10–6.
Entrance charges: 75p (which includes the cost of an information sheet); OAPs 50p; children free.
Parking: Free parking next to the house.
Wheelchair access: Not really possible; there are many steps and the house is small.
Guidebook: The small leaflet is mainly about the house, with a little information about the owners. It would be improved by the addition of a plan of the garden as it originally was.
Catering: None.
WCs: Yes.
Shop. None.

GILLING CASTLE Gilling East, nr Helmsley (Ampleforth Abbey Trustees)
Tel: Ampleforth (043 93) 238
Directions: 18 miles N. of York, 5 miles S. of Helmsley on the B1363; in the village of Gilling East take the unsigned road opposite the church

The castle stands on a hill above the village and the slopes of the hill have been landscaped to make a very pleasant garden. The long drive leads into a spacious courtyard enclosed by buildings which appear to date from the 18th century. In fact, the basement of the main part of the house includes part of a large square tower built in about 1350. Sir William Fairfax built a Tudor house around and on top of the older tower between 1575 and 1585 and this in turn was rebuilt at the beginning of the 18th century, when the wings on either side of the front courtyard were added and some of the rooms in the central block improved. The architect for the 18th century work was probably William Wakefield. Only two rooms inside the house are open to the public. The entrance hall is 18th century work and has plaster decoration by Giuseppi Cortese. Beyond it is the staircase and then the great chamber of the Tudor house, which was left untouched. It is a very fine room, with inlaid panellig and heraldic stained glass made for the room in 1585 by Baernard Dirickhoff, who engraved his name on one of the window panes. Both panelling and glass were sold and taken to America in the 1920s, but were brought back again in 1952. There are no guides and visitors may spend as long as they like in house and garden.

Opening times: House all year, daily except Sun 10–12, 2–4; gardens open July to Sept, same times.
Entrance charges: House free; gardens 20p.
Parking: In the courtyard of the house, free.
Wheelchair access: Very difficult, steps up to front door.
Guidebook: A small leaflet with a very brief history and a description of the great chamber.
Catering: None.
WCs: None.
Shop: None.

HELMSLEY CASTLE   Helmsley (Ancient Monument)
Directions: In the town of Helmsley, 20 miles N. of York

The castle stands on one edge of the small town, looking over fields. A steep grassed bank surrounds the castle. From the ticket office a footpath leads round the bank and up to the 13th century barbican which defends the bridge to the central enclosure. The walls of the main castle date from about 1200. On one side is the dramatic ruined keep, of which only one side was left standing after the Civil War. The other face was unusual in that it was semi-circular. Opposite the keep is the square West Tower and a range of domestic buildings next to it which were improved and given new windows in the 1570s. This range is roofed and floored and has glass in the windows, but the interior is a wreck, with the remains of plaster decoration and oak panelling. There is no furniture. The other buildings of the castle have been reduced to their foundations.

Opening times: Standard hours (SM), see page xii.
Entrance charges: 40p; children and OAPs 20p.
Parking: There is no car park, but free on-street parking can be found in Helmsley.
Wheelchair access: There are no steps between the ticket office and the castle, but there are some very steep grass slopes.
Guidebook: The Official Handbook contains a dry history, a description and a plan of the whole castle.
Catering: None.
WCs: None.
Shop: None.

KIPLIN HALL   nr Richmond
Tel: Richmond (0748) 818178
Directions: 7 miles E. of Richmond, 4 miles E. of the A1, on the B6271 between Bolton on Swale and Great Langton

Kiplin is a charming, small Jacobean house, built in about 1625 for George Calvert, First Lord Baltimore, the founder of the state of Maryland, USA. The identity of his architect is unknown. The original house is oblong with a square tower in the middle of each side. It is tall, with three storeys rising to a romantic skyline of gables, chimneystacks and domes. The walls are of red brick, enlivened by patterns in darker brick. A wing was added in 1874. The interior has a different character as a result of improvements carried out in about 1720. The great hall, the long gallery at the top of the house, and several other rooms were redecorated and a completely new staircase made to replace the original staircases in the north and south towers. The last owner left the house in trust, intending that the building should be repaired and opened to the public. The work of restoration is being slowly carried on. The rooms are filled with a motley collection of pictures and furniture including some charming water colours by Lady Waterford, but the arrangement of the furniture will doubtless alter as the rooms are finished.

At the moment everything about the house is a little ramshackle but this only adds to its charm.

Opening times: May to Sept, Wed and Sun 2–5.30; grounds 2–7.00.
Entrance charges: (1981) 50p; children 25p.
Parking: Free car parking in the stableyard, about 100 yards from the house.
Wheelchair access: The hall and major rooms on the ground floor and the whole of the exterior can be seen without difficulty.
Guidebook: A small leaflet gives a brief history of house and owners and appeals for money. There is a much larger pamphlet but this is about the estate not the house; neither contains a plan. There are three typed descriptions of the paintings and furniture in each room.
Catering: Extremely good home-made cakes and cups of tea are served in the great hall.
WCs: In the house; facilities for wheelchair-users on request.
Shop: None.

MARKENFIELD HALL nr Ripon (Lord Grantly)
Directions: 3 miles S. of Ripon on the W. side of the A61 Ripon–Harrogate road. The house is reached by a farm road which is not signposted

Markenfield Hall is hidden away in the fields behind some handsome Victorian farm buildings. A water-filled moat surrounds a grassed forecourt which is also a farmyard. The L-shaped house stands in one corner, flanked by a mixture of mediaeval and Victorian ranges, which are now farm cottages. The main house was probably built soon after 1310, with a great hall and chapel on the first floor and vaulted kitchen and store rooms underneath. In 1569 the owner of the house was forced to flee abroad after having rebelled against Queen Elizabeth I and the building was abandoned. A later owner carried out restorations in the 19th century, but the building has since been abandoned again. The empty rooms are an odd mixture of 13th century stonework and 20th century matchboarding. Visitors are given free run of the house.

Opening times: May to Sept, Mon 10–12.30, 2.15–5.
Entrance charges: 25p; children accompanied by an adult free.
Parking: By the farm buildings outside the moat.
Wheelchair access: Not possible to principal rooms but the forecourt and ground floor are accessible.
Guidebook: None.
Catering: None.
WCs: None.
Shop: None.

MIDDLEHAM CASTLE Middleham (Ancient Monument)
Directions: 17 miles N.E. of Ripon on the A6108 in the town of Middleham

The castle at Middleham is thoroughly ruined; many of the walls are still standing but no roofs or floors are left. The outer ward has disappeared under the houses of the pretty market town and what remains is the square keep and the rectangle of walls around it. The keep was built in about 1170. It is one of the largest in England and always contained the principal living rooms, so that Middleham unlike most other castles, has no separate hall or great chamber. The curtain wall enclosing the keep was built in the 13th century but much of it is hidden by the buildings added inside the walls in the 14th and 15th centuries, which contained bakehouses, store rooms and living rooms to supplement those in the keep.

Opening times: Standard hours (S), see page xii.
Entrance charges: 50p; childen and OAPs 25p.
Parking: Free parking in the road outside the castle.
Wheelchair access: All the castle can be seen from ground level, but there are some rough surfaces.
Guidebook: A cheap leaflet with a plan and a desription of the castle, which is doubtless accurate but makes dry reading.
Catering: None.
WCs: None.
Shop: None.

NEWBURGH PRIORY nr Coxwold (Capt. V.M. Wombwell)
Tel: Coxwold (034 76) 435
Directions: 7 miles S.E. of Thirsk, near Coxwold village

Newburgh Priory, as its name suggests, was originally a house of Augustinian monks which was founded in about 1145. In 1529 the buildings were sold to King Henry VIII's chaplain, Anthony Bellasis, who began to turn them into a mansion. His descendants still live here. Very little of the original Priory now remains. Instead, there is a large stone house whose outside is a confused mixture of Tudor, Jacobean and early and late 18th century buildings. The drainpipes on the east front are dated 1732 and the twin bow windows on the south front were rebuilt in 1766 after a fire, but the dates of the other parts of the building and the names of the various architects are not known. The guided tour of the inside includes the main rooms on the ground floor, with a diversion upstairs to see Oliver Cromwell's tomb. Are his bones really here? No one knows for sure. The best rooms come at the end of the tour. The dining room (originally the great hall) has an elaborate chimneypiece, carved by Nicholas Stone in 1615. A passage leads from the dining room to the two drawing rooms behind the bow windows of the south front. Both of these rooms have pretty mid-18th century plasterwork by Guiseppi Cortese. The small drawing room also has a mysterious row of arches along one wall, which must originally have opened into the entrance passage. The furniture of the house includes a good collection of family portraits and a set of mid-18th century tapestry chairs in the small drawing room. The building has been restored in recent years and there are extensive gardens, including a water garden.

Opening times: 19 May to 25 Aug, Wed 2–6.
Entrance charges: (1981) House and gardens 70p; children 30p. Garden only 30p and 10p.
Parking: Free parking on the grass in front of the house.
Wheelchair access: Not practicable to the interior, all the exterior can be seen.
Guidebook: Brief history of the house, family tree of the Bellasis and Wombwell family, room-by-room tour and illustrations which include two views of the house in 1700.
Catering: Tea and very good home-made cakes in the old kitchen.
WCs: Free, clean and modern facilities on the ground floor of the house; not suitable for wheelchairs.
Shop: None.

NEWBY HALL nr Ripon (R.E.J. Compton)
Tel: Boroughbridge (09012) 2583
Directions: 4 miles S.E. of Ripon, 3 miles W. of the A1, off the B6265

Profits from the family coal mines paid for this large red brick mansion, built for Sir Edward Blackett in the 1690s. The Weddell family bought the house in 1748. William Weddell employed the architect Robert Adam to enlarge and redecorate the building. Between 1770 and 1780 Adam altered the interiors of all the main rooms and added two wings to the east side of the house; one contains the kitchens, the other a sculpture gallery. 'Adam style' is a term so often taken in vain that is good to see the real thing for a change, and the interiors at Newby are among the finest of their date in Europe. Weddell was a collector and the furniture and objects which he acquired are still in the house. The entrance hall and dining room contain furniture designed by Adam, the tapestry room is lined with Gobelin's tapestries and furnished with chairs made by Thomas Chippendale, while the domed and richly decorated sculpture gallery still contains the Roman sculptures acquired by William Weddell in Italy. Other attractions include a collection of chamber pots on the back stairs and a Victorian billiards room in the Tudor style. Almost all of the main house is open to visitors, who follow a prescribed route along roped gangways. There are friendly but non-expert guides in each room. The garden of the house was created in this century. It is laid out as a number of small, seasonal gardens, divided by broad walks with two enormous herbaceous borders sloping down to the river. There is also a very fine stable block once thought to be by Robert Adam but now known to be by William Belwood (this is not open to the public).

Opening times: Gardens, 1 April to 30 Sept, daily except Mon 11–6; house, April, May and Sept, Wed, Thurs, Sat, Sun and all Bank Holidays; June, July and Aug, daily except Mon, but including Aug Bank Holiday 1.30–5.30; last admission 5.00.
Entrance charges: House and gardens £1.50. Gardens only 90p; children half price. (HHA)
Parking: Large car park 100 yards from the house.
Wheelchair access: Access is possible to all ground floor rooms, but peak visiting times are best avoided.
Guidebook: Good value, many illustrations, a full room-by-room guide, adequate history of the building and also a plan.

Catering: Large new cafeteria overlooking the garden serving meals and snacks.
WCs: Near the restaurant, new; facilities for wheelchairs.
Shop: Large souvenir shop at entrance to grounds.
Extras: Miniature railway (extra charge) and children's playground (free, but some distance from the house). For architectural enthusiasts there is a very good Victorian church at the edge of the park by William Burges.

NORTON CONYERS   nr Ripon (Sir Richard Graham)
Tel: The Administrator. Melmerby (0765 84) 252
Directions: 3½ miles N. of Ripon, 1½ miles W. of the A1 on a minor road near the village of Wath

Norton Conyers is an extremely pleasant medium-sized house. The entrance front, with its shaped gables, can be seen across the parkland from the road. On closer inspection the irregular windows suggest that this façade has been added to an earlier house and that the alterations to the original brickwork have been concealed behind a layer of 18th century rough cast. This is indeed the case. The original house was built in about 1500. Richard Graham (an ancestor of the present owner) bought the building in 1624 and over the next 50 years both he and his son made a number of alterations. The two main fronts were smartened up and a new front door added. The principal rooms were altered in the 1770s, but the moulded roof timbers of the original great hall survive above the present 18th century ceiling. The rooms shown are the three principal living rooms on the ground floor; they are largely furnished with 18th century pieces and there is a display of 19th century costume in the library. The James II bedroom on the first floor contains earlier furniture, including a splendid Jacobean bed. This room is reached by the magnificent 17th century oak staircase and a corridor with sporting prints and portraits. There are more portraits downstairs including two by Romney, one by Zoffany, and one by Batoni. Visitors are also free to wander round the very charming walled garden.

Opening times: 9 May to 12 Sept, Sun, also Sats in July and Bank Holidays 2–5.30
Entrance charges: House and gardens 90p; OAPs 80p; children 50p. (HHA)
Parking: Free parking near to the house.
Wheelchair access: Possible to all the ground floor rooms.
Guidebook: A small leaflet with a brief history and room-by-room guide. No plan of the house but still good value.
Catering: None.
WCs: In the house, unsuitable for wheelchairs.
Shop: Unusual garden plants and soft fruit produced on the estate are on sale as the season allows in a garden shop.

NUNNINGTON HALL   nr Helmsley (The National Trust)
Tel: Nunnington (043 95) 283
Directions: 4½ miles S.E. of Helmsley, 1½ miles N. of the B1257, on the edge of Nunnington village

Nunnington is a moderate sized house built of the local grey stone. Part of the house is Elizabethan, and the west side, which is the first to be seen by most visitors, probably dates from this period. The present character of the house is the result of the alterations made by Lord Preston, who was forced to retire from politics in 1688 and spent the last seven years of his life here. The main front dates from this time and many of the rooms behind this front have bold panelling, wooden doorcases and carved chimneypieces of the late 17th century. There is a large open staircase of the same period. Several blocked windows can be seen in the walls of the stair hall and elsewhere, but it is not known why they were blocked. The paintings, furniture, and porcelain in the rooms were collected by the last private owner, and many of them are of the same date as the house. Several rooms have been opened recently including a nursery and maid's bedroom; the attics now house the Carlisle Collection of 22 miniature rooms furnished in the style of different periods. There are refreshingly few restrictions on visitors, who may make their own way through the house.

Opening times: April to end Oct, Tues, Wed, Thurs, Sat, Sun 2–6; Bank Holiday Mon 11–6.
Entrance charges: £1.00; children 50p.
Parking: Free parking 50 yards from the house.
Wheelchair access: There are a number of internal steps which make access difficult.
Guidebook: A slim guide with a brief history and a tour of the rooms; a fuller, better-illustrated guide is in preparation. There is a separate guidebook to the Carlisle Collection.
Catering: One of the best features of the house is that tea is served in the small parlour, a panelled room overlooking the lawn. Waitress service, tea and cakes.
WCs: Inside the house, well-maintained; not suitable for wheelchairs.
Shop: The usual National Trust shop package with tasteful and educational gifts and souvenirs; it is placed at the beginning of the tour, for a change.

RICHMOND CASTLE Richmond (Ancient Monument)
Directions: In the centre of Richmond, 3 miles from the A1

Richmond is a pretty town with a sloping market place at its centre. The castle was built to guard the valley of the Swale and is perched on a triangular platform of rock above the river. The buildings have been more or less neglected for the last 600 years and the castle is now a ruin, but the remains of some very early buildings can still be seen. The walls on two sides of the grass-covered great courtyard were originally built in about 1080 (the walls of the third side have fallen away, giving a good view of the river). In one corner of the courtyard are the walls of the great hall of the castle, known as Scolland's Hall, which is possibly the earliest surviving hall in the country. The most conspicuous feature of the castle is the square keep built between 1150 and 1180 on top of the original gatehouse. It is very well preserved; all the walls are intact and modern floors have been put in. A fine view of the town can be had from the roof.

Opening times: Standard hours (SM), see page xii.

Entrance charges: 60p; children and OAPs 30p.
Parking: There is no car park, but it is not usually difficult to find parking space in the town.
Wheelchair access: Level access into the large grassed central area of the castle.
Guidebook: An Official Handbook of 1953, with a plan and a reliable description and history.
    The section on the owners of the castle makes heavy reading.
Catering: None.
WCs: In the castle, free; unsuitable for wheelchairs.
Shop: None.

RIPLEY CASTLE   Ripley, nr Harrogate (Sir Thomas Ingilby Bt)
Tel: Harrogate (0423) 770186
Directions: 3½ miles N. of Harrogate, off the A61 in the village of Ripley

The oldest part of Ripley Castle is the little 15th century gatehouse. The main house consists of a three storey tower of 1555 with the extensive additions made in the 1780s. There is also a very large courtyard, surrounded by stables and other buildings in the Gothick style. The rooms in the later part of the house have 18th century decoration and furniture of the same date. The drawing room boasts a statue of Venus by Antonio Canova. The tower rooms are more varied, with a library on the ground floor, a very pleasant panelled sitting room above it, with an ornamental plaster ceiling and a glory-hole cum museum on the top floor. The guided tours take over an hour. One of the best things about Ripley is the setting, which owes much to Sir William Amcotts Ingilby. He was responsible for creating the lake in the park and between 1820 and 1830 he replaced the old village at the castle gates with neat stone houses in the Gothick and Tudor styles and built a very French-looking town hall.

Opening times: Easter to end May, Sat and Sun 2–6; June to Sept, Tues, Wed, Thurs, Sat and
    Sun 2–6.
Entrance charges: £1.20; children 60p.
Parking: There is a new car park and plenty of space in the village.
Wheelchair access: Access possible to the downstairs rooms, which contain the best of the
    18th century furniture.
Guidebook: A recently-revised guide; much improved from the previous one.
Catering: Teas in a pleasant room in the outbuildings, self-service, tea by the pot, good cakes,
    also set teas and snacks.
WCs: In the outbuildings, free, clean; unsuitable for wheelchairs.
Shop: A few souvenirs and garden produce.

SHANDY HALL   Coxwold (The Laurence Sterne Trust)
Tel: Coxwold (034 76) 465
Directions: 7 miles S.E. of Thirsk on the edge of Coxwold village

In its earliest form, Shandy Hall was a very small 15th or 16th century timber-framed hall, but its main interest lies in the fact that it was the home of the author Laurence Sterne from 1760 to 1767. Here he wrote most of *Tristram Shandy* and *A Sentimental Journey*. He also made some alterations to the old house and may have added the 18th century red brick front. Visitors are conducted through the ground floor rooms, which are lived in by the curators. There are books and prints to do with Sterne and two objects which he once possessed, a small wooden table and a china cow.

Opening times: June to Sept, Wed 2–5.30.
Entrance charges: (1980) 80p.
Parking: Small free car park next to house.
Wheelchair access: It would be best to make a special appointment.
Guidebook: One about Sterne, another about the building and itself and the village.
Catering: None.
WCs: Yes.
Shop: Books, postcards and souvenirs.

SKIPTON CASTLE Skipton
Tel: Skipton (0756) 2442
Directions: In Skipton, at the top of the High Street

The long High Street slopes up to the main gate of the castle, which is flanked by massive round towers. A short distance behind the gate is the main building. It is in the shape of a D, with six round towers in the curved side. Most of these round towers date from the rebuilding of the castle in the early 14th century but two contain Norman work. Stretching away to the right is a less formidable looking range of buildings which was added in 1535; this part of the castle is not open to the public. Although the old castle is not occupied, it is in excellent condition, thanks to Lady Anne Clifford, who restored Skipton (and several other castles) after the Civil War. A tablet over the castle entrance records her work. This entrance leads into a very pretty small courtyard with a yew tree growing in the middle. All the rooms round the court are open to visitors, but they are completely empty, except for some kitchen fittings. Just downhill from the castle is a wreck of a building which used to be the chapel. There are optional guided tours at 10, 11, 12, 2, 3, and 4, but otherwise visitors are left to themselves.

Opening times: All year, daily except Good Friday and Christmas Day, Mon to Sat 10–7 or sunset, Sun 2–7 or sunset; last admission one hour before closing.
Entrance charges: 55p; children 30p (this includes an illustrated sheet of information), subject to revision.
Parking: There is no car park; it is usually possible to park in the High Street or behind the Town Hall near the castle.
Wheelchair access: Not possible to the interior.
Guidebook: The free information sheet is a good step-by-step guide. There is also a proper guidebook, which has many small illustrations and a plan and contains much about the occupants of the castle, but is short on hard facts about the building.
Catering: None.
WCs: Next to the castle, free but a bit primitive; not suitable for wheelchairs.

Shop: Postcards, pens and other souvenirs sold in the ticket office, which is a room in the gatehouse; it contains a very pretty shell mosaic, which is largely obscured by the souvenirs.

SUTTON PARK Sutton on the Forest (Mrs Sheffield)
Tel: Easingwold (0347) 810249
Directions: 8 miles N. of York on the B1363 in the village of Sutton

Sutton Park is a compact early Georgian house in the grand manner. The main block, of local brick, is only five windows wide but it has a giant pediment and elegant pedimented wings. The name of the architect is not known, but he was clearly enthusiastic for the Palladian style. The rooms are richly decorated. There is much good 18th century plasterwork and one room is lined with grand panelling brought from another Yorkshire house while the Tea Room is painted in imitation of tortoiseshell. The present owners came to Sutton in 1963 from a much larger house and brought the best of their furniture with them. There is 18th century English mahogany, Dutch and French furniture, good paintings and a room devoted to the display of porcelain. Visitors follow a set route and there are guides in each room who seem to be knowledgeable about the contents. The modern terraced garden and lily pond was laid out by Mrs Sheffield.

Opening times: Good Friday, Easter Sun and Mon, Suns 18 and 25 April; then 2 May to 26 Sept, Sun, Tues, Wed, Thurs and Bank Holiday Mon 2–6.
Entrance charges: House and garden £1.20; OAPs £1.00; children 50p. Garden only 60p and 30p. (HHA)
Parking: Free parking in the stable yard near the house.
Wheelchair access: There are steps to the front door but access is possible to the ground floor rooms which contain the best of the collection. The tea room is also accessible.
Guidebook: A history of the family, with a room-by-room guide, several colour illustrations but no plan. More reliable on the furnishings than on the house.
Catering: Self-service tea room near the stables; salad, teas and a set tea which is good value.
WCs: In the outbuildings, adequate but not suitable for wheelchairs.
Shop: There is a small antique shop and a more conventional shop next to the tea room selling mugs, lace, cooking aids and some garden produce.

YORK: TREASURER'S HOUSE Minster Yard (The National Trust)
Tel: York (0904) 24247
Directions: In the centre of York, on the N. side of York Minster

The Treasurer of York Minster was always a rich and powerful clergyman and the size of the house reflects this importance, but between 1547 and 1936 there was no Treasurer and the house passed through the hands of many private owners. The only part of the exterior which can be seen easily is the main front; the centre probably dates from the 1630s while the projecting wings with their Dutch gables and odd mixture of window shapes were added later. The whole building was completely restored in 1900 and several changes were made to the interior. In particular, the great hall was restored to its original height. Most of the rooms on either side of the hall have panelling, doorcases and chimneypieces of the 1730s or 1740s, though there is some earlier panelling. Two main staircases are needed to reach the upper floors on either side of the central hall. Many of the excellent furnishings were collected by Mr Frank Green, who also restored the house and presented it to the Trust. There are some particularly good Queen Anne pieces and, in one of the upstairs rooms, a George II tester bed, which probably came from Houghton in Norfolk. There are guides in most of the rooms and visitors have the run of the house.

Opening times: April to end Oct, daily 10.30–6, except Good Friday; last admission 5.30.
Entrance charges: £1.00; accompanied children 50p.
Parking: There is no car park for visitors; it is usually possible to park in the streets nearby.
Wheelchair access: The rather cramped entrance lobby makes this difficult.
Guidebook: A recent (1978) booklet with a history and a room-by-room guide and a plan; it does not say much about the dates of the house, perhaps because little is known.
Catering: None.
WCs: Fairly new facilities in the basement.
Shop: In the basement, the usual National Trust package.
Extras: Also in the basement is an audio visual display 'placing the property in the context of the City and the Minster'.

South Yorkshire

CANNON HALL nr Cawthorne (Barnsley Metropolitan Borough Council)
Tel: Barnsley (0226) 790270
Directions: 5 miles W. of Barnsley on the N. side of the A635 near Cawthorne

Cannon Hall might be described as a typical house of the lesser English gentry. It stands in the centre of a large and attractive park of 70 acres, with mature trees and a lake, which was first laid out in the 1760s. The house itself is built of stone. The five–bay central block was probably built in about 1700 for a member of the Spencer family. Two single-storey wings were added in 1764 under the direction of the Yorkshire architect John Carr, who returned in 1778, to make internal alterations and build a stable block. The inside of the house was also improved to Carr's designs, and the pretty ceiling in the dining room is one of his improvements. A panelled ballroom, in the Jacobean style, was added in the 1890s. Cannon Hall is now a country house museum. The elegant ground floor rooms are used to display furniture and paintings of the 18th century which have been purchased or acquired by the Corporation. Other parts of the house have been converted to display a very interesting collection of glassware, the regimental museum of the 13th/18th Hussars and the National Loan Collection of paintings, mostly by Dutch and Flemish masters.

Opening times: All year, except Christmas Day, Boxing Day, 27 Dec and Good Friday; weekdays 10.30–5, Sun 2.30–5.
Entrance charges: Free.
Parking: Large pay car park at the foot of the park.
Wheelchair access: Cars may drive to the front door of the house and access is possible to ground floor rooms.
Guidebook: A history of the house and its owners, with separate accounts of the different collections.
Catering: None.
WCs: Near the entrance to the house, reached by a steep flight of steps.
Shop: None.

CONISBROUGH CASTLE   Conisbrough (Ancient Monument)
Directions: 4 miles S.W. of Doncaster in the town of Conisbrough, off the A2063

The outer walls of the castle are ruinous, but they still make a good show at the top of a steep grassy bank. The gem of the castle is the keep, a tall cylinder of superb stonework with six buttresses carried above the top of the roof as turrets. It looks rather like a space-ship. Both the keep and the curtain walls which surround it were probably built in about 1180 by Hamelin Plantagenet. He built a castle at Mortemer in Normandy which has a keep exactly like that of Conisbrough. Although both the internal floors and the conical roof of the keep have been destroyed, it is still possible to climb to the top by means of passages in the thickness of the walls. The enormous fireplace of the Great Chamber can still be seen in the wall of the second floor and at third floor level there is a tiny Norman chapel built inside one of the buttresses. There are no other buildings standing inside the walls beside the keep, but the foundations of the living quarters can be seen in the grass.

Opening times: Standard hours (SM), see page xii.
Entrance charges: 40p, children and OAPs 20p.
Parking: Free parking on the roadside at the foot of the castle mound.
Wheelchair access: There is a shallow-graded path from the road into the inner ward of the castle.
Guidebook: Inexpensive leaflet with a learned history of ownership, a description and a plan.
Catering: None.
WCs: Free municipal lavatories by the road beneath the castle.
Shop: Postcards and guidebook only.

CUSWORTH HALL   Doncaster (Doncaster Metropolitan Borough)
Tel: Doncaster (0302) 782342
Directions: 2 miles N.W. of Doncaster centre, signposted from the A638

Cusworth Hall stands just on the edge of the suburbs of Doncaster, in a park which commands a panoramic view of the town. It is a pleasant small stone house, built for the Wrightson family in two stages. The main block and the two wings which enclose the small forecourt were built in 1741 to the designs of a little known architect called George Platt. Ten years later the small pedimented wings facing the garden were added by the more famous James Paine. The wings contain the chapel and the billiard room, which both have good plaster ceilings by Joseph Rose, one of the leading plasterers of the mid-18th century. The decoration in the other rooms is less elaborate, but there are a number of good marble chimneypieces. The entire house is filled with a variety of museum displays of Yorkshire life, but there is no furniture in the conventional sense.

Opening times: All year, weekdays except Fri 11–5, Sun 1–5; closes at 4 during winter months.
Entrance charges: Free.
Parking: Free parking near the house.
Wheelchair access: There are no special facilities, but after the steps up to the front door the principal rooms are all on one level.
Guidebook: None.
Catering: None.
WCs: A short distance from the house, adequate, but unsuitable for wheelchairs.
Shop: Postcards and souvenirs.

West Yorkshire

BOLLING HALL Bowling Hall Road, Bradford (Bradford Council)
Tel: Bradford (0274) 23057
Directions: 1½ miles S.E. of Bradford centre off the A6036 (Ring Road)

Bolling Hall is within the built-up area of Bradford and despite its garden and the park across the road the surroundings are not very attractive. The main front of the house faces the garden. On the left is a 15th century tower, the oldest part, which now forms part of one wing of the mainly 17th century house. The other wing was remodelled in 1779 by the architect John Carr of York. The house is built of rough stonework and was fairly drastically restored between 1912 and 1915. Windows of every shape and date are mixed together, the most notable being the enormous window of the great hall in the centre of the main front. The house is now a museum and most of the rooms inside are furnished in the style of different periods while a few are given over to displays of paintings or local life. The house is such a mixture of styles itself that the juxtaposition of a Victorian back kitchen, a 17th century great hall, and a late Georgian drawing room seems quite natural. As in many of these northern museums, the quality of the oak furniture is excellent, and there is some fine Chinese Chippendale furniture in the Georgian wing. Most of the rooms on both floors of the house are open to the public; one of the upstairs rooms has good 17th century panelling and furniture to match. Others have 19th century panelling and fittings.

Opening times: All year, daily except Mon, but open Bank Holiday Mon 10–5. Closed Good Friday, Christmas and Boxing Day.
Entrance charges: Free.
Parking: Free car park next to house.
Wheelchair access: There is one change of level on the ground floor, but otherwise access to the main rooms is straightforward.
Guidebook: A decent little guidebook with a plan of the house.
Catering: None.
WCs: In the east wing of the house, the gents entered from outside, free, small; unsuitable for wheelchairs.
Shop: Postcards and souvenirs.

BRAMHAM PARK   nr Wetherby (Mr and Mrs George Lane Fox)
Tel: Boston Spa (0937) 844265
Directions: 5 miles S. of Wetherby on the W. side of the A1, signposted locally

Neither the outside of this solid Queen Anne house nor the layout of the great park around it have changed very much since they were created for Robert Benson, First Lord Bingley. No architect is known for the house, which was built between 1700 and 1710, and it may very well have been designed by Benson himself, for he was knowledgeable about architecture. The massive central block is joined to the small wings by tall colonnades to produce a long and impressive front. To one side is a stable block of which the centre may have been designed by John Carr and the ends by James Paine, both of whom designed some of the small buildings in the park. In 1828 the main house was gutted by fire and abandoned until 1907, when it was restored by Detmar Blow. The great entrance hall still shows scars of the fire and many of the rooms have 20th century panelling and plasterwork. Visitors are guided through all the principal rooms which are still in family occupation and contain a good collection of animal and sporting paintings, English portraits and furniture. In the gallery, which Detmar Blow created out of three rooms on the garden front, there is a very grand Louis XV back-to-back desk. The park is one of the few in England which escaped 'Capability' Brown and Humphrey Repton. It is laid out with wide avenues flanked by tall clipped hedges, formal lakes and ponds, and punctuated by garden temples and obelisks in the French style of the late 17th century, which Robert Benson would have known from his travels abroad. The park suffered badly in a gale in 1962 when many full-grown trees were blown down, but it has been replanted.

Bramham Park, West Yorkshire

Opening times: House, garden and grounds, Easter to end Sept, Tues, Wed, Thurs, Sun and Bank Holiday Mon 1.15–5.30.
Entrance charges: House and grounds £1.20; OAPs £1.00; children 80p. Grounds only 60p, 50p, and 40p. (HHA)
Parking: Free car park by the stable block next to the house.
Wheelchair access: There is a broad flight of steps to the front door but all the main rooms are on the level. Tea room not directly accessible.
Guidebook: A well-written history of house, garden and owners, with good illustrations and a plan.
Catering: A self-service tea room in the basement of the garden front, tea by the cup, sandwiches and cakes; it is possible to sit outside.
WCs: Adequate.
Shop: In the stable block, jams and an attractive selection of souvenirs.

BRONTË PARSONAGE Haworth (The Brontë Society)
Tel: Haworth (0535) 42323
Directions: Haworth village is 4 miles S. of Keighley off the A6033; the parsonage is next to the village church

Haworth is a very popular tourist centre for besides the Brontë connections the Keighley & Worth Valley steam railway passes through the village. The Old Parsonage is an ordinary stone house of 1799 to which a wing was added in the 1870s. The building has a grim outlook over the forest of gravestones in the churchyard. In this house, the famous Brontë sisters, Charlotte, Emily and Anne, and their brother Branwell, were brought up by their overbearing father and all of them except Anne died here and are buried in Haworth church. The details of their life and their novels, *Jane Eyre*, *Wuthering Heights* and the rest, are probably familiar to many of the visitors. In 1929 the Parsonage was acquired as a public memorial to the sisters. The rooms have been restored to something like their original appearance and a modern extension at the rear contains the Bonnell Collection of manuscripts and other material.

Opening times: All year, weekdays 11–5.30 (Oct to March 11–4.30), Sun 2–5.30 (Oct to March 2–4.30). Closed last three weeks in Dec.
Entrance charges: 50p; OAPs and children 25p.
Parking: No parking space at the house; pay and display municipal car park in the centre of the village.
Wheelchair access: Possible with difficulty.
Guidebok: Either a cheap leaflet with a brief history and room-by-room guide, in fact all the causal visitor needs, or a souvenir guide with much fuller information about the village, the history of the collections etc.
Catering: None.
WCs: Public toilets in car park.
Shop: Near the exit, sells postcards, books and Brontë souvenirs.

EAST RIDDLESDEN HALL nr Keighley (The National Trust)
Tel: Keighley (0535) 607075

Directions: One mile N.E. of Keighley on the S. side of the A650

The main road to Bradford runs only a few hundred yards from the house but it is soon forgotten. The house has a pleasant setting with a fish pond, two old barns and plenty of mature trees. The stonework has endured years of atmospheric pollution and is now dark. The front of the house is long and irregular, the result of several different building campaigns, all in the 17th century. The oldest part is the insignificant centre which contains the great hall, known as the 'Banqueting House'. To its left is a good porch with a round window and a block with wide mullioned windows which was built for the Murgatroyd family in about 1638. To the right of the banqueting house is the front of another range of buildings dating from 1692, but now in ruins. East Riddlesden was owned by absentee landlords for most of the 19th century and escaped alteration. The ground floor rooms of the Murgatroyd wing have kept their original flagged floors, oak panelling and decorative plasterwork; furniture of the appropriate date has been provided by the National Trust. The banqueting hall has an enormous and elaborate fireplace and a good staircase dated 1668 which was imported from Guilsborough Grammar School, Northampton. The grounds overlooking the Aire valley are attractive and one of the barns in front of the house is a very fine timber-framed building, which contains a small collection of farm implements and vehicles.

Opening times: April to end Oct, Wed to Sun and Bank Holiday Mon 2–5; June to end Aug 10.30–6; closed Good Friday.
Entrance charges: 80p; children 60p.
Parking: Free car park in the grounds a short distance from the house.
Wheelchair access: It would be possible to see most of the main rooms in the house, all of the exterior, and the agricultural museum in the barn.
Guidebook: A history of owners and a room-by-room guide, but a plan would help clarify the evolution of the building.
Catering: None.
WCs: Modern, in the outbuildings in front of the house; unsuitable for wheelchairs.
Shop: Small National Trust shop.

HAREWOOD HOUSE Harewood (The Earl of Harewood)
Tel: Harewood (0532) 886225
Directions: 8 miles N. of Leeds, 7 miles S. of Harrogate; the entrance is at the junction of the A61 and A659 in Harewood village

Harewood can boast one of 'Capability' Brown's best landscapes, some of Robert Adam's best room decorations, and some of Chippendale's best furniture. The house is a solid Palladian building of local stone with a wide pediment in the centre and wings on each side. It was designed by John Carr of York and built between 1759 and 1771; Carr also designed the stables and the village at the gates. The building is larger than it seems for the wings are

Harewood House, West Yorkshire

really part of the main house. Several alterations were made in 1843 when Charles Barry remodelled the south front and added an extra storey to provide more bedrooms. He also laid out the formal garden on the south front, overlooking the lake. While the house was being built John Carr was replaced by the young architect Robert Adam, who provided the designs for the ceilings, walls, chimneypieces and other fittings. Some of his work was removed by Charles Barry and some has been repainted in the last few years, but Harewood is still one of the best places to see what 'Adam Style' should mean. The entrance hall is a sombre masculine room with giant half-columns and an enormous statue by Jacob Epstein. Other rooms have more delicate plasterwork by Joseph Rose, and the ceilings and walls of the long gallery and music room have pretty paintings by Angelica Kauffman and Antonio Zucchi. A large amount of superb furniture was made for Harewood by Thomas Chippendale and most of it survives, although many of the chairs have been re-upholstered. Among his most celebrated works are the pelmets in the gallery, carved in wood to imitate drapery. The long gallery also contains Chinese porcelain and a first class collection of English 18th century portraits, while the rose and green drawing rooms are hung with important Italian portraits (including two Bellinis) collected by the Sixth Lord Harewood. Visitors follow a set route round the edge of all the main rooms and there are guides on hand to answer questions.

Opening times: House and Bird Garden open 10 daily (house 11) 1 April to 31 Oct, and Sun, Tues, Wed & Thurs in Feb, March and Nov. Closing times variable (displayed at entrance). 26 Dec to 3 Jan, Bird Garden & Adventure Playground only open daily.

Entrance charges: Apply to D.P.S. Wrench Esq., The Estate Office, Harewood; Tel: Harewood (0532) 886225.

Parking: Free parking a short distance from the house.

Wheelchair access: Ramp to front door, then all rooms on the level; there is one narrow door; cafe and much of grounds also accessible.

Guidebook: Plush souvenir guide with most information contained in the room-by-room description; well-written, copiously illustrated, no plan.

Catering: Licensed Courtyard Restaurant open for morning coffee, lunch and afternoon tea; catering for parties booked in advance. There is also a self-service cafeteria with seats outside.

WCs: In car park, near stable block and in Bird Garden; facilities for the disabled near car park shop.

Shop: Main shop in stable block; another near the car park.

Extras: Bird Garden below the stable block with English and exotic species; Adventure Playground near the car park. In the stable block is a permanent exhibition about the building of the house, with original drawings and other material.

LOTHERTON HALL Aberford (Leeds Metropolitan District Council)
Tel: Aberford (0532) 813259
Directions: 10 miles E. of Leeds centre, 1 mile E. of the A1 on the B1217

There is little charm in the architecture of Lotherton Hall, which consists of a small 18th century house greatly extended between 1890 and 1910, and given token uniformity by a coat of grey rendering. The interior has been recast to form a suitable setting for the museum collections which it contains but some original decoration survives, as in the Adam revival drawing room of the 1890s and the sombre neo-classical boudoir, which dates from the 1820s when alterations were carried out by the architects Pritchett and Watson. The collections are extensive. They include the 18th century paintings and objects belonging to the Gascoigne family, who owned Lotherton until 1968, the Savery Collection of Chinese Ceramics, and a variety of 19th and 20th century furniture and art objects. The furniture includes modern work commissioned from John Makepiece and John Hardy and there is also a fashion collection which includes many designs of the 1970s and 1980s. These collections and the attractive Edwardian garden compensate for the ugliness of the house. There is also a small and much restored mediaeval church by the front door; it is open to the public and occasional services are held in it.

Opening times: All year, Tues to Sun 10.30–6.15 or dusk (Thurs, May to Sept 10.30–8.30), closed Mon except Bank Holiday Mon.
Entrance charges: 40p; OAPs 20p; children 15p; students free.
Parking: Free car parks about 100 yards from the house.
Wheelchair access: The ground floor rooms are accessible, but it is an uphill haul from the car park.
Guidebook: A cheap leaflet or an expensive souvenir guide; both of them are almost wholly concerned with the collections. An introductory slide programme with commentary is shown in the foyer.
Catering: There is a café in the outbuildings by the car park, but its opening times are erratic.
WCs: In the outbuildings, sordid.
Shop: Postcards, museum publications and a variety of souvenirs.

NOSTELL PRIORY   nr Wakefield (The National Trust)
Tel: Wakefield (0924) 863892
Directions: 6 miles S.E. of Wakefield off the A638

Originally an Augustinian Abbey, Nostell is now a large Palladian house built for Sir Rowland Winn. The massive main block, with its pedimented centre, was built between about 1735 and 1750. There were to have been four small pavilions joined to the house by quadrant walls; two were built and only one survives. It is not clear who provided the original design, but the building work was supervised by James Paine, who became one of the leading 18th century architects; he was also responsible for the original interiors. When Sir Rowland Winn died in 1765, his son turned to the fashionable architect Robert Adam to finish the house and the rooms at the north end of the building were decorated according to his designs. In 1776 Adam was asked to enlarge the house and made a scheme for replacing the old pavilions with four larger wings; only one of these was built on the north side and the main front of Nostell now has a lopsided appearance. As in most

Palladian houses, the principal rooms are all on the first floor, reached not by the grand outside staircase but by means of the lower hall. Visitors ascend the south staircase which was designed by Paine, and then are guided, or follow a prescribed route through most of the rooms. The Top Hall, Saloon, Tapestry Room, and Library have Adam's rather flat plaster decoration, which was re-coloured both in the 19th century and more recently, while the dining room and state bedroom have very attractive rococo plasterwork of Paine's time. The breakfast room, also Paine's work, was recently burnt out but is being restored. As at Harewood House, the decorations designed by Adam were combined with furniture by Chippendale and there is a large number of fully documented pieces still in the house. Perhaps the most beautiful are the two commodes in the saloon, but undoubtedly the most striking is the suite of bright green lacquered chinoiserie furniture in the state bedroom. For less elevated tastes, there is a dolls' house of about 1735 in the entrance hall. The stable quadrangle near the house was built to Adam's designs, though two of the sides were not completed until 1828. The large park provides some pleasant walks, although the lawn between the south front of the house and the lake is out of bounds.

Opening times: April, May, June, Sept, Oct, Sat 2–6, Sun 12–6; July, Thurs and Sat 2–6, Sun 12–6; Aug, every day except Fri 12–6; Bank Holidays, Sun, Mon and Tues 11–6. Guided tours only except Sat, Sun and Bank Holidays.

Entrance charges: House and grounds £1.40; children 70p. Grounds only 90p and 45p. No reductions on Sun or Bank Holiday Mon.

Parking: Free car park near the house.

Wheelchair access: Difficult as all main rooms are on the first floor. There is a service lift which may be used by appointment.

Guidebook: A good National Trust guide with a plan, full room-by-room guide and an account of the family and the building history. A long read but all the known facts are given.

Catering: In the stable block; self-service, seating in the stalls originally intended for the horses; hot and cold meals and traditional cream teas; the food has improved under new management.

WCs: In the stable block and in the surviving quadrant; access to those in the stable block is easier for the disabled.

Shop: A newish National Trust shop with the usual selection of tea-towels, educational games, olde englishe sweets etc.

Extras: An extra charge is made for a museum of veteran and vintage motor cycles, some aviation exhibits, a display of carts all in a complex near the main gate.

OAKWELL HALL Birstall (Kirklees Metropolitan Council)
Tel: Batley (0924) 474926
Directions: 6 miles S.W. of Leeds centre, off the A652 between Birstall and Batley. The house is reached from Cambridge Road

Oakwell Hall stands in a pocket of open country between Birstall and the motorway. The house is built of grimy local sandstone and follows a common late mediaeval arrangement with a single storey great hall in the centre and a two-storey wing on either side. The age of the building is problematical: 1583 is the date carved over the entance and the massive timber frame hidden under the panelling may be of this date, but much of the exterior and most of the interior fittings look 17th century. Almost the whole house is open to visitors. The most impressive room is probably the hall, with a huge 30-light window filling the whole of one side, but many other rooms have retained some of their 17th century panelling or decoration and the house is fully furnished with suitable furniture, mainly 17th century oak. The museum staff are very friendly, and will happily open hinged panels to show the timber frame behind, but during term-time school parties are a hazard for visitors to the house. Oakwell figures as 'Fieldhead' in Charlotte Bronte's novel *Shirley*.

Opening times: April to Oct, Tues to Sat 10–6, Sun 1–5, closd Mon; Nov to March, Tues to
   Sat 10–5, closed Sun and Mon.
Entrance charges: Free.
Parking: Small free parking area next to the house.
Wheelchair access: Possible to all ground floors.
Guidebok: Strong on genealogy, weak on building history; a brief room-by-room guide and a
   good plan of both floors.
Catering: None.
WCs: None.
Shop: None.

THE RED HOUSE Gomersal (Kirklees Metropolitan Council)
Tel: Cleckheaton (0274) 872165
Directions: 5 miles S.W. of Bradford on the A58 between Bradford and
   Heckmondwike

The house stands end-on to the main road and is screened from it by trees. There is nothing remarkable about this medium-sized late 18th century building except that it is of red brick in an area where most of the houses used to be of stone. The main front is two-storeyed with widely spaced windows, not in the least grand. The principal claim to distinction of the Red House is that it was lovingly described by Charlotte Brontë in her novel *Shirley*. The local Council, who now own the building, are gradually filling it with early 19th century furniture to recreate the appearance familiar to Charlotte on her frequent visits. There is not much to see which is outstanding but the house already has the feel of a comfortable late Georgian home. Visitors can wander about without restriction and the staff are conversational.

Opening times: April to Oct, Tues to Sat 10–6, Sun 1–5, closed Mon; Nov to March, Tues to
   Sat 10–5, closed Sun and Mon.
Entrance charges: Free.
Parking: Car park next to the house.
Wheelchair access: Possible to four downstairs rooms.
Guidebook: Written when the house served a community function and so restricted to a
   history of the building and the Brontë connection, with no details of the furniture.

Catering: None.
WCs: New lavatories inside the house, but unsuitable for wheelchairs.
Shop: None.

SHIBDEN HALL Halifax (Calderdale Corporation)

Tel: Halifax (0422) 52246
Directions: 1 mile N.W. of Halifax centre, off the A58 in Shibden Hall Road, well signposted locally

Shibden Hall is a timber-framed building, partly faced with stone. Most of it dates from about 1420, but additions and alterations were made in 1590 and also in the 17th and 19th centuries. The picturesque external appearance owes a lot to Anne Lister, who employed the architect John Harper to add a stone tower and make other alterations in the 1830s. She was also responsible for terracing the garden next to the house. The great hall, or 'housebody', is at the centre, with a two-storey wing on either side. The upper floors of the wings are connected by a gallery across the upper part of the hall. There is a great deal of panelling in the house, not all of it original and some dating from the 19th century. The panelling in the dining room is hinged and can be opened on request to show the original Elizabethan painted decoration on the plaster wall behind. Most of the rooms containing good 16th, 17th and 18th century furniture, which has been arranged to make the rooms like as if they are still occupied. This helps to bring the rooms alive, but the effect is spoiled by the roping off. The outbuildings behind the house are also open and they contain a collection of horse-drawn vehicles, agricultural equipment and craft workshops. The house is surrounded by a large sloping park.

Opening times: April to Sept, Mon to Sat 11–7, Sun 2–5; Oct, Nov and March 11–5, Sun 2:–5; Feb, Sun only 2–5; closed, Dec and Jan.
Entrance charges: 30p; OAPS and children 15p.
Parking: There is a car park at the rear of the house and another just by the entrance from the main road.
Wheelchair access: Difficult because of changes of level on the ground floor and some narrow openings.
Guidebook: A folder containing separate sections of 'The Architecture', 'The House', 'The Folk Museum', etc.; a good idea and full of information, but difficult to use when going round the building. There is a good plan of the house but no illustrations of the outside.
Catering: Cafe at the back of the house open 12–6; serves tea, coffee and biscuits.
WCs: At the back of the house, adequate; unsuitable for wheelchairs.
Shop: None.

TEMPLE NEWSAM HOUSE Leeds (Leeds Metropolitan District Council)

Tel: Leeds (0532) 641358
Directions: 5 miles E. of Leeds, 1 mile S. of the A63 near its junction with the A642, well signposted locally

Temple Newsam is a large Jacobean house in a vast park. It now houses the important collections belonging to the Leeds Art Galleries. The oldest part of the building is the central range, which formed one side of a courtyard house built before 1537 by Lord Darcy. In 1622 a new owner, Sir Arthur Ingram, knocked down three sides of the courtyard and built two long wings of his own. The house has an odd plan, with the main entrance in one of the wings, not in the central range. The exterior walls are of drab coloured brick, with large mullioned windows; the only ornaments are the Ingram family arms over the porch and the Latin inscription, cast in iron, which forms the parapet. The south wing was rebuilt in 1796 by a Mr Johnson, but he kept to the style of the older building. Little remains of the interior decoration of the 1620s. Between 1735 and 1745 the long gallery in the north wing was converted into a magnificent saloon and most of the rooms of the south wing were redone at the time of the 1796 rebuilding. In the 1890s a large amount of pseudo-Jacobean decoration was installed by the architect C.E. Kempe; this work is of the highest quality and includes a good oak staircase. There is some compensation for the lack of decoration properly belonging to the house; the Bretton Room contains 16th century panelling brought from Bretton Hall near Wakefield. It is just possible to imagine that the rooms in the south wing, which have fine furniture and paintings, are those of a house, but elsewhere the museum atmosphere is inescapable. The collections of art objects are outstanding and several visits would be needed to do them justice. The garden next to the house was laid out quite recently and beyond it is a large and attractive park.

Opening times: All year, Tues to Sun 10.30–6.15 or dusk; also May to Sept, Wed 10.30–8.30; closed Mon except Bank Holiday Mons.

Entrance charges: Park free. House 40p; children 15p; OAPs 20p.

Wheelchair access: There are six steps to the main entrance and about one quarter of the collection is on the ground floor. The garden has been designed to be accessible to wheelchairs.

Guidebook: Not really a guide to the house, but it contains a short account of the buildings as well as information about the collections; lavish colour illustrations make it expensive.

Catering: There is a proper restaurant in the handsome stable block, and also a café dispensing drinks in plastic cups and crisps (seasonal opening).

WCs: In the stable block, large and municipal; facilities for the disabled.

Shop: Shop adjoining the house sells postcards, publications and gifts.

Wales

Clwyd

BODRHYDDAN HALL Rhuddlan (Lord Langford)
Tel: Rhuddlan (0745) 590400
Directions: 4 miles S.E. of Rhyl, 1 mile E. of Rhuddlan off the A5151

The Conwy family have lived here, or hereabouts, for 600 years and this snug house is full of their family heirlooms. The tall red brick entrance front is in the Queen Anne style. It was designed in the 1870s by W.A. Nesfield as an improvement to the older house which lies behind and at right angles to it. This older part dates mainly from the late 17th and 18th centuries, though a single doorway of the previous Jacobean house survives at the back. The guided tours begin in Nesfield's entrance hall, which is full of armour; in a small room nearby are two very fine Egyptian mummy cases, one of which still contains the body for which it was made. The original great hall beyond was thoroughly re-fitted by Nesfield, but the furnishings are earlier and include two fine portraits by Geerhaerts. The main staircase leads up, past a stuffed bittern, to the room over the hall, formerly a library with dark carved woodwork, but painted a startling white by the present owner and now used to show a collection of china and family mementoes. The back stairs lead down to the two dining rooms, of which the larger doubles as a family portrait gallery with work by many respectable English painters including Hogarth. The tours are commendably thorough and they take about a hour. The gardens of Bodrhyddan are not particlarly elaborate but they contain several unusual or early types of rose and next to the house is a fine conservatory, an unusual survival these days.

Opening tims: June to Sept, Tues and Thurs 2–5.30.
Entrance charges: 75p; children 25p.
Parking: Free parking in the drive.
Wheelchair access: Would be possible to four of the five main rooms shown.

Catering: The tea room is in the house itself; waitress service with passable scones, home-made sponge cake etc.
Guidebook: Written by the present owner, with a friendly text and colour illustrations.
WCs: In the house for women; in the backyard for men; no facilities for the disabled.
Shop: None.

CHIRK CASTLE   Nr Wrexham (The National Trust)
Tel: Chirk (069 186) 7701
Directions: About 15 miles S. of Wrexham and ½ mile W. of Chirk village off the A5

The countryside round about Chirk is very attractive, and beyond the splendid wrought iron entrance gates, made for the castle in the 1720s, the drive winds for over a mile through rolling parkland. At first sight the building looks grim. A squat stone rectangle with bulging round towers round a bleak and stony central courtyard, it was built by Edward I to subdue the Welsh. The building was completed in 1301 and passed through many different hands in the next three hundred years. In 1595 it was bought by the Elizabethan adventurer Sir Thomas Myddleton, whose family have lived here ever since. The Myddletons converted their castle into a comfortable mansion, but left the exterior more or less in its original state. Visitors follow a set route through the main state rooms, where there are rope barriers and helpful guides. The entrance hall is mainly Victorian work by Augustus Pugin, who made several Gothic-style alterations to Chirk in the 1840s. Next to it is the great staircase, formed inside one of the round towers. It was designed by Joseph Turner and dates from the 1760s; its 18th century elegance introduces the three main first floor rooms which also belong to this period. The saloon and drawing room have notable blue and gold coffered ceilings and both they and the dining room are suitably furnished with 18th century paintings and furniture. Beyond the drawing room is the dark panelled long gallery, a survival of the 1670s. From the gallery visitors emerge suddenly high up on the wall of the Tudor chapel and then pass by way of a bedroom with a Charles II state bed back into the central courtyard. Opening directly off the courtyard is the servants' hall, splendidly grimy and authentic, and also Sir Thomas' Room and a genuine deep dungeon which convey something of the character of the castle before the 18th and 19th century improvements. Below the castle walls on the east side is an elegant formal garden with clipped yew hedges and Edwardian garden nymphs.

Opening times: 11 April to end Oct: April, May and Oct, Tues, Wed, Thurs, Sun 2–5; June to end Sept, Tues, Wed, Thurs 12–5.30, Sun 2–5.30, Bank Holiday Mon 12–5.30, closed Good Friday.
Entrance charges: Castle and garden £1.30; children 75p.
Parking: Free parking about 100 yards from the castle.
Wheelchair access: Possible to parts of the garden and castle.
Guidebook: An adequate room-by-room guide with coloured illustrations and a plan.

Catering: A small tea room has been formed in the base of one of the towers, serving tea, coffee and cakes

WCs: In the castle courtyard, down stairs; no facilities for the disabled.

Shop: A large standard National Trust shop, diversified by some local items like woollen shawls.

ERDDIG nr Wrexham (The National Trust)

Tel: Wrexham (0978) 55314

Directions: 1 mile S. of Wrexham off the A483; access for coaches off the A525

The Yorkes of Erddig tended their property and servants carefully and hated to throw things away. Thanks to them the workings of this great country estate can now be shown in every detail. The house itself is large and plain, and built of red brick. The centre was built for Joshua Erdisbury in the 1680s by an obscure mason named Thomas Webb. It was enlarged in the 1720s for John Mellor, a rich bachelor lawyer who was the next owner, and improved once more in the 1770s for the Yorke family. At this time the west front was re-faced in stone because the brickwork was decayed. The visitors' route to the house lies through the outbuildings with the carpenter's shop, stables kennels and laundry and the building is entered through the kitchen. These below-stairs rooms all have their proper fittings and are arranged as if in use. The principal rooms are of comfortable size but, apart from the severe dining room designed by Thomas Hopper in 1826, they make no great attempt at architectural show. The library is suitably brown and leathery, the saloon has late 17th century panelling, the hall and drawing room have rather ordinary plaster decoration designed by Samuel Wyatt. By contrast, the furniture is very good. The best pieces date from the early 18th century and were bought by John Mellor. Among them are two pier glasses in the saloon and a magnificent state bed on the first floor with Chinese embroidered silk hangings. The makers of many individual items are known and details are given in the guidebook. Almost the whole of the house is on show, from basement to attic, and visitors may take their own time in following the set route. One noticeable feature of many rooms is the small blue glass bottles hanging on the walls; they are primitive fire extinguishers. It is the little domestic details like these, now mostly swept away in other great houses, that make a visit to Erddig additionally interesting. The garden of the house looks rather bare at present; it has been re-planted in its early 18th century form and the plants are still young.

Opening times: April to end Oct, every day except Fri, but open Good Friday, 12–5.30, last admisson to house 4.30 (Oct 3.30).

Entrance charges: £1.50. Outbuildings and garden only 75p; children half price.

Parking: A large free car park with picnic facilities nearby.

Wheelchair access: Possible to the garden and some of the outbuildings only.

Guidebook: A good guide with an explanation of the outbuildings, a room-by-room tour of the house with itemised descriptions of paintings and furniture, illustrations and a plan.

Catering: A licensed restaurant in a large light room on the first floor of one of the outbuildings serves light lunches (salads, soup, etc.) as well as teas.
WCs: In the outbuildings; facilities for the disabled.
Shop: Under the restaurant, the full National Trust approved range.
Extras: Near the turning off the A483 is the Felin Puleston Agricultural Museum with a collection of mainly 19th and early 20th century agricultural machinery. Admission 50p, open at the same time as the house.

Dyfed

MANORBIER CASTLE   nr Pembroke
Tel: Manorbier (083 482) 421
Directions: 5 miles S.S.E. of Pembroke off the A4139 on the B4585 in Manorbier

Manorbier is a small castle which stands on a ridge in the middle of a valley running down to the sea. In 1170 the writer Gerald de Barry, better known as Giraldus Cambrensis, who lived at Manorbier, called it the pleasantest spot in Wales and one can still see why. Gerald's family owned Manorbier from about 1130 till 1360 and all the buildings were put up by them. Since the de Barrys were not wealthy the building work was done piecemeal as money became came available. Part of the original mediaeval house at the far end of the castle enclosure and a ruined tower by the gatehouse date from aout 1140, but the curtain wall was not added until the 1230s and the chapel next to the house in the 1260s. All these buildings are now ruined and uninhabited, but a more recent cottage stands within the walls and the inner ward shelters a fine flower garden, which makes a welcome change from the plain lawns favoured by the Welsh Office for the castles in their care.

Opening times: Easter for one week, then 19 May to 30 Sept, daily 11–6.
Entrance charges: 40p; children 15p.
Parking: Limited free parking in the village, a short distance from the castle.
Wheelchair access: Possible to the grounds.
Guidebook: A basic leaflet with a layout plan or a scholarly guide which bravely attempts to sort out the detailed history of the building and contains several plans and photographs.
Catering: None.
WCs: None.
Shop: None.

PEMBROKE CASTLE   Pembroke (The Castle Trustees)
Tel: Pembroke (06463) 4585
Directions: In Pembroke, at the W. end of the main street.

Pembroke Castle occupies a headland jutting out into the Pembroke river and its ruined walls still make a dramatic show. It was by far the strongest castle in south west Wales and served as the headquarters of successive Earls of Pembroke, who were usually military men. The natural harbour below the castle was the point of departure for several military expeditions against Ireland. The main building period was between 1189 and 1245 when William Marshal and his four sons were Earls of Pembroke, but there were many later additions and the whole castle was considerably restored in the 1930s. The earliest fortifications were at the very tip of the headland, which later became the inner ward. Here is the massive circular keep, the most prominent building of the castle, and the main living quarters, including two great halls, one of them built over a subterranean cavern. The buildings which must have stood in the outer ward have all gone, leaving it as an enormous grassy open space surrounded by massive walls. The ruins can be explored with the minimum of restriction.

Opening times: Winter 11–5.30; summer weekdays 10–6.30, Sat 10–6, Sun 11–6.30.
Entrance charges: (1981) 30p.
Parking: Free parking on the quay below the castle walls.
Wheelchair access: Would be possible.
Guidebook: A small book which unravels the complicated history of ownership and contains a plan and an explanation of the parts of the castle.
Catering: None.
WCs: In the outer ward, down steps.
Shop: None.

TENBY: THE TUDOR MERCHANT'S HOUSE Quay Hill (The National Trust)
Tel: Tenby (0834) 2279
Directions: In the centre of Tenby

Tenby is a pretty seaside town with many stuccoed early Victorian houses, although the mediaeval city wall still stands as a reminder of its mediaeval past. Another survival is the Merchant's House, one of the oldest small houses still standing in South Wales. It dates from about 1500 and has an irregular three storey stone front with a chimney thrusting up through the gable. Visitors can see all of the interior, which has some interesting features like the massive kitchen hearth at the rear of the ground floor and some early painted plasterwork. The rooms are fully furnished, mainly with heavy 17th and 18th century oak pieces and there are maps and prints of local scenes on the walls.

Opening times: Easter Sun to end Sept, Mon to Fri 10–1, 2.30–6; Sun 2–6; closed Good Friday.
Entrance charges: 45p; children 30p.
Parking: There are no adjacent parking facilities.
Guidebook: A slim illustrated booklet; it would be improved by a plan of the building.
Wheelchair access: Not practicable.
Catering: None.
WCs: None.
Shop: None.

Mid Glamorgan

CAERPHILLY CASTLE Caerphilly (Ancient Monument)
Tel: Caerphilly (0222) 883143
Directions Caerphilly is 7 miles N. of Cardiff by the A469 and 11 miles W. of Newport by the A468. The castle is in the centre of the town

The great strength of Caerphilly and its most memorable feature, is the great lake or mere surrounding the castle. It was formed by building two fortified dams on the eastern side of the castle and these give the building an impressively long main front. Caerphilly was built to protect the southern part of Glamorgan, which had been occupied and colonised by the Normans, from attacks by the Welsh under Llywelyn ap Gruffyd, Prince of independent Wales. The castle was begun in 1268, captured by Llywelyn, returned and begun again in 1271 and completed by about 1277. It consists of a double ring of walls strengthened by gatehouses and massive round towers (one of which now leans outward at a crazy angle, having been undermined in the Civil War). The principal living rooms were contained in the gatehouses, but there was also a separate great hall. Although the living accommodation is ruined Caerphilly is still a very impressive building. This is partly thanks to the restorations carried out in the late 19th and early 20th centuries by the Third and Fourth Marquesses of Bute, both castle enthusiastis as their restorations at Cardiff Castle and Castell Coch show. Several of the towers at Caerphilly were partly re-built by them, but always with the greatest respect for original work.

Opening times: Standard hours (SM), see page xii.
Entrance charges: 60p; children 30p.
Parking: In front of the entrance to the castle, limited space available.
Wheelchair access: Would be possible to the interior of the castle.
Guidebook: The Official Handbook is very thorough in its description, in fact so thorough as to be almost unreadable. There is also a very brief leaflet, which is also available in French and German.
Catering: None.
WCs: Inside the castle, free; no facilities for wheelchairs.
Shop: None.

CARDIFF CASTLE Cardiff (Cardiff City Council)
Tel: Cardiff (0222) 31033
Directions: In the centre of Cardiff; the main entrance is from Castle Street

Cardiff Castle stands in the heart of the town, with Bute Park stretching away behind it. The massive outer wall encloses a huge regular square which is the outline of a Roman fort. The Roman walls were re-used by the

Normans when they arrived in Glamorgan in the 1190s and a motte with a keep was built inside. South-east of the keep, against the outer wall, the main apartments were built. They were rebuilt and altered by successive owners — Despensers, Clares, Beauchamps, Nevilles and Herberts — all notable families. In 1766 the castle passed to the Earl of Bute who employed 'Capability' Brown and Henry Holland to rebuild the apartments in Gothick style, but with conventional 18th century interiors. His son the Second Marquess added to the already enormous family fortune by developing Cardiff as a coal port. The Third Marquess inherited in 1844 at the age of six months. He grew up to be sensitive, religious and keen on building and in 1865 he invited the architect William Burges to rebuild the apartment again. Burges was a wild, extravagant and playful man with a love of bright colours and his architecture is like him. He gave the exterior of the buildings an unruly mediaeval appearance and added the enormous Bute Tower which dominates Castle Street. Inside he created a memorable series of small rooms with opulent decoration, knobbly gilded ceilings, richly-inlaid woodwork and massive furniture. Some of this work is beautiful, some grotesque. Visitors are guided round the labyrinth by the reverent official guides and the tour takes about an hour. Most of the best rooms are on show, though the pretty summer smoking room at the top of the Bute Tower is only shown in summer. As well as the Burges work, visitors may see the mediaeval keep and the museum of the Welch Regiment which is housed in the Black Tower. Before leaving it is worth making a detour along Castle Street to see Burges' wall, crawling with carved stone animals.

Opening times: March, April, Oct, daily 10–5 (tours ½ hourly, Sun hrly); May to Sept, daily 10–6, Sun 10–5; Nov to Feb 10–4.

Entrance charges: (1981) £1.60; children 60p. Inner Ward, Keep and Museum only 85p and 40p.

Parking: No parking immediately next to castle entrance, nearest parking facilities in North Street.

Wheelchair access: Possible to the inner ward, but not to any of the buildings.

Guidebook: About half deals with the past owners of the castle, the rest with the Butes and their building work. There are colour illustrations and a useful plan, but it might have been better to describe rooms in the order that they are shown. It is also possible to hire a soundguide.

Catering: A rather basic cafeteria or a waitress service restaurant in the undercroft of the old great hall with Welsh food in sub-mediaeval style — surprisingly successful.

WCs: At the castle; not for wheelchairs.

Shop: Small souvenir shop by the gate.

Extras: No extra charge is made for admission to the well laid out museum of the Welch Regiment.

CASTELL COCH Tongwynlais (Ancient Monument)
Tel: Cardiff (0222) 810101
Directions: 5 miles N. of Cardiff centre off the A470

This little castle must be one of the most extraordinary Victorian houses in

Britain. It clings to a steep wooded hillside by the river Taff and looks like a miniature version of one of mad King Ludwig's Bavarian follies. But to those who know Cardiff Castle the style will be familiar, for this is another work by the architect William Burges for John Crighton-Stuart, Third Marquess of Bute. In 1872 Burges made a survey of the small ruined mediaeval castle here and suggested that it be rebuilt as a quiet retreat. Work began in 1875. The three bold round towers with their pointed roofs and the battlemented walls with fully-working arrow slits look convincingly mediaeval. Inside is a small galleried courtyard. There are four main living rooms, decorated in Burge's own rich and colourful mediaeval style. The giant fireplaces have figure carvings of almost life-size, the walls are covered with murals and these and other surfaces are ornamented with tiny butterflies, birds, animals and insects, both carved and painted. Most of the furniture was also designed by Burges and looks extravagant but uncomfortable. Visitors make their own through these and a few smaller plainer rooms and along the battlemented wall-walk. Taken all in all, Burges here got closer to the spirit of the Middle Ages than any other architect of his time.

Opening times: Standard Hours (SM), see page xii.
Entrance charges: 70p; OAPs and children 35p.
Parking: Free parking in the wood next to the castle.
Wheelchair access: Possible to the internal courtyard but not to any of the rooms; the whole exterior could be seen.
Guidebook: The Official Handbook is an instructing and entertaining account of the building, with plan and illustrations.
Catering: None.
WCs: Inside the castle on the upper floor.
Shop: None.

ST FAGAN'S CASTLE (The Welsh Folk Museum)
Tel: Cardiff (0222) 569441
Directions: 4¼ miles W. of the centre of Cardiff

St Fagan's is a famous folk museum, housed in a spacious new building surrounded by numerous smaller buildings including several farmhouses and a chapel which have been brought from other parts of Wales and re-erected here. However, the main purpose of this book is to describe historic houses and the original building at St Fagan's is a mansion of about 1570. It is a substantial Elizabethan house on an E-plan, with a long gabled front with roughcast whitewashed walls and stone window surrounds. Part of the wall of an earlier castle on the site survives in the garden. Visitors make their own way round the principal rooms on both floors, which are fully furnished with furniture from the museum's extensive collection. On the ground floor are the great hall, great kitchen and withdrawing room. The great staircase next to the drawing room leads to a rather narrow first floor long gallery serving the dining room, library, parlour and bedroom. The furniture in the house is pleasantly varied; the dining room, for example, has furniture of the 1860s. Beside the house is a large formal garden and beyond it the 100 acres of grounds dotted with the smaller buildings, from chapel to pigsty, which are a distinctive feature of St Fagan's. The modern museum building has a wide range of folk objects, from hay-wains to clocks, silver and costumes.

Opening times All year weekdays 10–5, Sun 2.30–5. Closed 3 May, 25 and 26 Dec and 1 Jan.
Entrance charges: 30p; OAPs and children 15p.
Parking: The large main car park next to the museum costs 20p for cars and 15p for coaches; Visitors whose main interest is the great house might find the free car park in the village more convenient.
Wheelchair access: Would be possible to most of the museum and to the ground floor of the main house.
Guidebook: A small guide covering the museum, main house and smaller buildings, with plans of the house and a bird's eye view of the estate which is most useful.
Catering: There is a tea shop beside the house and also a restaurant in the museum.
WCs: In the museum and at the house; facilities for the disabled at the museum.
Shop: Large shop in the museum selling principally publications.
Extras: None, everything is included in the cost of entry.

Gwent

CHEPSTOW CASTLE Chepstow (Ancient Monument)
Tel: Chepstow (029 12) 4065
Directions: Chepstow is on the W. bank of the River Wye where it is crossed by the main A48 from Gloucester to South Wales; the castle is visible from the road

Chepstow is a long thin castle, with its lower, middle and outer wards and a barbican ranged in a line along a narrow ridge, which drops steeply on one side to the river Wye. On the other side are the backs of houses in this pleasant town. The castle buildings have a complicated history of additions and alterations by a succession of different owners. The earliest part is the rectangular Great Tower between the middle and upper wards, which dates from about 1070. Though roofless, it is still impressive and there are traces of fine Gothic decoration on the walls. Broadly speaking, the enclosing walls of the castle were built between 1225 and 1245 by the famous soldier William Marshal and his four sons, who were also responsible for much of Pembroke Castle. The grand living quarters in the outer ward and also the massive Marten's Tower to the left of the main gate were added by Roger Bigod, Earl of Norfolk, between 1270 and 1300. Despite being beseiged in the Civil War, Chepstow escaped the usual 'slighting' which damaged so many castles and was kept as the home of a garrison until almost the end of the 17th century. Since that time it has not been occupied.

Opening times: Standard hours (SM), see page xii.
Entrance charges: 60p; children 30p.
Parking: Free parking near the castle entrance and the river.
Wheelchair access: Not really practicable, though it might be possible with really energetic
assistance.
Guidebook: The official handbook is clearly-written and contains a plan which helps to work
out the different stages of building; there is also a cheap leaflet with basic information and
a plan.
WCs: None.
Shop: None.

PENHOW CASTLE Nr. Newport (Stephen Weeks Esq.)
Tel: Penhow (0633) 400800
Directions: Midway between Newport and Chepstow on the A48, 7 miles
from the Severn Bridge

Unlike most Welsh castles open to the public, Penhow is still inhabited. It is
really a small fortified manor house whose buildings are grouped round a
tiny courtyard. The core of the castle is the square battlemented 12th
century tower or keep to which a wall enclosing the courtyard was added in
the 13th century. Most of this wall has now been built into other buildings
added over the years. The present owner purchased Penhow in 1973 and is
gradually restoring it for his own occupation. On arrival, visitors are issued
with a tape-recorded soundguide which gives a commentary by the owner
on the house in general and on the history and contents of each room. The
one disadvantage of this system is that the thick mediaeval walls keep the
rooms fairly cool and one does not always want to linger as long as the
commentary expects. The rooms shown in the hall wing and the keep are
only occasionally occupied and their contents are a casual mixture of
historically diverse and interesting objects. The present main living rooms
are across the courtyard in a building formed in the 17th century. From
outside it might be a farmhouse but the ground floor hall and parlour have
panelled decoration and a good carved staircase. There is also a Victorian
kitchen. The acoustiguide takes the visitors all round the building and back
to the entrance.

Opening times: Good Friday to end Sept, Wed to Sun & Bank Holiday 10–6.
Entrance charges: (1981) 80p; children 50p.
Parking: Free parking by the castle gate.
Wheelchair access: Possible to part of the ground floor only.
Guidebook: There is a leaflet with a bird's eye view of the castle supplementing the
acoustiguide (which is available in four languages).
Catering: Tea, coffee and snacks.
WCs: Yes.
Shop: A small souvenir shop.

RAGLAN CASTLE Raglan (Ancient Monument)
Tel: Raglan (0291) 690228
Directions: The village of Raglan lies about half way between Monmouth
and Abergavenny on the A40; the castle lies about ½ mile N. of the
village and is divided from it by the main road

The ruins of Raglan stand a little distant from the village, almost in open
country. This castle differs from most other large castles in Wales because it
is late in date and was intended from the first as a splendid fortified mansion
house. Soon after 1405 the old fort at Raglan, probably with timber
buildings, came by marriage to an ambitious Welsh gentleman named
William ap Thomas. In about 1430 he began rebuilding and was probably
responsible for the great hexagonal tower with its moat which stands boldly
in front of the other buildings. The rebuilding was continued by his son, a
friend and favourite of King Edward IV who was created Earl of Pembroke
in 1468. After his beheading in 1498 the castle passed to others, who made
alterations and improvements to the Earl's original house. The main
buildings at Raglan are ranged round two courtyards, the Pitched Stone
Court and the Fountain Court, which are divided by the range of buildings
containing the great hall and long gallery. The massive main gate leads into
the Fountain Court with the stately Tudor windows of the hall along one
side. Though ruined, the hall is still very impressive. The other buildings in
this outer court were of lesser importance and the principal apartments were
to be found in the Pitched Stone Court. From here a bridge leads across the
moat to the great tower which was intended as a last refuge. In its heyday the
castle had extensive pleasure gardens and some traces of these can still be
discerned under the turf.

Opening times: Standard hours (SM), see page xii.
Entrance charges: 60p; children 30p.
Parking: Free car park near the castle.
Guidebook: An official handbook with a good description and history of the castle; there is
   also a small leaflet with basic information and a plan.
Wheelchair access: Possible to much of the castle.
Catering: None.
WCs: In the castle; not for the disabled.
Shop: None.

TREDEGAR HOUSE Newport (Newport Borough Council)
Tel: Newport (0633) 62568
Directions: The house lies S.W. of Newport, near the junction of the M4
and A48

Tredegar is a substantial gentleman's house on the outskirts of Newport
with a large park only slightly blighted by the M4 motorway. The Morgan
family had a house here as long ago as 1400. Between 1664 and 1672 the old
family house was rebuilt by William Morgan, but he kept the general shape

and parts of the structure of the earlier building. The new house was very
grand and built of brick, a material rare in Wales at that time. It has been
little altered and still has the tall roof and cross-windows typical of the
1670s. The Morgans left in 1951 and after a period as a school the house and
estate were purchased by the local council who are gradually restoring them.
Visitors are guided round the inside of the house in tours which start at
regular intervals. On the ground floor are the family dining room, which has
panelling richly brown with varnish, and the three main state rooms which
fill the main front. The Brown room has richly-carved panelling and a
reproduction 17th century ceiling. The hall is also panelled but its ceiling is
modern. The best of the three is the Gilt Room, its gilt walls inset with oil
paintings, but at the time of writing (1981) it is being repaired. The original
contents were dispersed when the house was sold, but suitable paintings and
furniture are being acquired and placed in the rooms. A massive 17th
century staircase leads from the hall to the first floor, where a number of
panelled bedrooms are shown; the backstairs lead to the servants' quarters
and the wine cellar, where a running stream was ingeniously adapted for
cooling. In front of the house lies the splendid stable block, built in 1917–31
and around it is the park with the buildings of the home farm.

Opening times Grounds daily, 8 to sunset. House, Good Friday to last Sun in Sept, daily
except Mon and Tues, but including Bank Holiday, 2–5.30.
Entrance charges: (1981) Grounds free. House 75p; OAPs 50p; children 30p.
Parking: Free parking about 100 yds from the house.
Wheelchair access: Would be possible to ground floor rooms.
Guidebok: A simple leaflet with a very adequate historical account of the house.
Catering: Morgan's Bar in the courtyard of the house, licensed but fairly basic; there are also
kiosks in the grounds.
WCs: Being constructed in 1981.
Shop: None.
Extras: There are a number of 'attractions': boating on the lake, fishing, a children's farm,
donkey rides; all have their own charges.

WHITE CASTLE (Ancient Monument)
Tel: Llantilio (060 085) 380
Directions: 6 miles E. of Abergavenny and 9 miles W. of Monmouth, 1½
miles N.W. of Llantilio Crosseny, between the B4521 ad B4233, signed
from both

One of the chief attractions of White Castle is the peace and quiet of its
surroundings. The ruins command a tract of deep countryside and there do
not seem to be a great many visitors. It is difficult to imagine that in the 12th
and 13th centuries this border area needed constant policing against the
Welsh. The castle takes its name from the white plaster which once covered
the walls, but has now almost entirely gone. The layout of the castle is quite
conventional, with an inner ward defended by a tall stone curtain wall with
circular towers and also by a deep, steep-sided moat partly filled with water.

The outer ward has a lower wall and a dry ditch. There has probably been a fort of some kind here since the Normans first came to the area but the oldest surviving part now is the wall of the inner ward which probably dates from about 1180. The circular towers and gatehouse were added to the wall later, probably in the 1270s or 1280s. The living accommodation now survives only as a series of foot-high walls.

Opening times: Standard hours (S), see page xii.
Entrance charges: 40p; children 20p.
Parking: Free parking by the ticket office.
Wheelchair access: Would be possible, though the route from ticket office to castle is entirely on grass.
Guidebook: An official handbook with all the necessary information and a plan.
Catering: None.
WCs: None.
Shop: None.

Gwynedd

CONWY: ABERCONWY HOUSE Castle Street (The National Trust)
Tel: Conwy (049 263) 2246
Directions: In the centre of Conwy, at the junction of High Street and Castle Street

This small town house is the oldest surviving building in Conwy, after the church and the castle. There are some traces of 14th century work in the lower, stone-built, part of the house, but the timber-framed top floor probably dates from the early 16th century. For much of its life the building was the house of a prosperous merchant, conveniently near the quay, but it has also served as a temperance hostel and an antique shop. The National Trust has now taken over and made the sunken ground floor into a shop, which is probably what it was in the Middle Ages. The two upper floors are used to tell the story of Conwy with its famous castle and mussel-fishery by means of exhibits and audio-visual display. Much of the original structure of the house can be seen.

Opening times: April to end Sept, every day 10–5.30; closed Wed in April and May. Oct, Sat & Sun only 10–5.30; in low season closed for lunch 1–2.
Entrance charges: 45p; children 20p.
Parking: The house has no car park but there is a pay car park by the castle at the end of the street.
Wheelchair access: Impracticable; the shop is down steps and the house entrance is up steps.
Guidebook: A fold-out leaflet with a thorough history of the building, supported by plans and a cross-section.
Catering: None.
WCs: None.

Shop: The whole of the ground floor is a large National Trust shop selling books and a wide range of gifts.

BEAUMARIS CASTLE Beaumaris (Ancient Monument)
Tel: Beaumaris (0248) 810361
Directions: On the Isle of Anglesey, facing Bangor across the Menai Strait; Beaumaris town is 4 miles N.W. of the Menai Bridge on the A545

Beaumaris is now a small quiet waterside town but in the Middle Ages it was the commercial centre of North Wales. At one end of the town is the castle, built on flat, originally marshy, ground near the water's edge and half surrounded by a wide moat. This was the last of Edward I's series of great Welsh castles. It was begun in 1295 but never completed. By the 1330s the building was more or less in its present state; the walls virtually complete but the great gatehouse and other parts unfinished. The level site enabled the architect, Master James of St George, to build a castle which is almost perfectly symmetrical, something which can be best appreciated by looking at the plan in the guidebook. Beaumaris has a concentric layout: a great rectangular inner wall surrounded by a lesser outer wall with 16 towers defended by the moat. The inner ward is unusually large and was intended to have massive north and south gatehouses containing suites of royal apartments, in addition to the great hall and other buildings which once stood against the walls. Only one gatehouse survives, but its upper floor is missing. Visitors can reach the wall-walks and also thread through passages in the thickness of the walls and enter the delicate Gothic chapel in the west tower. Fewer visitors seem to go to Beaumaris than to the other castles on this coast and it is usually pleasantly quiet.

Opening times: Standard hours (SM), see page xii.
Entrance charges: 60p; children 40p.
Parking: Free car park near the castle entrance.
Wheelchair access: Would be possible to most parts of the castle at ground level.
Guidebook: A thorough and recent official guide.
Catering: None.
WCs: Municipal facilities directly outside the castle; not for wheelchairs.
Shop: None.

BRYN BRAS CASTLE Llanrug (Mrs M. Gray-Parry & Mr R.D. Gray-Williams)
Tel: Llanberis (028 682) 210
Directions: 4½ miles E. of Caernarfon off the A4086

Bryn Bras is an unusual castle-style house set in extensive landscaped grounds. The central section, with its three broad arches at ground floor level and four spindly towers is part of a building of about 1830. The two round stone towers flanking the centre were added in about 1833 and presumably the castle-style stables which can be glimpsed in the distance date from the same time. The house was built for a Bangor solicitor named Thomas Williams. There are many similarities with Penrhyn Castle, the Neo-Norman fantasy on the edge of Bangor designed by Thomas Hopper in 1827, such as some of the decoration, the fireplaces especially. Several ground floor rooms of this lived in home are open to visitors and they are chiefly remarkable for their Neo-Norman decoration (though the drawing room decoration is *Art Nouveau*). The furniture and paintings are mainly of the later 19th century. A circular room in the Flag Tower can be seen by appointment. There are pleasant lawns in front of the house, and a knot garden with a castellated wall.

Opening times: Spring Bank Holiday to mid-July and Sept, daily except Sat 1–5; mid-July to end Aug, daily except Sat 10.30–5.00.
Entrance charges: (1981) 80p; children 40p.
Parking: Outside the garden entrance, near the house. Free.
Wheelchair access: An entrance with no steps can be used on request.
Guidebook: An exhaustive investigation into the history of the building; there is also a room-by-room description and a plan and illustration.
Catering: Tea room in the garden; Bara Brith served.
WCs: Gents' tucked away in a labyrinth of paths at the rear of the house; ladies' nearer entrance.
Shop: A small selection of souvenirs sold in the tea room.

CAERNARFON CASTLE Caernarfon (Ancent Monument)
Tel: Caernarfon (0286) 3094
Directions: Caernarfon is at the southern end of the Menai Strait, 8 miles S.W. of Bangor

Caernarfon was intended by King Edward I to be the capital of North Wales and his castle here has polygonal towers decorated with bands of coloured stone which were probably copied from the walls of Constaninople, capital of the Roman Empire in its last years. The town walls, which still survive, have the more usual round towers. The fortification was began in 1283 under the direction of James of St George, architect in charge of all the North Welsh castles and by 1292 both the town walls and the walls of the castle towards the river were almost finished. After a short interval the land side walls of the castle were built between 1295 and 1301. Work continued sporadically until 1330 when the castle was left, still unfinished, but more or less in its present state. The plan of Caernarfon is like that of Conwy, with inner and outer wards of equal size placed end to end. Surrounding the two wards is a circuit of massive walls with nine towers; although there was a great hall in the lower ward, many of the main living rooms were contained in these towers. The largest of all, known as the Eagle Tower from the stone eagles on its triple turrets, housed the principal suite. Next to it is the Queen's Tower which now contains the Museum of the Welch Fusiliers. At

Caernarvon Castle, Gwynedd

the other end of the castle is the dramatic Queen's Gate which looms above the quayside. In recent time Caernarfon has become once again the centre of the Principality and the last two Princes of Wales have been invested here. One of the castle towers contains a display of photographs and objects connected with the investiture.

Opening times: Standard hours (SM), page xii.
Entrance charges: Summer £1.20; children 60p. Winter 80p; children 40p.
Parking: There is a large pay car park on the quay beneath the castle walls.
Wheelchair access: Not practicable to the interior of the castle, which is reached by steep steps.
Guidebook: A selection of different guides from the Official Handbook down to a simple leaflet.
Catering: None.
WCs: Inside the castle, down steps.
Shop: Principally publications and postcards.
Extras: An extra charge is made for admission to the Welch Fusiliers Museum.

CONWY CASTLE Conwy (Ancient Monument)
Tel: Conwy (049 263) 2358
Directions: In the centre of Conwy, on the A55 next to the Conwy Estuary

At Conwy can be found not only King Edward I's castle but also his town wall, complete with its 21 towers; together they make one of the most impressive mediaeval monuments in North Wales. Both were built in the incredibly short space of five years between 1283 and 1287 under the direct supervision of James of St George, Master of the Royal Works. The space enclosed by the town wall is roughly triangular and the castle stands at the apex on a rocky outcrop overlooking both town and river. Although the castle is ruined inside, its eight large round towers stand to their full height and still have their original battlements. The four towers at the corners of the inner ward which contained the royal apartments are marked out from the others by small turrets on top of the towers. A modern approach leads up the side of the castle mound to the old main gate and into the outer ward, with the ruins of the great hall on the right. A narrow gate through a cross-wall leads to the inner ward with the royal apartments, also ruined. Beyond the inner ward is the East Barbican, now a small grassy courtyard overlooking the river, but originally giving access to the postern or back gate. In the 19th century a railway was built directly alongside the castle and from the barbican may be seen George Stephenson's tubular iron railway bridge of 1848 ad Telford's earlier suspension bridge of 1817 carrying the road from Chester to Holyhead; both are early and important examples of their type. Conway is the nearest of Henry I's great castles to Llandudno and the holiday resorts and tends to get crowded in summer.

Opening times: Standard hours (SM), see page xii.

Entrance charges: 70p; children 35p.
Parking: There is a small pay car park next to the castle.
Wheelchair access: Not practicable; the approach is by a long flight of steps.
Guidebook: The official guide to the castle and the town walls is exhuastive; there is a smaller guide to the castle alone, written in a chattier style; both have black and white illustrations and plans.
Catering: None.
WCs: None.
Shop: Postcards and publications.

HARLECH CASTLE   Harlech (Ancient Monument)

Tel: Harlech (076 673) 552

Directions: 20 miles N. of Dolgellau along the coast road (A496) via Barmouth

Harlech is undoubtedly the most spectacular of the North Wales castles. Its rugged walls and towers are perched on a dramatic rock outcrop 200 feet above the sea with the mountains of Snowdonia behind. This compact and powerful castle was built for King Edward I by James of St George between May 1283 and December 1289. The massive walls and four round towers of the inner ward survive almost intact and also the gatehouse tower facing the town on the landwad side. But the outer walls tightly enclosing this inner ward are less well preserved. They suffered in repeated sieges in 1404, 1468 and finally in 1647 when Harlech was the last castle in Britain to fall to the Roundheads. The interior of the castle is ruinous and of the great hall, kitchen and chapel only the bases of the wall remain, but this does make it easier to appreciate the efficient simplicity of the architect's design. The usual entrance to the castle is from the town, but it can also be reached by a steep stairway leading down to sea-level which once connected Harlech with its water-gate.

Opening times: Standard hours (SM), see page xii.
Entrance charges: 60p; children 30p.
Parking: Free parking next to the castle.
Wheelchair access: Not possible to the interior, but the exterior can be seen from the car park.
Guidebook: A recent official handbook which is less drily written than many, or a cheap leaflet with basic information. Both have plans, the handbook also has black and white illustrations.
Catering: None.
WCs: None.
Shop: Postcards and publications sold in the ticket office.

PENRHYN CASTLE   Bangor (The National Trust)

Tel: Bangor (0248) 53084

Directions: 1 mile E. of Bangor at the junction of the A5 and A55

George Pennant spent part of the fortune he made from his slate quarries in

Penrhyn Castle, Gwynedd

building this enormous fantasy castle. From the long drive, winding through woods and shrubs, there are glimpses of a great keep and at last the long and picturesque entrance front is revealed. The castle, which incorporates an earlier house, was designed by the architect Thomas Hopper in a full-blooded Neo-Norman style, based on originals like Durham Cathedral and Castle Hedingham in Essex. Building began in 1827. The rooms inside are spectacular, and a little overpowering, for Hopper continued with his Neo-Norman and almost every room has heavily-carved arches, columns and decoration. The unassuming front door gives onto a long low entrance passage which opens abruptly into the three-storey great hall with its vaulted ceiling. Beyond is the library, curiously divided by heavy round arches, and the drawing room. Both of these have heavy furniture largely designed by Hopper, in Neo-Norman of course, and it needs only potted plants and the smell of cigar smoke to conjure up wealthy Victorian life in its full glory. Also on the ground floor is the sombre Ebony Room, which apparently served as a resting place for the coffins before family funerals. On the first floor are the bedrooms and the nursery, which has a good exhibition of toys and dolls at a convenient height for children to see. Some of the bedrooms shown are in the castle keep, and here can be found the slate four-poster bed which is one of the most curious objects in this curious house. The descent to the ground floor is by the main staircase, a weird and disturbing piece of architecture with writhing carved decoration, and the way out lies through the kitchen and the kichen courtyard. Immediately adjoining is the stable court which is now an industrial museum with several steam locomotives. The grounds immediately next to the house planted with shrubs and trees command views of the mountains and the Menai Strait while at some distance from the house is a more formal walled garden.

Opening times: April to end Oct, every day; April to 28 May and Oct 2–5; 29 May to end Sept and all Bank Holiday weekends 11–5.

Entrance charges: £1.60; children half price; dogs in grounds only.

Parking: Large car park near the house and industrial museum.

Wheelchair access: Possible to part of the ground floor.

Guidebook: A good room-by-room guide with a history of the Pennant family and information about the vogue for the Neo-Norman style; there is a plan and illustrations of a size to do justice to the house. There is also a braille guide.

Catering: A tea room in the house serving very adequate lunches and teas.

WCs: Near the tearoom; facilities for the disabled.

Shop: A large National Trust shop near the exit from the house.

CONWY: PLAS MAWR High Street (The Royal Cambrian Academy of Art)

Tel: Conwy (049 263) 3413

Directions: In the centre of Conwy, the entrance is in High Street

Plas Mawr (the name means 'Great House') is the most splendid house in Conwy. It was built in the later 16th century by Robert Wynne who had spent part of his life as a diplomat in Flanders and the house has some foreign features like the stepped gables. The earliest part is the north west wing (farthest from the street) which was built in 1756–7; the main block and the south east wing were added in 1580 and the large gatehouse fronting the High Street in 1595. Plas Mawr is now occupied by the Royal Cambrian Academy who leased the building in 1887 and have restored it to excellent condition. Visitors are free to wander through most of the rooms on the ground and first floors. There are two original kitchens with massive fireplaces and an unusual hanging bread-safe, and the main rooms contain some old oak furniture, but the chief feature of the interior is the very elaborate plasterwork on the walls and ceilings of the principal rooms. Furniture is minimal, but a exhibition of paintings by members of the Cambrian Academy is held in an annexe. The small courtyard at the rear of the house has the remains of an old cock-pit to one side.

Opening times: All year, daily 10–5.30 (winter 10–4).
Entrance charges: 40p; OAPs 20p; children 10p.
Parking: No car park; there is some street parking nearby or pay car parks outside the city walls.
Wheelchair access: The usual entrance route involves flights of steps but by using the original main entrance in a side-street it would be possible to reach the courtyard and ground floor rooms.
Guidebook: An inexpensive leaflet or a more costly guide with much information about the Wynne family, a room-by-room tour and plans of the house.
Catering: Good teas with home-made Bara Brith.
WCs: Yes.
Shop: None, but there is a small selection of souvenirs in the ticket office.

PLAS NEWYDD Isle of Anglesey (The National Trust)
Tel: Llandfairpwll (024 886) 714795
Directions: On the Isle of Anglesey, facing the Menai Strait, 1 mile S. of Llanfairpwll and the A5 on the A4080

The memorable things about Plas Newydd are its splendid waterside site and Rex Whistler's mural in the dining room. The visitor's route from the car park first passes the castellated stable block built in 1797, before reaching the house, which stands on lower ground than the stables and is screened from it by trees. Originally built in the 16th century for the Griffith family, the house was altered and enlarged in the 1750s for Sir Nicholas Bayly but took its present late Georgian Gothick form between 1783 and 1799. The architect James Wyatt and a Staffordshire carpenter named Joseph Potter were both involved in the designing; their client was Lord Paget of Beaudesert in Staffordshire, later Earl of Uxbridge. The entrance hall and the large music room (on the site of the 16th century great hall) are in the Gothic style but the other rooms, though of the same date, have more

conventional Classical decoration. Visitors make their own way round the
house and can see the main ground floor rooms and two first floor bedrooms.
Most of these rooms face directly across the Menai Strait towards
Snowdonia. There is much good furniture on the house, some of it brought
from Beaudesert, and many family portraits. In the 1930s the Sixth
Marquess of Anglesey and his wife made some alterations to Plas Newydd in
the cause of comfortable living. The chapel was replaced by a large dining
room with bedrooms and bathrooms on the floor above. The dining room
wall is filled with one of Rex Whistler's best murals — an architectural
fantasy with the artist himelf standing shyly in one corner. An adjoining
room has been made into a Whistler Musem and there is also a Cavalry
Museum in honour of the First Marquess of Anglesey, who was a
distinguished soldier, lost a leg at Waterloo and gave his name to a successful
type of artificial limb. The garden is chiefly composed of shrubs, which
flank the dramatic sweep of lawn between house and water.

Opening times: April to end Oct, every day except Sat 12–5. Gardens, tea room and shop,
  additional opening 18 July to 12 Sept 11–5.30.
Entrance charges: £1.30. Gardens only 65p.
Parking: Large car park near the main road and visitors' facilities but about 440 yds from the
  house.
Wheelchair access: Would be possible to ground floor: the park slopes steeply in places.
Guidebook: A thorough guide with illustrations and a plan of the house.
Catering: An attractive tea room in the Old Dairy; self service, salad lunches and acceptable
  cakes.
WCs: In the visitors' area; facilities for the disabled.
Shop: Large National Trust shop with books and gifts.

TY MAWR Wybrnant (The National Trust)
Directions: 3½ miles S.W. of Betys-y-Coed at the head of the Gwybernant
  valley off the B4406; it is possible to approach from the A470 but the road
  is unsigned

Ty Mawr is a small stone cottage of about 1560 in a remote valley. Here, or
in an earlier house on the same site, William Morgan was born in 1541.
Morgan, who became a priest and eventually Bishop of St Asaph, produced
the first complete translation of the Bible into Welsh. A partial translation
by Bishop Dacies and Richard Salesbury was published in 1567, but
Morgan's complete translation of 1588 was a masterpiece of Welsh prose and
can be seen as the equivalent of the splendid English Authorised Version
which has inspired so much English literature. During the 17th, 18th and
19th centuries when the Bible was the only written word for much of the
population, Morgan's translation did much to keep the Welsh language
alive. One room of the cottage is shown, the parlour of the house, with
simple Welsh furniture lent from St Fagan's Museum. The charming
custodian coaxes life and interest out of the simplest ingredients.

Opening times: April to end Oct, every day except Sat 12–5.
Entrance charges: 25p; children 10p.
Parking: Next to the cottage.
Wheelchair access: Would be possible.
Guidebook: A fully bi-lingual Welsh and English text describing both the building and the life and work of William Morgan.
Catering: None.
WCs: None.
Shop: None.

Powys

POWIS CASTLE Welshpool (The National Trust)
Tel: Welshpool (09389) 4336
Directions: 1 mile S. of Welshpool on the A483; pedestrian access through the park from High Street Welshpool

Powis, once known as Red Castle from its sandstone walls, began as a stronghold of Welsh princes. It stands on a rocky outcrop, from which the ground slopes steeply away on three sides; the eastern slope was transformed in the late 17th century into a magnificent terraced garden, which still exists and forms a memorable setting for the castle. The building has a lumpy and irregular outline; the shapes of its mediaeval towers can still be discerned but there have been many alterations and new windows have been punched through the walls. These alterations were begun by Sir Edward Herbert, who bought Powis in 1587 and at once added the long gallery with its painted panelling and plaster ceiling. In the late 17th century a splendid state bedroom was created, which still has its original silvered furniture and rich red Spitalfields velvet hangings, and at about the same time the great staircase was formed, with pompous wall and ceiling paintings by Lanscroon and Verrio. A number of minor changes were made in the 18th century and the Blue Drawing Room has painted panelling from this time, but most of the 18th century work was swept away in the 1890s by the architect G.F. Bodley, who formed a series of new living rooms with Jacobean-style panelling and plasterwork. All the rooms are tangled together inside the old castle keep and it is difficult to keep one's bearings — a plan in the guidebook would help. The rooms are filled with the accumulated furniture and paintings of the Herbert family and those of the family of Clive of India, which married into the Herberts and took their name. Visitors make their own way round; most rooms are partly-roped off and there are guides on hand. In addition to the rooms in the keep, the ballroom, on the first floor of a 14th century range of buildings on the north side of the castle courtyard, is open to visitors and contains the family

The State Bed, Powis Castle, Powys.

collection of stuffed animals and many objects collected in India. The house and garden together are popular and attract many visitors, but the garden is large enough to contain them and the surrounding park with its herd of deer is enormous.

Opening times: Castle and gardens, 10–18 April and May to 26 Sept, every day except Mon and Tues but open Bank Holiday Mon. Garden also open every day in July and Aug, Castle 2–6, garden 1–6; Bank Holiday Mon both open 11.30–6.
Entrance charges: Castle and Garden £1.50. Castle only £1.00. Garden only £1.00. Children half price. No charge for admission to park.
Parking: Free parking next to the castle.
Wheelchair access: Not possible to interior of castle or to the lower terraces of the garden.
Guidebook: A room-by-room guide with a full list of the pictures but a bit thin on the furniture and lacking a plan; it also contains sections on family and architectural history. There is also a separate guide to the garden.
Catering: A cheerful tea room in the 14th century wing, under the ballroom.
WCs: Near the tea room in the castle courtyard; not for wheelchairs.
Shop: A substantial National Trust shop in the same building as the tea room.

TRELYDAN HALL   nr Welshpool (Mr & Mrs J. Trevor-Jones)
Tel: Welshpool (0938) 2773
Directions: 1 mile N. of Welshpool, off the A490 and reached by a minor road

The first view of Trelydan is a long and showy black and white front, a mass of irregular gables and geometrical patterns. As so often, only the central part is timber-framed; the outer parts are of brick with half-timber patterns painted on. The timber house is a substantial building, once probably a wealthy farmer's house. It is H-shaped, with a tall porch at the front and a tall staircase-tower at the back. Nothing looks earlier than the 16th century, though the house may be on an earlier site. There have been many alterations and additions both inside and out. Visitors may inspect the ground floor of the old house, then ascend the handsome 18th century staircase to the attic floor, where there is a display of costume and also of artificial flowers. The flowers are here because Trelydan is the home of Iona Trevor Jones, 'a top International T.V. Flower Arranger'. There are some decent pieces of old oak furniture, as well as some 19th century imitations, and many modern comforts. The house has a small domestic garden.

Opening times: Easter to Christmas, daily 11–5; Great Christmas Exhibition third week in Nov.
Entrance charges: 75p.
Parking: Free parking in front of the house.
Wheelchair access: Not practicable to the interior.
Guidebook: A slight production with little hard information about the house or its past occupants; the text is in both Welsh and English.
Catering: By prior arrangement only.
WCs: Yes, but no facilities for the disabled.
Shop: Some craftwork and more especially artificial flowers for sale.

TRETOWER COURT nr Crickhowell (Ancient Monument)
Tel: Brecon (0874) 730279
Directions: 3½ miles N.W. of Crickhowell, between the A40 and the A479,
 signed from both

When the Normans seized this part of Wales in the 11th century they built a small fort here in the Usk valley to command a crucial road junction. Gradual improvements were made to the fort by the Picard family; they replaced the original wooden palisade with a stone wall and,in about 1230, built a tall round tower inside the wall. All this survives, though ruined; the outer ward of the castle is now covered by farm buildings. In about 1300 the Picards began to build a more comfortable house near the castle. At first it was a single building containing a great hall with rooms on either side. In th 15th century the building was reconstructed and all the main rooms were placed on the first floor and linked by an outside timber gallery. Shortly afterwards a whole new range was added with a much bigger great hall and space for the small private army which was an essential part of life in Wales at this time. At the end of the 15th century the L-shaped house was fortified by the building of an outer wall with a small gatehouse. The appearance of the mediaeval building was altered in the 17th century by new and larger windows, and many more drastic changes were made in the next two centuries when Tretower served as a farm. In recent years the building has been restored to show as many of its old features as possible, and parts have been competely rebuilt as they once were. To get the best from this house it is essential to absorb the information given in the official guidebook, which is very readable and brings these empty rooms to life.

Opening times: Standard hours (S), see page xii.
Entrance charges: 40p; children 20p.
Parking: In front of the gatehouse.
Wheelchair access: Would be possible to the courtyard and great hall in the west range; the outside could also be viewed.
Guidebook: The official handbook is well-written and essential reading.
Catering: None.
WCs: Near the ticket office; not for wheelchairs.
Shop: None.

Houses open by appointment

The houses in this section are open to visitors for a few days in each year or by appointment only. Many of them are buildings whose owners have agreed to allow public access in return for a grant from the Historic Buildings Council. Appointments should be made with the owner or occupier named in the individual entries. A charge is made for admission to some of these properties.

England

Avon

ASHTON COURT MANSION, Bristol (by appointment with Bristol City Council)
The former seat of the Lyons, Choke, Dawbney and Smith families, containing work of all ages from the 15th century to the present day. The most notable additions to the mediaeval and Tudor core are the long gallery wing remodelled in the 1630s in the classicising style of Inigo Jones and the Gothick library of the 1760s or 1770s.

BADMINTON HOUSE, nr Chipping Sodbury (house open June to Sept, Weds. 2.30–5; tel: Badminton (072 875) 202)
Started by the First Duke of Beaufort just after the Commonwealth and completed, to designs by William Kent, by the Third Duke in 1740, Badminton has been the family seat ever since. The interiors, one of them by Kent himself, are of the greatest splendour and contain important furniture by Chippendale and others. The house is magnificently situated amidst a 'Capability' Brown landscape.

BRISTOL: 6 DOWRY SQUARE, Hotwells (by written appointment with Mr J. Carlton or Mr G. Alexander)
A three-storey house of about 1730, with basement and attic storey, stone coping, string-course, rusticated pillars and keyed flat arches. Between 1799 and 1805 the house was the Pneumatic Institution, where Humphrey Davy worked.

BRISTOL: 9 DOWRY SQUARE, Hotwells (by written appointment with Elizabeth Vibert)
This building of five bays, with a wide cleft pedimented doorway, dates

from about 1730/40 and, as the centrepiece, is the most important building in this notable square.

BRISTOL: ST VINCENT'S PRIORY, Sion Hill, Clifton (by appointment with G. Melhuish Esq; tel: Bristol (0272) 39621)
A small Gothic Revival house with bowed windows on the facade. The first floor music room has a frieze modelled in relief from Pompeian murals.

CHIPPING SODBURY: TUDOR HOUSE, Hatter's Lane (by appointment with Mr F.C. Payne; tel: Chipping Sodbury (0454) 312065)
The oldest part of the house, the three western bays, was built about the middle of the 15th century. The house was extended in the 16th century and also contains some interesting Jacobean panelling, exposed roof framing and moulded beams.

CONGRESSBURY VICARAGE, nr Bristol (by appointment with the Rev. J. Simmonds; tel: Yatton (0934) 833126)
A small manor house of the mid 15th century, of stone, with an ornate porch, most of its original windows and roofs and a contemporary chimney-piece in the solar.

EASTWOOD MANOR FARM, East Harptree (by appointment with Mr A.J. Gay; tel: West Harptree (076 122) 237)
A very early example of a Victorian 'Model Farm', built in 1858 or 1859. It consists of a building which unites round two internal courtyards all the separate services and accommodation which are usually spread around the farmyard, thus giving advantages of cover, warmth and economy in time and motion.

LITTLE SODBURY MANOR, Chipping Sodbury (by appointment with Gerald Harford Esq; tel: Chipping Sodbury (0454) 312232)
A Cotswold manor house with work of several periods and in particular a fine late 15th century hall with an open timber roof.

TICKENHAM COURT, Clevedon (by appointment with Mrs Ruth Plant; tel: Nailsea (027 55) 2340)
A rubble-built hall of the late 14th century with an extensive range of high-end chambers, enlarged and remodelled in about 1500. The corresponding low-end offices have been lost, though the doorways are still visible. The Court is an important and remarkably complete building which has suffered little alteration.

WHITEHAVEN, Bathford (by written appointment with the

Whitehaven Trust Ltd)
High on the Downs near Bath stands the great columned facade of the elder John Wood's 'Titan Barrow', renamed Whitehaven. Many alterations have taken placed since this Palladian mansion was built in 1748, but internally and externally much remains of the original grandeur.

Bedfordshire

AVENUE HOUSE, Ampthill (by written appointment with Mr S. Houfe)
Built about 1780 for John Mars, the Ampthill brewer, and enlarged by Henry Holland in 1792 5. The house was the home of the late Sir Albert Richardson and contains several good fireplaces.

BEDFORD: ST JOHN'S RECTORY (by appointment with St John's Ambulance Brigade County Headquarters, 34 St John's St. Bedford)
This house is of considerably more interest than its outward appearance suggests. It is a mediaeval hall house and the cross range still preserves the open timber roof and the original hall, probably dating from the late 14th century. It is reasonably certain that the house is the refectory of the mediaeval Hospital of St John and was the original of Bunyan's 'Interpreter's House'.

MILTON ERNEST HALL (Hotel) (by appointment with the hotel; tel: Oakley (023 02) 4111)
Designed and built by William Butterfield in 1856 for his brother-in-law; an elaborate composition with projecting bays, dormers, arcading, chimneys and finials and notable for the use of contrasting materials and pointing for the exterior.

WARDEN ABBEY, Old Warden (by written appointment with The Secretary, The Landmark Trust, Shottesbrooke, Berks)
An impressive brick and stone fragment of the ambitious and costly house begun by the Warden of the Cistercian Abbey late in the monastic period.

Berkshire

HIGH CHIMNEYS, Hurst, Reading (by written appointment with Mr & Mrs K.E. Ayers)
A remarkably unaltered 17th century red brick house (dated 1661 on several bricks). The building has an H-plan with a recessed and gabled hall section; the windows still have wooden mullion and transom windows and the doorways canopies on carved brackets.

NEWBURY: THE CHESTNUTS (Hymac House), Bath Road
  (weekdays only by appointment with Mrs Ruth Smith, Hymac Ltd)
The Chestnuts is an unusually attractive example of the typical late 18th century Newbury brick house. The long south front is of five bays with a central pediment. The main walls use patterns of blue-grey and red bricks.

PURLEY HALL, nr Pangbourne (by appointment with Major and Mrs
  H.W.O. Bradley; tel: Pangbourne (073 57) 2028)
The house has an early 17th century front, though other fronts have some 19th century alterations. Inside is a fine small entrance hall with some grisaille wall paintings in the Thornhill manner and a delicate staircase. Both probably date from about 1720. The house was the home of Warren Hastings for seven years.

SANDLEFORD PRIORY, Newbury (School) (weekdays only by
  appointment with the Headmistress; tel: Newbury (0635) 40663)
The original Priory was founded about 1200 and the present building retains the old chapel which, under James Wyatt, was made into a drawing room. Above Wyatt's ceiling is a scissors-truss roof of about 1500. The finely decorated Octagon Room which has the external shape suggested by its name but is elliptical inside, connects the chapel with the main house.

WRAYSBURY: KING JOHN'S HUNTING LODGE (by written
  appointment with the owner)
A timber-framed building of about 1300, altered in subsequent centuries. The original central crown-post truss with long scissor-braces survives, together with part of the early trussed rafter roof with arcade plates. Substantial additions were made in about 1500, when the hall was reduced in width.

Buckinghamshire

BISHAM ABBEY, nr Marlow (by appointment with The Director, The
  Sports Council; tel: Marlow (062 84) 2818)
A mediaeval religious house of the Templars, Augustinians and Benedictines in turn, converted and modified for domestic use after the Reformation by the Hoby family. There is much good 13th century and later work surviving and the great hall has an impressive Elizabethan fireplace with a later overmantel.

IVER GROVE, Shreding Green, Iver (by written appointment with Mr &
  Mrs T. Stoppard)
A compact red brick Baroque house built in 1722, perhaps to the design of

John James. Five by three bays with giant pilasters and a pediment on the west front. On the north and south sides the central bay is framed by a giant arch. There are no original internal fittings except the staircase with its slim balusters.

PRINCES RISBOROUGH: MANOR HOUSE (by written appointment with the National Trust tenant)
A 17th century red brick house, five generous bays wide with broad brick pilasters in two orders between each bay, and a hipped roof. The interior has a spectacular Jacobean oak open-well staircase.

WOOTON HALL, Wooton, nr Aylesbury (open for a limited period each summer, or by appointment with the Administrator)
Built in 1704 on the same plan as Buckingham House (later Buckingham Palace). The interior was remodelled by Sir John Soane in 1820.

Cambridgeshire

BRAMPTON: SAMUEL PEPYS' HOUSE (by appointment only, Mon to Sat; tel: Huntingdon (0480) 53431)
The house, from an architectural point of view, is a modest building, originally a 16th century timber-framed house, three rooms long and without wings, to which later extensions were made at different times. It was Samuel Pepys' childhood home, to which he made several visits in later life.

BUCKDEN PALACE, Buckden (Sundays in July, Aug and Sept; or by appointment, tel: Huntingdon (0480) 810344)
A mediaeval palace of the Bishops of Lincoln; the surviving fragments include the gatehouse and the late 15th century tower.

ELY: 1 & 2 THE ALMONRY (by appointment with the Chapter Office; tel: Ely (0353) 2078)
The mediaeval monastic buildings of Ely among them the Almonry, are the most extensive and complete in England.

ELY: THE CHANTRY, Palace Green (by written appointment only with Mr T.A.N., Bristol)
An 18th century house of brick, five bays wide and two storeys high, with a good ironwork garden gate.

ELY: THE OLD PALACE (Palace School) (by written appointment with the Headmistress during term time only)

Bishop Alcock built a palace slightly south west of the cathedral, of which the chief remains today are the east tower, formerly the gatehouse, and the lower part of the west tower. The latter was completed in 1550, when the long gallery to the left was also added. *Circa* 1670 Bishop Laney demolished much of Alcock's palace and built instead a symmetrical brick house with recessed centre and two projecting wings leading to the existing towers. The interior was almost entirely remodelled in 1771, to which period also belongs the chapel.

KIMBOLTON CASTLE, Kimbolton (School) (open Spring and Summer Bank Holidays and some Sundays in summer; tel: Kimbolton (048 084) 505)
Little remains of the original 16th century house. The present courtyard facade dates from the late 17th century and the remainder of the house was spendidly remodelled by Vanbrugh in 1707. The Doric portico on the east front is by Alessandro Galilei, 1718–19. The gatehouse was designed by Robert Adam. The main staircase has painted decoration by Pellegrini.

LEVERINGTON HALL, nr Wisbech (by written appointment with Mr & Mrs S.G. Thompson)
The first building was probably Elizabethan and two massive chimney-breasts remain, but the hall was largely rebuilt *circa* 1650, with alterations in 1716. The interior belongs largely to the latter period.

PETERBOROUGH: ARCHDEACONRY HOUSE, Minster Precincts (by written appointment with the Rev Canon K.G. Routledge)
A mixture of monastic ruins, re-used material and 19th century restoration by Sir Giles Gilbert Scott. There is a mediaeval roof.

THORNEY ABBEY HOUSE, Thorney, Peterborough (by written appointment with owner)
An important small house built by John Lovin in 1661 for the Earl of Bedford. An earlier wing has been damaged by fire but this building retains much of its original interior.

Cheshire

BIDSTON HALL, nr Birkenhead (by appointment with Mr and Mrs J.V. Murphy; tel: Liverpool (051) 652 2023)
An early 17th century two-storey house with mullioned lights, associated with the Sixth Earl of Derby. Across the west front is a low terrace and walled forecourt entered through a wide stone gateway with a semi-circular moulded arch.

CHESTER: TUDOR HOUSE, 29-31 Lower Bridge Street (Art Gallery)
(by appointment with Oriel Galleries Fine Art; tel: Chester (0244) 20095)
One of the few original and unspoilt timber-framed buildings in Chester,
this early 17th century house is a single-bay jettied structure with one gable
facing onto the street.

THE OLD HALL, Willaston, Wirral (by appointment with Mrs Joanna
Wood; tel: Liverpool (051) 327 4779)
A building dating from 1558, of brick with sandstone dressings. The
interior contains a considerable amount of original detail including the
staircase and front door.

SHOTWICK HALL, Wirral (by appointment with Mrs J.A. Hewitt; tel:
Chester (0244) 880228)
Built in 1662, a small manor house of the period of Charles II which, apart
from a small later addition at the rear, has survived almost unaltered. The
mullion and transom windows are largely original, as are the staircase, the
Jacobean doorcases and the double-planked front door with iron locks and
bolts.

Cornwall

MEDROS FARM, Par (by written appointment with the owner)
A 15th century house retaining its original hall. It has a walled courtyard
adjoining a wing built a century later and now a separate dwelling. A well-
preserved and rare example of a Cornish hall-house.

TRECARREL MANOR (Hall and Chapel) (by appointment with Mr
N.H. Burden; tel: Coads Green (056 682) 286)
These were the only two buildings erected by Sir Henry Trecarrel, soon
after 1500, as part of an ambitious but abortive project for a large manor
house. The buildings are faced with coarse-grained granite and each has a
fine waggon roof covered with slates. Both hall and chapel contain features
of unusual interest, such as the tracery-headed windows and the arms of
Henry Trecarrel carved on a tympanum. The buildings are a mediaeval
monument of the first importance.

TRURO: THE MANSION HOUSE, Princes Street (open Mon to Fri 9–
5.30, on application at the house)
Built 1755–62 for Thomas Daniell by Thomas Edwards of Greenwich, with
a symmetrical front of Bath stone, of five bays and two and a half storeys
with a basement and a modillion cornice. The doorcases have Tuscan half-
columns supporting a pediment, the cornice of which is ingeniously

arranged and decorated with elaborate woodwork, ironwork and plasterwork of high quality.

Cumbria

CARLISLE: THE DEANERY TOWER (open Mon to Sat 10–5; ask in the cathedral for a guide)
A characteristic Cumbrian house consisting of a pele tower and a hall and service range. Built originally in the 15th century and partly remodelled in the 17th and 19th centuries. The pele tower has a very fine painted timber ceiling.

CONISHEAD PRIORY, Ulverston (by written appointment with the owners)
An Augustinian Priory was founded on the site in 1180–87 but nothing of it remains. The present house is a vast mansion built by Philip Wyatt in 1821–36 in an elaborate late Gothic style with many pointed, arched and traceried windows, pierced battlemented parapets, steep gables and panelled octagonal chimneys. Very fine interior with some woodwork from Samlesbury Hall (Lancs) and a fireplace dated 1638.

DACRE CASTLE, Penrith (by written appointment with E.H.A. Stretton Esq)
At first sight Dacre appears as a conventional keep with a large turret at each corner, but in fact it occupies a position midway between the ordinary fortified pele tower and the castle proper. The structure is basically of the 14th century but it was re-fenestrated and re-roofed in the 17th century. Otherwise it is little altered.

DACRE HALL, Lanercost (key available from the Custodian of the Priory ruins; tel: Brampton (069 77) 3030)
The hall is part of the conventual buildings of Lanercost Priory, which was founded as a house of Augustinian canons in about 1166. It was dissolved in 1537 and granted to Thomas Dacre, who converted the west range into the present house. Apart from the nave of the Priory, which is now the parish church, the other buildings have fallen into ruin.

HUTTON JOHN, Dacre, Penrith (by appointment with Mr N.F. Hudleston; tel: Greystoke (085 33) 326)
A house of which the nucleus is the sandstone tower dating from the 14th century when fortified pele towers were built all along the border. The additional buildings round the tower were erected in the 15th, 17th and succeeding centuries.

KENDAL: CASTLE DAIRY, Wildman Street (Restaurant) (May to Sept, Weds 2–4; tel: Kendal (0539) 21170)
Castle Dairy is a 14th century stone house of the hall-and-ends type. Its most attractive features are the stepped chimneystacks and semi-circular cusped heads below the hood-moulds of the mullioned windows.

NAWORTH CASTLE (by appointment with J.M. Clark & Ptnrs, Bute Ho, Rosehill, Carlisle; tel: Carlisle (0228) 44158/9)
One of the most important border strongholds, with many historical associations. The outer walls are substantially of mediaeval date; the interior was largely reconstructed after a fire in 1844. Lord William's Tower has the most important interiors, notably his bedroom, library and the chapel, which has a wall-painting of Flemish origin aid to have been imported from Kirkoswald. In the courtyard is a superb Byzantine-Romanesque well-head in silver-grey limestone.

PRESTON PATRICK HALL, Milnthorpe (by appointment with Mrs J. Pumphrey; tel: Crooklands (044 87) 200)
A good example of a small mediaeval manor house of the late 14th century with a central hall range with a cross-wing at each end, altered in about 1500 and later but retaining the original roofs in the wings and much other mediaeval work.

REDNESS HALL, Carlisle (by appointment with Carlisle City Council)
A timber-framed building dating from the 15th or early 16th centuries, considerably altered but a rarity in the area.

TYTUP HALL, Dalton in Furness (by appointment with Dr and Mrs Edge; tel: Dalton in Furness (0229) 62929)
An early Georgian five-bay house with a pretty doorway. It has a segmental pediment and a frieze with the typical motif of two concave curves leading up to a truncated middle.

WHITEHALL, Mealsgate (by written appointment with Mr S. Parkin Moore, 40 Woodsome Rd, London NW5)
A typical mediaeval pele tower of substantial size and proportions, altered in the late 16th century when two carved panels with shields of arms were introduced. Additions were made 1861-2 by Anthony Salvin.

Derbyshire

BREADSALL: THE OLD HALL (by appointment with the caretaker; tel: Derby (0332) 831714)

A small mediaeval hall house of stone with some timber-framing; altered and restored early in the 20th century.

FOREMARKE HALL, Milton (School) (by appointment with the Headmaster, during term time only; tel: Burton on Trent (0283) 703269)
This house was designed and built in 1760 by David Hiorne of Warwick for Sir Robert Burdett. It is a stone-faced building of three storeys with an attic floor, connected by quadrant walls to four small pavilions. The two most notable parts of the interior are the entrance and staircase halls, the former running the full width of the house, with a screen of Ionic columns at either end. The staircase has slender balusters, carved scroll stair-ends and Chinese fret to the first floor landing. The whole constitutes an impressive essay in the Palladian manner.

LOCKO PARK, Derby (Chapel only) (by appointment with Capt. P.J.B. Drury Lowe; tel: Derby (0332) 673517)
Locko Park itself is a large house of many periods, from the late 17th century to the late 19th century. The body of the house is of 1725–30 and has been ascribed to Francis Smith of Warwick. The earliest part is the chapel, built in 1669–73. It is a small rectangular box lit by round-headed windows and entered through a round-headed door. There are some good fittings.

NORBURY MANOR, Ashbourne (Great Hall only) (by written appointment to Mr M.B.B. Stapleton Martin)
The house is in two parts: the great hall which is a small two-storey building of the early 14th century and, at right angles to it, a much larger building of about 1700, but incorporating earlier parts.

NORTH LEES HALL, Hathersage (by appointment with The Estates Section, Alder House, Baslow Road, Bakewell; tel: Bakewell (062 981) 2881)
A 17th century stone house with semi-circular battlements and mullion and transom windows. Inside are the remains of original plaster friezes and other plaster decoration; a small internal porch has panelling of the period.

ST HELEN'S HOUSE, King Street, Derby (by written appointment with the owner)
A grand stone-fronted town mansion of the mid-1760s, attributed to the builder-architect Joseph Pickford. Inside, one room and the stairs are of particular note.

Devon

BINDON MANOR, Axmouth (by appointment with Mrs J.M. Loveridge, The White House, 82 Fitzjohn's Avenue, London NW3)
A small stone-built manor house of the early 15th century, incorporating the walls of a 12th century tower. The building was remodelled in about 1500 and again in the early 17th century. The exterior has windows of all three periods and the interior has some important examples of mediaeval woodwork and stonework.

BRIDWELL HOUSE, Uffculme, Cullompton (by written appointment with R.B.W. Clarke Esq)
A plain late 18th century building, rectangular in plan, of two-and-a-half storeys with five bays, the centre bay of the front stepped forward and capped by a small pediment. The main interest lies in the interior which retains the original decoration of the highest quality.

CASTLE HILL, Filleigh, Barnstaple (House by appointment with Lady Mary Fortesque; tel: Filleigh (059 86) 228. Gardens only by appointment with the Estate Office; tel: Filleigh (059 86) 336)
One of the stateliest mansions in Devon. Built in 1694, enlarged in the 1730s, further enlarged in 1841 by Blore, but rebuilt in the original pre-Victorian form in 1935. The house has a long and severe Palladian front with flanking nine-bay wings. The grounds are grandly landscaped.

DARTMOUTH: THE MANSION HOUSE (by appointment with W.H. Battarbee Ltd; tel: Dartmouth (080 43) 2272)
This is a plain red brick house of the mid-18th century. It is remarkable, for a house of this size, for the unusual splendour of its interior, which is virtually unaltered. The plasterwork is particularly fine.

EXETER: 7 THE CLOSE (by appointment with the Assistant Secretary of the Devon and Exeter Institution; tel: Exeter (0392) 74727)
Originally an important town house of about 1450 with a double courtyard, used as a prebendal residence but drastically remodelled on a reduced site in the early 19th century. The former entrance archway through the front range is the only surviving mediaeval feature. Two large early 19th century library rooms now occupy the site of the two courtyards and hall range.

HIGHER HARESTON, Brixton (by appointment, May to Sept, Mon, with Mr K.T. Bassett; tel: Plymouth (0752) 880426)
A chapel was licensed here as early as 1378, but the main building is a medium-sized early 16th century hall house on two sides of an enclosed

courtyard. Built of granite, the building is well preserved, though with various later alterations. The hall has a fine collar-braced roof with curved wind-braces and there are a number of good 17th century moulded stone fireplaces.

HILL FARM, Christow, Exeter (by appointment with the owners)
A late mediaeval hall house with decorative plaster ceilings of the early 17th century. The roof is partly thatched and slated and the casement windows date from the 19th century. These are virtually the only alterations since the 17th century.

THE OLD MANOR, Little Hempston, Totnes (by appointment with the owner)
This is a small stone-built courtyard house in a secluded, attractive setting. It was probably at one time a mediaeval priest's house and its most remarkable feature is a wall-painting of the resurrected Christ between censing angels.

OLD NEWNHAM, Plympton (by appointment with Mr & Mrs Cundy; tel: Plymouth (0752) 331127)
This is basically a 16th century house, but incorporated earlier features and has been in the possession of the Strode family since it was built. It is of irregular plan and the roofs of the hall and chapel are of particular interest.

PLYMOUTH: 33-33A LOOE STREET (by appointment with the Plymouth Barbican Association Ltd., 70 Mutley Plain, Plymouth)
These early 17th century houses are in the oldest part of the city. They are timber-framed and retain their original pole staircases. The canted bay windows retain the original glazing.

SHAPCOTT BARTON, Knowstone (by written appointment with the owner)
A mediaeval farmhouse containing Elizabethan plasterwork. The plaster designs are unusual and on one ceiling are used in conjunction with mediaeval beams. The earliest owners, the Shapcott family, can be traced back to the reign of Edward III.

SHUTE BARTON, Axminster (by appointment with Mrs Hurd; tel: Axminster (0297) 33682)
A large mediaeval house dating partly from the 14th century (the kitchen and hall are of this date) and partly from the late 15th century. Alterations and additions were made in the Elizabethan period, when the great entrance gatehouse was built.

SIDMOUTH: TUDOR COTTAGE (by appointment with Mrs F.R. Isen-Smith; tel: Sidmouth (039 55) 5976)
A simple building, possibly mediaeval in origin. Its special interest lies in a wall-painting, consisting of geometric patterns and naturalistic floral designs with the Elizabethan royal arms in the centre.

SOUTH YARDE, Bishops Nympton, South Molton (by appointment with Mr and Mrs H.J. Rolle; tel: Bishops Nympton (076 97) 409)
A small late mediaeval house, substantially unaltered with an elaborate open timber roof.

TIVERTON: THE GREAT HOUSE, 1 St Peter's Street (by appointment with the Mid Devon District Council; tel: Tiverton (088 42) 4911)
An early 17th century stone building of pink sandstone with two main storeys and a pair of coped gables to the attics on the street front. It adjoins Slee's almshouses and is said to have been built by the textile merchant George Slee.

WARLEIGH HOUSE, Tamerton Foliot (Great Hall only open by appointment with David Piper Esq.; tel: Plymouth (0752) 779432)
This is an E-plan house; to the north east is the kitchen, perhaps coaeval with the 16th century house, while at the north west corner is a Victorian wing. The north front contains much old material, some of it re-arranged in the early 19th century. The south front has elaborate embossed rainwater heads.

Dorset

BETTISCOMBE MANOR (by appointment with Mr M.A. Pinney; tel: Broadwindsor (030 86) 239)
A small red brick building of two storeys in the form of an elongated U. The main building dates from the late 17th century, although it incorporates the remains of a 16th century building and has some 18th century alterations. Much of the interior woodwork dates from the early 18th century and the staircase is particularly graceful.

BLANDFORD FORUM: COUPAR HOUSE, Church Lane (by appointment with The Hon. Sec., The British Legion, Legion House, Church Lane, Blandford; tel: Blandford Forum (0258) 53618)
For the most part this house dates from the rebuilding of Blandford after the great fire of 1731. It is a dignified brick and stone three-storey building with an imposing facade and an excellent staircase inside.

BLOXWORTH HOUSE, Bloxworth (by written appointment with T.A. Dulake Esq)
A picturesque group of brick buildings of the 17th and 18th centuries, comprising house, stables, brewhouse and ice house. The facade of the house, dated 1608, but with the appearance of the 18th century, conceals a symmetrical E-plan dating back to the later Middle Ages.

BUCKSHAW HOUSE, Holwell (by appointment with Sir George Paterson; tel: Bishops Caundle (096 323) 318)
A handsome two-storey house of the mid-18th century with a segmental pediment over the doorway. All the upper windows have raised stone aprons.

CAME HOUSE, Winterbourne Came, Dorchester (by appointment with Major and Mrs N.D. Martin; tel: Dorchester (0305) 3056)
This is one of the best 18th century houses in Dorset. It is of two storeys with an attic; the facade breaks forward in the centre to form a pediment and there is a balustraded parapet. An unusual feature is the conservatory; a fine example of Victorian skill in handling cast iron and glass.

MOIGNES COURT, Owermoigne (by written appointment with Mr A.M. Cree)
A 13th century manor house which, though partly rebuilt after a fire in the 19th century, retains its first floor hall with several important original features, including traceried windows.

WIMBORNE MINSTER: PRIESTS HOUSE, 5 High Street (by appointment with Miss H.M. Coles; tel: Wimborne Minster (0202) 2533)
This is the only surviving mediaeval house now visible in Wimborne. A ground floor room contains an interesting early 16th century ceiling with an inscription in the plaster frieze.

WINTERBOURNE CLENSTON MANOR (by appointment with Mrs J. Carlyle Clarke; tel: Milton Abbas (0258) 880230)
A small 15th century manor house of stone and flint with a fine open timber roof and an unusual staircase tower added in the 16th century. The house has been in the owner's family for several centuries. The great barn in Clenston with its hammerbeam roof is one of the best in the county.

WOODFORD CASTLE, Dorchester (by written appointment with the owner)
A fortified manor house, built after Sir William de Whitfield was granted license to crenellate in 1335; it was repaired after becoming ruinous in the 17th century. The main range survives, together with the service rooms on

the ground floor and a series of chambers with a chapel on the first floor.

Essex

BECKINGHAM HALL, Tolleshunt Major, Maldon (by written appointment with J.A. Hunter Esq)
A fine gatehouse of about 1540 is the most prominent surviving feature of the former mansion. The courtyard wall in which the gatehouse stands has typical 16th century diaper patterns of red and blue brickwork.

BELCHAMP HALL, nr Sudbury (by appointment with Mrs M.M.J. Raymond; tel: Sudbury (0787) 72744)
A dignified house built in the 1720s of yellow brick with rubbed brick dressings and giant pilasters at the corners. Inside there is original panelling and many articles associated with the family, which has been at Belchamp for 350 years.

BRADWELL LODGE, Bradwell juxta Mare (by written appointment with Mr James A. Mann)
Originally a rectory, Bradwell Lodge consists of an elegant house of 1781–6 by John Johnson, built onto the remains of an early 16th century house. It has a gazebo on top of the roof and a ceiling in one of the rooms which was designed by Smirke.

HORHAM HALL, Thaxted (by written appointment with A.T.B. Shand Esq)
A fine Tudor brick moated manor house, with an earlier wing; it was formerly of much greater extent and was restored in 1841. The great hall has a fine oriel window.

LITTLE CHESTERFORD MANOR, nr Saffron Walden (by appointment with Mr W.H. Mason; tel: Saffron Walden (0799) 30312)
A very impressive mediaeval house containing the only 13th century timber aisled hall so far known, together with a solar of the same date (*circa* 1275) and a service block of the early 13th century. The house was extensively altered in the 16th century, but many of the details of the original building survive.

RAYNE HALL, Braintree (by appointment with the owner)
An unusually interesting timber-framed house, re-modelled about 1500 and later, with some good early 16th century panelling.

SPAINS HALL, Finchingfield (open some summer weekends, or by

appointment with Col. Sir John Ruggles-Brise)
A harmonious late 16th century building of brick, L-shaped in plan, with curvilinear gables on its main fronts and pierced bargeboarding on the north west front. The interior decoration is of various periods, mainly early 17th century, Georgian and Victorian.

Gloucestershire

ALDERLEY GRANGE, Alderley, Wooton under Edge (by written
   appointment with Guy & The Hon. Mrs Acloge)
Alderley Grange was built in 1608 and has a handsome classical front added in about 1750. It has a Cotswold stone roof and three hipped dormers. The main feature of the interior is the fine mid-18th century staircase.

ASHLEWORTH COURT, nr Gloucester (parties only by appointment
   with Mr H.J. Chamberlayne; tel: Hartpury (045 270) 241)
A house of *circa* 1460, L-shaped in plan with a stone newel stair in the angle between hall and solar ranges. The hall has large traceried windows but some of the other windows in the house have been altered. The great hall, once rising the full height of the house, has been subdivided but its ornamental timber roof survives in the first floor room. The only really major alteration has been the substitution of tiles for the original thatch.

ASHLEWORTH MANOR, Ashleworth (by written appointment with
   Dr Jeremy Barnes)
The manor house, also known as the Old Vicarage, is a late 15th century timber-framed E-shaped building with an exceptionally rich and complete exterior. The interior has some fine timbering and a good fireplace.

BEVERSTON CASTLE, Tetbury (by written appointment with Mrs
   Laurence Rook)
The substantial remains of a 13th and 14th century castle of the Berkeleys, to which is attached a long low 17th century house. The castle contains two chapels, and the gatehouse to the courtyard also survives.

CASTLE GODWIN, Painswick (by written appointment with Mr and
   Mrs John Milne)
A wool merchant's house of *circa* 1720, possibly incorporating an earlier building. The stone front is of five bays and two storeys, with a central segmental pediment showing finely executed detail.

CHACELEY HALL, nr Tewkesbury (by appointment with W.H. Lane;
   tel: Tirley (045 278) 205)

A timber-framed building of the 15th century with 16th century additions on the north and south sides. One 16th century window survives in the north addition. The roof of the 15th century range is almost complete, four bays with arch-braces, collars and curved wind-braces.

CHELTENHAM: THIRLESTANE HOUSE (School) (by appointment with the Secretary to the Council, The Bursar's Office, Cheltenham College; tel: Cheltenham (0242) 22105)
One of the most important houses in Cheltenham. It was begun in 1893 and may have been designed by J.R. Scott, the first owner. It has a notable entrance hall, which is aisled with two Greek Ionic colonnades, and has a carved and rosetted ceiling.

CHURCH STANWAY: THE OLD VICARAGE (by appointment with The Estate Office, Stanway, Cheltenham; tel: Stanton (038 673) 469)
The Old Vicarage is a group of cottages built in a U-shaped plan with the entrance between the arms in a typical early 17th century Cotswold manner.

CORSE COURT, Hartpury (by written appointment with Mr and Mrs C.A. Barrett)
A timber-framed building of the late 14th or 15th century with four pairs of crucks and a bay and cross-wing added in the 17th century.

DANEWAY HOUSE, Sapperton (by written appointment with Sir Anthony Denny, Bt)
An attractive stone building. The oldest part is the hall range which was built in the later 13th century and subdivided in the 16th. The oratory was added in about 1339 and the high building at one end in about 1620. At the beginning of this century the house was lent to Ernest Gimson and the Barnsley brothers as a workshop and showroom for their furniture.

FRAMPTON COURT, Frampton on Severn (by written appointment with Mrs Clifford Saul)
Built in about 1730 to the designs of John Strahan, Frampton Court is an interpretation of Colen Campbell's Stourhead, largely in the style of Vanbrugh. The fine quality of the exterior elevation is matched by the contemporary interiors. A rectanguar canal to the north of the house is terminated by a delicious Gothick orangery by William Halfpenny.

LASBOROUGH PARK, Tetbury (by written appointment with Walter Curtis Esq)
A compact house designed in 1794 in a semi-Gothic castellated style with Tudor windows. The interiors are simple, with sparse classical decoration.

MATSON HOUSE, Matson (School) (by appointment with the Bursar, Selwyn School; tel: Gloucester (0452) 26572)
A 16th century stone building of three storeys with stone mullioned windows, and a Cotswold stone roof with finials. It has a pleasant 18th century wing and the interiors are exceptionally fine.

NAILSWORTH: STOKESCROFT, Cossack Square (access during office hours by appointment with A.E Smith & Sons Solrs; tel: Nailsworth (045 383) 2566)
A stone building dating from the period at the turn of the 17th century. The interior is almost intact: the staircase in particular is an excellent piece of work.

OWLPEN MANOR, Owlpen, nr Dursley (by written appointment with Mr & Mrs Mander)
A picturesque stone house. A new hall and great chamber were added in 1540 and the west wing in 1616. The interior has many good features, including some rare painted wall hangings in the great chamber.

SOUTHAM DELABERE, Cheltenham (School) (by written appointment with the Headmaster)
Built by Sir John Huddleston in the early 16th century but restored and extended by Lord Ellenborough in the mid-19th century. A considerable amount of the original house remains; the most noteworthy feature is the stone roof.

STANLEY PONTLARGE: THE COTTAGE (by appointment with Mrs S.M. Rolt)
This house consists of a late mediaeval two storey building, to the north end of which a slightly smaller Georgian building has been added.

Hampshire

CHARFORD MANOR, Breamore (by written appointment with E. Hardy Esq)
A fine brick building of *circa* 1600 with an unusual late 18th century facade overlying the gable end. An early hall range, probably of the 14th century, projects from one end.

EAST MEON: COURT HOUSE (by appointment with Mr Arthur D. Gill; tel: East Meon (173 087) 274)
The house was built about 1400 or a little later. The hall range and the service wing at the north end are preserved; the south wing has been

demolished. The house was restored between the wars by the architect Morley Horder.

HALE PARK, Fordingbridge (by written appointment with Mrs Patrick Hickman)
Thomas Archer rebuilt this house for his own use in about 1715 and Henry Holland partly remodelled it in 1770. The house is planned internally round an oblong double-storey staircase hall, having an oak staircase with graceful wrought iron balustrading.

HAMBLEDON: MANOR FARM HOUSE (by written appointment with Mr S.B. Mason)
This house contains the remains of a flint and chalk built 13th century structure probably the service and solar end of a house, the hall of which has vanished. The remains are of great rarity and archaeological value.

MARSH COURT, Stockbridge (School) (by appointment with the Headmaster; tel: Stockbridge (026 481) 503)
A spectacular early house by Sir Edwin Lutyens for Edward Johnson. Built 1901–4 almost entirely of hewn chalk; according to Christopher Hussey, 'a visual embodiment of the zestful vitality we associate with Elizabethan England and the revival of its spirit rather than its style.'

MOYLES COURT, Ellingham, Ringwood (School) (by appointment with the Headmaster; tel: Ringwood (042 54) 2856)
Basically, Moyles court is a 16th century house remodelled in Restoration times. Although the interior has not survived, externally the house looks much as it must have done 300 years ago; the attractive early 17th century stable block which adjoins it is little altered.

Hereford and Worcester

BRILLEY CWMMAU FARMHOUSE, Whitney on Wye (open summer Bank Holidays, or by appointment with Mr S.M. Joyce (National Trust tenant))
A Jacobean house with a two-storey porch.

CROOME COURT, Croome d'Abitot (School) (by appointment with the Besford Court School; tel: Pershore (038 65) 2074)
A large Palladian stone house begun in 1751; the architect was Lancelot Brown, perhaps with the assistance of Sanderson Miller. Most of the original interiors are now in the Metropolitan Museum in New York but some remain, including some Adam work, and the landscaped grounds

contain many small buildings and also a church designed by both Brown and Adam, which is now in the care of the Redundant Churches Fund.

DOWLES MANOR, Bewdley (by written appointment, for parties only, with Mrs M.C. Sholden)
A small but very complete Elizabethan timber-framed manor house with a central hall and two wings. Inside there are some very well-preserved wall-paintings in the three principal rooms.

EVESHAM: CHURCH HOUSE (by appointment with the Trustees of the Walker Hall & Church House)
In an important position in the town centre of Evesham, this house is of late 15th or early 16th century date and is a post-and-panel timber structure. Its original framing is intact and internally it has a late 15th century fireplace and the fragment of a mediaeval painting.

GRAFTON MANOR, Bromsgrove (by written appointment with Mr. J.W. Morris)
A manor house, of which most of the interesting surviving parts date from Sir John Talbot's rebuilding in the 16th century; the porch, dated 1567, bears the arms of Queen Elizabeth I.

HARTLEBURY CASTLE (by appointment with the Bishop's Secretary; tel: Hartlebury (029 96) 410)
It has been the seat of the Bishops of Worcester since before the Norman Conquest. The present building has a mediaeval hall and adheres to the mediaeval plan but is mainly of the 17th century with 18th century additions. The Great Hall, the shell of which is 15th century, was replanned in the late 17th century and is a most interesting example of the late survival of a mediaeval hall.

HEATH HOUSE, Leintwardine (by appointment with Mr Simon Dale ARIBA; tel: Bedstone 234)
Heath House was built in the early 17th century and is of two storeys in red brick with tiled roofs. Much of the original early 17th century work remains including panelling and plasterwork, but the outstanding feature is a remarkable staircase dating from about 1700; it has turned balusters, panelled risers, moulded rails and square panelled newels with moulded terminals.

HEREFORD: 24/5 CHURCH STREET (sometimes open for exhibitions, or key obtainable at 29 Church Street)
A timber-framed building of the late 16th century showing two identical gables towards the street, one with its original decorative bargeboards.

Internally, there is a stone-built cellar with a fine central barrel-vault and a 15th century doorway and an exceptionally fine early 17th century plaster ceiling in one of the upper rooms.

HUDDINGTON COURT, nr Droitwich (by written appointment with Dr Hugh D. Edmonson)
An early 16th century timber-framed house with many alterations. The main part of the building is L-shaped with a fanciful brick chimney in the angle. The porch is of 1584 and most of the interiors are also of that time.

KENTCHURCH COURT, Hereford (parties only by appointment with Lady Patricia Lucas Scudamore; tel: Golden Valley (0981) 240228)
Originally a 14th century castle, largely rebuilt by John Nash some time between 1795 and 1807. The remaining mediaeval parts are a gateway, the mighty north west tower and the north east range. Nash faced the original hall with ashlar and moved the porch. There is also work of the early 18th century and mid-19th century. The interior has some woodwork transferred from Holme Lacy and perhaps by Gibbons.

TEDGEWOOD FARM, Upton Bishop, nr Ross on Wye (by written appointment with Mr and Mrs A.T. Price; April to end Sept only)
An unusual type of timber-framed house of the second half of the 17th century with a central entrance and stair hall flanked by two rooms on either side.

UPPER WYTHALL, Walford, Ross on Wye (by appointment with Mrs Stratford McIntyre)
An early 16th century house, half-H in plan, with an open-roofed hall in the middle, extended in the latter part of the 16th century at the upper end, where an unusual jettied garderobe was added.

WEOBLEY: THE LEY (by appointment with Lt Col Sir Richard Verdin, Stoke Hall, Nantwich, Cheshire; tel: Wettenhall (027 073) 284)
Dates from about 1589, since when its external appearance has scarcely been changed — it is timber-framed and two storeys high with a Cotswold stone roof. As well as certain external details the house contains its original moulded ceiling beams and joists and some well-preserved panelling.

WOOLLAS HALL, Pershore (by written appointment with W. Clark, 1A Woollas Hall)
An early 17th century house on the slopes of Bredon Hill. It has been little altered externally and its porch bears the date 1611. Internally it has been divided into ten flats, but the hall retains its screen and gallery balustrading and the 18th century staircase survives.

WORCESTER: THE GREYFRIARS, Friar Street (open May to end Sept, first Wed in each month, or for parties by written appointment with the National Trust tenant, Mr Matley More)
A very fine timber-framed house of about 1480, possibly built as the guest house of the vanished Friary. The front courtyard is flanked by wings which are probably 16th century. The main front has a jettied first floor with a twelve-light window and two gables with bargeboards. The hall is on the ground floor but the best room is on the first floor and has a decorative 16th century plaster frieze.

Hertfordshire

ASHRIDGE, Berkhamsted (open certain summer week-ends; tel: Little Gaddesden (044 284) 3491)
James Wyatt's house, built for the Second Earl of Bridgewater, is one of the most spectacular works of the early Gothic revival. It was completed after Wyatt's death by his nephew Wyatville, but substantially in accordance with his plans. The entrance front consists of a central block, dominated by the staircase tower and flanked by two courtyards. On the other side of the house the central accent is the chapel tower of two stages surmounted by a spire.

LOCKLEYS, Welwyn (School) (by appointment with the Bursar, Sherrardswood School; tel: Welwyn (043 871) 4282)
Lockleys was built in 1717. Its chief feature, the west front, is provincial Baroque in style with remarkably fine brickwork. Most of the original panelling and chimneypieces survive throughout the two principal floors.

WOODHALL PARK, Watton at Stone (School) (by appointment with the Headmaster, Heath Mount School; tel: Ware (0920) 830230)
A house of 1777 by Thomas Leverton in which the staircase is decorated with allegorical paintings in the style of Angelica Kauffman and the Etruscan Hall with mythological scenes in the same style set in 'Etruscan' plasterwork.

Humberside

BOYNTON HALL, Bridlington (by written appointment with Mr W.S. Cook)
First built in the reign of Elizabeth I as an H-shaped three-storey mansion in red brick with stone quoins. Several alterations were made in the 18th century (the hall was, until recently, in the possession of the Strickland

family, who had been the owners for over four hundred years). The interior has handsome bolection panelling, a good oak staircase and enriched ceilings.

HULL: BLAYDES HOUSE, 6 High Street (by appointment only with Blackmore, Son & Co, Architects, Mon to Fri 10.30–1, 2–4; tel: Hull (0482) 26406)
A fine merchant's house of *circa* 1740 of two and a half storeys originally divided into five bays, with a plain exterior apart from the porch, which has a projecting pediment with enriched entablature and soffit standing on Doric columns with Doric pilaster responds. The interior is richly decorated, with a fine staircase, plaster decoration, enriched modillion cornices, panelling and pedimented doorcases.

Kent

BARMING PLACE, Maidstone (by appointment with Mr J.P. and Dr R. Bearcroft; tel: Maidstone (0622) 27844)
A handsome Georgian residence of three storeys and five bays, built in 1768. The house contains some fine 18th century fittings, including an oak staircase several fireplaces and much decorative plasterwork.

BETTESHANGER HOUSE, Deal (School) (by appointment with the Headmaster; tel: Eastry (030 486) 215)
At Betteshanger George Devey, the predecessor of Norman Shaw, Nesfield and Webb, revived in effect the 'Picturesque' mode of fifty years earlier, drawing for inspiration on a mixture of locally derived details. The original building was a late Georgian villa. From 1856 onwards by additions and alterations Devey created the impression of a building that had grown up over the years as a patchwork of different styles, dates and materials.

BUMPIT, Lynsted (by appointment with J.A.M. Vaughan and A.J.W. Vaughan; tel: (0795) 521610)
A small timber-framed building erected by WC in 1587. In plan the house is L-shaped, the rear wing being a relic of an earlier house. The chief interest lies in the extensive wall paintings and painted decoration also dating from about 1587.

FAIRFIELD HOUSE, Eastry, Sandwich (by appointment with Mr and Mrs Anthony Crane; tel: Eastry (030 486) 489 or (0304) 611489)
A small timber-framed hall and end house of about 1500, almost unaltered.

FAVERSHAM: 6 MARKET PLACE (by written appointment with Mr.

J.B. Kerr)
A quadrangular town house, probably of the 14th or 15th century. The two storey elevation of three plaster-faced gables has a Gothic arched entrance alongside the 18th century front of the 'Old Pharmacy' of which the gilded mortar sign projects above. The chapel room contains wall paintings datable from the costumes to about 1500.

HONEYWOOD HOUSE, Lenham (by appointment with the tenant)
A small sumptuous timber-framed house dated 1621. The symmetrical front is of two storeys with the first floor overhanging and two attic gables overhanging yet again. The whole is supported by grotesque figure brackets. Beneath the overhangs are oriel windows with similar brackets.

LUDDESDOWN COURT, Cobham (by appointment with Mr J.A. Williams; tel: Cobham (Kent) 359)
A 13th century building retaining its original L-shaped plan, with hall, solar, small chamber and dovecote. Much of the original wall decoration remains as well as a number of early graffiti.

MERSHAM LE HATCH, nr Ashford (School) (by appointment with the Caldecott Community; tel: Ashford (0233) 23954)
An important house by Robert Adam and the first to be designed by him from the foundations up. It was built in 1762-5. There are typical interiors by Adam, with stucco work by Joseph Rose and paintings by Antonio Zucchi.

NURSTEAD COURT, Meopham (by appointment with Major R.W. Edmeades; tel: Meopham (0474) 812121)
The west part of the building is all that remains of a 14th century hallhouse. The east part was demolished early in the 19th century and replaced by a Regency-style wing which has since been altered. This is a very rare example of an aisled domestic hall, where the aisles are formed with timber columns.

OTTERDEN PLACE, Faversham (by appointment with D.K. Merifield Esq; tel: Eastling (079 589) 341)
Originally a 16th century brick courtyard house, much of which was demolished or altered in the late 18th century. The fine first floor gallery has a timber bracketted cornice and a four-centred stone fireplace. There are also 16th and 18th century timber doorcases and an early 18th century fully panelled bedroom.

PARAMOUR GRANGE, nr Westmarsh (by appointment with the owner, through the Sandwich Local History Society, 42 High Street, Sandwich)

A house with Jacobean wall-paintings on the first floor. The decoration consists of interlocking shapes with square beds containing floral motifs; the overall effect recalling stained glass. A frieze running round the room is dated 1603 and marked with the initials IR (Jacobus Rex) and H, probably for Henry, Prince of Wales.

SHARSTEAD COURT, Newnham, nr Sittingbourne (by written appointment with Canon E.H. Wade)
An E-shaped building, mainly of the 18th century, of fine brickwork with rubbed dressings and a timber cornice, but with a mediaeval core.

Lancashire

BORWICK HALL, Carnforth (by appointment with The Warden; tel: Carnforth (052 473) 2508)
A late 16th century building which includes an earlier pele tower. There is also a 17th century gatehouse and a long range of 16th century stables and barns. The house has interesting interiors.

CONISTON HALL (by appointment with the National Trust tenant)
Built in the late 16th century of rubble with Lake District chimneys, wooden window frames and much timber-framing inside. The hall and solar are on the first floor.

JACKSONS HOUSE FARM, Worsthorne, Burnley (by appointment with Mrs Elsie Witt; tel: Burnley (0282) 28477)
Roughly T-shaped in plan; at the east end there is a two-storey solar wing and the remainder formed the hall or housebody. The latter was rebuilt in 1627. The solar is possibly half a century earlier.

PARROX HALL, Preesall, Fleetwood (by written appointment with D.H. Elleston)
An H-shaped house, probably of about 1600, constructed of brick rendered and painted white. Although much of the interior has been modernised, the hall is panelled and the drawing room has fluted Corinthian pilasters and a box cornice.

SCARISBRICK HALL, Ormskirk (School) (open to persons with a particular interest in architecture or in Victorian studies, by appointment with The Principal)
A.W. Pugin's most famous domestic building and a landmark in the Gothic revival. Pugin's work at Scarisbrick was begun in about 1837, but only completed many years after his death by his son E.W. Pugin. Much of

Pugin's decoration, which has parallels in the House of Lords, remains.

Leicestershire

APPLEBY MAGNA, THE MOAT HOUSE (by appointment with Mr
  H.S. Hall; tel: Measham (0530) 70301)
This consists of two distinct parts — a stone range probably of the mid or
late 15th century and a timber-framed range which appears to be 16th
century. They are the surviving fragments of a much larger house on the site
and the stone range was probably originally a gatehouse. The moat, from
which the house takes its name, can still be seen although it is now dry.

LOUGHBOROUGH: THE OLD RECTORY, Rectory Place (April to
  Oct, Thurs; contact The Parks & Recreation Office, Macaulay House, 5
  Cattle Market, Loughborough)
Within the walls of an otherwise undistinguished building are the remains of
a hall, with service block and great chamber, all belonging to the 14th
century. The remains of the hall include a group of three service doorways,
and the chamber block has its original ceiling beams and joists with parts of
the original partitions and fireplace still remaining. The hall is ruined but
the chamber block is a local museum.

NORTH LUFFENHAM HALL, nr Oakham (by written appointment
  with Mrs E. Cotton)
A composite building dating in part from the mid-16th century but greatly
remodelled in about 1600 and again in 1700.

SHENTON HALL GATEHOUSE, Shenton, nr Nuneaton (by
  appointment with Peter Hall Esq; tel: Hinckley (0455) 212253)
The gatehouse was built in 1629 of red brick and stone, square in plan with
straight gables to attics rising from each face. The interior is almost
completely of the 19th century.

STAUNTON HAROLD HALL, Ashby de la Zouch (Cheshire Home)
  (by appointment with The Warden; tel: Melbourne (033 16) 2571)
A brick mansion whose mainly 18th century exterior conceals an altered
Jacobean house. The Hall was the home of the Shirley family until the last
war, when it was converted into a Cheshire Home. There is a fine staircase,
the Justice Room contains some early 17th century panelling and there are
two good late 17th century gates. The celebrated church built during the
Civil War stands immediately in front of the east facade. The church now
belongs to the National Trust.

Lincolnshire

AUBORN HALL, nr Lincoln (open for a short period in the summer, or by appointment with H.N. Neville Esq)
An L-shaped house, originally Tudor but rebuilt by Sir John Meres some time between 1587 and 1628. There is also some artisan mannerist work of late 17th century date. The interior is also of two distinct periods; late 16th century and mid-17th century. The staircase has grotesque carved decoration of entwined foliage and serpents.

CAISTOR HOUSE, 19 Market Place, Caistor (by appointment with Mrs A.M. Frank; tel: Caistor (0472) 851434)
The most pretentious of the 17th and 18th century houses around the marketplace. Although dated 1682 the present three storey brick house with Ionic pilasters crowned by a pediment to the centre of the five bays appears to have been constructed about a century later.

CULVERTHORPE HALL, Grantham (by appointment with P.T.S. Bowlby Esq)
The original house was built in about 1679 for Sir John Newton and was subsequently altered and enlarged. There are two forecourt ranges: the east range probably mid-17th century and the west range contemporary with the 1679 hall.

FILLINGHAM CASTLE, nr Gainsborough (by written appointment with Mr W. Rose)
A mock castle believed to be the work of Carr of York, about 1760. The main building is square with rounded turrets at each corner and castellated parapets concealing the mansard roof. The entrance hall has a low-pitched barrel-vault ceiling of plaster with decorative ribs.

FULBECK MANOR, Grantham (by written appointment with Mr J.F. Fane)
Built in 1733 for Francis Fane, probably by a Stamford architect. The front is of five bays and two storeys divided by giant Doric pilasters. The three bay wing to the north was added shortly before 1800, although its upper storey is later. Inside there is good joinery to the hall and stairs, all of 1733.

GREAT PONTON RECTORY, Grantham (by appointment with The Rev H. Briggs; tel: Great Ponton (047 683) 251)
Built in the early 16th century, probably by Anthony Ellis, wool merchant of the staple of Calais, who built the west tower of the nearby church. It is a simple rectangular building of ashlar, three storeys high with gable ends,

one of which is crow-stepped. The roof has ten bays with unchamfered collars, purlins and wind-braces. On the first floor is a series of wall paintings of plant and animal motifs of French inspiration.

LINCOLN: 4 JAMES STREET (Deloraine Court South) (by appointment with Dr W.A. Maclure; tel: Lincoln (0522) 28480)
Deloraine Court is T-shaped in plan — the long cross bar being numbers 3 and 4 and the downstroke number 2. The latter appears to have been the open hall of the original mediaeval house, but there is early material in the basement of numbers 3 and 4.

LINCOLN: 18 JAMES STREET (The Cathedral School) (by appointment with the Headmaster; tel: Lincoln (0522) 28489)
Originally late 13th century lodgings consisting of an upper and a lower chamber used at one time as stables. The upper chamber has substantial remains of the original fireplace with brackets, joggle-jointed flat head and a semi-pyramidal hood. The open timber roof has a double braced crown post and double collars.

LINCOLN: 33-4 THE STRAIT (Dernstall House) (by appointment with the Lincoln Civic Trust; tel: Lincoln (0522) 24232)
This house is basically of interest as a rare specimen of a large town house of pre-1500 date. It includes the remains of a large first floor open-roofed hall or solar, with king-posttrusses.

MARSTON HALL, Grantham (by appointment with the Rev Henry Thorold; tel: Honington (040 04) 225)
An oblong block of two storeys, seemingly the central part of a large late 16th century H-shaped house. There are signs of considerable alterations which appear to date from about 1720.

SCRIVELSBY COURT, nr Horncastle (by written appointment with Lt Col J.L.M. Dymoke MBE DL)
Of the mid-16th century house of the Dymoke family — hereditary Champions of England — only the brick office range survives. The present house is mainly Georgian.

SEDGEBROOK MANOR, Grantham (by written appointment with Caroline Stuart)
Built about 1632 by Sir Robert Markham; of stone, in one long range with short projections at each end of the north side; refaced *circa* 1716 by the Thorold family. The low ground floor and the much taller *piano nobile* above seem to reflect in a crude form the Palladian style coming into fashion at that time.

SOMERTON CASTLE (by appointment with C.L. Thomasson Esq, but not during harvest))
Built by Anthony Bek, Bishop of Durham. The castle, surrounded by a large earthwork, consisted originally of an inner bailey of irregular rectangular form with circular towers of three storeys at the corners. There survive only the south east tower and the first storey of the north east and south west towers. The present house, which incorporated the south east tower, was probably rebuilt in about 1628, when the castle was acquired by the City of London.

SOMERSBY GRANGE (by written appointment with Lady Maitland, Harrington Hall, Spilsby, Lincs.)
A small simplified version of Vanbrugh's own house, Vanbrugh Castle, with sham machicolations, crenellations, corner turrets and round-headed windows; the interior arrangements are largely undisturbed.

WYBERTON PARK, Boston (by appointment with Mr F.C. Whitaker; tel: Boston (0205) 62194)
This house is built on a T-shaped plan. The main wing dates from 1761 and the secondary wing from about 1700. The interior contains a considerable number of good 18th century features, including a fine staircase.

Greater London

8 ADDISON ROAD, Kensington (by appointment with the Administrator, The Richmond Fellowship; tel: 01 603 6373)
Designed by Halsey Ricardo in 1906, and one of the innovating buildings of its period. Outside the walls are faced with green, blue and greenish-yellow tiles; the pilasters, arcading, cornices etc., are in a kind of white terra-cotta. The interior is mainly in Byzantine style, with mosaics and William de Morgan tiles.

50 ALBEMARLE STREET, W.1 (by written appointment with John Murray Ltd)
An early 18th century house, altered and stuccoed in the early 19th century, the home of the publishing house of Murray since the early 19th century. It houses considerable quantities of books and correspondence relating to Scott, Canning, Peel, Disraeli, Gladstone, Darwin, Coleridge and others, which are a valuable source of literary research.

ALL HALLOWS VICARAGE, Tottenham (by appointment with The Rev. R. Pearson; tel: 01 808 2470)

A modest early Georgian building which encases the early 17th century house of Joseph Fenton, a wealthy London merchant. Fittings include chimneypieces and dated plaster ceilings of the early 17th century, while the 18th century is represented by a striking rococo chimneypiece, a good staircase and other features.

ASGILL HOUSE, Richmond (by written appointment with Mr F. Hauptfuehrer)
Sir Robert Taylor built this house in 1760-70 for the Lord Mayor of London. The interior is arranged so that an octagonal room lies behind the front bay on each floor; the one on the upper floor has wallpaintings. There are fine chimneypieces throughout the house.

16 BUCKINGHAM GATE, Westminster (by appointment with The Principal, The British School of Osteopathy; tel: 01 828 9479)
A town house 1706 attributed to the architect William Winde, who was in charge of the building of Buckingham House, the predecessor of Buckingham Palace.

CARSHALTON HOUSE, Carshalton (School) (by appointment with the Sister Superior; tel: 01 642 0287)
Built in the late 17th century and altered 1715-21. One of the principal rooms has elaborate plaster decoration and another has early 18th century wall paintings. In the garden is a water pavilion in the Vanbrugh style and a small but elaborate grotto called The Hermitage.

11-13 CAVENDISH SQUARE, W.1 (by written appointment with the occupiers, Heythrop College)
This striking pair of mid-18th century houses forms part of the central feature of the north side of Cavendish Square. Fronted in Portland stone, they have Corinthian columns on the upper storeys and balustraded parapets.

CHARLTON HOUSE, Charlton, Greenwich (Day Centre) (by appointment with The Warden; tel: 01 856 3951)
One of the most important surviving Jacobean houses in London, with exuberant decoration to the centrepiece of the main front. The two-storey hall is placed at right angles to the main front — a notable innovation — and several of the other rooms have important chimneypieces.

CROMWELL HOUSE, 104 Highgate Hill (by appointment with The Rector, Mountford Missionaries; tel: 01 340 1108)
A long two-storey house with attics and basement, built in 1637–8; the carved and moulded brick front is one of the most important of its kind. The

interior has a fine carved oak staircase with statuettes of soldiers on the newels.

20 DEANS YARD, Westminster (Chapter (Office) (by appointment with the Receiver General, W.R.J. Pullen CVO JP LLB FCIS; tel: 01 222 5152)
The former rectory of St Margaret's, a mediaeval stone building on two floors with a fine vaulted ceiling on the ground floor. The early 18th century addition is of brick and tile. On the side facing the Abbey is the old, partly excavated misericord with original column bases.

EAGLE HOUSE, 224 London Road, Mitcham (Education Centre) (by appointment with the Vice Principal; tel: 01 640 7195)
Built *circa* 1705 in the Anglo-Dutch manner, possibly for Fernando Mendes, Physician in Ordinary to Catherine of Braganza. Two storeys of five bays above a semi-basement, with a high roof with dormers, timber eaves cornice, a balustrade to the roof platform and a tall glazed cupola.

EASTBURY HOUSE, Barking (by appointment with the London Borough of Barking; tel: 01 592 4500)
An important Elizabethan house built between 1550 and 1570. Of brick, on an H-plan, three storeys high. The exterior has been little altered, except that one of the rear staircase towers has been destroyed, but few of the interior features remain. One room has original panelling and the first floor great chamber over the hall has painted mural decoration.

KELMSCOTT HOUSE, 26 Upper Mall, Hammersmith (by appointment with The Secretary, William Morris Society; tel: 01 748 5618)
A late 18th century house in which William Morris lived from 1878 until 1891 and partly decorated by him.

LINLEY SAMBOURNE HOUSE, 18 Stafford Terace, W8 (open March to Oct, Wed 10–4 and Sun 2–5 by appointment with the Victorian Society, 1 Priory Gardens, London W4; tel: 01 994 1019)
A late Victorian town house, once the home of Edward Linley Sambourne, a leading cartoonist of the late 19th and early 20th century. The magnificent 'artistic' interior has survived largely unchanged, with original decorations, fixtures and fittings.

LITTLE HOLLAND HOUSE, 40 Beeches Avenue, Carshalton (open on the first Sunday in each month, March to Oct, or by appointment with the curator, Mrs Pat Shepherd; tel: 01 661 5050)
Built from 1902 onwards by the artist/craftsman F.R. Dickinson. Together

with its contents, most of which were designed and made by him, it is a unique record of the Arts and Crafts movement inspired by Ruskin and Morris. The house is now owned by the local authority.

THE PRESBYTERY, 66 Crooms Hill, Greenwich (by appointment with the Rev Mother Superior, Ursuline Convent; tel: 01 858 0779)
This is a small brick house of *circa* 1630 looking eastwards to Greenwich Park. Its interest is centred on its street elevation with its two plastered gables and the moulded brickwork of its cornice and first floor pilasters. It is one of the few examples of this type and date remaining in London.

RED HOUSE, Red House Lane, Bexleyheath (open on the first Sunday in each month 2.30–4.30 by written appointment with Mr and Mrs Hollamby)
There can be a few houses in recent times which were built under such distinguished auspices as this. Phillip Webb designed Red House for William Morris who lived in it and the decoration was by Rossetti and Burne-Jones. To all people interested in the preservation of buildings this house is a practical reminder of the spirit of an early enthusiast in the field.

THE ROUND HOUSE, Havering-atte-Bower (by written appointment with Mr Michael Heap)
An unusual late 18th century house which, despite its name, is not round but elliptical. The building has obvious links with John Plaw's Belle Isle on Lake Windermere.

STRAWBERRY HILL, Twickenham (Theological College) (by appointment with The Principal; tel: 01 892 0051)
Horace Walpole's famous 'Otranto Gothic' fantasy, one of the crucial buildings in the revival of the Gothic style with several important interiors.

Greater Manchester

SLADE HALL, Slade Lane, Longsight (by written appointment with Mr R.A. Fieldhouse)
The two-storey house, dated 1585 with the initials ES on the porch, is one of the few surviving timber-framed buildings in Manchester. A room on the first floor has enriched plaster frieze panels on the walls, that on the west wall consisting of two spirited hunting scenes with the Stanley crest; that on the east wall of three coats of arms and two small figures in niches.

West Midlands

CHEYLESMORE MANOR, Coventry (Registry Office) (by appointment with the Superintendent Registrar; tel: Coventry (0203) 255555 ext 2685)
The gatehouse and part of two adjoining wings are all that remain of what was once a royal manor house. Although the exterior is clad in rendering so that the superficial appearance is late Georgian, much of the original 14th to 16th century timber-framed structure remains.

Norfolk

GOWTHORPE MANOR, Swardeston (by appointment with Francis Horner & Sons Ltd., Queen St., Norwich; tel: Norwich (0603) 29871)
The house is built on the unusual plan of a cross of Lorraine and dates from 1574. It has interesting interiors which make up a harmonious mixture of original, late 17th century and early 18th century work.

GREAT CRESSINGHAM PRIORY (by written appointment with Mrs F. Chapman)
A fragment of a once sumptuous brick house of *circa* 1545, notable for the unique facing of moulded terra-cotta in a reticulated pattern with heraldic devices in relief in the centres of the panels.

HALES HALL, Loddon (by appointment with Mr and Mrs T.E. Read; tel: Raveningham (050 846) 395)
Originally a substantial mansion, now a farmhouse consisting of a very long brick range with diaper decoration and a large barn. These both belonged to the outer courtyard of the house.

HOVETON HOUSE, Wroxham (by written appointment with Mr T.R.C. Blofeld)
Built towards the end of the 17th century, a charming red brick house with a front eleven bays long and two storeys high with a steep three bay pediment on attentuated Corinthian giant pilasters. Inside are fine fireplaces of about 1740 and a good staircase of the same date.

HORSHAM ST FAITH: ABBEY FARM (by written appointment with Mr and Mrs R.W. Newell)
The farm house is a conversion of the north or Frater range of the 12th century Priory, the cloisters now forming the garden. A number of mediaeval details survive, including a large 12th century doorway and a rare example of a painted frater reredos.

LANGLEY HALL, Loddon (School) (open during the school holidays by appointment with the Headmaster)
Dating from 1740, by Matthew Brettingham the elder. The exterior is of red brick with stone dressings and is elaborately ornamented with urns and statues; the interior contains plasterwork by Charles Stanley, J.F. Clermont and Salvin.

LITTLE HAUTBOIS HALL, nr Norwich (by appointment with the Steward to the Trustees, c/o Francis Horner & Son, Queen St., Norwich)
A good example of an East Anglian type of house, built in the late 16th century. Of brick with a flat front, mullion and transom windows and dormers with pinnacles. The main gables also have pinnacles.

MANNINGTON HALL, Saxthorpe (open on Thursdays only, by written appointment with The Hon Robin Walpole)
A moated mediaeval house built of brick which was under construction in 1460. Parts of the original house have been destroyed and some alterations and additions were made by the second Earl of Orford in 1864.

METHWOLD: THE OLD VICARAGE (by written appointment with Mr and Mrs H.C. Dance)
Basically a timber-framed building, the Old Vicarage would be of note even without its chief claim to distinction, which is the spectacular west front — one of the richest examples of East Anglian moulded terra-cotta work. The interior retains much of its original plan and details.

RAINTHORPE HALL, Newton Flotman (by appointment with Mr G.F. Hastings; tel: Swainsthorpe (0508) 470618)
Most of the Hall dates from the second half of the 16th century and is of brick, except for the upper storey of the main range which is timber-framed with close studding. The interior contains a number of original 16th and 17th century features.

SHERRINGHAM HALL (by written appointment with Mr Thomas Upcher)
An unspoilt Repton house in an unspoilt Reptonian setting. It was designed in 1813–20 by John Adey Repton in association with his father who landscaped the gardens.

THORPE HALL, Diss (by written appointment with Mr and Mrs David Mlinaric)
This compact mid-16th century house is only one room thick and two rooms and a hall long, and was probably intended as a hunting lodge. An

ornamental stack and three-storeyed porches to the front and back, fenestrated like the house and reaching above the eaves, contribute to the striking appearance.

WILBY HALL, nr Quidenham (by appointment with Mr and Mrs C. Warner)
A house of about 1650 built of red brick with stepped gables and mullion and transom windows. The staircase with turned balusters is Elizabethan in appearance.

Northamptonshire

APETHORPE HALL, Peterborough (by appointment with The Principal, St John's County Home; tel: King's Cliffe (078 087) 263)
An early Tudor house, greatly extended in about 1680 and partly remodelled in the mid 18th century. The house is grouped round two courtyards and the east front is one of the best pieces of Jacobean work in the county. The interior has fine plaster ceilings and some good chimneypieces.

ASTWELL CASTLE FARMHOUSE, nr Brackley (by written appointment with Mr Graham Pidgeon)
The present buildings consist of a small stone manor house with mullioned windows and gables, standing beside and linked to a three storey crenellated gatehouse. The manor house probably dates from the late 16th century, the gatehouse is somewhat earlier. Originally the latter formed the approach to an imposing courtyard house of which only the humbler apartments remain as the present dwelling.

COURTEENHALL, Northampton (by written appointment with Sir Hereward Wake Bt. MC)
A late 18th century stone faced house designed for Sir William Wake by Samuel Saxon, a pupil of Sir William Chambers. The landscape design of the park is by Humphrey Repton.

DEENE PARK (open for a few days each summer; parties at other times by appointment with the Housekeeper; tel: Bulwick (078 085) 223)
Since 1514 Deene Park has been owned by the Brudenell family and it has been added to in nearly every century since; as a result the present house is large and complex. It is built round a courtyard with the Elizabethan hall range to the south and an earlier hall range to the east. There are some fine interiors.

DRAYTON HOUSE, Lowick, Ketting (by written appointment with
    L.G. Stopford Sackville Esq)
Simon de Drayton received license to crenellate in 1328 although the house
existed in some form before then. Alterations were made in the 15th
century, a north east wing was added in 1584 and important work was
carried out in the years after 1702 when William Talman remodelled the
great hall and added the courtyard colonnades and the stone staircase with
its painted wall decorations. Altogether an extremely interesting building.

EASTON ON THE HILL: PRIEST'S HOUSE (access by appointment
    only with the Rector; tel: Stamford (0780) 2616; or with Mr H. Overhall,
    Rock House, 2 Stamford Rd., Easton on the Hill; tel: Stamford (0780)
    2052)
Surviving examples of priests' houses are rare. This small two-storey
building of the late 15th or early 16th century shows what form the
parsonage house of a small benefice must have taken. It now contains a
small museum.

OUNDLE: PAINE'S COTTAGES (by written appointment with Mr.
    R.O. Barker)
The cottages were originally built as two houses in local coursed rubble with
ashlar quoins and dressings and Collyweston slate roofs. A picturesque wall
seals off the courtyard from a street on the north side and contains a fine
ornamental doorway. The building was brought into use as an almshouse at
the beginning of the 19th century.

Northumberland

CRASTER TOWER, Alnwick (by written appointment with Mr J.H.
    Craster, Mr O.E. Craster and Mrs Eadie)
Craster Tower was standing in 1415 and still stands today to its full height,
attached to an east wing of indeterminate date and a south wing which is in
the form of a three storey classical house of 1767–70.

ELSDON TOWER, Elsdon (by appointment with Mr G.N. Taylor; tel:
    Otterburn (0830) 20688)
A pele tower with the characteristic oblong plan, thought to have been
erected *circa* 1400 when the church was rebuilt. There are two principal
storeys over a tunnel-vaulted ground storey.

HARNHAM HALL, Belsay (by appointment with Mr J. Wake)
A 17th century farm house combined with a mediaeval pele tower. It is

situated on a hill top guarding a sheer tree-clad cliff. From 1667 to 1677 it was owned by Philip Babington and still contains relics of his family.

LANGLEY CASTLE, Langley on Tyne, nr Hexham (by appointment with the Manager; tel: Haydon Bridge (043 484) 481)
The castle was built in about 1350 by Sir Thomas de Lucy but is said to have been destroyed by Henry IV in 1405 and by the middle of the 16th century it was an abandoned ruin. However it was sympathetically restored at the end of the last century and remains one of the most impressive castles in the border counties.

Nottinghamshire

CARLTON HALL, Carlton on Trent, Newark (by written appointment with Lt Col G.H. Jere-Laurie DL JP)
A medium-sized Georgian country house. Three-storey centre block dated 1765, flanked by pedimented wings, all built of brick without stone dressings. One wing is wholly occupied by the drawing room whose walls and ceilings have elaborate decorative plasterwork in the Adam style. The architect for the building may have been Carr of York, or perhaps John Johnson of Leicester.

CLIFTON HALL, Clifton (by appointment with the owner)
Early 17th century house, remodelled by John Carr in 1779 onwards in a plain manner. The three-storey house is built of patched red brick with stuccoed dressings and has a roof balustrade. The interior has important work of the late 17th and early 18th centuries.

THRUMPTON HALL (by appointment for parties of twenty or more; tel: Nottingham (0602) 830333)
Built between 1609–17 by Gervase Pigot and modernised by his son in the 1660s. The house is H-shaped with an original loggia between the wings on the entrance side. The younger Pigot added Flemish gables and rebuilt the west wall to accommodate a new great staircase. There are good interiors of the early and late 17th century and the house has a pleasant lakeside setting.

Oxfordshire

ABINGDON: TWICKENHAM HOUSE (by written appointment with Mrs Marie Alex)
A brick town house of about 1760 occupying an important place in one of the

best streets in Abingdon: there is a good staircase hall and a fine garden stretching down to the Thames.

BANBURY: 85 HIGH STREET (by written appointment with Mrs E. Zwirn, Mr H. Cohen and Mrs S. Sherwood (Bennett's Estates))
A characteristic early 17th century timber-framed building of two main storeys with an ornate gabled attic and prominent jetties at each level on the street front. The overhang of the first floor is underbuilt by a 19th century shop front but the large bowed window on the first floor, the decorative bargeboards and the elaborate cornice are all original.

BUSCOT OLD PARSONAGE, nr Lechlade (open Wed 2–6 by written appointment with the Tenant)
A fine early 18th century stone house with a front of five bays.

COTE HOUSE, Aston (by written appointment with Mrs David Anderson)
This is a typical 16th century manor house of mellow appearance with old lime rendering and stone dressings. There is also a walled courtyard with four gateways, three of which have original iron gates.

DITCHLEY PARK, Enstone (Conference Centre) (open for a short period each summer; tel: Enstone (060 872) 346)
Built in 1720-5, this is the most important surviving country house designed by James Gibbs. The central block of the house is of four storeys, with low curving wings leading to side pavilions. The interior has some particularly fine plasterwork. The entrance hall was decorated by William Kent.

EDGECOTE HOUSE, nr Chipping Warden (by appointment with E.R. Courage Esq; tel: Enstone (029 586) 257)
A delightful Palladian house, built in 1747–52 for Richard Chaucey. The main interest of the interior is the plasterwork by J. Whitehead and the handsome carving in the stairhall by Abraham Swan.

HENLEY ON THAMES: THE CHANTRY HOUSE (by written appointment with The Rev Alan Pyburn)
A mediaeval timber-framed building with the first floor jettied to east and west. At the north and south ends are the original timber doorcases. The first floor room is aisled.

HINTON MANOR, Hinton Waldrist (by appointment with Nicholas Davenport CBE)
The house stands within a moat, which is supposed to have belonged to a mediaeval motte and bailey castle. The main front of the house dates from

the early 18th century but there is evidence of early 17th century work.

KELMSCOTT MANOR, Kelmscott, nr Lechlade (open on the first Wed in each month from April to Sept 11–1, 2–5)
This hamlet owes its fame to William Morris, who leased the manor house from 1871 until his death in 1896. Morris described the house as 'Elizabethan in appearance but much later in date', which indeed it is. The interior still has the pleasing George I panelling painted white which Morris described, together with a fine collection of his furniture and works of art.

KINGSTONE LISLE PARK, nr Wantage (by appointment with The Secretary; tel: Uffington (036 782) 223)
Apparently a substantial mid-Georgian house, to which wings were added in 1813 by Richard Pace. A number of internal alterations appear to have been made shortly after this, including the building of an extravagant and spectacular staircase.

STEVENTON: 39-43 THE CAUSEWAY (by written appointment with Mr and Mrs H.C. Dance, The Old Vicarage, Methwold, Norfolk)
This building dates from 1350. It is an outstanding example among the cruck houses of England and a remarkable survival of this mediaeval form of construction.

STEVENTON: 103-7 THE CAUSEWAY (by appointment with James Cobban Esq; tel: Steventon (0235) 831444)
This is one of a group of timber-framed buildings alongside The Causeway forming a remarkable collection of mediaeval building types. The Old Vicarage dates from the late 14th century and has a king post roof.

WOODSTOCK: HOPE HOUSE (by written appointment with Capt J. Marston Money RN)
This house is reputed to have been built by Sir John Vanbrugh when he was engaged at Blenheim Palace and is a remarkable instance of the Vanbrugh style applied to a small town house. Its grimness is offset by bow windows added later. It is ashlar faced with Cotswold stone.

WROXTON ABBEY, Wroxton, nr Banbury (Bank holidays in summer or by appointment with the Wroxton College of Farleigh Dickinson University; tel: Wroxton St Mary (029 573) 551)
Little remains of the Augustinian Priory founded here in the early 13th century except some walling concealed in the north wing. A house was begun in the 17th century but left incomplete in 1631. Sanderson Miller remodelled the chapel in 1747 and Sydney Smirke added a library in 1830. The building was restored in 1858 by John Gibson and much 16th and 17th

century carved woodwork was introduced. The fine hall gallery, however, is original.

WYTHAM ABBEY, Wytham, nr Oxford (by appointment with the agents L. Fink Ltd., 121 Princes Street, Manchester M1 7AD)
The Abbey is a rambling house grouped round a large staircase hall, which lies half hidden behind the picturesque group of buildings which comprises the village of Wytham. The mediaeval gate tower and the 16th and 17th century range to the north of it have considerable resemblance to some of the college buildings in nearby Oxford.

Shropshire

BEDSTONE COURT, Bucknell (School) (by appointment with the Headmaster; tel: Bucknell (054 74) 303)
Built by Thomas Harris between 1879 and 1884 for Sir Henry Rigley; of red brick, stone quoins and timber panels filled with plain plaster. The visual effect, combining a variety of parts with the unity of the whole, is carefully considered and pleasing. The interior decoration is restrained, with extensive use of natural wood and stained glass.

BROSELEY HALL, Broseley (by written appointment with the owner)
A mid-18th century red brick building of three storeys and five bays with stone quoins at the angles, rusticated stone lintels with keystones projecting upwards to the windows, stone cornices and plain parapets. The interior is relatively complete.

CRONKHILL, Atcham (by appointment with the National Trust tenant)
Built by John Nash in 1802 and forming part of the Attingham estate. A picturesque Italianate villa dominated by a massive round tower linked by a colonnade to a lower square tower.

CONDOVER HALL, Condover, nr Shrewsbury (during August only by written appointment)
An H-plan house, one of the most distinguished of its type, built of local stone in 1595-8 by the Shropshire mason Walter Hancock. The interior contains some good 18th century decoration. The house is used by the Royal National Institute for the Blind and only part of the house is open to view.

LONGNER HALL, Uffington, nr Shrewsbury (by written appointment with R.F.L. Burton Esq)
Built *circa* 1805 by John Nash in the Gothic manner with pictuesquely

irregular elevations. The interior is remarkably untouched, with plaster fan-vaults, gothic friezes and pelmets and stained glass by David Evans.

LONGNOR HALL, Longnor (by appointment with Major and Mrs Lawson; tel: Dorrington (074 373) 543)
Built *circa* 1670, a fine example of the home of a small well-to-do country gentleman under Charles II. The interior, which follows the typical plan of its date, survives almost intact: the staircase, derived from Coleshill, clearly resembles that of Powis Castle.

LUDLOW: 1 and 1A HIGH STREET (Shop) (ground floor open daily during shop hours; upper floor by appointment with Treasurer's Estates Ltd., Eagle House, Corve Street, Ludlow)
A timbered building adjoining the Butter Cross, historically of one build with number 2 though the latter now appears to be the older of the pair. The roof construction and single stack suggest that number 2 was the cross-wing of the house of which 1 and 1A originally formed the main range. Number 1 was re-modelled in the 18th century and given a stuccoed front.

MARKET DRAYTON: THE OLD HOUSE, 41 Shropshire Street (by appointment with B.D. Hilton Esq; tel: Mkt Drayton (0603) 2361)
An early 18th century building of red brick, two storeys with attic and dormers.

MAWLEY HALL, Cleobury Mortimer (by written appointment with A.M.G. Galliers-Pratt Esq)
The house was built in the 1730s for Sir Edward Blount and remained in his family until the Tenth Baronet died in 1958. The exterior of the house is dignified and sober. The interior is a treasury of craftsmanship which has few equals. The staircase with its serpentine balustrade, the richly modelled plasterwork, the veneered inlaid panelling and the marquetry floors are the principal features, all of the highest quality.

MORVILLE HALL, Bridgnorth (by appointment with Miss Bythell (National Trust tenant))
Basically of the 16th century, the house was altered both externally and internally in the 18th century. Flanked by pavilions with domed cupolas and elaborate iron weathervanes. The whole forms an attractive group with the parish church.

OAKLEY HALL, Market Drayton (by written appointment with Mrs P.G.H. Crosfield)
Built *circa* 1710 of brick with extensive stone dressings, eleven bays long by seven bays wide, surmounted by a parapet. The original serpentine parapet

with swags and cartouches was removed in 1930 and replaced by the present triangular version. The interior has been partly re-modelled.

PITCHFORD HALL (The Tree House) (by appointment with Mrs Oliver
    Colthurst; tel: Acton Burnell (06944) 205)
Pitchford Hall, built in about 1570 is a fine example of a large Elizabethan timber-framed house with gables. The Tree House was built about 1750, twenty-five feet off the ground in a huge lime tree. It has enriched plaster ceilings.

STANDWARDINE HALL, nr Ellesmere (by appointment with Mr D.J.
    Bridge; tel: Cockshutt (093 922) 212)
An Elizabethan mansion, probably built about 1560 and now used as a farmhouse. It is of brick, with stone facings and mullioned windows and has three storeys with three gables at the front.

WIGMORE ABBEY, Leintwardine, nr Craven Arms (by appointment
    with Mrs Scott; tel: Wigmore (058 886) 454)
Founded in 1179 by Hugh Mortimore for Augustinian Canons, Wigmore Abbey was largely reconstructed in 1379. The inner gatehouse is one of the best surviving early timber gatehouses and the former Abbot's lodging and the remains of the Abbey's outer gatehouse also survive.

Somerset

AXBRIDGE: THE OLD DRUG STORE (by written appointment with
    Mr and Mrs K.E.D.J. Schofield)
A sub-mediaeval building on three floors, oversailing at each level. The street front is plastered. Details and fenestration belong to the early 18th century, at which date the interior of the house was re-modelled.

COTHELSTONE MANOR, nr Taunton (by written appointment with
    Mrs E. Warmington, Lane Cottage, Lower Terhill, Cothelstone)
The original house was partly ruined in the Civil War and restored in 1855; conventional in plan but with a wealth of unusual trimmings, including mullions shaped like balusters and tapering columns placed around the courtyard walls and flanking the doorway of the hall. Beyond the house is a mediaeval structure now converted into cottages and two garden buildings.

CROSCOME: THE OLD MANOR HOUSE (by written appointment
    with L.J. Lusby Esq)
A secular building of the late Middle Ages, rich in sculptural detail. Of

particular interest is the oriel chamber which has a stone ceiling in the form of a flattened fan vault, in the centre of which are angels holding the initial HS of the mid-15th century Treasurer of Wells, Hugh Sayer.

DODINGTON HALL, nr Williton (by appointment with Mrs Webber; tel: Holford (027 874) 422)
This is externally a rambling late 16th century gabled building. Earlier work survives inside. The main feature is the great hall, probably 15th century in origin, with a chimneypiece of 1581 which contains detail reminiscent of Longleat.

FROME: ST JOHN'S VICARAGE (by appointment with the Vicar, The Rev Michael Higgin)
A small stone-built 18th century house with high-pitched and hipped stone roofs. The centre three bays of the entrance front are original and show good dressed stone features: the interior contains a beautifully carved rococo overmantel.

HALSWAY MANOR, Bicknoller, Crowcombe (Residential Centre) (by appointment with Mr and Mrs Cavill; tel: Crowcombe (098 48) 274)
Basically a mid-15th century manor house, but drastically altered and re-modelled in the early 16th and 17th centuries and again in the 1870s. The salient external features are the three embattled and pinnacled towers with gargoyles and a gable with copings and finial over a two-storeyed bay below.

HATCH COURT, Hatch Beauchamp (open for a few days each summer and by appointment with Commander and Mrs Berry Norton; tel: Hatch Beauchamp (0823) 480208)
A stone-built country house in the Palladian style to the designs of the amateur architect Thomas Prowse. The building has a fine interior.

HYMERFORD MANOR, East Coker (by appointment with Mr and Mrs Dudley; tel: West Coker (093 586) 2214)
A small mediaeval manor house, partly remodelled, of harled rubble with dressings of Ham Hill stone, and a thatched roof. Most of the roof timbers with moulded arch-braces survive.

MEARE: MANOR FARM (by written appointment with the tenant, Mr C.J. Look)
This important 14th century manor house originally belonged to the Abbots of Glastonbury and consists of two ranges, each containing a large hall, of which one in the west range contains a magnificent hooded fireplace and its original windows. The hall in the south range, the original great hall, has since been subdivided and altered.

MUCHELNEY: THE PRIEST'S HOUSE (by written appointment with
the National Trust tenant (only two rooms shown))
A small house of the 14th and 15th century. To the right of the door lies the
hall with a fireplace against the screens passage and a large four-light early
16th century window. To the right of the hall was a small study, to the left
the kitchen and offices.

NETTLECOMBE COURT (Field Study Centre) (open on Thursday
mornings May to Sept by appointment with The Warden; tel: Washford
(098 44) 320)
The Elizabethan house and the church stand together in agreeable isolation
since the village was swept away by landscaping. Inside the chief feature is
the plasterwork notable for both its quality and variety. The hall has one of
the most sumptuous ceilings in the country and elsewhere work of the mid
17th century, mid-18th century and in the Adam style is to be found.

WELLS: THE OLD DEANERY (access during office hours (9–1, 2–5) on
Wed and Fri by appointment with the Diocesan Office; tel: Wells (0749)
73308)
The north range was rebuilt by Dean Gawthorpe 1472–98, by which time
the south and west range had been added. The east range, dating from the
17th century, completed the present inner courtyard plan. The south range
is now largely 18th century Gothic in appearance but the stepped buttresses
and polygonal angle turrets show its earlier origin.

WEST BOWER MANOR, Durleigh, Bridgwater (by appointment with
Mrs Michael Martin; tel: Bridgwater (0278) 2895)
A late 14th century stone gatehouse subsequently altered for use as a
farmhouse with a wing added in the early 17th century. It was originally the
property of the Lord Protector Somerset's family, and is popularly, though
possibly erroneously, thought to have been Jane Seymour's birthplace.

WEST COMPTON HOUSE, Shepton Mallet (by appointment with Mr
Patrick Taylor; tel: Pilton (074 989) 264)
Built *circa* 1700 of harled rubblestone, of seven bays and two storeys above
vauled cellars. The interior has a fine staircase.

WHITELACKINGTON HOUSE, Ilminster (by appointment with the
Dillington Estate Office, Ilminster; tel: Dillington (046 05) 4614)
An Elizabethan building, remodelled in the 18th century, built of rust-
coloured sandstone. It has associations with the Monmouth Rebellion of
1685 and its staircase and panelling are among its noteworthy features.

Staffordshire

ABBOT'S BROMLEY: CHURCH HOUSE (by written appointment
with the Vicar, The Rev. R. Vaughan, The Vicarage, Abbot's Bromley)
This is a timber-framed L-shaped house consisting of a 16th century range
of hall, pantry and butter, some early 17th century improvements including
an elaborate framed gable and additional mid-17th century range.

BROUGHTON HALL, Eccleshall (Convent) (by written appointment
with The Superior)
Built *circa* 1630 by Thomas Boughton, added to in the late 17th century or
early 18th century and drastically altered and partially rebuilt in the 1920s
and 1930s. The most important surviving part of the original house is the
main timbered facade of three jettied storeys with gables at either end and a
balustraded parapet over the three middle bays. The principal posts on the
ground floor are carved with spiralled columns and shields.

CLANFORD HILL, Sleighford (by written appointment with Mr W.O.
Brown)
Built in the reign of Charles I, the Hall is a multi-gabled timber-framed
building. It has a huge central stack, some original fireplacs and a fine
staircase. William Woolaston, the philosophical writer, is said to have been
born here in 1660.

LICHFIELD: 45 JOHN STREET (Rural Council House) (open during
office hours; arrangements should be made with Mr Gavin; tel: Lichfield
(054 32) 22373)
Built in 1682 as the Master's house of the old Grammar School. The street
elevation is in brick with timber croise windows on the first floor. Inside is a
circular timber open-well staircase with turned balusters. The school's most
famous pupil was Dr Johnson.

LICHFIELD: LICHFIELD HOUSE, Bore Street (the Tudor Cafe)
(open during shop hours, Mon to Sat)
A timber-framed building of *circa* 1510. The upper two storeys overhang on
a deep moulded cornice and plain consoles. The three gables have
bargeboards, pendants and finials.

LITTLE WRYLEY HALL, Pelsall (by appointment with the owner)
The core of the house is timber-framed and may be 16th century. The
service wing was added in 1660 when the Tudor house was faced with brick,
and divers shaped gables constructed. The very fine staircase is early
Georgian and there is excellent panelling and door furniture of about 1690.

MARCHINGTON HALL, Uttoxeter (by written appointment with A.F. Bagshaw Esq)
A late 17th century building related in style to nearby Sudbury Hall. It is rectangular in plan, of brick with stone quoins and dressings. The front is of five bays with two tiers of cross windows and a broad low door surround, thick and coarse and surmounted by a rustic pen pediment with a pineapple. Over the central bay the cornice is interrupted by an open balustraded parapet: above the two parts of the cornice are steep gables surmounted by ball finials.

MAVESYN RIDWARE: THE OLD HALL FARMHOUSE (by appointment with Mr J.R. Eades; tel: Armitage (0543) 490312)
The house itself is early 18th century and is of brick with stone dressings. There is also a 14th century gatehouse whose upper room retains much of its original timber framing, which is of massive size. The gatehouse has a particularly fine king post roof.

PARK HALL, Leigh (by written appointment with Mr E.J. Knobbs)
A compact red brick 16th century house with elaborate entrance gates, surrounded by a moat.

PILLATON OLD HALL, Penkridge (by appointment with Mr R.W. and the Hon. Mrs Perceval; tel: Penkridge (078 571) 2200)
The gatehouse range of a courtyard house of which little now remains. Of three storeys, with circular turrets at the corners supported on triangular buttresses. Adjoining the east end of the range is a stone chapel with a low pitched roof behind a crenellated parapet. The gatehouse probably dates from the later 16th century and the chapel from the 15th century.

Suffolk

BELCHAMP HALL, Belchamp Water, nr Sudbury (May to Sept by appointment with M.M.J. Raymond Esq; tel: Sudbury (0787) 72744)
Built in 1720 of white brick with rubbed brick dressings, the house has a front of nine bays and two storeys with giant pilasters at the angles, and dormers with alternating pediments. There are some additions of about 1880, but original 18th century panelling and other fittings survive inside.

FLEMINGS HALL, Bedingfield, nr Eye (by appointment with Mr Angus McBean)
The outer shell of the present building is said to have been built by Thomas Bedingfield about 1500, though the evidence suggests a 17th century date. The long facade of brick below and close studding above is punctuated by

the two storey brick porch terminating in gables of Dutch curvilinear profile the whole surmounted by clusters of four octagonal brick stacks.

GREAT BRICETT HALL FARMHOUSE, nr Ipswich (by written appointment with Mr and Mrs R.B. Cooper)
A carved oak screen of the early 13th century came to light when the house was being altered in 1958. It is a remarkable survival both for its exceptionally early date and for the variety of its carving.

HADLEIGH: THE DEANERY TOWER (by appointment with the Dean of Bocking; tel: Hadleigh (0473) 822218)
This tower was built by Archdeacon Pykenham in 1495 when he was Rector of Hadleigh. It was originally the gatehouse to the Old Parsonage, which was later demolished and replaced by a house attached to the tower itself. It was at a conference held in a room in the tower in 1833 that the Oxford Movement had its beginnings.

HADLEIGH: 48 HIGH STREET (Shop) (Mon to Sat (except Wed) during shop hours)
A two storey timber-framed building with a 17th century mural decoration painted directly on a plaster wall.

HENGRAVE HALL, Bury St Edmunds (Ecumenical Centre) (by appointment with the Warden; tel: Culford (028 484) 722)
A house built between 1525 and 1538 for Sir Thomas Kytson, Merchant Adventurer in London. It is constructed partly of stone and partly of brick of a similar colour, round a courtyard, and has a triple-bayed window above the entrance with some of the earliest-known Renaissance decoration in England.

HINTLESHAM HALL (Restaurant) (open to patrons, or by appointment; tel: Hintlesham (047 387) 268)
Originally a Tudor red brick house, Hintlesham was much altered in the 18th century and much of the exterior is re-facing of the latter period. The two storey hall in the central range still has 16th century features, but also a Corinthian doorcase giving onto the main staircase, as well as an 18th century chimneypiece and overmantel. The entrance front is stuccoed. There are other good 18th century features and attractive outbuildings.

MOAT FARM, Chevington (by written appointment with Mr and Mrs Martin Lightfoot)
An almost perfect specimen of a small later mediaeval timber-framed hall house, enlarged and subdivided for greater space and comfort in the latter half of the 16th century.

MOAT HALL, Parham (by appointment with Mr. J.W. Gray; tel: Wickham Market (0728) 746317)
The surviving part of an early 16th century manor house, picturesquely sited in its moat.

NEWBOURNE HALL, Woodbridge (by written appointment with Mr and Mrs Stuart Somerville)
The hall and service end of a timber-framed house of the late 15th and early 16th centuries. A wing in red brick was added in the early 17th century and a small block in the Gothic style in the 19th century.

POLSTEAD HALL, Cosford (by written appointment with Guy B. Scott Esq)
A brick Georgian house with some 16th century work at the rear. There are fine 16th century wall paintings in a small room on the first floor.

ROOS HALL, Beccles (by appointment with Mr and Mrs H.W.N. Suckling; tel: Beccles (0502) 2115)
This red brick house built in 1583 has considerable value as a substantially unaltered specimen of a small late Elizabethan house. It is basically a rectangle with two near-symmetrical elevations; at each corner are octagonal buttresses diminishing in size as they rise to the top of the house, where they stand well above the battlemented parapets like chimneys.

SAXHAM HALL, Great Saxham (by written appointment with Lady Stirling)
A late 18th century house by Joseph Patience but with a number of 19th century additions. The interiors include a domed octagonal music room with painted arabesques and panels depicting the Muses.

WORLINGHAM HALL, Beccles (by written appointment with Viscount Colville of Culross)
Designed by France Sandys in 1800, Worlingham followed the contemporary fashion for geometric centrally-planned houses and more particularly for those in which the whole house, or some important part of it, in this case the staircase hall, is circular or elliptical.

THE WURLEIGH, Badwell Ash (by written appointment with Mr B.W. Belcher, Rickinghall, Diss, Norfolk)
The Wurleigh stands in the single street of Badwell Ash and is a very complete example of a 15th century hall house. It is E-shaped with some later additions; remains of a screens passage and a queen-post roof survive.

Surrey

ABINGER HAMMER: CROSSWAYS FARM (by written appointment
with the tenant, Mr C.T. Hughes)
A small but historically valuable 17th century farmhouse of sandstone
rubble with brick enrichments. The house's most prominent feature is its
double-storeyed porch which has moulded bargeboards and a pendant.

BREWERSTREET FARM, Bletchingley (by written appointment with
C.J. French)
An unusually complete timber-framed hall-and-ends house with a hall of
two bays between jettied and gabled wings.

EGHAM: GREAT FOSTERS (Hotel) (tel: Egham 33822)
Built in 1550, the home of Sir Robert Foster, Lord Chief Justice, enlarged
and embellished at the beginning of the 17th century and extensively remodelled *circa* 1866 and *circa* 1922. It now consists of a long straggling
gabled range of brick, the older portions at the north and subsequent
additions to the south. The interiors have rich decoration of different styles
and periods.

ELSTEAD: THE HILL HOUSE (by appointment with Mrs C.D.
Bentley; tel: Elstead (025 122) 3132)
This is basically a 16th century house with 17th and 18th century brick
cladding. It is a valuable part of an attractive group of buildings which
cluster about Elstead's mill — a handsome building and a local landmark.

FARNHAM CASTLE, Farnham (Conference Centre) (open Wed 2–4 or
by appointment with The Director; tel: Farnham (0252) 721194)
Farnham Castle was the property of the Bishops of Winchester from Saxon
times until 1927. It consists of a 12th century keep (see main guide) and the
Mediaeval Bishop's Palace, which is of various dates and incorporates
substantial parts of the bailey wall of the castle.

FARNHAM: RANGER'S HOUSE, Farnham Castle Park (open April to
Sept by appointment with Brooks Richards Esq; tel: Farnham (0252)
716764)
A small, almost square brick house of 1700. The form of the roof and the
fenestration are both of unusual design.

LINGFIELD: POLLARD COTTAGE, Old Town (by written
appointment with Miss K. Skinner)

A timber-framed building formed from two-thirds of a late mediaeval hall house.

THE NEWLAND, Western Green Road, Thames Ditton (Flats) (by appointment with The Housemother, Mrs Philbrick)
A late 17th century brick house, much altered internally and externally at the end of the 19th century and later, but retaining a 17th century room with plasterwork of exceptional quality.

NEW PLACE, Farnham Lane, Haslemere (by written appointment with H.C. Ziegler Esq)
Built by C.F.A Voysey in 1897, on a hillside above extensive steeply-terraced gardens which may also have been designed by him.

SUNBURY COURT, Sunbury on Thames (by appointment with The Manager; tel: Sunbury 82196)
An 18th century house, remodelled in the 19th century and now used by the Salvation Army. In the dining room are wall-paintings by Elias Martin, a Swedish artist who lived in England 1768–80 and again in 1788–91; he was a friend of Lord Pomfret, who owned the house. The paintings of pastoral, classical and gothic subjects are the only known wall decorations by Martin in either England or Sweden.

East Sussex

ASHDOWN HOUSE, Forest Row (School) (by appointment with the Headmaster; tel: Forest Row (034 282) 2574)
A stone built house of about 1790: one of the few known buildings in England by Benjamin Latrobe, who became famous as architect of the Capitol at Washington D.C.

BEECHES FARM, nr Uckfield (garden open all year, daily 10–5; house open by appointment with Mrs Vera Thomas)
A 16th century timber-framed and tile-hung farmhouse.

HAREMERE HALL, Etchingham (Bank holiday weekends 2.30–5.30 and parties by appointment with Lady Killearn; tel: Etchingham (058 081) 245)
A large symmetrical Jacobean stone house with two projecting bays in the front with shaped gables. At the back the fenestration is uneven and a date stone of 1682 must refer to later alterations. The staircase with twisted balusters may be of this date.

HORSTED PLACE, Little Horsted, nr Uckfield (garden open Easter to Sept; house open to parties by written appointment with Lord Rupert Nevill CVO JP)
The house was designed by Samuel Dawkes and built 1850–1. The builder was Myers, A.W.N. Pugin's favoured craftsman, and it is possible that much of the interior decoration is based on Pugin's designs. There is a pleasant landscaped garden.

West Sussex

CHICHESTER: THE DEANERY (by written appointment with The Dean of Chichester)
Built in 1725 of red brick with contrasting brick dressings in a box-like structure of two storeys with a depressed gable on each of the four sides. The entrance front has a slightly projecting central bay with a segmental pediment within the gable head. The interior was largely re-planned in about 1860.

LITTLE THAKEHAM, Pulborough (by written appointment with Mr S. Hanbury Aggs)
Built in 1903, this is an early example of the country houses of Sir Edwin Lutyens. It is in a composite 'Tudor Renaissance' style handled with originality and daring.

NEWBUILDINGS PLACE, Southwater (by written appointment with The Viscount Knebworth)
A late 17th century house of stone with brick dressings, formerly the seat of the Caryll family but best-known for its association with the poet Wilfrid Scawen Blunt, who is buried in the garden. The house contains many things associated with the poet.

NEWTIMBER PLACE, Newtimber (open May to Aug Thurs 2–5; tel: Hurstpierpoint 833104)
The house stands in a wide moat; the main front dates from the late 17th century although the north wing is earlier. The walls are of flint, with brick surrounds to the windows.

STEYNING: CHANTRY GREEN HOUSE (by appointment with Mr and Mrs G.H. Recknell; tel: Steyning (0903) 812239)
A good mid-18th century town house of five bays, built of grey and red brick with segmental windows and a delicate brick cornice.

Warwickshire

FOXCOTE, Shipston on Stour (by written appointment with Mr C.B. Holman)
A large 18th century house attributed to the Woodwards of Chipping Camden with interiors dating chiefly from about 1800.

SALFORD HALL, Abbot's Salford (Hotel) (Tel: Evesham (0386) 870561)
A large stone-built house with some timber framing in the west range. It is of the early mid-16th century and probably incorporates parts of an earlier building.

WARWICK: NORTHGATE HOUSE, Northgate (by written appointment with Mr R.E. Phillips)
The eleven bay front is made up of two brick houses of 1698 with a central carriageway under a pediment. Some of the original windows can be seen at the rear. The original staircase survives and there is one upper room with fine pilastered panelling.

Wiltshire

BRADFORD ON AVON: THE OLD MANOR HOUSE, Whiteheads Road (by written appointment with Mr John Teed)
The building is in two parts, one 18th century, built in ashlar with pilasters, cornice and pediment; the other 17th century built in coursed rubble with a central gable. Its importance lies mainly in its contribution to the townscape.

BRADFORD ON AVON: THE OLD CHURCH HOUSE, Church Street (by written appointment with Mr J. Gibson)
An early 16th century building, T-shaped in plan, built in rubble with ashlar quoins and a high-pitched stone-tiled roof; once the hall of the Weaver's Guild.

BRADFORD ON AVON: ORPINS (by written appointment with Salisbury Diocesan Council of Education)
Orpins takes its name from a former Parish Clerk who is now remembered largely because his portrait was painted by Gainsborough. The house dates from the late 17th or early 18th century. It is unusually elaborate for its size and contains a fine central Doric doorcase, gables and mullioned windows.

CORSHAM: THE GROVE (by written appointment with the Corsham Estate Office)
An attractive early 18th century house with an impressive pedimented doorway. The chief feature of the interior is the fine staircase.

DEVIZES: BROWNSTON HOUSE (by appointment with Kennet District Council, Bath Rd., Devizes)
A good house of 1720, two storeys and attic, built of dark red brick of fine quality, with a hipped tiled roof.

HEALE HOUSE, Woodford, nr Salisbury (by appointment with Major and Mrs David Rasch; tel: Middle Woodford (072 273) 207)
A fine brick house, originally of the late 17th century but sensitively enlarged after 1894 by Detmar Blow. The staircase is original 17th century work but does not belong to the house.

LITTLE CLARENDON HOUSE, Dinton (by written appointment with the National Trust tenant (Mrs Streader))
Near to Phillips House (see main guide), Little Clarendon is a building with an exterior of 16th century date with a gabled two-storey porch; the interior has some earlier, probably 15th century, features.

MALMESBURY: ABBEY HOUSE (by appointment with the Sister in Charge; tel: (066 62) 2216)
A 16th century building of rubble, faced with roughcast, with the undercroft of one of the monastic offices of the Abbey of Malmesbury used as the foundation.

MERE: THE CHANTRY (by written appointment with F. Newby Esq)
On 1424 the Chantry of the Blessed Virgin Mary acquired the site for the erection of a house for chantry priests. It was built some time afterwards and is an important and complete mediaeval building.

MILTON MANOR, Milton Lilbourne, nr Pewsey (by appointment with Mrs Rupert Gentle; tel: Pewsey (067 26) 3344)
This house, of the late 17th or early 18th century, is chiefly notable for its external features which include 'Gothick' glazing of the centre windows, the bolection architraves and the attractive use of blue vitrified headers in the brickwork.

POTTERNE: THE PORCH HOUSE (by written appointment with the occupier)
A late 15th century timber-framed hall house, carefully restored in 1874 by the painter George Richmond, who owned a house at that time. The main

feature is the survival of the very fine original roofs of the hall and solar: both are hammerbeam roofs, a rarity in small scale domestic architecture.

ROCHE OLD COURT, Winterslow (by written appointment with Major H.B. Trevor Cox)
A small mid-17th century mansion of brick with stone mullioned windows. The site was occupied in the Middle Ages by the royal falconer attendant upon Clarendon Palace close by.

SALISBURY: CHURCH HOUSE, Crane Street (May to Aug, Wed and Fri afternoons, by appointment with the Salisbury Diocesan Board of Finance; tel: Salisbury (0722) 3074)
A stone built 15th century merchant's house, with 16th and early 18th century additions and forming three sides of a courtyard. The great hall has a fine arch braced timber roof.

SALISBURY: 29 THE CLOSE (by written appointment with E.J.Bickersteth)
Basically a stuccoed timber-framed building, heavily restored and refenestrated in the 19th century, but with a part of a roof dating from the 14th century.

SALISBURY: 57 THE CLOSE (by written appointment with Major Gen. P.B. Foster MC)
Built in the 14th century, but re-fronted in the 18th century. Two-storeys of brick with stone quoins and a first floor string-course surmounted by a moulded and carved cornice. Old tile roof and dormered attics.

SALISBURY: MALMESBURY HOUSE, 15 The Close (by written appointment with Miss P. Richey, Curator, 17 Bouverie Ave, Salisbury)
Early in the 18th century the existing houses were transformed by the application of a two storey range seven bays wide across the length of their west fronts. Number 15 has tall sash windows and a high hipped roof. A small room on the first floor is decorated in the Gothick maner and there are examples elsewhere of fine rococo decoration.

SALISBURY: THE NORTH CANONRY, 60 The Close (by appointment with Mr and Mrs Cory; tel: Salisbury (0722) 5682)
Mainly 16th century with later alterations and additions, perhaps by Gilbert Scott. It has a late 13th century undercroft and fragments of mediaeval work.

SALISBURY: THE OLD BISHOP'S PALACE, 1 The Close (School) (by appointment with The Bursar, The Cathedral School; tel: Salisbury

(0722) 22652)
A complex straggling building greatly altered during its long history. It has a 13th century undercroft, a late 15th century tower, a chapel with enriched beams in a waggonhead ceiling, an 18th century saloon with Venetian windows and a timber staircase of Baroque plan.

SALISBURY: THE OLD DEANERY (by written appointment with the Chapter Clerk, 6 The Close)
The Old Deanery stands on the west side of the Cathedral Close. It is contemporary with the cathedral and has a very well-documented history. Restoration work discovered the ground plan of the hall and solar wing, a good deal of the mediaeval walls and the whole of the 13th century roof.

SWALLOWCLIFFE MANOR, Tisbury (by written appointment with Mr and Mrs James Leasor)
An Elizabethan two storey manor house, originally T-shaped, built in about 1600. It was extended early in this century, when the interior of the ground floor was altered.

North Yorkshire

BOLTON PERCY GATEHOUSE, Tadcaster (key available at The Crown Inn, Bolton Percy)
The present structure consists of three bays of a 16th century timber-framed building of two storeys; the upper storey and the gable end are jettied. Two of the ground floor timber posts and some of the internal posts, tie-beams and brackets of the principal trusses are richly carved.

BUSBY HALL, Carlton in Cleveland (by written appointment with Mr and Mrs G.C. Wilson)
The house stands on a spur of the Cleveland Hills. It is probably of the late 18th century and is of two storeys, built in grey stone. The best internal feature is a Baroque style staircase lit by Venetian windows.

FOSTON OLD RECTORY (by written appointment with Mr R.F. Wormald)
A plain comfortable Georgian house which was built for and probably designed by Sydney Smith, who was Rector of Foston from 1806 to 1829.

HAZLEWOOD CASTLE, Tadcaster (Carmelite Order) (free access for individuals, parties by appointment with The Guestmaster)
The home of the Vavasour family for eight hundred years until 1907. Sir William Vavasour began to build in 1286 but the house was extensively

altered and modernised 1740-50. It now appears as a rectangular block of limestone ashlar, battlemented, with square towers projecting on each side of the middle part of five bays. Some mediaeval features remain in the great hall amid fine 18th century decoration.

HOME FARMHOUSE, Old Scriven, Knaresborough (by written appointment with Mr G.T. Reece)
Built in the late Middle Ages as a timber-framed single aisled hall. In the early 17th century an upper floor was inserted and the outer walls were largely rebuilt in stone. The parlour is decorated with wall paintings of huge flowers and foliage.

MOULTON HALL, Richmond (by written appointment with The Hon J.D. Eccles (National Trust tenant))
Built about 1660-70, flat-fronted with three big Dutch gables to the entrance front and two to the side. The stonework on the front has many narrow raised bands. The three-light ground and first floor windows have alternating pediments and inside there is a splendid carved staircase.

RIPON: MINSTER HALL (by written appointment with The Dean of Ripon)
An early Georgian house with rusticated pilasters at the corners of the west front and a centrepiece in which the doorway forms part of a 'Venetian' feature. Some rooms have 18th century panelling and in others there is re-fixed panelling of the 17th century. The best feature is the open-well staircase with balusters of three patterns.

STOCKELD PARK, Wetherby (by written appointment with Mrs R.E.F. Gough)
An impressive house designed by James Paine and built 1758-63. The composition is dramatic, with a tall three-storey pedimented centre flanked by wings each of one very wide bay. Towards the garden these wings have great blank arches below their pediments. The interior is largely altered, but the staircase hall survives. The house was extended in the 19th century.

YORK: CUMBERLAND HOUSE, Cumberland Street (by appointment with the occupiers, Messrs Hague, Dixon and Burn (Solicitors); tel: York (0904) 27111)
An early 18th century house of two storeys, of brick on a stone plinth, built by William Cornwall, Sherrif of York in 1700 and twice Lord Mayor. In its craftmanship, externally and internally, the house displays exceptional quality. The building occupies a conspicuous position on the quay.

YORK: 111 WALMGATE (by appointment with the occupiers Lombard
   North Central Ltd.; tel: York (0904) 55455)
The house is of particular importance, both because it is an excellent
example of the timber-framed houses of York's prosperous mediaeval times,
and because it is now one of the few surviving mediaeval houses in this
quarter of the city. There have been later alterations and additions but the
original framework has survived very well, especially on the upper floor,
and the roof in particular is a fine example of the braced king post type
developed in York in the 14th century.

South Yorkshire

FERHAM HOUSE, Kimberworth, Rotherham (by appointment with the
   Rotherham Area Health Administrator; tel: Rotherham (0709) 63131)
A good example of the small anglo-palladian villa, built in 1787 by John
Platt of Rotherham.

HOWSAM HOUSE, Norton (by written appointment with J.A. Knock
   Esq during May and June only)
Built at the beginning of the 17th century, the many-windowed limestone
front is of the highest quality. Howsham Hall underwent considerable
conversions and extensions about 1770, the grafting of the later work onto
the Jacobean achieving a harmonious whole.

West Yorkshire

HEATH HALL, nr Wakefield (Exhibition Centre) (by appointment with
   Mr Cook or Mr Mitchell; tel: Wakefield (0924) 6646/7/8)
Heath Hall is mostly, though not entirely, by Carr of York. Built in the
second half of the 18th century, it includes part of a house of about 1700 and
consists of a symmetrical block flanked by two large pavilions with cupolas
and clock towers. The saloon and principal bedroom have elaborate rococo
ceilings.

LEDSTON HALL, Allerton Bywater (by appointment through the
   agents, Byron & Granger, 3 New St., York; tel: York (0904) 23008)
The oldest parts of Ledston Hall are remains of an early 13th century
monastic range. However, the house is now more obviously the work of later
periods and is, in the main, an outstanding example of the transition period
between Jacobean and Artisan Mannerism.

THORNTON HALL, Thornton nr Bradford (June to Sept Sunday
    afternoons by written appointment with Dr J.C. Douglas)
A typical late 17th century building with a flat three-bay front of three
storeys divided by string-courses. The windows are all of six lights on the
ground and first floors and five lights on the second floor.

Wales

Clwyd

ASTON HALL, Hawarden (by written appointment with Mrs R. Moore)
A 17th century house, altered externally in the 19th century. Many 17th century details survive inside, including a fine Jacobean carved mantel and painting dated 1615.

FFERM, Pontbyddyn, Mold (by appointment with the tenant; tel: Pontybodkin 371)
A small two-storey Elizabethan mansion. It is rubble-built with sandstone dressings to its doors and windows. The interior of the house on the ground floor contains a fine oak screen whose two wide openings give access to a partitioned chamber. Moulded ceiling beams provide evidence of a single large hall. The four bedrooms on the first floor follow their original plan. A contemporary outbuilding called the Brewhouse is set at right-angles to the main house.

HALGHTON HALL, Bangor on Dee (by appointment with the tenant, Mr Douglas Lewis; tel: Bangor on Dee 338)
A small moated manor house, for many years the home of the Lloyds of Halghton. The main part of the building dates from 1662. Original features of the interior include the staircase, a decorated plaster ceiling and several doors. The moat survives on two sides.

HEN BLAS, Llansa (by written appointment with D.H. Lawton Esq)
An imposing three-storey mansion built in 1645 with later alterations. Interesting interior including a Jacobean dog-leg staircase.

NERQUIS HALL, nr Mold (by written appointment with Mr A.W. Furse)
One of the best examples of Renaissance architecture in Wales. The many-gabled elevations are similar to Chastleton in Oxfordshire which is of the same date (c 1602). The house is a compact square block with slightly-projecting wings to the entrance front. The walls are of Ewloe stone. Internally, three of the rooms contain panelling and fireplaces which are Jacobean. On the second floor a long gallery extends the entire length of the house.

PLAS TEG, Hope (by appointment with Jones & Sons (Estate Agents), 33 High Street, Wrexham. This property is currently for sale)

A Jacobean country mansion built about 1610. The estate has for long belonged to the Trevor family. The mansion is a gaunt imposing building approximately square in plan with a recessed main front and corner towers capped with ogee roofs and small arched cupolas.

Dyfed

GUANDOVAN, Cilgerran (by written appointment with Mrs J.D.Drew-Smythe)
A square stone house with its outbuildings — an 18th century barn and stable range. The 19th century exterior conceals features of 200 years earlier, notably the fine oak open-well staircase; some of the moulded beams and doorways may be relics of the late 16th century house of the Vaughans.

HENLLYS, Llandovery (by written appointment with Mrs V. McGill, The Coach House, Henllys)
A 17th century house with 19th century outbuildings.

LAUGHARNE: CASTLE HOUSE (by written appointment with Miss A.M. Starke, Laugharne Castle, Carmarthen)
An 18th century house of three storeys adjoining Laugharne Castle.

NANTEOS, Llanilor, Aberystwyth (by written appointment with Mr and Mrs B.M. Jones, Nanteos Lodge)
A large early 18th century house of severe appearance, built of grey stone. The handsome and elaborate interior was decorated soon after the house was built and has been little altered. A fine contemporary main staircase runs from the entrance hall to the first floor. There are notable decorated ceilings.

RHYDARWEN, Llanarthney (by written appointment with Mr Rhys Roberts. This property is currently for sale)
A mediaeval house built in two sections, with a floor at first floor level inserted in the 16th century. The house was altered and largely re-faced in the 18th century. Its features include a stair turret at each end, an 18th century wooden porch and a massive fireplace. The study contains a 16th century wall-painting.

TALIARIS PARK, Llandeilo (by written appointment with Messrs J.H.S. & M.F. Williams)
The house dates from the 17th century and was the property of the Gwynne family until 1754. Some original features survive including the wide Jacobean staircase and the richly-modelled drawing room ceiling. Probably

early in the 19th century the house was re-faced and re-modelled. The exterior is now an attractive and refined example of Regency achitecture.

Gwent

BLACKBROOK HOUSE, Skenfrith (by appointment with Mr G.F.W. Buckland; tel: Skenfrith 238)
A substantial square house of rubble stone, rendered with stucco, built in the late 18th century by Lord Balcarres. A notable feature of the interior is a staircase contained in a spacious well to the full height of the house.

CWRT PORTH HIR, Llanover (by written appointment with the Coldbrook and Llanover Estate)
The building dates from 1500–1550 and was altered in the early and late 17th century. It shows the development of two parallel stone wings joined by a connecting link, irregular in plan and constructed of stone with a stone slate roof and a two-storey gabled porch.

GREAT CIL-ILWYCH, Llantilio Crosenny (by written appointment with Mr J.F. Ingledew)
A large stone building dating mainly from the 17th century and originally a small manor house of distinction. The elevations are generally plain but several original windows survive. There is an interesting gabled porch with a four-centred stone arch. Internally there are features of the late 16th century and the panelling, ceilings and main staircase are principally of the 17th. There are remains of earlier plasterwork in the east wing attic.

ITTON COURT, Chepstow (by written appointment with P.D. Carroll Esq)
This consists of a range of buildings round a rectangular courtyard. The main building known as the 'Queen Anne Block' dates from 1712 and faces outwards from the courtyard. Its face is lime-rendered. In front of the house are two terraces. The gatehouse tower is mediaeval, built about 1400, and possibly once part of a curtain wall enclosing the house.

KEMYS HOUSE, Kemys Inferior, Caerleon (by written appointment with Mr I.S. Burge)
A small square tower, possibly dating from the 15th century, is the earliest part of Kemys House. In Elizabethan times a rectangular building was added to the south side of the tower and a lean-to was built on the north side. Other parts of the house were added in the 17th century but most of the original windows were replaced in the 19th century. There are features

surviving from all these periods, including a fine 16th century plaster ceiling in the ground floor south east room.

LLANFIHANGEL COURT, Abergavenny (open on Bank Holidays and some Sundays in summer; for details apply to the Custodian)
This stone-built manor house dates from the 16th and 17th centuries. Its internal features include moulded plaster ceilings exposed timber-framing, oak panelling and a magnificent staircase. The house forms a group with other buildings including a contemporary stable block, an 18th century coach house and a 16th or 17th century timber-framed barn.

MONMOUTH: 3 & 4 PRIORY STREET (by written appointment with Mr H.R. Ludwig)
Early 19th century terrace houses with convex fronts, three storeys high with pilasters through the upper floors and a central attic pediment; an outstanding group.

MONMOUTH: ST JAMES' HOUSE (by written appointment with the Governors of Monmouth School)
An early 18th century house incorporating at the back some remains of its predecessor. The building has been adapted for use by Monmouth School.

OVERMONNOW HOUSE, Overmonnow (by written appointment with Mr J.R. Pangbourne)
A three-storey Georgian house situated near the famous Monnow Bridge in Monmouth. Internally the house has an interesting oak staircase and several panelled rooms.

TREOWEN, Wonastow (by written appointment with Mr R.H. Wheelock)
This house of local stone was built in 1623 and owned by the same family until 1946. The interior has survived almost intact and contains a magnificent open-well staircase and good panelling and plasterwork.

Gwynedd

BRYN NODOL, Tudweiliog, Pwllheli (by written appointment with Mrs B.M. Williams)
A 16th or 17th century farmhouse mostly remodelled in the first half of the 18th century. Constructed of rubble masonry it has a slate roof with skylights. Moulded panelling in ground and first floor rooms. There is an attic bedroom of *circa* 1600.

CAE'R BERLLAN, Llanfihangel Y Pennant (by written appointment with Major Corbett, Gesail, Bryncrug, Tywyn, Gwynedd)
An 18th century farmhouse with a slated roof and end stone stacks. Its architectural features include casements with transoms and leaded light. The house has a five window front and a rear wing.

COCHWILLAN OLD HALL, Talybont (by appointment with Lady Janet Douglas-Pennant; tel: Bangor 4608)
Cochwillan is probably the finest piece of late mediaeval domestic architecture surviving in North Wales. The great hall built in about 1450 retains its original open timber roof, timber screens, fireplaces, doorways and windows

CYMRYD, Conwy (by appointment with Miss D.E. Glynne, Llys Gwynedd Bangor; tel: Bangor 2315)
A former farmhouse built of stone with a slate roof. The west wing built about 1696 has two-storeys and an attic. The east wing built about 1500 is of one storey with an inserted attic and a modern entrance. This was the former residence of Henry and Katherine Lloyd and there is a stone in the gable inscribed 'LL HK DVWA DIGON 1696'.

DDUALLT, Tan y Bwlch, Blaenau Festiniog (by appointment with Col. A.H.K. Campbell, tel: Maentwrog 272)
A remote house built on high ground north of the vale of Maentwrog. It consists of two houses facing each other, their entrances being joined by a two-storey porch which provides an archway and a connecting passage over. The southern building dates from about 1600. The northern part is very similar in character and layout to a house known through documentary evidence to have been standing on the site in about 1500. In the 19th century a main entrance was formed on the south side.

DOLAUGWYN, Brancrug, Towyn (by written appointment with Mrs S. Tudor)
Dolaugwyn was built about 1620 by Lewis Gwynne and has retained its original form. It is L-shaped in plan, with a projecting porch, a turret for the stair and a second turret which may have housed a second stair. The ground and first floor windows have mullions and transoms. An interesting and dominating feature of the house is the crow-stepped parapet which surmounts all gables and dormer windows. The interior contains a fine 17th century panelled plaster ceiling and there are heraldic or floral panels over many of the fireplaces.

NANNAU, Llanfachreth, nr Dolgellau (by written appointment with Mr E. Bowen)

Nannau has been connected with the Vaughan and Nanney families for nine centuries. The present house dates from 1808 and incorporates portions of an earlier house. It stands in a fine situation above the town of Dolgellau with views of a lake and woods.

PLAS BERW, Holland Arms, Anglesey (by appointment with the Carrelglwyd Estate, Carr, Vincent, Trevor, Jones & Co Solrs., Bangor; tel: Bangor 2551)

Plas Berw consists of two adjacent structures; the older, now ruined, belongs to the late 15th century. The newer was built by Sir Thomas Holland in 1615. At the rear is a square tower containing the staircase. The house is built of rubble and consists of two storeys with attics and dormer and a roof of small Welsh slates. The original roof timbers remain and in the hall is late 17th century panelling of good quality.

PLAS COCH, Llanedwen, Llanfairpwll, Anglesey (by appointment with Mr A.M. Ripley; tel: Llanfairpwll (0248) 714272)

Plas Coch built in 1569 by David Hughes. He is said to have used stone from Porthamel Isaf. There have been later additions, but Plas Coch retains the appearance of an Elizabethan country house. It is built of red sandstone with stepped gables and carved finials.

PLAS YN RHIW, nr Pwllheli (by appointment, April to end June, Wed and Thurs 3–4.30; tel: Rhiw (075 888) 219)

A small manor house, partly mediaeval, with Tudor and Georgian additions. Also an ornamental garden and woodland down to the sea on the west shore of Porth Neigwl.

Mid-Glamorgan

LLANCAIACH FAWR FARM, Nelson (by appointment with Mr Edward T. Williams; tel: Nelson 278)

A massively-constructed Tudor house — one of the best examples of its period in South Wales. Except for the roof its structure has remained unaltered since it was built. The walls are built with a batter from bottom to top and this feature, together with the massive oak doors, show that solidity and strength were of importance when the house was built. The original Elizabethan staircase survives, though mutilated, and there is some fine panelling and much original timber.

South Glamorgan

FONMON CASTLE, Barry (by written appointment with Sir Hugo Boothby, Bt)
Fonmon is a crenellated castle of the early Middle Ages and is claimed to be the oldest continuouly inhabited dwelling in Wales. It belonged to the St John family from the 13th century until acquired during the Commonwealth by Col. Philip Jones. Extensive alterations were made by Robert Jones in 1750-60, but since 1800 there have been few changes to the building. The castle contains fine Georgian furniture and a remarkable collection of family portraits by masters of the 17th and 18th centuries.

LLANTWIT MAJOR: THE GREAT HOUSE (by appointment with Mr C. Baxter-Jones; tel: Llantwit Major 2483)
This was originally a small manor house of the 16th century and was for a long time unoccupied and derelict. It was made habitable in 1951.

West Glamorgan

PENRICE CASTLE, Gower (by written appointment with Mr. C. Methuen-Campbell)
Penrice comprises a high square Georgian house with low wings and a Victorian guest wing. The Georgian block was built in 1774 by Anthony Keck of Gloucestershire for Thomas Mansel Talbot and is sited close to the remains of the mediaeval castle and commands a magnificent view. The building is of four storeys, ashlar-faced, with a full height semi-circular bay facing southward. Inside, the well-proportioned rooms retain their fine original cornices, fireplaces and doors. The Victorian wing was added in 1894.

Powys

ABERCYNRIG, Llanfryach (by written appointment with Mr W.R. Lloyd)
A late 17th century house with many characteristic features of its period. The interior has original panelling and overmantels and a fine newel staircase.

BRECON: BUCKINGHAM PLACE (by written appointment with Mrs Meeres (No. 1) Mrs C. Sims (No. 2) and Mr and Mrs A. Whitley (No. 3))
Numbers 1, 2 and 3 Buckingham Place were built in 1547 as Buckingham

House by Dr Aubrey, but have subsequently been converted into three residences. Named after the Duke of Buckingham, the last Lord of the Lordship of Brecon, who was attainted for treason and beheaded in 1521 the house occupies a fine position inside the town walls and still retains several curvilinear stone mullion Tudor windows.

BURFA, Evenjobb, Presteigne (by written appointment with Michael J. Garner Esq)
A 15th or 16th century farmhouse with a stone-built plinth. The elevation facing the farmyard is picturesque as the house is built on a bank. The east wing is gabled and has close-set studding while the central gabled wing has square framing. The west wing is a granary with a stone-built gable end. The farm has casement windows, some with leaded lights.

MAESMAWR HALL, Caersws (by appointment with Mrs V.H.M. Kendal; tel: Caersws 255)
An early 17th century house, one of the finest surviving examples of a half-timbered Montgomeryshire house.

NEWTON FARM, Brecon (by written appointment with the tenant, D.L. Evans Esq)
A tall square stone building with prominent chimney-stacks and gables on three sides. There are traces of 14th century work but the house as a whole is of the 16th century. It was a manor house of the Games family and in the great hall a fireplace bears the date 1582 with a crest and inscription. At the east end is a Tudor oak screen with fragments of a minstrels' gallery above. There is also a large Tudor stair.

PEN-Y-LAN, Meifod (by appointment with Mr S.R.J. Meade; tel: Meifod 202)
An elegant Georgian building of about 1812, among the best of its period in Montgomeryshire. The staircase with its slender balusters and gold medallions on the outer end of each step is one of its most attractive features.

PLAS LLANGATTOCK, Crickhowell (by written appointment with Mr J.P.C. Sankey-Barker)
An attractive early 18th century house, altered a century later. There is some fine ironwork and an interesting balcony extending the whole width of the front façade. The interior contains a good oak staircase and some pleasing grates and mantelpieces. In the ground there is an early 19th century orangery of carved iron framework.

PLASAU DUON, Clatter (by written appointment with Mr C. Breese)
Plasau Duon is a yeoman's house dating from about 1600 with the original

timber framework virtually intact. Five or six ogee doorways, all differing in design, also survive and both the porch and the inlaid overmantel in the sitting room are good examples of 17th century rural craftmanship. A distinctive feature is the porch and the adjoining room has a fine patterned cobbled floor.

RHYDCARW, Trefeglwys (by appointment with Mr F. Davies; tel: Trefeglwys 226)
A good example of a characteristic Montgomeryshire timber-framed house with a projecting two-storey porch and a good oak staircase.

TREBARRIED, Llandefalle (by written appointment with Mr T. Hutton, Manor Farm, Wherwell, nr Andover)
A 16th and 17th century house built for a branch of the Vaughan family, together with a range of 17th and 18th century stable buildings round three sides of a courtyard to the rear of the house.

TREBERFYYD, Bwlch (by written appointment with Major R.D. Raikes)
A mid-19th century mansion designed by J.L. Pearson in Tudor style with stone mullioned windows and fortified by castellated towers; there are also contemporary stables and outbuildings.

TREVECCA FAWR, Talgarth (by written appointment with Major W.H. Lewis)
A good example of a Jacobean manor house, probably built soon after 1600 as a dower house for the Gwynne family. The house is built of random stonework in two storeys and is E-shaped. Notable interior features are three decorated plaster ceilings, panelling in the hall and drawing room and a good original stairway with balusters.

YDDERW, Llyswen (by written appointment with Mr D.P. Eckley)
An early Tudor stone building, formerly the seat of the Morgan family of Ystrad fellte. The house has the mediaeval layout of hall between two cross-wings and additional wings to complete an H-plan were added in the 17th century. Internal features include a 17th century stairway and an original fireplace in the parlour.

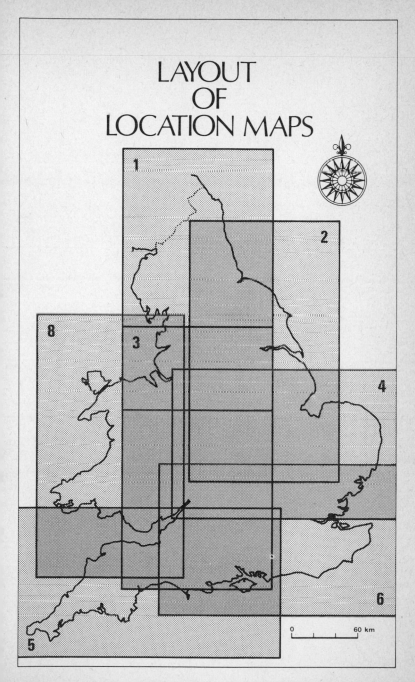

LAYOUT
OF
LOCATION MAPS

1

2

8

3

4

6

5

0   60 km

MAP 1: NORTHERN ENGLAND

1	Norham Castle B1	38	Leighton Hall B5
2	Lindisfarne Castle C2	39	Lancaster Castle B5
3	Bamburgh Castle C2	40	Thurnham Hall B5
4	Dunstanburgh Castle C2	41	Skipton Castle C5
5	Alnwick Castle C2	42	Broughton Hall C5
6	Callaly Castle C2	43	Browsholme Hall B5
7	Warkworth Castle C2	44	Harewood House C5
8	Cragside C2	45	East Riddlesden Hall C5
9	Brinkburn Priory C3	46	Clitheroe Castle B5
10	Wallington Hall C3	47	Bronte Parsonage C6
11	Seaton Delaval Hall C3	48	Braham Park C6
12	Carlisle Castle B3	49	Bolling Hall C6
13	Hylton Castle C3	50	Lotherton Hall D6
14	Washington Old Hall C3	51	Chingle Hall B6
15	Durham Castle C4	52	Temple Newsam D6
16	Hutton in the Forest B4	53	Gawthorpe Hall B6
17	Wordsworth House A4	54	Red House C6
18	Brougham Castle B4	55	Hoghton Tower B6
19	Dalemain B4	56	Oakwell Hall C6
20	Raby Castle C4	57	Samlesbury Hall B6
21	Appleby Castle B4	58	Shibden Hall C6
22	Barnard Castle C4	59	Towneley Hall B6
23	Brough Castle B4	60	Astley Hall B6
24	Dove Cottage A4	61	Turton Tower B6
25	Rydall Mount B4	62	Nostell Proiry C6
26	Townend B4	63	Smithills Hall B6
27	Hill Top B4	64	Rufford Old Hall B6
28	Brantwood A4	65	Hallith Wood B6
29	Belle Isle B5	66	Foxdenton Hall B6
30	Muncaster Castle A5	67	Heaton Hall B6
31	Abbot Hall B5	68	Ordsall Hall B6
32	Sizergh Castle B5	69	Croxteth Hall B6
33	Rusland Hall A5	70	Newton Hall C6
34	Bolton Castle C5	71	Platt Hall C6
35	Levens Hall B5	72	Fletcher Moss B6
36	Holker Hall B5	73	Speke Hall B7
37	Swarthmoor Hall A5	74	Dunham Massey Hall B7

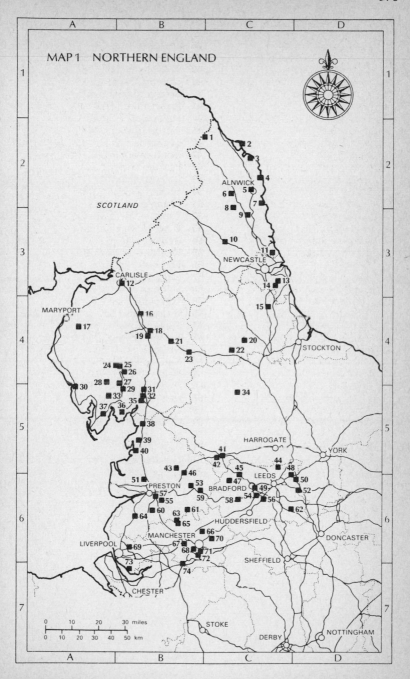

MAP 1   NORTHERN ENGLAND

SCOTLAND

ALNWICK

NEWCASTLE

CARLISLE

MARYPORT

STOCKTON

HARROGATE

YORK

LEEDS

BRADFORD

PRESTON

HUDDERSFIELD

DONCASTER

MANCHESTER

LIVERPOOL

SHEFFIELD

CHESTER

0   10   20   30 miles
0 10 20 30 40 50 km

STOKE

DERBY

NOTTINGHAM

MAP 2: NORTH-EAST ENGLAND

1	Ormesby Hall B2	27	Maister House C4
2	Richmond Castle A3	28	Wilberforce House & 23/4
3	Kiplin Hall B3		High Street C4
4	Constable Burton Hall A3	29	Carlton Towers B4
5	Bedale Hall A3	30	Normanby Hall C4
6	Ebberston Hall B3	31	Cannon Hall A4
7	Helmsley Castle B3	32	Epworth Old Rectory B4
8	Middleham Castle A3	33	Cusworth Hall B4
9	Nunnington Hall B3	34	Conisborough Castle B4
10	Shandy Hall B3	35	Gainsborough Old Hall B5
11	Newburgh Priory B3	36	Alford Manor House D5
12	Norton Conyers A3	37	Bishop's Palace C5
13	Gilling Castle B3	38	Harrington Hall D5
14	Newby Hall B3	39	Doddington Hall B5
15	Castle Howard B3	40	Thoresby Hall B5
16	Markenfield Hall A3	41	Gunby Hall D5
17	Sledmere House C3	42	Thorpe Tilney Hall C5
18	Sewerby Hall C3	43	Tattershall Castle C5
19	Sutton Park B3	44	Newstead Abbey B5
20	Burton Agnes Hall C3	45	Fydell House C5
21	Ripley Castle A3	46	Allington Manor House C5
22	Beningborough Hall B3	47	Nottingham Castle B5
23	Norman Man or House C3	48	Belton Hall C5
24	Treasurer's House B3	49	Wollaton Hall B5
25	Beverley Lairgate Hall C4	50	Holme Pierrepoint Hall B5
26	Burton Constable C4		

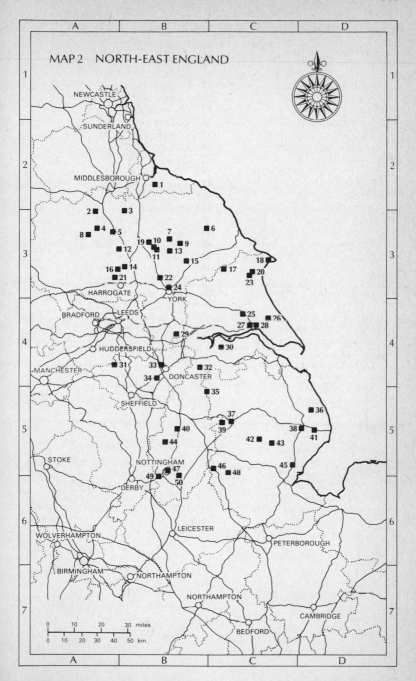

MAP 2   NORTH-EAST ENGLAND

MAP 3: WEST MIDLANDS

1   Bramhall Hall   C2
2   Tatton Park   B2
3   Lyme Park   C2
4   Adlington Hall   C2
5   Poever Hall   B2
6   Capesthorne   B2
7   Bolsover Castle   D2
8   Gawsworth Hall   B2
9   The Old House Museum   C2
10   Chatsworth   D2
11   Stanley Palace   B2
12   Haddon Hall   C2
13   Hardwick Hall   D2
14   Little Moreton Hall   B2
15   Dorfold Hall   B2
16   Churche's Mansion   B2
17   Alton Tower   C3
18   Kedleston Hall   C3
19   Tyn-y-Rhos Hall   A3
20   Sudbury Hall   C3
21   Isaak Walton Cottage   B3
22   Tutbury Castle   C3
23   Moreton Corbett Castle   B3
24   Melbourne Hall   C3
25   Shughborough   B3
26   Adcote   B3
27   Rowley's House   B3
28   Hanch Hall   C3
29   Attingham Park   B3
30   Boscobel House   C3
31   Dr Johnson's House   C3
32   Weston Park   B3
33   Benthall Hall   B3
34   Tamworth Castle   C3
35   Moseley Old Hall   B3
36   Acton Burnell Castle   B3
37   Chillington Hall   B3
38   Asbury Cottage   C3
39   Acton Round Hall   B3
40   Shipton Hall   B4
41   Wightwick Manor   B3
42   Wilderhope Manor   B4
43   Upton Cresset Hall   C4
44   Dudmaston Hall   B4
45   Dudley Castle   C4
46   Oak House   C4
47   Aston Hall   C4

48   Arbury Hall   C4
49   Selly Manor House   C4
50   The White House   B4
51   Hagley Hall   C4
52   Stokesay Castle   B4
53   Blakesley Hall   C4
54   Harvington Hall   B4
55   Kenilworth Castle   C4
56   Packwood House   C4
57   Croft Castle   B4
58   Witley Court   B4
59   Eye Manor   B4
60   Berrington Hall   B4
61   Hanbury Hall   C4
62   Coughton Court   C4
63   Warwick Castle   C4
64   Burton Court   B4
65   Tudor House   B4
66   mary Arden's House   C4
67   Charlecote Park   C4
68   Elgar's Birth Place   B4
69   The Commandery   B4
70   Lower Brockhampton
     House   B4
71   1 Ann Hathaway's
       Cottage   C4
     2 Hall's Croft   C4
     3 Harvard House   C4
     4 New Place   C4
     5 Shakespeare's
       Birthplace   C4
72   Ragley Hall   C4
73   Dinmore Manor   B4
74   Farnborough Hall   D4
75   Upton House   C4
76   Moccas Court   A4
77   Honington Hall   C4
78   Little Malvern Court   B5
79   The Old House   B5
80   Eastnor Castle   B5
81   Buckland Rectory   C5
82   Snowshill Manor   C5
83   Hellens, Much Marcle   B5
84   Sudeley Castle   C5
85   Upper Slaughter
     Manor House   C5
86   Pembridge Castle   B5

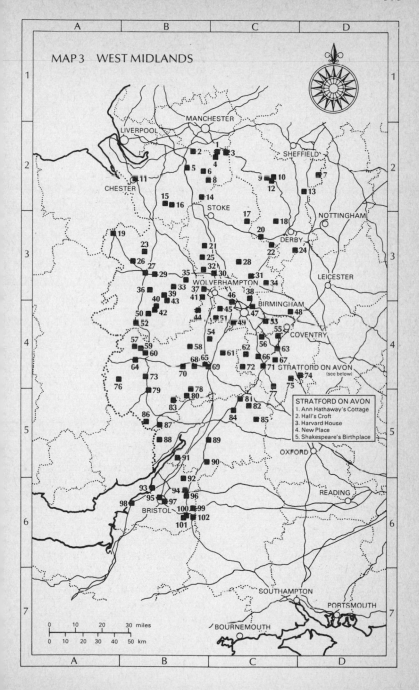

MAP 3   WEST MIDLANDS

STRATFORD ON AVON
1. Ann Hathaway's Cottage
2. Hall's Croft
3. Harvard House
4. New Place
5. Shakespeare's Birthplace

87 Goodrich Castle   B5
88 Clearwell Castle   B5
89 Painswick House   B5
90 Chavenage   B5
91 Berkeley Castle   B5
92 Horton Court   B6
93 Blaise Castle House   B6
94 Dodington House   B6

95 Red Lodge   B6
96 Dyrham Park   B6
97 The Georgian House   B6
98 Clevedon Court   B6
99 St. Catherine's Court   B6
100 1, Royal Crescent   B6
101 Prior Park   B6
102 Claverton Manor   B6

MAP 4: EAST MIDLANDS & EAST ANGLIA

1 Holkham Hall   A5
2 Felbrigg Hall   A6
3 Houghton House   B5
4 Belvoir Castle   B3
5 Baconsthorpe Castle   B5
6 Sandringham House   B5
7 Woolsthorpe Manor   B3
8 Blickling Hall   B6
9 Castle Rising   B5
10 The Red Hall   B3
11 Beeston Hall   B6
12 Stapleford Park   B3
13 Caister Castle   B6
14 Donnington le Heath
     Manor House   B2
15 Oakham Castle   B3
16 Norwich Castle   B6
17 Anna Sewell's House   B6
18 Quenby Hall   B3
19 Peckover House   B4
20 Stranger's Hall   B6
21 Merchant's House   B6
22 4 South Quay   B6
23 Belgrave Hall   B3
24 Burghley House   B3
25 Oxburgh Hall   B5
26 Kirby Muxloe Castle   B2
27 Wygston's House   B2
28 Lyddington Bede House   B3
29 Somerleyton Hall   B6
30 Southwick Hall   B3
31 Kirby Hall   B3
32 Langton Hall   B3
33 Rockingham Castle   B3
34 Lyveden New Bield   C3
35 Rushton Hall   C3
36 Stanford Hall   C2
37 Boughton House   C3
38 Kelmarsh Hall   C3
39 Euston Hall   C5
40 Lamport Hall   C3
41 Althorp   C3
42 Castle Ashby   C3
43 Delapre Abbey   C3

44 Hinchingbrooke House   C4
45 Ixworth Abbey   C5
46 Anglesey Abbey   C4
47 Angel Corner   C5
48 Framlingham Castle   C6
49 Ickworth   C5
50 Haughly Park   C5
51 Glemham Hall   C6
52 Little Hall   C5
53 Wimpole Hall   C4
54 Orford Castle   C6
55 Chicheley Hall   C3
56 Kentwell Hall   C5
57 Christchurch Mansion   C5
58 Sulgrave Manor   C5
59 Melford Hall   C5
60 Gainsborough's House   C5
61 Broughton Castle   C2
62 Houghton House   C3
63 Audley End   C4
64 Aynho   C2
65 Hedingham Castle   C5
66 Woburn Abbey   D3
67 Castle House, Dedham   D5
68 Winslow Hall   D3
69 Gosfield Hall   D5
70 Chasleton House   D2
71 Claydon House   D3
72 Ascott   D3
73 Knebworth   D4
74 Paycocke's   D5
75 Rousham Park   D2
76 Mentmore   D3
77 Luton Hoo   D3
78 Shaw's Corner   D4
79 Waddesdon Manor   D3
80 Layer Marney Tower   D5
81 St. Osyth's Priory   D5
82 Blenheim Palace   D2
83 Dorton House   D3
84 Minster Lovell   D2
85 Nether Winchendon
     House   D3

577

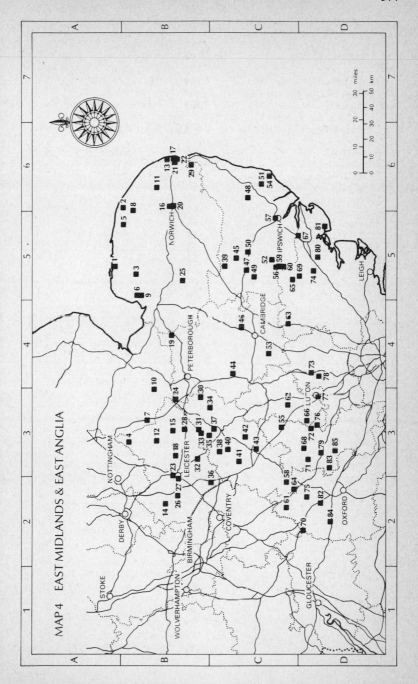

MAP 4 EAST MIDLANDS & EAST ANGLIA

578

MAP 5: SOUTH WEST ENGLAND

1 Farleigh   A5
2 King John's Hunting
  Lodge   A5
3 Oakhill Manor   B5
4 Old Manor House   A5
5 Nunney Castle   B5
6 Chambercombe Manor   B3
7 Bishop's Palace Wells   B5
8 Dunster Castle   B4
9 Arlington Court   B3
10 Halsway Manor   B4
11 Combe Sydenham Hall   B4
12 Coleridge Cottage   B4
13 Barford Park   B4
14 Gaulden Manor   B4
15 Tapeley Park   B3
16 Hestercombe House   B4
17 Lytes Carey   B5
18 Tintinhull House   B5
19 Poundisford Park   B4
20 Midelney Manor   B5
21 Barrington Court   B5
22 Purse Caundle Manor   B5
23 Montacute House   B5
24 Knightshayes Court   B4
25 Sherbourne Castle   B5
26 Tiverton Castle   B4
27 East Lambrook Manor   B5
28 Compton House   B5
29 Chettle House   B6
30 Brympton d'Evercy   B5
31 Bickleigh Castle   B4
32 Ebbingford Manor   B2
33 Milton Abbey   B5
34 Forde Abbey   B5
35 Parnham House   B5
36 Dewlish House   B5
37 Cadhay   B4
38 Killerton House   B4
39 Okehampton Castle   C3
40 Wolfeton House   B5
41 Atelhampton   B5
42 Lyford Castle   C3
43 Castle Drogo   C3
44 Tintagel Old Post Office   C2
45 Launceston Castle   C3
46 A la Ronde   C4
47 Powderham Castle   C4
48 Lawrence House   C3
49 Corfe Castle   C6
50 Welsley's Cottage   C2
51 Ugbrooke Park   C4
52 Smedmore   C6
53 Bradley Manor   C4
54 Buckland Abbey   C3
55 Pencarrow House   C2
56 Cotehele House   C3
57 Torre Abbey   C4
58 Compton Castle   C4
59 Kirkham House   C4
60 Oldway Mansion   C4
61 Dartington Hall   C2
62 Lanhydrock   C3
63 Restormel Castle   C2
64 Berry Pomeroy Castle   C3
65 Trerice   C2
66 Elizabethan House   C3
67 Merchant's House   C3
68 Prysten House   C3
69 Totnes Castle   C4
70 Anthony House   C3
71 Mount Edgcumbe   C3
72 Saltram   C3
73 Flete   C3
74 Dartmouth Castle   C4
75 Trewithen   C2
76 St. Mawes Castle   D2
77 Godolphin House   D1
78 Pendennis Castle   D2
79 St. Michael's Mount   D1
80 Trelowarren   D2

579

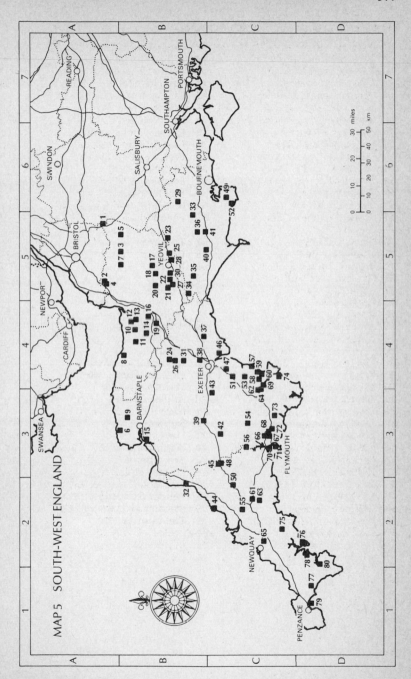

MAP 5   SOUTH-WEST ENGLAND

MAP 6: SOUTHERN ENGLAND

1 Piccott's End   A4
2 Hatfield House   A4
3 Gorhambury   A4
4 Kingston House   B2
5 Buscot Park   B2
6 Forty Hall   B4
7 Chenies Manor House   B4
8 Hughenden Manor   B3
9 Milton Manor House   B3
10 Moor Park Mansion   B4
11 Milton' Cottage   B4
12 West Wycombe Park   B3
13 Stonor Park   B3
14 Ashdown House   B3
15 Cliveden House   B3
16 Lydiard Mansion   B2
17 Grey's Court   B3
18 Mapledurham House   B3
19 Dorney Court   B3
20 Basildon Park   B3
21 Windsor Castle   B4
22 Sheldon Manor   B2
23 Bowood   B2
24 Avebury Manor   B2
25 Littlecote House   B2
26 Donnington Castle   B3
27 Corsham Court   B2
28 Lacock Abbey   B2
29 Cobham Hall   B5
30 Temple Manor   B5
31 Owletts   B5
32 Swallowfield Park   B3
33 Great Chalfield Manor   B2
34 Lullingstone Castle   B5
35 Rochester Castle   B5
36 Tudor House   B6
37 Quex Park   B6
38 Claremont   B4
39 Stratfield Saye   B3
40 Westwood Manor   B1
41 West Green House   B3
42 Allington Castle   B5
43 Maisdon Dieu   B5
44 Old Soar Manor   B5
45 Knole   B5
46 Hatchlands   C4
47 Eyhorne Manor   B5

48 Leeds Castle   B5
49 The Vyne   B3
50 Polesdon Lacey   B4
51 Detillens   B4
52 Igtham Mote   C5
53 Stonacre   C5
54 Deal Castle   B6
55 Quebec House   B4
56 Boughton Monchelsea   C5
57 Chalcot House   C1
58 Long Barn   B5
59 Clandon Park   B4
60 Squerryes Court   C4
61 Losely House   C4
62 Roydon Hall   B5
63 Walmer Castle   B6
64 Chartwell   B5
65 Albury Park   C4
66 Longleat   C2
67 Farnham Castle   C3
68 Hever Castle   C5
69 Chiddingstone Castle   C5
70 Penhurst Place   C5
71 Godington Park   C5
72 Greathead Manor   C4
73 Dover Castle   C6
74 Sissinghurst Castle   C5
75 Jane Austen's House   C3
76 Stourhead   C1
77 Phillips House   C2
78 Finchcocks   C5
79 Pattydenne Manor   C5
80 Standen   C4
81 Wilton House   C2
82 Avington Park   C3
83 Lympe Castle   C6
84 Saltwood Castle   C6
85 Mompesson House   C2
86 Great Maytham Hall   C5
87 Port Lympne   C6
88 Pythouse   C1
89 Mottisfont Abbey   C2
90 Smallhythe Place   C5
91 Wardour Old Caslte/
      Wardour Castle   C2
92 Newhouse   C2
93 Bodiam Castle   C5

581

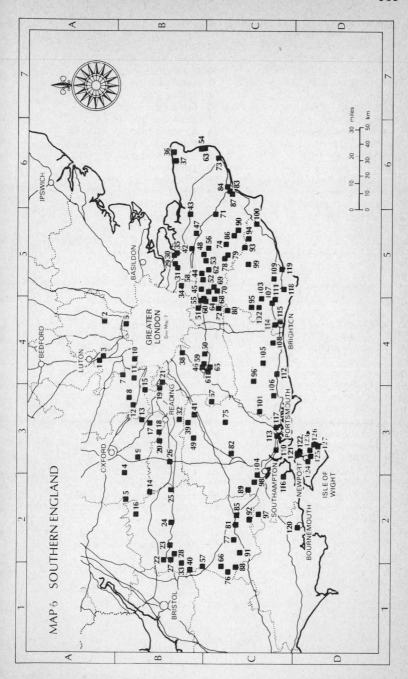

MAP 6   SOUTHERN ENGLAND

94 Great Dixter   C5
95 Sheffield Park   C4
96 Petworth House   C4
97 Breamore House   C2
98 Broadlands   C2
99 Batemans   C5
100 Lamb House   C5
101 Uppark   C3
102 Anne of Cleves' House   C4
103 Bentley Wildfowl   C4
104 Grove Place   C2
105 Parham   C4
106 Goodwood House   C3
107 Glynde Place   C4
108 St. Mary's   C4
109 Michelham Priory   C5
110 Titchfield Abbey   C3
111 Firle Place   C4

112 Arundel Castle   C4
113 Portchester Castle   C3
114 Preston Manor   C4
115 Brighton Pavillion   C4
116 Beaulieu Abbey   C2
117 Charles Dickens' House   C3
118 Alfriston Clergy House   C5
119 Pevensey Old Mint
      House   C5
120 Russell Coates Museum   D2
121 Norris Castle   D3
122 Osborne House   D3
123 Arreton Manor   D3
124 Carisbrooke Castle   D3
125 Hazeley Manor   D3
126 Morton Manor   D3
127 Appledurcombe House   D3

MAP 7: LONDON

1 Kenwood House   A4
2 Fenton House   A3
3 The Dickens House   B4
4 Apsley House   B4
5 Sir John Soane's Museum   B4
6 Dr Johnson's House   B4
7 Kensington Palace   B4
8 The Tower of London   B4
9 Lancaster House   B4
10 Hogarth's House   B3
11 Chiswick House   B3
12 Carlyle's House   B4
13 Osterley Park House   B2
14 Syon Park   B2
15 The Queen's House   B5
16 Ranger's House   B5
17 Kew Palace (Dutch House)   B5
18 Eltham Palace   B6
19 Hall Place   C6
20 White Lodge   C3
21 Marble Hill House   C2
22 Ham House   C2
23 Hampton Court Palace   C2
24 Down House   D6

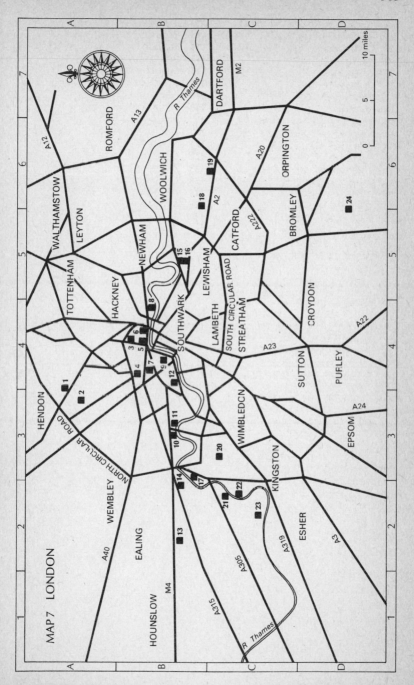

584

MAP 8: WALES

1 Bodrhyddan   C2
2 Beaumaris Castle   B2
3 Aberconway House   C2
4 Conwy Castle   C2
5 Plas Mawr   C2
6 Penrhyn Castle   B2
7 Plas Newydd   B3
8 Caernarfon Castle   B3
9 Bryn Bras Castle   B3
10 Ty Mawr   C3
11 Erdigg   D3
12 Chirk Castle   D3
13 Harlech Castle   B3
14 Trelydan Hall   D4
15 Powis Castle   D4
16 Tretower Court   C5
17 White Castle   D5
18 Pembroke Castle   A6
19 Tenby   A6
20 Raglan Castle   D5
21 Manorbier Castle   A6
22 Penhow Castle   D6
23 Caerphilly Castle   C6
24 Chepstow Castle   D6
25 Tredegar House   D6
26 Castell Coch   C6
27 Cardiff Castle   D6
28 St. Fagan's   C6

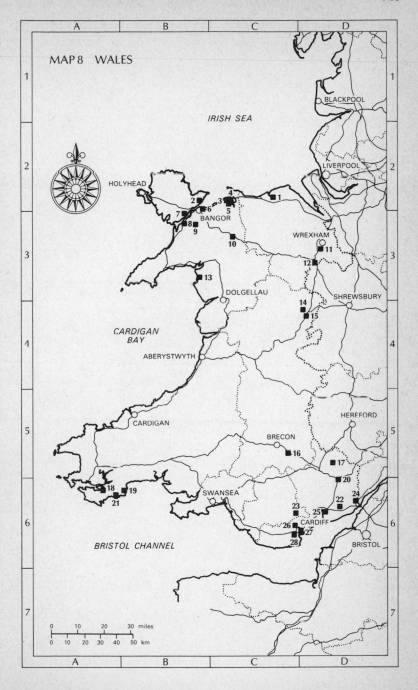

MAP 8 WALES

IRISH SEA

A B C D

BLACKPOOL

LIVERPOOL

HOLYHEAD

2
3 4
7 6 5 1
8 BANGOR
9

10

WREXHAM
11

12

13

DOLGELLAU

14
15

SHREWSBURY

CARDIGAN
BAY

ABERYSTWYTH

CARDIGAN

HEREFORD

BRECON
16

17

20

18 19
21

SWANSEA

23
22

24

25
26 CARDIFF
27
28

BRISTOL

BRISTOL CHANNEL

0   10   20   30 miles
0 10 20 30 40 50 km

Index of houses

A La Ronde 87-8
Abbot Hall 62-3
Abbot's Bromley: Church House 545
Aberconwy House, Conwy 487-8
Abercynrig 565
Abingdon: Twickenham House 537-8
Abinger Hammer: Crossways Farm 549
Acton Burnell Castle 333
Acton Round Hall 333-4
Adcote 334-5
8 Addison Road 529
Adlington Hall 38
50 Albermarle Street 529
Albury Park 380-1
Alderley Grange 516
Alford Manor House Folk Museum 232-3
Alfriston Old Clergy House 388
All Hallows Vicarage 529-30
Allington Castle 182-3
Allington Manor House 223
Alnwick Castle 305-6
Althorp 294-5
Alton Towers 360-1
Anglesey Abbey 32-3
Ann Hathaway's Cottage, Stratford On
    Avon 420
Ann of Cleves, Lewes 396-7
Antony House 48-9
Apethorpe Hall 535
Appleby Castle 63-4
Appleby Magna, Moat House 526
Appuldurcombe House 176
Apsley House Museum 241-2
Arbury Hall 410-12
Mary Arden's House 417-18
Arlington Court 88-9
Arreton Manor 176-8
Arundel Castle 400-2
Asbury Cottage 272
Ascott 19
Asgill House 530
Ashdown House (Oxon) 321
Ashdown House (E Sussex) 550
Ashleworth Court 516
Ashleworth Manor 516
Ashridge 522
Ashton Court Mansion 501
Astley Hall 211
Aston Hall (Birmingham) 272-3
Aston Hall (Clwyd) 559
Astwell Castle Farmhouse 535
Athelhampton Hall 111
Attingham Park 335

Auborn Hall 527
Audley End 124
Jane Austen's House, Chawton 141
Avebury Manor 425
Avenue House 503
Avington Park 137
Axbridge: King John's Hunting Lodge 343
Axbridge: The Old Drug Store 542
Axbridge: The Old Manor House 344
Aynhoe Park 295-6

Baconsthorpe Castle 281
Badminton House 501
Bakewell: The Old House Museum 78-9
Bamburgh Castle 306-8
Banbury: 85 High Street 538
Barford Park 344-5
Barming Place 523
Barnard Castle 121-2
Barrington Court 345-6
Basildon Park 15-16
Batemans 388-9
Bath: 1 Royal Crescent 1
Beaulieu Abbey 137-9
Beckingham Hall 515
Bedale Hall 444
Bedford: St John's Rectory 503
Bedstone Court 540
Beeches Farm 550
Beeston Hall 281-2
Belchamp Hall (Essex) 515
Belchamp Hall (Sussex) 546
Belgrave Hall 222-24
Belle Isle 64
Belton House 233-4
Belvoir Castle 222
Beningbrough Hall 444-5
Benthall Hall 336
Bentley 389-90
Berkeley Castle 130
Berrington Hall 148-9
Berry Pomeroy Castle 89-90
Bettiscombe Manor 513
Betteshanger House 523
Beverley: Langate Hall 168
Beverston Castle 516
Bickleigh Castle 89
Bidston House 506
Bindon Manor 511
Bisham Abbey 504
Blackbrook House 561
Blaise Castle House 2
Blakesley Hall 273-4

Index

Blandford Forum: Coupar House 513
Blenheim Palace 321-3
Blickling Hall 282-3
Bloxworth House 514
Bodiam Castle 390-1
Bodryhyddan Hall 475-6
Bolling Hall 463-4
Bolsover Castle 79
Bolton Castle 445-6
Bolton Percy Gatehouse 555
Borwick Hall 525
Boscobel House 336-7
Boughton House 296-8
Boughton Monchelsea Place 183-4
Bourne: The Red Hall 234-5
Bowood 426-7
Boynton Hall 522-3
Bradford on Avon: The Old Church House 552
Bradford on Avon: The Old Manor House 552
Bradford on Avon: Orpins 552
Bradley Manor 90-1
Bradwell Lodge 515
Bramall Hall 39
Bramham Park 464-6
Brampton: Samuel Pepy's House 505
Brantwood 65
Breadsall: The Old Hall 509-10
Breamore House 139-40
Brecon: Buckingham Palace 565-6
Brewerstreet Farm 549
Bridwell House 511
Brighton: The Royal Pavilion 391-3
Brilley: Cwmmau Farmhouse 519
Brinkburn Priory 308-9
Bristol: 6 Dowry Square 501
Bristol: 9 Dowry Square 501-2
Bristol: The Georgian House 2-3
Bristol: The Red Lodge 3-4
Bristol: St Vincent's Priory 502
Broadlands 140-1
Bronte Parsonage 466
Broseley Hall 540
Brough Castle 65-6
Brougham Castle 66-7
Broughton Castle 323-4
Broughton Hall (Staffs) 545
Broughton Hall (N Yorks) 446-7
Broughton House 296-8
Browsholme Hall 212
Brympton d'Evercy 346-8
Bryn Bras Castle 488-9
Bryn Nodol 562
Buckden Palace 505
16 Buckingham Gate 530
Buckland Abbey 91
Buckland Rectory 131
Buckshaw House 514
Bumpit 523

Burfa 566
Burghley House 33-5
Burton Agnes Hall 169
Burton Agnes Old Hall 170
Burton Constable Hall 170-1
Burton Court 149
Bury St Edmunds: Angel 369
Busby Hall 555
Buscot Old Parsonage 538
Buscot Park 324-5

Cadhay 92
Cae'r Berllan 563
Caerphilly Castle 480
Caernarfon Castle 489-91
Caister Castle 283
Caistor House 527
Callaly Castle 309
Came House 514
Cannon Hall 461-2
Capesthorne Hall 39-40
Cardiff Castle 480-1
Carisbrooke Castle 178-9
Carlisle Castle 67
Carlisle: The Deanery Tower 508
Carlton Hall 447
Carlton Towers 447
Carlyle's House 242
Carshalton House 530
Castell Coch 481-2
Castle Ashby 298-9
Castle Drogo 92-4
Castle Godwin 516
Castle Hill 511
Castle House 125
Castle Howard 448-9
Castle Rising 284
11-13 Cavendish Square 530
Chaceley Hall 516-17
Chalcot House 427
Chamercombe Manor 94-5
Charford Manor 518
Charlecote Park 413
Charlton House 530
Chartwell 184
Chastleton House 325-7
Chatsworth House 80-2
Chavenage House 131-2
Chawton: Jane Austen's House 141
Cheltenham: Thirlestane House 517
Chenies Manor House 20
Chepstow Castle 483-4
Chester: Tudor House 507
Chettle House 111-12
Cheylesmore Manor 533
Chicheley Hall 20-1
Chichester: The Deanery 551
Chiddingstone Castle 185
Chillington Hall 361-2
Chingle Hall 212-13

Chipping Sodbury: Tudor House 502
Chirk Castle 476-7
Chiswick House 244-5
Churche's Mansion 40-1
Church Stanway: The Old Vicarage 517
Clandon Park 381-21
Clanford Hall 545
Claremont House 382-3
Claverton Manor 4-5
Claydon House 21-2
Clearwell Castle 132-3
Clevedon Court 5
Clifton Hall 537
Clitheroe Castle 213
Cliveden House 22-4
Cobham Hall 185-6
Cochwillan Old Hall 563
Coleridge's Cottage 348
Combe Sydenham Hall 348-9
Compton Castle 95-6
Compton House 112-13
Condover Hall 540
Congressbury Vicarage 502
Conisbrough Castle 462
Conishead Priory 508
Coniston Hall 525
Constable Burton Hall 450
Conwy: Aberconwy House 487-8
Conwy Castle 491-2
Conwy: Plas Mawr 494-5
Corfe Castle 113
Corse Court 517
Corsham Court 477-8
Corsham: The Grove 553
Cote House 538
Cotehele 49 51
Cothelstone Manor 542
Coughton Court 414-15
Courteenhall 535
Craster Tower 536
Cragside 310
Croft Castle 150
Cromwell House 530-1
Cronkhill 540
Croome Court 519-20
Croscombe: The Old Manor House 542-3
Croxteth Hall 270
Culverthorpe Hall 527
Cusworth Hall 462-3
Cwrt Porth Hir 561
Cymrd 563

Dacre Castle 508
Dacre Hall 508
Dalemain 67-8
Daneway House 517
Dartington Hall 96
Dartmouth: Agincourt House 96-7
Darmouth Castle 96-7
Dartmouth: The Mansion House 511

Ddaullt 563
Deal Castle 186
20 Deans Yard 531
Deene Park 535
Delapré Abbey 299-300
Detillens 383
Devizes: Brownston Houses 553
Dewlish House 113-14
The Dickens House Museum 244-5
Dinmore Manor 150-1
Ditchley Park 538
Doctor Johnson's House 245
Doddington Hall 543
Dodington Hall 235-6
Dodington House 6
Dolangwyn 563
Donnington Castle 16
Donnington-le-Heath Manor House 225
Dorfold Hall 41
Dorney Court 24-5
Dorton House 25
Dove Cottage 68-9
Dover Castle 186-7
Dowles Manor 520
Down House 246
Dunham Massey Hall 264-5
Drayton House 536
Dudley Castle and Zoo 274-5
Dudmaston 337-8
Dunham Massey Hall 264-5
Dunstanburgh Castle 310-11
Dunster Castle 349-50
Durham Castle 122-3
Dyrham Park 8

Eagle House 531
Eastbury House 531
East Lambrock Manor 350-1
East Meon: Court House 518-19
East Riddlesden Hall 466-7
Eastnor Castle 151-1
Easton On the Hill: Priests House 536
Eastwood Manor Farm 502
Ebberston Hall 450-1
Ebbingford Manor 51
Edgcote House 538
Egham: Great Fosters 549
Elgar's Birthplace 152
Elsdon Tower 536
Elstead: The Mill House 549
Eltham Palace 246-7
Ely: 1 & 2 The Almonry 505
Ely: The Chantry 505
Ely: The Old Palace 505-6
Epworth Old Rectory 171-2
Erddig 477-8
Euston Hall 369-70
Evesham: Church House 520
Exeter: 7 The Close 511
Eye Manor 152-3

Index

Eyhorne Manor 187-8

Fairfield House 523
Farleigh Hungerford Castle 351-2
Farnborough Hall 415
Farnham Castle 384, 549
Farnham: Ranger's House 549
Faversham: 6 Market Place 523-4
Felbrigg Hall 284-5
Fenton House 247-8
Ferham House 557
Fferm 559
Fillingham Castle 527
Finchcocks 187
Firle Place 393-4
Flemings Hall 546-7
Fletcher Moss Art Gallery 265
Flete 97-8
Fonmon Castle 565
Forde Abbey 114-16
Foremarke Hall 510
Forty Hall 248
Foston Old Rectory 555
Foxcote 552
Foxdenton House 265-6
Framlingham Castle 370
Frampton Court 517
Frome: St John's Vicarage 543
Fulbeck Manor 527
Fydell House 236

Gainsborough: The Old Hall 236-7
Gainsborough's House 370-1
Gaulden Manor 352
Gawsworth Hall 42
Gawthorpe Hall 213-14
Gilling Castle 451
Glemham Hall 371-2
Glynde Place 394-5
Godington Park 189
Godolphin House 52
Goodrich Castle 153-4
Goodwood House 402-3
Gorhambury 161
Gosfield Hall 126
Gowthorpe Manor 533
Grafton Manor 520
Great Bricett Farm House 547
Great Chalfield Manor 428-9
Great Cil-Ilwych 561
Great Cressingham Priory 533
Great Dixter 395-6
Great Maythem Hall 189-90
Great Ponton Rectory 527-8
Great Yarmouth: The Old Merchant's
    House 286-7
Great Yarmouth: Anna Sewell's House
    285-6
Great Yarmouth: 4 South Quay 287
Greathed Manor 384-5

Grey's Court 327
Grove Place 141-2
Guandovan 560
Gunby Hall 237-8

Haddon Hall 82-3
Hadleigh: The Deanery Tower 547
Hadleigh: 48 High Street 547
Hagley Hall 275-7
Hale Park 519
Hales Hall 533
Halghton Hall 559
Hall ith Wood 266
Hall Place 248-9
Halsway Manor 352-3, 543
Ham House 249-50
Hambledon: Manor Farm House 519
Hampton Court Palace 250-1
Hanbury Hall 154
Hanch Hall 362-3
Hardwick Hall 83-4
Haremere Hall 550
Harewood House 467-9
Harlech Castle 492
Harnham Hall 536-7
Harrington Hall 238-9
Hartlebury Castle 520
Harvington Hall 154-5
Haseley Manor 179-80
Hatch Court 543
Hatchlands 385-6
Hatfield House 162-4
Haughley Park 372
Hazlewood Castle 555-6
Heale House 553
Heath Hall 557
Heath House 520
Heaton Hall 266-7
Hedingham Hall 126-7
Hellen's 155-6
Helmsley Castle 452
Hen Blas 559
Hengrave Hall 547
Henley: The Chantry House on Thames
    538
Hereford: 24/5 Church Street 520-1
Hereford: The Old House 156-7
Hestercombe House 353-4
Hever Castle 190-2
High Chimneys 503
Higher Hareston 511-12
Hill Farm 512
Hill Top 69
Hinchingbrooke House 35-6
Hintlesham Hall 547
Hinton Manor 538-9
Hogarth's House 251-2
Hoghton Tower 214-15
Holkham Hall 288-90
Holker Hall 70

Holme Pierrepont Hall 316-17
Home Farmhouse 556
Honeywood House 524
Honington Hall 415-16
Hope House, Woodstock 539
Horham Hall 515
Horsham St Faith: Abbey Farm 533
Horsted Place 551
Horton Court 8-9
Houghton House 12
Houghton Hall 290-1
Hoveton House 533
Howsham House 557
Huddington Court 521
Hughenden Manor 25-6
Hull: Maister House 172
Hull: Wilberforce House 172-3
Hull: Blaydes House 523
Hutton In the Forest 70-1
Hutton John 508
Hylton Castle 409
Hymerford Manor 543

Ickworth 372-3
Ightham Mote 192
Ipswich: Christ Church Mansion 373-4
Itton Court 561
Iver Grove 504-5
Ixworth Abbey 374-5
Izaak Walton Cottage 363

Jackson's House Farm 525
Dr Johnson's House 245

Kedleston Hall 84-5
Kelmarsh Hall 300
Kelmscott House 531
Kelmscott Manor 539
Kemys House 561-2
Kendal: Castle Dairy 509
Kenilworth Castle 416-17
Kensington Palace 252
Kentchurch Court 521
Kentwell Hall 375-6
Kenwood House 253
Kew Palace 253-4
Killerton House 98-9
Kimbolton Castle 506
Kingstone Lisle Park 539
Kingston House 328
Kiplin Hall 452-3
Kirby Hall 301-2
Kirby Muxloe Castle 225-6
Knebworth House 165-6
Knightshayes Court 99
Knole 193-4

Lacock Abbey 429-30
Lamb House 396
Lamport Hall 301-2

Lancaster Castle 215-16
Lancaster House 254-5
Langley Castle 534
Langley Hall 537
Langton Hall 226-7
Lanhydrock House 52-3
Lasborough Park 517
Laugharne: Castle House 560
Launceston Castle 53-4
Launceston: Lawrence House 54
Lavenham: Little Hall 376
Layer Marney Tower 127-8
Ledston Hall 557
Leeds Castle 194
Leicester: Wygston's House 227
Leighton Hall 216-17
Levens Hall 71-2
Leverington Hall 506
Lewes: Ann of Cleves House 396-7
Lichfield: Dr Johnson's Birthplace 363-4
Lichfield: 45 John Street 545
Lichfield: Lichfield House 545
Lincoln: 33/4 The Strait 528
Lincoln: 4 James Street 528
Lincoln: 18 James Street 528
Lincoln: The Old Bishop's Palace 239
Lindisfarne Castle 311-12
Lingfield: Pollard Castle 549-50
Linley Sambourne House 531-2
Little Chesterford Manor 515
Little Clarendon House 553
Little Hautbois Hall 534
Little Holland House 531-2
Little Malvern Court 157
Little Moreton Hall 42-4
Little Sodbury Manor 502
Little Thakeham 551
Little Wryley Hall 545
Littlecote House 430-1
Llancaiach Fawr Farm 564
Llanfihangel Court 562
Llantwit Major: The Great House 565
Lockleys 522
Locko Park 510
Long Barn 196
Longleat House 431-3
Longner Hall 540-1
Longnor Hall 541
Loseley Park 386
Lotherton Hall 469-70
Loughborough: The Old Rectory 526
Lower Brockhampton House 157-8
Luddesdown Court 524
Ludlow: 1 & 1a High Street 541
Lullingstone Castle 196-7
Luton Hoo 12-13
Lyddington Bede House 228
Lydford Castle 100
Lydiard Park 433-4
Lyme Park 44-5

Index

Lympne Castle 197-8
Lytes Carey 354-5
Lyveden New Bield 302-3

Maesmawr Hall 566
Malmesbury: Abbey House 553
Mannington Hall 534
Manorbier Castle 478
Mapledurham House 328-9
Marble Hill House 255-6
Marchington Hall 546
Margate: Tudor House 198
Markenfield Hall 453
Market Drayton: The Old House 541
Marsh Court 519
Marston Hall 528
Mary Arden's House 417-18
Matson House 518
Mavesyn Ridware: The Old Farmhouse
  546
Mawley Hall 541
Meare: Manor Farm 543
Medros Farm 507
Melbourne Hall 85-6
Melford Hall 376-7
Mentmore 26-7
Mere: The Chantry 553
Mersham le Hatch 524
Methwold: The Old Vicarage 534
Michelham Priory 397-8
Middleham Castle 453-4
Midelney Manor 355
Milton Abbey 116-17
Milton Ernest Hall 503
Milton Manor (Oxon) 329-30
Milton Manor (Wilts) 553
Milton's Cottage 27-8
Minster Lovell Hall 330-1
Moat Farm 547
Moat Hall 548
Moccas Court 158
Moignes Court 514
Mompesson House Salisbury 434-5
Monmouth: 3 & 4 Priory Street 562
Monmouth: St James' House 562
Montacute House 356
Moor Park 166-7
Moreton Carbet Castle 338
Morton Manor 180
Morville Hall 541
Moseley Old Hall 277
Mottisfont Abbey 142-3
Moulton Hall 556
Mount Edgcumbe 54-5
Moyles Court 519
Muchelney: The Priest's House 544
Muncaster Castle 72-3

Nailsworth: Stokescroft 518
Nannan 562-3

Nanteos 560
Naworth Castle 509
Nerquis Hall 559
Nether Wichendon House 28-9
Nettlecombe Court 544
New Place 550
Newbourne Hall 548
Newbuildings Place 551
Newburgh Priory 454-5
Newbury: The Chestnuts 504
Newby Hall 455-6
Newhouse 435-6
The Newland 550
Newstead Abbey 317-18
Newtown Farm 566
Newtimber Place 551
Newton Hall 267-8
Norbury Manor 510
Norham Castle 312
Normanby Hall 173-4
Norris Castle 180-1
North Lees Hall 510
North Luffenham Hall 526
Norton Conyers 456
Norwich: Castle Museum 291
Norwich: Strangers' Hall 292
Nostell Priory 470-1
Nottingham Castle Museum 318-19
Nunney Castle 356
Nunnington Hall 456-7
Nurstead Court 524

Oak House 277-8
Oakham Castle 228-9
Oakhill Manor 356-7
Oakley Hall 541-2
Oakwell Hall 471-2
Okehampton Castle 100-1
Old Hall 507
The Old Manor 512
Old Newnham 512
Old Soar Manor 198-9
Ordsall Hall 268
Orford Castle 377-8
Ormesby Hall 47-8
Osborne House 181-2
Ospringe: Maison Dieu 199
Osterley Park House 256-7
Otterden Place 524
Oundle: Paine's Cottages 536
Overmonnow House 562
Owletts 199-200
Owlpen Manor 518
Oxburgh Hall 292-3

Packwood House 418-19
Paignton: Kirkham House 101
Paignton: Oldway Mansion 101-2
Painswick House 133-4
Paramour Grange 524-5

Parham Park 403-4
Park Hall 546
Parnham House 117
Parrox Hall 525
Pattyndenne Manor 200
Paycocke's 128-9
Peckover House 36-7
Pembridge Castle 159
Pembroke Castle 478-9
Pencarrow 55-6
Pendennis Castle 56-7
Penhow Castle 484
Penrhyn Castle 492-4
Penrice Castle 565
Pen-y-lan 566
Penshurst Place 201
Peover Hall 45
Samuel Pepy's House Brampton 505
Peterborough: Archdeaconry House 506
Petworth House 404-5
Phillips House 436
68 Piccotts End 167
Pillaton Old Hall 546
Pitchford Hall (Tree House) 542
Plas Llangattock 566
Plasandnon 566-7
Plas Berw 564
Plas Coch 564
Plas Newydd 495-6
Plas Teg 559-60
Plas Yn Rhiw 564
Platt Hall 268-9
Plymouth: Elizabethan House 102-3
Plymouth: 33-34a Looe Street 512
Plymouth: Merchant's House Museum 103
Plymouth: Prysten House 103-4
Polesdon Lacey 387-8
Polstead Hall 548
Port Lympne 202
Portchester Castle 143
Portsmouth: Charles Dickens Birthplace
    Museum 143-4
Potterne: The Porch House 553-4
Poundisford Park 358
Powderham Castle 104-6
Powis Castle 497-9
The Presbytery 532
Preston Manor 509
Preston Patrick Hall 398-9
Princes Risborough: Manor House 505
Prior Park 9-11
Purley Hall 504
Purse Caundle Manor 117-18
Pyt House 436-7

Quebec House 202-3
The Queen's House 257-8
Quenby Hall 229-30
Quex Park 203-4

Raby Castle 123-4
Raglan Castle 485
Ragley Hall 419-20
Rainthorpe Hall 534
Ranger's House 258
Rayne Hall 515
Red House *(London)* 532
The Red House *(W Yorks)* 472-3
Redness Hall 509
The Round House 532
Restormel Castle 57
Rhydarwen 560
Rhydcarw 567
Richmond Castle 457-8
Ripley Castle 458
Ripon: Minster Hall 556
Roche Old Court 554
Rochester Castle 204
Rockingham Castle 303-4
Roos Hall 548
The Round House 532
Rousham Park 331
Roydon Hall 204-5
Ruffold Old Hall 217
Rushton Hall 304-5
Rusland Hall 73
Russell-Cotes Art Galley 118-19
Rydal Mount 74

St Catherine's Court 11-12
St Fagan's Castle 482-3
St Helens House, Derby 510
St Mary's 405-6
St Mawes Castle 57-8
St Michael's Mount 58
St Osyth's Priory 129
Salford Hall 552
Salisbury: Church House 554
Salisbury: 29 The Close 554
Salisbury: 57 The Close 554
Salisbury: Malmesbury House 554
Salisbury: The North Canonry 554
Salisbury: Mompesson House 434
Salisbury: The Old Bishop's Palace 554
Salisbury: The Old Deanery 555
Saltram 106
Saltwood Castle 205-6
Samlesbury Hall 219
Sandleford Priory 504
Sandringham House 293-4
Saxham Hall 548
Scarisbrick Hall 525-6
Scrivelsby Court 528
Seaton Delaval Hall 314
Sedgebrock Manor 528
Selly Manor 278-9
Sewerby Hall 174
Shandy Hall 458-9
Shapcott Barton 512
Sharstead Court 525

Index

Shaw's Corner 167-8
Sheffield Park 399-400
Sheldon Manor 437-8
Shenton Hall Gatehouse 526
Sherborne Castle 119
Sherringham Hall 534
Shibden Hall 473
Shipton Hall 338-9
Shotwick Hall 507
Shrewsbury: Rowley's House 339-40
Shugborough 364-6
Shute Barton 512
Sidmouth: Tudor Cottage 513
Sissinghurst Castle 206
Sizergh Castle 74-5
Skipton Castle 459-60
Slade Hall 532
Sledmere House 175
Smallhythe Palace 206-8
Smedmore House 120
Smithills Hall 269
Snowshill Manor 134
Sir John Soane's Museum 259
Somerleyton Hall 378-80
Somersby Grange 529
Somerton Castle 529
Southam Delabere 518
South Yarde 513
Spains Hall 515-16
Speke Hall 271
Squerrys Court 208-9
Standen 406-8
Stanford Hall 230-1
Stanley Palace 46
Stanley Pontlarge: The Cottage 518
Stanwardine Hall 542
Stapleford Hall 231-2
Staunton Harold Hall 526
Steventon: 39-43 The Causeway 539
Steventon: 103-107 The Causeway 539
Steyning: Chantry Green House 551
Stockeld Park: Strangers Hall 556
Stokesay Castle 340
Stoneacre 209
Stonor Park 332
Stourhead 438-9
Stratfield Saye House 144-6
Stratford-on-Avon: Ann Hathaway's
    Cottage 420
Stratford-on-Avon: Hall's Croft 420-1
Stratford-on-Avon: Harvard House 421-2
Stratford-on-Avon: Nash's House and New
    Place 422
Stratford-on-Avon: Shakespeare's
    Birthplace 422-3
Strawberry Hill 532
Sudbury Hall 86-7
Sudeley Castle 135
Sulgrave Manor 305
Sunbury Court 550

Sutton Park 460
Swallocliffe Manor 555
Swallowfield Park 16-17
Swarthmoor Hall 75
Syon House 259-61

Taliaris Park 560-1
Tamworth Castle 366-7
Tapeley Park 107-8
Tattershall Castle 239-40
Tatton Park 46-7
Tedgewood Farm 520
Temple Manor 209-10
Temple Newsam House 473-4
Tenby: The Tudor Merchant's House 479
Thoresby Hall 319
Thorney Abbey House 506
Thornton Hall 558
Thorpe Hall 534-5
Thorpe Tilney Hall 240-1
Thrumpton Hall 537
Thurnham Hall 219-20
Tickenham Court 502
Tintagel: The Old Post Office 59
Tintinhull House 359
Titchfield Abbey 146
Tiverton Castle 108
Tiverton: The Great House 513
Torquay: Torre Abbey 108-9
Totnes Castle 109
The Tower of London 262-3
Towneley Hall Art Gallery and Museum
    220-1
Townend 76
Trebarried 567
Treberfydd 567
Trecarrel Manor 507
Tredegar House 485-6
Trelowarren 59-60
Trelydan Hall 499
Treowen 562
Trerice 60-1
Tretower Court 500
Trevecca Fawr 567
Trewint: Wesley''s Cottage 61
Trewithen 61-2
Truro: The Mansion House 507-8
Turton Tower 221
Tutbury Castle 367
Twickenham Court 502
Ty Mawr 496-7
Tyn-y-Rhos Hall 340-1
Tytup Hall 509

Ugbrooke 110
Uppark 408-9
Upper Slaughter Manor House 136
Upper Wythall 520
Upton Crescett Hall 341
Upton House 423-4

The Vyne 146-7

Waddesdon Manor 30
Wallington 314-15
Walmer Castle 210
Izaak Walton Cottage 363
Warden Abbey 503
Wardour Castle 439-40
Wardour Old Castle 440-1
Warkworth Castle 315-16
Warleigh House 513
Washington Old Hall 410
Warwick Castle 424-5
Warwick: Northgate House 552
Wells: The Old Deanery 544
Wells: The Bishop's Palace 359-60
Weobley: The Ley 521
West Bower Manor 544
West Compton House 544
West Green House 147-8
West Wycombe Park 31
Weston Park 368
Westwood Manor 441
White Castle 486-7
The White House 342
White Lodge 263
Whitehall 509
Whitehaven 502-3
Whitclackington House 544
Wightwick Manor 279-81
Wigmore Abbey 542
Wilby Hall 535
Wilderhope Manor 342-3

Wilton House 441-3
Wimborne Minster: Priests House 514
Wimpole Hall 37-8
Windsor Castle 17-19
Winslow Hall 32
Winterbourne Clenston Manor 514
Witley Court 159-60
Woburn Abbey 13-14
Woodhall Park 522
Woodford Castle 514-15
Woodstock: Hope House 539
Wooton Hall 505
Wollaton Hall 320
Woollas Hall 521
Wolveton House 120-1
Woolsthorpe Manor 241
Worcester: The Commandery 160-1
Worcester: The Grey House 522
Worcester: Tudor House 161
Wordsworth House 76-8
Worlingham Hall 548
Wraysbury: King John's Hunting Lodge
    504
Wroxton Abbey 539-40
The Wurleigh 548
Wyberton Park 529
Wytham Abbey 540

Ydderw 567
York: Cumberland House 556
York Treasurer's House 460-1
York: 111 Walmgate 557